HUMAN DEVELOPMENT REPORT 1998

Published
for the United Nations
Development Programme
(UNDP)

New York   Oxford
Oxford University Press
1998

Oxford University Press

Oxford   New York

Athens   Auckland   Bangkok   Bombay
Calcutta   Cape Town   Dar es Salaam   Delhi
Florence   Hong Kong   Istanbul   Karachi
Kuala Lumpur   Madras   Madrid   Melbourne
Mexico City   Nairobi   Paris   Singapore
Taipei   Tokyo   Toronto

and associated companies in
Berlin   Ibadan

Published by Oxford University Press, Inc.
198 Madison Avenue, New York, New York, 10016

Oxford is a registered trademark of Oxford University Press

ISBN 0-19-512458-8 (cloth)
ISBN 0-19-512459-6 (paper)

9 8 7 6 5 4 3 2 1
Printed in the United States of America on elemental chlorine free, recycled paper (30% postconsumer waste) using soy-based ink.

Cover and design: Gerald Quinn, Quinn Information Design, Cabin John, Maryland

Editing, desktop composition and production management: Communications Development Incorporated, Washington DC and New York

Foreword

The *Human Development Report,* since its launch in 1990, has defined human development as the process of enlarging people's choices. This year's Report examines consumption from the perspective of human development. It concludes that despite a dramatic surge in consumption in many countries, all is not well: more than a billion people lack the opportunity to consume in ways that would allow them to meet their most basic needs. Other consumers—including me and most likely you and the societies in which we live—are consuming in ways that cannot be long sustained environmentally or socially and that are quite often inimical to our own well-being.

It is a truism that bears repeating: more is not invariably better. Consumption has grown at an unprecedented pace in this century, reaching some $24 trillion in 1998, but that growth has not yielded only benefits. Yet we appear to be on a runaway consumption train. For the more than one billion people living at or near the margin, increased consumption is essential. For those at the top, increased consumption has become a way of life. Yet we know, and this year's Report shows, that some aspects of consumption are undermining the prospects of sustainable human development for all.

When consumption erodes renewable resources, pollutes the local and global environment, panders to manufactured needs for conspicuous display and detracts from the legitimate needs of life in modern society, there is justifiable cause for concern.

Those who call for changes in consumption, for environmental or other reasons, are often seen as hair-shirt ascetics wishing to impose an austere way of life on billions who must pay for the waste of generations of big consumers. Advocates of strict consumption limits also are confronted with the dilemma that for more than one billion of the world's poor people increased consumption is a vital necessity and a basic right—a right to freedom from poverty and want. And there is the ethical issue of choice: how can consumption choices be made on behalf of others and not be seen as a restriction on their freedom to choose?

The Report poses these hard questions and concludes that the need is not so much for more consumption or for less, but for a different pattern of consumption—consumption for human development. It marshals environmental, developmental, technological and moral arguments to present a critique of consumption patterns that are inimical to human development, and an agenda for action to create an enabling environment for sustainable consumption for human development.

Poor people and poor countries need to accelerate the growth of their consumption, but they need not follow the path trodden by the rich and high-growth economies. Production techniques can be made more environmentally friendly. Environmental damage can be reversed. The global burden of reducing environmental damage and underdevelopment can be shared more equitably. And patterns of consumption that harm society and reinforce inequalities and poverty can be changed. Above all, we must make a determined effort to eradicate poverty and expand the consumption of the more than one billion desperately poor people who have been left out of the global growth in consumption.

The Report contains a message of qualified optimism. Awareness of the damaging effects of consumption has been increasing, and the momentum for consumption for human development growing. Poverty has been declining, sometimes rapidly. Many of the approaches and technologies needed to make consumption more sustainable are already in use or are on the drawing board—though they need to be applied far more broadly. The challenge is to accelerate these actions. Ways must be found to provide stronger international support for poor countries and to moderate the growing inequity between and within countries.

As in previous years, this year's *Human Development Report* is the fruit of a collaborative effort by a team of eminent consultants and advisers and the Human Development Report team. Richard Jolly, my special adviser, together with Sakiko Fukuda-Parr, Director of the Human Development Report Office, led the effort.

The analysis and policy recommendations in this Report do not necessarily reflect the views of the United Nations Development Programme, its Executive Board or its Member States. The independence of views and the professional integrity of its authors ensure that the conclusions and recommendations offered here will have the greatest possible audience.

As always, this is an innovative and thought-provoking report. I welcome the publication of *Human Development Report 1998* as an important contribution to the international debate on consumption and human development. I look forward to the Report's serving as an inspiration to the many national human development reports that our programme countries are preparing with the support of UNDP country offices. I hope in particular that it serves as a useful stimulus to the many non-governmental and community movements that have long led the way on issues of consumption, poverty, environment and human development. The Report ends by emphasizing the need for new and stronger alliances among these groups. Such alliances are vital for defining a more human vision of consumption and for generating the action required to achieve it in the 21st century.

James Gustave Speth

New York
May 1998

Team for the preparation of
Human Development Report 1998

Principal Coordinator
Richard Jolly

UNDP team
Director: Sakiko Fukuda-Parr
Deputy Director: Selim Jahan
Members: Håkan Björkman, Laura Mourino-Casas, Kate Raworth, A. K. Shiva Kumar and Gül Tanghe-Güllüova, in collaboration with Özer Babakol, Eliane Darbellay, Pia Nyman and Nadia Rasheed
Editors: Geoffrey Lean and Bruce Ross-Larson
Design: Gerald Quinn

Panel of consultants
Anil Agarwal, Galal Amin, Sudhir Anand, Graciela Chichilnisky, Allen Hammond, Bruce Hutton, Martin Khor, Michael Lipton, Emily Matthews, Norman Myers, Theodore Panayotou, Charles Perrings, Robert Prescott-Allen, Juliet Schor, Amartya Sen, Anuradha Seth, Vandana Shiva, Frances Stewart, Herbert Wulf, Simon Zadek and the originator of the *Human Development Report,* Mahbub ul Haq

Acknowledgements

The preparation of the Report would not have been possible without the support and valuable contributions of a large number of individuals and organizations.

Many international organizations generously shared their experience, research materials and data: the Food and Agriculture Organization, International Fund for Agricultural Development, International Labour Organisation, International Telecommunication Union, Inter-Parliamentary Union, Joint United Nations Programme on HIV/AIDS (UNAIDS), Office of the United Nations High Commissioner for Human Rights, Office of the United Nations High Commissioner for Refugees, Organisation for Economic Co-operation and Development, United Nations Centre for Social Development and Humanitarian Affairs, United Nations Children's Fund, United Nations Department of Economic and Social Affairs, United Nations Development Fund for Women (UNIFEM), United Nations Division for the Advancement of Women, United Nations Economic Commission for Europe, United Nations Educational, Scientific and Cultural Organisation, United Nations Environment Programme, United Nations Population Fund (UNFPA), United Nations Research Institute for Social Development, World Bank and World Health Organization.

Several research institutions and non-governmental organizations also generously shared their experience, research materials and data: the Bread for the World Institute, International Food Policy Research Institute, International Institute for Democracy and Electoral Assistance, International Institute for Strategic Studies, Oxfam International, Social Watch, Stockholm International Peace Research Institute, University of Pennsylvania and World Resources Institute.

Some private corporations also generously shared information and data: the Coca-Cola Company, McDonald's and Nike, Inc.

The Report benefited greatly from intellectual advice and guidance provided by the external Advisory Panel of eminent experts, which included Lourdes Arizpe, Noel Brown, Gretchen Daily, Herman Daly, Meghnad Desai, Paul Ekins, Diane Elson, Everett Elting, Jeremy Eppel, Nancy Folbre, Claude Fussler, Dharam Ghai, José Goldemberg, Heba Handoussa, Hazel Henderson, Ryokichi Hirono, Maria Elena Hurtado, Louka Katseli, Ashok Khosla, Jacqueline Aloisi de Laderel, Fu Chen Lo, Santosh Mehrotra, Benno Ndulu, Bishnodat Persaud, Rubens Ricupero, Leslie Roberts, Kenneth Ruffing, Wolfgang Sachs, Akligpa Sawyerr, Paul Streeten and Anders Wijkman.

The Report also benefited greatly from discussions with and kind contributions from Sultan Ahmad, Yonas Biru, Erik Brandsma, Nitin Desai, Clarence Dias, Shareen Hertel, Alan Heston, Kenneth Hill, Karl Hochgesand, Julio Hurtado, Alfred Kahn, Sheila Kamerman, Lawrence Klein, Jonathan Lash, Nyein Nyein Lwin, Robert Lynch, Alex MacGillivray, Jim MacNeill, Daniel Miller, Marc Miringoff, Geraldo Nascimento, William Prince, John Quelch, Stephen Rayner, Syuichi Sasaki, Timothy Smeeding, Karen Stanecki, Andrew Steer, Maurice Strong, Lawrence Summers, Alice Tepper Marlin, Kazuhiro Ueta, Joke Waller-Hunter, Michael Ward,

Tessa Wardlow, Kevin Watkins and Ernst Ulrich von Weizsäcker.

The Report benefited greatly from country case studies prepared by Jorio Abdeljaouad, Anil Agarwal, Galal Amin, Nadira Barkallil, Luis Camacho, David Crocker, Samir Halaoui, Rachid Hamimaz, Magdi Ibrahim, Stefan Larenas, Dow Mongkolsmai, Njuguna Mwangi, Sunita Narain, Ramón Romero, Marcelo Gomes Sodré, Somchai Suksiriserekul and Amei Zhang.

The Report drew on short papers and other contributions by Dean Abrahamson, Lourdes Arizpe, Rajat Chaudhuri, Hazel Henderson, Thomas Johansson, Alan Kay, Jon Lane, Kishore Mahbubani, John Mason, Ranjini Mazumdar, Patricia de Mowbray, Prasannan Parthasarathi, Albert Tuijnman and Robert Wild.

The team expresses its special thanks for the contribution of John Kenneth Galbraith.

Colleagues in UNDP provided extremely useful comments, suggestions and inputs during the drafting of the Report. In particular, the authors would like to express their gratitude to Gilbert Aho, Thelma Awori, Sarah Burd-Sharps, Marcia de Castro, Georges Chapelier,* Desmond Cohen, Djibril Diallo, Moez Doraid, Juliette El Hage, Fawaz Fokeladeh, Isabelle Grunberg,* Soheir Habib, Noeleen Heyzer,* Nay Htun,* Thomas Johansson, Karen Jorgensen,* Judith Karl, Inge Kaul,* Gladson Kayira, Normand Lauzon, Thierry Lemaresquier,* Roberto Lenton,* Carlos Lopes,* Khalid Malik, Susan McDade, Herbert M'Cleod,* Saraswathi Menon,* Omar Noman,* John Ohiorhenuan,* Kirit Shantilal Parikh,* Jonas Rabinovitch, Marta Ruedas, Yves de San, Nessim Shallon, R.

Sudarshan, Jerzy Szeremeta,* Sarah Timpson,* Antonio Vigilante, Eimi Watanabe and Fernando Zumbado.

Several offices in UNDP provided support and information. They include many UNDP country offices, UNDP's Regional Bureaux and the Bureau for Development Planning. The United Nations Office for Project Services provided the team with critical administrative support. Particular thanks go to Ingolf Schuetz-Mueller, Serene Ong and Martha Barrientos.

The Report also benefited from the dedicated work of interns. Thanks are due to Catherine Byrne, Poornima Paidpaty and Nasheeba Selim.

Secretarial and administrative support for the Report's preparation were provided by Oscar Bernal, Renuka Corea-Lloyd, Chato Ledonio-O'Buckley, U Thiha and Marjorie Victor. And as in previous years, the Report benefited from the design of Gerald Quinn and the editing and pre-press production of Communications Development Incorporated's Bruce Ross-Larson, with Heidi Gifford, Paul Holtz, Daphne Levitas, Terra Lynch, Heidi Manley, Glenn McGrath, Jessica Moore, Laurel Morais and Alison Strong.

The team expresses sincere appreciation to the peer reviewers, José Goldemberg, Maria Elena Hurtado, Solita Monsod, Jim MacNeill and Paul Streeten.

The authors also wish to acknowledge their great debt to James Gustave Speth, UNDP Administrator. His deep commitment to human development and his support for an independent Report are most appreciated.

Thankful for all the support that they have received, the authors assume full responsibility for the opinions expressed in the Report.

* Also members of the Advisory Panel.

Contents

BOXES

TABLES

FIGURES

AIDS	Acquired immunodeficiency syndrome
CIS	Commonwealth of Independent States
CO_2	Carbon dioxide
DAC	Development Assistance Committee of the OECD
EU	European Union
GDI	Gender-related development index
GDP	Gross domestic product
GEM	Gender empowerment measure
GNP	Gross national product
HDI	Human development index
HIPC	Heavily Indebted Poor Countries
HIV	Human immunodeficiency virus
HPI	Human poverty index
IMF	International Monetary Fund
NGO	Non-governmental organization
OECD	Organisation for Economic Co-operation and Development
PPP	Purchasing power parity
UNDP	United Nations Development Programme
UNICEF	United Nations Children's Fund
WHO	World Health Organization
WTO	World Trade Organization

Changing today's consumption patterns —for tomorrow's human development

World consumption has expanded at an unprecedented pace over the 20th century, with private and public consumption expenditures reaching $24 trillion in 1998, twice the level of 1975 and six times that of 1950. In 1900 real consumption expenditure was barely $1.5 trillion.

The benefits of this consumption have spread far and wide. More people are better fed and housed than ever before. Living standards have risen to enable hundreds of millions to enjoy housing with hot water and cold, warmth and electricity, transport to and from work—with time for leisure and sports, vacations and other activities beyond anything imagined at the start of this century.

How do these achievements relate to human development? Consumption is clearly an essential means, but the links are not automatic. Consumption clearly contributes to human development when it enlarges the capabilities and enriches the lives of people without adversely affecting the well-being of others. It clearly contributes when it is as fair to future generations as it is to the present ones. And it clearly contributes when it encourages lively, creative individuals and communities.

But the links are often broken, and when they are, consumption patterns and trends are inimical to human development. Today's consumption is undermining the environmental resource base. It is exacerbating inequalities. And the dynamics of the consumption-poverty-inequality-environment nexus are accelerating. If the trends continue without change—not redistributing from high-income to low-income consumers, not shifting from polluting to cleaner goods and production technologies, not promoting goods that empower poor producers, not shifting priority from consumption for con-

spicuous display to meeting basic needs—today's problems of consumption and human development will worsen.

But trend is not destiny, and none of these outcomes is inevitable. Change is needed—and change is possible.

In short, consumption must be shared, strengthening, socially responsible and sustainable.

• *Shared*. Ensuring basic needs for all.
• *Strengthening*. Building human capabilities.
• *Socially responsible*. So the consumption of some does not compromise the well-being of others.
• *Sustainable*. Without mortgaging the choices of future generations.

Human life is ultimately nourished and sustained by consumption. Abundance of consumption is no crime. It has, in fact, been the life blood of much human advance. The real issue is not consumption itself but its patterns and effects. Consumption patterns today must be changed to advance human development tomorrow. Consumer choices must be turned into a reality for all. Human development paradigms, which aim at enlarging all human choices, must aim at extending and improving consumer choices too, but in ways that promote human life. This is the theme of this report.

Trend is not destiny—change is possible

The 20th century's growth in consumption, unprecedented in its scale and diversity, has been badly distributed, leaving a backlog of shortfalls and gaping inequalities.

Consumption per capita has increased steadily in industrial countries (about 2.3%

annually) over the past 25 years, spectacularly in East Asia (6.1%) and at a rising rate in South Asia (2.0%). Yet these developing regions are far from catching up to levels of industrial countries, and consumption growth has been slow or stagnant in others. The average African household today consumes 20% less than it did 25 years ago.

The poorest 20% of the world's people and more have been left out of the consumption explosion. Well over a billion people are deprived of basic consumption needs. Of the 4.4 billion people in developing countries, nearly three-fifths lack basic sanitation. Almost a third have no access to clean water. A quarter do not have adequate housing. A fifth have no access to modern health services. A fifth of children do not attend school to grade 5. About a fifth do not have enough dietary energy and protein. Micronutrient deficiencies are even more widespread. Worldwide, 2 billion people are anaemic, including 55 million in industrial countries. In developing countries only a privileged minority has motorized transport, telecommunications and modern energy.

Inequalities in consumption are stark. Globally, the 20% of the world's people in the highest-income countries account for 86% of total private consumption expenditures—the poorest 20% a minuscule 1.3%. More specifically, the richest fifth:

• Consume 45% of all meat and fish, the poorest fifth 5%.

• Consume 58% of total energy, the poorest fifth less than 4%.

• Have 74% of all telephone lines, the poorest fifth 1.5%.

• Consume 84% of all paper, the poorest fifth 1.1%.

• Own 87% of the world's vehicle fleet, the poorest fifth less than 1%.

How rewarding is today's pattern of consumption in terms of human satisfaction? The percentage of Americans calling themselves happy peaked in 1957—even though consumption has more than doubled in the meantime.

Despite high consumption, poverty and deprivation are found in all industrial countries and in some they are growing. This year's Report presents a new index of poverty in industrial countries—a multidimensional measure of human deprivation, on the same lines as the human poverty index presented in *Human Development Report 1997* for developing countries but more appropriate to the social and economic conditions of the industrial countries.

The new human poverty index (HPI-2) shows that some 7–17% of the population in industrial countries is poor. These levels of deprivation have little to do with the average income of the country. Sweden has the least poverty (7%), though ranked only thirteenth in average income. The United States, with the highest average income of the countries ranked, has the highest population share experiencing human poverty. And countries with similar per capita incomes have very different levels of human poverty. The Netherlands and the United Kingdom, for example, have HPI-2 values of 8% and 15%, despite similar income levels.

HPI-2 shows conclusively that underconsumption and human deprivation are not just the lot of poor people in the developing world. More than 100 million people in rich nations suffer a similar fate. Nearly 200 million people are not expected to survive to age 60. More than 100 million are homeless. And at least 37 million are without jobs, often experiencing a state of social exclusion. Many conclusions about deprivation apply to them with equal force.

Ever-expanding consumption puts strains on the environment—emissions and wastes that pollute the earth and destroy ecosystems, and growing depletion and degradation of renewable resources that undermines livelihoods.

Runaway growth in consumption in the past 50 years is putting strains on the environment never before seen.

• The burning of fossil fuels has almost quintupled since 1950.

• The consumption of fresh water has almost doubled since 1960.

• The marine catch has increased fourfold.

• Wood consumption, both for industry and for household fuel, is now 40% higher than it was 25 years ago.

The new human poverty index (HPI-2) shows that some 7–17% of the population in industrial countries is poor

Rapid consumption growth for some, stagnation for others, inequality for all—with mounting environmental costs

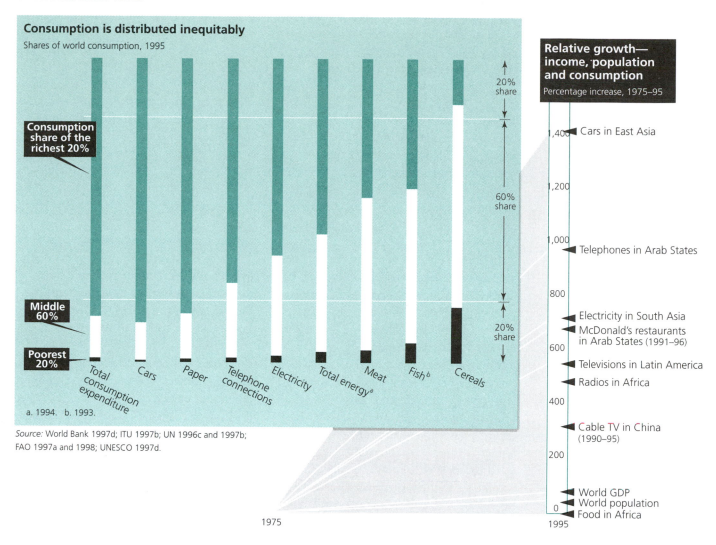

Consumption is distributed inequitably
Shares of world consumption, 1995

Consumption share of the richest 20%

Middle 60%

Poorest 20%

Total consumption expenditure
Cars
Paper
Telephone connections
Electricity
Total energy[a]
Meat
Fish[b]
Cereals

a. 1994. b. 1993.

Source: World Bank 1997d; ITU 1997b; UN 1996c and 1997b; FAO 1997a and 1998; UNESCO 1997d.

Relative growth—income, population and consumption
Percentage increase, 1975–95

20% share
60% share
20% share

1,400 — Cars in East Asia
1,200
1,000 — Telephones in Arab States
800 — Electricity in South Asia
— McDonald's restaurants in Arab States (1991–96)
600 — Televisions in Latin America
— Radios in Africa
400
— Cable TV in China (1990–95)
200
— World GDP
— World population
0 — Food in Africa

1975   1995

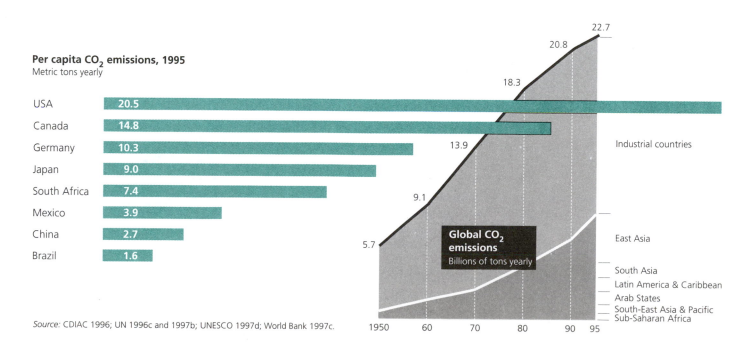

Per capita CO$_2$ emissions, 1995
Metric tons yearly

USA	20.5
Canada	14.8
Germany	10.3
Japan	9.0
South Africa	7.4
Mexico	3.9
China	2.7
Brazil	1.6

22.7
20.8
18.3
13.9
9.1
5.7

Industrial countries

Global CO$_2$ emissions
Billions of tons yearly

East Asia
South Asia
Latin America & Caribbean
Arab States
South-East Asia & Pacific
Sub-Saharan Africa

1950   60   70   80   90   95

Source: CDIAC 1996; UN 1996c and 1997b; UNESCO 1997d; World Bank 1997c.

Yet growth in the use of material resources has slowed considerably in recent years, and much-publicized fears that the world would run out of such non-renewable resources as oil and minerals have proved false. New reserves have been discovered. The growth of demand has slowed. Consumption has shifted in favour of less material-intensive products and services. Energy efficiency has improved. And technological advance and recycling of raw materials have boosted efficiency in material use, now growing more slowly than economies. Call this dematerialization. The per capita use of basic materials such as steel, timber and copper has stabilized in most OECD countries—and even declined in some countries for some products.

So, non-renewables are not the urgent problem. It is two other crises that are nudging humanity towards the "outer limits" of what earth can stand.

First are the pollution and waste that exceed the planet's sink capacities to absorb and convert them. Reserves of fossil fuels are not running out, but use of these fuels is emitting gases that change the ecosystem— annual carbon dioxide (CO_2) emissions quadrupled over the past 50 years. Global warming is a serious problem, threatening to play havoc with harvests, permanently flood large areas, increase the frequency of storms and droughts, accelerate the extinction of some species, spread infectious diseases— and possibly cause sudden and savage flips in the world's climates. And although material resources may not be running out, waste is mounting, both toxic and non-toxic. In industrial countries per capita waste generation has increased almost threefold in the past 20 years.

Second is the growing deterioration of renewables—water, soil, forests, fish, biodiversity.
• Twenty countries already suffer from water stress, having less than 1,000 cubic metres per capita a year, and water's global availability has dropped from 17,000 cubic metres per capita in 1950 to 7,000 today.
• A sixth of the world's land area—nearly 2 billion hectares—is now degraded as a result of overgrazing and poor farming practices.

• The world's forests—which bind soil and prevent erosion, regulate water supplies and help govern the climate—are shrinking. Since 1970 the wooded area per 1,000 inhabitants has fallen from 11.4 square kilometres to 7.3.
• Fish stocks are declining, with about a quarter currently depleted or in danger of depletion and another 44% being fished at their biological limit.
• Wild species are becoming extinct 50–100 times faster than they would naturally, threatening to tear great holes in the web of life.

The world's dominant consumers are overwhelmingly concentrated among the well-off—but the environmental damage from the world's consumption falls most severely on the poor.

The better-off benefit from the cornucopia of consumption. But poor people and poor countries bear many of its costs. The severest human deprivations arising from environmental damage are concentrated in the poorest regions and affect the poorest people, unable to protect themselves.
• A child born in the industrial world adds more to consumption and pollution over his or her lifetime than do 30–50 children born in developing countries.
• Since 1950 industrial countries, because of their high incomes and consumption levels, have accounted for well over half the increase in resource use.
• The fifth of the world's people in the highest-income countries account for 53% of carbon dioxide emissions, the poorest fifth for 3%. Brazil, China, India, Indonesia and Mexico are among the developing countries with the highest emissions. But with huge populations, their per capita emissions are still tiny—3.9 metric tons a year in Mexico and 2.7 in China, compared with 20.5 metric tons in the United States and 10.2 in Germany. The human consequences of the global warming from carbon dioxide will be devastating for many poor countries—with a rise in sea levels, Bangladesh could see its land area shrink by 17%.

- Almost a billion people in 40 developing countries risk losing access to their primary source of protein, as overfishing driven by export demand for animal feed and oils puts pressure on fish stocks.
- The 132 million people in water-stressed areas are predominantly in Africa and parts of the Arab states—and if present trends continue, their numbers could rise to 1–2.5 billion by 2050.
- Deforestation is concentrated in developing countries. Over the last two decades, Latin America and the Caribbean lost 7 million hectares of tropical forest, Asia and Sub-Saharan Africa 4 million hectares each. Most of it has taken place to meet the demand for wood and paper, which has doubled and quintupled respectively since 1950. But over half the wood and nearly three-quarters of the paper is used in industrial countries.

The poor are most exposed to fumes and polluted rivers and least able to protect themselves. Of the estimated 2.7 million deaths each year from air pollution, 2.2 million are from indoor pollution, and 80% of the victims are rural poor in developing countries. Smoke from fuelwood and dung is more dangerous to health than tobacco smoke, but every day women have to spend hours cooking over smoky fires.

Leaded petrol, used more in developing and transition economies than in industrial countries, is crippling human health, permanently impairing the development of children's brains. In Bangkok up to 70,000 children are reported to be at risk of losing four or more IQ points because of high lead emissions. In Latin America around 15 million children under two years of age are at similar risk.

These environmental challenges stem not only from affluence but also from growing poverty. As a result of increasing impoverishment and the absence of other alternatives, a swelling number of poor and landless people are putting unprecedented pressures on the natural resource base as they struggle to survive.

Poverty and the environment are caught in a downward spiral. Past resource degradation deepens today's poverty, while today's poverty makes it very hard to care for or restore the agricultural resource base, to find alternatives to deforestation, to prevent desertification, to control erosion and to replenish soil nutrients. Poor people are forced to deplete resources to survive; this degradation of the environment further impoverishes them.

When this reinforcing downward spiral becomes extreme, poor people are either forced to move in increasing numbers to ecologically fragile lands. Almost half the world's poorest people—more than 500 million—live on marginal lands.

The poverty–environmental damage nexus in developing countries must be seen in the context of population growth. In the developing world pressures on the environment intensify every day as the population grows. The global population is projected to be 9.5 billion in 2050, with more than 8 billion in developing countries. To feed this population adequately will require three times the basic calories consumed today, the equivalent of about 10 billion tons of grain a year. Population growth will also contribute to overgrazing, overcutting and overfarming.

How people interact with their environment is complex. It is by no means simply a matter of whether they are poor or rich. Ownership of natural resources, access to common properties, the strength of communities and local institutions, the issue of entitlements and rights, risk and uncertainty are important determinants of people's environmental behaviour. Gender inequalities, government policies and incentive systems are also crucial factors.

In recent times environmental awareness has been increasing in both rich and poor countries. The rich countries, with greater resources, have been spending more on environmental protection and clean-up. The developing countries, though they have fewer resources, have also been adopting cleaner technologies and reducing pollution, as in China.

The world community has also been active on environmental problems that directly affect poor people. Such areas include desertification, biodiversity loss and exports of hazardous waste. For example, the Convention on Biological Diversity has

Competitive spending and conspicuous consumption turn the affluence of some into the social exclusion of many

near-universal signature, with over 170 parties. The Convention to Combat Desertification has been ratified by more than 100 countries. But the deterioration of arid lands, a major threat to the livelihoods of poor people, continues unabated.

And there are other immediate environmental concerns for poor people, such as water contamination and indoor pollution, that have yet to receive serious international attention. Global forums discuss global warming. But the 2.2 million deaths yearly from indoor air pollution are scarcely mentioned.

Globalization is creating new inequalities and new challenges for protecting consumer rights

---

Rising pressures for conspicuous consumption can turn destructive, reinforcing exclusion, poverty and inequality.

Pressures of competitive spending and conspicuous consumption turn the affluence of some into the social exclusion of many. When there is heavy social pressure to maintain high consumption standards and society encourages competitive spending for conspicuous displays of wealth, inequalities in consumption deepen poverty and social exclusion.

Some disturbing trends:
• Studies of US households found that the income needed to fulfil consumption aspirations doubled between 1986 and 1994.
• The definition of what constitutes a "necessity" is changing, and the distinctions between luxuries and necessities are blurring. In the 1980s Brazil, Chile, Malaysia, Mexico and South Africa had two to three times as many cars as Austria, France and Germany did when they were at the same income level 30 years earlier.
• Household debt, especially consumer credit, is growing and household savings are falling in many industrial and developing countries. In the United States households save only 3.5% of their incomes, half as much as 15 years ago. In Brazil consumer debt, concentrated among lower-income households, now exceeds $6 billion.

Many voice concerns about the impact of these trends on society's values—and on

human lives. Do they further deepen poverty as households compete to meet rising consumption standards—crowding out spending on food, education and health? Do these patterns motivate people to spend more hours working—leaving less time for family, friends and community?

And is globalization accelerating these trends in competitive spending and rising standards?

Globalization is integrating consumer markets around the world and opening opportunities. But it is also creating new inequalities and new challenges for protecting consumer rights.

Globalization is integrating not just trade, investment and financial markets. It is also integrating consumer markets. This has two effects—economic and social. Economic integration has accelerated the opening of consumer markets with a constant flow of new products. There is fierce competition to sell to consumers worldwide, with increasingly aggressive advertising.

On the social side local and national boundaries are breaking down in the setting of social standards and aspirations in consumption. Market research identifies "global elites" and "global middle classes" who follow the same consumption styles, showing preferences for "global brands". There are the "global teens"—some 270 million 15- to 18-year-olds in 40 countries—inhabiting a "global space", a single pop-culture world, soaking up the same videos and music and providing a huge market for designer running shoes, t-shirts and jeans.

What are the consequences? First, a host of consumption options have been opened for many consumers—but many are left out in the cold through lack of income. And pressures for competitive spending mount. "Keeping up with the Joneses" has shifted from striving to match the consumption of a next-door neighbour to pursuing the life styles of the rich and famous depicted in movies and television shows.

Second, protecting consumer rights to product safety and product information has become complex. Increasingly, new products with higher chemical content, such as foods and medicines, are coming on the market. When information is not adequate, or safety standards are not strictly enforced, consumers can suffer—from pesticides that are poisonous, from milk powder that is contaminated.

At the same time the consumer receives a flood of information through commercial advertising. An average American, it is estimated, sees 150,000 advertisements on television in his or her lifetime. And advertising is increasing worldwide, faster than population or incomes. Global advertising spending, by the most conservative reckoning, is now $435 billion. Its growth has been particularly rapid in developing countries—in the Republic of Korea it increased nearly threefold in 1986–96, in the Philippines by 39% a year in 1987–92. In 1986 there were only three developing countries among the 20 biggest spenders in advertising. A decade later there were nine. And in spending relative to income, Colombia ranks first with $1.4 billion, 2.6% of its GDP.

Poor countries need to accelerate their consumption growth—but they need not follow the path taken by the rich and high-growth economies over the past half century.

Not only have consumption levels been too low to meet basic needs for more than a billion people, their growth has often been slow and interrupted by setbacks. In 70 countries with nearly a billion people consumption today is lower than it was 25 years ago. It cannot be raised without accelerating economic growth—but growth has been failing many poor people and poor countries. Despite the spectacular growth of incomes for many people in Asia, only 21 developing countries worldwide achieved growth in GDP per capita of at least 3% each year between 1995 and 1997—the rate needed to set a frame for reducing poverty.

Some suggest that developing countries should restrain their consumption in order to limit environmental damage. But this would mean prolonging the already scandalously deep and extensive deprivation for future generations.

Developing countries today face a strategic choice. They can repeat the industrialization and growth processes of the past half century, and go through a development phase that is inequitable, and creates an enormous legacy of environmental pollution. Or they can leapfrog to growth patterns that are:
• Pro-environment, preserving natural resources and creating less pollution and waste.
• Pro-poor, creating jobs for poor people and households and expanding their access to basic social services.

If poor countries can leapfrog in both consumption patterns and production technologies, they can accelerate consumption growth and human development without the huge costs of environmental damage. They can incorporate many of the available technologies that are not only less environmentally damaging but clean—solar energy, less energy-intensive crop production, cleaner paper production technologies.

Leapfrogging technologies will enhance the prospects for development by saving the huge costs of environmental clean-up that many countries are now incurring. The cost savings will go beyond the direct costs of cleaning up old toxic sites, scrubbing coal power plants and so on. Health care costs linked to environmental damage can also be saved. And leapfrogging will bypass the lock-in that can result from inappropriate infrastructure development.

Some argue that the scope for cheap, effective and politically less contentious antipollution policies is very limited in poor countries. This is a myth. Many actions have already been taken. And further options exist:
• Higher yields can be achieved through more intensive agricultural methods rather than more fertilizers and pesticides.
• Phasing out lead in petrol costs only 1–2 cents per litre for the refinery, as Mexico and Thailand have shown.
• Solar power and compact fluorescent lightbulbs can increase efficiency fourfold and reduce the need for rural electricity grids.

Developing countries today can leapfrog to growth patterns that are pro-environment and pro-poor

- Clean four-stroke engines can be made compulsory for motorcycles and three-wheelers, as Thailand has done.

These show what is possible. But to realize the potential, more needs to be done to develop and apply innovations.

Affluent societies in industrial countries also face strategic choices. They can continue the trends in consumption of the past decade. Or they can shift to consumption that is pro-people and pro-environment.

Continuing past trends would increase industrial countries' consumption by four- to fivefold over the next half century. Some argue that growth must be slowed and consumption downsized. But the real issue is not growth of consumption but its impacts on people, the environment and society. If societies adopt technologies that diminish the environmental impact of consumption, if patterns shift from consuming material goods to consuming services, growth can help, not hinder, moves to sustainability. The strategic choices of rich countries as the world's dominant consumers, will be critical in determining the future.

AGENDA FOR ACTION

Five goals are central:
- Raise the consumption levels of more than a billion poor people—more than a quarter of humanity—who have been left out of the global expansion of consumption and are unable to meet their basic needs.
- Move to more sustainable consumption patterns that reduce environmental damage, improve efficiency in resource use and regenerate renewable resources—such as water, wood, soils and fish.
- Protect and promote the rights of consumers to information, product safety and access to products that they need.
- Discourage patterns of consumption that have a negative impact on society and that reinforce inequalities and poverty.
- Achieve more equitable international burden-sharing in reducing and preventing global environmental damage and in reducing global poverty.

The key is to create an enabling environment for sustainable consumption—where both consumers and producers have the incentives and options to move towards consumption patterns that are less environmentally damaging and less socially harmful. People care about the impact of consumption on their own health and safety—and the broader impact on the environment and society. But they are caught up in a system of limited choices and opportunities and perverse incentives. Here's a seven-point agenda for action.

1. Ensure minimum consumption requirements for all—as an explicit policy objective in all countries.

"Everyone has the right to a standard of living adequate for the health and well-being of himself and his family, including food, clothing, housing and medical care and necessary social services … Everyone has the right to education" (Universal Declaration of Human Rights). These principles of universalism and human rights acknowledge the equal rights of everyone—women, men and children—without discrimination. They demand governance that ensures that all have enough to eat, that no child goes without education, that no human being is denied access to health care, safe water and basic sanitation and that all people can develop their potential capabilities to the full extent.

Strong public action is needed to meet these goals. This means a mix of public provisioning in basic social services and an enabling environment and incentive system for private and voluntary action. It means:
- Strong public policies to promote food security—ranging from conducive monetary, fiscal, commercial and pricing policies to institutions and incentives to promote local production and distribution.
- Priority public expenditures for basic social services—education, health, safe water, basic sanitation. Not only should services be expanded, but access should be made more equitable. Studies in many countries show that access favours the better-off rather than the poor, and urban rather than rural populations.
- Infrastructure for transport and energy to provide affordable and efficient services

Consumption levels of over a billion poor people must be raised

for people, not just economic growth. This means, for example, public transport, paths for bicycles and pedestrians and energy from renewable sources in rural areas.

- Incentives to develop "poor people's goods"—low-cost housing materials, energy-saving equipment and food storage systems.
- Institutions and legal frameworks that secure people's rights to housing, to common property, to credit.

John Kenneth Galbraith wrote 40 years ago about private affluence amid public squalor. Far from narrowing, the contrasts have grown, and to them are added private and environmental squalor.

---

2. Develop and apply technologies and methods that are environmentally sustainable for both poor and affluent consumers.

Human development can be sustained with purposeful action. The challenge is not to stop growth. It is to change the patterns of consumption and production, using new technologies to achieve greater efficiency and to reduce waste and pollution. Many such technologies are already in production or on the drawing board.

Sustainable growth of consumption and production depends on major advances in cleaner, material-saving, resource-saving and low-cost technologies. Also needed are consumption options that are environmentally friendly and low cost and affordable for the poor. But many do not yet exist— these need to be invented. And those that exist need to be better marketed—goods that use less energy and fewer renewables (water and wood), that create less waste and pollution and that are low in cost. Such options may be available in some countries—the zero-emission car, for example— but not worldwide, or they may be only at the experimental stage. Public expenditure on research and development in energy has declined by a third in real terms since the early 1980s. Moreover, less than 10% goes to energy efficiency improvements. The rest goes largely to fossil fuel and nuclear energy development. The case is strong for firms and governments to support more technological development and application.

Rather than attempting to pick and promote winning technologies, governments can help create a dynamic marketplace to perform that task more effectively. The state can require all energy providers— public and private—to supply a fixed minimum share of energy from renewable sources—either by generating it themselves or by purchasing it from other providers. This approach both ensures the introduction of renewable energy sources in the market and stimulates innovation of more efficient and lower-cost technologies.

The benefits of cleaner technologies have been well demonstrated, as with the reduction of material use in OECD countries. Many technological solutions already exist for environmentally friendly goods, but current pricing structures undervalue environmental costs and benefits—and thus reduce market incentives. Increased public support for further research and development could accelerate the pace of technological progress.

There is a particular need for technologies to meet the requirements of the poor. About 2 billion people in developing countries lack access to electricity. Meeting this need through clean, renewable sources of energy can reduce poverty and indoor air pollution. The sun and wind are available at no cost to villages that have little hope of being connected to electricity grids. Windpower, now the world's fastest-growing source of energy, meets only 1% of global demand. India aims by 2012 to provide 10% of its electricity from renewables, which could provide half the world's energy by the middle of the next century.

Perhaps most important among technologies for the poor are those for agricultural production in ecologically marginal environments. Improvements in food production in much of Asia and Latin America would not have been possible without the green revolution—the scientific breakthroughs that provided high-yielding varieties of rice, wheat and maize. The world average yield of these crops has more than doubled over the past 20 years. But this did not happen in areas of lower rainfall and in the more fragile ecological zones, where

A second green revolution is needed—primarily to benefit the world's poorest

people subsist on millet and sorghum—and on cattle, sheep and goats. The world average yield of millet and sorghum increased by only 15% over the past two decades.

A second green revolution is needed for these people, among the world's poorest. But this should not just repeat the first revolution—it needs to aim both at increasing yields and incomes and at preserving and developing the environmental base.

The private sector has a critical role too—not just to meet the challenges of social responsibility but to produce environmentally friendly, poverty-reducing goods. The market for environmental goods alone is estimated at $500 billion. But for the private sector to act, it needs the right signals from prices and incentives in the market.

3. Remove perverse subsidies and restructure taxes to shift incentives from consumption that damages the environment to consumption that promotes human development.

Many developing countries use subsidies—on staple foods and basic energy supplies, for example—to help poor people survive and reduce poverty. Yet at the same time, most countries tax employment and subsidize pollution and environmental damage directly and indirectly. Such "perverse" subsidies are particularly common in the sectors of energy, water, road transport and agriculture. Total subsidies worldwide in these four sectors are estimated at $700–900 billion a year. They are also often distributionally regressive, benefiting mostly the wealthy—often political interest groups—while draining the public budget.

The absolute amount of subsidies is about twice as large in the OECD countries as in the rest of the world. In the OECD countries agriculture is most heavily subsidized (more than $330 billion), followed by road transport ($85–200 billion). In developing and transition economies the largest subsidies go to energy ($150–200 billion) and water ($42–47 billion). In the words of the Earth Council, "the world is spending hundreds of billions of dollars annually to subsidize its own destruction."

Environmental taxes—charging for pollution, congestion and depletion—have proved highly effective in both industrial and developing countries. They have been widely used in Western Europe and are the well-accepted core of green tax reforms—the Swedish air pollution tax and the Dutch water pollution tax, for example. But not just in Europe. Malaysia's effluent charges and Singapore's automobile taxes are well established and effective.

In Europe the social costs of environmental damage, unaccounted and unpaid, are estimated to average more than 4% of GDP. Estimates for the United States range from 2% to 12%. Users are encouraged to make excessive and wasteful use of road transport, with private cars most underpriced and most environmentally damaging.

Removing perverse subsidies that encourage environmental damage, lower economic efficiency and benefit the wealthy—and imposing environmental taxes instead—can be a catalyst for reducing inequalities and poverty and improving the prospects for equitable growth. Environmental taxes raise revenues that can be used to spend on environmental protection, to reduce taxes on labour, capital and savings or to improve access to social services for poor people.

The policy instruments described above present a win-win opportunity for changing consumption patterns to reverse environmental damage and increase the consumption of the poor. Removing water subsidies, for example, would reduce water use by 20–30%—and in parts of Asia by as much as 50%. That would make it possible, without large, environmentally destructive water development projects, to supply safe drinking water to most of the 1.3 billion people now lacking it.

Another example: congestion charges can finance improvements in public transport and expand transport options. They can ease congestion, save time, lower the costs of public transport and, usually, improve the distribution of income. Road transport subsidies in developing countries amount to $15 billion. The increased involvement of the private sector in financing, building and operating public transport systems in the

Removing perverse subsidies and imposing environmental taxes can promote equitable growth

1990s is creating pressure to reduce road subsidies and increase user fees. Argentina cut subsidies to suburban rail systems by $25 million between 1993 and 1995 when it privatized the operation of urban transport.

The benefits of a shift from taxing employment to taxing pollution and other environmental damage could be considerable. An OECD study on Norway suggests that a revenue-neutral shift would reduce unemployment while encouraging recycling and reducing environmental damage.

More and more countries are realizing that old policies and subsidies have adverse consequences. Thus energy subsidies in developing countries have fallen from more than $300 billion in the early 1990s to about $150–200 billion today. Environmental taxes are multiplying. But perverse subsidies are still huge, and environmental taxes have reached nowhere near their potential. Even in the Nordic countries, where some of the most interesting experiments are being carried out, pollution taxes and congestion charges raise only about 7% of government revenues.

---

4. Strengthen public action for consumer education and information and environmental protection.

The expansion of consumer choice has little significance if choices are based on wrong or misleading information. Strong public action to protect consumer rights is needed to offset vastly unbalanced information flows dominated by commercial advertisements.

Consumer rights must be defended through:
• Strict standards for consumer health and safety.
• Product labelling about the content and proper use of products and their environmental and social impact.
• Information and awareness campaigns about potential health hazards, such as smoking tobacco and the improper use of feeding formula for infants.

Advertising can serve positive purposes, but controls are needed, especially on television advertising targeting young children.

Sweden bans television advertising directed at children under 12.

Where price incentives are inadequate, environmental laws and regulations are needed. Skilfully devised, controls can be enabling for the consumer, not restricting. But implementation is as important as legislation. Strong institutions, free from corruption, are needed to enforce regulations in such areas as rights to land, security of tenure in housing and accurate information on consumer goods to protect the interests of poor people.

Regulation and market interventions can be mutually reinforcing. Sometimes regulation is needed to initiate action that can later be taken further with price incentives. At other times price incentives can be used to make a start—with regulation later to ensure wider compliance, especially after fostering social acceptance.

A new approach that has gained considerable interest and momentum in recent years is self-regulation through publicizing information on industrial polluters. This encourages the production of information about pollution generation, both as a source of incentive for behavioural change and as a benchmark for subsequent regulation. A well-known example is the US Toxic Release Inventory, which requires businesses to report the amounts of toxic materials that they put into the environment. Many companies respond by reducing pollution to preserve their reputations.

---

5. Strengthen international mechanisms to manage consumption's global impacts.

Environmental damage crosses borders. So do shifts in consumption patterns and habits. Poverty and inequality are issues of global magnitude and thus cannot be tackled by nations singly. They require international action.

International responsibilities for ensuring the sustainability of natural resource use have been debated in numerous forums. The Kuala Lumpur Meeting of the Parties to the Basel Convention on the Ban on Hazardous Waste agreed to ban the export

Consumer rights must be protected from unbalanced information flows

of such waste to poor countries. Both the Convention on Biological Diversity and the Convention on International Trade in Endangered Species of Wild Flora and Fauna have been quite successful.

Although some of these agreements sometimes fall short of expectations and ideals, they are steps in the right direction. The recent Kyoto Meeting on the United Nations Framework Convention on Climate Change has set industrial country targets for emissions of carbon dioxide and proposed a Clean Development Mechanism to assist developing countries. Both the financing and the institutional arrangement for this mechanism must be dealt with by the global community. Another problem that needs to be addressed: the continuing decline of official development assistance and the mounting unsustainable debt of poor countries.

Many global instruments to tackle environmental and poverty issues are underdeveloped—such as environmental trading permits, debt swaps and fair trade schemes. These instruments tend to be double-edged swords, however, and need to be carefully negotiated so that they do not penalize poor nations and make them even poorer. Trading environmental permits should not mean permanently giving away the rights of developing countries. A coordinating global institution in the form of the proposed international bank for environmental settlements is needed to develop and manage these instruments equitably.

6. Build stronger alliances among the movements for consumer rights, environmental protection, poverty eradication, gender equality and children's rights.

Consumer groups have been a powerful force for protecting consumer rights worldwide. They have helped remove unsafe products from the market and promote proper labelling and the supply of safe and low-cost goods.

Now consumers increasingly are using the power of their purses to push the interests of communities even halfway around the globe. Studies in Europe show that consumers are willing to pay price premiums of 5–10% for products that are more environmentally sound (in production, operation and disposal).

Businesses are responding to consumer demand for cleaner, safer products. Evidence from Eastern Europe shows that firms exporting to the European Union tend to have cleaner production processes than firms that produce for the domestic markets, which are less environmentally demanding.

Conventional wisdom assumes that environmental damage is a necessary consequence of economic growth. This is wrong. Environmental damage is a drain on economic growth, and it is possible to pursue a path to growth that does not damage the environment.

Poverty eradication, environmental sustainability, consumer rights protection—all these build on one another. Eradicating poverty does not require growth that ignores consumer rights or destroys the environment. Quite the opposite. Protecting consumer rights and protecting the environment are necessary for eradicating poverty and reducing inequalities.

There is great potential for building closer alliances among the environmental movement, the women's movement, the movement for children, consumer groups and pressure groups against poverty. Already their central concerns show great convergence. Stronger alliances are needed—and possible—if each movement emphasizes the common need for human development. United and mobilized together, these groups can achieve much more.

7. Think globally, act locally. Build on the burgeoning initiatives of people in communities everywhere and foster synergies in the actions of civil society, the private sector and government.

The growing number and strength of consumer and environmental movements around the world—including the 2,000 town and city Agenda 21s that have been prepared—reflect the commitment of people to taking collective action. Many opinion surveys show that people place a higher

Strong civil society alliances should be built to protect consumer rights

value on community and family life than on acquiring material possessions. And many people are asking how they can give more emphasis to human concerns.

Some 100 countries have prepared national human development reports, assessing their present situations and drawing conclusions on actions to achieve more human patterns of development. Most of these plans have analysed needs in the critical areas of education, health and employment, often linking them with opportunities for generating resources from reduced military spending.

These initiatives in many cases are the outcomes of successful alliances of the government, institutions of civil society and international organizations.

Progress has also been made in the area of sustainable consumption and a cleaner environment as a result of civil pressure, public action and private sector responses. The instruments: eco-taxes and subsidy removal, stiff environmental regulations backed by penalties, community efforts for better management of common resources (erosion control, reforestation) and more equitable provisioning of public infrastructure and services.

This shows what is possible. It also shows that support exists for a cleaner environment, a more equitable society and the eradication of poverty. Individuals, households, civil society groups, governments and private businesses—all have a role, and together their complementary efforts can build even more energy and synergy for action.

•　•　•

In the poorer countries many priorities in consumption still need to be addressed.

Increases in consumption should be planned and encouraged—but with attention to nurturing the links, to making sure that the increases contribute to human development and to avoiding extremes of inequality. Forward-looking perspectives are also needed—to avoid infrastructure and institutions that may lock a country into unsustainable or socially dysfunctional consumption.

In the better-off countries—most of the industrial countries and some of the richer developing countries—the challenge is different. The priority to eradicate poverty and ensure the basic needs of all remains. Indeed, the failure of the richest countries to do that is a scandal. But as general living standards rise and the proportion in poverty falls, the balance of attention in economic and social policy needs to shift. Increasingly, the policy focus needs to move towards enlarging the options for patterns of consumption in which human creativity can be lived out and carried forward with diversity and fulfilment, with most of the population at comfortable levels of consumption, well above the margins of subsistence. These policies need to be combined with those of the environment and human development.

Recent experiences give considerable hope, with more evidence showing that changes in consumption patterns towards sustainable poverty reduction are possible.

Hope brings challenge. The high levels of consumption and production in the world today, the power and potential of technology and information, present great opportunities. After a century of vast material expansion, will leaders and people have the vision to seek and achieve more equitable and more human advance in the 21st century?

Increases in consumption must also nurture links to human development

Human development is a process of enlarging people's choices. Enlarging people's choices is achieved by expanding human capabilities and functionings. At all levels of development the three essential capabilities for human development are for people to lead long and healthy lives, to be knowledgeable and to have access to the resources needed for a decent standard of living. If these basic capabilities are not achieved, many choices are simply not available and many opportunities remain inaccessible. But the realm of human development goes further: essential areas of choice, highly valued by people, range from political, economic and social opportunities for being creative and productive to enjoying self-respect, empowerment and a sense of belonging to a community.

Income is certainly one of the main means of expanding choices and well-being. But it is not the sum total of people's lives.

Current global concerns and human development

Here is how human development relates to current global concerns:

• *Human rights.* Human development leads to the realization of human rights—economic, social, cultural, civil and political. The human development perspective takes an integrated view of all human rights—not the narrow and exclusive focus on civil and political rights. It provides a framework in which advancing human development is commensurate with realizing human rights.

The 1948 Universal Declaration of Human Rights affirms that "everyone has the right to a standard of living adequate for the health and well-being of himself and his family, including food, clothing, housing and medical care and necessary social services ... Everyone has the right ... to education ... to work ... [and] to social security." Subsequent international human rights instruments reaffirmed people-centred development as a universal right—identifying as additional dimensions the right to security, participation, freedom of association, freedom from discrimination and exclusion from development.

• *Collective well-being.* Individual rights, choices and opportunities cannot, however, be unlimited. One person's freedom can constrain or violate the freedom of many others. As the reaction to the excessive individualism of the free market shows, there is a need for socially responsible forms of development. Individual and collective well-being are intertwined, and human development requires strong social cohesion and equitable distribution of the benefits of progress to avoid tension between the two. And the power of collective action is an essential driving force in the pursuit of human development.

• *Equity.* Concerns for equity take centre stage in the human development perspective. The notion of equity is most often applied to wealth or income. But human development emphasizes equity in basic capabilities and opportunities for all—equity in access to education, in health, in political rights.

• *Sustainability.* Sustainability means meeting the needs of present generations without compromising the abilities and opportunities of future generations. It thus implies both intra-generational and intergenerational equity. Sustainability is an important dimension of human development. Human development is a process of enlarging people's choices. But such enhancement must be for both present and future generations without sacrificing one for the other.

In the 1990s there have been major global debates on sustainable development (United Nations Conference on Environment and Development in Rio, 1992) and for people-centred sustainable development (World Summit for Social Development in Copenhagen, 1995). These have a common core, not to be missed, with human development. Human development is not a concept separate from sustainable development—but it can help to rescue "sustainable development" from the misconception that it involves only the environmental dimension of development.

All these approaches have emphasized the need for people-centred development, with concerns for human empowerment, participation, gender equality, equitable growth, poverty reduction and long-term sustainability.

Measuring human development—human development index

Human Development Reports, since the first in 1990, have published the human development index (HDI) as a measure of human development. Recognize, however, that the concept of human development is much broader than the HDI. It is impossible to come up with a comprehensive measure—or even a comprehensive set of indicators—because many vital dimensions of human development are non-quantifiable. But a simple composite measure of human development can draw attention to the issues quite effectively. The HDI is not a substitute for the fuller treatment of the richness of the concerns of the human development perspective.

The HDI measures the overall achievements in a country in three basic dimensions of human development—longevity, knowledge and a decent standard of living. It is measured by life expectancy, educational attainment (adult literacy and combined primary, secondary and tertiary enrolment) and adjusted income.

Human poverty index

While the HDI measures overall progress in a country in achieving human development, the human poverty index (HPI) reflects the distribution of progress and measures the backlog of deprivations that still exists. The HPI measures deprivation in the same dimensions of basic human development as the HDI.

HPI-1

The HPI-1 measures poverty in developing countries. The variables used are the percentage of people expected to die before age 40, the percentage of adults who are illiterate and deprivation in overall economic provisioning—public and private—reflected by the percentage of people without access to health services and safe water and the percentage of underweight children under five.

HPI-2

Introduced in this year's Report, the HPI-2 measures human poverty in industrial countries. Because human deprivation varies with the social and economic conditions of a community, this separate index has been devised for industrial countries, drawing on the greater availability of data. It focuses on deprivation in the same three dimensions as HPI-1 and one additional one, social exclusion. The variables are the percentage of people likely to die before age 60, the percentage of people whose ability to read and write is far from adequate, the proportion of people with disposable incomes of less than 50% of the median and the proportion of long-term unemployed (12 months or more).

Gender-related development index

The gender-related development index (GDI) measures achievements in the same dimensions and variables as the HDI, but captures inequalities in achievement between women and men. It is simply the HDI adjusted downward for gender inequality. The greater the gender disparity in basic human development, the lower a country's GDI compared with its HDI.

Gender empowerment measure

The gender empowerment measure (GEM) reveals whether women can take active part in economic and political life. It focuses on participation, measuring gender inequality in key areas of economic and political participation and decision-making. It tracks the percentages of women in parliament, among administrators and managers and among professional and technical workers—and women's earned income share as a percentage of men's. Differing from the GDI, it exposes inequality in opportunities in selected areas.

HDI, GDI, HPI-1, HPI-2—Same components, different measurements

	Longevity	Knowledge	Decent standard of living	Participation or exclusion
HDI	Life expectancy at birth	1. Adult literacy rate 2. Combined enrolment ratio	Adjusted per capita income in PPP$	–
GDI	Female and male life expectancy at birth	1. Female and male adult literacy rate 2. Female and male combined enrolment ratio	Female and male earned income share	–
HPI-1	Percentage of people not expected to survive to age 40	Illiteracy rate	Deprivation in economic provisioning, measured by: 1. Percentage of people without access to water and health services 2. Percentage of underweight children under five	–
HPI-2	Percentage of people not expected to survive to age 60	Functional illiteracy rate[a]	Percentage of people living below the income poverty line (50% of median disposable income)	Long-term unemployment rate (12 months or more)

a. Based on level 1 prose literacy according to the results of the OECD International Adult Literacy Survey.

CHAPTER 1

The state of human development

The human development perspective has moved into the mainstream of global debate

The state of human development is improving. But the overall progress is marked by great inequalities between people and countries and is threatened by setbacks. Human development—a process of expanding human choices by enabling people to enjoy long, healthy and creative lives (see pages 14 and 15)—faces constant challenges, new problems to overcome and achievements reversed.

This chapter provides a general overview of advances and setbacks in human development—with the theme of consumption patterns addressed in subsequent chapters. The highlights of this chapter:

• The rapid spread of national human development reports as a tool for advocacy and policy dialogue reflects the growing recognition of the need for a people-centred policy focus in national development. Their impact is described.

• Advances are contrasted with setbacks and slowdowns, providing a comprehensive view of the state of human development.

• Human poverty and deprivation remain a formidable challenge in both rich and poor countries. A new human poverty index measures the extent of human poverty in industrial countries.

• Gender inequalities and persisting disparities between rich and poor, between urban and rural and among ethnic groups are illustrated. Results from this year's gender-related development index and gender empowerment measure are presented.

• Human development remains fragile and reversible, as shown by evidence presented on the current threats from armed conflicts, economic setbacks and the AIDS epidemic.

Wider recognition of human development

The human development perspective has moved into the mainstream of the global development debate. The concept of human development provides an alternative to the view of development equated exclusively with economic growth. Human development focuses on people. And it sees economic growth and higher consumption not as ends in themselves but as means to achieve human development.

Nonetheless, concern with economic growth as an end in itself continues to dominate policy choices—often measuring success and failure in terms of changes in GDP and stock market performance rather than focusing on how economic growth can promote human development in a sustainable and equitable manner. Human development has yet to enter into many aspects of policy-making and frameworks for action.

But many years of popular action for social justice—intensified by the growth of civil society movements and the globalization of information—have set the stage for the humanization of development priorities. In nearly every country people are increasingly mobilizing—through their actions, organizations and movements—to push for human development. And they are having a significant impact on the policy focus of governments and international institutions. The democratic space for people's action is expanding in most countries—with freedom of association, freedom of the media, stronger judicial activism, more opportunities for public-private partnership and growing social and political awareness. Inevitably, the demand for human development will continue to intensify.

100 countries with national human development reports

Bangladesh, Cameroon, Pakistan and the Philippines published the first national human development reports in 1992. Today more than 100 countries have issued national human development reports with UNDP support (table 1.1). There also are four regional reports, each covering several countries, including the South Asia report prepared by the first non-governmental institute focused exclusively on human development—the Human Development Centre in Pakistan. This explosive growth is clear evidence of the growing commitment to shifting development towards people-centred, multifaceted approaches.

The global *Human Development Report,* published annually since 1990, triggered extensive national debate about the importance of focusing on people and their capabilities and opportunities as the goal of development efforts. It also has drawn attention to the formidable challenges in many developing countries in accelerating human development. Guinea is probably the most striking example. Its ranking as lowest in human development in 1993 prompted a "national soul-searching" about the lack of progress. This led to the formulation of a national human development policy framework, a national human development programme and the publication of a national human development report.

The longest-running series of annual reports is from Bangladesh, starting in 1992. Almost all countries in Eastern Europe and the Commonwealth of Independent States (CIS) have produced annual reports since 1995. Even subnational reports have been produced—for the Indian state of Madhya Pradesh, for La Paz, Cochabamba and Santa Cruz in Bolivia and for Sofia in Bulgaria. All these reports offer in-depth, focused perspectives on local circumstances and country-specific strategies for advancing human development.

National teams prepare these reports through a process of consultation with the government and its development partners. New and unique as a focus for dialogue, the reports assess the state of human develop-

TABLE 1.1

Countries and regions that have produced human development reports

Sub-Saharan Africa

Angola, *1996, 1997*
Benin, *1997*
Botswana, *1993*
Burkina Faso, *1997*
Burundi, *1997*
Cameroon, *1992, 1993, 1996*
Cape Verde, *1997*
Central African Rep., *1996*
Chad, *1998*
Comoros, *1997*
Côte d'Ivoire, *1998*
Equatorial Guinea, *1997*
Ethiopia, *1997*
Gambia, *1997*
Ghana, *1997*
Guinea, *1997*
Guinea-Bissau, *1997*
Kenya, *1998*
Lesotho, *1998*
Liberia, *1998*
Madagascar, *1996, 1997*
Malawi, *1997*
Mali, *1995*
Mauritania, *1996*
Namibia, *1996, 1997*
Niger, *1997*
Nigeria, *1996, 1997*
Sierra Leone, *1996*
Swaziland, *1998*
Tanzania, U. Rep. of, *1998*
Togo, *1994, 1995*
Uganda, *1996, 1997*
Zambia, *1997*

Regional
Africa, *1995*

Asia and the Pacific

Bangladesh, *1992, 1993, 1994, 1995, 1996, 1997*
Cambodia, *1997*
China, *1998*
Indonesia, *1997*
Iran, Islamic Rep. of, *1998*
Korea, Rep. of, *1998*
Lao People's Dem. Rep., *1998*
Madhya Pradesh, India,[a] *1995*
Mongolia, *1997*
Myanmar, *1997*
Nepal, *1997*

Pakistan, *1992*
Papua New Guinea, *1998*
Philippines, *1992, 1994, 1997*
Sri Lanka, *1998*
Thailand, *1998*
Viet Nam, *1998*

Regional
Pacific Islands, *1994*
South Asia, *1997, 1998*

Eastern Europe and CIS

Albania, *1995, 1996, 1997, 1998*
Armenia, *1995, 1996, 1997, 1998*
Azerbaijan, *1995, 1996, 1997, 1998*
Belarus, *1995, 1996, 1997, 1998*
Bosnia and Herzegovina, *1998*
Bulgaria, *1995, 1996, 1997, 1998*
  Sofia[a], *1997*
Croatia, *1997, 1998*
Czech Republic, *1996, 1997, 1998*
Estonia, *1995, 1996, 1997, 1998*
Georgia, *1995, 1996, 1997, 1998*
Hungary, *1995, 1996, 1998*
Kazakhstan *1995, 1996, 1997, 1998*
Kyrgyzstan, *1995, 1996, 1997, 1998*
Latvia, *1995, 1996, 1997, 1998*
Lithuania, *1995, 1996, 1997, 1998*
Macedonia, FYR, *1997, 1998*
Malta, *1996, 1998*
Moldova, Rep. of, *1995, 1996, 1997, 1998*
Poland, *1995, 1996, 1997, 1998*
Romania, *1995, 1996, 1997, 1998*
Russian Federation, *1995, 1996, 1997, 1998*
Slovakia, *1996, 1997, 1998*

Tajikistan, *1995, 1996, 1997, 1998*
Turkey, *1995, 1996, 1997, 1998*
Turkmenistan, *1995, 1996, 1997, 1998*
Ukraine, *1995, 1996, 1997, 1998*
Uzbekistan, *1995, 1996, 1997, 1998*
Yugoslavia, *1996, 1997, 1998*

Regional
Europe and CIS, *1995, 1996*

Latin America and the Caribbean

Argentina, *1995, 1996*
Belize, *1996*
Bolivia, *1998*
  La Paz,[a] *1995*
  Cochabamba,[a] *1995*
  Santa Cruz,[a] *1996*
Brazil, *1996, 1998*
Chile, *1996, 1998*
Colombia, *1998*
Costa Rica, *1995, 1996, 1997*
Cuba, *1998*
Dominican Rep., *1997*
El Salvador, *1997*
Guatemala, *1998*
Guyana, *1996, 1997*
Honduras, *1998*
Paraguay, *1995, 1996*
Peru, *1997*
Trinidad and Tobago, *1997*
Uruguay, *1996*
Venezuela, *1995, 1997*

Arab States

Bahrain, *1997*
Egypt, *1994, 1995, 1996*
Iraq, *1994, 1995, 1996*
Kuwait, *1997*
Lebanon, *1997*
Morocco, *1997*
Qatar, *1997*
Sudan, *1997*
United Arab Emirates, *1997*
Yemen, *1997*

Occupied Palestinian territory,[b] *1997*

a. Subnational report.
b. Human development profile.
Source: Human Development Report Office.

ment in a country and advocate a policy environment for achieving human development goals. Many have had a significant impact (box 1.1).

What role do these reports play in promoting human development? Their scope and nature—and the processes for their preparation and follow-up—vary greatly

BOX 1.1

National human development reports—making an impact

National human development reports can be an effective tool for governments, civil society organizations, citizens, political representatives and academics in their joint efforts to promote human development. They bring people together and help build consensus. And with a degree of editorial independence, they open the door to new thinking and policy perspectives—essential for facing the challenges of human development and poverty eradication.

The Philippines—advocating human development as a national priority

The Philippine reports have changed development planning in the country.. Through an effective, transparent and consultative process, the reports have been prepared by a human development network—a partnership of academics, NGO representatives and government officials acting in their personal capacity. After the launch of the 1997 report President Fidel Ramos directed all local government units to devote at least 20% of their internal revenue to human development priorities. He asked the National Statistical Coordination Board to include the human development index regularly in the system of statistics used to track variations across provinces. He requested the Department of Budget and Management to provide budgetary support for a human development database. And he directed the Department of Interior and Local Government to closely monitor provincial and municipal human development indices—and to institute rewards for good performance.

Benin—monitoring human development for planning purposes

Benin's 1997 report informs policy-makers about progress and setbacks in human development and poverty—and provides policy analysis and recommendations. A new "observatory of social change" combines sophisticated indicator databases, household surveys, small strategic participatory assessments and a social accounting matrix to monitor human development and poverty and to analyse policy options and impacts. The national human development report has synthesized the results of all these research initiatives. The observatory's wide range of quantitative and qualitative information enabled the report to

maintain a sharp focus on the multidimensional aspects of human poverty. The report provided a critical contribution to the National Development Plan for 1998–2002, making poverty eradication the nation's top priority.

Egypt—addressing socio-economic disparities

Egypt's reports—analysing rural-urban dichotomies, regional disparities and gender gaps—became effective decision-support tools for national and subnational policy-making, for resource allocation and for the monitoring of progress. Since the country published its first report, all 26 of its governors have been meeting to jointly examine disparities in human development among and within governorates, and they have come up with fresh strategies to reduce them. They shifted developmental priorities and reallocated resources to underserved areas. They established a platform for action and monitoring to assess progress in reducing human development disparities using the national reports' findings and indicators as the basis for analysis. The People's Assembly and the Shora Council, the two houses of parliament, also use the reports for policy analysis.

Latvia—advocating social integration and poverty alleviation

The Latvian human development reports have addressed difficult issues common to many countries in transition—falling standards of living, rising poverty and growing income disparities—while also focusing on development issues of particular relevance to Latvia. Because of Latvia's ethnically and linguistically diverse population, the reports have given special emphasis to the challenge of social cohesion in the context of consolidating democracy and the shift to a market-based economy. Policy recommendations relate to the protection of human rights, good governance and the need for a fair judicial system, as well as the need to develop a national antipoverty strategy. The reports have contributed to the development of a national programme for protecting and promoting human rights, as well as a national programme for Latvian language training as a means for social integration. The government has also begun developing a national poverty alleviation strategy, again

prompted and inspired by the findings of the Latvian reports.

Brazil—allocating budgets for human development needs

Brazil's experience shows how a national human development report can receive high-profile attention and significantly change the way a government allocates its resources for development. The production of the 1996 report involved researchers from 25 institutions—government, NGOs, UN agencies and universities—and provided comprehensive, disaggregated information about human development in all 27 Brazilian states. The report led to several interesting initiatives. The state of Minas Gerais, for example, further disaggregated the human development index for all its municipalities. It then introduced the "Robin Hood law", to ensure that more tax revenues are allocated to municipalities that rank low on the index and perform poorly on other social and environmental indicators. Allocations to municipalities are also based on the successful adoption of concrete programmes to overcome the shortcomings detected. No longer will geographic area, economic power and population size be the only parameters for determining resource allocations to municipalities. Now the budgets also depend on the level of human development.

Russia—focusing academic attention on human development

The Russian human development reports—published annually since 1995—draw attention to the growing inequality, the spread of poverty and the withering of social protection in the country. The people-centred approach to assessing the impact of economic and social transition inspired many academics in Russia, and the economics department of the State University of Moscow has introduced a master's course on human development as a permanent part of its curriculum. The university has also organized a national seminar on human development in Russia, bringing together academics, students, researchers, government policy-makers and representatives from UN agencies. It is hoped that more such academic research will be initiated to provide an essential input into policy dialogue and development planning.

Source: UNDP 1995b, 1997b, 1997d and 1997e; UNDP and Instituto de Pesquisa Econômica Aplicada 1996; Egypt, Institute of National Planning 1996.

from country to country. And these are still the early stages. But a review of their uses reveals four main impacts:

- *Advocating human development.* The national reports bring human development concerns into the limelight, advocating a more people-centred approach to policy-making. They fill an important niche in the policy dialogue among development partners, complementing other government-led planning as well as civil society initiatives and donor-supported studies and reports.

- *Highlighting critical concerns.* In most countries the first national human development report provides a general profile of the state of human development, and subsequent reports address specific themes. Benin, Cambodia, Cameroon, Madagascar, Namibia, Nigeria, Sierra Leone and the Indian state of Madhya Pradesh have all issued reports focusing on poverty. Many of the reports in Eastern Europe and the CIS have had as their theme the transition from centrally planned to free market economies. And they are now beginning to focus on issues related to governance and human rights. The latest report from Namibia focused on HIV/AIDS and poverty. Bangladesh and the Philippines have issued reports on women and development—and Armenia, Lithuania and Poland reports on human settlements.

- *Focusing on equity when planning for development.* By providing comprehensive human development indicators and indices, the reports help to monitor progress and setbacks in human development and poverty. One of the most exciting features of many of the national reports is the disaggregation of the human development indices (HDI, GDI and HPI) by region, province, urban or rural residence or ethnic group, providing a practical focus on equity. This has proved useful as a planning tool for governments—to target development programmes and public spending to areas with shortfalls in human development.

- *Articulating people's perceptions and priorities.* Some reports provide interesting insights into people's perceptions of human development and their concerns and priorities and incorporate them into policy analysis. This was especially the case for the 1996 Bangladesh report, which gives equal weight to two different approaches to assessing poverty—an analytical study by academics based on data and survey results, and a comprehensive participatory appraisal by poor people themselves.

Progress and setbacks in human development

A child born today in a developing country can expect to live 16 years longer than a child born 35 years ago. Developing countries have covered as much distance in human development during the past 30 years as the industrial world managed over more than a century (figures 1.1, 1.2 and 1.3). Their infant mortality rate has been more than halved since 1960. The lives of more than 3 million children are being saved each year thanks to the extension of basic immunization over the past two decades. Child malnutrition rates have declined by a quarter. Combined primary and secondary school enrolment has more than doubled. And the share of rural families with access to safe water has risen from 10% to about 60%.

Every region made progress in human development—as measured by the human development index—over the past three decades. This index, worked out for 174 countries having comparable data, measures the overall progress of a country along three dimensions of human development—health, knowledge and a decent standard of living.

What does this year's HDI reveal?

- Canada, France, Norway and the United States rank at the top on the HDI (table 1.2). Among developing countries Cyprus and Barbados are at the top—with HDIs of 0.913 and 0.909, only marginally lower than those of Greece, Italy and Israel (table 1.3).

- Some regions of the world have more ground to cover in making up shortfalls than others. Among developing regions South Asia has almost twice as much distance to cover as East Asia—and more than three times as much as Latin America and the Caribbean.

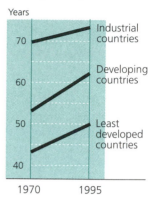

FIGURE 1.1
Life expectancy

Source: Human Development Report Office.

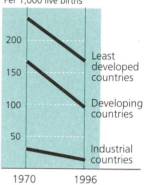

FIGURE 1.2
Under-five mortality rate

Source: Human Development Report Office.

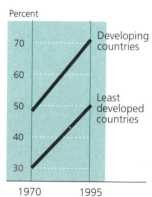

FIGURE 1.3
Adult literacy rate

Source: Human Development Report Office.

FIGURE 1.4
Similar HDI, different income

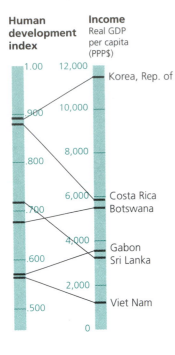

Source: Human Development Report Office.

FIGURE 1.5
Similar income, different HDI

Source: Human Development Report Office.

• Wide disparities in human development persist. Canada's HDI value of 0.960 is more than five times Sierra Leone's 0.185. Thus Canada has to make up a shortfall in human development of only 4%, Sierra Leone one of 82%.

• Of the 174 countries, 98 rank higher on the HDI than on GDP per capita (PPP$), suggesting that they have converted economic prosperity into human capabilities very effectively. This achievement is noteworthy for such low-income countries as Lesotho, Madagascar, the United Republic of Tanzania and Viet Nam.

• For 73 countries the ranking on the HDI is lower than that on GDP per capita (PPP$), suggesting that they have failed to translate economic prosperity into correspondingly better lives for their people. This is particularly disturbing for some of the more affluent (Brunei Darussalam, Kuwait, Mauritius and Qatar) and equally so for some of the poorest (Angola, Iraq, Lao People's Democratic Republic, Senegal and Uganda).

The link between economic prosperity and human development is thus neither automatic nor obvious (figures 1.4 and 1.5).

Progress in human development can be further illuminated by an assessment of some of its essential dimensions—health, knowledge, participation and human security.

Health—improving

During the past 36 years life expectancy at birth has increased in developing countries, from 46 to 62 years. But while East Asia and Latin America and the Caribbean have achieved a life expectancy of nearly 70 years, in Sub-Saharan Africa it is still only 50 years. The world's fastest progress in raising life expectancy since 1970 has been in Oman, Yemen, Saudi Arabia and Viet Nam (table 1.4). But in Uganda, Zambia and Zimbabwe the spread of HIV/AIDS has set back the average to less than 50 years.

Much of the progress reflects improvements in the life expectancy for women in developing countries, up by 10 years in the past 25 years, 20% more than for men.

TABLE 1.2
HDI ranking for industrial countries, 1995

Country	HDI value	HDI rank	Real GDP per capita (PPP$) 1995	Real GDP per capita (PPP$) rank minus HDI rank[a]
Canada	0.960	1	21,916	10
France	0.946	2	21,176	12
Norway	0.943	3	22,427	5
USA	0.943	4	26,977	−1
Iceland	0.942	5	21,064	10
Finland	0.942	6	18,547	17
Netherlands	0.941	7	19,876	11
Japan	0.940	8	21,930	2
New Zealand	0.939	9	17,267	17
Sweden	0.936	10	19,297	12
Spain	0.935	11	14,789	19
Belgium	0.933	12	21,548	0
Austria	0.933	13	21,322	0
United Kingdom	0.932	14	19,302	7
Australia	0.932	15	19,632	5
Switzerland	0.930	16	24,881	−12
Ireland	0.930	17	17,590	8
Denmark	0.928	18	21,983	−9
Germany	0.925	19	20,370	−3
Greece	0.924	20	11,636	15
Italy	0.922	21	20,174	−4
Israel	0.913	22	16,699	6
Luxembourg	0.900	26	34,004	−25
Malta	0.899	27	13,316	5
Portugal	0.892	33	12,674	1
Slovenia	0.887	37	10,594	1
Czech Rep.	0.884	39	9,775	2
Slovakia	0.875	42	7,320	9
Hungary	0.857	47	6,793	6
Poland	0.851	52	5,442	17
Bulgaria	0.789	67	4,604	8
Belarus	0.783	68	4,398	11
Russian Federation	0.769	72	4,531	5
Romania	0.767	74	4,431	4
Croatia	0.759	76	3,972	10
Estonia	0.758	77	4,062	5
Lithuania	0.750	79	3,843	12
Macedonia, FYR	0.749	80	4,058	3
Latvia	0.704	92	3,273	8
Kazakhstan	0.695	93	3,037	11
Armenia	0.674	99	2,208	24
Ukraine	0.665	102	2,361	16
Turkmenistan	0.660	103	2,345	17
Uzbekistan	0.659	104	2,376	13
Albania	0.656	105	2,853	3
Georgia	0.633	108	1,389	33
Kyrgyzstan	0.633	109	1,927	18
Azerbaijan	0.623	110	1,463	28
Moldova, Rep. of	0.610	113	1,547	23
Tajikistan	0.575	118	943	43

a. A positive figure indicates that the HDI rank is better than the real GDP per capita (PPP$) rank, a negative the opposite.
Source: Human Development Report Office.

TABLE 1.3
HDI ranking for developing countries, 1995

Country	HDI value	HDI rank	Real GDP per capita (PPP$) 1995	Real GDP per capita (PPP$) rank minus HDI rank[a]	Country	HDI value	HDI rank	Real GDP per capita (PPP$) 1995	Real GDP per capita (PPP$) rank minus HDI rank[a]
Cyprus	0.913	23	13,379	8	Guatemala	0.615	111	3,682	−16
Barbados	0.909	24	11,306	13	Egypt	0.612	112	3,829	−20
Hong Kong, China	0.909	25	22,950	−19	El Salvador	0.604	114	2,610	−2
Singapore	0.896	28	22,604	−21	Swaziland	0.597	115	2,954	−10
Antigua and Barbuda	0.895	29	9,131	16	Bolivia	0.593	116	2,617	−6
					Cape Verde	0.591	117	2,612	−6
Korea, Rep. of	0.894	30	11,594	6					
Chile	0.893	31	9,930	9	Honduras	0.573	119	1,977	7
Bahamas	0.893	32	15,738	−3	Gabon	0.568	120	3,766	−26
Costa Rica	0.889	34	5,969	28	São Tomé and Principe	0.563	121	1,744	11
Brunei Darussalam	0.889	35	31,165	−33	Viet Nam	0.560	122	1,236	26
					Solomon Islands	0.560	123	2,230	−2
Argentina	0.888	36	8,498	11					
Uruguay	0.885	38	6,854	14	Vanuatu	0.559	124	2,507	−9
Trinidad and Tobago	0.880	40	9,437	3	Morocco	0.557	125	3,477	−27
Dominica	0.879	41	6,424	15	Nicaragua	0.547	126	1,837	3
Bahrain	0.872	43	16,751	−16	Iraq	0.538	127	3,170	−25
					Congo	0.519	128	2,554	−14
Fiji	0.869	44	6,159	16					
Panama	0.868	45	6,258	14	Papua New Guinea	0.507	129	2,500	−13
Venezuela	0.860	46	8,090	2	Zimbabwe	0.507	130	2,135	−6
United Arab Emirates	0.855	48	18,008	−24	Myanmar	0.481	131	1,130	22
Mexico	0.855	49	6,769	5	Cameroon	0.481	132	2,355	−13
					Ghana	0.473	133	2,032	−8
Saint Kitts and Nevis	0.854	50	10,150	−11					
Grenada	0.851	51	5,425	19	Lesotho	0.469	134	1,290	12
Colombia	0.850	53	6,347	4	Equatorial Guinea	0.465	135	1,712	−1
Kuwait	0.848	54	23,848	−49	Lao People's Dem. Rep.	0.465	136	2,571	−23
Saint Vincent	0.845	55	5,969	6	Kenya	0.463	137	1,438	2
					Pakistan	0.453	138	2,209	−16
Seychelles	0.845	56	7,697	−6					
Qatar	0.840	57	19,772	−38	India	0.451	139	1,422	1
Saint Lucia	0.839	58	6,530	−3	Cambodia	0.422	140	1,110	14
Thailand	0.838	59	7,742	−10	Comoros	0.411	141	1,317	3
Malaysia	0.834	60	9,572	−18	Nigeria	0.391	142	1,270	5
					Dem. Rep. of the Congo	0.383	143	355	31
Mauritius	0.833	61	13,294	−28					
Brazil	0.809	62	5,928	1	Togo	0.380	144	1,167	6
Belize	0.807	63	5,623	1	Benin	0.378	145	1,800	−14
Libyan Arab Jamahiriya	0.806	64	6,309	−6	Zambia	0.378	146	986	11
Suriname	0.796	65	4,862	9	Bangladesh	0.371	147	1,382	−4
					Côte d'Ivoire	0.368	148	1,731	−15
Lebanon	0.796	66	4,977	7					
Turkey	0.782	69	5,516	−2	Mauritania	0.361	149	1,622	−14
Saudi Arabia	0.778	70	8,516	−24	Tanzania, U. Rep. of	0.358	150	636	20
Oman	0.771	71	9,383	−27	Yemen	0.356	151	856	12
Ecuador	0.767	73	4,602	3	Nepal	0.351	152	1,145	−1
					Madagascar	0.348	153	673	15
Korea, Dem. People's Rep. of	0.766	75	4,058	8					
Iran, Islamic Rep. of	0.758	78	5,480	−10	Central African Rep.	0.347	154	1,092	2
Syrian Arab Rep.	0.749	81	5,374	−10	Bhutan	0.347	155	1,382	−13
Algeria	0.746	82	5,618	−17	Angola	0.344	156	1,839	−28
Tunisia	0.744	83	5,261	−11	Sudan	0.343	157	1,110	−3
					Senegal	0.342	158	1,815	−28
Jamaica	0.735	84	3,801	9					
Cuba	0.729	85	3,100	18	Haiti	0.340	159	917	3
Peru	0.729	86	3,940	2	Uganda	0.340	160	1,483	−23
Jordan	0.729	87	4,187	−6	Malawi	0.334	161	773	5
Dominican Rep.	0.720	88	3,923	1	Djibouti	0.324	162	1,300	−17
					Chad	0.318	163	1,172	−14
South Africa	0.717	89	4,334	−9					
Sri Lanka	0.716	90	3,408	9	Guinea-Bissau	0.295	164	811	0
Paraguay	0.707	91	3,583	5	Gambia	0.291	165	948	−5
Western Samoa	0.694	94	2,948	12	Mozambique	0.281	166	959	−7
Maldives	0.683	95	3,540	2	Guinea	0.277	167	1,139	−15
					Eritrea	0.275	168	983	−10
Indonesia	0.679	96	3,971	−9					
Botswana	0.678	97	5,611	−31	Ethiopia	0.252	169	455	4
Philippines	0.677	98	2,762	11	Burundi	0.241	170	637	−1
Guyana	0.670	100	3,205	1	Mali	0.236	171	565	1
Mongolia	0.669	101	3,916	−11	Burkina Faso	0.219	172	784	−7
					Niger	0.207	173	765	−6
China	0.650	106	2,935	1	Sierra Leone	0.185	174	625	−3
Namibia	0.644	107	4,054	−22					

a. A positive figure indicates that the HDI rank is better than the real GDP per capita (PPP$) rank, a negative the opposite.
Source: Human Development Report Office.

TABLE 1.4

**Fastest progress and biggest setbacks:
life expectancy in developing countries, 1970–95**
(years)

Country	Life expectancy at birth 1970	Life expectancy at birth 1995	Percentage change 1970–95	Country	Life expectancy at birth 1995
Fastest progress				*Highest life expectancy*	
Oman	47	70	50	Hong Kong, China	79
Yemen	41	57	39	Cyprus	77
Saudi Arabia	52	71	36	Singapore	77
Viet Nam	49	66	35	Costa Rica	77
Indonesia	48	64	34	Barbados	76
Nepal	42	56	33	Cuba	76
Bolivia	46	61	32	Kuwait	75
Honduras	53	69	31	Chile	75
Bhutan	40	52	30	Brunei Darussalam	75
Lao People's Dem. Rep.	40	52	29	United Arab Emirates	74
Slowest progress—and setbacks				*Lowest life expectancy*	
Uganda	46	41	–12	Rwanda	28
Zambia	46	43	–8	Sierra Leone	35
Zimbabwe	50	49	–3	Liberia	40
Botswana	52	52	0	Uganda	41
Sierra Leone	34	35	1	Malawi	41
Burundi	44	45	2	Zambia	43
Malawi	40	41	2	Guinea-Bissau	43
Paraguay	66	69	6	Afghanistan	45
Uruguay	69	73	6	Burundi	45
Iraq	55	59	6	Guinea	46

Source: Human Development Report Office.

TABLE 1.5

**Fastest and slowest progress:
under-five mortality rate in developing countries, 1970–95**
(per 1,000 live births)

Country	Under-five mortality rate 1970	Under-five mortality rate 1995	Percentage change 1970–95	Country	Under-five mortality rate 1995
Fastest progress				*Lowest under-five mortality rate*	
Oman	200	18	–91	Korea, Rep. of	7
United Arab Emirates	150	19	–87	Singapore	5
Korea, Rep. of	55	7	–87	Cuba	10
Brunei Darussalam	78	11	–86	Cyprus	10
Chile	96	14	–85	Brunei Darussalam	11
Saudi Arabia	185	32	–83	Barbados	12
Tunisia	201	37	–82	Jamaica	13
Singapore	27	5	–82	Malaysia	13
Iran, Islamic Rep. of	208	40	–81	Chile	14
Malaysia	63	13	–79	Kuwait	14
Slowest progress				*Highest under-five mortality rate*	
Zambia	181	202	12ª	Niger	320
Niger	320	320	0	Angola	292
Angola	301	292	–3	Sierra Leone	284
Iraq	127	122	–4	Afghanistan	257
Nigeria	200	191	–5	Guinea-Bissau	227
Papua New Guinea	130	112	–14	Liberia	235
Dem. Rep. of the Congo	245	207	–16	Mali	225
Myanmar	178	150	–16	Mozambique	220
Guyana	101	84	–17	Malawi	219
Sierra Leone	345	284	–18	Guinea	215

a. Setback.
Source: Human Development Report Office.

Contrary to biological expectations (women normally live longer), women's life expectancy in the Maldives and Nepal is lower than men's—and in Bangladesh and India it is almost the same. In Asia and North Africa more than 100 million women are estimated to be "missing" because of such neglect.

In Eastern Europe and the CIS life expectancy is only one year higher than it was 35 years ago—68 years today, compared with 67 in 1960. This reflects the sharp decline in life expectancy after 1989 because of social and economic upheavals, especially the effect on men. In Russia male life expectancy is down by more than five years since 1989.

Life expectancy in the industrial countries continues to increase, contributing to a significant ageing of the population. Today around 150 million of their people, 13% of the total, are aged 65 and over—and more than 35 million are 80 years or older. This remarkable success presents a major challenge to provide enough health and other care for people as they age and become less self-reliant. But older people have experience and skills to enrich society. Societies must recognize them as assets rather than burdens.

The infant mortality rate in developing countries during the past 35 years has been more than halved—from 149 per 1,000 live births in 1960 to 65 in 1996—and the share of underweight children has declined from 40% to 30%.

Oman, the United Arab Emirates, the Republic of Korea and Brunei Darussalam have achieved the fastest progress in reducing under-five mortality since 1970 (table 1.5). The slowest progress is found in Zambia, Niger, Angola and Iraq.

Broader access to health services, safe water and sanitation—and the mobilization of public action, as for immunization—have made the difference. Today four-fifths of the people in developing countries have access to health services, and more than 70% to safe water. Nearly 90% of the one-year-olds in developing countries are now immunized against tuberculosis, and about 80% against diphtheria, pertussis, tetanus, polio and measles.

Knowledge—spreading

Between 1970 and 1995 adult literacy rates in developing countries increased by nearly half—from 48% to 70%. But compare nearly 90% in South-East Asia and the Pacific—and in Latin America and the Caribbean—with 51% in South Asia.

The improvements in female literacy have been similar. The rate increased by more than two-thirds in the past two decades, and in the Arab States it more than doubled, from 20% in 1970 to 44% in 1995.

Since 1970 the fastest progress in increasing adult literacy has been achieved in the Central African Republic, Mali, Benin and Nigeria (table 1.6). The slowest progress—among countries with literacy rates below 70%—has taken place in Nicaragua, Comoros, Mauritania and Malawi.

What accounts for the progress in literacy? Big improvements in school enrolment. Between 1960 and 1991 net primary enrolment rose from 48% to 77%, and net secondary from 35% to 47%. In South Asia the gains were more at the primary and secondary levels—in East Asia and in Latin America and the Caribbean, more at the secondary and tertiary levels.

Some of the biggest advances have been for women. Between 1970 and 1992 the female primary and secondary enrolment ratio in developing countries almost doubled, from 38% to 68%. And in East Asia (83%) and Latin America and the Caribbean (87%) it is approaching that of the industrial countries. South Asia (55%) has a long way to go.

Countries of Eastern Europe and the CIS have always prided themselves on high standards of education, but they have recently lost ground. In the past five years the primary and secondary enrolment ratio fell by 4% in Russia and by 6% in Bulgaria.

Industrial countries have achieved nearly 100% literacy rates and 85% enrolment ratios. But new surveys show that many people—18% of adults on average in 12 European and North American countries—though "literate", have such low levels of skills that they cannot meet even the basic reading requirements of a modern society.

Another 29% do not have the ability to be trained in skilled employment (box 1.2). Industrial countries may even start falling behind the fast-growing developing countries, especially in technical education. Fewer than a third of students in the industrial countries now enrol for applied or natural science—in Norway and the Netherlands only 1 student in 5. But in Chile, China, the Republic of Korea and South Africa the proportion is 1 in 2 or 1 in 3.

People's participation—broadening

About two-thirds of the world's people live under fairly democratic regimes. In Eastern Europe and the CIS almost all countries have held multiparty elections since 1990. In South Asia 15 parliamentary elections have taken place since 1990. In Latin America and the Caribbean nearly 90 general elections were held between 1987 and 1997. Democracy in this region has been strengthened and consolidated to the extent that no military coups have taken place in the past seven years.

TABLE 1.6

**Fastest and slowest progress:
adult literacy rate in developing countries, 1970–95**
(percent, age 15 and over)

Country	Adult literacy rate 1970	Adult literacy rate 1995	Percentage change 1970–95	Country	Adult literacy rate 1995
Fastest progress				*Highest adult literacy rate*	
Central African Rep.	13	60	380	Bahamas	98
Mali	7	31	331	Guyana	98
Benin	10	37	256	Korea, Rep. of	98
Nigeria	21	57	169	Trinidad and Tobago	98
Côte d'Ivoire	16	40	152	Barbados	97
Mozambique	16	40	152	Uruguay	97
Algeria	25	62	148	Argentina	96
Burkina Faso	8	19	146	Cuba	96
Sierra Leone	13	31	143	Chile	95
Gabon	26	63	142	Costa Rica	95
Slowest progress[a]				*Lowest adult literacy rate*	
Nicaragua	57	66	15	Niger	14
Comoros	42	57	37	Burkina Faso	19
Mauritania	27	38	40	Nepal	28
Malawi	38	56	48	Mali	31
Guatemala	44	65	48	Sierra Leone	31
India	34	52	55	Afghanistan	32
Bangladesh	25	38	55	Senegal	33
Botswana	44	70	59	Burundi	35
Egypt	32	51	60	Ethiopia	36
Uganda	37	62	68	Guinea	36

a. Among countries with an adult literacy rate of less than 70%.
Source: Human Development Report Office.

BOX 1.2

Adult literacy in OECD countries

Low literacy levels are usually thought of as a problem of developing, not industrial countries. Yet shortcomings in literacy skills limit the opportunities of a large proportion of people living in OECD countries. At least a quarter of the adult population in these countries lacks the minimum level of literacy needed to cope adequately with the complex demands of everyday life and work (failing to reach level 3, as explained below). This is all the more disquieting as societies move into the information age at breakneck speed, leaving many people behind and excluded from the benefits of progress.

Literacy is a powerful determinant of an individual's life choices and opportunities. This holds true in all countries, developing or industrial. Yet in many OECD countries policy-makers have tended not to recognize low literacy as a problem. Until fairly recently policy emphasis was placed mainly on "illiteracy", defined as the percentage of people without a minimum of four years of schooling. This approach proved unhelpful, not only because it used a proxy measure that effectively assigned literacy rates of 99–100% to many OECD countries, but also because it failed to draw attention to the dynamic nature of literacy. At issue in all countries is the ability to read with increased levels of competence, to keep up with the evolving demands of a competitive and knowledge-based society.

The first International Adult Literacy Survey, coordinated by the OECD, aimed to measure the degree of literacy in a country from this perspective. For this survey literacy was defined as a continuum of proficiency levels denoting how well adults use written information to function in society. Literacy is a particular skill—the ability to understand and use printed information in daily activities at home, at work and in the community.

The survey assessed literacy proficiency in three domains:

• Prose literacy—the knowledge and skills needed to understand and use information from printed texts, including editorials, news stories, poems and fiction.

• Document literacy—the knowledge and skills required to locate and use information in different formats, such as job applications, payroll forms, transportation schedules, maps, tables and charts.

• Quantitative literacy—the knowledge and skills required to apply arithmetic operations, either alone or sequentially, to numbers embedded in printed materials, such as balancing a cheque-book, figuring out a tip, completing an order form or determining the interest on a loan from an advertisement.

In each domain scores were grouped into five levels. Level 1 indicates very poor skills, such as when an individual might be unable to determine the correct amount of medicine to give a child from information printed on the package. Level 4/5 describes respondents who demonstrate the capacity to use more complex thinking and information processing skills.

BOX TABLE 1.2
Adult population at each prose literacy level, 1994–95
(percent, age 16–65)

Country	Level 1	Level 2	Level 3	Level 4/5
Sweden	7.5	20.3	39.7	32.4
Netherlands	10.5	30.1	44.1	15.3
Germany	14.4	34.2	38.0	13.4
Canada	16.6	25.6	35.1	22.7
Australia	17.0	27.1	36.9	18.9
Switzerland (French speaking)	17.6	33.7	38.6	10.0
Belgium (Flanders speaking)	18.4	28.2	39.0	14.3
New Zealand	18.4	27.3	35.0	19.2
Switzerland (German speaking)	19.3	35.7	36.0	8.9
USA	20.7	25.9	32.4	21.1
United Kingdom	21.8	30.3	31.3	16.6
Ireland	22.6	29.8	34.1	13.5
Poland	42.6	34.5	19.8	3.1

Source: OECD, Human Resources Development Canada and Statistics Canada 1997.

Sub-Saharan Africa has also been swept by democratic reforms, an event just as dramatic as the political changes in the former Soviet Union, though it has received much less attention from the world community. Nearly all countries in the region have undertaken democratic reforms and legalized opposition parties, changes often championed by students, labour unions and other civil society movements. Between 1990 and 1994, 38 of the region's 47 countries held competitive legislative elections. But democracy in Africa is still in its infancy and is vulnerable to setbacks. Some countries are taking a step back, with military take-overs and political unrest. The big challenge remains to consolidate democracy—by strengthening civil society organizations, freeing the media of all constraints and providing real opportunities for people to participate in politics at all levels.

Despite the wave of democracy, women everywhere do not enjoy the same opportunities for participating in public life as men. They constitute fewer than a third of administrators and managers—and occupy only 12% of parliamentary seats and 7% of cabinet positions.

A majority of governments have made a legally binding commitment to respect the civil and political rights of their citizens. So far, 140 countries have ratified the International Covenant on Civil and Political Rights. Three countries are at the door—having signed but not yet ratified (see indicator table 48). Forty-two countries have signed the optional protocol of the covenant, recognizing the authority of the United Nations Human Rights Committee to consider claims from alleged victims of violations.

People are taking a bigger part in civil society movements as NGOs and people's movements in developing countries increase in number and take on bigger roles in voicing people's aspirations and working as pressure groups. This grass-roots progress towards greater participation is probably even more significant than the number of elections.

Human security—under siege

Human security—another essential dimension of human development—involves safety from such chronic threats as hunger, disease and repression. It also involves protection from sudden and hurtful disruptions in people's daily lives—in the home, workplace and community.

In poor nations and rich, human life is under threat from crime, accidents and violence. Reported crimes worldwide were increasing by 5% a year in the late 1970s and early 1980s—faster than the growth in population. Recently, however, some countries with disturbingly rampant crime have been witnessing improvements. In the United States incidents of violent crime have fallen three years in a row, and between 1995 and 1996 the number declined from 3 million to 2.7 million, the lowest level since surveying began 24 years ago.

Industrial and traffic accidents also present great risks. In most industrial countries the number one killer of people aged 15–30 is accidental injury. In developing countries traffic injuries account for at least half of accidental deaths, and in Thailand, for example, the death rate due to traffic accidents quintupled between 1962 and 1992, from 4 per 100,000 people to 20.

Another threat to human security: inadequate and illegal housing. More than a billion people live in inadequate shelter, without piped water, electricity, roads or, in most cases, security of tenure. Between 30% and 60% of the people in developing countries live in illegal settlements, and around 100 million are thought to be homeless. Such conditions leave people constantly exposed to overcrowding, chronic diseases, environmental disasters, evictions and other sudden new threats, undermining progress in human development.

Domestic violence—an often hidden but universal scourge—causes physical and persistent mental suffering, disrupts women's lives and blocks their personal growth and participation in society. In Thailand a study shows that more than 50% of married women living in Bangkok's biggest slum are regularly beaten by their husbands. In Santiago, Chile, 80% of women acknowledged being victims of violence in their homes. Every nine seconds in the United States a woman is physically abused by her partner.

Human poverty and deprivation

Despite the remarkable progress in human development, the backlog of human poverty remains pervasive.

Human poverty, a concept introduced in *Human Development Report 1997,* sees impoverishment as multidimensional. More than a lack of what is necessary for material well-being, poverty can also mean the denial of opportunities and choices most basic to human development. To lead a long, healthy, creative life. To have a decent standard of living. To enjoy dignity, self-esteem, the respect of others and the things that people value in life.

Human poverty thus looks at more than a lack of income. Since income is not the sum total of human lives, the lack of it cannot be the sum total of human deprivation.

Measuring human poverty in developing countries

Human Development Report 1997 introduced the human poverty index (HPI) in an attempt to bring together in a composite index the different dimensions of deprivation in human life. The HPI provides an aggregate human measure of the prevalence of poverty in a community. It is important to keep in mind that the *concept* of human poverty is much bigger than the *measure,* for it is difficult to reflect all dimensions of human poverty in a single quantifiable composite indicator. Lack of political freedom, lack of personal security, inability to participate freely in the life of a community and threats to sustainability can hardly be measured and quantified. The HPI nonetheless draws attention to deprivations in three essential elements of human life already reflected in the HDI—longevity, knowledge and a decent living standard.

What's the difference between the HDI and the HPI? The HDI measures progress in a community or country as a whole. The HPI measures the extent of deprivation, the proportion of people in the community who are left out of progress.

Estimates of the HPI for developing countries (HPI-1) have been worked out for 77 countries with comparable data (see

Since income is not the sum total of human lives, the lack of it cannot be the sum total of human deprivation

TABLE 1.7
Human poverty index (HPI-1) for developing countries

Country	Human poverty index (HPI-1) value (%)	HPI-1 rank	HPI-1 rank minus HDI rank[a]	HPI-1 rank minus $1-a-day poverty rank[a]	Country	Human poverty index (HPI-1) value (%)	HPI-1 rank	HPI-1 rank minus HDI rank[a]	HPI-1 rank minus $1-a-day poverty rank[a]
Trinidad and Tobago	3.3	1	−4	..	Papua New Guinea	29.8	40	−1	..
Chile	4.1	2	0	−13	Namibia	30.0	41	11	..
Uruguay	4.1	3	−1	..	Iraq	30.1	42	3	..
Singapore	6.5	4	3	..	Cameroon	30.9	43	−1	..
Costa Rica	6.6	5	2	−15	Congo	31.5	44	4	..
Jordan	10.0	6	−15	−1	Ghana	31.8	45	0	..
Mexico	10.7	7	−1	−9	Egypt	34.0	46	14	16
Colombia	11.1	8	−1	−4	India	35.9	47	−3	−11
Panama	11.1	9	3	−13	Zambia	36.9	48	−7	−14
Jamaica	11.8	10	−9	0	Lao People's Dem. Rep.	39.4	49	2	..
Thailand	11.9	11	1	7	Togo	39.8	50	−4	..
Mauritius	12.1	12	1	..	Tanzania, U. Rep. of	39.8	51	−8	14
Mongolia	14.0	13	−15	..	Cambodia	39.9	52	1	..
United Arab Emirates	14.5	14	7	..	Morocco	40.2	53	16	28
Ecuador	15.3	15	1	−16	Nigeria	40.5	54	2	8
China	17.1	16	−13	−14	Central African Rep.	40.7	55	−7	..
Libyan Arab Jamahiriya	17.4	17	5	..	Dem. Rep. of the Congo	41.1	56	3	..
Dominican Rep.	17.4	18	−4	−7	Uganda	42.1	57	−10	−2
Philippines	17.7	19	−8	−9	Sudan	42.5	58	−6	..
Paraguay	19.1	20	−4	..	Guinea-Bissau	42.9	59	−10	−10
Indonesia	20.2	21	−4	1	Haiti	44.5	60	−6	..
Sri Lanka	20.6	22	−1	8	Bhutan	44.9	61	−2	..
Syrian Arab Rep.	20.9	23	7	..	Mauritania	45.9	62	4	8
Bolivia	21.6	24	−10	7	Pakistan	46.0	63	14	24
Honduras	21.8	25	−10	−16	Côte d'Ivoire	46.4	64	7	20
Iran, Islamic Rep. of	22.2	26	11	..	Bangladesh	46.5	65	9	15
Peru	23.1	27	7	−16	Madagascar	47.7	66	5	−3
Tunisia	23.3	28	10	13	Malawi	47.7	67	−1	9
Zimbabwe	25.2	29	−13	−10	Mozambique	48.5	68	−2	..
Lesotho	25.7	30	−16	−16	Senegal	48.6	69	4	1
Viet Nam	26.1	31	−5	..	Yemen	48.9	70	10	..
Nicaragua	26.2	32	−6	−10	Guinea	49.1	71	0	21
Botswana	27.0	33	7	−6	Burundi	49.5	72	−1	..
Algeria	27.1	34	17	20	Mali	52.8	73	−1	..
Kenya	27.1	35	−13	−11	Ethiopia	55.5	74	2	15
Myanmar	27.5	36	−7	..	Sierra Leone	58.2	75	−2	..
El Salvador	27.8	37	4	..	Burkina Faso	58.2	76	1	..
Oman	28.9	38	25	..	Niger	62.1	77	1	3
Guatemala	29.3	39	8	−12					

Note: HDI and $1-a-day poverty ranks have been recalculated for the universe of 77 countries.
a. A negative figure indicates that the HPI-1 rank is better than the other, a positive the opposite.
Source: Human Development Report Office.

technical note 2). The HPI-1 value reflects the proportion of people affected by the three key deprivations—providing a comparative measure of the prevalence of human poverty. Here's what the HPI-1 reveals (table 1.7):

• The HPI-1 ranges from 3% in Trinidad and Tobago to 62% in Niger.

• Other countries with an HPI-1 of less than 10% are Chile, Uruguay, Singapore and Costa Rica.

• The HPI-1 exceeds 50% in Mali, Ethiopia, Sierra Leone, Burkina Faso and Niger.

• The HPI-1 exceeds 33% in 32 countries, implying that an average of at least a third of the people in these countries suffer from human poverty.

A comparison of HDI and HPI-1 values shows how well—or poorly—the average achievements in a country are distributed. China and Egypt have similar levels of overall human development, but the HPI-1 for China is only 17%, while that for Egypt is 34%. Similarly, Kenya and Pakistan are at par in the HDI, but the HPI-1 for Kenya is less than 30% and that for Pakistan is more than 45%. This reveals that the fruits of human development are distributed more inequitably in Egypt and Pakistan than in China and Kenya.

The HPI-1 also reveals deprivation that would be masked in the income measure of poverty. Egypt and Pakistan have reduced their income poverty to less than 15%. But human poverty in these countries remains much higher, at 34% and 46%. The HPI-1 also shows progress masked by the income measure of poverty. In Zimbabwe and Nicaragua, for example, income poverty is severe, at nearly 50%. But these countries have made much more progress in reducing human poverty, achieving HPI-1 values of 25% and 26%.

Measuring human poverty in industrial countries

Poverty and deprivation are not only a problem of the developing countries.
• On the basis of an income poverty line of 50% of the median personal disposable income, more than 100 million people are income-poor in OECD countries.
• At least 37 million people are without jobs in OECD countries, often deprived of adequate income and left with a sense of social exclusion from not participating in the life of their communities.
• Unemployment among youth (age 15–24) has reached staggering heights, with 32% of young women and 22% of young men in France unemployed, 39% and 30% in Italy and 49% and 36% in Spain.
• About 8% of the children in OECD countries—including half or more of children of single parents in Australia, Canada, the United Kingdom and the United States—live below the income poverty line of 50% of median disposable personal income.
• Nearly 200 million people are not expected to survive to age 60.
• More than 100 million are homeless, a shockingly high number amid the affluence.

To capture the multiple dimensions of poverty in a composite measure, an HPI for industrial countries (HPI-2) is introduced here, focusing on deprivation in the same three dimensions of human life as the HPI-1, but replacing the measures with ones that better reflect social and economic condi-

tions in these countries. And it adds a fourth dimension—social exclusion—for which the HPI-1 does not include a quantitative measure because no reliable data could be found. For industrial countries appropriate data are available.

The nature of deprivation in human life varies with the social and economic conditions of a community or country. Studies of poverty in the developing countries—with low levels of resources and human development—focus on hunger, epidemics, illiteracy and lack of health services and safe water. These issues are less dominant in industrial countries, where hunger is not as pervasive, primary schooling is nearly universal, most epidemics are well controlled, health services are typically widespread and safe water is easily available. Not surprisingly, typical studies of poverty in the more affluent countries concentrate on social exclusion, a complex and persistent deprivation difficult to eliminate in all countries, industrial and developing alike.

Although the dimensions used in the HPI-1, for developing countries, are equally relevant to industrial countries, the indicators used are not. A second index is needed, using indicators that reflect the way poverty is manifested in industrial countries.

The HPI-2 comprises:
• Deprivation in survival, measured by the percentage of the population likely to die before age 60.
• Deprivation in knowledge, measured by the percentage of the population functionally illiterate—lacking an ability to read and write adequate for the most basic demands of modern society, such as reading instructions on a medicine bottle or reading stories to children.
• Deprivation in economic provisioning, measured by the proportion of people whose disposable personal income is less than 50% of the median, leaving them unable to achieve the standard of living necessary to avoid hardship and to participate in the life of the community.
• Social exclusion, measured by one of its most critical aspects—the percentage of long-term unemployed (those out of work 12 months or more) in the total labour force.

The HPI-2 uses the same measures as the HPI-1 for survival and knowledge,

Poverty and deprivation are also major problems in industrial countries

applying a higher cut-off point. For economic provisioning and exclusion, new measures are used. These require explanation.

Social exclusion takes many forms, varies considerably from one community to another and is difficult to measure. But long-term unemployment, which is consistently monitored in most industrial countries, is a suitable proxy for exclusion. It reflects exclusion from the world of work and the social interaction associated with employment, which is an important part of social exclusion in most communities.

For economic provisioning the HPI-1 uses a combination of malnourishment and lack of access to water and health services, while the HPI-2 uses a headcount measure of income poverty. These divergent approaches were followed for three reasons.

First, the HPI-1 incorporates economic provisioning from both public and private income. Public provisioning is an important source of consumption for poor households, and key deprivations in this area are captured in lack of access to such services as health care and water. Deprivation in private provisioning focuses on food consumption, since by far the largest proportion of personal incomes of the poorest households in the poorest countries goes to food—more than 50%, sometimes more than 80%. For the HPI-2 these would not have been the most suitable measures because in industrial countries food is not the principal component of private income and because most people already have access to such basic public services as water.

Second, deprivation in income is a more appropriate measure for industrial countries because it reflects deprivation in the material means that people require. But the use of a single international poverty line can be misleading—because of variations in what are defined as "essential" commodities. Differences in the prevailing patterns of consumption—of clothing, housing and such means of communication as radios, televisions and telephones—mean that

TABLE 1.8
Human poverty index (HPI-2) for industrial countries

Countries	DEPRIVATION IN SURVIVAL — People not expected to survive to age 60 (%) 1995	DEPRIVATION IN KNOWLEDGE — People who are functionally illiterate[a] (% age 16–65) 1995	DEPRIVATION IN INCOME — Population below the income poverty line[b] (%) 1990	SOCIAL EXCLUSION — Long-term unemployment, 12 months or more (as % of total labour force) 1995[c]	HUMAN POVERTY INDEX — Human poverty index (HPI-2) for industrial countries Value (%)	HPI-2 rank	Real GDP per capita (PPP$) rank
Sweden	8	7.5	6.7	1.5	6.8	1	13
Netherlands	9	10.5	6.7	3.2	8.2	2	10
Germany	11	14.4	5.9	4.0	10.5	3	8
Norway	9	—[d]	6.6	1.3	11.3	4	2
Italy	9	—[d]	6.5	7.6	11.6	5	9
Finland	11	—[d]	6.2	6.1	11.8	6	14
France	11	—[d]	7.5	4.9	11.8	7	7
Japan	8	—[d]	11.8	0.6	12.0	8	4
Denmark	12	—[d]	7.5	2.0	12.0	9	3
Canada	9	16.6	11.7	1.3	12.0	10	5
Belgium	10	18.4[e]	5.5	6.2	12.4	11	6
Australia	9	17.0	12.9	2.6	12.5	12	11
New Zealand	10	18.4	9.2[f]	1.3	12.6	13	16
Spain	10	—[d]	10.4	13.0	13.1	14	17
United Kingdom	9	21.8	13.5	3.8	15.0	15	12
Ireland	9	22.6	11.1	7.6	15.2	16	15
United States	13	20.7	19.1	0.5	16.5	17	1

a. Based on prose level 1, as reported in the International Adult Literacy Survey (IALS). Data are for 1995 or a year around 1995.
b. Poverty is measured at 50% of the median disposable personal income. Data are for 1990 or a year around 1990.
c. Standardized unemployment rates calculated by the International Labour Organisation.
d. No data available. For calculating the HPI-2 value, the average of 16.8% of all countries (except Poland) included in the International Adult Literacy Survey has been used.
e. Data refer to Flanders.
f. The unweighted average of the industrial countries (excluding Eastern Europe and CIS).
Source: column 1: UN 1994e; column 2: OECD, Human Resource Development Canada and Statistics Canada 1997; column 3: Smeeding 1997; column 4: OECD 1997d.

many goods considered essential for social participation in one community might not be seen as essential in another. Thus the minimum income needed to avoid social exclusion can be quite different across countries. For this reason 50% of the country's median personal disposable income was used as the poverty line, reflecting what is appropriate for each country. Moreover, this measure of income poverty is now the standard used in the European Union for making international comparisons.

Third, data availability and quality are an important concern. Income poverty data are available for only 48 developing countries and rely on many estimates. Data on malnourishment and access to public services have broader coverage. In industrial countries comparable data on income poverty are available.

What does the HPI-2 reveal?

Among 17 industrial countries Sweden has the lowest incidence of human poverty as measured by the HPI-2, with 6.8%, followed by the Netherlands and Germany (table 1.8). The countries with the most poverty are the United States, with 16.5%, followed by Ireland and the United Kingdom at 15.2% and 15%.

The extent of human poverty has little to do with the average level of income. The United States, with the highest per capita income measured in purchasing power parity (PPP) among the 17 countries, also has the highest human poverty. Sweden ranks first in the HPI-2, with the least poverty, but only 13th in average income. And the Netherlands and the United Kingdom have similar average incomes but very different human poverty levels, at 8.2% and 15%. One might expect that the higher a country's GDP, the fewer poor people there would be. But comparing GDP per capita with the HPI-2 suggests the opposite: poverty rates in higher-income countries are the same as—or higher than—rates in lower-income industrial countries (figure 1.6).

The level of the HPI-2 does not correlate with the overall human development achieved by a country. All 17 countries ranked on the HPI-2 have reached high lev-

els of human development, with HDI values of more than 0.900. But the top HDI countries—Canada and France—have significant problems of poverty, and their progress in human development has been poorly distributed. Canada ranks tenth in the HPI-2 because 17% of its people lack adequate literacy skills, more than twice the proportion in Sweden (figure 1.7).

Human poverty is deprivation in multiple dimensions, not just income. Industrial countries need to monitor poverty in all its dimensions—not just income and unemployment, but also lack of basic capabilities such as health and literacy, important factors in whether a person is included in or excluded from the life of a community.

Human poverty is one side of the story of the backlog of human deprivation. The other side is persisting disparities—often the result of uneven progress in human development, but reinforced by the backlog of human poverty.

Persisting disparities

The inequalities that persist between poor people and rich, women and men, rural and urban, and among different ethnic groups are seldom isolated—instead, they are interrelated and overlapping.

Income and wealth—stark inequality

In 1960 the 20% of the world's people who live in the richest countries had 30 times the income of the poorest 20%—by 1995 82 times as much income. Consider the extraordinary concentration of wealth among a small group of the ultra-rich (box 1.3).

Disparities are just as stark within countries. In Brazil the poorest 50% of the population received 18% of national income in 1960, falling to 11.6% in 1995. The richest 10% received 54% of national income in 1960, rising to 63% in 1995. In Costa Rica during the 1980s the richest 20% enjoyed a per capita income of PPP$14,400, while the poorest 20% had an average income of PPP$1,340.

Income distribution in industrial countries also shows wide disparities between rich and poor. In the worst case, Russia, the

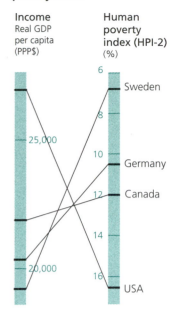

FIGURE 1.6
Incomes do not predict poverty levels

Source: Human Development Report Office.

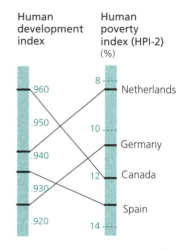

FIGURE 1.7
No pattern between the HDI and human poverty

Source: Human Development Report Office.

The ultra-rich

New estimates show that the world's 225 richest people have a combined wealth of over $1 trillion, equal to the annual income of the poorest 47% of the world's people (2.5 billion).

The enormity of the wealth of the ultra-rich is a mind-boggling contrast with low incomes in the developing world.

• The three richest people have assets that exceed the combined GDP of the 48 least developed countries.

• The 15 richest have assets that exceed the total GDP of Sub-Saharan Africa.

• The wealth of the 32 richest people exceeds the total GDP of South Asia.

• The assets of the 84 richest exceed the GDP of China, the most populous country, with 1.2 billion inhabitants.

Another striking contrast is the wealth of the 225 richest people com-

pared with what is needed to achieve universal access to basic social services for all. It is estimated that the additional cost of achieving and maintaining universal access to basic education for all, basic health care for all, reproductive health care for all women, adequate food for all and safe water and sanitation for all is roughly $40 billion a year. This is less than 4% of the combined wealth of the 225 richest people in the world.

The country with the biggest share of the world's 225 richest people is the United States, with 60 (combined wealth of $311 billion), followed by Germany, with 21 ($111 billion), and Japan, with 14 ($41 billion). Industrial countries have 147 of the richest 225 people ($645 billion combined), and developing countries 78 ($370 billion). Africa has just two ($3.7 billion), both from South Africa.

BOX TABLE 1.3
The ultra-rich, by origin, 1997

Region or country group	Distribution of the 225 richest people	Combined wealth of the ultra-rich (US$ billions)	Average wealth of the ultra-rich (US$ billions)
OECD	143	637	4.5
Asia	43	233	5.4
Latin America and the Caribbean	22	55	2.5
Arab States	11	78	7.1
Eastern Europe and CIS	4	8	2.0
Sub-Saharan Africa	2	4	2.0
Total	225	1,015	4.5

Source: Forbes Magazine 1997.

FIGURE 1.8
Urban-rural HPI disparity in Namibia, 1991–94
(percent)

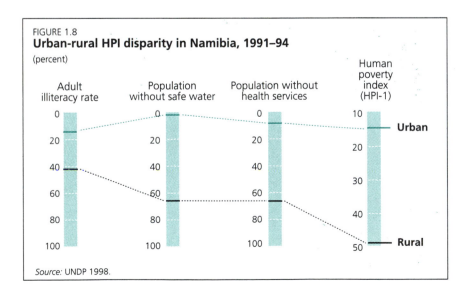

Source: UNDP 1998.

income share of the richest 20% is 11 times that of the poorest 20%. In Australia and the United Kingdom it is nearly 10 times as much. The United Kingdom stands out for its particularly sharp rise in income inequality over the 1980s.

Rural-urban disparities—pronounced

In developing countries 43% of rural men are illiterate, more than twice the percentage in urban areas. The urban literacy rate in El Salvador is 88%, the rural 66%. Nearly 90% of people have access to safe water in urban areas, only 60% in rural areas. In Romania 12% of urban dwellings are without piped water, 84% of rural dwellings.

The HDI and the HPI, when disaggregated along the rural-urban divide, also highlight the rural-urban disparity in human progress and deprivation. In Botswana the urban HDI is comparable to Russia's, while the rural is closer to Nicaragua's. In Namibia human poverty in rural areas is three times that in urban areas. Its urban HPI is comparable to the United Arab Emirates', its rural HPI close to Guinea's (figure 1.8).

Regional disparities within countries

Significant regional disparities in countries are sometimes reflected in access to social services, other times in human development outcomes.

• In Turkey the secondary enrolment ratio in the Aegean and Marmara regions is 62%, compared with 34% in East and South-East Anatolia.

• In the Gambia the under-five mortality rate in Mansadonko, at 162 per 1,000 live births, is almost twice the 85 in Banjul.

• In Romania unemployment in Botosane County, at 16%, is nearly four times the 4.5% in Bucharest.

• In Mongolia less than 9% of people are income-poor in the Alimag of Erdenet, 35% in Khusvel.

Disaggregated HDIs and HPIs point to regional disparities in human progress and deprivation (figures 1.9, 1.10 and 1.11). In the Philippines the gender-related development index (GDI) of the National Capital Region is four times that of the region of

Western Mindanao, where women are doubly disadvantaged—because of gender disparities and because they live in a disadvantaged region.

Gender inequalities

Societies have made real progress over the past 30 years in achieving more equitable distribution between women and men of the benefits of development. Gender gaps in education and health have narrowed rapidly. Female life expectancy has increased 20% faster than male life expectancy over the past two decades. Education levels have been steadily rising for women in developing countries. The gaps between women and men in adult literacy and school enrolment were halved between 1970 and 1990. In primary schools the enrolment of girls, once 75% that of boys, is now about 90%.

Human Development Report 1995 introduced the gender-related development index, which measures the same dimensions, using the same variables, as the HDI, to show the inequalities in achievement between women and men. The greater the gender disparity in human development, the lower the country's GDI relative to its HDI.

This year the GDI has been calculated for 163 countries (table 1.9). The human development achievements of women fall below those for men in every country, and the shortfall in the GDI relative to the HDI reflects this inequality. Other interesting features of the GDI:

• For 60 of the 163 the GDI rank (not the value) is lower than the HDI rank. This shows the unequal opportunities that women face relative to men. For several countries the GDI rank falls short of the HDI rank by 20 points or more: Oman, Saudi Arabia, the Islamic Republic of Iran, the Syrian Arab Republic, Algeria, Libya and the United Arab Emirates, in descending order.

• The GDI rank falls short of the HDI rank by 10 points or more in such industrial countries as Ireland and Malta.

• For 82 countries the GDI rank exceeds the corresponding HDI rank. The countries with a GDI rank more than 10 points higher than the HDI rank include 12 in Eastern

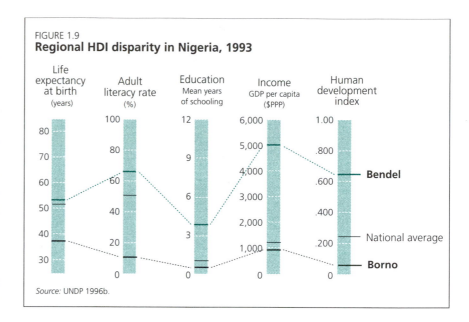

FIGURE 1.9
Regional HDI disparity in Nigeria, 1993

Source: UNDP 1996b.

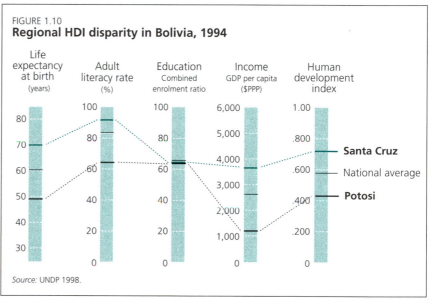

FIGURE 1.10
Regional HDI disparity in Bolivia, 1994

Source: UNDP 1998.

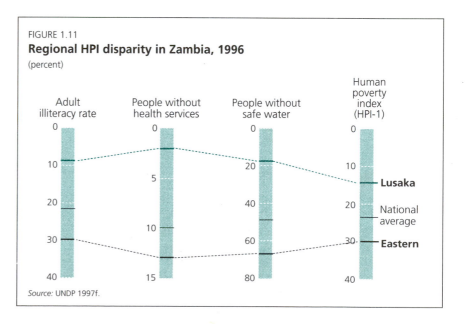

FIGURE 1.11
Regional HPI disparity in Zambia, 1996
(percent)

Source: UNDP 1997f.

Europe and the CIS. Only three countries outside this region—Thailand, Jamaica and Sri Lanka—have a GDI rank more than 10 points greater than the HDI rank.

Progress in building women's capabilities has been significant, but there is a seri-ous delay in creating real opportunities for women. The lack of equal opportunities for women to participate in economic and political life is partly captured by the gender empowerment measure (GEM), estimated for 102 countries (see technical note 2). It

TABLE 1.9
Gender disparity—GDI and HDI ranks

GDI rank	HDI rank	HDI rank minus GDI rank	GDI rank	HDI rank	HDI rank minus GDI rank	GDI rank	HDI rank	HDI rank minus GDI rank
1 Canada	1	0	56 Brazil	55	−1	110 Bolivia	108	−2
2 Norway	3	1	57 Romania	67	10	111 Egypt	104	−7
3 Sweden	10	7	58 Korea, Dem. People's			112 Gabon	112	0
4 Iceland	5	1	Rep. of	68	10	113 Guatemala	103	−10
5 Finland	6	1	59 Estonia	70	11	114 Honduras	111	−3
6 USA	4	−2	60 Bahrain	41	−19	115 Nicaragua	116	1
7 France	2	−5	61 Croatia	69	8	116 Morocco	115	−1
8 New Zealand	9	1	62 Lithuania	72	10	117 Congo	118	1
9 Australia	15	6	63 Suriname	58	−5	118 Zimbabwe	120	2
10 Denmark	18	8	64 Macedonia, FYR	73	9	119 Papua New Guinea	119	0
11 United Kingdom	14	3	65 Jamaica	77	12	120 Myanmar	121	1
12 Netherlands	7	−5	66 United Arab Emirates	46	−20	121 Ghana	123	2
13 Japan	8	−5	67 Qatar	51	−16	122 Kenya	127	5
14 Belgium	12	−2	68 Lebanon	59	−9	123 Lesotho	124	1
15 Austria	13	−2	69 Cuba	78	9	124 Cameroon	122	−2
16 Barbados	24	8	70 Sri Lanka	83	13	125 Lao People's Dem. Rep.	126	1
17 Germany	19	2	71 Latvia	85	14	126 Equatorial Guinea	125	−1
18 Switzerland	16	−2	72 Belize	56	−16	127 Iraq	117	−10
19 Spain	11	−8	73 Kazakhstan	86	13	128 India	129	1
20 Greece	20	0	74 South Africa	82	8	129 Cambodia	130	1
21 Bahamas	31	10	75 Armenia	91	16	130 Comoros	131	1
22 Israel	22	0	76 Tunisia	76	0	131 Pakistan	128	−3
23 Italy	21	−2	77 Maldives	87	10	132 Dem. Rep. of the Congo	133	1
24 Slovenia	36	12	78 Ecuador	66	−12	133 Nigeria	132	−1
25 Czech Rep.	38	13	79 Libyan Arab Jamahiriya	57	−22	134 Zambia	136	2
26 Slovakia	40	14	80 Peru	79	−1	135 Benin	135	0
27 Ireland	17	−10	81 Dominican Rep.	81	0	136 Togo	134	−2
28 Portugal	32	4	82 Philippines	90	8	137 Tanzania, U. Rep. of	140	3
29 Singapore	28	−1	83 Ukraine	94	11	138 Mauritania	139	1
30 Cyprus	23	−7	84 Mongolia	93	9	139 Madagascar	143	4
31 Uruguay	37	6	85 Botswana	89	4	140 Bangladesh	137	−3
32 Luxembourg	26	−6	86 Uzbekistan	96	10	141 Côte d'Ivoire	138	−3
33 Hong Kong, China	25	−8	87 Turkmenistan	95	8	142 Central African Rep.	144	2
34 Hungary	45	11	88 Indonesia	88	0	143 Yemen	141	−2
35 Poland	48	13	89 Paraguay	84	−5	144 Haiti	149	5
36 Brunei Darussalam	34	−2	90 Jordan	80	−10	145 Angola	146	1
37 Korea, Rep. of	29	−8	91 Albania	97	6	146 Uganda	150	4
38 Trinidad and Tobago	39	1	92 Iran, Islamic Rep. of	71	−21	147 Bhutan	145	−2
39 Costa Rica	33	−6	93 China	98	5	148 Nepal	142	−6
40 Thailand	52	12	94 Syrian Arab Rep.	74	−20	149 Senegal	148	−1
41 Colombia	49	8	95 Guyana	92	−3	150 Malawi	151	1
42 Panama	43	1	96 Algeria	75	−21	151 Sudan	147	−4
43 Venezuela	44	1	97 Kyrgyzstan	101	4	152 Chad	152	0
44 Malta	27	−17	98 Georgia	100	2	153 Guinea-Bissau	153	0
45 Malaysia	53	8	99 Namibia	99	0	154 Gambia	154	0
46 Chile	30	−16	100 Azerbaijan	102	2	155 Eritrea	157	2
47 Bulgaria	60	13	101 Moldova, Rep. of	105	4	156 Mozambique	155	−1
48 Argentina	35	−13	102 Saudi Arabia	63	−39	157 Guinea	156	−1
49 Mexico	47	−2	103 El Salvador	106	3	158 Ethiopia	158	0
50 Kuwait	50	0	104 Oman	64	−40	159 Burundi	159	0
51 Belarus	61	10	105 Swaziland	107	2	160 Mali	160	0
52 Fiji	42	−10	106 Tajikistan	110	4	161 Burkina Faso	161	0
53 Russian Federation	65	12	107 Cape Verde	109	2	162 Niger	162	0
54 Mauritius	54	0	108 Viet Nam	113	5	163 Sierra Leone	163	0
55 Turkey	62	7	109 Solomon Islands	114	5			

Note: HDI ranks have been recalculated for the universe of 163 countries. A positive difference between a country's HDI and GDI ranks indicates that it performs relatively better on gender equality than on average achievements.
Source: Human Development Report Office.

measures women's participation in decision-making in professional, economic and political domains.

At the top of the GEM ranking are three Nordic countries—Sweden, Norway and Denmark, each with high levels of human capabilities and many opportunities for women to participate in economic and political activities (table 1.10). Some developing countries do even better than indus-trial countries on the GEM. Trinidad and Tobago and Barbados are ahead of the United Kingdom and Ireland. Cuba and Costa Rica are ahead of France and Israel. China and Mexico are ahead of Japan.

Ethnic and racial disparities

Ethnic and racial disparities are serious in many areas of human development. In

TABLE 1.10
Gender disparity—GEM, GDI and HDI ranks

GEM rank		GDI rank	HDI rank	GEM rank		GDI rank	HDI rank
1	Sweden	3	10	52	Latvia	57	68
2	Norway	2	3	53	Suriname	53	51
3	Denmark	10	18	54	Peru	63	62
4	New Zealand	8	9	55	Mozambique	99	99
5	Finland	5	6	56	Zimbabwe	83	84
6	Iceland	4	5	57	Cape Verde	78	81
7	Canada	1	1	58	Dominican Rep.	64	64
8	Germany	17	19	59	Uruguay	31	33
9	Netherlands	12	7	60	Thailand	38	46
10	Austria	15	13	61	Chile	43	28
11	USA	6	4	62	Venezuela	41	39
12	Australia	9	15	63	Swaziland	77	79
13	Switzerland	18	16	64	Romania	51	55
14	Luxembourg	32	25	65	Bolivia	79	80
15	Bahamas	21	29	66	Cyprus	30	23
16	Spain	19	11	67	Paraguay	68	67
17	Trinidad and Tobago	36	35	68	Brazil	50	49
18	Barbados	16	24	69	Ecuador	62	54
19	Belgium	14	12	70	Indonesia	67	70
20	United Kingdom	11	14	71	Haiti	95	96
21	Ireland	27	17	72	Mali	100	100
22	Portugal	28	30	73	Georgia	75	75
23	South Africa	59	65	74	Tunisia	60	60
24	Czech Rep.	25	34	75	Kuwait	46	45
25	Cuba	55	61	76	Maldives	61	69
26	Italy	23	21	77	Burkina Faso	101	101
27	Slovakia	26	36	78	Fiji	47	37
28	Costa Rica	37	31	79	Syrian Arab Rep.	72	58
29	Poland	34	43	80	Bangladesh	93	92
30	Hungary	33	40	81	Zambia	90	91
31	France	7	2	82	Morocco	82	82
32	Israel	22	22	83	Korea, Rep. of	35	27
33	China	71	74	84	Sri Lanka	56	66
34	El Salvador	76	78	85	Turkey	49	53
35	Guatemala	81	76	86	Cameroon	86	85
36	Slovenia	24	32	87	Iran, Islamic Rep. of	70	57
37	Mexico	45	42	88	Egypt	80	77
38	Japan	13	8	89	Malawi	96	97
39	Guyana	73	73	90	Equatorial Guinea	87	87
40	Belize	58	50	91	Papua New Guinea	84	83
41	Colombia	39	44	92	United Arab Emirates	54	41
42	Singapore	29	26	93	Algeria	74	59
43	Bulgaria	44	52	94	Gambia	98	98
44	Panama	40	38	95	India	88	89
45	Malaysia	42	47	96	Sudan	97	95
46	Philippines	65	72	97	Jordan	69	63
47	Estonia	52	56	98	Central African Rep.	94	94
48	Botswana	66	71	99	Togo	91	90
49	Mauritius	48	48	100	Pakistan	89	88
50	Lesotho	85	86	101	Mauritania	92	93
51	Greece	20	20	102	Niger	102	102

Note: GDI and HDI ranks have been recalculated for the universe of 102 countries.
Source: Human Development Report Office.

FIGURE 1.12
The legacy of AIDS—a growing population of orphans

AIDS orphans as a percentage of the population under 15

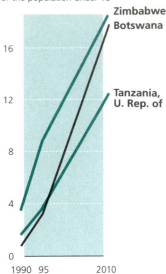

Zimbabwe
Botswana

Tanzania, U. Rep. of

Note: AIDS orphans are HIV-negative children who lost their mother or both parents to AIDS when they were under the age of 15.
Source: Stanecki and Way 1997.

South Africa whites had a life expectancy of 68 years in the early 1990s, 14 years more than the 54 years for blacks. In Malaysia the incidence of income poverty among ethnic Malays, at 24%, is nearly four times that among the ethnic Chinese, at 6%. In Canada 35% of Inuit men are unemployed, compared with 10% of other Canadian men. And in the United States 31% of Hispanics aged 25–65 have not completed the ninth grade, compared with only 6% of whites.

Disaggregating the HDI for South Africa in 1994 gives a value for whites of 0.878, almost twice the 0.462 for blacks. The white South Africans rank next to Spain, the blacks next to Congo. In Namibia the incidence of human poverty among the San-speakers, at 65%, is more than eight times that among English-speakers and six times that among German-speakers (table 1.11). The human poverty index of the English-speakers in Namibia puts them next to Singapore and Costa Rica—while that of the people who speak Lozi/Caprivi, Oshiwambo and Rukavango puts them next to the Democratic Republic of the Congo, Uganda and Sudan. The HPI of the San group is 65%—worse than in Niger, the lowest-ranking country in the HPI.

The uneven progress in human development over the years and the existence of a significant backlog of human deprivation have not only resulted in persisting disparities. They have also generated forces that are reversing human progress in several areas.

TABLE 1.11
Human poverty by language group in Namibia, early 1990s

Rank	Language group	HPI-1 value (%)
1	English	8
2	German	10
3	Afrikaans	11
4	Tswana	21
5	Nama/Damara	31
6	Otjiherero	34
7	Lozi/Caprivi	41
8	Oshiwambo	43
9	Rukavango	44
10	San	65

Source: UNDP 1997d.

Reversibility of human development

Making progress in human development is like negotiating an obstacle course—with constant challenges, with new problems to overcome and with achievements reversed by such forces as epidemics, armed conflict and economic turmoil.

HIV/AIDS

Global epidemics threaten not just the health of the world's people but the achievements in human development. So far HIV/AIDS has been one of the most devastating, claiming nearly 12 million lives since it started 18 years ago. The most devastating aspect of the HIV/AIDS epidemic compared with other epidemics is that it usually affects people in their most productive years. Some experts claim that we are only "10%" into the epidemic in infections and mortality, with the real impact on people, communities and economies still to come. No affordable cure or vaccine is in sight, so the only option is to prevent its further spread, minimize its impact and provide a caring and compassionate environment for those infected.

At the end of 1997 nearly 31 million people were living with HIV, up from 22.3 million the year before. This tremendous increase reflects the epidemic's momentum, with 16,000 new infections a day. It is now estimated that 40 million people will be living with HIV in 2000, just two years away.

Of the 16,000 people who become infected each day, 90% are in developing countries, 40% are women and 50% are between 15 and 24 years old.

There are now 8.2 million AIDS orphans—HIV-negative children who lost their mother or both parents to HIV/AIDS while still under age 15. There will be an estimated 16 million by 2000. Households headed by children have begun to appear in some African villages, and in an increasing number of communities the strain is proving too great for traditional coping systems. In many countries with a high prevalence of HIV/AIDS, more than 10% of all children under the age of 15 will have lost at least one parent to HIV/AIDS 5–10 years from now (figure 1.12).

In the urban centre of Francistown, in Botswana, 48% of pregnant women are HIV-positive—at Beit Bridge, Zimbabwe, nearly 60% are. More than two in every five adult deaths in rural Uganda are related to HIV/AIDS. In Namibia more than twice as many people of all ages die of HIV-related illness as die of malaria, the country's number two killer.

But the epidemic is not, as some suggest, a problem only in Africa. India has the largest number of people living with HIV—3–5 million—and Thailand has three-quarters of a million, 2.3% of the adult population.

The progress in improving life expectancy over the past three decades is now under threat in many countries as HIV/AIDS reduces the expected life span. The epidemic is raising both under-five mortality and mortality in the age group 20–49 (where mortality is normally quite low). In Botswana—where 25–30% of people between 15 and 49 are infected with HIV—life expectancy is already at levels last seen in the late 1960s. By 2010 life expectancy in Zimbabwe will be shorter by 25 years—in some parts of Uganda it has already been cut by 16 years (figure 1.13).

HIV/AIDS increases child mortality both because children are dying directly from HIV-related illnesses and because uninfected children are dying of malnutrition and lack of health care as the impact of the disease impoverishes families and communities. As is well documented, infant and child mortality is directly related to maternal mortality, so HIV-related mortality of mothers is an important factor in the rising rates of child mortality already observed in some countries. It is estimated that in 1998 the epidemic will have pushed up the child mortality rate by about 150% in Zimbabwe and 100% in Guyana and Kenya.

But the impact of HIV/AIDS on human development goes far beyond reduced life expectancy brought about by higher child and adult mortality. Besides the unspeakable tragedy for families and communities when the disease takes its toll, the economic and social effects can be catastrophic. Since most people who die of HIV/AIDS are in their most productive years, the epidemic affects the sustainability of households and the socio-economic prospects of communities.

Just as poverty fuels the epidemic, the epidemic intensifies poverty. HIV/AIDS is having a significant impact on economies, creating shortages of skilled labour in such sectors as health, education and transport and adding to the burden on already overstretched health budgets. It is reversing years of investment in training and education. Striking the poorest countries of the world—already burdened with other socio-economic problems, low resources and inadequate social services—the HIV/AIDS epidemic is becoming one of the main development challenges facing the world community.

Conflict

Civilian fatalities have climbed from 5% of war-related deaths at the turn of the century to more than 90% in the wars of the 1990s. Recent times have witnessed new weapons and patterns of conflict, including the indiscriminate use of land-mines and antipersonnel cluster bombs, as well as the proliferation of light weapons. As a result many of the casualties are women and children, with an incalculable impact on human development. Over the past decade armed conflict has killed 2 million children, disabled 4–5 million, and left 12 million homeless, more than 1 million orphaned or separated from their parents and some 10 million psychologically traumatized.

More than 110 million active mines are scattered in 68 countries, with an equal number stockpiled around the world. Every month more than 2,000 people are killed or maimed by mine explosions. In 1994, although around 100,000 mines were removed, an additional 2 million were planted. But recently efforts to deal with this problem have intensified, and in 1997 more than 120 countries agreed to ban land-mines by signing the Convention on the Prohibition of the Use, Stockpiling, Production and Transfer of Antipersonnel Mines and their Destruction.

It is estimated that half a million children under five died as a result of armed conflict in 1992, and many more were wounded or deprived of essentials. In

FIGURE 1.13
Projected human development setbacks due to AIDS

Life expectancy at birth (years)

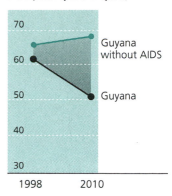

Life expectancy at birth (years)

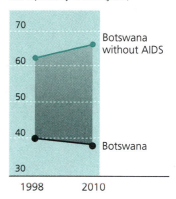

Life expectancy at birth (years)

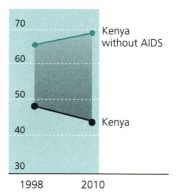

Life expectancy at birth (years)

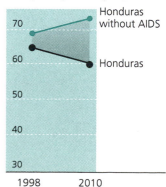

Source: US Bureau of the Census forthcoming.

Chechnya children made up 40% of all civilian casualties between February and March 1995. In Sarajevo, Bosnia, almost one child in four has been wounded. In Somalia half or more of all children under five who were alive at the beginning of January 1992 were dead by the end of the year. In Mozambique wartime damage to schools left two-thirds of the 2 million primary-school-age children with no access to education.

It is estimated that nearly 100 million people are caught in a cycle of civil strife and hunger. About 50 million people have been forced to flee their homes.

Conflict destroys years of progress in building social infrastructure, establishing functioning government institutions, fostering community-level solidarity and social cohesion and promoting economic development. When conflicts finally peter out and the death tolls are tallied up, countries face formidable challenges of reconstruction and reconciliation requiring resources far beyond their reach as they emerge from years of destruction.

Many conflicts go on for years, with only temporary let-ups. By 1998 armed conflicts had been running for 20 years in Afghanistan, 10 in Somalia, 14 in Sri Lanka and 15 in Sudan.

But the number of conflicts worldwide fell from 21 in 1996 to 18 in 1997. Nearly all are being fought within countries, where they tend to be smaller but more violent. They can take a variety of forms. First are random acts of violence by individuals or groups and among rival criminal gangs, with no aspiration to control the state. Second are sporadic incidents of violence by organized groups seeking greater political participation, cultural autonomy and economic benefits. Third is sustained resort to violence over long periods by organizations and movements that aim to take over the government or part of the country's territory. And fourth are intense acts of extreme violence by groups operating during a partial or total breakdown of the state.

The near eradication of international conflicts—and the increase in internal ones—show up in military spending, which is down by about a third since its cold war peak in 1987. The reductions in many countries conceal the fact that it remains very high, or is increasing, in some. Military spending fell by a third in member countries of the North Atlantic Treaty Organization (NATO) between 1987 and 1996. But it increased by 13% in South Asia and by 11% in several countries in the Middle East—the Islamic Republic of Iran, Iraq, Israel, Jordan and the United Arab Emirates. In the largest South-East Asian countries—Indonesia, Malaysia, the Philippines and Thailand—it has soared by 35% since 1987.

Economic decline

Continuing economic stagnation and decline in many developing countries poses

---

BOX 1.4

The East Asian crisis—can it be turned to opportunity?

Undoubtedly the biggest setback to human development in the past year has been the East Asian economic crisis. The five countries most affected—Indonesia, the Republic of Korea, Malaysia, the Philippines and Thailand—had made huge economic and social strides in the previous 20–30 years, including impressive improvement in human development indicators. Although there were increasing signs of economic vulnerability, the triggers for the crisis were financial—a sudden and dramatic reversal of short-term commercial bank flows, from an inflow of more than $50 billion in 1996 to an outflow of $20 billion-plus in 1997.

The effects: falling GDPs, soaring unemployment, deep cuts in public expenditure, rapid inflation and severe declines in consumption. These have resulted from both the initial causes of the crisis and from actions taken to deal with it. The human setbacks could be enormous, with health care and education declining and poverty projected to double in Indonesia.

The international community has made great efforts to respond. The International Monetary Fund and other multilateral and bilateral lenders mobilized $100 billion or so of financial support.

Although it is too early to draw final lessons, some things are clear:

• The international response needs to be strengthened, both to prevent such crises and to do more to protect people from the consequences of economic collapse.
• From the beginning the response should focus on the human dimensions of such crises with at least the same intensity as on the financial and economic issues.

Many actions are possible to protect people: public employment schemes, food provision for the vulnerable, credit allocations for small businesses and low-income households and subsidies for community groups to provide meals for those thrown into poverty.

International agencies and regional development banks have a part to play in encouraging and supporting such actions and in monitoring human indicators as seriously as they do economic and financial ones. And in the long run newly industrializing countries need to create systems of insurance for the unemployed, as the Republic of Korea was doing.

Recession in the industrial countries in the 1930s was the catalyst for fundamental social and political rethinking of national and international economic strategy. The Asian crisis provides a similar opportunity. Will it be taken?

Source: Ranis and Stewart 1998.

another formidable obstacle to human development. No fewer than 100 countries—all developing or in transition—have experienced serious economic decline over the past three decades. As a result per capita income in these 100 countries is lower than it was 10, 15, 20, even 30 years ago, depriving their economies of the resources for improving human development.

Globally, economic growth was nevertheless strong by the mid-1990s, and 109 countries recorded positive growth in per capita income during 1995. Though the growth was welcome, there were still worrying signs in human development.

• Among 124 developing countries, only 21—12 of them in Asia—had a per capita growth rate of 3% or more each year between 1995 and 1997; projections for 1998 show the number falling to 20, with only 6 in Asia.

• Among the 48 least developed countries, only 6 had a per capita growth rate of 3% or more between 1995 and 1997. This does not bode well, since 3% annual growth has been set as the minimum required for rapidly reducing poverty.

• In many countries the growth appears to be pro-rich—not pro-poor. Honduras grew 2% per capita a year in 1986–89—but income poverty doubled. New Zealand, the United Kingdom and the United States all experienced good average growth between 1975 and 1995—yet the proportion of their people in income poverty rose.

Add to this the major doubts about sustainability sowed by the crisis in East and South-East Asia (box 1.4).

The burden of debt repayment and servicing is so great for many countries that it cripples their ability to make advances in human development or inroads in eradicating poverty (see box 5.12 in chapter 5). For 27 heavily indebted poor countries debt is greater than GNP. Countries of Sub-Saharan Africa spent an average $12 billion annually on debt repayments in 1990–95, while their debt stock increased by $33 billion. For some, debt payments are equivalent to almost all the official development assistance coming into the country. Mozambique has an external debt burden nine times the value of its annual exports, and it allocates almost half its budget to servicing debt, four times what it spends on health.

Facing the challenge

The world has more than enough resources to accelerate progress in human development for all and to eradicate the worst forms of poverty from the planet. Advancing human development is not an exorbitant undertaking. For example, it has been estimated that the total additional yearly investment required to achieve universal access to basic social services would be roughly $40 billion, 0.1% of world income, barely more than a rounding error. That covers the bill for basic education, health, nutrition, reproductive health, family planning and safe water and sanitation for all.

Why are so few financial resources dedicated to advancing human development in countries where the need is greatest? Donor countries allocate a mere $55 billion to development cooperation—only 0.25% of their total GNP of $22 trillion. Official development aid is now at its lowest since statistics started. Moreover, the share to the least developed countries is declining. There is still an urgent need for most donors to double the share going to basic social services, as part of the 20:20 initiative commitment to the most essential human development priorities.

To see that ample resources are available but not used for human development, compare the additional annual cost of universal access to basic social services with consumer spending (table 1.12). The comparisons here are, of course, illustrative, but they provide a striking view of how we use the world's resources.

Accelerating progress in human development and eradicating the worst forms of human poverty are within our reach, despite challenges and setbacks. We know what to do. And the world has the resources needed to do it. Success is now to be found in strengthening partnerships, building political momentum for reform and pledging strong commitments for action—followed by real action.

TABLE 1.12
The world's priorities?
(annual expenditure)

Basic education for all	$6 billion[a]
Cosmetics in the USA	$8 billion
Water and sanitation for all	$9 billion[a]
Ice cream in Europe	$11 billion
Reproductive health for all women	$12 billion[a]
Perfumes in Europe and the USA	$12 billion
Basic health and nutrition	$13 billion[a]
Pet foods in Europe and the USA	$17 billion
Business entertainment in Japan	$35 billion
Cigarettes in Europe	$50 billion
Alcoholic drinks in Europe	$105 billion
Narcotic drugs in the world	$400 billion
Military spending in the world	$780 billion

a. Estimated additional annual cost to achieve universal access to basic social services in all developing countries.
Source: Euromonitor 1997; UN 1997g; UNDP, UNFPA and UNICEF 1994; Worldwide Research, Advisory and Business Intelligence Services 1997.

CHAPTER 2

Consumption from a human development perspective

FIGURE 2.1
Consumption inputs for human development

Goods and services from

Consumption of goods and services is a constant activity in daily life—yet it is not the ultimate end of the lives that people lead. We consume for a purpose, or for various purposes simultaneously. Thus the role of consumption in human lives cannot be comprehended without some understanding of the ends that are pursued through consumption activities. Our ends are enormously diverse, ranging from nourishment to amusement, from living long to living well, from isolated self-fulfilment to interactive socialization.

Concepts of consumption

The human development perspective focuses on the many different ways in which consumption of goods and services affects people's lives. From such a people's perspective consumption is a means to human development. Its significance lies in enlarging people's capabilities to live long and to live well. Consumption opens opportunities without which a person would be left in human poverty.

• Food, shelter, water, sanitation, medical care and clothing are necessary for leading a long and healthy life.

• Schooling and access to information through books, radio, newspapers—and, increasingly, electronic networks—are necessary to acquire language, literacy, numeracy and up-to-date information.

• Transport and energy are critical inputs to all these things and virtually all other human activity. There is growing evidence that lack of mobility and access lie at the heart of economic and social disempowerment of women.

Consumption is also a means of participating in the life of a community, for goods are the words of a social language. As Marcel Mauss pointed out in his classic work *The Gift*, we offer gifts to express sentiments and to establish a need for reciprocity, cementing a relationship between giver and receiver. Furthermore, communities each have standards of dress, food, housing, transport and communications, without which a person would be excluded from full participation in society.

From the human development perspective consideration is not limited to material consumption by individuals using their personal incomes; this approach would capture only a fraction of the goods and services that contribute to human development. Equally important in the life of a community are many collective and non-material goods and services supplied through public provisioning, such as social security, health care, education and transport. The human development approach goes further still, embracing consumption that lies outside the monetized economy: goods and services supplied through unpaid work—especially by women—and those supplied from the natural resources of the environmental commons. When all these are taken into account, a far broader perspective is gained of a community's consumption levels and patterns (figure 2.1).

Consumption clearly contributes to human development when it enlarges the capabilities of people without adversely affecting the well-being of others, when it is as fair to future generations as to the present ones, when it respects the carrying capacity of the planet and when it encourages the emergence of lively and creative communities.

Yet even though consumption is critical for some human development advances, it is not always necessary. A family does not have to own many possessions to respect the rights of each of its members. A nation does not have to be affluent to treat men and women equally. Artistic creativity—in literature, dance, music and many other modes of expression—can flourish even with minimal material resources, so long as people enjoy freedom of expression, freedom of thought and freedom of time.

At the foundation of human development is the principle of the universalism of life claims, acknowledging the life claims of everyone—women, men and children—without discrimination. It demands a world where consumption is such that all have enough to eat, no child goes without education, no human being is denied health care, and all people can develop their potential capabilities to the full extent. The human development perspective values human life for itself. It does not value people merely because they can produce material goods, important though that might be. Nor does it value one person's life more than another's.

The principle of universalism demands both intragenerational and intergenerational equity. Sustainable development may sometimes be interpreted carelessly to mean that the present level and pattern of development and consumption should be sustained for future generations as well. This is clearly wrong. The inequities of today are so great that sustaining the present patterns of development and consumption would mean perpetuating similar inequities for future generations. Development and consumption patterns that perpetuate today's inequities are neither sustainable nor worth sustaining.

It is from this perspective of the universalism of life claims—as reflected in many declarations and covenants, starting with the Universal Declaration of Human Rights—that we need to explore the linkages between consumption and human development. Addressing consumption shortfalls is of fundamental importance. If every member of society—woman, man and child—must be able to consume a minimum amount of goods and services essential for ensuring the development of their

---

BOX 2.1

Consumption hypotheses—from Veblen to Sen

Veblen

Thorstein Veblen (1899) initiated the study of consumption as a social phenomenon and of the way individual tastes are influenced by others. Veblen clarified the two major means by which the relatively small leisure class extended its influence over society through its tastes. First, refined or cultivated taste became associated with distance from the world of work; objects suggesting practical necessity could be dismissed as cheap. Second, the process of emulation, by which each group seeks to copy those above itself, extended conspicuous consumption and upper-class standards throughout society.

Weber

Max Weber (1920) introduced the notion of a "status group" sharing a common life style. This provided a wider framework for analysing class and social differentiation, incorporating criteria based on consumption patterns rather than just property ownership and incomes.

Mauss

Marcel Mauss (1925) saw reciprocity in exchange and consumption of goods as the social glue binding individuals and communities to one another.

Keynes

John Maynard Keynes (1936) mainly looked at consumption from a macroeconomic perspective. He saw aggregate consumption expenditures as important components of national income. Keynes argued that with rises in income, consumption would also increase, but not as fast. When income rises, the marginal propensity to consume would go down as consumer needs are satisfied. Keynes regarded effective demand by the consumer as the principal vehicle of economic growth.

Samuelson

The impossibility of observing and measuring the utility of consumption was an awkward feature of neoclassical theory from the start. Economists sought to escape this embarrassment by showing that the theory could still be derived

without actually measuring utility. Paul Samuelson's revealed preference hypothesis (1938) is a classic example of this thinking. Samuelson believed that no utility function, cardinal or ordinal, was required; it was enough for consumers to reveal their preferences through their purchases in the marketplace.

Duesenberry

The issue of copying the neighbours in consumption behaviour—keeping up with the Joneses—was taken up by James Duesenberry in the late 1940s. The notion is that individuals' preferences are influenced by the consumption preferences of admired neighbours, so they try to keep up. The relative income hypothesis of Duesenberry (1949) provides the analytical framework for this view. Duesenberry considered the major determinant of consumption to be relative income—not absolute income, as proposed by Keynes.

Scitovsky

Tibor Scitovsky (1976) distinguishes between comfort and stimulation and emphasizes in particular the role of culture in generating durable pleasure from stimulation. He emphasizes the need for acquiring "the consumption skills that will give us access to society's accumulated stock of past novelty and so enable us to supplement at will and almost without limit the currently available flow of novelty as a source of stimulation."

Douglas

Mary Douglas (1979) describes consumption of goods as a medium of communication particularly central to the establishment of people's personal identity and social standing.

Sen

Amartya Sen (1985) focuses not on the ownership of commodities but on the uses to which they can be put in extending people's capabilities. Commodities are important for enriching human lives, but their effectiveness depends on personal characteristics and social circumstances, variations in which contribute to inequalities in a society.

Source: Human Development Report Office.

Revolt against consumer materialism in religion

Restraint in consumption has been recognized as a virtue throughout the ages by many religions, as is reflected in their texts and teachings.

In Hinduism:
"When you have the golden gift of contentment, you have everything."

In Islam:
"It is difficult for a man laden with riches to climb the steep path that leads to bliss."

"Riches are not from an abundance of worldly goods, but from a contented mind."

In Taoism:
"He who knows he has enough is rich."

"To take all one wants is never as good as to stop when one should."

In Christianity:
"Watch out! Be on your guard against all kinds of greed: a man's life does not consist in the abundance of his possessions."

In Confucianism:
"Excess and deficiency are equally at fault."

In Buddhism:
"By the thirst for riches, the foolish man destroys himself as if he were his own enemy."

"Whoever in this world overcomes his selfish cravings, his sorrow falls away from him, like drops of water from a lotus flower."

Source: Parthasarathi 1997c.

---

capabilities and for enjoying a decent standard of living, then high priority must be given to eliminating those shortfalls that perpetuate human deprivations.

This human development perspective on consumption draws on diverse disciplines and ideas put forward by many key thinkers (box 2.1).

In economics the focus is typically on consumption of final goods and services. Mainstream economics tends to concentrate at the microeconomic level on individual utility and satisfaction derived from consumption and at the macroeconomic level on the generation and use of national income. The alternative activity to consumption is savings, which is related to deferred consumption. Many economists differentiate between consumption of necessities, which are required to meet basic human needs, and consumption of luxuries, which go beyond that.

In sociology and anthropology consumption activities are analysed in the context of social relations and institutions. People's consumption decisions are influenced by their social commitments—that is, the social class to which they belong, the social norms within that class and the relationships that they have with others. Following from this, consumption is a means for social communication, and without it, one becomes socially non-interacting. For example, apart from meeting the biological need of hunger, sharing a meal is a form of collective participation.

In environmental studies the focus with regard to consumption is on the level and depletion of natural resources. Natural resources are categorized as renewables, such as water, wood and fish, or non-renewables, such as metals and minerals. Consumption entails depleting both kinds of natural capital. In addition, what is consumed is ultimately disposed of—creating waste and pollution problems.

For philosophers, social commentators and theologians concern with consumption relates to the tension between the values embodied in materialism and those of simpler life styles. Major world religions have commented on materialism, giving guidance to their followers (box 2.2).

Given the contrasting approaches taken to consumption, each of these fields of study debates very different issues. Economics discusses utility maximization, optimization of aggregate demand and present versus deferred consumption. Issues in sociology and anthropology include how consumption is used for group identity, inclusion and exclusion, since objects are given symbolic meaning. There is increasing interest in the interaction of local and global cultures in developing societies through the consumption of goods and services. In the environmental field the debate is over the problems of natural resource scarcity and environmental unsustainability.

These are diverse perspectives on consumption, focused on contrasting issues. But they are not necessarily conflicting—in fact, they complement one another. This Report uses the understanding generated by all the perspectives to explore the impact of consumption on human lives from many angles.

Factors affecting consumption options

Individual consumers are assumed to be in the best position to judge their own needs and preferences and to make their own choices. It is fair to presume that people know what they are seeking and have reasons for their preferences when they opt for one consumption pattern over another. Even when a person may not be all that well informed, the idea that another person could judge her decisions better than she can is not, as a general rule, easy to accept.

Before being able to make any such decisions, however, the consumer must at least be presented with choices. Yet millions of people face too narrow a range of consumption options, which prevents them from enlarging their capabilities. The existing distribution of consumption options points to serious shortfalls affecting people in every society who lack access to a range of essential goods and services. They may not be able to get enough food, may lack health care services or may have little access to transport beyond their own feet. There are many factors causing these constraints on consumption options. Income is not the only one. Other factors include the availability and infrastructure of essential goods and services, time use, information, social barriers and the household setting.

Income

Income is an important means of widening the range of consumption options, especially as economies around the world become increasingly monetized. Income gives people the ability to buy diverse, nutritious foods instead of eating only their own crops, to pay for motorized transport instead of walking, to pay for health care and education for their families, to pay for water from a tap instead of walking for many hours to collect it from a well.

The increasing dependence of much consumption on private income means that changes in income have a dominant influence on changes in consumption. When incomes rise steadily—as they have in most industrial countries over the past few decades—consumption rises for most of the population. But for the same reason, when incomes decline, consumption also falls sharply, with devastating consequences for human well-being.

Availability and infrastructure of essential goods and services

Consumption options depend on the range of goods and services available—from the market and state provisioning, from home production and common resources. Many of the most basic essential goods and services—water, sanitation, education, health care, transport and electricity—cannot be provided without an infrastructure, without laying down water pipes, drains and electricity cables, without establishing a school or health centre, without building roads for vehicles. Money is of little use if there is no health dispensary within miles for buying medicine, no school that children can reach, no way to get electricity in the home.

Traditionally, these services have been provided first by the community and then by the state. As markets develop and technology improves, the services increasingly are being provided by the private sector in areas where profit can be made. In less profitable areas community organizations are stepping in to raise funds and provide for their needs themselves. Yet it is still the state that must ensure that, by whatever means, access is available to all—rural as well as urban, poor as well as rich.

Even as markets increasingly take over services previously supplied by the state, there is complementarity between public and private goods. Privately owned cars and buses need well-maintained roads to run effectively. Private companies supplying water services still expect the state to provide the underlying infrastructure. And despite the growth of private schools, there must also be state schools for those who cannot afford to pay the fees. A balance must be maintained between public and private goods. Yet in many countries and regions there is now a large and unhealthy imbalance, leading to great social inequity. This was the forceful thesis presented by John Kenneth Galbraith in his seminal work *The Affluent Society* about 40 years ago. Galbraith revisits the scene now and finds that "the contrast between needed public services and affluent private consumption has become much greater" in those 40 years (box 2.3).

Across countries and regions there is a large and unhealthy imbalance between public and private goods

Opportunities to consume can be severely limited by lack of time. Women in Africa and Asia spend many hours a day meeting the household's needs for energy and water and have no time left for education, better health care or community activities. Similarly, overworked labourers may receive an adequate wage, but they often work long hours and are denied the opportunity of regular leave. Women frequently

On the continuing influence of affluence
John Kenneth Galbraith

It is now 40 years and something more since I surveyed the scene in the economically advanced countries, especially the United States, and wrote *The Affluent Society*. The book had a satisfying reception, and I'm here asked about its latter-day relevance. That should not be asked of any author, but the mistake having been made, I happily respond. The central argument in the book was that in the economically advanced countries, and especially in the United States, there has been a highly uneven rate of social development. Privately produced goods and services for use and consumption are abundantly available. So available are they, indeed, that a large expenditure on talented advertising and salesmanship is needed to persuade people to want what is produced. Consumer sovereignty, once governed by the need for food and shelter, is now the highly contrived consumption of an infinite variety of goods and services.

That, however, is in what has come to be called the private sector. There is no such abundance in the services available from the state. Social services, health care, education—especially education—public housing for the needful, even food, along with action to protect life and the environment, are all in short supply. Damage to the environment is the most visible result of this abundant production of goods and services. In a passage that was much quoted, and which I thought myself at the time was perhaps too extravagant, I told of the family that took its modern, highly styled, tail-finned automobile out for a holiday. They went through streets and countryside made hideous by commercial activity and commercial art. They spent their evening in a public park replete with refuse and disorder and dined on delicately packaged food from an expensive portable refrigerator.

So it seemed 40 years ago; in the time that has since elapsed the contrast between needed public services and affluent private consumption has become much greater.

Every day the press, radio and television proclaim the abundant production of goods and the need for more money for education, public works and the desolate condition of the poor in the great cities. Clearly affluence in the advanced countries is still a highly unequal thing.

All this, were I writing now, I would still emphasize. I would especially stress the continuing unhappy position of the poor. This, if anything, is more evident than it was 40 years ago. Then in the United States it was the problem of southern plantation agriculture and the hills and hollows of the rural Appalachian Plateau. Now it is the highly visible problem of the great metropolis.

There is another contrast. Were I writing now, I would give emphasis to the depressing difference in well-being as between the affluent world and the less fortunate countries—mainly the post-colonial world. The rich countries have their rich and poor. The world has its rich and poor nations. When I wrote *The Affluent Society,* I was becoming more strongly aware of this difference on the world scene and had started at Harvard one of the first courses on the problems in the poor countries. I went on to spend a part of my life in India, one of the most diversely interesting of the post-colonial lands. There has been a developing concern with these problems; alas the progress has not kept pace with the rhetoric.

The problem is not economics; it goes back to a far deeper part of human nature. As people become fortunate in their personal well-being, and as countries become similarly fortunate, there is a common tendency to ignore the poor. Or to develop some rationalization for the good fortune of the fortunate. Responsibility is assigned to the poor themselves. Given their personal disposition and moral tone, they are meant to be poor. Poverty is both inevitable and in some measure deserved. The fortunate individuals and fortunate countries enjoy their well-being without the burden of con-

science, without a troublesome sense of responsibility. This is something I did not recognize writing 40 years ago; it is a habit of mind to which I would now attribute major responsibility.

This is not, of course, the full story. After the Second World War decolonization, a greatly civilized and admirable step, nonetheless left a number of countries without effective self-government. Nothing is so important for economic development and the human condition as stable, reliable, competent and honest government. This in important parts of the world is still lacking. Nothing is so accepted in our times as respect for sovereignty; nothing, on occasion, so protects disorder, poverty and hardship. Here I'm not suggesting an independent role for any one country and certainly not for the United States. I do believe we need a much stronger role for international action, including, needless to say, the United Nations. We need to have a much larger sense of common responsibility for those suffering from the weakness, corruption, disorder and cruelty of bad government or none at all. Sovereignty, though it has something close to religious status in modern political thought, must not protect human despair. This may not be a popular point; popularity is not always a test of needed intelligence.

So I take leave of my work of 40 years ago. I am not entirely dissatisfied with it but I do not exaggerate its role. Books may be of some service to human understanding and action in their time. There remains always the possibility, even the probability, that they do more for the self-esteem of the author than for the fate of the world.

Author of The Affluent Society (1958)

face a triple constraint that severely affects their consumption choices. Not only is much of their work unpaid, but their domestic obligations on top of their responsibilities for bearing and raising children leave them with little time to do much else. And families in the industrial world find that their overbusy life styles prevent them from enjoying leisure time activities, despite their high incomes. Even though the choice to work long hours is often voluntary, many workers also face pressure to do so. And they may be motivated by a perception of "need" for money that can only be met by working so many hours that they end up with little time and opportunity to use the money they earn.

Information

Information is the key to raising awareness of the range of consumption options available and enabling the consumer to decide which choices are best. Without information, there is no way of knowing what goods and services are available in the market, and what services are being provided by the state and are, by right, available to all. Advertising and public information campaigns play an important role in this respect. As with all things, a balance is required. Commercial information needs to be complemented by public education to make consumers aware of both the benefits and the potential drawbacks of the choices they face. As products become more sophisticated—especially foods, medicines and chemical-based goods—information on how to use them correctly is essential for protecting the health of the consumer and of others.

Social barriers

Income cannot always remove barriers to access to opportunities. This is particularly so when considerations of gender, class, caste or ethnicity limit people's freedom to consume the goods and services they want. For example, people belonging to certain ethnic groups might be denied equal access to education, employment and other basic social services by the state, regardless of how much they earn. Women often face social barriers. In Afghanistan today they are denied the opportunity to pursue formal education and to participate in many economic activities.

The household—decision-making and upbringing

Much analysis of consumer decision-making assumes that the person making the decision is the one who will directly benefit from the consumption. This is far from the truth in many cases. A great deal of household consumption decision-making is in the hands of one person—often the mother or the father of the family. Although this may lead to good outcomes, it can also be a source of inequity within the family—with girls being given less chance to get an education than boys and women being overworked. Sometimes the father controls the money for his own use, not for the family's benefit.

Household values have a wider effect on the consumption options of individual members. The education and upbringing given to children early in life play a critical part in establishing their ability to make good use of the options available for living a full and fulfilling life. The remarkable expansion and diversification in consumption options have made it more difficult for consumers to make informed choices. People are sometimes unaware of the consequences of their decisions. If an infant is not fed adequately, if a child is not sent to school, if an adolescent is not made aware of reproductive health care, if a youth is not given the opportunity to develop a sense of community, they will not have the same ability as others to make choices that maximize their best interests and those of the community.

Consumption and the links with human development

There is a complex chain of links between consumption and human development. Those links can be strong, creating positive impacts for many people. But the links can also break down, producing some negative

Information is the key to raising awareness of the range of consumption options available

impacts—on the consumer and on others, near and far.

Impacts on the consumer

As consumption levels have risen over the past few decades, there have been many positive and previously unimagined impacts on the lives of millions of people. Increased consumption of nutritious food by the undernourished has reduced hunger and improved health. Improved access to medicines and the introduction of new drugs have reduced morbidity and mortality. Massive improvements in transport have greatly increased people's mobility—leading to opportunities for employment and social interaction. The technology revolution in information and telecommunications has made it possible for people living in remote areas to interact with others all over the world—for example, enabling health workers in remote villages to call for emergency help. The impressive advances in refrigeration and packaging technology have greatly improved people's access to nutritious and convenient foods. The increasing availability of such goods and services has transformed the quality of people's lives all over the world.

Yet consumption can sometimes have harmful effects on consumers. Drinking water that is not clean causes disease and can even be fatal. Using cow dung and wood as a cooking fuel produces a smoke that can cause lung disease. Traveling in overcrowded buses or in poorly maintained cars can lead to fatal road accidents. Foods can be contaminated—through poor household hygiene or through substandard production. Electrical products may be faulty and unsafe to use, and toys can contain small parts that cause babies to choke. Although intended to promote health, medicines can be extremely dangerous if they are contaminated, if they are past the expiry date or if instructions are not provided or are not followed. When consumed in large quantities, some foods are unhealthy, causing obesity, heart disease and cancer. And consumers can become addicted to drugs, alcohol or gambling, to the point at which their judgement, health,

self-respect and social standing are impaired.

Impacts on others

Although consumption decisions are made by individuals, they have impacts on others—not only at the household level but in the community and even globally. These impacts—or "externalities"—can be positive or negative.

Positive externalities abound and make an important contribution to human development. Ownership of a telephone by one person in a village can bring information to all. Educating a woman not only opens opportunities to her but also has positive benefits for the health of her family. Vaccinating someone against an infectious disease reduces the health risks for others. A beautiful garden can be enjoyed by all passers-by. And the stronger are community ties, the more opportunities there are for those positive impacts to be spread to others.

Consumption can also have negative effects on other people, breaking the links with human development. These impacts occur both locally and globally, through the environment and through society.

Impacts on others through the environment

Each person's consumption is linked, mainly through production and disposal processes, with environmental impacts that can ultimately cover the globe.

• Use of non-renewable resources (metals, minerals and fossil fuels) depletes their stocks and future availibility.

• Intensive use and abuse of renewable resources (soil, water, wood and fish) degrades their condition and increases scarcity for present and future generations.

• Emissions of pollutants create unhealthy local conditions: cigarette smoke fills a room and traffic fumes hang over a city, harming the health of all around.

• Generation of pollution and waste beyond the earth's capacity to absorb them causes critical changes in the temperature and acidity of the earth, affecting the future of all.

Impacts on others through social inequality and exclusion

The consumption of some goods and services is linked, through production processes, to circumstances that are exploitative of workers. This occurs particularly in poorly regulated markets where the state fails to intervene and protect the rights of workers and small producers. Consumption can also have a negative impact on society when it is used for social rivalry. Pressure to consume "status goods" can be high, leading to debt and the sacrifice of essential goods for the household. Failure to consume a symbolic brand of goods can lead to social exclusion. Lack of access to the technology—especially transport and communications—widely used in the community can exclude individuals from effective participation.

The links between consumption and human development are clearly neither automatic nor always positive. This Report focuses on the question of how and why those links break down. How can they be restored and maintained? What policy actions should be taken? And by whom? This chapter has outlined a conceptual framework within which the links between consumption and human development can be explored. Chapter 3 looks at global trends and illustrates both positive and negative links. Chapter 4 focuses on the impact of consumption patterns on natural resources, examining the links between consumption, environmental impacts and inequality. Finally, chapter 5 discusses the policy options that societies face in restoring and nurturing positive links between consumption and human development.

The links between consumption and human development are neither automatic nor always positive

CHAPTER 3

Consumption in a global village— unequal and unbalanced

Global real consumption expenditure has doubled in the past 25 years

World consumption expenditures, private and public, have expanded at an unprecedented pace, doubling in real terms in 25 years to reach $24 trillion in 1998. This expansion has propelled considerable advances in human development.

• Steady expansions in health care, safe water and sanitation—and quantitative and qualitative improvements in food consumption—have strengthened the capabilities of people for a long and healthy life. These advances range from access to safe water for the millions who would otherwise depend on open ponds and rivers to the most advanced scientific discoveries in medicine, such as cancer treatments. Since 1960 life expectancy has increased from 46 to 62 years in developing countries and from 69 to 74 years in industrial countries—while infant mortality in developing countries has declined from 149 per 1,000 live births to 65, and that in industrial countries from 39 to 13.

• Broadening access to schooling, information and communications technology has vastly expanded the knowledge base and the potential of people—critical in the rise in adult literacy in developing countries from 48% in 1970 to 70% in 1995.

• Expanding consumption of energy, an input to all human activities, has opened myriad opportunities—for cooking, heating and lighting and for transport, production, communications and technological development. Quadrupling in the past half century, global energy consumption is growing faster than the population.

• Growth in transport is opening possibilities for employment and marketing and making it easier to reach schools and dispensaries. While the world population has doubled since 1950, means of transport have increased over eightfold—passenger cars from 53 million to 456 million, and bicycles from 11 million to 109 million (table 3.1).

The past decade of accelerating globalization, and the integration of the global consumer market, have brought rapid changes in consumption patterns, from toothpaste to refrigerators, and led to the spread of global "brand-name" goods. Global merchandise imports grew rapidly from $2 trillion in 1980 to more than $5 trillion in 1995. The share of manufactures in total imports rose in almost every country between 1980 and 1995—from 19% to 54% in Japan, from 40% to 71% in Brazil, from 51% to 81% in Thailand and from 50% to 79% in the United States. Imports of televisions more than doubled in Asia in just the four years between 1990 and 1994, while imports of household equipment more than tripled in Latin America.

The rise in the consumption of manufactured products has been particularly rapid in high-growth economies in Asia and Latin America. Take China. Urban family spending on new durables nearly doubled between 1980 and 1994, while that on traditional durables declined by nearly 10%. With per capita incomes in urban areas increasing 50% between 1981 and 1985, purchases of washing machines, refrigerators and television sets rose 8–40 times—supplied both by imports and by skyrocketing domestic production. By the mid-1980s China was the largest manufacturer of television receivers, with 23% of world output.

The spread of consumer products is reaching more than the urban elite and middle classes. In India in 1994, for example, a survey by the National Council of Applied Economic Research found that more than 70% of rural households owned a portable radio, a bicycle and wrist watches—and

TABLE 3.1
Long-term trends in private consumption of selected items, by region

Item	Year	World	Industrial countries	Developing countries	Sub-Saharan Africa	Arab States	East Asia	South-East Asia and the Pacific	South Asia	Latin America and the Caribbean
Meat (millions of tons)	1970	87	57	29	3	2	8	3	3	10
	1995	199	95	103	6	5	53	8	8	23
Cereals (millions of tons)	1970	473	91	382	27	20	142	41	112	33
	1995	866	160	706	56	49	236	82	212	57
Total energy (millions of tons of oil equivalent)	1975	5,575	4,338	1,237	139	67	407	102	180	306
	1994	8,504	5,611	2,893	241	287	1,019	296	457	531
Electricity (billions of kilowatt-hours)	1980	6,286	5,026	1,260	147	98	390	73	161	364
	1995	12,875	9,300	3,575	255	327	1,284	278	576	772
Petrol (millions of tons)	1980	551	455	96	10	12	11	8	6	48
	1995	771	582	188	15	27	38	19	13	72
Cars (millions)	1975	249	228	21	3	2	0.5	2	2	12
	1993	456	390	65	5	10	7	7	6	27
Bicycles produced (millions)	1970	36	..	..	..	..	..	..	..	..
	1995	109	..	..	..	..	..	..	..	..
McDonald's restaurants	1991	12,418	11,970	448	0	0	123	113	0	212
	1996	21,022	19,198	1,824	17	69	489	409	3	837

Source: FAO 1998; McDonald's Corporation 1997; UN 1996a, 1996c and 1997b.

more than 20% refrigerators. Households owning a sewing machine increased from 39% to 64% in 1988–94, and those owning televisions from 31% to 57%. The upsurge in purchases of consumer durables and products reached even the 90 million lowest-income households in India. Although two-thirds of them had incomes below the official poverty line, more than 50% owned wrist watches, 41% bicycles, 31% transistor radios and 13% fans.

So, there have been many achievements in consumption that are propelling human development. But the current patterns and growth of consumption raise problems:

• The expansion of consumption is badly distributed, with about a fifth of the world's people left out.

• Consumption growth and patterns are environmentally damaging. Thus the consumption of some harms the well-being of others, in both present and future generations.

• Consumption growth and patterns have social impacts that deepen inequalities and social exclusion.

• Consumer rights to information and product safety are difficult to defend in the context of the global consumer market.

Consumption shortfalls and poverty

The poor distribution of the growth of global consumption has left an enormous backlog of shortfalls in areas of consumption essential to human development.

Although consumption is an essential means to human development, not all consumption has the same value. We focus here on those areas of consumption that are most essential to achieving basic capabilities to live long, healthy and creative lives and to enjoy a decent standard of living. These include such basics as food, shelter, clean water, schooling, health care, energy and transport as well as means of communication and freedom of creative and cultural expression (figures 3.1 and 3.2).

Uneven growth and increasing inequalities

Global consumption expenditure, private and public, has grown an average 3% a year since 1970. But this overall figure masks enormous disparities in growth that have widened inequalities.

In low-income countries (except China and India) private consumption expenditure per capita has declined by about 1%

FIGURE 3.1

Growth of consumption has been dramatic, but severe disparities remain

ENERGY AND TRANSPORT

Electricity
Kwh per capita yearly

Industrial countries

7,000
6,000
5,000
2,000
1,000
0

Latin America & Caribbean
Arab States
East Asia
South-East Asia & Pacific
Sub-Saharan Africa
South Asia

1970   1995

Total consumption expenditure
1995 $21.7 trillion

1990
$19.5 trillion

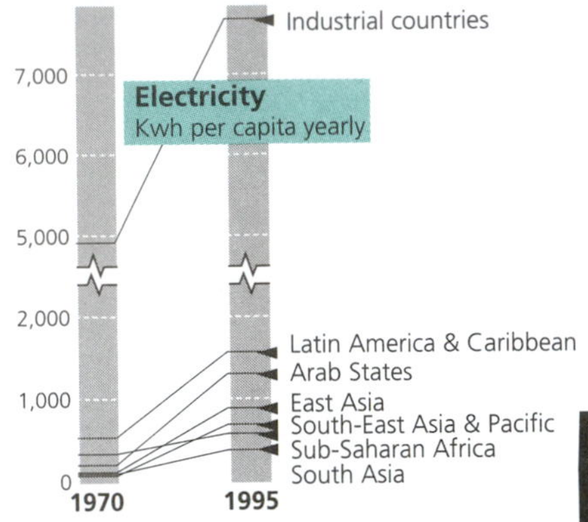

	Total energy Kg of oil equiv. per capita		Cars Per 1,000 people		Petrol Kg per capita	
	1975	1994	1975	1993	1970	1995
Sub-Saharan Africa	455	458	..	11	22	27
Arab States	491	1,215	16	42	32	113
South Asia	216	360	2	5	5	10
East Asia	413	794	1	6	5	29
South-East Asia and Pacific	312	619	7	18	19	39
Latin America and Caribbean	969	1,144	40	61	99	152
All developing countries	420	670	8	16	21	43
Industrial countries	4,240	4,568	289	405	554	500

1980
$15.0 trillion

COMMUNICATIONS

Televisions
Per 1,000 people

Industrial countries

500
400
300
200
100
0

East Asia
Latin America & Caribbean
South-East Asia & Pacific
Arab States
South Asia
Sub-Saharan Africa

1970   1995

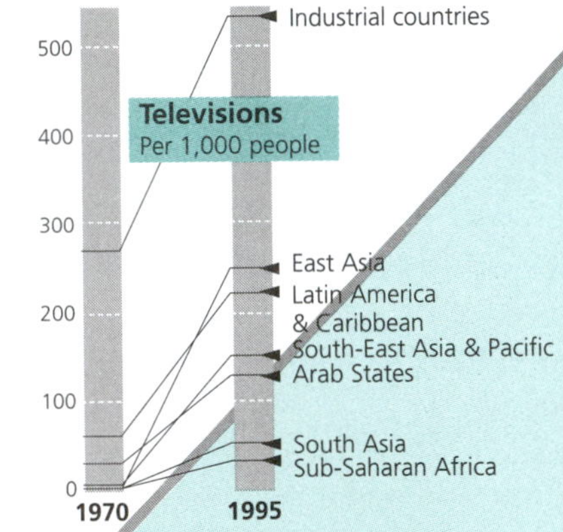

	Printing and writing paper Kg per capita yearly		Telephones Per 1,000 people	
	1970	1995	1975	1995
Sub-Saharan Africa	2.2	1.6	6	12
Arab States	2.1	2.9	8	49
South Asia	1.2	1.9	2	16
East Asia	1.6	7.5	4	49
South-East Asia and Pacific	1.6	6.8	3	29
Latin America and Caribbean	7.2	10.7	34	86
All developing countries	2.2	5.2	8	39
Industrial countries	45.7	78.2	178	414

Total consumption expenditure
1970 $10.2 trillion (1995 prices)

FOOD

Meat
Kg per capita yearly

80
60
40
20
0

Industrial countries

Latin America & Caribbean

East Asia

Arab States
South-East Asia & Pacific
Sub-Saharan Africa

South Asia

1970   1995

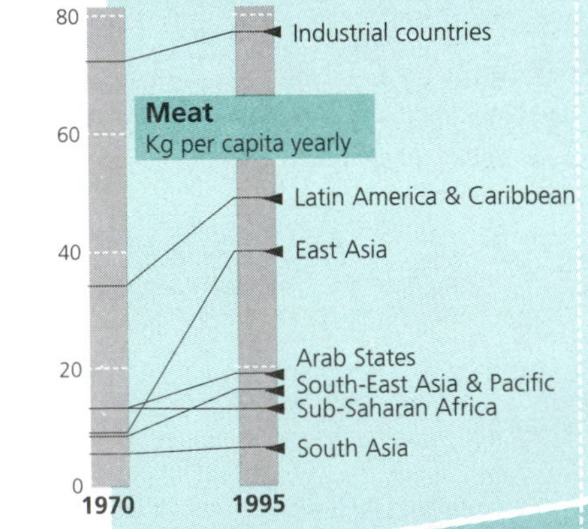

	Calories per capita per day	
	1970	1995
Sub-Saharan Africa	2,225	2,237
Arab States	2,206	2,903
South Asia	2,094	2,385
East Asia	2,041	2,717
South-East Asia and Pacific	1,957	2,533
Latin America and Caribbean	2,491	2,781
All developing countries	2,131	2,572
Industrial countries	3,016	3,157

Industrial countries $16.5

Total consumption
expenditure, 1995:
$21.7 trillion (1995 prices)

Developing countries $5.2[a]

Latin America & Caribbean $1.3

East Asia $1.0

Eastern Europe & CIS $0.8

South-East Asia & Pacific $0.5

South Asia $0.4

Arab States $0.3

Sub-Saharan Africa $0.2

Total consumption expenditure (US$ trillions; 1995 prices)

	1970	1980	1990	1995
Industrial countries	8.3	11.4	15.2	16.5
Developing countries	1.9	3.6	4.3	5.2

Note: Eastern Europe and the CIS countries are not included among industrial countries.

1970   1980   1990   1995

a. Developing country total includes countries not in regional aggregates.

Source: FAO 1997b and 1998; ITU 1997b; UN 1996c and 1997b; UNESCO 1997d; World Bank 1997d.

FIGURE 3.2

The environmental cost is also growing, and many basic deprivations remain

STEADY GROWTH IN CONSUMPTION

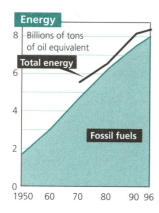

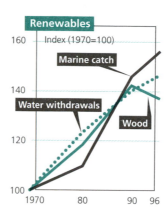

ENVIRONMENTAL COST

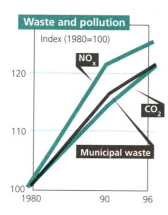

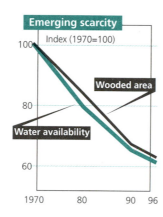

LOSS OF BIODIVERSITY
- About 12% of mammal species, 11% of bird species and almost 4% of fish and reptile species are classified as threatened.
- Between 5% and 10% of the world's coral reefs and half the world's mangroves have been destroyed.
- About 34% of the world's coasts are at high potential risk of degradation, and another 17% are at moderate risk.

DECLINING FISH STOCK
- About 25% of fish stocks for which data are available are either depleted or in danger of depletion, and another 44% are being fished at their biological limit.

SOIL DEPLETION
- Nine million hectares are extremely degraded, with their original biotic functions fully destroyed, and 10% of the earth's surface is at least moderately degraded.

BASIC CAPABILITIES, CONSUMPTION REQUIREMENTS AND DEPRIVATION

Long, healthy life
(freedom from premature mortality and avoidable morbidity)

Requirement	Backlog of deprivation
Clean water	1.3 billion deprived of access to safe water
Shelter	1 billion without adequate shelter
Food and nutrition	841 million malnourished
Health care	880 million without access to health services
Sanitation	2.6 billion without access to sanitation
Energy	2 billion deprived of electricity
Transport	3 cars per 1,000 people in least developed countries, 16 in developing countries, 405 in industrial countries

Knowledge
(freedom from illiteracy, innumeracy and lack of acquired basic skills)

Requirement	Backlog of deprivation
Schooling	109 million (22% of primary-school-age children) out of school
Information	885 million illiterate adults (age 15 and above)
	4 copies of daily newspapers circulated per 100 people in developing countries, 26 in industrial countries
Communication	3 telephone lines per 1,000 people in least developed countries, 40 in developing countries, 414 in industrial countries

Decent standard of living well distributed among members of society

Requirement	Backlog of deprivation
Secure access to material resources	1.3 billion people in developing countries living on less than $1 a day, 32% in transition economies on less than $4 a day and 11% in industrial countries on less than $14.40 a day

Creative life

Requirement	Backlog of deprivation
Culture—language, arts, traditions, philosophy	3,000 of the world's 6,000 languages endangered
Freedom from political and civil constraints	13.2 million refugees
Freedom from time constraints	6–8 hours a day spent by rural women in developing countries in fetching fuelwood and water

Source: CDIAC 1996; FAO 1995, 1996b and 1997c; ITU 1997b; OECD 1997e; Shiklomanov 1996; UN 1996b and 1996c; UNESCO 1997d; World Bureau of Metal Statistics 1996; Worldwatch Institute 1997b; WRI 1994 and 1996a.

TABLE 3.2A

Inequalities in consumption: the world's highest and lowest consumers

Telephone services, 1995

Top 5 countries	Lines per 1,000 people
Sweden	681
USA	626
Denmark	613
Switzerland	613
Canada	590

Bottom 5 countries	Lines per 1,000 people
Cambodia	1
Dem. Rep. of the Congo	1
Chad	1
Afghanistan	1
Niger	2

Meat consumption, 1995

Top 5 countries	Kilograms per capita a year
USA	119
New Zealand	119
Cyprus	108
Australia	107
Austria	105

Bottom 5 countries	Kilograms per capita a year
Bangladesh	3
Guinea	4
Malawi	4
Burundi	4
India	4

Source: FAO 1998; ITU 1997b.

annually over the past 15 years. Both public and private consumption per capita are about 20% lower in Africa today than in 1980.

For the world, average per capita food consumption rose dramatically in the past 25 years. The developing country average—only 2,131 calories per person in 1970, well below the minimum requirement of 2,300 calories—is now 2,572 per person, well above the minimum. But in Sub-Saharan Africa it rose only from 2,225 calories to 2,237. As a result Sub-Saharan Africa was the only region not to see a steady decline in malnutrition: the number of undernourished people more than doubled, from 103 million in 1970 to 215 million in 1990.

Inequalities in consumption patterns and levels are huge (see figure 3.1; tables 3.2a and 3.2b):

• Per capita private consumption expenditure is $15,910 (1995 prices) in industrial countries (excluding Eastern Europe and the CIS), but $275 in South Asia and $340 in Sub-Saharan Africa. And public consumption per capita is $3,985 in industrial countries, but $183 in developing countries.

• Industrial countries, with 15% of the world population, account for 76% of global consumption expenditure. Allowing for differences in purchasing power (using a $PPP measure) would moderate some of these consumption expenditure gaps—however the gaps are still very wide.

• The fifth of the world's people who live in the highest-income countries consume 58% of the world's energy, 65% of electricity, 87% of cars, 74% of telephones, 46% of meat and 84% of paper—86% of total expenditure. In each of these areas the share of the bottom fifth, in the lowest-income countries, is less than 10%.

• The average protein consumption per person is 115 grams a day in France, but only 32 grams in Mozambique. And while annual energy consumption per person is more than 4,500 kilograms of oil equivalent in industrial countries, it is less than a tenth of that in South Asia (300 kilograms).

• For the world the average number of cars per 1,000 people is 90—but it is 405 in industrial countries, only 11 in Sub-Saharan Africa, 6 in East Asia and 5 in South Asia.

• More than 600 telephone lines serve every 1,000 people in such countries as Sweden, the United States and Switzerland, but in Cambodia, Democratic Republic of the Congo, Chad and many other developing countries there is only one line per 1,000 people.

These huge inequalities remain even though consumption has expanded more rapidly in developing countries than in industrial countries, especially in such basic essentials as food and energy. The initial disparities were so large that even with spectacular increases, consumption levels in developing countries have not caught up with those in industrial countries.

• Per capita petrol consumption has increased sixfold in East Asia and ninefold in South Asia since 1950. But while it averages 500 kilograms per capita a year in industrial countries, it is still only 29 kilograms in East Asia and 10 in South Asia.

• Total meat consumption has risen more than fivefold in East Asia since 1970 but is still only 41 kilograms per capita a year, compared with 77 kilograms in industrial countries.

Pervasive consumption shortfalls

Of the 4.4 billion people in developing countries, nearly three-fifths lack access to sanitation, a third have no access to clean water, a quarter do not have adequate housing and a fifth have no access to modern health services of any kind (see figure 3.2). A fifth of primary-school-age children are out of school. About a fifth do not have enough dietary energy and protein, and micronutrient deficiencies are even more widespread—with 3.6 billion suffering iron deficiency, 2 billion of whom are anaemic. This, despite poor households spending at least half their incomes on food (table 3.3). And 2 billion people lack access to commercial energy such as electricity.

These consumption shortfalls hold back human development and lead to human poverty. About 17 million people in developing countries die each year from such curable infectious and parasitic diseases as diarrhoea, measles, malaria and tuberculosis. Micronutrient deficiencies reduce physical strength, intellectual functioning and resistance to disease. Malnourished mothers pass these deficiencies on to their children, making them less alert at school and more prone to sickness. More than 850 million people in developing countries are illiterate, excluded from a wide range of information and knowledge. And in this day of ever-expanding global communications and networking, the poor in developing countries are isolated—economically, socially and culturally—from the burgeoning information and progress in the arts, sciences and technology.

Shortfalls in essential consumption are not just a problem of poor countries. In industrial countries too, many cannot meet their basic needs and the life choices of millions are limited. The United States may have among the highest levels of per capita food consumption in the world—fourth in calorie intake—yet 30 million of its people, including 13 million children under 12, are hungry because of difficulty getting the food they need. In Canada 2.5 million people (9% of the population) received food assistance in 1994—and in the United Kingdom more than 1.5 million families could not afford an adequate diet in 1994. Remarkably, iron deficiency anaemia affects 55 million people in industrial countries.

In Eastern Europe and the CIS the process of transition gave rise to many consumption shortfalls. Malnutrition rose to levels similar to those in many low-income countries. In Russia stunting affected 15% of children two years of age in 1994. In Romania the share of infants who were underweight at birth increased to 10% in 1993, and in Bulgaria in 1991, 17% of children aged three to six were undernourished.

Constraints to meeting basic needs

These inequalities and shortfalls in basic consumption reflect the unequal distribution of income and assets and the uneven rate of economic growth—globally and nationally. About 1.3 billion people still live on less than $1 a day (1985 PPP$), and almost 3 billion on less than $2 a day. In recent decades economic growth has been both qualitatively and quantitatively inadequate. In about 100 countries incomes today are lower in real terms than they were a decade or more ago. These issues are analysed in detail in *Human Development Report 1996* (on economic growth) and *Human Development Report 1997* (on poverty).

Apart from the basic constraints of income and economic growth, several other constraints limit poor people's options for meeting their basic needs: lack of access to public provisions, failure of the market to supply poor people's goods, intrahousehold power relations and the enormous amounts of time the poor must spend walking and carrying.

Public provisioning of basic social services is inadequate—and access is inequitable. Many essentials—schooling, transport, modern energy, health facilities—are provided publicly. For low-income groups public provisioning is often an important source for consumption. Yet the poor suffer consumption shortfalls because they lack access—to water supply, modern energy, sanitation, health, education, public transport and road infrastructure. Access is often highly inequitable, favouring high-income

TABLE 3.2B
Inequalities in consumption: the world's highest and lowest consumers

Private and public health expenditure, 1990

Top 5 countries	Expenditure per capita (US$)
USA	2,765
Switzerland	2,520
Sweden	2,343
Finland	2,046
Canada	1,945

Bottom 5 countries	Expenditure per capita (US$)
Viet Nam	3
Sierra Leone	4
Tanzania, U. Rep. of	4
Lao People's Dem. Rep.	5
Mozambique	5

Public expenditure on education (preprimary, first and second levels), 1992

Top 5 countries	Expenditure per pupil (US$)
Luxembourg	15,514
Finland	11,720
USA	11,329
Austria	9,065
Belgium	8,143

Bottom 5 countries	Expenditure per pupil (US$)
Sri Lanka	38
Nepal	44
Mozambique	46
China	57
Madagascar	60

Source: WHO 1995b; UNESCO 1995.

TABLE 3.3
The lower the household income, the larger the share spent on food and energy, the smaller the share spent on transport, health and education
(as a percentage of household expenditure)

Country	Lowest income quintile					Highest income quintile				
	Food	Energy	Transport	Health	Education	Food	Energy	Transport	Health	Education
Sierra Leone	67.9	6.6	1.9	2.7	1.8	53.9	3.3	8.9	4.7	3.2
Costa Rica	54.4	9.4	4.2	2.1	0.7	29.1	7.5	19.5	4.8	1.0
Thailand	52.8	5.0	3.8	2.6	1.2	25.2	2.9	20.3	4.8	1.0
Jordan	43.4	7.6	3.5	2.4	1.3	32.1	4.1	16.8	2.0	4.7

Note: Data are from household surveys conducted in 1987–94.
Source: Sierra Leone, Central Statistics Office 1993; Costa Rica, General Office of Statistics 1988; Thailand, National Statistical Office 1995; Jordan, Department of Statistics 1993.

FIGURE 3.3
**Public provisioning
is not equitable provisioning**
Percentage of population quintile
with access to public goods and services

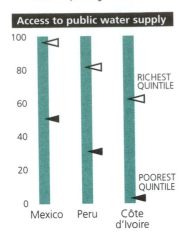

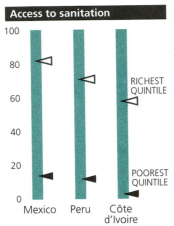

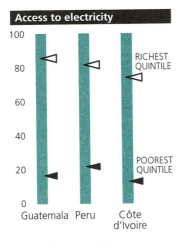

Source: World Bank 1994.

groups and leaving the poor with little or without (figure 3.3). Access also heavily favours urban communities, leaving great deprivation in rural areas (figure 3.4). In Brazil disparities in access due to regional inequalities are marked: in the Central West region 98% of children aged 7–14 are enrolled in school, while in the lower-income North-East region 50% of children are not enrolled.

Even when the poor have access, pricing can undercut them. In Lima a poor family pays more than 20 times what a middle-class family pays for water. Unregulated water markets in the Indian state of Tamil Nadu lead to grotesque inequities: tubewell owners pump groundwater, often using subsidized electricity, and sell it to intermediaries, who then sell it to poor households. The mark-up can be 1,000%!

The increasing "marketization" of education and health services—with growing use of private facilities and private tutors, often accompanied by declining quality in public services—has added to disparities. In Egypt access to basic education has improved, but public spending on education per student has declined. In 1991 non-personnel expenditures were a fifth of what they had been 10 years before. To make up for the declining quality, middle-class parents send their children to fee-charging private schools, which are expanding rapidly.

Supplies of poor people's goods in the market are inadequate. Often, the goods most needed for human development—goods that are affordable for the poor, that meet basic needs, that are environmentally friendly, that create productive work for the needy—are not available in the market. Market incentives for innovation are much stronger for rich people's goods than for poor people's—because profits are larger. The incentives are also stronger for environmentally destructive goods than for environmentally friendly goods—because production costs are lower. And they are stronger for socially negative than for socially positive goods—again, because production costs are lower.

Provision of the goods essential for human development requires technological innovation and product development. Public investment has driven much of the progress in increasing the availability of such goods—oral rehydration salts, seeds of high-yielding varieties of rice, wheat and maize and many other products that have led to better health, improved food security and a cleaner environment.

New incentives are needed to accelerate the provision of poor people's goods—starting with pricing incentives, especially the removal of perverse subsidies, and support for technological development.

Intrahousehold power relations lead to inequitable access and consumption. Households are often assumed to be harmonious units of cooperation, and public policies often target the household as the beneficiary of assistance. But gender research consistently reveals flaws in this assumption. In reality power relations in households often favour boys over girls, and young adults over the aged—in nutrition, education and many other resources. Research shows evidence of boys receiving more food than girls in regions of India and Pakistan. Gender gaps in schooling may be narrowing in all regions of the world, but enrolment of girls still falls short of that of boys in developing countries as a whole—girls' enrolment is 88% of boys' at the primary level, and 78% at the secondary. And when user fees are introduced, it is the girls who are taken out of school, as studies in many countries show, including Côte d'Ivoire and Zambia.

When women retain control over household income, more resources tend to be channelled to the health, education and nutrition of children. Many empirical studies show that women spend their incomes for the entire household, while men spend more on items for themselves—such as entertainment, alcohol and cigarettes. A study in Jamaica shows that compared with male-headed households, female-headed households consume foods of a higher nutritional quality and spend less on alcohol. In Kenya and Malawi a smaller percentage of children in female-headed

households are malnourished. In Côte d'Ivoire research shows that doubling the income under women's control would lead to a 2% rise in the share of the budget for food—and a 26% decline in the share for alcohol, 14% for cigarettes. And a study in Guatemala shows improvements in children's nutritional status when the mother earns a higher share of the income.

Intrahousehold resource allocation shows bias not only by gender, but also by age and by sibling hierarchy. The point: intrahousehold power relations determine claims to consumption. The policy implication: assuming that equity reigns in the household is unrealistic, and policies that target household heads may well be ineffective. Food stamps and assistance to women, for example, are likely to be more effective in securing household food security than are income subsidies for the entire household.

Unequal claims on time restrict consumption choices. Consumption requires time, and each day's 24 hours need to accommodate a variety of consumption objectives. Everyone has those same 24 hours—but gender and differences in access to amenities and resources determine how much time is available—and how much is required—to meet a consumption objective. Just as food takes up the most resources for the poorest families in poor countries, walking—especially to collect firewood and water—takes up the most time resources for poor households, both urban and rural. As recent studies attest, time is the critical constraint people face in meeting all their needs—and in lifting themselves out of poverty.

A study in Ghana shows that a farmer spends 43 minutes a day collecting firewood, 25 minutes collecting water, 48 minutes walking to the farm, 28 minutes to reach the grinding mill and 2 hours and 8 minutes walking to the market—a total of almost five hours. So much time spent walking leaves little time for activities that might enhance health, knowledge and productivity, such as improving care of children and of the aged, improving cultivation of crops and preparing better food.

The time spent working is unequally distributed—with women spending much more time than men in work—paid and unpaid—in virtually every society for which time use studies exist. As *Human Development Report 1995* documented, women take on a larger share of the work—53% on average in developing countries, and 51% in industrial. But the disparities are particularly marked in rural areas of developing countries, where women's work burden is significantly larger than men's—35% more in Kenya, 21% in the Philippines, 17% in Guatemala (figure 3.5). In most industrial countries the disparity is less—but women still take on 28% more in Italy, 11% more in France and 6% more in the United States. A study of rural areas in the United Republic of Tanzania shows able-bodied women carrying 86 ton-kilometres a year, compared with only 11 ton-kilometres for able-bodied men. Women in these areas spend 1,842 hours a year walking—to markets, to fields, to fetch water—but men only 492 hours (figure 3.6).

Policies for securing basic consumption needs

Securing entitlements for all people to the basic essentials has long been an international commitment. The Universal Declaration of Human Rights set the objective 50 years ago: "Everyone has the right to a standard of living adequate for the health and well-being of himself and his family, including food, clothing, housing and medical care and necessary social services." In any country's poverty eradication strategy meeting basic consumption requirements should be an important goal.

Such an objective would make a substantial difference in many sectoral policies. Transport and energy investments are considered primarily as "economic infrastructure" driven by the goal of economic growth rather than the needs of people for mobility and communications. Construction of walkways and bicycle lanes in cities receives little public attention—even though walking is how most people get about, and cycling is the first accessible improvement over walking. More equitable access to such

FIGURE 3.4
Rural populations are poorly served by public provisioning

Index (urban population served=100)

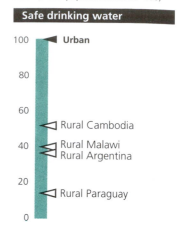

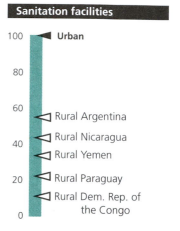

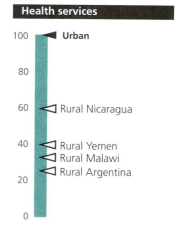

Source: UNICEF 1997.

FIGURE 3.5
Women work longer than men

Index (men's work time=100)

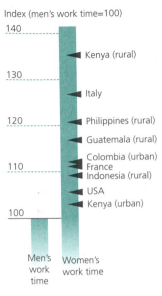

Men's work time

Women's work time

Source: UNDP 1995a.

FIGURE 3.6

Rural transport activities in the United Republic of Tanzania—who carries the load?

TIME SPENT

Hours spent in transport activities yearly

Grinding
169

Marketing
248

Firewood collection
324

Agriculture
441

Water collection
587

Health
73

Total for all activities
492

Women   Men

BURDEN TRANSPORTED

Ton-kilometres yearly

85.6

10.6

Women   Men

Source: Howe 1998.

public infrastructure as clean water, energy, roads and public transport is a key criterion for assessing the performance of a state in democratic governance.

Housing also receives little public attention and is generally left to the private sector. But with the pace of urbanization outstripping the development of sites and services, families have little option but to resort to squatter settlements, where they face the constant threat of eviction. Singapore, in its vision of development and poverty elimination in the early 1960s, had explicit goals to meet needs for housing, transport and a clean environment in addition to schooling and health (box 3.1).

Achieving equitable access—through public investments, fair pricing of services and an enabling environment for private investment—should be a public policy goal in each sector in each country. The post-apartheid government in South Africa has articulated a comprehensive policy for assuring equitable access to basic services (box 3.2).

Rising consumption puts stress on the environment

Almost any human consumption activity produces environmental impacts throughout the life cycle of the product—from production to consumption to waste disposal. The impacts:
• Depletion of the stock of non-renewable resources (like metals and minerals).
• Mismanagement of renewable resources, leading to depletion and degradation—such as overfishing, overexploiting forests, over-exploiting groundwater and exposing soils to erosion.
• Emissions of pollutants that create an unhealthy environment: cigarette smoke filling a room, traffic fumes hanging over a city, industrial effluents choking river life.
• Generation of pollution and waste beyond the sink capacity—the earth's capacity to absorb them—both locally and globally. Toxic waste builds up in landfills, and pollution from oil-burning industries releases carbon dioxide (CO_2), causing global warming.

The unprecedented growth in world consumption is leading to environmental stress through impacts that are both global and local. What are the principal environmental problems affecting human development? Contrary to the fears of the 1960s and 1970s, the problem is not the scarcity of non-renewables, such as metals and minerals. Quite the opposite. There is no immediate shortage, prices for these resources have been falling, and demand is depressed. Consumption of ores and minerals as a proportion of reserves has actually declined with the discovery of new reserves. Far more urgent: the scarcity of renewable resources and the generation of emissions and waste that exceed the sink capacity.

The crisis of renewable resources

The world is facing a growing scarcity of renewable resources essential for sustaining the ecosystem and for human survival—from deforestation, soil erosion, water depletion, declining fish stocks and lost biodiversity.

Deforestation. Since 1970 the world's wooded area has fallen from 11.4 square kilometres per 1,000 inhabitants to 7.3. Only 40 years ago most deforestation was in the industrial countries. Now it is concentrated in the developing world. Over the past decade at least 154 million hectares of tropical forest—three times the area of France—have been cut, and every year an area the size of Uruguay is lost. Latin America and the Caribbean fell 7 million hectares a year, and Asia and Sub-Saharan Africa 4 million each. These estimates tell only part of the story, for they count only land that has lost more than 90% of its forest cover—only a quarter of Africa's loss in the 1980s. Despite rapidly growing global demand for timber, the lost stocks are not being replenished. Worldwide, only 1 hectare of tropical forest is replanted for every 6 cut down—in Africa, 1 for every 32. India, a notable exception, now plants 4 hectares for every 1 felled.

Deforestation has many human and environmental consequences, from scarcity

of fuelwood and building materials to microclimate changes and loss of biodiversity through loss of habitat.

Soil degradation and desertification. Since 1945 nearly 2 billion hectares have been degraded—more than a sixth of the world's productive land—reducing the earth's capacity to support human life. On about two-thirds of this area—equal to a China and an India—agricultural productivity has been greatly reduced or destroyed, with developing countries bearing more than 80% of the damage, most severely in Africa and Asia. Nearly half the world's degraded lands are in Asia, and about half a billion hectares in Africa are moderately to severely degraded—two continents that together have two-thirds of the world's poorest people. Overcultivation, overgrazing and the felling of forests each account for around 30% of the damage—and overexploitation of firewood for another 7%.

Water. Since 1950 water withdrawals have nearly tripled, from 1,365 cubic kilometres a year to 3,760 in 1995. Water availability has declined dramatically, from about 16,800 cubic metres per capita a year in 1950 to 7,300 in 1995 (see figure 3.2). Currently 20 countries with 132 million people suffer from water scarcity, having less than 1,000 cubic metres per capita yearly, a benchmark below which lack of water is considered to constrain development and harm human health. If present trends continue, 25 more countries would be in this situation by 2050, and the total population of all affected countries would grow to 1–2.5 billion.

Water depletion is becoming irreversible as a result of groundwater overpumping and aquifer depletion. Northern China now has eight regions of water "overdraft", covering 1.5 million hectares, much of it productive, irrigated farmland. In Beijing the water table has dropped 37 metres in the past 40 years. In and around Bangkok overpumping has caused land to subside at 5–10 centimetres a year for the past two decades. In the Arabian Peninsula water is being used at nearly three times the rate of recharge—at current depletion

rates, the exploitable groundwater reserves will be empty in about 50 years.

Fish stocks. During the past four decades the world marine catch has increased nearly fourfold, from 19 million tons in 1950 to 91 million tons in 1996. New species of fish and new fishing grounds are being exploited. A growing number of the world's fisheries are at or near the point where yields decline and fish become scarce.

The crisis of pollution and waste

Generated faster than the earth's natural ability to absorb them, pollutants are causing critical changes in the climate and the acidity of the ecosystem. Sulphur dioxide emissions have more than doubled, from 30 million tons in 1950 to 71 million tons in 1994. These emissions are converting rain into acid, crossing national boundaries, destroying forests, degrading soil. Toxic waste from industry and chemical agriculture can seep into the water supply, pollut-

BOX 3.2

The new South Africa—ending apartheid in consumption

Under apartheid, consumption patterns of black and white South Africans were kept separated—not only by the unequal distribution of income, but by unequal access to basic services and suppression of living standards.

People were housed according to colour. There was a shortage of housing and lack of choice for black South Africans. Most houses were government owned and allocated with no consideration of the social standing of the occupant. Row upon row of matchbox houses provided adequate but sparse and soulless accommodation. Only in limited self-build areas were blacks allowed to construct the dwellings of their choice. Government house building came to a halt in the early 1980s at a time when the housing backlog was estimated to be around 600,000 units. Now it is about 2.5 million units.

Added to this was the extremely unequal access to public infrastructure, which left the black population barely able to meet basic needs. A 1993 household survey shows the contrast between the richest 20% (mostly white) and the poorest 40% (mostly black; box table 3.2).

Among the top objectives for the new South Africa is to meet basic needs for all—housing, water, transport, electricity, telecommunications, a clean and healthy environment, nutrition, health care and jobs. In 1995 alone there was a marked increase in access to services among black households: the share with electricity increased from 37% to 51%, those with a telephone from 12% to 14%, those with piped water from 27% to 33%, those with a flush toilet or latrine from 46% to 51% and those with refuse removal by the local authority from 37% to 43%.

The black South African population is a growing market for consumer products. A study by the South African Advertising Research Foundation shows a marked decline in "have nots" among the black population in the past three years.

Yet there is no room for complacency. Progress in service delivery has been positive but much slower than targeted. And where electricity has been brought to households, the consumption is low, as households are not equipped with (or do not shift to) electric appliances. In one survey, however, pensioners said electricity might consume up to a quarter of their income, yet they could no longer imagine living without it. And because other spending could not be cut, they sought credit.

Only a few years ago a cartoon neatly captured the stereotypical viewpoints of the problems of South Africa's divided society. A white family was picnicking on the roadside surrounded by an impressive array of equipment—coolers, camping tables, radio—virtually a portable household. Passing on foot was a rural black family. The woman had a small bundle on her head, her baby on her back and a toddler by her side. The caption: "too many children," thought the white picnickers; "too many things," went through the heads of the black passers-by. This kind of cartoon may one day be a historical curiosity.

BOX TABLE 3.2
Apartheid in consumption in the old South Africa

	Poorest 40%	Richest 20%
People per room	2.0	0.5
Percentage of households with:		
Electricity	21.4	97.5
Piped water in house	27.5	97.6
Flush toilet or improved latrine	18.4	97.5
Wood as main source of fuel for cooking	47.6	0.2

Note: Data are from a 1993 household survey.

Source: Moller 1997.

1950 to 22,660 million tons in 1995. The burning of fossil fuels—oil, coal and gas—has grown nearly fourfold since 1950 and is the prime cause of the carbon dioxide emissions responsible for the greenhouse effect and global warming. These emissions already exceed the capacity of the world's forest vegetation to absorb them. And with rising emissions and declining forest areas, that capacity is being squeezed on both ends. Scientists predict dire human consequences: declining crop yields, increasing infectious diseases, changing monsoons and more flooding, forever taking land from people.

Waste generation too has grown exponentially. In OECD countries per capita municipal waste grew 30% in the past two decades, reaching 510 kilograms in 1995, two to five times the level in developing countries.

The uneven geography of consumption, environmental damage and human impact

The nature and full magnitude of these environmental impacts can only be appreciated through life-cycle analysis of a product. Such analyses show the full environmental impacts, including all materials that are moved, processed or wasted during extraction, production, distribution and disposal. Because of global integration in production, trade and consumption, these impacts are distributed around the world.

Who gains and who loses? The world's dominant consumers—the beneficiaries—are concentrated among the well-off. The fifth of the world's people in the highest-income countries account for 86% of the $21.7 trillion in total global consumption expenditure in 1995. The costs of environmental damage are more broadly shared, with the poor suffering more acutely than the better-off.

The crises of renewables, a major source of global poverty, endanger the livelihoods of millions, especially the rural people who derive their livelihood directly from the natural environment around them. They are the poorest, in Asia, Africa, Latin America and the Arab States. By even the most conservative estimates, at least 500 million of the

ing the soil and entering the food chain. Carbon dioxide (CO_2) emissions have quadrupled, from 5,740 million tons in

world's poorest people live in ecologically marginal areas. Environmental degradation means that they must go further in search of water and firewood, and they suffer falling land productivity, which adds to the threat to their livelihoods. Population growth is an obvious source of this pressure, but it is only one element in the population-environment-poverty nexus that drives the growing scarcity. Growing demand as the incomes of the affluent increase is another source. Today's upward trend in fish catch is for exported non-food use, mainly animal feed and oils. The consequence is pressure on a natural resource that provides low-cost, nutritious food for almost a billion people in 40 developing countries who rely on fish as their primary source of protein. And deforestation meets the demand of industry.

The geography of global warming also illustrates the uneven shares of the rich and poor in environmental damage and impact. Some 60% of carbon dioxide emissions come from the industrial countries. But it is the climate of the developing world that is most at risk of change, and studies project that the impact will fall largely on developing countries. Bangladesh, for example, will lose huge areas of land if global warming leads to rising sea levels. But Bangladesh now emits only 183 kilograms of carbon dioxide per capita annually, compared with the industrial country average of 11,389 kilograms. There could also be a serious threat to the very existence of the Maldive Islands. In addition, the poor are less able to defend themselves against these harmful effects. Poor countries cannot afford to build extensive sea walls—and poor people cannot afford to pay for increasingly scarce water and productive agricultural land (see chapter 4).

Rapid economic growth and rapid urbanization have put several developing countries on a steep curve of rising resource use and pollution. Acid deposition has been particularly high in such industrial areas as south-east China, north-east India, the Republic of Korea and Thailand. And within 15 years 60% of the annual carbon dioxide emissions will come from the developing world, intensifying the damage if urgent and innovative action is not taken globally.

Even though consumption in developing countries is growing rapidly on a per capita basis, it is still far below the levels of the industrial countries and in some basic commodities, such as food, energy and clean water, it is below minimum requirements. The per capita use of six common metals was 31 kilograms in the industrial countries in 1990—only 3 kilograms in the developing world. The per capita consumption of commercial energy in the industrial world in 1994 (4,452 kilograms of oil equivalent) was eight times that in the developing world (568 koe).

On a per capita basis, annual carbon dioxide emissions in industrial countries still far exceed levels in the developing countries. While per capita emissions are 2,981 kilograms in East Asia and 1,549 in South-East Asia and the Pacific, they are 11,389 kilograms in industrial countries. Average per capita petrol consumption in industrial countries is 500 kilograms a year, more than 10 times the 43 for developing countries on average, the 29 kilograms for East Asia and the 39 for South-East Asia.

The extension of agricultural land adds to soil erosion, changes ecosystems and reduces biodiversity. But growth in food consumption and intensification of agriculture are needed in poor countries, where 841 million people suffer consumption shortfalls in food and billions suffer deficiencies in iron and other micronutrients.

Prospects

Environmental damage is an important source of global poverty and is deepening inequality (see chapter 4). But in the past decade enormous efforts have been made to address many of the environmental impacts of modern consumption growth and patterns. Results have been very positive.

First, growth in the use of material resources has slowed as a result of shifts in demand towards less material-intensive products such as services. Technological innovations have led to improved efficiency in energy and material use. Recycling rates for many key raw materials have increased, and bulk materials have been progressively

The geography of global warming illustrates the uneven shares of the rich and poor in environmental damage and impact

replaced by lighter materials. World demand for metals and minerals rose by 120% between 1961 and 1990, but the growth rate has declined—from 6% in the 1960s to 2% in the 1990s. Material use has begun to grow more slowly than the global economy—thus there has been dematerialization. Per capita use of steel, timber and copper, for example, has stabilized or even declined in OECD countries.

Second, emissions have been brought under control with tighter regulations and incentives. Shifting to cleaner technologies and switching away from sulphur-heavy solid fuels towards oil and natural gas have led to sharp declines in sulphur emissions. Pollution loads from pulp and paper making have been dramatically reduced at many large mills with the advent of non-chlorine bleaching processes and strict environmental regulation.

Third, although the volume of municipal waste has continued to rise in most countries, the increase has begun to slow or to decline in some areas with improved waste management.

These trends are promising, but there is still a long way to go. If current trends in consumption patterns continue, global environmental pollution will increase and the degradation of the earth's renewable resource base will accelerate.

To achieve a more sustainable pattern of development and preserve the natural ecosystems for future generations, environmental damage must be reversed. The challenge is twofold:

• *Addressing natural resource scarcity for the poor.* This requires a variety of measures to redistribute public provisioning and private incomes, to ensure land tenure for poor people and improve community management of the local environment. It also requires a series of measures to address the profound economic, political and social causes of poverty.

• *Reversing the rising environmental damage from emissions and waste,* generated largely by high-income consumption patterns. This requires technological solutions to reduce energy and material intensity; institutional solutions to manage common resources such as air, water, fisheries,

forests and pasture; regulatory measures and standards for emissions and waste management; and market-based mechanisms, especially prices that internalize environmental externalities.

The challenge is particularly acute for the poorer countries facing the double problem of having to accelerate consumption growth to lift people out of poverty but needing to do so in the most environmentally friendly way. The growth patterns of the postwar industrial countries and the rapid growth in Asia and elsewhere in recent decades are too environmentally damaging. Alternative models need to be developed that rely on more environmentally friendly technologies that leapfrog the steps followed by industrial countries.

Impacts of consumption on society

The levels, patterns and growth of consumption have major impacts on employment—and thus on society. When consumption falls, demand falls and economic growth falters—disastrous for the lowest-income countries.

But social and economic impacts do not stop there. Consumption incurs side-effects—or external costs—on society through the production process. Those effects depend on who is employed and how they are involved in production and marketing—on who profits and who loses in the competition for markets. Some goods can generate fair employment for the poor and contribute to equitable development— as with the garment production that empowers women through wage employment in Bangladesh, and the coffee grown by smallholders and traded through cooperative networks.

In contrast, the consumption of goods whose production exploits the wage labourer or the smallholder hurts global society and works against development that is equitable, participatory and sustainable. Carpets produced by child labour deprive the children of an education and a childhood.

Consumer advocates are highlighting these impacts and promoting fair trade through social labelling and alternative trading organizations. As the interconnectedness

Alternative models need to be developed that rely on more environmentally friendly technologies

of consumers and producers becomes more recognized, consumer movements are shifting from self-interest to global social goals. For many years consumer groups mobilized mainly to demand better and cheaper products. Now they are directing more attention to the social impacts of production and marketing. And with the global integration of consumer markets, this mobilization is becoming international. Consumers in Sweden demand clothing made without child labour. The Seikatsu club in Japan is forging "people-to-people" dialogues with producers in Bangladesh. And Dutch consumers are forming alliances with small farmers in Costa Rica (see box 5.11).

Conspicuous consumption, social exclusion and inequality

Commodities serve as a means of social identity and social communication, and their social symbolism heavily influences consumption patterns. Food is sought not only for nutrition and survival but also for entertainment, communication and community activities. What food is served depends on the needs of nutrition and on the social occasion and the social composition of those present—family meals are intended to be simple and nutritious but at weddings elaborately prepared luxury foods are served.

Economists and social scientists have explored these social dynamics in different ways. While early writers focused on property and income as determinants of class, Max Weber was the first to show that consumption patterns and life styles are powerful determinants of social class and status. Thorstein Veblen pointed out the importance of conspicuous consumption—of achieving social status within a community as a motivation for consumption of visible "status goods". Contemporary anthropologists explain consumption decisions as driven by "social commitments" (see box 2.1).

The social symbolism of consumption is central to the cultural traditions of all people, even as early as 40,000 years ago among the Cro-Magnons (box 3.3). The creativity in producing beautiful designs for everyday objects—dishes, furnishings, clothing, architecture, landscapes—is part of a flour-

ishing culture. The use of commodities for strengthening social ties brings joy and subtleties to social relations and builds social cohesion (box 3.4).

Yet the symbolic power of consumption can also turn destructive. For just as consumption can create social bonds, it can be a powerful source of exclusion. Examples abound from all communities in all times. A teenager without fashionable brand-name shoes may feel ashamed among his peers at school. In rural India a young woman can be excluded from marriage where standards for dowry are beyond the means of her family.

Unequal income distribution translates into social exclusion if a society's value system places too much importance on what a person possesses rather than what a person is or can do. And if social standards are rising faster than incomes, consumption patterns can become unbalanced. Household spending for conspicuous consumption can crowd out such essentials as food, education, health care, child care and saving for a secure future.

The new era of global consumption is bringing new trends in competitive and conspicuous consumption, as standards are upscaled, as consumer credit grows and as consumerism dominates values.

Upscaling social standards—faster than income growth. Social standards of consumption—the kind of clothing, housing and transport one uses—are rising every-

The social symbolism of consumption is central to the cultural traditions of all people

BOX 3.3

40,000 years ago—the first consumers?

The rapid emergence of personal ornamentation may have marked not a difference in mental capabilities between Cro-Magnons and Neanderthals but new forms of social organization that demanded the communication and recording of ideas.

Significant innovations in technology were developed not so much to improve efficiency in hunting or gathering as to achieve aesthetic goals. In the Aurignacian period (about 40,000 to 28,000 years ago) the Cro-Magnons devised various techniques for working ivory, including the preparation and use

of metallic abrasives for polishing. They used ivory to create beads, pendants and figurines—but rarely to manufacture tools and weapons.

The Cro-Magnons also made objects from mammal bones and teeth, antlers, fossil, freshwater shells, coral, limestone and many other stones. They did not choose these raw materials at random. Some materials came from sources hundreds of miles away, through trade. And only a dozen or so of the thousands of shell species available on the Atlantic and Mediterranean shores became personal ornaments.

Source: White 1993.

The community feast builds social solidarity

In many traditional societies the surplus of goods was redistributed through celebrations. In one of the most famous the north-western Indians of Canada destroyed beautifully produced objects in a community ritual called the potlatch. Although those objects were lost, giving them as gifts to the community created goodwill among all. This was a form of investment in social solidarity.

In other cultures such occasions of redistribution were aimed at creating greater equality of incomes. For example, in many Mexican Indian cultures social structure was based on a "cargo system" in which the heads of affluent households held community positions such as mayor. They would finance the annual feast of the village and employ members of poorer households as musicians, dancers, decorators, cooks,

embroiderers and messengers. They would pay the people in cash or in kind—use of oxen for ploughing, or permission to cut reeds for basket making. *Viva la fiesta!* Everyone was invited to eat and drink at the feast, which helped support local widows and orphans. Such consumption was also an investment for the village heads, who could then count on reciprocity of favours.

This use of consumption for redistributing incomes and creating social solidarity is disrupted, however, when these economically isolated communities are brought into the market economy. Both the goods consumed and the services needed for the feast are brought in from outside the community, so the wealth flows out rather than being redistributed within the community.

Source: Arizpe 1997.

FIGURE 3.7
Declining rates of savings

Savings as a percentage of disposable household income

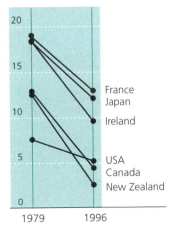

Source: OECD 1997b.

where. What was considered a luxury 20 years ago is now a necessity—a private car for every middle-class family in France, a wrist watch for every rural family in India, a refrigerator for every family in China. For the same income, the consumption of luxury items is increasing. Take the private car—with a price out of reach for most people in developing countries. Owning a car was exceptional in the 1940s and 1950s in almost all countries but is now the norm for middle-class families everywhere. In the 1940s there were 16 cars per 1,000 people in Germany, 27 in Austria, 30 in Italy and 36 in France. When the same level of income was reached in Japan in the 1960s, car ownership was low, at 16 per 1,000. But by the 1980s, when Brazil, Chile, Malaysia and Mexico reached this income, car ownership had become the norm and it was 50–64 per 1,000 in these countries—two, three or four times what it had been in other countries at similar income levels in earlier years.

Whatever the causes, this rising consumption reveals the rising standards. Other studies indicate the same trends. Studies of US households found that the income needed to fulfil consumption aspirations doubled between 1986 and 1994—

to more than twice the median income (boxes 3.5 and 3.6).

Rising consumer credit—declining household savings. The rising consumption of luxuries has gone hand in hand with income growth and increased savings in many countries. In India the aspiration to own household durables is thought to be an important motive for the rise in the household savings rate. But when the rising aspirations are not matched by rising incomes, the spending on luxuries and visible status symbols—the latest brand of shoe or shirt, the lavish wedding, the fast car—can squeeze household budgets, leaving little for savings.

There are signs that consumers are stretching their incomes to buy more and more, with consequent increases in consumer debt and declines in household savings. The average American household saves only 3.5% of its disposable income, about half the rate of a decade and a half ago, and the median value of household financial assets was only $13,000 in 1995. One survey in the United States found that only 55% of households did any saving in the previous year. Concurrently, indebtedness has been rising relentlessly for a decade—to $5.5 trillion in 1997. Much of this growth is driven by credit card debt, which doubled between 1990 and 1996. In almost all other OECD countries household savings have been declining (figure 3.7).

Household debt has been on the rise in many countries. Liabilities as a percentage of disposable income rose from 74% to 101% in the United States, from 85% to 113% in Japan, from 58% to 70% in France and from 8% to 33% in Italy between 1983 and 1995. In Chile credit and cheque defaults are on the rise. In Brazil a popular form of consumer financing is through cheques without cover—they rose sixfold as a percentage of cheques from 1994 to 1996. And in 1996 alone bank consumer credit increased by 28%. Of 1.5 million Brazilian families with incomes of less than $300 a month, two-thirds had debts.

An important element in this picture is that it is increasingly easier to spend because of the expansion of consumer credit. Between 1992 and 1996 the number of credit cards in circulation increased by 83% in Germany, 62% in France, 48% in the United States and 42% in Italy.

Consumerism and values—divergent trends and questions. Are people overconcerned with possessions? Many studies show that people care more about the environment, the common good, their relationships with others. Yet there is also a rise in pathological behaviour—clearly exceptional rather than the norm, but a major concern for society. It includes the growth in shoplifting, the rise in violent crime to obtain status goods (athletic shoes, leather jackets, designer sunglasses) and the greater incidence of compulsive buying.

To encourage the use of consumption to build social solidarity, foster creativity and cement relationships—rather than to exclude people and undermine social solidarity—will require conscious efforts to foster positive values. Opinion leaders—in the media, politics, government, business, religious organizations, community, family—all need to work together to ensure that people are valued for what they are, not what they possess.

Impacts on consumer health— consumer rights to product safety and information

Many products can jeopardize consumers' health and safety because they are intrinsically harmful: car seatbelts that do not hold up, food with salmonella, tinned foods past their expiry dates.

Other products, not harmful in themselves, become so when abused or put to inappropriate use. Cigarette addiction compromises the lives of many millions. About 3.5 million deaths a year are attributed to smoking. The "affluent diet" is rich in salts, sugar and saturated fats and contains much less fibre and complex carbohydrates than the traditional diet. It carries its own dangers—of cancer, heart disease and diabetes, especially later in life. Obesity is rising rapidly, especially among the poor in industrial countries and the middle classes in developing countries of Asia and Latin America. In the United States it is esti-

BOX 3.5

Upscaling the American dream

"I used to think of the American dream as the house with the little picket fence and the two-car garage, two kids and a dog and a cat.... If you look at the old *Beaver* movies, they didn't show these huge mansions. What's different now? Just the whole thing of *more*. I'm not saying that's bad and I'm not saying I'm not in that category. I'm just saying that the American dream … I think it's expanding."

The upscaling of the American dream started in the 1980s, prompted by the escalating life styles of the most affluent. Between 1979 and 1989 the top 1% of households in the United States increased their incomes from an average of $280,000 a year to $525,000. The rich and the super-rich took conspicuous consumption to new heights. This is the group that is now widely watched and emulated, whose visible consumption is the life style to which most Americans aspire. A recent survey of American consumers found that a third would someday like to be a member of the group that "really made it", a category representing the top 6% of American society.

And how much income would they need to "fulfil all their dreams"? The answer was $50,000 in 1986. By 1994 it had doubled to $102,000.

But keeping up is increasingly hard. Between 1979 and 1994 families in the top 20% increased their share of income from 42% to 46%, while the share of every group beneath them fell. All along the line, the gaps between the groups grew larger.

BOX TABLE 3.5
Survey of consumption wants and needs
(percentage of respondents)

	1975	1991	Percentage change
What makes a "good life"?			
Vacation home	19	35	+84
Swimming pool	14	19	+36
Job that pays more	45	60	+33
Interesting job	38	38	0
Happy marriage	84	77	−8
What is a necessity?	1973	1996	
Second television	3	10	+233
Home air conditioning	26	51	+96

Source: Schor 1998.

mated that a third of adults above age 20 suffer from obesity.

With the rapid shifts in consumption to more and more manufactured goods, including many chemical-based products, consumer safety and protection become increasingly complex and important. Developing countries are vulnerable to the dumping of commercial imports that could be hazardous: countries report imports of powdered milk at bargain prices but past expiry dates, and imports of milk contaminated with high radioactive content after the Chernobyl disaster. Many countries have banned DDT but others still manufacture and use it. How many other products are banned where standards are high but sold where standards are lacking?

Consumer groups worldwide have successfully campaigned for government regulations and standards in the interest of consumers—for stricter limits on additives

and pesticide residues in foods and higher safety standards in cars. They have lobbied against powerful commercial pressures to relax standards. Their years of public campaigns resulted in the recognition of the deadly environmental impact of factory effluents that caused the "Minamata disease" in Japan, and the effects of the thalidomide widely prescribed in Europe, which caused birth defects in thousands of children.

Another example: the Bangladesh national drug policy, enacted in 1982 after considerable pressure from civil society groups. The main purpose is to protect the rights of consumers by restricting the marketing of harmful drugs, ensuring quality control and making quality medicines available to people at fair prices. The policy also sought to break the monopoly of multinational companies and encourage local producers. And it introduced the use of generic names for essential medicines, avoiding enticing brand names.

The benefits have been substantial. By 1992 the share of essential drugs in local drug production increased from 30% to 80%. Drug prices stabilized, increasing only 20%, compared with a 180% increase in the consumer price index. Local companies increased their share of production from 35% to more than 60%, and overall production more than tripled. Meanwhile, the proportion of substandard drugs fell from 36% to 9%.

Information imbalances

Information and awareness are always essential, but the need becomes even more imperative in the new global markets—not just for accurate information but also for balanced information covering the potential harm of products as well as their attraction. Globalization is bringing a constant stream of new products, produced far away in unknown conditions (box 3.7).

The abuse of unfamiliar "goods" has long been a source of social disaster. Alcohol brought to the Americas in the 17th century led to widespread and entrenched alcoholism. Tinned food brought to Nauru led to unbalanced diets, obesity and malnutrition. Infant formula brought to villages without access to clean water has threatened infant survival, leading to the deaths of an estimated 1.5 million babies a year. And then there is tobacco, brought back from the Americas in the 17th century. Tobacco consumption is a growing problem in Africa, Asia, Latin America and the Arab States, even as it declines in Europe and North America, the result of massive public awareness campaigns and the requirement to include warnings in all advertisements and packaging (box 3.8).

The predominant source of product information is now commercial advertising. If unchecked, commercial advertising can be deceptive. Companies can claim qualities with no scientific basis—and products can arrive in a country before health warnings are made known. Advertising can provide incomplete information—not disclosing the risks associated with tobacco, for example. And it can be particularly deceptive for those with few alternative sources of information—children, those with little schooling, those who read little.

Advertising is now a $435 billion business. But that's a conservative estimate of annual global expenditures. If all forms of marketing are included, the figure rises to nearer $1 trillion. Global advertising spending—up sevenfold since 1950, growing a third faster than the world economy—is still concentrated in North America, Europe and Japan. But growth has been faster in Asia and Latin America, especially since the mid-1980s and early 1990s. Over the past 10 years individual countries in these regions have shown spectacular advertising growth: for China more than 1,000%, for Indonesia 600%, for Malaysia and Thailand more than 300% and for India, the Republic of Korea and the Philippines more than 200%. And compared with GDP levels, the advertising expenditures in developing countries are particularly high (table 3.4 and box 3.9).

The revolution in information technology and telecommunications has dramatically altered the geography of information and intensified the unbalanced flow of information. A village in China is as likely to be linked to Hollywood movies and advertising on satellite television as by road or railroad to a village 50 kilometres away. Growth in global communications and media products has skyrocketed. China had 11 million cable television subscribers in 1990—35 million in 1995 (3 per 100 people). India had 7 million in 1993, and 16 million in 1995. Mexico's 610,000 in 1990 doubled to 1.2 million in 1995. Annual sales of televisions in Brazil, Chile and the Republic of Korea are now at or above the levels in most industrial countries (around four to six sets per 100 inhabitants). Annual sales of personal computers are now 35 per 1,000 people in the Republic of Korea, higher than in Norway (16) and the United Kingdom (19). For Malaysia the figure is 9 per 1,000, the same as in Denmark, and higher than in Spain and Sweden, at 8 per 1,000. And for Brazil it is 6 per 1,000, higher than in Greece (3) and Ireland (4). Many other countries are rapidly catching up, with the number of personal computers doubling in the past few years, or even increasing tenfold, as in Ghana, Pakistan and Romania.

Access to information through the global media and global advertising now rivals access to information through

The revolution in information technology and telecommunications intensified the unbalanced flow of information

BOX 3.8

Tobacco—the emerging crisis in the South

The World Health Organization estimates that 3.5 million people die annually from causes related to tobacco use, with more than half these deaths occurring in industrial countries. By the 2020s, however, when the death toll is likely to reach 10 million each year, 70% of tobacco-related deaths will be in developing countries.

Smoking is the primary cause of lung cancer. It is associated with heart disease, stroke, emphysema and lung diseases. Children who are regularly exposed to second-hand smoke are prone to respiratory illnesses. Smoking during pregnancy can increase the risk of miscarriage, result in low infant birthweight and impede child development. Tobacco consumption is the leading cause of preventable death in many countries. In both industrial and developing countries half of regular smokers die from causes related to their tobacco use. Smokers are three times as likely to die between the ages of 35 and 69 as are non-smokers.

Since the 1970s vigorous antismoking campaigns have been mounted in most industrial countries—banning tobacco advertising in the media, increasing cigarette taxes, requiring health warnings on cigarette packages, banning cigarette sales to minors and disseminating information.

But in most developing countries information campaigns lag far behind, while marketing and advertising campaigns have intensified. Per capita cigarette consumption fell by 10% between the early 1970s and early 1990s in industrial countries. But in the same period consumption increased by 64% in developing countries. Per capita consumption more than doubled in Haiti, Indonesia, Nepal, Senegal and Syria, and tripled in Cameroon and China.

Source: WHO 1996a and 1998; Worldwatch Institute 1997a.

TABLE 3.4
The spread of advertising to the developing world—top 10 countries in advertising expenditure as a share of GDP, 1986 and 1996

	1986				1996		
Country	Advertising as a percentage of GDP	Education as a percentage of GDP	Total advertising expenditure (US$ billions)[a]	Country	Advertising as a percentage of GDP	Education as a percentage of GDP	Total advertising expenditure (US$ billions)[a]
USA	1.6	5.0	94.6	Colombia	2.6	3.4	1.4
Australia	1.4	5.4	4.3	United Kingdom	1.4	5.5	16.6
United Kingdom	1.4	4.9	13.0	New Zealand	1.4	6.4	1.0
New Zealand	1.1	4.4	0.7	Hong Kong, China	1.4	2.8	2.2
Hong Kong, China	1.1	2.8	1.1	Korea, Rep. of	1.4	3.7	6.7
Switzerland	1.0	5.1	2.7	Venezuela	1.4	5.0	1.0
Colombia	1.0	2.8	0.5	USA	1.3	5.4	101.2
Spain	1.0	3.3	4.2	Taiwan, China	1.2	..	3.4
Venezuela	1.0	5.0	0.6	Brazil	1.2	..	8.2
Finland	0.9	5.3	1.0	Australia	1.2	5.4	4.7

a. In constant 1996 dollars.
Source: Hutton 1997 and UNESCO 1997d.

schools, books and newspapers. Hungarian primary school children, for example, now spend 1,000 hours a year watching television, and 1,100 hours in school. In Japan the ratio is 800 to 1,300, and in the United States it is 1,300 to 1,400. And while television sales in emerging economies have skyrocketed, newspaper circulation has stagnated or even fallen. In Brazil television sales doubled from 1990 to 1994, while newspaper circulation declined by 8%.

Societies need to consider the powerful impact of advertising on young children, for whom all information has an educational and formative impact. Children constitute an important market for consumer products, but society has a responsibility to educate them, not exploit them. Sweden has legislated a ban on advertising targeted at children and is advocating the same for all European countries (box 3.10). Such protection of consumer interests is possible only in an environment that encourages a free press, open dialogue and political activism.

Civil action has almost always led the way in pressuring for government action for consumer protection. But against the $435 billion in advertising spending, civil action will always be underfinanced.

Consumers would benefit if some of this spending could be set aside for alternative, more balanced information and education. If incentives for advertising to keep itself in check could be built in, such set-asides could be even more effective (see box 5.3).

The same global environment that leads to negative impacts from consumption also presents opportunities to tackle them. The communications revolution has opened contacts and fostered networks among disparate groups around the world. This has increased

BOX 3.9

China—advertising in a socialist market economy

Advertising is a tool of commercial business marketing. But it can also be used by governments or NGOs. In China it is used by the state for transformation of the economy into a "socialist market economy".

During the Cultural Revolution advertisements disappeared from newspapers. All shop windows were pasted with big character posters. Only political slogans were on billboards. Party policy concluded that advertising was a "capitalist tool", a "societal waste" and "not adding any value to commodities."

Since the economic reforms of the 1970s advertising has made a dramatic comeback. It is now officially "an accelerator for the economic development of China" as a "means of promoting trade, earning foreign exchange and broadening the horizons of the masses". On 15 March 1979 the *Wenhui Daily* featured the first foreign advertisement in China after the Cultural Revolution—for the Swiss watch Rado. Advertising expenditures grew more than 40% yearly between 1981 and 1992, far faster than GNP. By 1993 China had climbed to 15th place in the ranking of countries by volume of advertising business.

Modernity, emphasized in so many commercials, is a pillar of Chinese national ideology driving economic progress. An analysis of 570 magazine advertisements in 1982–92 showed modernity, technology and quality as three predominant cultural values reflected. Chinese television commercials emphasize modernity (32%), youth (8%), family (7%), technology (7%) and tradition (5%).

But modernity does not mean westernization. From the inception of the "Four Modernizations" programme, a line was drawn between modernization and westernization. While promoting western technology and management skills, the programme prohibits western life styles and political systems.

According to national regulations for advertising introduced in 1982, advertising is to "serve the needs of socialist construction and promote socialist moral standards". It prohibits advertising that is "reactionary, obscene, superstitious, or absurd in content".

Source: Zhang 1997.

information and understanding about the distant consequences of consumption. It has also forged new partnerships for creating a system of checks and balances among consumers, producers and governments.

• • •

These changing patterns of consumption in the global village of the 1990s show increasing imbalances with human development. Links between consumption growth and human development have not been automatic.

Consumption has propelled advances in human development, yet there are growing trends in consumption that are harmful to the health and safety of the consumer and to the well-being of others through environmental and social impacts. The links between consumption and human development are being broken as:

• Rising global consumption has not spread to those most in need. Consumption growth has been rapid for the rich, but more than a billion have been left out, suffering shortfalls in basic essentials for human development—clean water, food with adequate energy, protein and micronutrients, housing, schooling, health care, energy and means of transport and communication. And despite rising consumption among many in poor countries, disparities remain huge.

• Globalization has integrated consumer markets, making available a wide variety of consumer goods all over the world and spreading global consumption standards. But it has marginalized many whose incomes have not kept up, and the risks of spreading harmful consumption have intensified as product safety standards and information campaigns have failed to keep up with the spread of products. And the information revolution, the media revolution and the spectacular rise of advertising

in developing countries have all brought great imbalances in information to consumers.

• The pressures of competitive spending and rising social standards of consumption continue, with worrying trends showing the consumption of "luxuries" rising faster than the consumption of "necessities", and the social power of consumption leading to exclusion rather than inclusion.

• Rising consumption puts stress on the environment. And these environmental stresses hurt the poor most severely. The next chapter explores these links between environmental damage and poverty, looking at how the burdens of the damage to the environment from consumption are shared and at how environmental damage and poverty interact, often caught in a reinforcing downward spiral.

CHAPTER 4

Unequal human impacts of environmental damage

Environmental damage almost always hits those living in poverty the hardest. The overwhelming majority of those who die each year from air and water pollution are poor people in developing countries. So are those most affected by desertification—and so will be those worst affected by the floods, storms and harvest failures caused by global warming. All over the world poor people generally live nearest to dirty factories, busy roads and waste dumps.

There is an irony here. Even though poor people bear the brunt of environmental damage, they are seldom the principal creators of the damage. It is the rich who pollute more and contribute more to global warming. It is the rich who generate more waste and put more stress on nature's sink.

Yet there are also environmental challenges that stem not from growing affluence but from growing poverty. As a result of increasing impoverishment and the absence of alternatives, a swelling number of poor and landless people are putting unprecedented pressure on the natural resource base as they struggle to survive.

Poor people and environmental damage are often caught in a downward spiral. Past resource degradation deepens today's poverty, while today's poverty makes it very hard to care for or restore the agricultural resource base, to find alternatives to deforestation to prevent desertification, to control erosion and to replenish soil nutrients. People in poverty are forced to deplete resources to survive, and this degradation of the environment further impoverishes people.

When this self-reinforcing downward spiral becomes extreme, poor people are forced to move in increasing numbers to ecologically fragile lands. Almost half the world's poorest people—more than 500 million—live on marginal lands.

The poverty–environmental damage nexus in developing countries must be seen in the context of population growth as well. In the developing world pressures on the environment intensify every day as the population grows. United Nations projections indicate that the global population in 2050 will be 9.5 billion, with 8 billion in developing countries. By 2050 the population of Africa will be three times that of Europe, and China's will be four times North America's.

To feed this projected 9.5 billion human beings adequately will require three times the basic calories consumed today, the equivalent of about 10 billion tons of grain a year. To produce that much, all the world's current cropland would have to be farmed at three times the current global average productivity.

Yet each year almost 15 million acres of drylands are added to the 3.2 billion acres that have already been moderately or severely desertified. And population growth will contribute further to land degradation—the rough overgrazing, overcutting and overfarming. The situation can be expected to get worse.

The issue of the poverty–environmental damage nexus is complex, and explaining it in terms of income levels only is too simple. Questions of the ownership of natural resources, of access to common resources, of the strength or weakness of communities and local institutions, of the way information about poor people's entitlements and rights to resources is shared with them, of the way people cope with risk and uncertainty, of the way people use scarce time—all these are important in explaining people's environmental behaviour (box 4.1).

Some kinds of environmental degradation are truly global concerns, such as global warming and the depletion of the ozone layer. Others are international—acid rain, the state of the oceans, the condition of rivers that run through several countries. Others still are more localized, though they may occur worldwide—air pollution, water pollution, soil degradation.

And regardless of the categorization, the costs of environmental degradation for human well-being are enormous (table 4.1). Fewer than a fifth of poor households in developing countries have water connections to their houses, so poor people bear the brunt of water pollution. The rural poor suffer too because they are at the bottom of the energy ladder: of the 2.7 million deaths related to air pollution each year, 1.8 million are caused by indoor pollution in rural areas, most among poor households relying on traditional fuels. And the degradation of 1.5 billion hectares of land in developing countries ruins the lives and livelihoods of poor people. In all these cases the damage falls disproportionately on those least able to bear it.

This chapter analyses the disproportionate consequences of local and global environmental damage for poor people, presenting the geography of environmental impacts. It also presents a scenario for

future environmental degradation, recognizing positive developments, concluding with some relevant policy issues and pointing to the recommendations in chapter 5.

Local environmental damage hurts poor people most

Local environmental concerns—water pollution and contamination, air pollution, waste disposal—have immediate and

TABLE 4.1

Estimated costs of environmental degradation in selected Asian countries

Country	Year or period	Environmental damage	Annual cost (US$ billions)	Cost as a percentage of GDP
China	1990	• Productivity losses caused by soil erosion, deforestation and land degradation; water shortage and destruction of wetlands	13.9–26.6	3.8–7.3
		• Health and productivity losses caused by environmental pollution in cities	6.3–9.3	1.7–2.5
Indonesia	1989	• Health effects of particulate and lead levels above WHO standards in Jakarta	2.2	2.0
Pakistan	Early 1990s	• Health impacts of air and water pollution and productivity losses from deforestation and soil erosion	1.7	3.3
Philippines	Early 1990s	• Health and productivity losses from air and water pollution in the vicinity of Manila	0.3–0.4	0.8–1.0
Thailand	1989	• Health effects of particulate and lead levels above WHO standards	1.6	2.0

Source: ADB 1997.

FIGURE 4.1
**Access to safe water
and basic sanitation
in developing countries**
Number of people, 1996 (billions)

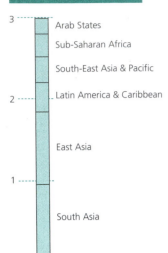

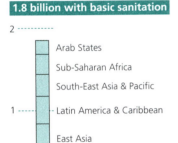

Source: Human Development Report Office.

directly attributable effects on people. Dirty water causes disease; air pollution and inadequate waste disposal make people sick. They affect not only human health, but people's livelihoods and survival.

Water pollution and contamination

Water pollution and contamination affect people the world over, but by far the greatest impact on human well-being is in developing countries, especially in the poorest. Concerns about the effects of toxic chemicals and minerals, such as pesticides and lead, in drinking water in industrial countries are serious and well founded, but the effects seem small beside the widespread illness from simple contamination by sewage in developing countries.

Recent years have seen big improvements in access to safe water and adequate sanitation (figure 4.1). In developing countries nearly 2 billion people have gained access to safe water and 400 million people to basic sanitation during the past one and a half decades. But these gains in many cases have passed by the poor.

As a result nearly 30% of the population of developing countries, more than 1.3 billion people, lack access to safe water—and nearly 60%, or over 2.5 billion, to basic sanitation (table 4.2). Excrement ends up in ponds, streams and ditches and on open ground. More than 90% of the waste water of the developing world is discharged directly into streams, open drains, rivers, lakes and coastal waters without treatment. On average, Asian rivers carry 50 times as

much bacteria from human excrement as do those in industrial countries (box 4.2). Water pollution as measured by organic pollutants and suspended solids is most serious in Asia and Africa (figure 4.2).

As a result of this pollution, water-borne diseases—diarrhoea, dysentery, intestinal worms and hepatitis—are rife in developing countries, particularly among poor people. Diarrhoea and dysentery account for an estimated 20% of the total burden of disease in developing countries. Every year polluted water produces nearly 2 billion cases of diarrhoea in the developing world, and diarrhoeal diseases cause the deaths of some 5 million people (including 3 million children). Contaminated water also leads to 900 million cases of intestinal worms and 200 million cases of schistosomiasis. If everyone had access to safe water and basic sanitation, 2 million young lives would be saved every year.

Fisheries, one of the main sources of livelihood for poor people—and of protein for many more—are being damaged by sewage. Major declines in fish catches have been documented in rivers near cities in China, India, Senegal and Venezuela. And in Manila Bay, heavily polluted by vast quantities of sewage carried by two major rivers, fish yields have declined by nearly 40% during the past decade. About 100 million of the world's poorest people depend on fishing for all or part of their livelihoods.

In industrial countries the overuse of fertilizers causes great water pollution problems. Over the years nitrates from overloaded fields work their way through the groundwater supplies. Nearly a quarter of the groundwater in Europe—west and east—has contamination levels above the European Union's maximum permissible concentration. Meanwhile, nutrients from fertilizers wash off the land into inland waters and the sea, causing blooms of toxic algae. Fertilizers are less of a problem in developing countries, though nitrates have been found in the water supply of both São Paulo and Buenos Aires. High levels of arsenic, linked to heavy use of phosphatic fertilizers, have appeared in groundwater in six districts in West Bengal, India, and one in Bangladesh— killing some of those who drink the water.

TABLE 4.2

Lack of access to safe water and basic sanitation—a regional profile, 1990–96
(percent)

Region	People without access to safe water	People without access to basic sanitation
Arab States	21	30
Sub-Saharan Africa	48	55
South-East Asia and the Pacific	35	45
Latin America and the Caribbean	23	29
East Asia	32	73
East Asia (excluding China)	13	..
South Asia	18	64
Developing countries	29	58
Least developed countries	43	64

Source: Human Development Report Office.

In industrial countries a third of waste water is discharged untreated. Rivers generally are becoming cleaner in OECD countries, but there still are major problems in Eastern Europe and the former Soviet Union. Four-fifths of water samples from 200 rivers in the former Soviet Union were found to be dangerously contaminated, and the water of the river Vistula is too dirty over much of its length even for industrial use.

In developing countries public water utilities have often failed to serve people because of inefficiency and leakages. As a result in many parts of the developing world the private sector and communities are launching initiatives to provide safe water to people (box 4.3).

Air pollution

Air pollution from industrial emissions, car exhaust and the burning of fuels at home kills more than 2.7 million people every year—mainly from respiratory damage, heart and lung disease and cancer (table 4.3). The toll is heaviest where it is most overlooked.

Although air pollution is normally seen as predominantly a problem of industrial countries, more than 90% of the deaths occur in the developing world. Although it is normally seen as affecting the air outdoors, more than 80% of the casualties are from indoor pollution. And although it is normally seen as affecting towns and cities, more than two-thirds of the mortalities are in rural areas.

Poor people in developing countries, at the bottom of the energy ladder, must burn dung, wood and crop residues indoors for their cooking and heating, especially in Sub-Saharan Africa, the region with the majority of the least developed countries. In most other regions traditional fuel use has declined substantially during the past two decades (figure 4.3). Traditional fuels are much more polluting than modern alternatives such as kerosene, propane, biogas and electricity. Burning such fuel fills houses with smoke swirling with hundreds of toxic substances, killing 2.2 million people a year, mostly in rural areas, where most of the poor live. Both indoor air pollution and

poor nutrition increase susceptibility to respiratory infections in the developing world.

Nearly two-thirds of the deaths from indoor air pollution are in Asia. In Latin America, where a large proportion of the poorest people live in city slums, nearly two-fifths of the deaths from causes related to indoor pollution are in urban areas. Women and children, particularly girls, spend the most time indoors and are disproportionately affected.

Outdoor air pollution—once almost entirely concentrated in the industrial countries—is now growing rapidly in the developing world. Rapid industrialization in many countries has greatly increased pollution, and the spread of motorized vehicle ownership is raising emissions all over the world. Vehicle exhaust, coal burning and smoke from factories form small particles in the air that cause serious health damage.

High vehicle densities also lead to congestion, noise, rising traffic accident rates and lost time—all at significant cost (table 4.4).

FIGURE 4.2
Water pollution

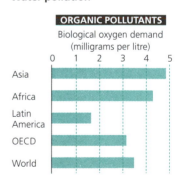

ORGANIC POLLUTANTS
Biological oxygen demand (milligrams per litre)

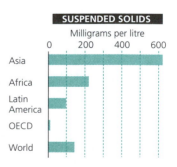

SUSPENDED SOLIDS
Milligrams per litre

Source: ADB 1997.

Improving access to safe water—public-private alliance in Guinea

In the 1980s less than 15% of the population in Guinea had access to safe water. By 1996 that share had increased almost fourfold to 55%. In a decade Guinea had brought one of the least developed water supply services in Sub-Saharan Africa to the point at which it could provide safe water to more than half the population. Guinea still has a long way to go, but its progress is impressive.

These significant achievements in the provision of safe water are the result of a public-private alliance. After 1989 Guinea restructured the water sector, transferring the water supply authority and responsibility for planning and investment to a new autonomous authority, SONEG. A new company, SEEG, was created to operate and maintain the facilities. SEEG is a joint venture, 49% owned by the government and 51% by a foreign private consortium.

The strength of the Guinean arrangement lies in the clarity of responsibilities and incentives. Under a 10-year lease contract SEEG operates and maintains the system at its own risk, with remuneration based on the user charges it collects as well as new connections. SEEG can increase its profits by improving the collection rate and reducing operating costs and unaccounted-for water.

The collection rate has increased dramatically, from 20% to 70%, and technical efficiency and coverage have improved. Tariff collection has increased from 60 Guinean francs per cubic metre before the lease contract to 680 Guinean francs in 1993 and is expected to reach full cost recovery this year.

SONEG has steadily increased the number of customers in Conakry and other cities. Between 1989 and 1993 it added 8,000, raising the total from 13,000 to 21,000. Since SONEG has ultimate responsibility for capital financing, it also has incentives to seek adequate tariffs and invest prudently.

Source: World Bank 1995a.

Lead, often added to petrol and so emitted by car exhaust, has been eliminated from petrol in some OECD countries and is being phased out in others, but it is still used heavily in developing and transition economies (figure 4.4). In these countries it continues to harm human health, permanently impairing children's development. In 1990 in Bangkok 30,000–70,000 children were reported to be at risk of losing four or more IQ points because of high lead emissions. In Latin America and the Caribbean, where almost three-fourths of the people live in urban areas, nearly 15 million children below two years of age are particularly at risk. The children of the poorest urban dwellers often are worst affected, because they tend to live near busy roads.

Studies suggest that outdoor air pollution causes 2–3% of all urban deaths in the Czech Republic, Poland and the United States. Particulates alone—tiny particles in black smoke—are estimated to kill 24,000 Britons each year, and several times as many Americans. Some parts of Eastern Europe and the CIS are affected even more. Nearly 5% of deaths and 4% of disabilities in Hungary are attributed to air pollution. More than 70% of the deaths from outdoor air pollution are in developing countries.

Although few studies have been done on the effects of air pollution in developing country cities, estimates in Mexico City suggest that particulates kill 6,400 residents a year. Air pollution caused more than 175,000 premature deaths in China in 1995 and nearly 2 million cases of chronic bronchitis. Damage to health and buildings from air pollution may cost Bangkok $1 billion a year. The total health costs of particulate air pollution in developing country cities were estimated to be nearly $100 billion in 1995, with chronic bronchitis accounting for $40 billion. Many municipalities, from Los Angeles to cities in Eastern Europe and the CIS—such as Katowice, Poland—are implementing broad-based strategies to

FIGURE 4.3

Changing reliance on traditional fuel sources

Traditional fuel as a percentage of total fuel use

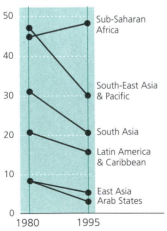

Source: Human Development Report Office.

TABLE 4.3

Air pollution takes its toll—a regional picture, 1996
(thousands)

Region or country	Deaths from indoor pollution		Deaths from outdoor pollution in urban areas	Total
	Rural	Urban		
India	496	93	84	673
Sub-Saharan Africa	490	32	..	522
China	320	53	70	443
Other Asian countries	363	40	40	443
Latin America and the Caribbean	180	113	113	406
Industrial countries	..	32	147	179
Arab States	..	..	57	57
Total	1,849	363	511	2,723

Source: WHO 1997a.

TABLE 4.4
Estimated losses due to traffic jams in selected cities, 1994

City	Annual cost of time delay (US$ millions)	Cost as a percentage of local GNP[a]
Bangkok	272	2.1
Kuala Lumpur	68	1.8
Singapore	305	1.6
Jakarta	68	0.9
Manila	51	0.7
Hong Kong	293	0.6
Seoul	154	0.4

a. GNP in the region in which the city is located.
Source: WRI 1996a.

curb pollution. Some cities in developing countries are successfully managing their air quality (box 4.4).

Besides harming human health, air pollution causes direct economic losses. Germany loses an estimated $4.7 billion in agricultural production every year as a result of air pollution, Poland $2.7 billion, Italy $1.8 billion and Sweden $1.5 billion. The adverse effects from crop damage hit the poor particularly hard.

Domestic solid waste

Domestic solid waste continues to increase worldwide in both absolute and per capita terms (table 4.5). With affluence, the composition of waste changes from primarily biodegradable organic materials to plastic and other synthetic materials, which take much longer to decompose, if they do at all.

In developing country cities an estimated 20–50% of the domestic solid waste generated remains uncollected, even with up to half of local government recurrent spending going for waste collection. In most

TABLE 4.5
Domestic solid waste generation— a regional picture, early 1990s

Region or country group	Per capita waste generated annually (kg)	Population served by municipal waste services (%)
Developing countries	100–330	50–70
OECD	510	96
European Union	414	99
North America	720	100

Source: UNCHS 1997.

industrial countries the entire urban population is served by municipal waste collection, but with rising consumption, cities confront ever-growing mounds of garbage.

Poorly managed domestic solid waste seriously threatens health. In areas lacking sanitation, waste heaps become mixed with excreta, contributing to the spread of infectious diseases. Again, the poor suffer most. They live near waste disposal sites, and their children are the waste-pickers.

Uncollected domestic waste is the most common cause of blocked urban drainage channels in Asian cities, increasing the risk of flooding and water-borne diseases. But in the developing world there is increasing concern about dealing with domestic solid waste. Innovative attempts have even been made to transform waste into fertilizer (box 4.5).

Industrial hazardous waste

Toxic effluents from mines, chemical producers, pulp and paper plants and leather tanning factories are playing an increasing

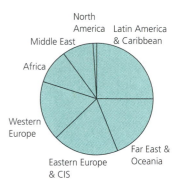

FIGURE 4.4
Lead emissions from petrol consumption, 1990
Regional shares of total lead emissions

Source: Matthews and Hammond 1997.

BOX 4.4
Successful air quality management—the Chilean story

Air pollution in Santiago, the capital of Chile, is the most obvious environmental problem in the country. About 5.5 million people, 40% of the country's population, live in the metropolitan area. The urban transport system must handle 8.5 million trips a day within greater Santiago. The nation's fleet of motor vehicles doubled between 1985 and 1996, from 284,000 to 561,000. Now Santiago is one of the most polluted population centres in the world.

But recently the government has been quite successful in combating the problem through legislation and enforcement of laws. New legislation is based on the Framework Environmental Law, which provides the basis for a gradual improvement in environmental quality, while avoiding conflict between industry, government and pressure groups.

Earlier, Santiago had been characterized by unregulated public transport services and unlimited air pollution. In response, a bidding system for route concessions was introduced in the early 1990s. The system established a scheme allowing only modes of transport that meet certain requirements to use the busiest streets.

To encourage more environmentally sound use of automobiles, the Pollution Prevention and Clean-Up Plan for the Metropolitan Region proposes such measures as toll roads, the elimination of parking lots and changes in their rate structures. The ultimate goal of the plan, which was drafted by the National Environment Commission, is to reduce the levels of certain pollutants to acceptable standards by 2011. The steps include revamping private and public transport fleets, using improved fuels, curbing urban sprawl and establishing sustainable mechanisms for controlling airborne emissions from industry.

As a result of these efforts, Chile today has good and improving air quality management capabilities with an excellent monitoring network, an emissions inventory and strengthening regulatory and administrative structures.

Source: Larenas 1997.

role in environmental pollution. The typical contaminants are organo-chlorines, dioxins, pesticides, grease and oil, acid and caustic and heavy metals such as cadmium and lead. Most are generated in industrial countries (table 4.6).

Workers in facilities that produce toxic materials and people living close to waste disposal sites are the main victims of the effects of these contaminants. Illegal dumping and improper disposal are common in many developing countries, allowing wastes to leach into and contaminate water supplies. Asia's rivers contain 20 times as much lead on average as those in industrial countries. Jakarta Bay, where some 30,000 small industries discharge untreated waste, has a high accumulation of toxic heavy metals. In Peru 20,000 tons of mining waste laden with cyanide washed into the Pacoy River last year.

In addition to causing health-related risks, contamination of water threatens shipping and fishing industries. In China most toxic solid wastes are disposed of in the municipal waste streams without treatment—contaminating soils and waterways

with such heavy metals as lead, arsenic and mercury and threatening or destroying marine life. Recently, however, there have been initiatives to control industrial effluents in the developing world through the use of fees, as has been done in Malaysia.

Pesticides are used most widely in industrial countries. Indeed, the effects in industrial countries may be more widespread than in developing countries, if more subtle. As many as 50 million Americans may be drinking water polluted by pesticides, and the US National Research Council has estimated that up to 20,000 may die each year from the effects of the relatively low levels in food.

But again it is the world's poor who suffer the most acute effects from pesticides. They pose a major occupational health hazard for poor farmers and farm workers, who are easily exposed to dangerous levels. These workers use pesticides without training or protective clothing and are often unable to read even simple instructions. As many as 25 million agricultural workers in the developing world—11 million of them in Africa—may be poisoned each year, and hundreds of thousands die. In recent years, however, alternatives to pesticides have sometimes been used to reduce the adverse effects of pesticide use in Africa and Asia (box 4.6).

The poor are most at risk, too, from accidents and discharges involving factories—for they tend to live nearest to them. Population growth, increasing urbanization and rural-urban migration have given rise to large squatter settlements in developing countries—*favelas* in Brazil, *juggias* in India and *barrios* in Venezuela. Squatter housing accounts for more than 50% of the total housing stock in Caracas and Dar-es-

---

BOX 4.5

Managing solid waste—the experience in Alexandria, Egypt

Alexandria, the second largest city in Egypt, generates around 1,700 tons a day of domestic solid waste. And with nearly 40% of Egypt's industry, Alexandria also generates nearly 800 tons of industrial waste a day.

The high percentage of domestic waste in total solid waste creates problems because of its high moisture content. It contaminates water and pollutes the environment, spreading disease and posing health risks. In the short run industrial wastes produce toxicity by ingestion, inhalation and skin absorption or corrosivity. And in the long run they pose a potential carcinogenic hazard through polluted underground and surface water.

But Alexandria found an innovative way to deal with its solid waste—turning it into organic fertilizer, or compost. That takes care of the waste itself and in the process produces something useful

for agriculture. The idea has received strong support from the national government.

In the mid-1980s a composting plant was established in the city's central district, Abbis. The processing technology is window-type fermentation. At first the plant was running a deficit, but within two years it started generating profits as prices for compost increased.

The Abbis compost plant produces 160 tons of fertilizer every day, at a price per ton of about $8. There is a heavy demand for compost among farmers, who have found that it boosts agricultural productivity.

The Abbis plant has shown that waste can have productive uses. With the demand for compost in Egypt estimated to be as high as 8 million tons a year, many observers have recommended replicating the experiment on a larger scale.

Source: Serageldin, Cohen and Sivaramakrishnan 1995.

TABLE 4.6

Hazardous waste in industrial regions, early 1990s
(thousands of metric tons)

Region or country group	Hazardous waste produced
OECD	258,000
North America	220,000
European Union	27,000
Nordic countries	1,300

Source: Human Development Report Office.

Salaam, more than 40% in Karachi and between 25% and 30% in Tunis. In Asia a quarter of the urban population lives in slums. These slums are made of cardboard and scrap materials, poorly served with water and sewerage and built on hazardous landfills.

The Bhopal disaster in India in 1984—when a cloud of lethal gases swept out of the Union Carbide factory—was particularly severe because a squatter settlement was pressed up against the factory grounds. It killed nearly 8,000 people and injured more than 50,000. In the aftermath the lawsuit was moved to India from the United States so that a smaller compensation could be negotiated. After a long drawn-out legal process the victims were reportedly paid a meagre amount. Thus the Bhopal disaster was not just a severe industrial accident—it was also a case of environmental injustice.

The rising costs of responsible toxic waste management (now up to $3,000 a ton) have encouraged the export of toxic waste from industrial to developing countries, where it can be buried untreated for as little as $5 a ton. In the late 1980s it was reported that several African countries—in urgent need of foreign currency as commodity prices plunged and their debt soared—became dumping grounds for industrial country waste.

Between 1984 and 1986 the former Soviet Union dumped tons of hazardous waste in Benin. Between the late 1980s and early 1990s Paraguay and Uruguay were reported to be destinations for waste shipments from Europe and the United States. But in early 1998, in a meeting in Malaysia of the Parties to the Basel Convention on the Ban on Hazardous Waste, more than 100 countries agreed to ban such exports.

Soil degradation and desertification

Water contamination, air pollution and indiscriminate waste disposal have the most immediate human impact—and their effects are relatively easy to quantify. But in the longer term the effects of the degradation of the world's natural systems are just as serious, for they both further impoverish hundreds of millions of poor people and

BOX 4.6

Alternatives to pesticide use

Integrated pest management and biological control have proved to be successful alternatives to pesticides. The first method relies on such techniques as crop rotation and intercropping to inhibit the proliferation of weeds, pests and pathogens. Biological control relies on nature's own checks and balances. Natural predators are introduced to keep pest populations to a minimum, or pest breeding is disrupted by the release of sterilized males.

Integrated pest management has produced good results in Brazil, China and India. In Brazil its introduction in soyabean production has reduced pesti-

cide use by more than 80% over seven years. In cotton production in Jiangsu Province in China, pesticide use decreased by 90%, pest control costs were reduced by nearly 85% and increases in yields were reported. The introduction of integrated pest management in Orissa, India, has cut insecticide use by 30–50%.

Biological control has worked well in Sub-Saharan Africa and Costa Rica. In Africa it has brought mealy bug pests under control in some 65 million hectares of land planted with cassava. And in Costa Rica it has reduced banana pest populations.

Source: Lean 1992.

undermine the very basis of development. They also are much harder to reverse. It is generally easier to provide safe drinking water or to clean up dangerous waste dumps than it is to restore badly degraded land—and given the political will, it can be done much faster.

Nearly a third of the world's people—almost all of them poor—depend directly on what they can grow, gather or catch. And while everyone on earth ultimately depends on its natural systems, the poor are particularly vulnerable to degradation of those systems.

The geography of soil degradation shows that the problem is severest in Asia and Africa, where two-thirds of the world's poor people live (figure 4.5). Population growth has often been identified as the driving force behind soil degradation. But increasing population density need not undermine environmental sustainability (box 4.7).

Soil degradation affects human life in three main ways:
• It reduces the availability of agricultural land per capita and agricultural productivity. Pressure on arable land stemming in part from soil degradation has reduced per capita farmland in developing countries to a tenth of a hectare, compared with half a hectare in industrial countries.
• It reduces the fodder available for cattle.

FIGURE 4.5

The magnitude of soil degradation

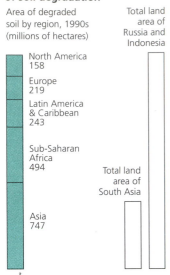

Area of degraded soil by region, 1990s (millions of hectares)

North America 158
Europe 219
Latin America & Caribbean 243
Sub-Saharan Africa 494
Asia 747

Total land area of Russia and Indonesia

Total land area of South Asia

Source: Matthews and Hammond 1997.

• It turns people into environmental refugees searching for more fertile land.

The crisis is worst in the drylands, which stretch across a third of the world's land surface. Here the soils are particularly fragile, vegetation is sparse, the climate is especially harsh—and land degradation is defined as desertification. Patches of degraded land erupt and spread like a skin disease, joining up to produce desertlike conditions over vast areas.

Desertification already costs the world $42 billion a year in lost income—Africa alone, $9 billion a year. But the human cost is even higher. Some 250 million people, and the livelihoods of a billion, are at risk from slashed crop yields. The poor people on the drylands of developing countries are among the most marginalized on earth—economically, politically and geographically. Extraordinarily vulnerable, they rarely have rights to their land. Traditional methods of managing the ecologically sensitive soils are being edged out as more and more good land is used for monoculture, often for export, pushing poor farmers onto ever more marginal territory.

This is not just a developing country phenomenon. The continent with the greatest share of dryland suffering moderate to severe desertification is North America, with 74%, just beating Africa, with 73%. In all, more than 110 countries are at risk.

Drought can cause disaster. One person in six in Burkina Faso and Mali has had to leave land as it turns to dust. About 135 million are in danger of becoming environmental refugees.

Deforestation

About a third of the earth's original forests have disappeared, and about two-thirds of what is left has been fundamentally changed (figure 4.6).

Deforestation has significant human costs. Forests have been a major source of food, fodder, fuel, fibre, timber, dyes and oils for medicine. Cutting them can rob poor people of their livelihood as well as their medicines. In many parts of the developing world poor communities able to draw at least half their food from forest products have never had famine. That ability is now diminishing. In the Philippines, for example, 50% of the forest was lost to commercial logging during the Marcos regime; a few hundred families shared the $42 billion in revenue, leaving 18 million forest dwellers impoverished.

Forests do wonderful things. They bind soil to the ground, regulate water supplies and help govern the climate. Cutting them seriously impairs these attributes. Two-fifths of the world's people depend on water absorbed by the forests of mountain ranges. But when the trees have been felled, rainwater sheets off the land, causing first floods, then drought. Tens of millions of hectares in India have become more vulnerable to flooding as a result of deforestation.

BOX 4.7

Population growth and environmental sustainability—the Machakos miracle

Many people believe that rapid population growth is incompatible with sustainable management of the environment. But the experience of Machakos District in Kenya clearly demonstrates that this need not be so. In some cases increasing population density is required for environmental sustainability.

Between 1932 and 1990 the population of Machakos increased from 240,000 to 1.4 million. Until the late 1930s significant soil degradation and erosion had been observed in the district, most of which is semi-arid and often subject to moisture stress. This suggests the likelihood of population-induced degradation on a large scale, and that was the assessment in the 1930s. But the population-environment nexus affected the situation positively—in two ways.

First, the concern about soil degradation and erosion led to such measures as bench terracing to conserve soils. The activity was rooted in the community through a variant of the traditional work party, *mwethya*. In the 1950s more than 40,000 hectares of land were terraced, a success described as the Machakos miracle. In the 1980s more than 8,500 kilometres of terraces were constructed annually, compared with a peak of about 5,000 kilometres earlier.

Second, increasing population density has had positive effects in Machakos. The increasing scarcity (and rising value) of land promoted investment, both in conservation and in high-yielding improvements. Integrating crop and livestock production improved the sustainability of the farming system.

Many social and institutional factors—a good policy framework, better physical infrastructure, a secure land tenure system, indigenous technology, an improved health and education system—facilitated the agricultural changes in the Machakos District. More and more women took on leadership roles. In this setting farmers were receptive to suggestions regarding soil conservation, moisture retention and tree planting.

The results have been impressive. Between 1930 and 1987 the productivity of food and cash crops increased more than sixfold. Horticulture productivity grew fourteenfold.

The Machakos experience offers an alternative to the Malthusian models. It clearly demonstrates that even in an area vulnerable to land degradation, a large population can be sustained through a combination of endogenous and exogenous technological change supported by a conducive policy framework and much local initiative.

Source: Montimore and Tiffen 1994.

Perverse economic incentives, political motives and insecurity of land tenure often cause deforestation. Poor people are encouraged to clear forests and build settlements, only to find later that the soil quality is not good for agriculture. That leads to further deforestation. People are also encouraged to build new settlements as a wall of defense against rebels or invaders. Insecurity of land tenure also leads to deforestation, by promoting uncontrolled cattle ranching.

Forests are now generally replanted in industrial countries, with tree cover increasing slightly in Europe, Australia and New Zealand. But many of the original ecologically rich forests have been felled, and the new plantations are usually far poorer mixes of at best a few species. Only 1% of Europe's original forest remains, and such "old-growth" forests are still being cut. Temperate rain forests are thus far more endangered than their more celebrated tropical counterparts.

But in recent times increasing awareness about deforestation has led to serious reforestation efforts in some countries. China increased its forest area by more than 7 million hectares in the 1980s—and India, by more than 6 million hectares. Other countries—for example, Brazil—have formulated laws and regulations to reverse deforestation. Communities also have been playing an increasing role in conserving forests for economic and environmental benefits (box 4.8). Such measures may slow deforestation so that forests may thrive again in the lives and livelihoods of poor people.

Loss of biodiversity

Biodiversity refers to diversity of species of life forms. Biodiversity is important for everybody. It is an important factor in safeguarding the world's food supplies. Medicines developed from wild species have saved countless lives, and every year drugs worth more than $100 billion are derived largely from forest plants and animals. Exports of palm nuts, kernels and rattan are worth $2 billion a year.

But more important, biodiversity is the means of livelihood and the means of production for poor people who have no access to other assets and productive resources. For food and medicine, for energy and fibre, for ceremony and craft, poor people depend on the wealth of biological resources and their knowledge of a diverse biosphere. Biodiversity helps poor people survive in times of scarcity.

The erosion of biodiversity thus has more than ecological consequences. It also translates into destroyed livelihoods and unfulfilled basic needs for the poorer two-thirds of humanity living in a biodiversity-based economy. An estimated 3 billion people depend on traditional medicine as the principal source of cures for illness.

In today's world biodiversity is lost through various processes. Biopiracy is on the rise (box 4.9). In developing countries it can cause poor people to lose access to their livelihoods, means of production and sources of energy and medicine. Their survival and sustenance may be endangered as

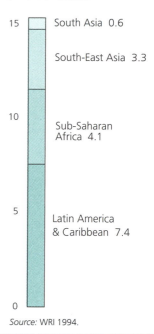

FIGURE 4.6

More than 15 million hectares of forest area were consumed during the 1980s

Decrease in forest area, 1980–90 (millions of hectares)

South Asia 0.6
South-East Asia 3.3
Sub-Saharan Africa 4.1
Latin America & Caribbean 7.4

Source: WRI 1994.

BOX 4.8

Forest conservation in Zanzibar—community action

Jozani Forest is the largest remaining natural forest on the main island of Zanzibar in the United Republic of Tanzania. In the surrounding community livelihoods depend on supplying firewood and charcoal to the town and timber for building. As a result of rapid growth in local communities, in the town and in tourism, demand for wood products—poles, firewood and charcoal—is rising on all sides. This threatens the sustainability of the forest as a renewable resource as well as its potential to raise revenue from visiting tourists.

Past conflict between the government and communities, poorly defined property rights and weak community organizations have led to a situation of rapid degradation of the forest's resources. The Jozani Chwaka Bay Conservation Project was set up in 1995 to reduce community dependence on forest products, improve community livelihoods, encourage common resource management and develop a protected forest area.

The villages set up committees to produce plans for managing their surrounding forest resources. Local forest guards were recruited to curb wood cutting without licences. Workshops have helped to educate villagers about the wider issues involved, and visits to other villages with very degraded resources have alerted the communities to the need to preserve their own.

Jozani is probably the most visited forest in East Africa. In 1997 it attracted 18,000 tourists, generating $40,000 in entrance fees. The government, lobbied to share these revenues with local communities, has allowed the retention of 30% of revenues for a community development fund. The communities have chosen to use this money to improve schools and health centres, repair wells and upgrade roads. Alternative micro-enterprise is promoted both to diversify income generation away from dependence on timber and to increase the value added of those resources used.

The Jozani experience is also an example of an effective alliance between local communities, the government and international organizations. The Commission for Natural Resources in Zanzibar and CARE Tanzania are partners in the project and are actively working with village communities around Jozani.

Source: Wild 1998.

a result. In addition, global consumption patterns encourage developing countries to export commodities, the production of which results in environmental damage and loss of biodiversity. And globally mobile investments may bring resource- and pollution-intensive industries to developing countries, activities that may adversely affect biodiversity.

Consider the explosion in shrimp and prawn production in developing countries and in their export to the industrial world. In the past decade annual production of giant tiger prawns in Thailand has gone from 900 tons to 277,000. In 1996 alone Thailand exported 235,000 tons of shrimp and prawns, mostly to Europe and North America. This production has serious environmental, economic, social and political consequences.

The most serious environmental impact is the large-scale pumping of sea water into the shrimp farms, which causes salinization of ponds. The extraction of large volumes of fresh water from underground aquifers to control salinity is another problem. Still another is the seeping or overflow of saline water onto neighbouring agricultural farms—and into the water table. The degraded ponds can rarely be used for agriculture. That is why shrimp farming is termed a rape-and-run industry.

But more important, shrimp farming is directly linked to the loss of mangroves—the nurseries of marine life (table 4.7). In Thailand 200,000 hectares of mangroves have been lost to shrimp farming, in Ecuador 120,000 and in Viet Nam almost 70,000. The result is eroding coastal land and dwindling shelter and habitat for fish and other marine life.

Shrimp farming has two distinct economic effects on poor people. First, in most cases shrimp farms have been developed on productive agricultural lands, and the activities monopolized by rich local farmers, big exporters and multinationals. So poor people find themselves facing constraints in producing staples for their families. Second, to produce each ton of industrial shrimp requires 10 tons of marine fish, limiting the access of poor people to a low-priced but nutritious source of animal protein.

Shrimp farming also leads to social and political problems. Land takeovers for shrimp production and actions to safeguard against shrimp theft have resulted in local conflicts and deaths.

The act of robbing poor people of their resources and livelihoods at the global level is repeated at the national level, particularly against indigenous people (box 4.10). It makes people extremely vulnerable.

BOX 4.9

Biopiracy

Biopiracy refers to the appropriation and pirating, through the enforcement of the intellectual property rights of scientists and corporations, of the intrinsic worth of diversified species and the community rights and innovations of indigenous people.

The intellectual property right implies four things: private rights as opposed to common rights; recognition of knowledge and innovation only when they generate profits, not when they meet social needs; innovation in a formal institutional setting rather than embodiment of indigenous knowledge; and international perspective rather than domestic and local use. Immediately it becomes apparent that the intellectual property right excludes all kinds of knowledge, ideas and innovations that arise in intellectual commons—in villages among farmers, in forests in tribes. It excludes all sectors that produce and innovate outside the industrial mode of organization of production.

Today a process is under way to strengthen enforcement of intellectual property rights. As a result, in many cases the collective and cumulative innovation of millions of people over thousands of years can be pirated and claimed as an innovation of professional scientists or corporations. This is happening for two reasons. The first is the idea that science is unique to formal institutions and indigenous knowledge systems cannot be treated as scientific. The second is that many countries do not recognize existing knowledge of other countries as intellectual property.

Such biopiracy inevitably leads to intellectual and cultural impoverishment, since it displaces other ways of knowing, other objectives for knowledge creation and other modes of knowledge sharing. It denies creativity, collective well-being and informal ways of knowledge creation and dissemination. But more important, it makes poor people poorer as their resources and knowledge are appropriated and privatized.

Source: Shiva 1997b.

TABLE 4.7

Relationship between mangrove loss and shrimp production

Country	Mangrove area loss by 1989 (thousands of hectares)	Shrimp production in 1995 (thousands of tons)
Thailand	200	280
Ecuador	120	90
Viet Nam	67	37
India	35	96
Bangladesh	9	34

Source: Shiva 1997a.

International environmental problems are also a burden for the poor

The international and truly global environmental issues, such as the changes in the earth's atmosphere, are the hardest to quantify. The effects, usually occurring long after the pollution that causes them, cannot be observed, only estimated. Yet they may be the most devastating of all to human well-being—and some cannot be reversed within human time-scales.

Acid rain and forest fires may originate in one country but have an effect on others. Ozone depletion and global warming pertain to the whole globe. All these phenomena have impacts, direct and indirect, on human well-being. And even though their ultimate consequences for human lives and livelihoods cannot be well quantified, they are believed to impose a greater burden on poor people than on rich.

Acid rain

Polluted air drifts inexorably across national frontiers, with emissions of sulphur dioxide and other gases in one country raining acid on another. Only 7% of the polluting sulphur in Norway originates in that country. In Sweden it is 10%. The environmental damage from acid rain—to forests and agriculture, critical for the livelihoods of poor people—is more fundamental and longer-lasting than first believed.

Acid rain is causing heavy damage in industrial countries, particularly in Canada, Poland and the Nordic countries. About 60% of Europe's commercial forests suffer damaging levels of sulphur deposition. In Sweden about 20,000 of the 90,000 lakes are acidified to some degree—in Canada 48,000 lakes are acidified.

Acid rain also is becoming a major problem in the developing world. Acid depositions are particularly high in such industrial areas as South-East China, North-East India, the Republic of Korea and Thailand. The effects are already being felt in agriculture. In India wheat yields have been cut in half in areas close to large sources of sulphur dioxide emissions.

Over the years most industrial countries have reduced their sulphur dioxide emissions drastically. Japan reduced its emissions from nearly 5 million tons in 1970 to 900,000 in 1993. Canada, Norway, Sweden and the United Kingdom have been quite successful too, though the last two started from a lower base. Yet sulphur dioxide emissions are still serious in some industrial countries. The United States alone emitted 20 million metric tons in 1993—compared with 38 million metric tons for 20 Asian countries.

There have also been attempts in some developing countries to reduce emissions of sulphur dioxide. In Chile a decree adopted in 1992 is aimed at reducing industrial emissions of air pollutants—and cutting sulphur dioxide emissions drastically. Early estimates show a reduction of 20–30% in sulphur dioxide emissions.

Forest fires

Forest fires are also a transnational environmental problem. They originate in one coun-

---

BOX 4.10

Invading the environmental resources of indigenous people—the Brazilian case

Today in Brazil indigenous people account for only 0.2% of the total population, and their lands for about 12% of national territory. During the past few years their existence has become ever more precarious as a result of increasing invasion of their territory through land confiscation and exploitation of natural resources. The invaders are mostly dispossessed marginal workers who engage in illicit activities on indigenous land, illegally mining gold or extracting luxury woods such as mahogany, cherry and cedar. Their numbers are estimated at 45,000. Another type of invasion is by the public sector, to build highways, hydroelectric power plants and other infrastructure projects.

The number of invasions nearly doubled in 1996, affecting around 43% of the indigenous population. More than two-fifths of the invasions were motivated by illegal exploration for and theft of timber, mostly in the states of Amazon and Pará. But illegal logging activity on indigenous land was also carried out in more than half the Brazilian states. In Rondônia 40% of indigenous lands were subject to illegal activities. In Maranhão about 37% of the territories were invaded by loggers, and in the states of Pará and Mato Grosso there was exploration for luxury species of hardwoods on 33% of indigenous lands.

Cases of environmental damage on indigenous land increased eightfold in 1996, including illegal exploitation and degradation of natural resources and usurpation of indigenous land. The outcome: devastation of vegetation, contamination of products from mining and agriculture and endangered fish species. Also during 1996 nearly 33% of all illnesses were linked to environmental degradation. Invasion of indigenous territory in Brazil has aggravated the survival conditions of nearly a third of the country's indigenous population.

Source: Sodré 1997.

try, but the smoke and air pollution they create travel to others, affecting human health and economic well-being. The Indonesian forest fire in 1997 exported smoke haze to Malaysia, the Philippines and Singapore. By mid-October nearly 1.7 million hectares had burned, though this was only the fifth largest fire in the past two decades. Poor visibility due to smoke caused major accidents and left drought victims without aid. And thousands of tourists cancelled trips to the region. Economic losses to some of the countries in the region have been estimated at 2% of GDP.

It was the fire in Indonesia that captured international headlines, but every continent experienced large blazes. Annual forest fires in the Amazon increased by nearly 30% in 1997. Unusually dry conditions in Africa and pressure for land led to vast fires in Kenya, Senegal and the United Republic of Tanzania. And fires burned out of control in Australia, Colombia and Papua New Guinea. Worldwide in 1997, fires destroyed at least 5 million hectares of forest and other land.

In health and in livelihoods these fires affected poor people most. In the Indonesian fire more than 1,000 people died and more than 20 million suffered smoke-related respiratory problems; most of these victims were poor. Yet poor people often have little to do with causing the fires. Logging by multinational corporations and clearing to speed development are the primary culprits, causing negative economic effects that will be felt for years. Sometimes forest fires are an outcome of tension between poor settlers in forest areas who are not given proper territorial rights and multinationals that are provided logging concessions. Small farmers burn trees planted by the multinationals, which in turn burn land to drive out the smallholders.

Depletion of the ozone layer

Ozone—a molecule of oxygen with three atoms instead of the normal two—is a troublesome pollutant near the earth's surface, but a lifesaver far overhead. Scattered so finely through the stratosphere, 15–50 kilometres up, that if collected it would form a shell around the earth no thicker than the sole of a shoe, it filters out the harmful ultraviolet rays of the sun. Without it, no terrestrial life would be possible.

The small amount of ultraviolet light that does get through damages health. It is the main cause of skin cancers, which have been fast increasing. The incidence of melanoma, the most dangerous, increased 80% in the United States during the 1980s alone. The ultraviolet light is also a major cause of cataracts, which cause more than half the blindness in the world and claim the sight of 17 million people a year. And it may suppress the immune system, helping cancers to become established and grow and increasing people's susceptibility to such diseases as malaria.

Even the slightest damage to the ozone layer would increase this toll on human health. It would also affect food supplies. More than two-thirds of crop species are damaged by ultraviolet light, which also penetrates the surface of the sea, killing the plankton so vital in the marine food chain.

Today the ozone layer has thinned by about 10% over temperate regions. Ozone depletion may provide one exception—at least among global issues—to the general rule that the poor suffer most from environmental degradation. It mainly affects temperate and polar regions, and ultraviolet light has its most severe effects on people with light skin. Yet in industrial countries the poor—who are less able to afford protection and more likely to work outdoors—may be more vulnerable.

Global warming

Global warming may be considered one of the most serious of all the environmental challenges. It threatens to disrupt the remarkably stable climate the world has enjoyed since the beginning of settled agriculture some 10,000 years ago—a climate that has made possible the growth of all civilizations and the expansion of human numbers from a few million to nearly 6 billion. Global warming is likely to aggravate most other environmental problems, and could exceed both what the planet can take and what human societies can stand.

Although the industrial world accounts for most of the emissions that lead to global warming, the effects will be felt all over the globe. A rate of climate change faster than at any time in the past 10,000 years is expected, and it is likely to cause widespread economic, social and environmental destruction over the next century. Developing countries, particularly their poorest people, are expected to be hit hardest by the failing harvests, growing water shortages and rising seas that will accompany global warming.

By the best estimates the world's harvests will be slightly reduced in the next century. This in itself is likely to increase food prices and hunger. More important, the effects will be distributed in a way that will generally worsen existing inequalities and patterns of poverty and hunger. Some areas, such as Europe and Canada, are expected to benefit from better harvests. But yields are expected to fall in Africa, South Asia and Latin America, where most of the world's poor and hungry live. A recent study predicts that harvests will decline by more than 30% in India and Pakistan by 2050.

It is the same story for rainfall. By and large the haves, who get enough now, are expected to get more, while the have nots will get less. Water shortages are expected to increase, with Sub-Saharan Africa, the Arab States, South Asia and Europe particularly affected. Deserts are expected to spread in all these regions except Europe.

Rising seas may threaten the lives of millions in developing countries. With a one-metre rise in sea level, due in part to global warming, Bangladesh could see its land area shrink by 17%, though it produces only 0.3% of global emissions. Egypt could see 12% of its territory, home to 7 million people, disappear under the waves. Rising seas threaten to make several small island nations—such as the Maldives and Tuvalu—uninhabitable and to swamp vast areas of other countries.

Human impacts of environmental damage—a summary

This discussion of the human impact of environmental damage establishes three appalling facts:

- Whether it is pollution, degradation or waste, environmental damage has serious consequences for human heath, livelihoods and human security. An attempt has been made to estimate such costs in India (box 4.11).
- The geography of environmental damage indicates that the rich contribute more, with larger shares in outdoor pollution, global warming, acid rain, solid waste and toxics. But the poor bear the brunt in loss of lives and risks to health from pollution and toxics—and in loss of livelihoods from soil degradation, desertification, deforestation and biodiversity loss. And among the poor, women face greater risks, largely because of their social and economic roles (box 4.12).
- Environmental damage threatens both the earth's carrying capacity and people's coping capacity. And it may have serious consequences for future generations.

The future need not be gloomy

During the next 20 years the worldwide demand for energy, under various scenarios, is projected to increase by 30–55%, with developing countries accounting for four-fifths of the growth. But with energy-saving measures, this demand growth could be limited to 30%.

Air pollution, on past trends, will rise with energy use—and so will its toll.

Rising seas may threaten the lives of millions in developing countries

---

BOX 4.11

Costs of environmental degradation—estimates for India

Economic development has been the watchword in India's march into the 21st century. But the country may be paying an enormous price for this march, which has brought in its wake ecological devastation and numerous health problems. A conservative estimate of environmental damage in India puts the figure at more than $10 billion a year, or 4.5% of GDP in 1992. If higher estimates are used, the total environmental costs would be $13.8 billion, or 6% of GDP.

A breakdown of the conservative cost estimate of about $10 billion shows that urban air pollution costs India $1.3 billion a year. Water degradation leads to health costs amounting to $5.7 billion every year, nearly three-fifths of the total environmental costs. Soil erosion affects 83–163 million hectares of land every year. Land degradation causes productivity loss equal to 4–6.3% of total agricultural output every year—a loss amounting to $2.4 billion. And deforestation, which proceeded at the rate of 0.6% a year between 1981 and 1990, leads to annual costs of $214 million.

These estimates, however, do not include the major environmental costs that arise out of biodiversity loss or pollution due to hazardous wastes.

Source: Agarwal 1996.

Sulphur dioxide emissions in Asia will overtake those in industrial countries in 2010, causing extensive damage through acid rain, particularly in South China. In another 25 years the number of cars in the world, now more than 500 million, may well double to top a billion. With much of this increase in countries that still use lead in petrol—most of them developing—emissions of lead could increase fivefold between 1990 and 2030.

Adding to global warming, energy-related carbon dioxide emissions are projected to rise between 30% and 40% by 2010 under moderate growth conditions. Much of the growth in these emissions will occur in the developing world. During the early 1990s carbon dioxide emissions in OECD countries were projected to increase some 24% by 2010 from their levels in 1990. Annual emissions in developing countries are projected to more than double, though from a much smaller base. If current trends continue, developing countries, with four-fifths of the world's population, will account for nearly half the annual global carbon dioxide emissions, up from a third today. China and India will account for more than half the developing world total. The issue of carbon dioxide emissions must be seen in a historical context, however, and from the perspective of cumulative accumulation over many years.

The renewable natural resources on which we all depend—the poor disproportionately more—will become scarcer. Today nearly a third of the world's people depend directly on renewable resources for much of their livelihoods. And in 2025 much of the population of Sub-Saharan Africa and South Asia might still be highly dependent on such resources—as might many people in rural Latin America and the Caribbean, given the extreme disparities in income and land ownership.

The use of firewood and other traditional fuels—indeed, the use of most renewable resources—is driven by expanding populations. Within 40 years the amount of cropland available per person is projected to fall by half from today's already meagre 0.27 hectare. By 2050 more than 2 billion people will live in regions facing land scarcity, with extensive and increasing desertification and land degradation, particularly in parts of South Asia and Sub-Saharan Africa.

Worldwide, water use is expanding rapidly, and by 2025 it will have risen by 40%. By then, three-quarters of the world's available freshwater run-off could be pressed into service, up from half today. By 2050 the number of people short of water may rise from 132 million to 1–2.5 billion. Regions home to nearly two-thirds of the world's people will face moderate to high water scarcity. Many authorities predict that water will become an important cause of war and human conflict in the 21st century.

If trends continue, the world may see a fivefold increase in waste generation by 2025, adding to pollution and the related health risks in developing countries.

BOX 4.12

Environmental deterioration and women—a disproportionate burden

In developing countries women are doubly affected by environmental deterioration, first because of poverty and second because they are women. Environmental degradation places a disproportionate burden on women largely because of their social and economic roles, which expose them to greater numbers of environmental hazards.

Women have primary responsibility for household chores, activities that keep them inside the house most of the time. As the household food preparers, women are often exposed to high levels of smoke for long periods. Thus it is no wonder that the majority of the 2.2 million deaths every year from indoor air pollution occur among women. They also take primary responsibility for obtaining water and washing the family's clothes—activities that can be hazardous where sanitation is poor, washing facilities are inadequate and water supplies are contaminated. And women are usually responsible for caring for sick children, increasing their exposure to disease-causing organisms.

Moreover, the kind of employment that women have access to often puts them at risk as well. In rural areas many women work in agricultural fields, where they are exposed to toxics from fertilizers and pesticides. Many urban women work in small-scale industries, where toxic chemicals are often used without adequate safeguards. Another common source of income for women is piece work done at home, such as fabricating sandals or articles of clothing, which can involve the use of dangerous adhesives and other flammable or toxic materials.

In poor households women have the responsibility of collecting fuelwood and cow dung to meet the family's energy requirements. In an environmentally degraded setting that may mean long hours of walking to collect fuel. These activities significantly reduce women's time for other activities, as well as exposing them to health risks. Moreover, girls often help their mothers fetch water and fuelwood, depriving them of education.

Physiological factors also play a part in making women's health more vulnerable. Women are particularly at risk during pregnancy and after childbirth, when they are more vulnerable to such diseases as malaria.

Source: WRI 1996a.

The possible result of all this: poor people will be pushed more and more onto ecologically fragile lands, increasing their vulnerability. By the end of the next decade a billion poor people may be living on such lands, twice the number today. Scarce resources and unequal access to natural resources and sinks will make it difficult for them to escape impoverishment. This continuing disproportionate impact of environmental degradation will hamper their health, lives and livelihoods.

Is humankind heading for doomsday? Yes and no. The future is bleak if we continue with business as usual. But there are alternatives and we can shape the future accordingly—with big commitments, big changes in policies, institutions and values and a big sense of collective responsibility. New patterns of consumption, new technologies and greater efficiency in resource use can make resources available to poor people and minimize damage to the environment.

Progress has already been made in the dematerialization of production and consumption—in reducing the natural resource content per unit of production and thus consumption. Suggestions have also been put forward for knowledge-based societies to ensure sustainable development (box 4.13). This will ease pressure on resources and reduce environmental damage. Both would be good for poor people.

Dematerializing production and consumption

Economic growth has been directly linked to increasing use of resources. If this link could be weakened by reducing the materials required for production and using resources more efficiently, there would be many advantages for both industrial and developing countries.

Could this delinking of growth and natural resource use be applied throughout economies? To some extent it already is. Energy use no longer necessarily parallels economic growth. Japan reduced the energy used to produce each (constant) dollar of GNP by nearly a third between 1973 and 1985. But in most countries

energy use continues to rise because consumption has increased faster than efficiency. The amount of steel, timber and copper used per person in industrial countries has generally stabilized or declined, even as their economies have grown—showing some delinking (figure 4.7). But in most cases the absolute amounts have increased.

Much more will have to be done if the environmental crises of our time are to be avoided—and it can be done. Energy consumption can be cut by up to half in present industrial installations and by up to 90% in new ones—using technologies already available. *Factor Four,* the 1997 report to the Club of Rome, shows how output can be doubled while halving resource use, and describes concrete techniques to achieve this. Beyond cuts in energy consumption, there are possibilities for heavily reducing the use of wood, water and minerals while increasing living standards.

A broad consensus is growing, however, that industrial countries must go far beyond such delinking, to embrace the dematerialization of their economies. Both sustainability and equity demand that they reduce their use of resources—such as fisheries

FIGURE 4.7
Delinking economic growth and natural resource use

Economic growth and per capita consumption Index (1960=100)

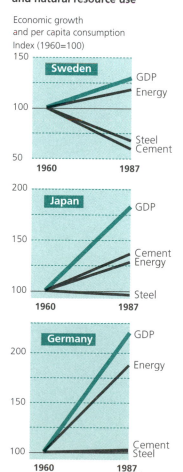

and natural forests—and their emissions by more than tenfold in the coming decades. This target for sustainability, "Factor Ten," has been broadly endorsed by a group of ministers from both industrial and developing countries.

Recycling can help, by reducing the use of new materials. If France doubled its reuse and recycling of non-renewable materials, it would reduce natural resource use by three-fifths. Every ton of recycled steel saves more than a ton of iron ore, half a ton of coal and 9 kilograms of limestone—as well as several tons of hidden material flows associated with mining and processing. Recycling can also save energy—recycling aluminium requires only 5% of the energy needed to refine and smelt new aluminium from bauxite. In industrial countries today, the recycling rate for paper is about 45%—and that for glass 50%. In the mid-1980s the rates were 33% and 26%. Recycling on a large-scale commercial basis is not yet significant in developing countries.

But recycling is only one option for dematerialization. Reusing products, repairing them and increasing their durability are also part of the package. So is cleaner production—designing the production process to minimize raw material use and waste and thus reducing pollution at the source (box 4.14). There is also increasing evidence that transforming effluents into commercial products, such as fertilizer, can be profitable for private firms.

Just as environmental damage seriously limits the well-being of poor people, these solutions can enhance it. Technologies that use fewer resources and create less pollution generally employ more people. Recycling waste, for example, creates jobs, particularly for women (box 4.15). Many studies show that ecological tax reform—which substitutes taxes on resource use and pollution for taxes on jobs and income—could help. One study by the European Union suggests that such tax reform could produce 4 million new jobs in the EU countries.

Technology is crucial

But dematerialization should not undermine the technologies needed to meet the requirements of poor people. Renewable sources of energy offer particular promise both for reducing poverty and for reducing indoor pollution for poor people—and for cutting the use of polluting forms of energy by the rich.

Technology is one of the make-or-break factors in the delinking of economic growth and natural resource use:

- Clean production processes must be broadly introduced so that industry becomes less polluting. And clean and efficient technologies must be developed for waste management.
- Efficient "next-generation" technologies must be made available to developing countries so that their pollution levels do not rise as they industrialize and develop. These countries should advance to better

---

BOX 4.14

Cleaner production—prevention is better than cure

Cleaner production marks a new approach to enlisting technology to protect the environment. It reflects the old adage: "prevention is better than cure".

This approach aims to eliminate pollution at the source and to conserve raw materials such as energy and water through efficient production processes. It also aims to reduce the environmental impact of products throughout their life cycle, from the first extraction of raw materials to their ultimate disposal. This proactive, preventive approach contrasts sharply with traditional pollution control or waste management, which aims to mitigate damage after it occurs. It is more effective and much cheaper.

There are many examples of successful implementation of cleaner production in both industrial and developing countries. In the industrial world Dow Chemical's WRAP (Waste Reduction Always Pays) programme has cut emissions of 58 pollutants by more than half since 1985, and is continuing to bring about further reductions. Pollution by 3M has been cut 90% worldwide. In New Zealand companies that have reduced waste have saved 50–100% of

annual costs and where reuse is involved, have produced extra income. Payback times in many cases are only days or weeks.

Eastern Europe and the CIS are also beginning to take clean production seriously. In Lithuania only about 4% of companies had started cleaner production in the 1960s; that proportion increased to 35% in the 1990s. In the Czech Republic 24 case studies of clean production found that generation of industrial waste had been reduced by nearly 22,000 tons a year, including nearly 10,000 tons of hazardous waste. Waste water had been reduced to 12,000 cubic metres a year. The economic benefits have been estimated at more than $2.4 million every year.

In the developing world a cement company in Indonesia is saving $350,000 a year by using cleaner production techniques. The payback period of the investment was less than a year. Pilot projects in China, in 51 companies spanning 11 industries, found that cleaner production techniques cut pollution by 15–31% and were five times as effective as traditional methods.

Sources: Hillary 1997.

technology by leapfrogging phases of technological development rather than progressing gradually.

• Low-cost, simple but efficient technology should be developed to meet the requirements of poor people. Without access to such technology, it will be difficult for them to break out of the poverty trap.

Developing countries are important arenas for innovation and leapfrogging. There is potential for leapfrogging in both processes and products, and often a synergy between the two. For example, lighting in isolated villages is predominately kerosene lanterns and candles. Switching to a compact fluorescent lightbulb (CFL), which is four times as efficient as a conventional incandescent bulb, would make it economical to supply power from a solar photovoltaic (PV) panel. Connecting to an electric grid—probably required if inefficient bulbs are used—would be unnecessary, allowing vast savings in capital equipment. These savings could be reflected in improved education, health and livelihoods. The PV-CFL solution leapfrogs over its alternative: a large, expensive electricity generating system.

A second dividend from leapfrog technologies derives from the avoided costs of long-term environmental clean-up, such as mopping up old toxic sites and scrubbing coal power plants. Using leapfrog technologies minimizes clean-up costs, as well as health care costs linked to environmental pollution and degradation.

Leapfrog technologies are not only ideas—they are a reality (box 4.16). And they are being used in many developing as well as industrial countries.

But technology alone is not the solution. It must be supplemented with policy reforms, institutional arrangements and changes in collective responsibility.

Policy issues

Reversing and minimizing the human impacts of environmental damage, particularly the unequal impacts on poor people, and ensuring environmental sustainability raise a number of important policy questions. These cover efficiency in resource use, clean production, reduction of waste generation, poor people's access to natural resources, their rights and entitlements to common property, low-cost next-generation technologies for poor people and changes in production and consumption patterns. And in several areas public provisioning of goods and services for poor people is critical.

Another important issue is environmental management. Strengthening it will require a role for communities as well as the state and a stronger alliance between local communities, institutions of civil society and governments. Inspiration can be drawn from grass-roots environmental movements in alliance with antipoverty and women's movements.

Addressing all these issues effectively requires first exposing five myths that often surround policy discussion on the poverty-environment nexus.

BOX 4.15

Waste recycling—women in Ho Chi Minh City

Over the past six years the amount of garbage generated annually in Ho Chi Minh City has quadrupled, from 198,000 tons to 839,000. Each person produces three-fourths of a kilogram of waste per day. Non-decomposable garbage makes up about a third of the total. Of this, about 62 tons a day enter the recycling chain, mainly through women.

The urban waste recycling chain of Ho Chi Minh City involves several links for the collection of waste products, their transformation into low-priced consumer items and their sale, predominantly to poor people. Women are involved in all these links as buyers, shopkeepers and recyclers.

Women waste buyers ply their trade by walking door to door in self-designated areas where they know the clientele. Walking approximately 15 kilometres daily, they collect an average of 41 kilograms of waste, such as newspapers, old books, shoes, bottles, tin and aluminium. On average, buyers earn a daily income of VN$14,000 (US$1.30); in most cases this represents the largest share in their household income.

Women make up a little more than half of all shopkeepers dealing in waste. On average, a medium-size shop buys about 523 kilograms of waste and 115 bottles daily, while the big shops can buy up to 30 tons a day. Shopkeepers enjoy a fairly high living standard. The average monthly income per shop is VN$3–4 million (US$280–370) and can go as high as VN$10 million (US$930).

The waste recycling activities by women in Ho Chi Minh City have brought three distinct benefits. First, they relieve some of the pressure posed by the large amount of solid waste that must be collected by the city's public works department. Second, they transform waste into consumer goods purchased by poor people. Third, they create employment and income. About 10,000 people are employed in these activities, most of them women. More than 5,000 women are engaged in buying waste from households, more than 500 work as shopkeepers and more than 40% of the workers in recycling factories are women. Even though their earnings are not high, they contribute an important share of household incomes.

Source: Ngoc and others 1994.

Leapfrog technologies

In developing countries there have been many attempts to develop technologies that can help leapfrog over steps in the traditional development path followed by industrial countries. These technologies include engine fuel from ethanol, electricity from biomass and zero-emission cars.

Ethanol produced from fermented sugar cane juice is used as a substitute for petrol to fuel cars in Brazil. Around 200,000 barrels a day of ethanol are used, reducing the petrol needed for the 10 million Brazilian automobiles by 50%. Although ethanol has lower caloric content than petrol, it is an excellent motor fuel, it has a motor octane of 90, exceeding that of petrol, and it is suitable for use in high-compression engines. The development of high-compression motors in Brazil is itself an example of technological leapfrogging. Nearly 400 processing plants have been established for ethanol production, creating more than 700,000 jobs. The substitution of ethanol for petrol avoids emissions of nearly 10 million tons of carbon dioxide a year.

Burning fuelwood, bagasse and other agricultural residues to generate electricity is a proven technology used in many countries. In the United States some 8,000 megawatts of electricity is generated from biomass. But generation efficiency is less than 10%. Using an integrated gasifier–gas turbine system would increase efficiency to more than 45%. This emerging technology is two and a half times as efficient as the conventional way of producing electricity (steam cycle), and the cost of the electricity from this system would be 5 cents per kilowatt-hour, compared with more than 8 cents per kilowatt-hour in the traditional system.

The zero-emission cars will operate on electricity. Two options exist—using energy stored in batteries and generating electricity on-board, for example, in fuel cells using hydrogen as fuel and yielding only water as a by-product. Buses are probably the ideal first candidate for zero-emission vehicles (see box 5.7).

Source: Goldemberg 1997.

First myth: subsidies on resources are always for the benefit of poor people. This myth becomes exposed when one looks at water and energy. In most cases, throughout the world, the cost of providing water to consumers exceeds what they pay. The average price paid covers only a third of the cost, and government subsidies make up the difference. Since water prices are too low to recover investment costs, new connections are not seen as profitable and poor people remain unserved as a result.

Energy also receives significant subsidies in developing countries. Even in the early 1990s the average price paid per unit of electricity was only 40% of its production cost. But such subsidies are not passed on to poor people, because they are not connected to the grid. In developing countries it is the urban middle class that enjoys access to such facilities.

Not only have subsidies failed to benefit poor people. They have often provided incentives to the rich for wasting resources rather than conserving them.

Second myth: poor people are unable or unwilling to contribute to costs. This myth too is false. Most poor people already pay for the basics. Many poor families lacking a connection to piped water must purchase water from private vendors—at a cost that is sometimes 10–12 times what a middle-class family with a connection pays. More positively, poor people are willing to contribute their time and effort to improving community water supply and sanitation systems. In low-income parts of Haiti and Nigeria more than a fifth of household expenditure goes to the purchase of water.

Third myth: developing countries should simply imitate what industrial countries have done in dealing with the environment. Developing countries can certainly learn from the experiences of industrial countries. But that does not mean that they should adopt their practices wholesale. During the past decade and a half most OECD countries have been quite successful in reducing lead, carbon monoxide and sulphur dioxide emissions and in cleaning up their lakes and rivers. They have also increased forest cover. But their approach may not be the least-cost one. In seeking to reduce emissions, for example, governments have often imposed technologies on firms and industries, rather than looking for the cheapest solutions. And they have introduced emissions standards late in industrialization, after significant investments had already been made in polluting processes. Developing countries should avoid these mistakes.

Fourth myth: developing countries should restrain their consumption, industrialization and development, because these will contribute to further environmental damage. Developing countries face a fundamental choice. They can mimic the industrial countries, and go through a development phase that is dirty and wasteful and creates an enormous legacy of pollution. Or they can leapfrog over some of the steps followed by industrial countries and incorporate modern, efficient technologies into their development process. Leapfrogging would allow them to increase their consumption, industrialization and development without contributing to environmental damage. Their consumption is still so low that the issue should not be restraining it, but seeing how they can advance technologically to increase consumption without the adverse environmental impacts.

Fifth myth: the scope for cheap, effective and politically acceptable antipollution policies is very limited in developing countries. This contention also is incorrect. There are many such policy options for developing countries. For example, to ensure clean air, governments can introduce measures to phase lead out of petrol. Or they can tax unleaded fuel less heavily, to give drivers more incentive to use it. The cost of taking lead out of petrol is minimal, and the belief that using unleaded petrol harms engines has been found to be false. With a large share of the emissions in many developing countries caused by motorcycles and three-wheelers, another important option would be to encourage the use of four-stroke engines through differential taxation, as has been done in Thailand. In the extreme, the use of such engines could be made mandatory.

• • •

All environmental issues, particularly the unequal impacts of environmental damage on poor people, demand urgent attention, for the time lags built into the world political system ensure that medium- and long-term threats require action just as immediate as that demanded by short-term threats. The millions of deaths each year from dirty water and indoor air pollution cry out for action without delay. But desertification and deforestation also have to be tackled now to avert disasters that would affect many millions of lives. And the inertia built into the world's climate system is so great that immediate steps to reduce greenhouse gas emissions are essential if runaway global warming is to be avoided.

All this would mean big changes and a big shift from business as usual. The changes would encompass structural shifts in natural resource use, in the production and consumption patterns of societies and in values and the sense of collective responsibility. All these shifts call for serious policy actions, discussed in chapter 5.

The millions of deaths each year from dirty water and indoor air pollution cry out for immediate action

Agenda for action

The 20th century's explosion in consumption has largely bypassed many of the world's poorest people

The 20th century's explosion in consumption has brought immense benefits to humanity, greatly advancing human development. But it has largely bypassed many of the world's poorest people. Inequalities are growing, and the natural systems on which all people depend are more endangered.

Challenges ahead

What would happen if the trends in consumption of the past 25 years were to continue for another 50? Where would that leave the world in the mid-21st century?
• Global consumption expenditure would rise to levels four to five times those of 1995.
• Average annual consumption expenditure in the industrial countries would surpass $55,000 a person, compared with $20,000 today.
• The consumption of the fifth of the people in the world's poorest countries would still be well under $2,000—not even 3% of the rich country average at that time and under 10% of rich country levels today.
• Discharges of carbon dioxide, fluorocarbon gases and many other toxic wastes would continue to mount—with carbon emissions, for example, more than doubling.
• Fish stocks would decline, soil erosion would increase, deforestation would continue and water scarcity would become much more acute.

Continuing past trends, with little change in consumption patterns or production technologies, would thus reinforce some of today's most basic human problems. Poverty would not be eradicated. Inequalities would widen. And the environment would be pushed even further beyond its limits.

But trend is not destiny. None of these outcomes is inevitable. The challenge for the global community in the 21st century is to adopt new directions in the growth and patterns of consumption. To reverse today's trends, we need to focus on five goals:
• Raising consumption levels among the poorest to meet basic consumption needs, eliminating shortfalls in areas critical for human development.
• Moving to sustainable, environmentally friendly consumption patterns and levels that reduce environmental damage, improve efficiency in resource use and regenerate renewable resources—such as water, wood, soils and fish.
• Achieving more equitable international burden sharing in meeting the costs of reducing and reversing global environmental damage—such as global warming, acid rain and loss of biodiversity.
• Discouraging patterns of consumption that have a negative impact on society and reinforce inequalities and poverty.
• Protecting and promoting the rights of consumers to information, product safety and access to products that they need.

There are good examples to build on for all five goals. In each critical area of consumption—energy, education, water, transport, health care, housing—we know how consumption patterns can achieve stronger links to human development, and how new patterns of consumption can be more equitable and less environmentally damaging (box 5.1).

Consumption policy—agenda for action

Consumption is sometimes seen as an inappropriate area for policy. It is argued that consumption choices are the sovereign decisions of consumers and should not be interfered with.

This logic is mistaken. First, consumer choices are often constrained by social barriers, inadequate incomes, unavailability of goods and lack of time and information. Consumers thus do not have the full range of choices that would match their real preferences.

Second, consumer choices have impacts on others. When information is misleading, when prices fail to capture environmental costs and when regulations fail to prevent harmful side-effects, the impacts of consumption can be negative. Individual choices may be legal, affordable and socially acceptable—yet the cumulative consequences can be devastating for human development on a global scale. Consumers are then caught in an irrational system.

The goods and bads of consumption will not automatically right themselves; the impacts of consumption—on the individual and on others—will not automatically be positive. To end such irrationality, and to realize the full potential of consumption for human development, the framework within which people make their consumption choices needs policy attention.

Policy for consumption needs to address our economic, social and regulatory frameworks to reforge the links between consumption and human development. The shift to more satisfactory and sustainable consumption patterns must be promoted by favourable pricing, enforced by effective regulations and supported by shifts in social norms and values. All levels of society need to be involved—individuals, community organizations, NGOs, the private sector, local and national government and international institutions.

The key actions for change:
• Improving information and raising awareness.
• Taking actions to ensure minimum consumption for all.
• Promoting technological innovation.
• Tackling market distortions by removing perverse subsidies and introducing eco-taxes.
• Establishing and enforcing adequate laws and regulations.

• Strengthening mechanisms for international cooperation.

Improving information—raising awareness

Consumers, faced with inadequate information and education, are often poorly prepared to resist the onslaughts of advertising and consumerism. The freedom and expansion of consumer choices have little significance if those choices are based on wrong or misleading information. Price signals are one important form of information, but accurate labelling and other product information are equally important. The information now available to consumers, provided mostly by commercial advertisements, is grossly unbalanced. Other information—about the contents and hazards of products—is lacking.

Consumers need to be provided with correct and clear information, especially on the basics of food, drink, medicines, health care, household appliances and transport safety. Consumer education is important in this, including school education on good diet, fitness and health. In these and other areas government has an important role—to provide quality education, to enforce controls on misleading advertising, to ensure proper labelling of goods and to clarify their effects on health and safety.

Strengthening social awareness and individual responsibility among young people—their values and their life skills—is a high priority. In all cultures this has long been one of the most important concerns in bringing up children. Parents and families have a major role, but so do schools and community organizations. Children and young people need to develop their values, skills, self-awareness and self-confidence, together with a sense of community. These will ultimately affect their consumption choices and increase their awareness of the impacts of these choices on others.

Eco-labelling and social labelling are further steps in supplying information that consumers need to assess the impact of their choices on others. And some consumers are now using the power of their purses to promote the interests of their communities as a whole, even extending their concerns to the lives of others far across the globe. Studies

Individual choices may be legal, affordable and socially acceptable—yet the consequences can be devastating for human development

BOX 5.1

Towards sustainable consumption patterns and poverty reduction

Reducing poverty

Goal
The World Summit for Social Development (1995) agreed that each country should prepare strategies geared to reducing overall poverty in the shortest possible time, reducing inequalities and eradicating absolute poverty by a target date to be specified in each country in its national context.

Priority needs
An average of 25% of people in developing countries are affected by human poverty. Around 1.3 billion people there live on less than $1 a day. Between 1995 and 1997, only 21 out of 124 developing countries had a per capita growth rate of 3% or more each year—this being the minimum required for rapidly reducing poverty. At least half the world's poorest people live in ecologically fragile areas. In transition economies, 32% of people live below an income poverty line of $4 a day and in industrial countries, 11% of people live on less than $14.40 a day. In the OECD countries 34 million are unemployed.

The way forward: six priorities
If poverty is to be ended and unemployment kept low, a long-run strategy of sustained, pro-poor, pro–human development actions will be needed in both macroeconomic policy and sectoral programmes. *Human Development Report 1997* set out a six-point agenda for reducing poverty worldwide:
• Empowering women and men—to ensure their participation in decisions that affect their lives and enable them to build on their strengths and assets.
• Achieving gender equality as an imperative for empowering women—and for eradicating poverty.
• Fostering pro-poor growth in all countries—and faster growth in the hundred or so developing and transition economies where growth has been failing.
• Managing globalization carefully, with more concern for global equity.
• Creating an enabling political environment to ensure broad-based support and alliances for pro-poor policies and markets.
• Providing special international support for countries in special situations—to reduce debt faster in the poorest countries, to increase their share of aid and to open agricultural markets for their exports.

Food and nutrition—an end to hunger

Goal
An end to hunger and malnutrition, ensuring healthy diets and life styles, especially for vulnerable groups. As a step towards this, the World Food Summit (1996) set the target of halving the number of malnourished people in the world by 2015. In parallel, action is needed to slow the growth in obesity—a rapidly growing problem in both developing and industrial countries.

Priority needs
About 840 million people are malnourished in developing countries—almost a fifth of the population. Around 30% of children under five are underweight—in South Asia this share is as high as 50%. Food intake in terms of calories has stagnated in Sub-Saharan Africa over the past 25 years. Micronutrient deficiencies are still serious, affecting more than 2 billion people, especially women and children.

The way forward: food and health care
Policies are needed to increase the food security of the poor while reducing environmental stress. Actions include:
• Strengthening agricultural research and extension systems in developing countries, especially in fragile areas and in Africa.
• Establishing clear, long-term property rights over land, and access to credit.
• Promoting sustainable intensification of agriculture and sound management of natural resources, especially in areas with fragile soils, limited rainfall and widespread poverty.
• Developing low-cost markets and transport networks for inputs and outputs.
• Expanding and improving assistance in food and agricultural development.
    Improved nutrition is a matter of health and child care as well as adequate food and diet. Further actions needed:
• Ensuring that primary health care services have a comprehensive outreach and a strong focus on nutrition, especially on priority actions for ending malnutrition of young children and women.
• Encouraging breast-feeding as the priority action for infant nutrition.
• Ensuring family and community support for mothers when pregnant, when breast-feeding and with young children.
• Using the school system to promote nutritional priorities (see box 5.4).

Energy—a key link between poverty and the environment

Goal
Access to clean and modern energy services for all—essential not only for household uses but also in opening opportunities in communications, transport and production.

Priority needs
Deprivation in energy services hits the poor in three ways: indoor smoke pollution (a major cause of lung disease in women and children), lack of energy for income-generating activities and lost time in collecting wood and dung for fuel.
    Two billion people still depend entirely on biomass for cooking, while some 1.5–2 billion have no access to electricity.
    Current patterns of energy use are probably the single most environmentally damaging form of resource exploitation. Total energy use has increased fourfold during the past 50 years and is projected to double again in the next 50. Thus there is a priority need to combine energy expansion with environmental protection.

The way forward: new technologies
Technologies for decentralized renewable energy sources, such as wind and solar power and modern biomass technologies, have enormous potential. Not only can they bring access to modern energy for all, but they can create employment and provide opportunities for rural entrepreneurship and supply generation. Measures needed to promote their development include:
• The political commitment to promoting access to modern energy services for all.
• Indigenous capacity building in the development of appropriate and environmentally sound technologies.
• Systematic development and introduction of a mix of the next generation of cleaner fossil-fuel-using technologies, renewable sources and efficiency improvements.
• The elimination of permanent fuel subsidies and the introduction of pricing to reflect the social and environmental costs of fuels.
• New roles for a competitive, regulated private sector.
• The involvement in policy-making of stakeholders such as environmentalists and current and potential consumers, especially women.

Water and sanitation—critical consumption for health

Goal

Safe water and sanitation for all. This has long been the goal, reinforced in the global conferences of the 1990s.

Priority needs

Despite a more than doubling of the number of people with access to safe water since 1980, some 1.3 billion people still lack access to safe water, and some 2.5 billion access to adequate sanitation. Polluted water is still a major cause of diarrhoeal disease. This crisis is exacerbated by growing water scarcity, already affecting 132 million people in 20 countries.

The way forward: community solutions

Access to water and sanitation for all cannot be achieved by the state alone—there is a key role for the private sector to play in devising community-level solutions. Yet privatized services—as in the United Kingdom—have generally been introduced only after the state had ensured that full coverage was established. Although the private sector can provide some service delivery and maintenance, only the state can ensure that access to infrastructure is made available to all.

When only the rich are connected to water supplies, subsidies perpetuate inequity. First, subsidies encourage wasteful use of a scarce resource. Second, they limit investment in infrastructure that could extend coverage and reduce leakage. Pricing that reflects costs reduces household water and energy use and the need for waste treatment. It also raises revenue to create infrastructure for all.

Policy development needs a public-private participatory approach, involving planners and users—especially women, who play a central part in the provision, management and safeguarding of water supplies. Key measures include:
- A commitment to providing access to clean water and sanitation services for all, with special emphasis on reaching rural and peri-urban areas.
- Demand management with pricing that better reflects the cost of water, improving agricultural and industrial efficiency in use.
- Investment in infrastructure to cut leakage and extend coverage to all households.
- Community participation in devising solutions and setting up local water services.

Housing—adequate shelter as a universal human right

Goal

Adequate shelter for all. This is a universal human right, recognized in the Habitat II Conference (1996). But the right to housing goes beyond the right to a roof over one's head. It includes access to the systems essential to a healthy home: safe water and sanitation, waste disposal, modern energy, transport and proximity to social services.

Priority needs

More than a billion people in developing countries lack adequate shelter. An estimated 100 million are homeless. Children are worst affected—with many living on the streets. And homelessness has become a growing problem in many industrial countries.

The way forward: state support, local action

As urbanization and population growth accelerate in developing countries, new partnerships are needed to provide housing. Participatory solutions must be found, with the state creating an enabling environment for commercial, community and self-help initiatives. Policy measures needed include:
- Promoting the use of low-cost materials and labour-intensive construction techniques.
- Encouraging public-private cooperation to facilitate community-based, self-help solutions.
- Developing local designs and construction technology.
- Promoting environmentally sound technologies for extraction and processing of building materials.
- Providing urban land use planning and infrastructure.
- Creating security of occupancy.

Construction and improvement of shelter and housing is a universal activity—and people everywhere demonstrate ingenuity and creativity in doing it. Provided there is security of tenure and occupancy, people are willing to invest great effort in their homes—adding to savings and investment while improving living standards. Such work is also open to the unemployed, and its hours can accommodate other obligations. Most of this can be done without direct government support—but governments, especially local authorities, have an obligation to ensure an enabling environment to release this creativity, and to provide land use planning and basic infrastructure.

Transport—the road to empowering the poor

Goal

Access for all to safe and low-cost transport services—essential for access to education, health services, employment, markets and community life.

Priority needs

Deprivation in transport particularly affects the poor even in their everyday lives. Around the world, they travel less far and less frequently, yet spend more time travelling than others. And safety is compromised: half a million people are killed on the roads each year, many of them poor and many children. The range of transport options must be expanded, especially to introduce options that are low cost, save time, reduce pollution and minimize congestion.

The way forward: technology, community and planning

In rich countries and poor, many exciting new approaches provide ideas and lessons for application elsewhere:
- Curitiba, in Brazil, has shown the benefits and savings of a low-cost "subway bus" providing mass transport and fast service (see box 5.5).
- Expensive vehicles can be replaced with a combination of bicycles, motorbikes and simpler vehicles, mobilizing a health or agricultural outreach team at lower operating and capital costs.
- Informal sector minibuses often provide efficient, low-cost transport, but need regulation to ensure safety.
- Imaginative and early town planning can create fast and safe routes for pedestrians and cyclists.

The big pay-off comes when such options are combined with broader and bolder measures to phase out subsidies and charge for road use and pollution, using the fiscal gains for improving roads and public transport. A further pay-off comes with new technologies to develop more efficient vehicles, better adapted to public transport needs and achieving both less fuel consumption and less pollution. The necessary actions:
- End perverse subsidies on fossil fuels.
- Promote development and production of low-polluting vehicles.
- Phase out leaded petrol.
- Introduce and enforce vehicle emissions and fuel economy standards.

Source: Hammond 1998b; Nigam and Rasheed 1998; Pinstrup-Andersen, Pandya-Lorch and Rosegrant 1997; Rabinovitch and Hook 1998; Reddy, Williams and Johansson 1997; Serageldin, Cohen and Sivaramakrishnan 1995; UN 1995a, 1996c, 1997b, 1997e, 1998; UNCHS 1996; UNDP 1997a; UNICEF 1998b.

Socially responsible shopping

A powerful movement of consumers buying "fair trade" goods has gained momentum in Europe and North America. In 1994 Europeans spent more than $300 million on fairly traded coffee, tea, honey, sugar, nuts, textiles and other products—and sales are growing by 10–25% each year. But what is fair trade? It is an alternative way of buying from producers in developing countries. Alternative trading organizations buy products directly from small-scale producer groups, paying a stable price that enables the producers to make an adequate living. These organizations also assist with prefinancing, product development, marketing and cooperative skills. Started on a modest scale by churches and charity organizations in the 1960s and 1970s, fair trade has grown into a large consumer movement. There are more than 100 such organizations following the same broad principles, selling products through 45,000 specialist shops. It is estimated that fair trade practices are helping gain income for 800,000 households, or 5 million people, in developing countries.

A remarkably successful example is fairly traded coffee—CafeDirect—in the United Kingdom, a joint venture involving Equal Exchange, Oxfam Trading, Traidcraft and Twintrading (all alternative trade organizations). After oil, coffee is the most important traded commodity. Around 25 million people in developing countries depend on coffee for their livelihood; 60–80% of the world's coffee plantations are family owned. These producers are extremely vulnerable to price volatility and exploitative practices of middle men. CafeDirect buys directly from farmer organizations, with a fixed minimum price, prepayment of orders and a commitment to a long-term trading partnership. But the benefits to the producers do not end there. Many producer cooperatives invest their profits in community development. For example, the Kagera Co-operative Union in the United Republic of Tanzania, one of CafeDirect's partners, has used profits to build and finance a secondary school in its community.

CafeDirect is now sold in 1,700 supermarkets in the United Kingdom and has reached a market share of 5%. It is the sixth best-selling coffee, linking thousands of UK consumers with nearly half a million coffee-growing households in developing countries. People are realizing that their shopping choices can affect the lives of millions of people around the world and contribute to more socially responsible and sustainable consumption patterns in their own communities. The potential for expanding into other products is great.

In recent years the fair trade movement has gained further momentum by using labelling, both for environmentally friendly products and for fairly traded goods. Labelling products is an essential step in expanding sales of fair trade goods, which are now found in regular supermarkets and thus reaching more consumers. Eco-labelling—first introduced in Germany's Blue Angel scheme in 1977—guides consumers to products with lower environmental impact and induces industry to develop more environmentally friendly products. By 1994 the Blue Angel scheme covered 3,500 products. The Nordic eco-labelling scheme was launched in 1989, and the Environmental Choice Australia eco-labelling scheme in 1991. Several developing countries, including China, Costa Rica, the Republic of Korea and Peru, are now joining the movement.

Source: European Fair Trade Association 1995j; Zadek, Lingayah and Murphy 1997.

quality and safety. Now the lens is widening to awareness of broader development priorities. One group in Tamil Nadu, India, has captured this shift by changing its slogan from "value for money" to "value for people". Others are joining forces with consumer groups in industrial countries and with those working on issues relating to poverty, women, indigenous people, the environment and human rights. With such a broad spectrum of information and opinions being brought together, these partnerships are an important way of making the impacts of consumption better known and understood—by consumers and producers alike.

Consumers' interest in a cleaner environment—in their community, in their country, in their world—can be a significant factor in the market competitiveness of firms. There is powerful potential for further shaping and channelling the pressures of such awareness to meet objectives for sustainable consumption patterns in the 21st century—especially those of a cleaner environment and more equitable patterns of development (box 5.2).

Advertising can serve positive purposes. But controls are needed—on advertising of tobacco or infant formula and, more generally, on advertising targeted at young children. Sweden has legislated a ban on television advertising targeted at children and is advocating the same for all European countries (see box 3.10). Such protection of consumer interests works best in an environment that encourages a free press, open dialogue and political activism.

The power of advertising techniques can also be used for civil action and for public campaigns to put across information, opinions and values not in the mainstream of commerce or politics. Yet against the billions of dollars spent by the private sector, civil and public action will always be underfinanced. Consumers would benefit from more balanced information and education if some of this money could be set aside for alternative views (box 5.3).

Ensuring minimum consumption for all

To ensure minimum consumption for all, strong public action is needed in several

show that consumers in Europe are willing to pay 5–10% more for products that are more environmentally sound in production, operation or disposal.

In developing countries too, consumer movements are gathering power. These movements first emerged among the better-off, urban populations, with a focus on information about value for money, product

areas, starting with setting and maintaining a framework for national policy that creates an enabling environment. Pro-poor growth is a key part of this, as are policies that create employment opportunities. Incentives are also needed for expanding production to meet consumption needs in a wide range of sectors (boxes 5.1 and 5.4).

Several consumption requirements essential for human development—clean water, energy, transport—are drawn from resources that are either community common property or publicly provided. Access is often highly skewed, discriminating against the poor. These inequalities of access deepen poverty and inequalities in capabilities—fueling the downward spiral of environmental degradation and poverty.

In many areas the challenge is for government to play an enabling and supporting role in ensuring creative and effective private sector or community action. In transport government must provide a framework of planning and often much of the infrastructure of roads, especially with towns and cities growing rapidly. But within this frame the incentives must be in place to encourage a dynamic contribution from the private sector and communities, to provide the trucks and buses, the taxis and minibuses, the cycles and handcarts that together create a comprehensive and responsive public transport system (box 5.5).

Promoting technological innovation

Technological innovation is the key to meeting basic needs. Among its past achievements are the miracle seeds of the green revolution, immunization, low-cost water pumps and new forms of public transport. Simply devising new approaches can also be an important form of innovation, as with low-cost ways of improving maternal nutrition (box 5.6).

Technological leapfrogging is essential to allow advances in consumption without exceeding environmental limits. Advances in technological efficiency of more than tenfold are needed to reduce environmental damage and poverty at the same time. The dematerialization of consumption goes

BOX 5.3

Truth in advertising set-aside—a proposal for the United States

Watching television is the number one preferred activity in the United States. The typical American spends more than 1,000 hours in his or her lifetime watching some 150,000 advertisements. The importance of television as a means of communication creates the opportunity to put across information to millions of people—and corporations take full advantage of that opportunity. In 1997 American companies spent more than $100 billion on television advertising, paying up to $8,000 per second of airtime. The result is a heavy dominance of commercial information, all with one underlying message: "buy more stuff". Other ideas—on alternative life styles and environmental awareness—are not heard because their supporters do not have the financial backing to pay for airtime. Moreover, advertising expenditures in the United States are tax deductible. With an average corporate tax of 30%, this amounts to a 30% subsidy on the cost of advertising, increasing the volume of commercial information presented.

Consumer groups in the United States are proposing a solution to this imbalance: the truth in advertising assurance set-aside. Under the proposal companies would be required to set aside a small percentage—less than 3%—of their television advertising tax exemption for a special fund. This money would then be used to fund certified, qualified public interest television producers to prepare and air counter-advertising that broadens the messages and views in advertising.

Refunds could be given to companies whose advertisements are realistic and promote products that are healthy, non-polluting and energy efficient. This would give an incentive to cut back on misleading advertisements.

A precedent for this scheme exists: in the state of California tobacco companies must contribute funds to anti-smoking campaigns.

Source: Kay and Henderson 1997.

hand in hand with the shift from resource-intensive goods to service-intensive and knowledge-intensive goods.

Current technological development and application are far below their potential for creating consumption patterns with environmentally friendly impacts. Why? The pricing and profitability of energy-saving cars or of better public transport systems do not reflect their benefits in reducing environmental damage and avoiding congestion or their social benefits for the health of present and future generations. Similarly, public resources and public action are inadequate to provide the help poor people need to meet their consumption needs—through low-cost building materials, public transport and agricultural research and extension for ecologically fragile environments.

Many of the most important options do not yet exist. They need to be invented, especially consumption options that would require fewer inputs of such scarce renewables as safe water and wood—or options that would create less waste and pollution. Some options may be available in the mar-

BOX 5.4

School meals—some nutritious, some not

Increasingly, evidence confirms the importance of nutrition habits developed early in life. School meals are an important part of the hidden curriculum in school and sometimes—but by no means always—nutrition education is part of the school curriculum. Experience across countries differs widely.

In Norway it has long been the tradition for students to bring sandwiches to school. Recently the Norwegian Nutrition Council set the goal of doubling the intake of fresh fruit and vegetables eaten by school-age children. That led schools to introduce a scheme in which fresh fruit and vegetables are distributed every day to schoolchildren between the ages of 6 and 14. Parents pay an annual cost of $100 a student— or about 0.5% of the average annual salary. Low-fat or skim milk is usually sold at a lower price than whole milk, and discussions are under way to reduce taxes on nutritious food. But even this does not go as far as Finland, where, by law, fresh salad is provided every day in schools, canteens and all restaurants.

Britain is a stark contrast. After many years of providing free milk and nutritiously balanced school meals, the government in the early 1980s introduced free-choice cafeteria service in schools. The cafeterias are run for profit, with a share going to the school administration as a small contribution to school budgets, which were exceptionally squeezed. The result is that many students now eat a poorly balanced lunch with too much fat and sugar. The problem is compounded by eating habits outside school—nearly a third of schoolchildren go to school with-

out breakfast and as many as a third have no family meal in the evening, but snacks instead. Economies in school budgeting have also cut back on physical education in schools, encouraging the likelihood of a sedentary life style. Not surprising, obesity in the United Kingdom has more than doubled since 1981.

Kenya shows yet another contrast, with a tradition of school feeding. But this programme has been adversely affected by increasing poverty due to falling incomes since the early 1980s and school fee increases. For years there has been a school lunch programme in arid and semi-arid areas, supported by the World Food Programme and the Kenyan government. The World Food Programme has given notice that it will withdraw from this programme, however, because of lack of resources. The government has supported a milk programme for primary school children, but now lacks the funds to run it effectively. In rural areas, home to more than 80% of schoolchildren, students go home for lunch. In some schools parents organizations work with school administrations to provide lunch at school.

Chile provides another example. Beginning in the mid-1970s a few far-sighted nutritionists lobbied the government to concentrate resources on a targeted food scheme, providing meals to children from poorer families at all levels of schooling. Management was good, and targeting efficient. Malnutrition fell impressively, along with child mortality rates, even though the proportion of families in income poverty rose markedly in the 1980s.

Source: Human Development Report Office.

ket in some countries, but not worldwide. Some may be at the experimental stage, but not yet in commercial production. Others may not have gone beyond the drawing board. Whatever the situation, there is tremendous need for more technological development and application, and for more government support. One example of the potential: the zero-emission car (box 5.7).

The scope for environmental markets is growing, with new opportunities created by tightening regulations, changes in price

incentives and shifts in consumers' values. By 2000 the global market for environmental goods and services could reach $500 billion a year, approaching 2% of world GDP.

Although this market is now dominated by the OECD countries, the share of developing countries is rapidly increasing. In East Asia, Latin America and the Carribbean and Central and Eastern Europe there are fast-growing markets for air and water pollution control. The market for air pollution control is expected to reach $1 billion by 2000 in China alone. Energy conservation, including energy-efficient technologies, will also be a major source of investment opportunities— the US Agency for International Development estimates that this global market will be worth $250 billion between 1995 and 2015. About half the market is expected to be in developing countries.

To promote this technology often takes government investment in research and development. But in the industrial countries this is perversely on the decline—a trend that must be reversed. The private sector too—national and transnational— must push forward into the new and innovative markets. Priority areas for innovation:

• Agricultural technology for ecologically fragile areas.

• Clean and efficient technologies to save energy and reduce pollution.

• Low-cost household equipment and efficient hand tools—beneficial across the whole range of informal and household activities, urban and rural, especially those easing the burden on women.

• Inexpensive building materials and water and sanitation equipment—to upgrade housing in rural and peri-urban areas.

Although many of the needed technologies are close at hand, the current level of application is far below what is required, both in the industrial countries and in many of the poorest ones. The policy shift to turn this around will not be easy.

Tackling market distortions—removing perverse subsidies, imposing eco-taxes

One of the highest priorities for changing today's consumption patterns is to end damaging market distortions—now large and widespread in both industrial and developing countries—so that consumers are faced with the true costs and implications of their consumption choices.

In theory subsidies aim to increase the supply of a social good. Yet in practice everywhere, perverse subsidies—on energy, agriculture, roads and water—are harmful environmentally and socially. Such subsidies militate against the long-run interests of the community by accelerating the depletion of natural resources and degrading the environment. They are often distributionally regressive, benefiting the wealthy—often political interest groups—while draining the public budget.

The global cost of subsidies in these four sectors is estimated at $700–900 billion a year, with about two-thirds in the OECD countries and one-third in the rest of the world. In OECD countries agriculture is the most heavily subsidized ($335 billion), followed by road transport ($85–200 billion). In the rest of the world energy ($150–200 billion) and water ($42–47 billion) receive the largest subsidies (table 5.1). As a report for the Earth Council says, "The world [is] spending hundreds of billions of dollars annually to subsidize its own destruction."

The removal of perverse subsidies in these sectors would save budgetary resources and increase public savings, while reducing environmental damage and inequality. Even if the savings were not spent on the environment or other sustainability-enhancing investments, development would still be advanced by the reduction in environmental damage and the shift of resources from high- to low-impact activities. Both production and consumption would be modified towards more environmentally sustainable patterns. To illustrate, removing water subsidies would reduce world water use by 20–30%—and in parts of Asia by as much as 50%—saving money, reducing waste and encouraging conservation of the precious resource.

In recent years there has been a welcome trend towards reducing perverse subsidies, especially in developing countries. Energy subsidies in developing countries

The Curitiba bus system—successful innovation in urban transport

The bus system in Curitiba, the capital of Brazil's Paraná State, demonstrates how transport can combine financial self-sufficiency, high-quality service and low fares. This required an integrated approach that involved changing the zoning system, diversifying the public transit service, concentrating residential development, creating dedicated road facilities, introducing an innovation—preboarding tubes—and developing a special relationship between the public and private sectors. And making it all possible politically required involving community groups directly in the planning process.

At the base of the transport system is a three-level transit grid. Numerous small buses ply lower-density areas. These serve as a feeder system to a dedicated busway network that provides high-speed, high-volume service along key corridors. The express bus and feeder networks are complemented by interdistrict routes that connect the axes of the express lines without passing through the city centre.

The zoning system is built around this transit grid. High-density development is allowed immediately adjacent to the express busway network, and permissible densities decline in relation to the distance from the network. The 1990 Municipal Housing Act allowed developers to pay additional fees to build up to two stories above the allowable limits on land sufficiently served by the bus network. This helped to raise funds for Curitiba's Municipal Housing Agency. With considerable foresight, the land along the busway had already been purchased for the agency to build 17,000 units of high- and moderate-density low-income housing, further increasing the viability of the public transit system. As a result of these zoning changes, population in the busway corridors increased 98% in the first five years after the system was implemented, compared with 26% for the city overall. Thus these efforts together have successfully encouraged development to concentrate on corridors served by the busway.

A further innovation was preboarding tubes. One of the major obstacles to increasing bus speeds is the time taken in paying fares, alighting and boarding. Many recent studies show that this slows bus travel as much as roadway congestion in many cities. Providing free transfers without slowing down boarding and alighting was a further complication. Curitiba solved this problem by constructing preboarding tubes that mimic the functioning of a subway station, but at about 1% of the cost. Passengers pay to enter the tubular station; once in, they can board the bus at all of its doors at once.

These integrated changes—in zoning, urban development, road-space allocation and tubular bus station construction—have led to a public transport system that has seen ridership increase at 2.4% a year for more than two decades, while trends in much of the world continue downward. Moreover, the system is fully self-financing and receives no state subsidies. The financial viability of the system has allowed the city to contract out bus service to private contractors, which can earn a profit while ensuring low fares and sufficient service to low-income neighborhoods.

Source: Rabinovitch and Hoehn 1995; Rabinovitch and Leitmann 1993.

TABLE 5.1
Subsidies in environmentally damaging sectors
(estimated totals; US$ billions a year; annual average in early 1990s)

Sector	OECD countries	Non-OECD countries	Total
Agriculture	335	10[a]	345
Energy	70–80	150–200	220–280
Road transport	85–200	15	100–215
Water	..[b]	42–47[c]	42–47
Total	490–615	217–272	710–890[d]

a. Includes food and input subsidies but not irrigation.
b. No estimate available. Subsidies average 30–50% of total costs.
c. Includes subsidies for drinking water and sanitation.
d. Rounded.
Source: de Moor and Calamai 1997.

The Gambia shows how supplementing mothers' consumption can reduce low birth-weight and infant mortality

In the Gambia a five-year trial in 28 villages has demonstrated that supplementing the daily diet of pregnant women with a high-energy, locally produced biscuit providing 1,000 calories a day can reduce the incidence of low birth-weight by 40% and still birth and perinatal mortality rates by 50%. The biscuits were made from local ingredients and baked by two local bakers in traditional clay ovens. For a six-month period the cost was about $10 for each pregnant woman.

In addition to these remarkable results, the study refuted the idea prevailing in some circles that improving the diet of pregnant women will add to obstetrical complications during childbirth by enlarging the head of the newborn. Birth-weight was higher in children of women who received the biscuit, but head circumference was only slightly larger and there was no increase in obstetrical complications.

Worldwide, more than 24 million babies born each year are below the low birth-weight threshold of 2.5 kilograms. Not surprising, the incidence of low birth-weight is higher among economically deprived mothers than among the better-off, often because inadequate maternal nutrition suppresses fetal growth. Women's nutritional needs increase during breast-feeding, so they need extra food at this time as well as during pregnancy.

Supplementary feeding programmes for mothers along the lines of the Gambian programme could most usefully be started six months before birth and continued for 12 months after. The total cost might then be about $30 per birth. On a global scale the cost per year of such a programme might be around $700 million—which would do much to improve the nutritional status of infants, at birth and even as they grow up.

Source: UNICEF 1998b.

Driving towards a zero-emission car

The first generation of zero-emission cars has been launched in response to two concerns: the need to reduce urban air pollution and its costs for health and the environment, and the need to reduce emissions of carbon dioxide and noxious gases that have regional and global impacts.

What makes a vehicle zero-emission? First, it must operate on electricity, not fossil fuels. But more is required—it matters how that electricity is generated. If it is produced by a coal-fired power plant, there will be heavy emissions of carbon dioxide, methane, heavy metals and many other pollutants. Instead, it must come from a renewable energy source—hydropower, windpower or photovoltaic cells, for example. Alternatively, the car's electricity can be generated on-board in hydrogen fuel cells, yielding only water as a by-product.

Making zero-emission cars happen will require establishing a market for the vehicles and developing widespread use of renewable energy sources to produce the electricity or hydrogen for the vehicles. This market was given a major stimulus when, in 1990, the Air Resources Board of California adopted a requirement that zero-emission cars be phased into sales in the state. Under current law 10% of all new vehicles sold in 2003 must be zero-emission. The California market is sufficiently large to have captured the attention of the major manufacturers, and now the introduction of electric cars is gaining momentum. The Kyoto Protocol to the UN Framework Convention on Climate Change has added global impetus to this market.

Battery-powered cars are still constrained by battery technology, limiting travel distances. Fuel-cell vehicles, regarded by many as the ideal propulsion system, are in the prototype stage of development and are expected to be put on the market in 5–10 years by automakers in Japan, Europe and the United States.

Source: Abrahamson and Johansson 1998b.

have declined from more than $300 billion in the early 1990s to about $150–200 billion today. Coal subsidies in China, for example, fell from $750 million in 1993 to $250 million in 1995. It is estimated that complete removal of energy subsidies in developing countries would yield $35 billion in economic, environmental and social benefits.

Pesticide subsidies, $2 billion in the developing countries in the late 1980s, have also declined. The most notable example is Indonesia, which cut pesticide subsidies from $128 million (82% of the retail price) to zero in the 1990s.

And what about taxes? Environmental taxes and charge systems are particularly effective for internalizing environmental costs directly into the prices of products and services that generate them. They provide incentives for consumers and producers to change to more efficient and sustainable use of resources (figure 5.1). They also raise revenues that can be used for environmental expenditures or to reduce taxes on labour, capital and savings.

Eco-taxes can be levied on products or pollutants. Product taxes are simply levied on each unit of the good produced, giving consumers an incentive to buy cheaper, less-polluting alternatives. Pollution taxes, in contrast, are based on the volume of emissions and so have the advantage of giving producers the incentive to shift to cleaner production. But the required monitoring makes them complex and costly to implement. Other charge mechanisms include deposit refund systems, which induce producers and consumers to return product waste for recycling or safe disposal. Many countries use such systems for batteries, bottles, cans and pesticide and chemical containers.

Environmental taxes have been used most extensively in Western Europe, where they began as cost-recovery charges in the 1960s and 1970s, evolving into fiscal incentives in the 1980s and 1990s. Today environmental taxes are used for green tax reforms and for the partial replacement of distortionary taxes (on labour, capital, savings) by corrective taxes (on energy, pollution, chemicals). Energy taxes account for 5.2% of EU taxes, and as much as 10% in

Greece and Portugal. Non-energy environmental taxes represented only 1.5% of EU taxes in 1993 but more than 4% in Denmark and 5% in the Netherlands.

In Norway energy taxes have helped cut carbon dioxide emissions in some industrial sectors by more than 20% since 1991, and in Denmark they helped increase the share of recycled and reused waste from 35% in 1985 to 61% in 1995. In Sweden—which gets 10% of its revenue from energy and environmental taxes—a tax on sulphur dioxide helped reduce emissions by 80% from 1980 to 1994, six years ahead of the target date—though taxes on carbon dioxide emissions have been less successful (box 5.8).

The United Kingdom introduced the Fossil Fuel Levy and the Non–Fossil Fuel Obligation. The levy—charged on every electric bill, and with the revenues used to finance the obligation—is thus a double subsidy for renewable energy. In 1996 it raised $145 million from fossil fuel users, all channelled to the development of renewable energy.

Germany used a somewhat analogous scheme to reduce vehicle emissions and promote unleaded petrol. Starting in 1985 a tax differential of DM 0.04 per litre—later raised to DM 0.10—favoured unleaded petrol to change consumer behaviour. It worked. Unleaded petrol today accounts for 90% of the petrol purchased in Germany.

Such taxes are also being used in developing countries. Thailand, for example, introduced a differential tax in the early 1990s to encourage a shift to unleaded petrol and reduce the impacts of lead emissions.

The oldest and best-known use of pollution charges in a developing country is the Malaysian effluent charge system, introduced more than 20 years ago. The Malaysian Environmental Quality Act of 1974 requires all firms discharging effluents pay a fee for a licence to discharge waste into public bodies of water. The results were dramatic. Despite a 50% increase in the number of palm oil mills between 1980 and 1982 and a steady increase in palm oil production, the effluents released in public bodies of

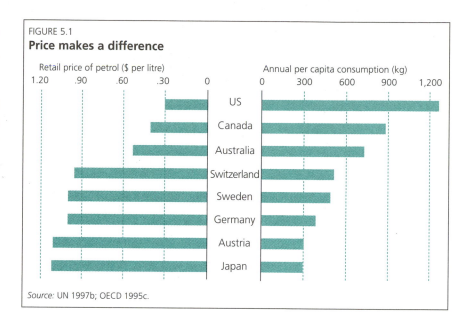

FIGURE 5.1
Price makes a difference

Retail price of petrol ($ per litre)   Annual per capita consumption (kg)

Source: UN 1997b; OECD 1995c.

water dropped from 222 tons of biochemical oxygen demand a day in 1978 to 59 tons in 1980, 18 tons in 1982 and 5 tons in 1984—all the more remarkable because the

BOX 5.8

Eco-tax—the Swedish success

Economic instruments have long been part of Swedish environmental policy, but they did not achieve a major breakthrough until the late 1980s. The Environmental Charges Commission, appointed in 1987, issued reports that resulted in the introduction of new eco-taxes. By 1997 environmental taxes and charges covered several activities and sectors of the Swedish economy: a sulphur dioxide tax and differential fuel tax in energy and transport, fertilizer and pesticide taxes in agriculture and other eco-taxes, such as differential refuse collection charges.

Notwithstanding some difficulties, eco-taxes have been a clear success in Sweden. For example, the Swedish Parliament had set a target of four-fifths reduction between 1980 and 2000 in sulphur dioxide emissions (the major cause of acid rain), but Sweden reached that target in 1994. The eco-tax on sulphur dioxide emissions was estimated to be responsible for 30% of the reduction in these emissions between 1989 and 1995. Differential charges on leaded and unleaded petrol were introduced in Sweden in 1986. By 1994 unleaded petrol had totally replaced leaded

petrol. By contrast, a complex tax structure and a concern about maintaining industry's international competitiveness meant that eco-taxes on carbon dioxide did not have the desired effect.

In 1995 the total government revenue from energy and environmental taxes amounted to $5.5 billion, nearly 3% of the Swedish GDP and more than 10% of its total tax revenue.

From an environmental perspective, the Swedish experience with eco-taxes and charges has been largely positive. Administration of the taxes was not as costly as originally feared. The major problem with eco-taxes is international. Sweden could not opt for much higher environmental taxes because its industries would then choose to move elsewhere. High unemployment in Sweden makes this a politically sensitive issue.

In today's world environmental problems are no longer just national, but also regional and global. Thus the Swedish success with eco-taxes in dealing with environmental problems cannot be sustained unless these taxes are part of international agreements and international action.

Source: Human Development Report Office.

output of crude palm oil more than tripled. Despite inefficiencies of this pioneering measure, it did not hurt the competitiveness of the Malay palm oil industry.

Charge and fee systems also have much potential for urban transport—to control congestion and air pollution and to produce revenue to help finance improvements in public transport. This should expand transport options, ease congestion, save time, lower the costs of public transport and, usually, improve income distribution. With wide applicability, charge and fee systems have been used to great effect in Singapore. And they are spreading to other countries—road tolls in China and area licensing in Singapore are beginning to reduce congestion and improve cost recovery. The Netherlands, Norway and Sweden have introduced or planned road charging in many cities to ease congestion and generate revenues for expanding public transport.

The increased private involvement in financing, building and operating public transport systems in the 1990s is creating further pressure to reduce road subsidies and increase user fees. Argentina cut subsidies to its suburban road system by $25 million between 1993 and 1995 after privatizing the operation of urban transport.

Establishing and enforcing adequate regulation and legislation

The market alone is inadequate—environmental legislation, land use planning, promotion of consumer rights and regulation of harmful substances are also needed. And when skilfully devised, these controls and regulations are enabling, not restricting. But institutions must be fair and free from corruption in implementation, especially in ensuring rights to land, guaranteeing security of tenure in housing and requiring accurate information on consumer goods.

Command and control regulation uses fines, licences, end-of pipe standards and specific government orders to stop pollution. Sometimes the regulation comes in the form of environmental quality standards for air and water.

The Philippines has air and water quality standards that apply to all industrial establishments and power generation facilities. Chile has the Framework Environmental Law, which provides the basis for a gradual improvement in environmental quality. In 1976 the California legislature created the South Coast Air Quality Management District, giving it the responsibility of regulating air quality in the greater metropolitan area of Los Angeles.

One building block of the Malaysian Environmental Quality Act was to set standards limiting industrial effluents, first at 5,000 milligrams per litre and not mandatory, then at 200 milligrams per litre and mandatory and later at 100 milligrams per litre. China has a complex system of environmental responsibility contracts between factories and local governments that set targets for reducing pollution.

In Brazil in 1997 an environmental crimes law was passed to protect natural resources, particularly the Amazon rain forest. The law imposes fines of up to $44 million or prison terms of four years for illegal logging or killing of wild animals.

A new approach that has gained considerable interest and momentum in recent years is self-regulation through public disclosure of information on industrial pollution. This method is a low-cost alternative to formal enforcement of regulations. It provides an incentive for behavioural change and a benchmark for subsequent regulation. A well-known example is the US Toxic Release Inventory, which requires businesses to report the amounts of toxic materials they put into the environment. This system enables firms to compare their performance against the benchmark of other firms. Firms can use good performance in controlling and reducing pollution to enhance their reputations and market advantage.

The best-known developing country example is the public disclosure programme in Indonesia. In the face of 10% annual growth in manufacturing, weak enforcement of formal regulation and mounting pollution damage, Indonesia's National Pollution Control Agency introduced a programme for rating and publicly disclosing the environmental performance of factories.

The market alone is inadequate—regulation is also needed

The programme, launched in June 1995, rated each polluter based on the agency's evaluation of environmental performance. During the pilot phase 187 plants were rated, with only five meeting standards. All plants were given six months to improve their performance before full disclosure. By that time, when factories that met national standards were publicly announced, half the plants had upgraded their status. More interesting, one of the facilities initially given a high ranking was downgraded in response to protests by a nearby community.

Preliminary assessment of this programme suggests that industrial polluters respond to regulation through information. Why? For two reasons. Public disclosure empowers local communities, which use the government-certified performance ratings to negotiate pollution control agreements with factories in their vicinity. And public disclosure works through the market as an incentive through reputational effects, which penalize low achievement and reward good performance.

Regulation and market interventions can be mutually reinforcing. On some occasions regulation is needed to initiate action, which later can be carried further with price incentives. On other occasions price incentives can be used to make a start, with regulation brought in later to ensure wider compliance, especially after social acceptance has been shown to be possible.

Strengthening mechanisms for international cooperation

Environmental impacts on the global commons—acid rain, global warming, holes in the ozone layer, the loss of biodiversity—cut across national boundaries and can be addressed only by international action. Yet the mechanisms of global governance are inadequate for managing these critical environmental issues. Just as governments need to create an enabling environment at the national level, so international action is needed, with new and responsive mechanisms.

There are some signs of progress. Newly negotiated international environ-

mental treaties under the United Nations are offering hope that the world may start to come to grips with these issues. Six examples:

BOX 5.9

After Kyoto, the challenge for Buenos Aires

The Kyoto Protocol to the United Nations Framework Convention on Climate Change is a major step on the long road towards achieving one element of global sustainability: "the stabilization of greenhouse gases in the atmosphere at a level that would prevent dangerous anthropogenic interference with the climate system".

The Kyoto Protocol, adopted at the Third Meeting of the Conference of the Parties to the Convention in December 1997, added to the convention mandatory reductions in emissions of carbon dioxide, methane, nitrous oxide and other powerful greenhouse gases. The target is an overall reduction in annual emissions from industrial (Annex I) countries by 5% from 1990 levels in the first commitment period, 2008–12.

The agreed 5% reduction in greenhouse gas emissions can be viewed from two angles: it is only a small step towards the 60–80% reductions necessary to meet the objective of the convention, yet it is still a significantly lower level than the projected increase of 20–30% by 2010 under a business-as-usual scenario.

So, the Kyoto conference did not achieve much in a quantitative, technical sense. But it was a significant step forward in that it represented agreement that business as usual is not acceptable, and that vigorous measures must be taken that will, within the next century, transform economies and means of production.

Reducing global emissions by 60–80% from the 1990 level is not possible without limiting and, eventually, reducing emissions in developing countries. These countries are therefore in a position where development is in danger of being limited by global environmental concerns. It is projected that developing countries' annual emissions will equal emissions from Annex I countries around 2010. Considering the cumulative nature of emissions in building up atmospheric concentrations, however, the more relevant measure is cumulative

emissions. Cumulative emissions from developing countries are not expected to equal cumulative emissions from Annex I countries until well after 2050. Moreover, per capita emissions in developing countries are now much lower than those in industrial countries.

Is there a way of ensuring that development needs are met at the same time that emissions are reduced? The answer appears to be yes—provided new technologies are employed, especially for much more efficient use of energy and utilization of renewable sources of energy. These technologies help address local social, economic and environmental problems, including indoor and urban air pollution, job creation, improvement in women's health and time use and other problems linked to how energy is provided and used. Meeting development needs while reducing emissions will require a focus on the performance of new technologies in energy use and emissions as they enter the capital stock. Global cooperation and partnerships are clearly needed.

The next step may be taken at the Fourth Meeting of the Conference of the Parties to the Convention, in Buenos Aires in November 1998. The general agreement on the establishment of a Clean Development Mechanism, emissions trading among Annex I parties and policies for emissions reductions have to be made operational, and the rules and procedures established. And then preparations for a second commitment period will start.

Industrial and developing countries alike need to recognize the local environmental and economic benefits of adopting energy-efficient and renewable energy technologies. And they need to recognize that everybody is in this together—emissions in one country affect all countries. Strong political commitment will be needed to ensure the financing and institutional framework needed for successful implementation of the proposed initiatives .

Source: Abrahamson and Johansson 1998.

International action on global warming—a need for a new institution?

In 1992, at the Rio Earth Summit, 100 nations agreed to consider implementing a treaty to reduce the threat of global warming by rolling back emissions of greenhouse gases in industrial countries to the 1990 level by the year 2000. Despite broad interest, implementation has been slow—not only due to scientific uncertainty about the impact of greenhouse gases on the atmosphere, but also because of disagreement about how such reductions should be achieved. There are many possible ways.

Joint implementation

One proposal is for "joint implementation", whereby countries can achieve reductions either within their own borders or pay for the same reduction to be made in another country. Experiments of this kind are under way in Mexico and Poland. Some developing countries feel, however, that this is a way for the industrial nations to avoid the consequences of a problem that they have largely created.

Tradable permits

A popular suggestion is to establish tradable permits for emissions so that countries can buy or sell the right to emit carbon dioxide. This market solution is certainly more flexible than command and control methods and gives incentives to develop cleaner technologies. The market alone is not always an appropriate tool, however. Since the quality of the atmosphere is a public

good—in that it affects everyone, no matter who pollutes—it should not be treated or traded as a private good. Since public goods are typically undersupplied by the market, this would result in too little reduction in greenhouse gases. Moreover, developing countries could find that they are selling their permits at an initial low price, then buying them back later at a higher price—or perhaps not being able to afford them at all. Borrowing and lending of rights might be a preferable path.

An environment bank?

To make tradable permits effective—not only for emissions but for many other environmental public goods—one proposal is to create an international bank for environmental settlements. The bank would act as a clearing house for the global environmental market, matching parties in environmental trade, mediating borrowing and lending and ensuring the integrity of market transactions and their settlement. The bank could provide the necessary institutional framework for the lending and borrowing of emissions rights. It could use as its collateral the world's environmental resources—its forests, bodies of water and atmosphere—thereby realizing the value of these assets without destroying them. It would balance the positions of large and small traders by offering a neutral trading base and an anonymous process in which several small sellers could meet large buyers.

Source: Chichilnisky 1997c.

• The Montreal Protocol, adopted in 1987 and now with 165 party countries, required industrial countries to phase out the use of many ozone-depleting chemicals by the end of 1995. Developing countries are being given financial help to meet this obligation after a 10-year grace period but many have already substantially reduced their use of these chemicals. These measures will lead to the gradual repair of the ozone layer and prevent an estimated 2 million cases of skin cancer.

• Governments took steps to tackle global warming in Kyoto in December

1997, reaching an agreement that will lead to a 5.2% cut in carbon dioxide emissions by 2012 (box 5.9).

• The newly negotiated Convention to Combat Desertification has now been ratified by more than 100 countries, providing a new framework for tackling desertification and drought, which affect more than 1.5 billion people globally.

• At the 1998 Kuala Lumpur Meeting of the Parties to the Basel Convention on the Ban on Hazardous Waste, more than 100 countries agreed to a ban on exports of hazardous waste to poor countries.

• The Convention on International Trade in Endangered Species of Wild Fauna and Flora, adopted in 1973 and now ratified by 135 nations, regulates trade in wildlife and plant species. Trade is prohibited in more than 600 species in danger of extinction and regulated for more than 20,000 animal and plant species at less risk.

• The Convention on Biological Diversity, born out of the Rio Earth Summit, has now been ratified by 172 countries. The convention represents an important step forward in the conservation of biological diversity, the sustainable use of its components and equitable sharing of benefits arising from the use of genetic resources.

Market-based mechanisms have been proposed to ensure environmental sustainability, such as tradable pollution permits, which countries can use to buy and sell the right to pollute (box 5.10). A second instrument is the debt-for-nature swap (box 5.11).

It is not only for environmental issues that international coordination is needed. The fundamental problems of poverty and inequality must also be tackled at this level, through a range of international mechanisms. International action is an essential complement to national action to raise consumption in the poorer countries.

As the recent setbacks in South-East Asia show, all countries, strong and weak, are vulnerable to international forces in the world today. For many of the same reasons all countries, strong and weak, will gain from a more stable, more dynamic and better-managed global economy. Avoiding extremes of inequality is an important requirement for stability and better management—for political and humanitarian reasons as well as economic ones.

To this end, issues of international governance need to be revisited.

• Measures are needed to control surges of financial speculation.

• Actions are needed to strengthen the bargaining position of poorer and weaker countries as a first step to offset their continuing marginalization within the global economy. Measures are needed to encourage a better flow of private capital to the poorest countries. At present 80% of such capital flows to the developing world go to just 12 countries.

• Debt relief is urgently needed by the 50 or so highly indebted low-income countries that need much more support, much more rapidly (box 5.12).

• With aid levels stagnant and even falling, much more serious efforts are needed to restructure aid in favour of the neediest countries and the priority programmes within them. The OECD has adopted a series of targets to help cut the proportion of people living in absolute poverty in half by 2015. The 20:20 guideline (proposing that 20% of domestic resources and 20% of external aid go to meet basic human priorities), encouraged for all interested countries at the World Summit for Social Development in Copenhagen in 1995, would greatly increase support for basic social services for all, but it needs much stronger follow-up.

In the past few years the international economic environment has seen a surge of activity and new initiatives, especially in trade, capital flows and financial liberalization. Many changes are positive—but they are driven overwhelmingly by the economic interests of the rich and powerful countries. Much less attention is being given to the needs of the poorer and weaker countries. Their interests have become even more marginalized. Global inequalities have grown even more extreme.

Nothing short of major reconsideration of mechanisms to offset these tendencies to global inequality is needed.

BOX 5.11

Planning for environmental sustainability in Costa Rica

Since the early 1980s Costa Rica has been working hard to transform its consumption patterns to rationalize human uses of natural resources and the environment.

In 1996 the country outlawed leaded petrol and has since cut its lead levels by two-thirds. All vehicles must now pass an annual emissions inspection, new imported cars must have catalytic converters, and industries are required to have systems to treat the contaminants that they produce. Last year the government, responding to citizens' protests, closed the Placer Dome Company's open-pit gold mine because of harm caused to the environment and local inhabitants.

Negative incentives are also used, such as higher import taxes on used imported vehicles without catalytic converters and fines for loggers who cut timber illegally. The hundred cleanest companies in Costa Rica are named annually, and a green seal of quality is given to gas stations with the best records in preventing air and water pollution and in treating waste water. A red stamp is for those with the worst records.

The government and civil society also apply moral suasion by using ad campaigns to convince people that a healthy environment is good in itself, contributes to human well-being and is good for tourism. Civil society, responding to a governmental programme, has organized 36 natural resource vigilance committees nationwide. These groups provide more than 3,000 citizens to serve as voluntary inspectors of natural resource use and compliance with environmental statutes.

In the late 1980s, in one year alone, Costa Rica felled 10 million cubic metres of forest, with an estimated timber value of $422 million. In 1988 the Netherlands purchased part of Costa Rica's external debt at a cost of $5 million and then wrote it off on the condition that Costa Rica spend an equivalent amount in local currency on forestry redevelopment. In 1989 Sweden purchased a further $5.5 million of Costa Rica's debt for a similar purpose. Such debt-for-nature swaps are helpful but need to be pursued on a much broader scale.

Home to about 5% of the world's species of flora and fauna, Costa Rica has been a global leader in environmental sustainability, setting aside about 25% of the country as conservation or protected areas and arranging debt-for-nature swaps.

Source: Crocker, Camacho and Romero 1997.

Combining the instruments

All these instruments can reshape the framework for consumption choices—in order to improve their outcomes for individuals and their impacts on others, especially through the environment. They are most effective when integrated in a coherent package, using regulations backed by price incentives and raising awareness on the need for those changes through information campaigns. Costa Rica shows how one country has combined the available tools (see box 5.11). Even among economic instruments alone, there is a wide array of tools for environmental protection that are being put into practice in industrial and developing countries alike (tables 5.2 and 5.3).

There is now a consensus in many industrial countries that policies for reducing perverse subsidies, raising taxes

Debt—$100 billion raised in a few months, while $7 billion takes years

A fast and sustainable solution to the crippling debt in many poor countries is long overdue, for debt is one of the biggest obstacles to further human development. The Heavily Indebted Poor Countries (HIPC) initiative, launched in 1996, was initially received with much optimism and anticipation. It was a major breakthrough in international efforts to resolve the debt problems of low-income countries. Creditors acknowledged the need to establish a sustainable debt threshold and agreed to a comprehensive and integrated approach to debt reduction, covering all categories of debt and creditors.

But after two years of slow progress, anticipation has turned to disappointment for countries that have gone through the HIPC framework.

Despite a decade of good compliance with the IMF conditions, Uganda had to wait an additional year until it qualified for the initiative; Bolivia faced a similar problem.

Most countries will not benefit from debt relief until after 2000. For example, the United Republic of Tanzania is not expected to be eligible for debt relief until 2002. In the meantime the country is spending three times as much on debt relief as on primary education and nine times as much as on primary health care.

The initiative needs to pick up speed. Required is accelerated action to integrate debt relief in an ambitious and internationally coordinated strategy for human development and poverty reduction. Ideas on how this could be achieved are worthy of serious attention and debate.

• *Adopting shorter, more flexible eligibility criteria.* Under the current HIPC arrangements countries need to undergo two successive IMF programmes, which can mean a time lapse of up to six years. Reducing the eligibility period from six to three years would help to accelerate progress and offer earlier benefits to eligible countries. The inflexibility of the conditionalities is becoming clear in the case of Ethiopia. Despite great strides in macroeconomic performance, fully recognized by donor governments, Ethiopia's entry into the HIPC initiative has been further delayed because of disagreements over policies on monetary and fiscal targets.

• *Broadening and deepening the debt relief.* The debt sustainability ratios to qualify for relief are too high. The ratio of present value debt stock to exports (200–250%) needs to be lowered to 100–150%, and the ratio of debt service to exports (20–25%) to 10–15%.

• *Linking debt relief with human development strategies.* HIPC debt relief needs to be linked to social priority initiatives converting debt burden into finance for human development and poverty reduction.

In 1996 member countries of the Development Assistance Committee of the OECD agreed to targets for human development for 2005 and 2015. A huge financial resource gap must be filled if these statements are to be turned from expressions of hope into plans of support. Debt relief could help to fill that gap.

Reallocating even a small proportion of debt repayment could achieve significant gains for human development. A compact between creditors and debtors could be developed to use accelerated debt relief to provide enhanced financial support for expansion of basic education and health, water and sanitation and poverty eradication programmes in countries benefiting from debt relief.

Political leadership is needed to restore the credibility of the debt initiative. The financial commitments needed to accelerate the HIPC initiative are not unachievable. In 1997 the Group of Seven countries responded to East Asia's crisis with extraordinary resolve, mobilizing in a few months more than $100 billion of loans. Equal resolve is now needed for finding the mere $7 billion needed to implement the HIPC initiative in more than 20 African countries.

Source: Oxfam International 1997 and forthcoming.

---

structure of the market have already had some good results—one important result being technological innovation. For example, taxes on pollution and the removal of energy subsidies have in many cases resulted in the introduction of catalytic converters in cars to control emissions. Such measures have also led to the use of solar energy technologies in primary health care in a number of countries. Similarly, taxes on pesticide use have encouraged integrated pest management and biological control as successful alternatives in agriculture.

The most comprehensive proposal for reform is to shift taxes from taxing employment to taxing pollution and other environmental damage. Although the idea is in its infancy, initial studies are promising. An OECD study for Norway suggests that a revenue-neutral shift of this sort might reduce unemployment by roughly one percentage point while substantially reducing environmental damage. Studies in both Germany and the United Kingdom have suggested that well-designed measures would provide at least half a million new jobs over 10 years, while a major investigation by the European Union predicted that such measures would raise employment in its member states by 4.4 million.

Such initiatives are pioneering steps in the right direction, but they do not go nearly far enough—nor are they sufficiently widespread. Even in the Nordic countries, where some of the most interesting experiments are being carried out, pollution taxes and congestion charges raise only about 7% of government revenues. More extensive use of taxes is constrained by concern about their effects on competitiveness. But combined with removal of perverse subsidies, revenue neutrality, gradual implementation and coordination among industrial countries, environmental taxes can be more acceptable and more implementable.

Alliances for a new vision

Achieving these changes will not be easy. It will require action by five important groups of actors:

• Individuals and households.
• Community organizations and NGOs.

and creating charge systems should be combined in a coherent package of reform measures. Such changes in the incentive

- Producers in the private sector.
- Government—local, regional and national.
- International institutions.

Each of these groups is already involved in some actions in most countries. But the result is often much less than could be achieved with more synergistic interaction among the actors—combining the push for change from individual decisions with collective action from civil society groups, producers operating in the market and the government at local, state and international levels (figure 5.2).

The power of each group of actors to force a change reflects their comparative advantages. Global concerns—desertification, global warming and toxic waste disposal—need international commitment and action. Local crises—water pollution and inadequate sanitation—are responsibilities of states, which must ensure provision or, at the very least, empower community organizations to step in. Privately produced public goods, such as technological innovations, need support from the state plus dynamism in the private sector to ensure that "poor people's technology" and environmentally friendly technology are produced and marketed. Monitoring the private sector's performance is best done by civil society, which can maintain an active and critical lobby—but only if government legislates for disclosure, requiring corporate information to be available for scrutiny. Likewise, civil society can be close to the community and so is more effective in conducting public education and awareness campaigns.

True to the saying "think globally, act locally", the most direct action an individual can take is to alter his or her consumption patterns—starting by reducing unnecessary energy and water use, recycling where possible and choosing fairly traded and environmentally friendly goods. People can vote with their wallets and purses, whether brimming with notes or just a few coins. When faced with choices, individuals and households can change their consumption patterns and pioneer life styles that are creative and fulfilling.

United through organized groups, consumers constitute the aggregate demand of the market—a powerful force in the economy. This highlights the importance of organized civil society in uniting consumers into a critical mass to push for change at the corporate and governmental levels.

Civil society organizations can lobby governments to take action on behalf of consumers and monitor the implementation of policies and the enforcement of regulations. They can also encourage changes in producer behaviour through direct action and by influencing consumer values and behaviour through awareness campaigns. The consumer movement in Zimbabwe has had success across this range of activities (box 5.13).

Many of the impacts of consumption are determined at the level of production,

FIGURE 5.2
Alliances for the new vision

Source: Human Development Report Office.

TABLE 5.2
Economic instruments for environmental protection

Sector	Property rights	Market creation	Fiscal instruments	Charge systems	Financial instruments	Liability systems	Bonds and deposit refund systems
Land and soils	Land titles, use rights	Tradable land permits	Property taxes, land use taxes	Pollution charges	Soil conservation incentives (loans)	Enforcement incentives	Land reclamation bonds
Water resources	Water rights	Water shares	Capital gains taxes	Water pricing, water protection charges	Green (blue) funds		Environmental accident bonds
Oceans and seas	Turf licensing	Fishing rights	Pollution taxes				Oil spill bonds
Forests	Communal rights	Concession bidding	Taxes and royalties	User charges, access fees	Reforestation incentives (subsidies)	Natural resource damage liability	Reforestation bonds, forest management bonds
Minerals	Mining rights	Tradable resource shares	Taxes and royalties	User charges	Sectoral funds	Liability insurance	Land reclamation bonds
Wildlife	Stewardship			Impact fees, access fees	Location and relocation incentives	Natural resource damage liability	
Biodiversity	Patents, prospecting rights	Transferable development rights	Product taxes, input taxes	Charges for scientific tourism	Eco-funds	Natural resource damage liability	
Water pollution		Tradable offsets and credits, tradable effluent permits	Effluent taxes	Water treatment fees, pollution charges	Low-interest loans	Non-compliance charges	Waste delivery bonds, environmental accident bonds
Air pollution		Tradable emissions permits	Emissions taxes	Pollution charges, betterment charges	Technology subsidies, low-interest loans	Non-compliance charges	Environmental accident bonds
Solid waste			Property taxes	Collection charges, impact fees		Liability insurance	Deposit refund systems, waste delivery bonds
Hazardous waste (zero assimilative capacity)			Differential taxation, product taxes	User charges, collection charges	Waste delivery incentives	Joint and several liability, liability insurance	Bonds, deposit refund systems
Toxic chemicals			Differential taxation, product taxes	User charges, impact fees		Legal liability, natural resource liability, liability insurance	Deposit refund systems
Human settlements and land use congestion	Land rights, buy-own-transfer (BOT) arrangements	Tradable development quotas, transferable development rights.	Property taxes, land use taxes	Betterment charges, development charges, land use charges, road tolls	Location and relocation incentives		Development completion bonds
Global climate		Tradable CO_2 permits, carbon offsets, tradable emissions rights, tradable forest protection obligations	Carbon taxes, BTU (British thermal unit) taxes	Pollution charges	Chlorofluoro-carbon (CFC) replacement incentives, forest compacts		

Source: Panayotou 1997.

TABLE 5.3
Examples of countries using innovative economic instruments for sustainable development

Sector	Property rights	Market creation	Fiscal instruments	Environmental charges	Financial instruments	Subsidy reduction	Bonds and deposit refund systems	Resource pricing	Offset systems
Biodiversity	Costa Rica Madagascar	Costa Rica USA (Maine, New Jersey, Puerto Rico)		Costa Rica Madagascar Nepal		Brazil		Costa Rica Kenya Thailand	Belize Costa Rica
Forests	Congo	Costa Rica Côte d'Ivoire	Brazil Central African Republic Colombia Venezuela	Brazil Costa Rica Indonesia	Costa Rica	Brazil Central America	Malaysia Panama Philippines Thailand	Indonesia Malaysia	Costa Rica Guatemala Malaysia
Fragile ecosystems		Costa Rica USA (Puerto Rico)		Brazil Costa Rica Indonesia					
Fresh water sources	Chile Hungary India USA	Australia Chile India New Zealand		Brazil China Costa Rica Korea, Rep. of Malaysia Several OECD countries	Indonesia Thailand	China Eastern Europe Morocco		Brazil Chile	Germany
Land resources	Papua New Guinea Thailand	USA (including Puerto Rico)	Germany Japan	Korea, Rep. of Mexico	USA	Brazil France	Australia Malaysia		Korea, Rep. of
Sustainable agriculture	Argentina Mexico Sri Lanka					Indonesia Many OECD countries		Germany Korea, Rep. of Peru	
Atmosphere	Philippines	Chile China Kazakhstan Poland Singapore USA	China Switzerland Most OECD countries Many developing countries	China France Korea, Rep. of Sweden USA	China Thailand		Sweden		Argentina Germany Norway Poland Russian Federation USA
Oceans and fisheries	Bangladesh Brazil Mauritania Sri Lanka	Australia New Zealand				Philippines	USA		
Hazardous waste and toxic chemicals	USA	Korea, Rep. of	Many developing countries	Europe	Thailand	Indonesia		USA	
Solid waste	Brazil		Nordic countries	Denmark Most OECD countries Netherlands USA (some states)			Chile Japan Korea, Rep. of Netherlands Norway Philippines USA		
Urban environment		Chile Singapore Thailand USA	Germany Netherlands	Europe Korea, Rep. of Singapore USA	Turkey	Thailand	Korea, Rep. of Netherlands	China Singapore USA Viet Nam	Korea, Rep. of

Source: Panayotou 1997.

Sustainable production and consumption

In 1995 Norway hosted a ministerial roundtable to explore policies of sustainable consumption. This was defined as "the use of goods and services that respond to basic needs and bring a better quality of life, while minimizing the use of natural resources, toxic materials and emissions of waste and pollutants over the life cycle, so as not to jeopardize the needs of future generations." Among the conclusions:

• Getting the world onto a sustainable consumption trajectory will take decades. Physical infrastructure—for example, in housing, energy, transport and waste management—can lock societies into unsustainable patterns of consumption, over which individual consumers have little influence. Moreover, many unsustainable patterns of consumption are deeply rooted in cultural habits, despite increasing evidence that many citizens are now ready to re-examine their life styles.

• Political reality in democratic societies will make it much easier to change consumption patterns than consumption volumes (or levels), although both issues need to be addressed.

• Governments have to provide the overarching framework of incentives, infrastructure, regulation and leadership that will enable other actors to take up their part of the chain from production to consumption and final disposal.

• The business sector has a major responsibility for managing the environmental impacts of the goods and services it supplies.

• Trade unions can help to promote new production and consumption patterns that unite employment and environmental concerns.

• Citizens too have a big part to play in changing consumption patterns in their multiple roles as consumers, householders, workers and voters. Women have a particularly powerful role in influencing sustainable consumption decisions.

Source: Oslo Ministerial Roundtable 1995.

so change in the private sector is essential in production, marketing and investment practices. Socially responsible business is small but growing, and it is gaining attention. Companies take on social commitments either through the personal motivation of board members or as a competitive marketing edge appealing to a new breed of consumers—or even as self-regulation to avoid more stringent measures from government and civil society.

Such commitments are, of course, far from universal. Increasing competition and tough-minded management styles often make maximizing profit the overwhelming objective. When these are combined with monopoly power on the global stage, consumer and social interests still get sacrificed. External pressures are needed to keep them in the picture. The state's disclosure law is essential in making information available for monitoring and accountability. In using this information, civil society is often most effective by emphasizing incentives for good performance—such as awards and publicity—over more confrontational approaches.

Aside from their economic and regulatory policy functions, governments have the task of enabling the other actors: setting standards, certifying eco-labelling, legislating access to information and allowing civil society to flourish. In this, government institutions naturally need to be able to enforce laws and regulations.

Inner and outer limits

Barbara Ward, one of the pioneers of sustainable development, called 20 years ago for action to tackle what she termed the inner and outer limits of sustainability. Environmental stress sets the outer limits, beyond which the economic conditions for sustainable production break down. Inequality sets the inner limits—the extremes within which social cohesion breaks down. The two sets of limits are related, not separate. A breakdown of social cohesion can lead to environmental destruction, as often happens today in countries of conflict. In contrast, when there is social harmony, good governance and democracy, efforts to protect and even improve the environment can be more readily explored politically.

The global economy over the next 50 years will need to respond to the challenges set by both sets of limits. It will need to adjust to a different pattern of consumption growth, achieving faster consumption growth and enhanced human development in the poorer countries and improved income distribution within all countries. The world population is expected to grow from about 6 billion to 9 or 10 billion—somewhat lower if education for all is rapidly achieved.

As the new millennium dawns, a progressive vision is needed. The focus and priorities of human development can contribute to such a vision, emphasizing the need for people to be at the centre of the vision and for priorities to focus on enlarging the opportunities and human capabilities of all.

Every country and community—whether rich or poor, large or small—needs its own vision of human development and needs to set its own goals as a framework for policy and action.

Key elements of the vision:

• Patterns of consumption that are environmentally and socially sustainable.

• Equitable societies without sharp dividing lines of exclusion.

• Consumption choices allowing a wide diversity of activities and life styles, encouraging creativity and sensitivity.

• People educated and well informed, driven by human values, not by material acquisition or the dictates of the market.

• Enlarged opportunities for people to choose and determine the lives they lead—and to participate in the key decisions that affect them and their families—in a context of freedom and democracy.

• A world without extremes of human poverty and deprivation.

Such a vision may be more within reach than many realize. The spread of democracy, the human advances in many countries, the expansion of information and the media—all these have enormously increased worldwide awareness of choices and impacts. Indeed, many countries and communities have begun creating their own visions.

Visionaries have long dreamed of a world in which the basic needs of all are met, and increasing consumption of material goods gradually gives way to a more human pattern of activities. John Maynard Keynes, whose economic theories laid much of the foundation for 25 years of economic prosperity and poverty reduction after the Second World War, wrote of *The Economic Consequences for Our Grandchildren* as follows: "A point may soon be reached, much sooner perhaps than all of us are aware of, when (our absolute) needs are satisfied, in the sense that we prefer to devote our further energies to non-economic purposes."

Following the Earth Summit in Rio in 1992, some 2,000 groups around the world prepared Agenda 21 documents, including many cities, towns, communities and even some countries. These plans and proposals for the future sketch out ways to achieve better life styles and consumption patterns on a sustainable basis. Some envisage only modest change; others are more radical (box 5.15).

Communities are also increasingly involved in the monitoring of economic and

---

Local Agenda 21s

At the Earth Summit in Rio de Janeiro in 1992, more than 178 governments adopted Agenda 21—a programme of action for sustainable development worldwide. Its first principle: "Human beings are at the centre of concerns for sustainable development. They are entitled to a healthy and productive life in harmony with nature." Tackling these concerns, however, cannot be the responsibility of national governments alone. As the tenth principle states, "environmental issues are best handled with the participation of all concerned citizens."

Taking on this challenge, by 1997 more than 2,000 local authorities worldwide had drawn up local Agenda 21s through consultation with local people, communities, groups, industrial associations and NGOs. The actions coming out of these initiatives vary widely across regions, reflecting the needs and visions of the local people.

In Kangawa, Japan, activities have included large-scale planting of trees, educational environmental events throughout the region, the development of a model of "eco-housing" and the founding of the Japan International Ecology Centre to promote international cooperation on environmental issues.

In Albertslund, Denmark, there have been two main initiatives. The municipality set many goals within a specific time frame, including reducing resource use and carbon dioxide emissions, introducing organic food in public institutions, developing new areas for outdoor recreation and setting up a business forum on the environment. At the grass-roots level an agenda centre was established to encourage households in Albertslund to tackle such issues as energy conservation and waste disposal.

The city of Santos, Brazil, has a wide range of programmes. To tackle poverty, the municipality is improving housing and sanitation and social services for residents in deprived areas. On the environmental front it is encouraging eco-tourism to protect biodiversity. And it is addressing urban decline through a plan to rejuvenate the old colonial centre through a stakeholder group of businesses, residents and city administrators.

The variety of examples shows the strengths and potential of the Agenda 21 blueprint. Not only has it succeeded in prompting local initiatives, but communities around the world have managed to adapt its guidelines to suit their very different needs—yet all in pursuit of the common goal of sustainable development.

Source: UN 1994a; WWF 1986; ICLEI, UNCHS and Secretariat of the Commission on Sustainable Development 1995.

---

social progress. The multi-indicator cluster surveys, supported by UNICEF, to assess progress towards the goals of the World Summit for Children have involved communities and districts in well over 60 countries. Far from shying away from such assessments, governments have found them useful both for monitoring progress and for identifying further problems to be tackled.

As reported in chapter 1, more than 100 countries have prepared national human development reports, analysing the present situation and drawing conclusions on actions needed to achieve more human patterns of development. Most of these plans have analysed needs in the critical areas of education, health and employment, often linking these needs with opportunities for

Consumption and life styles in national and subnational human development reports

The preparation of national or local human development reports provides a great opportunity to explore issues of consumption and life styles. It is often at the level of the town, village and community that the specifics come alive in considering how to expand opportunities for women and men, young and old.

Key items for the agenda:
• Developing more people-friendly environments.
• Promoting consumer groups, pushing for more equitable access to basic social services and protecting consumers from harmful products.
• Providing community support for parents with young children.
• Making better use of the talents and time of older people.
• Expanding transport options, especially in rural areas.
• Greening and cleaning the neighbourhood, and cutting pollution and waste.
• Discouraging high-pressure and harmful advertising focused on children—for cigarettes, for example.
• Keeping schools drug free.
• Expanding opportunities for youth—in sports, training and jobs.
• Ensuring safety—community efforts to reduce crime, parks should be safe from violence and cycle paths safe from cars.

Many of the items raise difficult issues—conflicts of interest, shortage of finance, competing priorities. Yet experience in many parts of the world shows that enormous reserves of creativity and human energy can be released when local problems are faced. "Where there's a will, there's often a way" to mobilize energy and resources.

So far, only a few national human development reports have dealt with this level of action. Many opportunities are open and could be linked to local Agenda 21s. Industrial countries too could gain from preparing national human development reports.

Source: Human Development Report Office.

generating the resources required through reductions in military expenditure. So far, few of the national human development reports have looked at consumption patterns and life styles. This could be an important theme for future national reports on human development (box 5.16).

In the poorer countries many priorities in consumption still need to be addressed. Increases in consumption should be planned and encouraged—but with attention to ensuring that they contribute to human development and avoid extremes of inequity. Forward-looking perspectives are also needed—to avoid patterns of infrastructure or institutions that in the long run may lock the country into unsustainable or socially dysfunctional consumption.

In the better-off countries—most of the industrial countries and some of the richest developing countries—the challenge is different. The need to eradicate poverty and ensure the basic needs of all remains. Indeed, the failure to do that in the richest countries is a scandal. But as general living standards rise and the proportion in poverty falls, the balance of attention in economic and social policy needs to shift. Increasingly, the policy focus needs to move towards enlarging options for patterns of life and consumption in which human creativity can be lived out and carried forward with diversity and fulfilment, and most of the population is at comfortable levels of consumption, well above the margins of subsistence. This focus needs to be combined with issues of environment and sustainability.

Human development will always be a voyage of human discovery. The high levels of consumption and production in the world today present great opportunities. After a century of vast material expansion and much human progess, will leaders have the vision to seek and achieve more equitable advances in the 21st century?

Technical note. Computing the indices

The human development index

The HDI is based on three indicators: longevity, as measured by life expectancy at birth; educational attainment, as measured by a combination of adult literacy (two-thirds weight) and the combined first-, second- and third-level gross enrolment ratio (one-third weight); and standard of living, as measured by real GDP per capita (PPP$).

For the construction of the index, fixed minimum and maximum values have been established for each of these indicators:

- Life expectancy at birth: 25 years and 85 years
- Adult literacy: 0% and 100%
- Combined gross enrolment ratio: 0% and 100%
- Real GDP per capita (PPP$): $100 and $40,000 (PPP$).

For any component of the HDI, individual indices can be computed according to the general formula:

$$\text{Index} = \frac{\text{Actual } x_i \text{ value} - \text{minimum } x_i \text{ value}}{\text{Maximum } x_i \text{ value} - \text{minimum } x_i \text{ value}}$$

If, for example, the life expectancy at birth in a country is 65 years, then the index of life expectancy for this country would be:

$$\text{Life expectancy index} = \frac{65 - 25}{85 - 25} = \frac{40}{60} = 0.667$$

The construction of the income index is a little more complex. The world average income of $5,990 (PPP$) in 1995 is taken as the threshold level (y^*), and any income above this level is discounted using the following formulation based on Atkinson's formula for the utility of income:

$$W(y) = y^* \text{ for } 0 < y < y^*$$
$$= y^* + 2[(y - y^*)^{1/2}] \text{ for } y^* < y < 2y^*$$
$$= y^* + 2(y^{*1/2}) + 3[(y - 2y^*)^{1/3}] \text{ for } 2y^* < y < 3y^*$$

To calculate the discounted value of the maximum income of $40,000 (PPP$), the following form of Atkinson's formula is used:

$$W(y) = y^* + 2(y^{*1/2}) + 3(y^{*1/3}) + 4(y^{*1/4}) + 5(y^{*1/5})$$
$$+ 6(y^{*1/6}) + 7[(40,000 - 6y^*)^{1/7}]$$

This is because $40,000 (PPP$) is between $6y^*$ and $7y^*$. With the above formulation, the discounted value of the maximum income of $40,000 (PPP$) is $6,311 (PPP$).

The construction of the HDI is illustrated with two examples—Greece and Gabon, an industrial and a developing country.

Country	Life expectancy (years)	Adult literacy rate (%)	Combined gross enrolment ratio (%)	Real GDP per capita (PPP$)
Greece	77.9	96.7	82	11,636
Gabon	54.5	63.2	60	3,766

Life expectancy index

$$\text{Greece} = \frac{77.9 - 25}{85 - 25} = \frac{52.9}{60} = 0.882$$

$$\text{Gabon} = \frac{54.5 - 25}{85 - 25} = \frac{29.5}{60} = 0.492$$

Adult literacy index

$$\text{Greece} = \frac{96.7 - 0}{100 - 0} = \frac{96.7}{100} = 0.967$$

$$\text{Gabon} = \frac{63.2 - 0}{100 - 0} = \frac{63.2}{100} = 0.632$$

Combined first-, second- and third-level gross enrolment ratio index

$$\text{Greece} = \frac{82 - 0}{100 - 0} = 0.820$$

$$\text{Gabon} = \frac{60 - 0}{100 - 0} = 0.600$$

Educational attainment index

$$\text{Greece} = [2(0.967) + 1(0.820)]/3 = 0.918$$

$$\text{Gabon} = [2(0.632) + 1(0.600)]/3 = 0.621$$

Adjusted real GDP per capita (PPP$) index

Greece's real GDP per capita (PPP$) at $11,636 is above the threshold level, but less than twice the threshold. Thus the adjusted real GDP per capita for Greece would be $6,140 (PPP$) because $6,140 = [5,990 + 2(11,636 - 5,990)^{1/2}]$.

Gabon's real GDP per capita at $3,766 (PPP$) is less than the threshold level, so it needs no adjustment.

Thus the adjusted real GDP per capita (PPP$) indices for Greece and Gabon would be:

$$\text{Greece} = \frac{6,140 - 100}{6,311 - 100} = \frac{6,040}{6,211} = 0.972$$

$$\text{Gabon} = \frac{3,766 - 100}{6,311 - 100} = \frac{3,666}{6,211} = 0.590$$

Human development index

The HDI is a simple average of the life expectancy index, educational attainment index and adjusted real GDP per capita (PPP$) index, and so is derived by dividing the sum of these three indices by 3.

Country	Life expectancy index	Educational attainment index	Adjusted real GDP per capita (PPP$) index	Sum of indices	HDI
Greece	0.882	0.918	0.972	2.772	0.924
Gabon	0.492	0.621	0.590	1.703	0.568

The gender-related development index and the gender empowerment measure

For comparisons among countries, the GDI and the GEM are limited to data widely available in international data sets. For this year's Report we have endeavoured to use the most recent, reliable and internally consistent data. Collecting more extensive and more reliable gender-disaggregated data is a challenge that the international community should squarely face. We continue to publish results on the GDI and the GEM—based on the best available estimates—in the expectation that it will help increase the demand for such data.

The gender-related development index

The GDI uses the same variables as the HDI. The difference is that the GDI adjusts the average achievement of each country in life expectancy, educational attainment and income in accordance with the disparity in achievement between women and men. (For a detailed explanation of the GDI methodology see technical note 1 in *Human Development Report 1995*.) For this gender-sensitive adjustment we use a weighting formula that expresses a moderate aversion to inequality, setting the weighting parameter, $\in$, equal to 2. This is the harmonic mean of the male and female values.

The GDI also adjusts the maximum and minimum values for life expectancy, to account for the fact that women tend to live longer than men. For women the maximum value is 87.5 years and the minimum value 27.5 years; for men the corresponding values are 82.5 and 22.5 years.

Calculating the index for income is fairly complex. Female and male shares of earned income are derived from data on the ratio of the average female wage to the average male wage and the female and male percentage shares of the economically active population aged 15 and above. Where data on the wage ratio are not available, we use a value of 75%, the weighted mean of the wage ratio for all countries with wage data. Before income is indexed, the average adjusted real GDP per capita of each country is discounted on the basis of the disparity in the female and male shares of earned income in proportion to the female and male population shares.

The indices for life expectancy, educational attainment and income are added together with equal weight to derive the final GDI value.

Illustration of the GDI methodology

We choose Japan to illustrate the steps for calculating the gender-related development index. The parameter of inequality aversion, $\in$, equals 2. (Any discrepancies in results are due to numbers' being rounded up.)

Percentage share of total population
Females   51
Males   49
Life expectancy at birth (years)
Females   82.8
Males   76.7
Adult literacy rate (percent)
Females   99
Males   99
Combined first-, second- and third-level gross enrolment ratio (percent)
Females   77
Males   79

STEP ONE
Computing the equally distributed life expectancy index

Life expectancy index
Females $(82.8 - 27.5)/60 = 0.922$
Males $(76.7 - 22.5)/60 = 0.904$

The equally distributed life expectancy index
{[female population share × (female life expectancy index)$^{-1}$] + [male population share × (male life expectancy index)$^{-1}$]}$^{-1}$
$[0.51(0.922)^{-1} + 0.49(0.904)^{-1}]^{-1} = 0.913$

STEP TWO
Computing the equally distributed educational attainment index

Adult literacy index
Females $(99 - 0)/100 = 0.990$
Males $(99 - 0)/100 = 0.990$
Combined gross enrolment index
Females $(77 - 0)/100 = 0.770$
Males $(79 - 0)/100 = 0.790$
Educational attainment index
2/3(adult literacy index) + 1/3(combined gross enrolment index)
Females $2/3(0.990) + 1/3(0.770) = 0.917$
Males $2/3(0.990) + 1/3(0.790) = 0.923$

The equally distributed educational attainment index
{[female population share × (educational attainment index)$^{-1}$] + [male population share × (educational attainment index)$^{-1}$]}$^{-1}$
$[0.51(0.917)^{-1} + 0.49(0.923)^{-1}]^{-1} = 0.920$

STEP THREE
Computing the equally distributed income index

Percentage share of the economically active population
Females   40.8
Males   59.2

Ratio of female non-agricultural wage to male non-agricultural wage: 0.750

Adjusted real GDP per capita: PPP$6,231 (see the section above on the HDI)

A. Computing proportional income shares

Average wage (W) = (female share of economically active population × female to male wage ratio) + (male economically active population × 1)
$(0.408 \times 0.750) + (0.592 \times 1) = 0.898$

Female to male wage ratio to average wage (W)
$0.750/0.898 = 0.835$

Male wage to average wage (W)
$1/0.898 = 1.114$

Share of earned income
Note: [(female to male wage ratio/average wage) × female share of economically active population] + [(male wage/average wage) × male share of economically active population] = 1
Females
Female to male wage ratio to average wage × female economically active population
$0.835 \times 0.408 = 0.341$

Males
Male wage × male economically active population
$1.114 \times 0.592 = 0.659$

Female and male proportional income shares
Females
Female share of earned income/female population share
$0.341/0.51 = 0.669$

Males
Male share of earned income/male population share
$0.659/0.49 = 1.343$

B. Computing the equally distributed income index

The weighting parameter ($\in$ = 2) is applied.
{[female population share × (female proportional income share)$^{-1}$] + [male population share × (male proportional income share)$^{-1}$]}$^{-1}$
$[0.51 (0.669)^{-1} + 0.49 (1.343)^{-1}]^{-1} = 0.888$
$0.888 \times 6,231 = 5,532$
$(5,532 - 100)/(6,311 - 100) = 0.874$

STEP FOUR
Computing the gender-related development index (GDI)

$1/3(0.913 + 0.920 + 0.874) = 0.902$

The gender empowerment measure
The GEM uses variables constructed explicitly to measure the relative empowerment of women and men in political and economic spheres of activity.

The first two variables are chosen to reflect economic participation and decision-making power: women's and men's percentage shares of administrative and managerial positions and their percentage shares of professional and technical jobs. These are broad, loosely defined occupational categories. Because the relevant population for each is different, we calculate a separate index for each and then add the two together. The third variable, women's and men's percentage shares of parliamentary seats, is chosen to reflect political participation and decision-making power.

For all three of these variables we use the methodology of population-weighted $(1 - \in)$ averaging to derive an "equally distributed equivalent percentage" (EDEP) for both sexes taken together. Each variable is indexed by dividing the EDEP by 50%.

An income variable is used to reflect power over economic resources. It is calculated in the same manner as for the GDI except that unadjusted rather than adjusted real GDP per capita is used. The maximum value for income is thus PPP$40,000 and the minimum PPP$100.

The three indices—for economic participation and decision-making, political participation and decision-making, and power over economic resources—are added together to derive the final GEM value.

Illustration of the GEM methodology
We choose Peru to illustrate the steps in calculating the GEM. The parameter of inequality aversion, $\in$, equals 2. (Any discrepancies in results are due to numbers' being rounded up.)

STEP ONE
Calculating indices for parliamentary representation and administrative and managerial, and professional and technical, positions

Percentage share of parliamentary representation
Females   10.8
Males   89.2
Percentage share of administrative and managerial positions
Females   23.8
Males   76.2
Percentage share of professional and technical positions
Females   41.3
Males   58.7
Percentage share of population
Females   50.33
Males   49.67

Calculating the EDEP for parliamentary representation
$[0.5033(10.8)^{-1} + 0.4967(89.2)^{-1}]^{-1} = 19.2$
Calculating the EDEP for administrative and managerial positions
$[0.5033(23.8)^{-1} + 0.4967(76.2)^{-1}]^{-1} = 36.1$

Calculating the EDEP for professional and technical positions
$[0.5033(41.3)^{-1} + 0.4967(58.7)^{-1}]^{-1} = 48.4$

Indexing parliamentary representation
$19.2/50 = 0.384$

Indexing administrative and managerial positions
$36.1/50 = 0.722$

Indexing professional and technical positions
$48.4/50 = 0.969$

Combining the indices for administrative and managerial, and professional and technical, positions
$(0.722 + 0.969)/2 = 0.846$

STEP TWO
Calculating the index for share of earned income

Percentage share of economically active population
Females   29.4
Males   70.6

Ratio of female non-agricultural wage to male non-agricultural wage: 0.750

Unadjusted real GDP per capita: PPP$3,940

Ratio of female wage to average wage (W) and of male wage to average wage (W):
$W = 0.294(0.75) + 0.706(1) = 0.927$
Female to male wage ratio to average wage: $0.750/0.927 = 0.810$
Male wage to average wage: $1/0.927 = 1.079$

Share of earned income
Note: [(female to male wage ratio/average wage) × female share of economically active population] + [(male wage/average wage) × male share of economically active population] = 1

Females $0.810 \times 0.294 = 0.238$
Males $1.079 \times 0.706 = 0.762$

Female and male proportional income shares
Females $0.238/0.5033 = 0.473$
Males $0.762/0.4967 = 1.534$

Calculating the equally distributed income index
$[0.5033(0.473)^{-1} + 0.4967(1.534)^{-1}]^{-1} = 0.721$
$0.721 \times 3,940 = 2,839$
$(2,839 - 100)/(40,000 - 100) = 0.069$

STEP THREE
Computing the GEM
$1/3(0.384 + 0.846 + 0.069) = 0.433$

The human poverty index

Computing the human poverty index for developing countries

The human poverty index for developing countries (HPI-1) concentrates on deprivations in three essential dimensions of human life already reflected in the HDI—longevity, knowledge and a decent standard of living. The first deprivation relates to survival—the vulnerability to death at a relatively early age. The second relates to knowledge—being excluded from the world of reading and communication. The third relates to a decent living standard in terms of overall economic provisioning.

In constructing the HPI-1, the deprivation in longevity is represented by the percentage of people not expected to survive to age 40 (P_1), and the deprivation in knowledge by the percentage of adults who are illiterate (P_2). The deprivation in a decent living standard in terms of overall economic provisioning is represented by a composite (P_3) of three variables—the percentage of people without access to safe water (P_{31}), the percentage of people without access to health services (P_{32}) and the percentage of moderately and severely underweight children under five (P_{33}).

The composite variable P_3 is constructed by taking a simple average of the three variables P_{31}, P_{32} and P_{33}. Thus

$$P_3 = \frac{(P_{31} + P_{32} + P_{33})}{3}$$

Following the analysis in chapter 1 of this Report and technical note 1 in *Human Development Report 1997*, the formula of the HPI-1 is given by:

$$\text{HPI-1} = [1/3(P_1^3 + P_2^3 + P_3^3)]^{1/3}$$

As an example, we compute the HPI-1 for Egypt.

STEP ONE
Calculating P_3

Country	P_1 (%)	P_2 (%)	P_{31} (%)	P_{32} (%)	P_{33} (%)
Egypt	13.0	48.6	13	1	15

$$P_3 = \frac{13 + 1 + 15}{3} = \frac{29}{3} = 9.67$$

STEP TWO
Constructing the HPI

$$\begin{aligned}
\text{HPI-1} &= [1/3(13.0^3 + 48.6^3 + 9.67^3)]^{1/3} \\
&= [1/3(2{,}197.0 + 114{,}791.3 + 904.2)]^{1/3} \\
&= [1/3(117{,}892.5)]^{1/3} \\
&= (39{,}297.5)^{1/3} \\
&= 34.0
\end{aligned}$$

Computing the human poverty index for industrial countries

The human poverty index for industrial countries (HPI-2) concentrates on deprivations in four dimensions of human life, quite similar to those reflected in the HDI—longevity, knowledge, a decent standard of living and social exclusion. The first deprivation relates to survival—the vulnerability to death at a relatively early age. The second relates to knowledge—being deprived of the world of reading and communication. The third relates to a decent living standard in terms of overall economic provisioning. And the fourth relates to non-participation or exclusion.

In constructing the HPI-2, the deprivation in longevity is represented by the percentage of people not expected to survive to age 60 (P_1), and the deprivation in knowledge by the percentage of people who are functionally illiterate as defined by the OECD (P_2). The deprivation in a decent living standard in terms of overall economic provisioning is represented by the percentage of people living below the income poverty line set at 50% of the median disposable personal income (P_3). And the fourth deprivation, in non-participation or exclusion, is measured by the rate of long-term (12 months or more) unemployment (P_4) of the labour force.

Following the analysis in chapter 1 of this Report and technical note 1 in *Human Development Report 1997*, the formula of the HPI-2 is given by:

$$\text{HPI-2} = [1/4(P_{13}^3 + P_{23}^3 + P_{33}^3 + P_{43}^3)]^{1/3}$$

As an example, we compute the HPI-2 for the United States.

Country	P_1 (%)	P_2 (%)	P_3 (%)	P_4 (%)
USA	13.0	20.7	19.1	0.5

STEP ONE
Constructing the HPI-2

$$\begin{aligned}
\text{HPI-2} &= [1/4(13.0^3 + 20.7^3 + 19.1^3 + 0.5^3)]^{1/3} \\
&= [1/4(2{,}197.0 + 8{,}869.7 + 6{,}987.9 + 0.125)]^{1/3} \\
&= [1/4(18{,}034.7)]^{1/3} \\
&= (4{,}508.7)^{1/3} \\
&= 16.5
\end{aligned}$$

References

Background papers, country studies and background notes for Human Development Report 1998

Background papers

Anand, Sudhir, and Amartya Sen. 1997. "Consumption and Human Development: Concepts and Issues."

Banuri, Tariq. 1997. "The Case of the Environmental Kuznets Curve."

Belser, Patrick. 1997. "Globalization, Consumers and Working Conditions."

Brzoska, Michael, and Herbert Wulf. 1997. "Dynamics of Military Procurement: Changes in Military Consumption Patterns."

Chichilnisky, Graciela. 1997a. "Financial Instruments for Human Development."

———. 1997b. "The Knowledge Revolution: Its Impact on Consumption Patterns and Resource Use."

CUTS (Consumer Unity and Trust Society). 1997. "The Role and the Impact of Advertising in Promoting Sustainable Consumption: The Case of India."

Darbellay, Eliane. 1997. "Consumption Patterns of Highest to Lowest Quintiles."

Haq, Mahbub ul. 1998. "Consumption and Human Development."

Hutton, Bruce. 1997. "The Role and Potential of Marketing and Advertising on Global Human Development."

Khor, Martin. 1997. "Globalization, Income Distribution, Consumption Patterns and Effects on Human and Sustainable Development."

Lipton, Michael, and Arjan de Haan. 1997. "Population, Consumption and Human Development."

Lipton, Michael, Arjan de Haan and Eliane Darbellay. 1997. "Food Security, Food Consumption Patterns and Human Development."

Matthews, Emily, and Allen Hammond. 1997. "Natural Resource Consumption."

Myers, Norman. 1997a. "Consumption and Sustainable Development: The Role of Perverse Subsidies."

Nyman, Pia. 1997a. "Global Marketing—A Literature Review."

Panayotou, Theodore. 1997. "Market Instruments and Consumption and Production Patterns."

Perrings, Charles. 1997. "Income, Consumption and Human Development: Environmental Linkages."

Prescott-Allen, Robert. 1997. "Consumption Patterns, Ecosystem Stress and Human Development."

Rasheed, Nadia, and Poornima Paidipaty. 1997. "Cultural Globalization and Consumption—A Literature Review."

Schor, Juliet. 1997. "A Structural Critique of Consumption: Inequality, Globalization and the Aspirational Gap."

Seth, Anuradha. 1997. "Intra-Household Consumption Patterns: Issues, Evidence and Implications for Human Development."

Shiva, Vandana. 1997a. "Biodiversity, Consumption Patterns and Globalization."

Stewart, Frances. 1997. "Consumption, Globalization and Theory: Why There Is a Need for Reform."

Zadek, Simon, Sanjiv Lingayah and Sara Murphy. 1997. "Consumer Works! Civil Action for Human Development."

Country studies

Abdeljaouad, Jorio, Samir Halaoui, Nadira Barkallil and Rachid Hamimaz. 1997. "Tendances de l'Evolution des Modes de Consommation dans le Contexte de Libéralisation Economique au Maroc."

Agarwal, Anil, and Sunita Narain. 1997. "Economic Globalization and Its Impact on Consumption, Equity and Sustainability: The Indian Case."

Amin, Galal. 1997. "Globalization, Consumption Patterns and Human Development: The Case of Egypt."

Crocker, David, Luis Camacho and Ramón Romero. 1997. "Globalization, Consumption Patterns and Human Development: The Cases of Costa Rica and Honduras."

Larenas, Stefan. 1997. "Globalization and Changes in the Patterns of Consumption in Chile."

Mongkolsmai, Dow, and Somchai Suksiriserekul. 1997. "Linkages between Globalization, Consumption Patterns and Human Development in Thailand."

Mwangi, Njuguna. 1997. "Linkages between Globalization, the Resultant Consumption Patterns and the Impact on Human Development: Country Study on Kenya."

Sodré, Marcelo Gomes. 1997. "Globalization and Changes in Consumer Patterns: The Case of Brazil."

Zhang, Amei. 1997. "Globalization, Consumption and Human Development in China."

Background notes

Abrahamson, Dean, and Thomas B. Johansson. 1998a. "After Kyoto: The Challenge for Buenos Aires."
———. 1998b. "The Zero-Emission Car."
Arizpe, Lourdes. 1997. "The Community Feast."
Consumer Council of Zimbabwe. 1998. "Sustainable Consumption and Environmental Health."
Galbraith, John Kenneth. 1997. "On the Continuing Influence of Affluence."
Kay, Alan, and Hazel Henderson. 1997. "Truth in Advertising Assurance Set-Aside: A Proposal to Help Steer the U.S. Economy toward Sustainability."

Mahbubani, Kishore. 1997. "Singapore—Eliminating Consumption Shortfalls on a Crowded Planet."
Mason, John. 1997. "Nutrition and Human Development."
Nyman, Pia. 1997b. "Environmental Taxes: The Case of Sweden."
Parthasarathi, Prasannan. 1997a. "The Global Middle Class."
———. 1997b. "On the Middle Classes."
———. 1997c. "Religion and Consumption."
Tuijnman, Albert. 1998. "Adult Literacy in OECD Countries."
Wild, Robert. 1998. "The Jozani-Chwaka Bay Conservation Project, Zanzibar."

Bibliographic note

Chapter 1 draws on the following: Bratton and van de Walle 1997, Bread for the World Institute 1996 and 1998, de Haan and Maxwell 1998, Egypt, Institute of National Planning 1996, *The Economist* 1998, Euromonitor 1997, *Forbes Magazine* 1997, OECD and Human Resource Development Canada and Statistics Canada 1997, IILS 1996, Jaura 1997, Mongkolsmai and Suksiriserekul 1997, Ranis and Stewart 1998, Rodgers, Gore and Figueiredo 1995, Stanecki and Way 1997, Tuijnman 1998, UN 1994b, 1997e and 1997g, UNAIDS 1997, UNDP 1995a, 1996a, 1996b, 1997b, 1997c, 1997d, 1997e, 1997f, and 1998, UNDP and the Government of El Salvador 1997, UNDP and the Government of Niger 1997, UNDP and Instituto de Pesquisa Econômica Aplicada 1996, UNDP, UNFPA and UNICEF 1994, UNICEF 1996, 1997, 1998a and 1998b, US Bureau of the Census forthcoming and Worldwide Research, Advisory and Business Intelligence Services 1997.

Chapter 2 draws on the following: Anand and Sen 1997, Bourdieu 1984, Douglas and Isherwood 1979, Duesenberry 1949, Galbraith 1997, Haq 1998, Keynes 1936, Mauss [1925] 1990, Miller 1995, Parthasarathi 1997a, 1997b and 1997c, Samuelson 1938, Schor 1991 and 1998, Scitovsky 1976, Sen 1985, Stewart 1997 and Veblen [1899] 1967.

Chapter 3 draws on the following: Agarwal and Narain 1997, Amin 1997, Arizpe 1997, Bank for International Settlements 1997, Bjurström 1994, Bread for the World Institute 1998, CDIAC 1996, Crocker, Camacho and Romero 1997, Consumers International 1996, CUTS 1997, Durning 1992, Euromonitor 1997, FAO 1995, 1996b, 1997a, 1997c, 1998, Government of Costa Rica 1988, Government of Jordan 1993, Government of Sierra Leone 1993, Government of Thailand 1995, Hawken 1993, Howe 1998, Hutton 1997, Ingelhart 1997, ITU 1997b, Khor 1997, Larenas 1997, Lipton, de Haan and Darbellay 1997, Mahbubani 1997, Matthews and Hammond 1997, McDonald's Corporation 1997, Moller 1997, Murray and Lopez 1996, Myers 1997b, OECD 1997b, 1997e, Parthasarathi 1997a, 1997b, Pearce 1993, Prescott-Allen 1997, Rabinovitch and Hook 1998, Redclift 1996, Reddy Williams and Johansson 1997, Riches 1997, Schor 1991, 1997, 1998, Seth 1997, Shiklomanov 1996, Shiva 1997a,

Sodré 1997, Stewart 1997, UN 1996a, 1996b, 1996c, 1997b, UNCTAD 1996 and 1997, UNDP 1995a, UNESCO 1995, 1997a, 1997b, UNHCR 1996, 1997, UNICEF 1997, 1998b, USDA 1997, WHO 1995b, 1996a, 1997c, 1998, World Bank 1992, 1994, 1997c, 1997d,1997e, World Bureau of Metal Statistics 1996, Worldwatch Institute 1997a, 1997b, WRI 1994, 1996a, 1996b, 1998 and Zhang 1997.

Chapter 4 draws on the following: Agarwal 1996, ADB 1997, Bernardini and Galli 1993, Crocker, Camacho and Romero 1997, Goldemberg 1997, Hillary 1997, Janicke, Monch, Ranneberg, and Simonis 1989, Larenas 1997, Lean 1992, Matthews and Hammond 1997, Montimore and Tiffen 1994, Myers 1997a and 1997b, Ngoc and others 1994, OECD 1997a and 1997e, Panayotou 1997, Prescott-Allen 1997, Raskin and others 1996, Reddy, Williams and Johansson 1997, Sampat 1996, Serageldin, Cohen and Sivaramakrishnan 1994, Shiva 1997a and 1997b, Sodré 1997, UN 1997a, UNCHS 1997, UNEP 1996, 1997a, 1997b, von Weizsäcker, Lovins and Lovins 1997, Welch 1997, WHO 1997a, Wild 1998, World Bank 1995a, WRI 1994 and 1996a and Zhang 1997.

Chapter 5 draws on the following: Abrahamson and Johansson 1998a and 1998b, Chichilnisky 1997a and 1997b, The Consumer Council of Zimbabwe 1998, Crocker, Camacho and Romero 1997, European Fair Trade Association 1995, FAO 1997b, Hammond 1998, ICLEI, UNCHS and Secretariat of the Commision on Sustainable Development 1995, Kay and Henderson 1997, Keynes 1930, Matthews and Hammond 1997, de Moor 1997, de Moor and Calamai 1997, Nigam and Rasheed 1998, Nyman 1997b, OECD 1995c, 1997g, 1997j, Oslo Ministerial Roundtable 1995, Oxfam International 1997 and forthcoming, Panayotou 1997, Pinstrup-Andersen, Pandya-Lorch and Rosegrant 1997, Rabinovitch and Hoehn 1995, Rabinovitch and Hook 1998, Rabinovitch and Leitmann 1993, Reddy, Williams and Johansson 1997, Robins and Roberts 1997, Roodman 1996 and 1997, Serageldin, Cohen and Sivaramakrishnan 1994, UN 1994a, 1995a, 1996c, 1997b, 1997e, 1998, UNCHS 1996, UNDP 1997a, UNICEF 1998b, WEC and IIASA 1995, WHO 1997a, Worldwatch Institute 1997b, WWF 1986 and Zadek, Lingayah and Murphy 1997.

References

ADB (Asian Development Bank). 1997. *Emerging Asia—Changes and Challenges.* Manila.

Agarwal, Anil. 1996. "Pay-offs to Progress." *Down to Earth* (Centre for Science and Environment, New Delhi) 5(10): 31–39.

ARF (Addiction Research Foundation). 1994. "Statistical Information, International Profile 1994." Ontario, Canada.

Bank for International Settlements. 1997. "Statistics on Payment Systems in the Group of Ten Countries—Figures for 1996." Basel.

Bernardini, Oliviero, and Ricardo Galli. 1993. "Dematerialization: Long-term Trends in the Intensity of Use of Materials and Energy." *Futures* 25(4): 431–48.

Bjurström, Erling. 1994. *Children and Television Advertising: A Critical Study of International Research Concerning the Effects of TV Commercials on Children.* Report 1994/95:8. Stockholm: National Swedish Board for Consumer Policies.

Bourdieu, Pierre. 1984. *Distinction: A Social Critique of the Judgement of Taste.* Cambridge, Mass.: Harvard University Press.

Bratton, Michael, and Nicolas van de Walle. 1997. *Democratic Experiments in Africa: Regime Transitions in Comparative Perspective.* New York: Cambridge University Press.

Bread for the World Institute. 1996. *Hunger 1996: Countries in Crisis.* Silver Spring, Md.

———. 1998. *Hunger 1998: Hunger in a Global Economy.* Silver Spring, Md.

Brewers and Licensed Retailers Association. 1997. *Statistical Handbook 1997.* London.

CDIAC (Carbon Dioxide Information Analysis Center), Environmental Sciences Division, Oak Ridge National Laboratory. 1996. "Estimates of CO_2 Emissions from Fossil Fuel Burning and Cement Manufacturing Based on the United Nations Energy Statistics and the US Bureau of Mines Cement Manufacturing Data." Oak Ridge, Tenn.

———. 1998. Data available at http://www.cdiac.ESD. ORNL.GOV/ftp/ndp001r7. January.

Chichilnisky, Graciela. 1997c. "Development and Global Finance: The Case for an International Bank for Environmental Settlements." Office of Development Studies Discussion Paper 10. UNDP, New York.

Consumers International. 1996. *A Spoonful of Sugar—Television Food Advertising Aimed at Children: An International Study.* London.

Costa Rica, General Office of Statistics. 1988. *Income and Expenditure Survey 1987.* San José.

de Haan, Arjan, and Simon Maxwell, eds. 1998. "Poverty and Social Exclusion in North and South." *IDS Bulletin* (Sussex) 29(1).

de Moor, André. 1997. *Perverse Incentives.* The Hague, Netherlands: Institute for Research on Public Expenditure.

de Moor, André, and Peter Calamai. 1997. *Subsidizing Unsustainable Development: Undermining the Earth with Public Funds.* San José, Costa Rica: Institute for Research on Public Expenditure and the Earth Council.

Douglas, Mary, and Baron Isherwood. 1979. *The World of Goods: Towards an Anthropology of Consumption.* New York: Basic Books.

Duesenberry, James S. 1949. *Income, Saving and the Theory of Consumer Behaviour.* Cambridge, Mass.: Harvard University Press.

Durning, Alan. 1992. *How Much Is Enough? The Consumer Society and the Future of the Earth.* London: Earthscan.

The Economist. 1998. "AIDS in Kenya: Serial Killer at Large." 7 February, pp. 97–176.

Egypt, Institute of National Planning. 1996. *Egypt Human Development Report 1996.* Cairo.

Euromonitor. 1997. *World Consumer Markets 1997/98.* CD-ROM. London.

European Fair Trade Association. 1995. *Fair Trade Yearbook 1995.* Maastricht, Netherlands.

Eurostat and UN (United Nations). 1995. *Women and Men in Europe and North America.* Geneva.

FAO (Food and Agriculture Organization of the United Nations). 1994. *1994 Country Tables: Basic Data on the Agriculture Sector.* Economic and Social Policy Department. Rome.

———. 1995. *Yearbook of Fishery Statistics: Catches and Landings.* Rome.

———. 1996a. *Production Yearbook.* FAO Statistics Series. Rome.

———. 1996b. *The Sixth World Food Survey.* Rome.

———. 1997a. Correspondence on daily per capita calorie supply. Received July. Rome.

———. 1997b. *Report of the World Food Summit.* Rome.

———. 1997c. *The State of the World's Forests 1997.* Rome.

———. 1998. Food Balance Sheets. Available at http://apps.fao.org/lim500/nphwrap.pl?FoodBalanceSheet&Domain=FoodBalanceSheet. February.

Forbes Magazine. 1997. "The Global Power Elite." 28 July, pp. 49–50.

Galbraith, John Kenneth. 1958. *The Affluent Society.* Boston, Mass.: Houghton Mifflin.

Goldemberg, José. 1997. *Leapfrog Energy Technologies.* San Francisco: Energy Foundation.

Hammond, Allen. 1998a. "Natural Resource Consumption: North and South." In David Crocker and Toby Linden, eds., *The Ethics of Consumption: The Good Life, Justice and Global Stewardship.* Oxford: Rowman and Littlefield.

———. 1998b. *Which World: Scenarios for the 21st Century.* Washington, DC: Island Press.

Haq, Mahbub ul. 1997. *Human Development in South Asia.* Karachi: Oxford University Press.

Haq, Mahbub ul, and Khadija Haq. 1998. *Human Development in South Asia: The Education Challenge.* Karachi: Oxford University Press.

Hawken, Paul. 1993. *The Ecology of Commerce: A Declaration of Sustainability.* New York: Harper Business.

Hillary, Ruth, ed. 1997. *Environmental Management Systems and Cleaner Production.* New York: John Wiley and Sons.

Howe, John. 1998. Correspondence on transport in the United Republic of Tanzania. Received March. Delft, Netherlands.

ICLEI (International Council for Local Environmental Initiatives), UNCHS (United Nations Centre for Human Settlements) and Secretariat of the Commission on Sustainable Development. 1995. "The Role of Local Authorities in Sustainable Development: 14 Case Studies on the Local Agenda 21 Process." Department for Policy Coordination and Sustainable Development. New York.

IDEA (Institute for Democracy and Electoral Assistance). 1997. *Voter Turnout from 1945 to 1997: A Global Report.* Stockholm.

IILS (International Institute for Labour Studies). 1996. "Social Exclusion and Anti-Poverty Strategies." International Labour Organisation, Geneva.

IISS (International Institute for Strategic Studies). 1993. *The Military Balance 1993–94.* London: Brasseys.

———. 1997. *The Military Balance 1997–98.* London: Oxford University Press.

ILO (International Labour Office). 1994. *World Labour Report 1994.* Geneva.

———. 1995a. *World Labour Report 1995.* Geneva.

———. 1995b. *Yearbook of Labour Statistics 1995.* Geneva.

———. 1996. *Estimates and Projections of the Economically Active Population, 1950–2010.* 4th ed. Diskette. Geneva.

———. 1997a. *World Labour Report 1997–98.* Geneva.

———. 1997b. *Yearbook of Labour Statistics 1997.* Geneva.

IMF (International Monetary Fund). 1995. *Government Finance Statistics Yearbook.* Washington, DC.

Ingelhart, Ronald. 1997. *Modernization and Postmodernization: Cultural, Economic, and Political Change in 43 Societies.* Princeton, N.J.: Princeton University Press.

International Federation of Red Cross and Red Crescent Societies. 1997. *World Disasters Report 1997.* New York: Oxford University Press.

IPU (Inter-Parliamentary Union). 1997a. Data available at http://www.ipu.org. December.

———. 1997b. *Democracy Still in the Making.* Geneva.

———. 1998. Correspondence on political participation. Received February. Geneva

ITU (International Telecommunication Union). 1996. *World Telecommunication Indicators.* Diskette. Geneva.

———. 1997a. *World Telecommunication Development Report 1996–97.* Geneva.

———. 1997b. *World Telecommunication Indicators.* Diskette. Geneva.

Janicke, Martin, Harald Monch, Thomas Ranneberg and Udo E. Simonis. 1989. "Economic Structure and Environmental Impacts: East-West Comparisons." *The Environmentalist* 9(3): 171–83.

Jaura, Ramesh. 1997. "South Still Arming Heavily for 1998." Inter Press Service, New York.

Jordan, Department of Statistics. 1993. *Household Expenditure and Income Survey 1992.* Amman.

Keesing's Worldwide (formerly Worldwide Government Directories). 1995. *Worldwide Government Directory with International Organizations.* Bethesda, Md.

Keynes, John Maynard. 1930. "The Economic Possibilities for Our Grandchildren." Reprinted in John Maynard Keynes, *Essays in Persuasion* (London: Macmillan, 1994).

———. 1936. *The General Theory of Employment, Interest and Money.* London: Macmillan.

Lean, Geoffrey. 1992. *WWF Atlas of the Environment.* Oxford: Helican.

Mauss, Marcel. [1925] 1990. *The Gift: The Form and Reason for Exchange in Archaic Societies.* London: Routledge.

McDonald's Corporation. 1997. *1996 Annual Report.* Oak Brook, Ill.

Miller, Daniel. 1995. *Acknowledging Consumption: A Review of New Studies.* London: Routledge.

Moller, Valerie. 1997. "Aspirations, Consumption and Conflict in the New South Africa." Paper presented to the conference Population, Consumption and Development, Cambridge.

Montimore, Michael, and Mary Tiffen. 1994. "Population Growth and Sustainable Development: The Machakos Story." *Environment* 36(8): 10–31.

Murray, Christopher, and Alan Lopez. 1996. *Global Health Statistics.* Cambridge, Mass.: Harvard University Press.

Myers, Norman. 1997b. "Consumption in Relation to Population, Environment and Development." *The Environmentalist* 17: 33–44.

Ngoc, Du, and others. 1994. "Women and Waste Recycling in Ho Chi Minh City." ICRW Report in Brief. International Centre for Research on Women, Washington, DC.

Nigam, Ashok, and Sadig Rasheed. 1998. "Financing of Freshwater for All—A Rights-Based Approach." Paper presented at expert group meeting on strategic approaches to freshwater management, Harare, Zimbabwe.

OECD (Organisation for Economic Co-operation and Development). 1994. *Development Co-operation: Development Assistance Committee Report 1994.* Paris.

———. 1995a. *Development Co-operation: Development Assistance Committee Report 1995.* Paris.

———. 1995b. *Employment Outlook.* Paris.

———. 1995c. *Energy Prices and Taxes.* Fourth quarter. Paris.

———. 1995d. *Environmental Data: Compendium 1995.* Paris.

———. 1995e. *OECD Health Data 1995.* Paris.

———. 1996a. *Economic Outlook.* 60th issue. Paris.

———. 1996b. *Education at a Glance 1996.* Paris.

———. 1996c. *Employment Outlook.* Paris.

———. 1997a. *Economic Globalisation and Environment.* Paris.

———. 1997b. *Economic Outlook.* 61st issue. Paris.

———. 1997c. *Education at a Glance 1997.* Paris.

———. 1997d. *Employment Outlook.* Paris.

———. 1997e. *Environmental Data: Compendium 1997.* Paris.

———. 1997f. *Geographical Distribution of Financial Flows to Aid Recipients.* Paris.

———. 1997g. *Reforming Energy and Transport Subsidies.* Paris.

———. 1997h. *Short-term Economic Indicators: Transition Economies.* Paris.

———. 1997i. *Sustainable Consumption and Production.* Paris.

———. 1997j. *The World in 2020: Towards a New Global Age.* Paris.

———. 1998. *Development Co-operation: Development Assistance Committee Report 1997.* Paris.

OECD (Organisation for Economic Co-operation and

Development) and Statistics Canada. 1995. *Literacy, Economy and Society.* Paris and Ottawa.

OECD (Organisation for Economic Co-operation and Development), Human Resource Development Canada and Statistics Canada. 1997. *Literacy Skills for the Knowledge Society: Further Results from the International Adult Literacy Survey.* Paris and Ottawa.

Oslo Ministerial Roundtable. 1995. "Report of the Conference on Sustainable Production and Consumption." Oslo, 6–10 February.

Oxfam International. 1997. "Beyond the HIPC Initiative: An Appraisal and Proposal for Converting Debt into Educational Opportunity." Policy Department. Washington, DC.

———. Forthcoming. "Tanzania: The Case for Debt Reduction." Policy Department. Washington, DC.

Pearce, David. 1993. *Blueprint 3: Measuring Sustainable Development.* London: Earthscan.

Pinstrup-Andersen, Per, Rajul Pandya-Lorch and Mark Rosegrant. 1997. *The World Food Situation: Recent Developments, Emerging Issues, and Long-term Prospects.* 2020 Vision Food Policy Report. Washington, DC: International Food Policy Research Institute.

Psacharopolous, George, and Zafiris Tzannatos, eds. 1992. *Case Studies on Women's Employment and Pay in Latin America.* Washington, DC: World Bank.

Rabinovitch, Jonas, and John Hoehn. 1995. "A Sustainable Urban Transportation System: The 'Surface Metro' in Curitiba, Brazil." Michigan State University, East Lansing.

Rabinovitch, Jonas, and Walter Hook. 1998. "Transport and Sustainable Human Settlements." A UNDP Policy Overview. Draft. New York.

Rabinovitch, Jonas, and Josef Leitmann. 1993. "Environmental Innovation and Management in Curitiba, Brazil." Urban Management Programme Working Paper 1. UNDP, United Nations Centre for Human Settlements and World Bank, New York.

Ranis, Gustav, and Frances Stewart. 1998. "A Pro-Human Development Adjustment Framework for the Countries of East and South-East Asia." UNDP, Regional Bureau for Asia and the Pacific, New York.

Raskin, Paul, and others. 1996. *The Sustainability Transition—Beyond Conventional Development.* POLESTAR Series Report No. 1. Stockholm: Stockholm Environment Institute.

Redclift, Michael. 1996. *Wasted: Counting the Costs of Global Consumption.* London: Earthscan.

Reddy, Amulya, Robert H. Williams and Thomas B. Johansson. 1997. *Energy after Rio: Prospects and Challenges.* New York: UNDP in collaboration with International Energy Initiative, Energy 21 and Stockholm Environment Institute.

Riches, Graham, ed. 1997. *First World Hunger: Food Security and Welfare Politics.* New York: St. Martin's Press.

Robins, Nick, and Sarah Roberts, eds. 1997. *Unlocking Trade Opportunities.* New York: International Institute for Environment and Development/United Nations Department of Policy Co-ordination and Sustainable Development.

Rodgers, Gerry, Charles Gore and Jose B. Figueiredo, eds. 1995. *Social Exclusion: Rhetoric, Reality, Responses.* Geneva: International Labour Office.

Roodman, David Malin. 1996. "Paying the Piper: Subsidies, Politics and the Environment." Worldwatch Paper 133. Worldwatch Institute, Washington, DC.

———. 1997. "Getting the Signals Right: Tax Reform to Protect the Environment and the Economy." Worldwatch Paper 134. Worldwatch Institute, Washington, DC.

Sampat, Payal. 1996. "The River Ganges' Long Decline." *Worldwatch* 9(4): 24–32.

Samuelson, Paul A. 1938. "A Note on the Pure Theory of Consumer Behavior." *Economica* 5.

Schor, Juliet. 1991. *The Overworked American: The Unexpected Decline of Leisure.* New York: Basic Books.

———. 1998. *The Overspent American.* New York: Basic Books.

Scitovsky, Tibor. 1976. *The Joyless Economy.* Oxford: Oxford University Press.

Sen, Amartya. 1985. *Commodities and Capabilities.* Amsterdam: North-Holland.

Serageldin, Ismail, Michael A. Cohen and K.C. Sivaramakrishnan. 1995. *The Human Face of the Urban Environment.* Environmentally Sustainable Development Proceedings. Washington, DC: World Bank.

Shiklomanov, Igor A. 1996. "Assessment of Water Resources and Water Availability in the World." Background paper for United Nations, *Comprehensive Assessment of the Freshwater Resources of the World.* United Nations, New York.

Shiva, Vandana. 1997b. *Biopiracy—The Plunder of Nature and Knowledge.* Boston, Mass.: South End Press.

Sierra Leone, Central Statistics Office. 1993. *Report on Survey of Household Expenditure and Household Economic Activities 1989–1990.* Freetown.

SIPRI (Stockholm International Peace Research Institute). 1997. *SIPRI Yearbook 1997.* New York: Oxford University Press.

Smeeding, Timothy. 1997. *Financial Poverty in Developed Countries: The Evidence from the Luxembourg Income Study (LIS).* Final report to UNDP. Luxembourg.

Stanecki, Karen A., and Peter O. Way. 1997. "The Demographic Impacts of HIV/AIDS: Perspectives from the World Population Profile, 1996." US Bureau of the Census, Washington, DC.

Summers, Robert, and Alan Heston. 1991. "Penn World Tables (Mark 5): An Expanded Set of International Comparisons, 1950–1988." *Quarterly Journal of Economics* 106: 327–68.

Thailand, National Statistical Office. 1995. *Report of the 1994 Household Socio-Economic Survey.* Bangkok.

UN (United Nations). 1993. "Statistical Chart on World Families." Statistical Division and the Secretariat for the International Year of the Family. New York.

———. 1994a. *Agenda 21: The United Nations Programme of Action from Rio.* New York.

———. 1994b. Economic and Social Council, Commission on Human Rights, Fiftieth Session. New York. E/CN.4/1995/42.

———. 1994c. *Statistical Yearbook 1992.* 39th issue. Statistical Division. New York. ST/ESA/STAT/SER.S/15.E/F/94.XVII.1.

———. 1994d. *Women's Indicators and Statistics Database.* CD-ROM Version 3. Statistical Division. New York.

———. 1994e. "World Population Prospects 1950–2050: The 1994 Revision." Database. Population Division. New York.

———. 1994f. "World Urbanization Prospects: The 1994

Revision." Database. Population Division. New York.

———. 1995a. "Progress Made in Providing Safe Water Supply and Sanitation for All During the First Half of the 1990s." Report of the Secretary-General. New York.

———. 1995b. *The World's Women 1970–95: Trends and Statistics.* New York.

———. 1996a. *Industrial Commodity Statistics Yearbook 1994.* New York.

———. 1996b. *International Trade Statistics Yearbook 1994.* New York.

———. 1996c. *Statistical Yearbook 1994.* 41st issue. Statistical Division. New York.

———. 1996d. "World Population Prospects 1950–2050: The 1996 Revision." Database. Population Division. New York.

———. 1996e. "World Urbanization Prospects: The 1996 Revision." Database. Population Division. New York.

———. 1997a. *Critical Trends: Global Change and Sustainable Development.* Department for Policy Coordination and Sustainable Development. New York.

———. 1997b. *Energy Statistics Yearbook 1995.* New York.

———. 1997c. "Landmines Factsheet." Department of Humanitarian Affairs, Mine Clearance and Policy Unit. New York.

———. 1997d. *Multilateral Treaties Deposited with the Secretary-General.* New York. Available at http://www.un.org/Depts/Treaty.

———. 1997e. "The World Conferences: Developing Priorities for the 21st Century." UN Briefing Papers. Department of Public Information. New York.

———. 1997f. *World Contraceptive Use 1997.* Population Division. New York.

———. 1997g. *World Drug Report.* International Drug Control Programme. New York: Oxford University Press.

———. 1997h. "World Population Monitoring—Issues of International Migration and Development: Selected Aspects." Population Division. New York.

———. 1997i. "World Population Prospects: The 1996 Revision." Population Division. New York.

———. 1998. *The Third Report on the World Nutrition Situation.* Administrative Committee on Coordination–Sub Committee on Nutrition. Geneva.

UNAIDS and WHO (Joint United Nations Programme on HIV/AIDS). 1997. *Report on the Global HIV/AIDS Epidemic.* Geneva (December).

UNCHS (United Nations Centre for Human Settlements). 1996. *An Urbanising World: Global Report on Human Settlements.* Nairobi.

———. 1997. "Changing Consumption Patterns in Human Settlements: Waste Management." Settlement Infrastructure and Environment Programme, Nairobi.

UNCSDHA (United Nations Centre for Social Development and Humanitarian Affairs). 1995a. "Results of the Fourth United Nations Survey of Crime Trends and Operations of the Criminal Justice System (1986–90)—Interim Report by the Secretariat." Vienna.

———. 1995b. "Interim Report by the Secretariat." Vienna.

UNCTAD (United Nations Conference on Trade and Development). 1996. *Handbook of International Trade and Development Statistics 1995.* New York and Geneva.

———. 1997. *Trade and Development Report 1997.* New York and Geneva.

UNDP (United Nations Development Programme). 1994. *Human Development Report 1994.* New York: Oxford University Press.

———. 1995a. *Human Development Report 1995.* New York: Oxford University Press.

———. 1995b. *Human Development Report 1995: Russian Federation.* Moscow.

———. 1996a. *Human Development Report 1996.* New York: Oxford University Press.

———. 1996b. *Human Development Report Nigeria 1996.* Lagos.

———. 1996c. *UNDP's 1996 Report on Human Development in Bangladesh: A Pro-Poor Agenda.* Dhaka.

———. 1997a. *Human Development Report 1997.* New York: Oxford University Press.

———. 1997b. *Latvia Human Development Report 1997.* Riga.

———. 1997c. *Namibia Human Development Report 1997.* Windhoek.

———. 1997d. *Philippine Human Development Report 1997.* Jakarta.

———. 1997e. *Rapport sur le Développement Humain au Benin.* Cotonou.

———. 1997f. *Zambia Human Development Report 1997.* Lusaka.

———. 1998. *Desarrollo Humano en Bolivia 1998.* La Paz.

UNDP (United Nations Development Programme) and the Government of El Salvador. 1997. *Informe sobre Indices de Desarrollo Humano en El Salvador.* San Salvador.

UNDP (United Nations Development Programme) and the Government of Niger. 1997. *Premier Rapport National sur le Développement Humain.* Niamey.

UNDP (United Nations Development Programme) and Instituto de Pesquisa Econômica Aplicada. 1996. *Relatório Sobre o Desenvolvimento Humano no Brazil 1996.* Brasilia.

UNDP (United Nations Development Programme), UNFPA (United Nations Population Fund) and UNICEF (United Nations Children's Fund). 1994. *The 20:20 Initiative.* New York: UNDP.

UNECE (United Nations Economic Commission for Europe). 1995. *Trends in Europe and North America: The Statistical Yearbook of the Economic Commission for Europe.* New York and Geneva.

———. 1996. Database. Geneva.

———. 1997a. *Statistics of Road Traffic Accidents in Europe and North America.* New York and Geneva.

———. 1997b. *Trends in Europe and North America 1996–97.* New York and Geneva.

UNEP (United Nations Environment Programme). 1996. *Our Planet* (Nairobi) 7(6).

———. 1997a. *Global Environment Outlook.* Nairobi.

———. 1997b. *Our Planet* (Nairobi) 8(6).

UNESCO (United Nations Educational, Scientific and Cultural Organization). 1993. *World Education Report 1993.* Paris.

———. 1994. "Statistics on Illiteracy, 1994 Estimates and Projections." Paris.

———. 1995. *World Education Report 1995.* Paris.

———. 1997a. Correspondence on adult literacy. Division of Statistics. Received July. Paris.

———. 1997b. Correspondence on combined primary, secondary and tertiary enrolment. Division of Statistics. Received November. Paris.

———. 1997c. *Education Policy Analysis.* Paris.

———. 1997d. *Statistical Yearbook 1997.* Paris.

———. 1998. *World Education Report 1998.* Paris.

UNHCR (United Nations High Commissioner for Refugees). 1994. "Populations of Concern to UNHCR: A Statistical Overview." Division of Programmes and Operational Support, Food and Statistical Unit. Geneva.

———. 1996. "Refugees and Others of Concern to UNHCR: 1996 Statistical Overview." Geneva.

———. 1997. *UNHCR by Numbers 1997.* Geneva.

———. 1998. *The State of the World's Refugees 1997–98: A Humanitarian Agenda.* New York: Oxford University Press.

UNICEF (United Nations Children's Fund). 1996. *The State of the World's Children 1996.* New York: Oxford University Press.

———. 1997. *The State of the World's Children 1997.* New York: Oxford University Press.

———. 1998a. "Information: Impact of Armed Conflict on Children." Data available at http://www.unicef.org. January.

———. 1998b. *The State of the World's Children 1998.* New York: Oxford University Press.

United Nations Centre for Human Rights. 1996. "Human Rights: International Instruments—Chart of Ratifications as of 31 December 1996." Geneva. ST/HR/4/Rev.13.

US Bureau of the Census. Forthcoming. *World Population Profile: 1998.* Washington, DC.

USDA (US Department of Agriculture). 1997. Correspondence on obesity in the United States. Received December. Riverdale, Mass.

Veblen, Thorstein. [1899] 1967. *The Theory of the Leisure Class.* New York: Macmillan.

von Weizsäcker, Ernst, Amory B. Lovins and L. Hunter Lovins. 1997. *Factor Four: Doubling Wealth, Halving Resource Use.* London : Earthscan.

WEC (World Energy Council) and IIASA (International Institute for Applied Systems Analysis). 1995. *Global Energy Perspectives to 2050 and Beyond.* London: WEC.

Welch, Wilford. 1997. "A World Standard for Measuring Information Societies." *On the Internet* (March/April): 41–45.

White, Randall. 1993. "The Dawn of Adornment." *Natural History* (May): 62–66.

WHO (World Health Organization). 1993. *World Health Statistics Annual 1993.* Geneva.

———. 1994. *World Health Statistics Annual 1994.* Geneva.

———. 1995a. *Global Database on Child Growth 1995.* Nutrition Unit. Geneva.

———. 1995b. *The World Health Report 1995.* Geneva.

———. 1995c. *World Health Statistics Annual 1995.* Geneva.

———. 1996a. "Tobacco Alert." Special issue. Geneva.

———. 1996b. *The World Health Report 1996.* Geneva.

———. 1997a. *Health and Environment in Sustainable Development: Five Years after the Earth Summit.* Geneva.

———. 1997b. *Health for All in the 21st Century.* Geneva.

———. 1997c. *Tobacco or Health: A Global Status Report.* Geneva.

———. 1997d. *The World Health Report 1997.* Geneva.

———. 1998. "Tobacco Alert." World No-Tobacco Day Advisory Kit. Geneva.

WHO (World Health Organization), WSSCC (Water Supply and Sanitation Collaborative Council) and UNICEF (United Nations Children's Fund). 1996. *Water Supply and Sanitation Sector Monitoring Report.* Geneva.

World Bank. 1992. *World Development Report 1992.* New York: Oxford University Press.

———. 1993. *World Development Report 1993.* New York: Oxford University Press.

———. 1994. *World Development Report 1994.* New York: Oxford University Press.

———. 1995a. *A Continent in Transition: Sub-Saharan Africa in the Mid-1990s.* Washington, DC.

———. 1995b. *World Data 1995.* CD-ROM. Washington, DC.

———. 1995c. *World Development Report 1995.* New York: Oxford University Press.

———. 1996. *World Development Report 1996.* New York: Oxford University Press.

———. 1997a. Correspondence on unpublished World Bank data on GNP per capita estimates using the GDP/GNP ratio for 1995. International Economics Department. Received July. Washington, DC.

———. 1997b. *Global Development Finance 1997.* Washington, DC.

———. 1997c. *World Development Indicators 1997.* Washington, DC.

———. 1997d. *World Development Indicators 1997.* CD-ROM. Washington, DC.

———. 1997e. *World Development Report 1997.* New York: Oxford University Press.

World Bureau of Metal Statistics. 1996. *World Metal Statistics.* Ware, England.

Worldwatch Institute. 1997a. "The Nicotine Cartel." *Worldwatch* (July/August): 19–27.

———. 1997b. *Vital Signs 1997.* New York: Norton.

Worldwide Research, Advisory and Business Intelligence Services. 1997. Data available at http://www.findsvp.com. December.

WRI (World Resources Institute). 1994. *World Resources 1994–95.* New York: Oxford University Press.

———. 1996a. *World Resources 1996–97.* New York: Oxford University Press.

———. 1996b. *World Resources 1996–97.* Diskette. Washington, DC.

———. 1998. *World Resources 1998–99.* New York: Oxford University Press.

WWF (World Wildlife Fund). 1986. *Spotlight on Solutions: A People's Agenda—A Handbook of Case Studies on Local Implementation of Agenda 21.* Toronto, Canada.

KEY TO COUNTRIES

HUMAN DEVELOPMENT INDICATORS

Indicators

TABLE 32 Profile of people in work   191

Industrial countries

- Labour force as % of total population
- Women's share of adult labour force
- Percentage of labour force in agriculture
- Percentage of labour force in industry
- Percentage of labour force in services
- Future labour force replacement ratio
- Real earnings per employee annual growth rate
- Labour force unionized
- Weekly hours of work
- Expenditure on labour market programmes

TABLE 33 Unemployment   192

Industrial countries

- Unemployed people
- Total unemployment rate
- Male unemployment rate
- Female unemployment rate
- Male youth unemployment rate
- Female youth unemployment rate
- Incidence of long-term unemployment, 6 months or more
- Incidence of long-term unemployment, 12 months or more
- Discouraged workers
- Involuntary part-time workers
- Unemployment benefits expenditure

TABLE 34 Access to information and communications   193

Industrial countries

- Radios
- Televisions
- Daily newspapers
- Printing and writing paper consumed
- Main telephone lines
- Public pay phones
- International telephone calls
- Fax machines
- Cellular mobile telephone subscribers
- Internet users
- Personal computers

TABLE 35 Profile of political life   194

Industrial countries

- Date of last elections for lower or single house
- Members elected or appointed to lower or single house
- Date of last elections for upper house or senate
- Members elected or appointed to upper house or senate
- Voter turnout at last elections
- Parties represented
- Year women received right to vote
- Year women received right to stand for election
- Year first woman elected or nominated to national parliament

TABLE 36 Social stress and social change   195

Industrial countries

- Prisoners
- Young adult prisoners
- Intentional homicides by men
- Drug crimes
- Reported adult rapes
- Injuries and deaths from road accidents
- Suicides
- Divorces
- Single-female-parent homes
- Births to mothers aged 15–19
- One-person-households headed by women aged 65 and above

TABLE 37 Aid flows   196

Industrial countries

- Net official development assistance (ODA) disbursed
- ODA as % of GNP
- ODA as % of central government budget
- ODA per capita of donor country
- Multilateral ODA as % of GNP
- Share of ODA through NGOs
- Aid by NGOs as % of GNP
- Aid to least developed countries
- Net official aid received
- Net official aid received as % of GNP
- Net official aid received per capita
- External debt
- External debt as % of GNP
- Debt service ratio

TABLE 38 Military expenditure and resource use imbalances   197

Industrial countries

- Defence expenditure
- Defence expenditure as % of GDP
- Defence expenditure per capita
- Military expenditure as % of combined education and health expenditure
- ODA disbursed as % of defence expenditure
- Exports of conventional weapons
- Total armed forces

TABLE 39 Financial inflows and outflows   198

Industrial countries

- Export-import ratio
- Export growth rate as % of import growth rate
- Terms of trade
- Net foreign direct investment
- Trade as % of GDP
- Net workers' remittances from abroad
- Gross international reserves
- Current account balance before official transfers

The *Human Development Report* has presented data on broad aspects of human development since its inception in 1990. This has required a far-ranging array of statistics that reflect people's well-being and the opportunities that they actually enjoy.

As a standard practice, this year's Report, like earlier ones, relies on national estimates reported by the United Nations and its agencies and by other internationally recognized organizations, and thus on the standardization and consistency of data produced by these offices. The few exceptions in which data from other sources have been used are noted in the relevant tables.

Data standards and methodology

Even when standardized international sources are used, a number of problems remain for any user of statistical data.

First, despite the considerable efforts of international organizations to collect, process and disseminate social and economic statistics and to standardize definitions and data collection methods, limitations remain in the coverage, consistency and comparability of data across time and countries. Second, significant shifts and breaks in statistical series can occur when statistical bodies and research institutions update or improve their estimates using new sources of data, such as censuses and surveys.

Such concerns arise in preparing the human development index (HDI). For example, for the 1996 revision of the United Nations database "World Population Prospects 1950–2050" (UN 1996d), released on 15 November 1996, the United Nations Population Division derived estimates and projections from population censuses—supplemented with information from national survey data—using specialized demographic techniques. It made significant adjustments to the 1994 revision to incorporate the demographic impact of HIV/AIDS and to accommodate the extensive migratory movements within Europe and elsewhere and the rapid growth in the number of refugees in Africa and elsewhere

(UN 1996d).[1] And it incorporated newly available data reflecting significant changes in the demographic profiles of countries in Eastern Europe and the Commonwealth of Independent States (CIS).

Changes in the population estimates have an effect on other indicators—such as enrolment ratios for different levels of schooling published by UNESCO. These are defined as the ratio of the number of children enrolled in a schooling level to the number of children in the relevant age group. The age group indicator depends on the estimates of age- and sex-specific populations published by the United Nations Population Division. Data on enrolment are affected by the methodology and timing used by the administrative registries, population censuses and education surveys at the national level. In addition, independent of the variations in population estimates and enrolment data, UNESCO may periodically revise the methodology used for its projections and estimations of literacy and enrolment. Consequently, the reader must take into account the potential for fluctuation in both literacy and enrolment rates when making comparisons across time and countries.

Estimates of income used in the HDI are GDP converted to international dollars by using purchasing power parities (PPP) established by the World Bank, based on the results of surveys by the International Comparison Programme (ICP). Revision and updating of the PPP-based income estimates lead to fluctuations across time and country series. The real GDP per capita (PPP$) estimates used in this year's Report integrate the 1993 results from the ICP, which cover the OECD member countries and Eastern Europe and the CIS countries, and the most recent version of the Penn World Tables (Mark 5.6).

Another problem is uneven data availability across country groups. Some issues, such as literacy, are well documented in the developing countries but less so in the industrial countries, or vice versa. In such cases the Report presents the limited data available, primarily from official national reporting systems and compiled by the

United Nations, with the caveat that these data may not be readily used for international comparisons.

Recently a group of major industrial countries undertook the International Adult Literacy Survey to assess the literacy profiles of their adult populations. They used a consistent methodology and a common definition of literacy based on the ability to use "printed and written information to function in society, to achieve one's goals, and to develop one's knowledge and potential." Although results published so far cover only Australia, Belgium (Flanders), Canada, Germany, Ireland, the Netherlands, New Zealand, Poland, Sweden, Switzerland, the United Kingdom and the United States, an increasing number of industrial and developing countries are expected to take part in this effort (OECD and Statistics Canada 1995).

The transition in Eastern Europe and the CIS countries has led to a break in most of their statistical series, so the data available for recent years present problems of reliability, consistency and comparability at the international level and are often subject to revision.

The quality of data also suffers in countries in which there is war or civil strife. Where the availability and quality of estimates have become extremely limited, reporting of the data in the *Human Development Report* has been interrupted. But other countries are included when data become available.

Improving human development statistics

A major goal of the Report is to encourage national governments, international bodies and policy-makers to improve statistical indicators of human development.

The importance of strengthening data collection and reporting to monitor progress in human development at the national and international levels cannot be overstated. As the symbols for unavailable data in the indicator tables in this Report demonstrate, there are many gaps in the coverage of human development data. Lack of data is a particular constraint in monitoring gender equality and poverty eradication. Coverage of the gender-related development index (GDI) is limited to 163 countries, the gender empowerment measure (GEM) to 102 countries and the human poverty index (HPI-1 and HPI-2) to 77 developing and 17 industrial countries. Reliable data are essential for assessing the progress towards national goals in poverty reduction, gender equality, environmental sustainability and many other priorities for human development. Internationally comparable series help national bodies compare achievements with progress in other countries. They aid in international monitoring of progress towards the goals of the global United Nations conferences. And they are necessary for policy analysis.

The *Human Development Report,* in striving to overcome the shortcomings of data on important human development issues, has received valuable and generous assistance from many colleagues in international and national organizations. They have made special efforts to provide additional data and guidance in their fields of specialization, especially for the purposes of constructing time series and improving consistency and comparability of human development indicators across countries.

Country classification

The main criterion for classifying countries is the HDI. Countries are classified into three groups: high human development, with HDI values of 0.800 and above; medium human development, with HDI values of 0.500 to 0.799; and low human development, with HDI values below 0.500. For analytic purposes, aggregate measures for the medium and low human development countries are also computed after excluding China and India from their respective groups because the magnitudes of their populations, GDP and other measures overwhelm those of the smaller countries.

The regional classification of countries corresponds to the Regional Bureaux of UNDP and the income classification to the definitions in the World Bank's *World*

Development Report 1997 (1997) except as otherwise noted.

For analytic purposes and statistical convenience, the designations *developing countries* and *industrial countries* are also used in the text and the tables. These designations do not necessarily express a judgement about the stage reached by a particular country or area in the development process.

The term *country* as used in the text and the tables refers, as appropriate, to territories or areas.

Indicator tables

In the indicator tables countries and areas are ranked in descending order by their HDI value. Where estimates have been calculated using established international statistical series, the estimates are footnoted and the sources given in the notes at the end of each table. These notes also give the data sources for each column. The first source listed is the main international source for the indicator. The indicator tables no longer include estimates derived from sources other than the documented sources, except for table 1 (human development index). Short citations of sources are given, corresponding to the full references in the complete list of data sources used in preparing the indicator tables. This list appears after the indicator tables.

Not all countries have been included in the indicator tables, owing to lack of comparable data.

Unless otherwise stated, aggregate data for the human development, income and regional groups of countries are weighted by population subgroups or other requisite indicators. Aggregates are not presented in cases where there were no data for the majority of countries in a group or appropriate weighting

procedures were unavailable. Where appropriate, aggregate data are presented as the sum for the region rather than as a weighted average. To present a consistent set of aggregates, summary measures calculated for the variables used in the HDI for the universe of 174 countries, and in the GDI for the universe of 163 countries, have been used throughout the Report. For other indicators the summary measures presented have been calculated on the basis of the majority of countries for which data are available.

Unless otherwise indicated, multiyear averages of growth rates are expressed as compound annual rates of change. Year-to-year growth rates are expressed as annual percentage changes.

In the absence of the phrase "annual", "annual rate" or "growth rate", a hyphen between two years indicates that the data were collected during one of the years shown. A slash between two years indicates an average for the years shown, such as 1993/94. The following signs have been used:

.. Data not available
(.) Less than half the unit shown
(..) Less than one-tenth the unit shown
— Not applicable
T Total

Note

1. The 1996 revision incorporates the demographic impact of HIV/AIDS in the population estimates and projections for the 28 developing countries where HIV seroprevalence had reached 2% in 1994 or where the absolute number of infected adults was large: Benin, Botswana, Brazil, Burkina Faso, Burundi, Cameroon, the Central African Republic, Chad, the Congo, Côte d'Ivoire, Democratic Republic of the Congo, Eritrea, Guinea-Bissau, Haiti, India, Kenya, Lesotho, Malawi, Mozambique, Namibia, Rwanda, Sierra Leone, the United Republic of Tanzania, Thailand, Togo, Uganda, Zambia and Zimbabwe.

1 Human development index

HDI rank	Life expectancy at birth (years) 1995	Adult literacy rate (%) 1995	Combined first-, second- and third-level gross enrolment ratio (%) 1995	Real GDP per capita (PPP$) 1995	Adjusted real GDP per capita (PPP$) 1995	Life expectancy index	Education index	GDP index	Human development index (HDI) value 1995	Real GDP per capita (PPP$) rank minus HDI rank[a]
High human development	73.5	95.7	79	16,241	6,193	0.81	0.90	0.98	0.897	–
1 Canada	79.1	99.0	100 [b]	21,916	6,231	0.90	0.99	0.99	0.960	10
2 France	78.7	99.0	89 [c]	21,176	6,229	0.90	0.96	0.99	0.946	12
3 Norway	77.6	99.0	92 [c]	22,427	6,232	0.88	0.97	0.99	0.943	5
4 USA	76.4	99.0	96 [c]	26,977	6,259	0.86	0.98	0.99	0.943	-1
5 Iceland	79.2	99.0	83 [c]	21,064	6,229	0.90	0.94	0.99	0.942	10
6 Finland	76.4	99.0	97 [c]	18,547	6,219	0.86	0.98	0.99	0.942	17
7 Netherlands	77.5	99.0	91 [c]	19,876	6,226	0.88	0.96	0.99	0.941	11
8 Japan	79.9	99.0	78 [c]	21,930	6,231	0.91	0.92	0.99	0.940	2
9 New Zealand	76.6	99.0	94 [c]	17,267	6,197	0.86	0.97	0.98	0.939	17
10 Sweden	78.4	99.0	82 [c]	19,297	6,223	0.89	0.93	0.99	0.936	12
11 Spain	77.7	97.1 [d]	90 [c]	14,789	6,187	0.88	0.95	0.98	0.935	19
12 Belgium	76.9	99.0	86 [c]	21,548	6,230	0.87	0.95	0.99	0.933	0
13 Austria	76.7	99.0	87 [c]	21,322	6,230	0.86	0.95	0.99	0.933	0
14 United Kingdom	76.8	99.0	86 [c]	19,302	6,223	0.86	0.95	0.99	0.932	7
15 Australia	78.2	99.0	79 [c]	19,632	6,225	0.89	0.92	0.99	0.932	5
16 Switzerland	78.2	99.0	76 [c]	24,881	6,254	0.89	0.91	0.99	0.930	-12
17 Ireland	76.4	99.0	88 [c]	17,590	6,198	0.86	0.95	0.98	0.930	8
18 Denmark	75.3	99.0	89 [c]	21,983	6,231	0.84	0.96	0.99	0.928	-9
19 Germany	76.4	99.0	81 [c]	20,370 [e]	6,227	0.86	0.93	0.99	0.925	-3
20 Greece	77.9	96.7 [d]	82 [c]	11,636	6,140	0.88	0.92	0.97	0.924	15
21 Italy	78.0	98.1 [d]	73 [c]	20,174	6,227	0.88	0.90	0.99	0.922	-4
22 Israel	77.5	95.0 [f]	75 [c]	16,699	6,195	0.88	0.88	0.98	0.913	6
23 Cyprus	77.2	94.0 [f]	79	13,379 [g,h]	6,178	0.87	0.89	0.98	0.913	8
24 Barbados	76.0	97.4	77 [i]	11,306	6,136	0.85	0.91	0.97	0.909	13
25 Hong Kong, China	79.0	92.2	67	22,950	6,233	0.90	0.84	0.99	0.909	-19
26 Luxembourg	76.1	99.0	58 [c,j]	34,004	6,287	0.85	0.85	1.00	0.900	-25
27 Malta	76.5	91.0 [f]	76 [c]	13,316 [g,h]	6,178	0.86	0.86	0.98	0.899	5
28 Singapore	77.1	91.1	68 [i]	22,604	6,232	0.87	0.83	0.99	0.896	-21
29 Antigua and Barbuda	75.0 [f]	95.0 [f]	76	9,131 [g]	6,102	0.83	0.89	0.97	0.895	16
30 Korea, Rep. of	71.7	98.0	83	11,594	6,140	0.78	0.93	0.97	0.894	6
31 Chile	75.1	95.2	73	9,930	6,116	0.84	0.88	0.97	0.893	9
32 Bahamas	73.2	98.2	72 [i]	15,738	6,191	0.80	0.90	0.98	0.893	-3
33 Portugal	74.8	89.6 [d]	81 [c]	12,674	6,171	0.83	0.87	0.98	0.892	1
34 Costa Rica	76.6	94.8	69	5,969	5,969	0.86	0.86	0.95	0.889	28
35 Brunei Darussalam	75.1	88.2	74 [i]	31,165 [g,h]	6,283	0.84	0.84	1.00	0.889	-33
36 Argentina	72.6	96.2	79 [i]	8,498	6,090	0.79	0.91	0.96	0.888	11
37 Slovenia	73.2	96.0	74	10,594 [k]	6,126	0.80	0.89	0.97	0.887	1
38 Uruguay	72.7	97.3	76	6,854	6,049	0.79	0.90	0.96	0.885	14
39 Czech Rep.	72.4	99.0	70 [c]	9,775	6,113	0.79	0.89	0.97	0.884	2
40 Trinidad and Tobago	73.1	97.9	65 [i]	9,437	6,107	0.80	0.87	0.97	0.880	3
41 Dominica	73.0 [f]	94.0 [f]	77	6,424 [g]	6,032	0.80	0.88	0.96	0.879	15
42 Slovakia	70.9	99.0	72 [c]	7,320 [k]	6,063	0.77	0.90	0.96	0.875	9
43 Bahrain	72.2	85.2	84	16,751	6,195	0.79	0.85	0.98	0.872	-16
44 Fiji	72.1	91.6	78 [i]	6,159	6,016	0.79	0.87	0.95	0.869	16
45 Panama	73.4	90.8	72	6,258	6,023	0.81	0.84	0.95	0.868	14
46 Venezuela	72.3	91.1	67 [i]	8,090	6,082	0.79	0.83	0.96	0.860	2
47 Hungary	68.9	99.0	67 [c]	6,793	6,047	0.73	0.88	0.96	0.857	6
48 United Arab Emirates	74.4	79.2	69 [i]	18,008 [g,h]	6,209	0.82	0.76	0.98	0.855	-24
49 Mexico	72.1	89.6	67 [i]	6,769	6,046	0.79	0.82	0.96	0.855	5
50 Saint Kitts and Nevis	69.0 [f]	90.0 [f]	78	10,150	6,119	0.73	0.86	0.97	0.854	-11
51 Grenada	72.0 [f]	98.0 [f]	78	5,425 [g]	5,425	0.78	0.91	0.86	0.851	19
52 Poland	71.1	99.0	79 [c]	5,442	5,442	0.77	0.92	0.86	0.851	17
53 Colombia	70.3	91.3	69	6,347	6,028	0.76	0.84	0.95	0.850	4
54 Kuwait	75.4	78.6	58	23,848	6,234	0.84	0.72	0.99	0.848	-49
55 Saint Vincent	72.0 [f]	82.0 [f]	78	5,969 [g]	5,969	0.78	0.81	0.95	0.845	6
56 Seychelles	72.0 [f]	88.0 [f]	61	7,697 [g]	6,073	0.78	0.79	0.96	0.845	-6
57 Qatar	71.1	79.4	71 [i]	19,772 [g]	6,225	0.77	0.77	0.99	0.840	-38
58 Saint Lucia	71.0 [f]	82.0 [f]	74	6,530 [g]	6,036	0.77	0.79	0.96	0.839	-3
59 Thailand	69.5	93.8	55	7,742	6,074	0.74	0.81	0.96	0.838	-10
60 Malaysia	71.4	83.5	61	9,572	6,110	0.77	0.76	0.97	0.834	-18
61 Mauritius	70.9	82.9	61 [i]	13,294	6,178	0.77	0.76	0.98	0.833	-28
62 Brazil	66.6	83.3	72 [i]	5,928	5,928	0.69	0.80	0.94	0.809	1
63 Belize	74.2	70.0 [f]	74 [i]	5,623	5,623	0.82	0.71	0.89	0.807	1
64 Libyan Arab Jamahiriya	64.3	76.2	90 [i]	6,309	6,026	0.66	0.81	0.95	0.806	-6

HDI rank	Life expectancy at birth (years) 1995	Adult literacy rate (%) 1995	Combined first-, second- and third-level gross enrolment ratio (%) 1995	Real GDP per capita (PPP$) 1995	Adjusted real GDP per capita (PPP$) 1995	Life expectancy index	Education index	GDP index	Human development index (HDI) value 1995	Real GDP per capita (PPP$) rank minus HDI rank[a]
Medium human development	67.5	83.3	66	3,390	3,390	0.71	0.77	0.53	0.670	–
65 Suriname	70.9	93.0	71	4,862	4,862	0.77	0.86	0.77	0.796	9
66 Lebanon	69.3	92.4	75	4,977 [g,h]	4,977	0.74	0.86	0.79	0.796	7
67 Bulgaria	71.2	98.0 [f]	66 [c]	4,604	4,604	0.77	0.87	0.73	0.789	8
68 Belarus	69.3	97.9	80 [c]	4,398	4,398	0.74	0.92	0.69	0.783	11
69 Turkey	68.5	82.3	60 [i]	5,516	5,516	0.72	0.75	0.87	0.782	-2
70 Saudi Arabia	70.7	63.0 [f]	57	8,516	6,091	0.76	0.61	0.96	0.778	-24
71 Oman	70.3	59.0 [f]	60	9,383	6,106	0.75	0.59	0.97	0.771	-27
72 Russian Federation	65.5	99.0 [f]	78 [c]	4,531	4,531	0.68	0.92	0.71	0.769	5
73 Ecuador	69.5	90.1	71 [i]	4,602	4,602	0.74	0.84	0.73	0.767	3
74 Romania	69.6	98.0 [f]	62 [c]	4,431	4,431	0.74	0.86	0.70	0.767	4
75 Korea, Dem. People's Rep. of	71.6	95.0	75	4,058 [g,h]	4,058	0.78	0.88	0.64	0.766	8
76 Croatia	71.6	98.0 [f]	67 [c]	3,972 [e]	3,972	0.78	0.88	0.62	0.759	10
77 Estonia	69.2	99.0	72 [c]	4,062	4,062	0.74	0.90	0.64	0.758	5
78 Iran, Islamic Rep. of	68.5	69.0 [f]	67 [i]	5,480	5,480	0.72	0.68	0.87	0.758	-10
79 Lithuania	70.2	99.0 [f]	70 [c]	3,843	3,843	0.75	0.89	0.60	0.750	12
80 Macedonia, FYR	71.9	94.0	60 [c]	4,058 [g,h]	4,058	0.78	0.83	0.64	0.749	3
81 Syrian Arab Rep.	68.1	70.8	62	5,374	5,374	0.72	0.68	0.85	0.749	-10
82 Algeria	68.1	61.6	66	5,618	5,618	0.72	0.63	0.89	0.746	-17
83 Tunisia	68.7	66.7	69	5,261	5,261	0.73	0.67	0.83	0.744	-11
84 Jamaica	74.1	85.0	67 [i]	3,801	3,801	0.82	0.79	0.60	0.735	9
85 Cuba	75.7	95.7	66	3,100	3,100	0.85	0.86	0.48	0.729	18
86 Peru	67.7	88.7	79	3,940	3,940	0.71	0.86	0.62	0.729	2
87 Jordan	68.9	86.6	66	4,187	4,187	0.73	0.80	0.66	0.729	-6
88 Dominican Rep.	70.3	82.1	73	3,923	3,923	0.75	0.79	0.62	0.720	1
89 South Africa	64.1	81.8	81	4,334	4,334	0.65	0.82	0.68	0.717	-9
90 Sri Lanka	72.5	90.2	67	3,408	3,408	0.79	0.83	0.53	0.716	9
91 Paraguay	69.1	92.1	63 [i]	3,583	3,583	0.74	0.83	0.56	0.707	5
92 Latvia	68.0	99.0	67 [c]	3,273	3,273	0.72	0.88	0.51	0.704	8
93 Kazakhstan	67.5	99.0	73 [c]	3,037	3,037	0.71	0.90	0.47	0.695	11
94 Samoa (Western)	68.4	98.0 [f]	74 [i]	2,948 [g]	2,948	0.72	0.90	0.46	0.694	12
95 Maldives	63.3	93.2	71	3,540	3,540	0.64	0.86	0.55	0.683	2
96 Indonesia	64.0	83.8	62 [i]	3,971	3,971	0.65	0.77	0.62	0.679	-9
97 Botswana	51.7	69.8	71 [i]	5,611	5,611	0.45	0.70	0.89	0.678	-31
98 Philippines	67.4	94.6	80	2,762	2,762	0.71	0.90	0.43	0.677	11
99 Armenia	70.9	98.8	78 [c]	2,208	2,208	0.77	0.92	0.34	0.674	24
100 Guyana	63.5	98.1	64 [i]	3,205	3,205	0.64	0.87	0.50	0.670	1
101 Mongolia	64.8	82.9	53	3,916	3,916	0.66	0.73	0.61	0.669	-11
102 Ukraine	68.5	98.0 [f]	76 [c]	2,361	2,361	0.73	0.91	0.36	0.665	16
103 Turkmenistan	64.9	98.0 [f]	90 [c]	2,345 [k]	2,345	0.67	0.95	0.36	0.660	17
104 Uzbekistan	67.5	99.0 [f]	73 [c]	2,376	2,376	0.71	0.90	0.37	0.659	13
105 Albania	70.6	85.0	59 [c]	2,853 [g,h]	2,853	0.76	0.76	0.44	0.656	3
106 China	69.2	81.5	64	2,935	2,935	0.74	0.76	0.46	0.650	1
107 Namibia	55.8	76.0 [f]	83	4,054	4,054	0.51	0.78	0.64	0.644	-22
108 Georgia	73.2	99.0 [f]	69 [c]	1,389	1,389	0.80	0.89	0.21	0.633	33
109 Kyrgyzstan	67.9	97.0 [f]	73 [c]	1,927	1,927	0.72	0.89	0.29	0.633	18
110 Azerbaijan	71.1	96.3	72 [c]	1,463	1,463	0.77	0.88	0.22	0.623	28
111 Guatemala	66.1	65.0	46	3,682	3,682	0.68	0.59	0.58	0.615	-16
112 Egypt	64.8	51.4	69 [i]	3,829	3,829	0.66	0.57	0.60	0.612	-20
113 Moldova, Rep. of	67.8	98.9 [d]	67 [c]	1,547 [e]	1,547	0.71	0.88	0.23	0.610	23
114 El Salvador	69.4	71.5	58	2,610	2,610	0.74	0.67	0.40	0.604	-2
115 Swaziland	58.8	76.7	77	2,954	2,954	0.56	0.77	0.46	0.597	-10
116 Bolivia	60.5	83.1	69 [i]	2,617	2,617	0.59	0.78	0.41	0.593	-6
117 Cape Verde	65.7	71.6	64 [c]	2,612	2,612	0.68	0.69	0.40	0.591	-6
118 Tajikistan	66.9	99.0 [f]	69 [c]	943	943	0.70	0.89	0.14	0.575	43
119 Honduras	68.8	72.7	60 [i]	1,977	1,977	0.73	0.69	0.30	0.573	7
120 Gabon	54.5	63.2	60 [c]	3,766 [g]	3,766	0.49	0.62	0.59	0.568	-26
121 São Tomé and Principe	69.0 [f]	75.0 [l]	57	1,744 [g]	1,744	0.73	0.69	0.27	0.563	11
122 Viet Nam	66.4	93.7	55	1,236 [g,h]	1,236	0.69	0.81	0.18	0.560	26
123 Solomon Islands	71.1	62.0 [f]	47	2,230	2,230	0.77	0.57	0.34	0.560	-2
124 Vanuatu	66.3	64.0 [f]	52 [c]	2,507 [g]	2,507	0.69	0.60	0.39	0.559	-9
125 Morocco	65.7	43.7	48	3,477	3,477	0.68	0.45	0.54	0.557	-27
126 Nicaragua	67.5	65.7	64 [i]	1,837 [g]	1,837	0.71	0.65	0.28	0.547	3
127 Iraq	58.5	58.0	52 [i]	3,170 [g,h]	3,170	0.56	0.56	0.49	0.538	-25
128 Congo	51.2	74.9	68	2,554	2,554	0.44	0.73	0.40	0.519	-14
129 Papua New Guinea	56.8	72.2	37	2,500	2,500	0.53	0.61	0.39	0.507	-13
130 Zimbabwe	48.9	85.1	69	2,135	2,135	0.40	0.80	0.33	0.507	-6

HDI rank	Life expectancy at birth (years) 1995	Adult literacy rate (%) 1995	Combined first-, second- and third-level gross enrolment ratio (%) 1995	Real GDP per capita (PPP$) 1995	Adjusted real GDP per capita (PPP$) 1995	Life expectancy index	Education index	GDP index	Human development index (HDI) value 1995	Real GDP per capita (PPP$) rank minus HDI rank[a]
Low human development	56.7	50.9	47	1,362	1,362	0.53	0.50	0.20	0.409	–
131 Myanmar	58.9	83.1	48	1,130 [g,h]	1,130	0.57	0.71	0.17	0.481	22
132 Cameroon	55.3	63.4	45 [i]	2,355	2,355	0.51	0.57	0.36	0.481	-13
133 Ghana	57.0	64.5	44 [i]	2,032	2,032	0.53	0.58	0.31	0.473	-8
134 Lesotho	58.1	71.3	56 [i]	1,290	1,290	0.55	0.66	0.19	0.469	12
135 Equatorial Guinea	49.0	78.5	64 [i]	1,712 [g,h]	1,712	0.40	0.74	0.26	0.465	-1
136 Lao People's Dem. Rep.	52.2	56.6	50 [i]	2,571 [g]	2,571	0.45	0.54	0.40	0.465	-23
137 Kenya	53.8	78.1	52 [i]	1,438	1,438	0.48	0.69	0.22	0.463	2
138 Pakistan	62.8	37.8	41	2,209	2,209	0.63	0.39	0.34	0.453	-16
139 India	61.6	52.0	55	1,422	1,422	0.61	0.53	0.21	0.451	1
140 Cambodia	52.9	65.0 [f]	62 [i]	1,110 [g,h]	1,110	0.46	0.64	0.16	0.422	14
141 Comoros	56.5	57.3	39 [i]	1,317	1,317	0.53	0.51	0.20	0.411	3
142 Nigeria	51.4	57.1	49 [i]	1,270	1,270	0.44	0.55	0.19	0.391	5
143 Dem. Rep. of the Congo	52.4	77.3	41 [i]	355 [g]	355	0.46	0.65	0.04	0.383	31
144 Togo	50.5	51.7	60 [i]	1,167	1,167	0.42	0.54	0.17	0.380	6
145 Benin	54.4	37.0	38 [i]	1,800	1,800	0.49	0.37	0.27	0.378	-14
146 Zambia	42.7	78.2	52 [i]	986	986	0.30	0.70	0.14	0.378	11
147 Bangladesh	56.9	38.1	37 [i]	1,382	1,382	0.53	0.38	0.21	0.371	-4
148 Côte d'Ivoire	51.8	40.1	38	1,731	1,731	0.45	0.39	0.26	0.368	-15
149 Mauritania	52.5	37.7	38	1,622	1,622	0.46	0.38	0.25	0.361	-14
150 Tanzania, U. Rep. of	50.6	67.8	33	636	636	0.43	0.56	0.09	0.358	20
151 Yemen	56.7	38.0 [l]	49 [i]	856 [g,h]	856	0.53	0.42	0.12	0.356	12
152 Nepal	55.9	27.5	56 [i]	1,145	1,145	0.52	0.37	0.17	0.351	-1
153 Madagascar	57.6	45.8 [m]	31	673	673	0.54	0.41	0.09	0.348	15
154 Central African Rep.	48.4	60.0	27 [i]	1,092	1,092	0.39	0.49	0.16	0.347	2
155 Bhutan	52.0	42.2	*31*	1,382	1,382	0.45	0.39	0.21	0.347	-13
156 Angola	47.4	42.0 [f]	30 [i]	1,839	1,839	0.37	0.38	0.28	0.344	-28
157 Sudan	52.2	46.1	32	1,110 [g,h]	1,110	0.45	0.41	0.16	0.343	-3
158 Senegal	50.3	33.1	33	1,815	1,815	0.42	0.33	0.28	0.342	-28
159 Haiti	54.6	45.0	29 [i]	917	917	0.49	0.40	0.13	0.340	3
160 Uganda	40.5	61.8	38 [i]	1,483	1,483	0.26	0.54	0.22	0.340	-23
161 Malawi	41.0	56.4	76 [i]	773	773	0.27	0.63	0.11	0.334	5
162 Djibouti	49.2	46.2	20	1,300 [g,h]	1,300	0.40	0.37	0.19	0.324	-17
163 Chad	47.2	48.1	27	1,172	1,172	0.37	0.41	0.17	0.318	-14
164 Guinea-Bissau	43.4	54.9	29 [c]	811	811	0.31	0.46	0.12	0.295	0
165 Gambia	46.0	38.6	39 [i]	948	948	0.35	0.39	0.14	0.291	-5
166 Mozambique	46.3	40.1	25	959	959	0.35	0.35	0.14	0.281	-7
167 Guinea	45.5	35.9	25	1,139 [g]	1,139	0.34	0.32	0.17	0.277	-15
168 Eritrea	50.2	25.0 [m]	29	983 [g,h]	983	0.42	0.26	0.14	0.275	-10
169 Ethiopia	48.7	35.5	20	455	455	0.40	0.30	0.06	0.252	4
170 Burundi	44.5	35.3	23 [i]	637	637	0.33	0.31	0.09	0.241	-1
171 Mali	47.0	31.0	18 [i]	565	565	0.37	0.27	0.08	0.236	1
172 Burkina Faso	46.3	19.2	19 [i]	784	784	0.36	0.19	0.11	0.219	-7
173 Niger	47.5	13.6	15 [i]	765	765	0.38	0.14	0.11	0.207	-6
174 Sierra Leone	34.7	31.4	30 [i]	625	625	0.16	0.31	0.08	0.185	-3
All developing countries	62.2	70.4	57	3,068	3,068	0.62	0.66	0.48	0.586	–
Least developed countries	51.2	49.2	36	1,008	1,008	0.44	0.45	0.15	0.344	–
Industrial countries	74.2	98.6	83	16,337	6,194	0.82	0.93	0.98	0.911	–
World	63.6	77.6	62	5,990	5,990	0.64	0.72	0.95	0.772	–

Note: Figures in italics are Human Development Report Office estimates. Countries with the same HDI value are ranked on the basis of the fourth decimal place, not shown here.
a. A positive figure indicates that the HDI rank is better than the real GDP per capita (PPP$) rank, a negative the opposite.
b. Capped at 100.
c. Carried over from UNDP 1997a.
d. UNESCO 1998.
e. UNECE 1996.
f. UNICEF 1998b.
g. Preliminary update of the Penn World Tables using an expanded set of international comparisons, as described in Summers and Heston 1991.
h. Provisional.
i. First- or second-level data, or both, have been estimated by UNESCO.
j. Most students in secondary and higher education pursue their studies in nearby countries.
k. OECD 1997h.
l. World Bank 1997d.
m. Human Development Report Office estimate based on national sources.
Source: Column 1: calculated on the basis of data from: UN 1996d; *column 2:* UNESCO 1997a; *column 3:* UNESCO 1997b; *column 4:* unless otherwise noted, calculated on the basis of estimates from World Bank 1997a.

HDI rank	Gender-related development index (GDI) rank	Life expectancy at birth (years) 1995		Adult literacy rate (%) 1995		Combined first-, second- and third-level gross enrolment ratio (%) 1995		Share of earned income (%) 1995[a]		GDI value 1995	HDI rank minus GDI rank[b]
		Female	Male	Female	Male	Female	Male	Female	Male		
High human development	–	76.8	70.3	95.3	96.2	79.2	75.9	34.4	65.6	0.861	–
1 Canada	1	81.8	76.3	99.0	99.0	100.0 [c,d]	100.0 [c,d]	38.0 [e]	62.0 [e]	0.940	0
2 France	7	82.6	74.4	99.0	99.0	91.0 [d]	87.0 [d]	39.1	60.9	0.925	-5
3 Norway	2	80.5	74.7	99.0	99.0	93.0 [d]	92.0 [d]	42.4	57.6	0.935	1
4 USA	6	79.7	73.0	99.0	99.0	98.0 [d]	93.0 [d]	40.3	59.7	0.927	-2
5 Iceland	4	80.9	77.4	99.0	99.0	81.0 [d]	82.0 [d]	41.9	58.1	0.932	1
6 Finland	5	80.0	72.6	99.0	99.0	100.0 [c,d]	92.0 [d]	42.0	58.0	0.929	1
7 Netherlands	12	80.4	74.5	99.0	99.0	88.0 [d]	93.0 [d]	34.1	65.9	0.905	-5
8 Japan	13	82.8	76.7	99.0	99.0	77.0 [d]	79.0 [d]	34.1 [e]	65.9 [e]	0.902	-5
9 New Zealand	8	79.4	73.9	99.0	99.0	96.0 [d]	91.0 [d]	38.8	61.2	0.920	1
10 Sweden	3	80.8	75.9	99.0	99.0	84.0 [d]	81.0 [d]	44.7	55.3	0.932	7
11 Spain	19	81.3	74.1	96.1 [f]	98.2 [f]	94.0 [d]	87.0 [d]	29.7 [e]	70.3 [e]	0.877	-8
12 Belgium	14	80.3	73.5	99.0	99.0	86.0 [d]	86.0 [d]	33.6	66.4	0.893	-2
13 Austria	15	79.8	73.3	99.0	99.0	85.0 [d]	88.0 [d]	33.6 [e]	66.4 [e]	0.891	-2
14 United Kingdom	11	79.4	74.2	99.0	99.0	86.0 [d]	85.0 [d]	37.6	62.5	0.907	3
15 Australia	9	81.1	75.3	99.0	99.0	80.0 [d]	77.0 [d]	40.0	60.0	0.918	6
16 Switzerland	18	81.6	74.8	99.0	99.0	73.0 [d]	78.0 [d]	32.5	67.5	0.887	-2
17 Ireland	27	79.1	73.7	99.0	99.0	89.0 [d]	87.0 [d]	26.8	73.2	0.859	-10
18 Denmark	10	78.0	72.7	99.0	99.0	90.0 [d]	87.0 [d]	41.8	58.2	0.917	8
19 Germany	17	79.5	73.0	99.0	99.0	79.0 [d]	83.0 [d]	34.8	65.2	0.888	2
20 Greece	20	80.5	75.3	95.3 [f]	98.3 [f]	80.0 [d]	83.0 [d]	31.8	68.2	0.876	0
21 Italy	23	81.0	74.7	97.6 [f]	98.6 [f]	74.0 [d]	72.0 [d]	31.2 [e]	68.8 [e]	0.868	-2
22 Israel	22	79.2	75.5	93.0 [g]	97.0 [g]	76.0 [d]	74.0 [d]	33.1 [e]	66.9 [e]	0.873	0
23 Cyprus	30	79.4	75.0	91.0 [g]	98.0 [g]	80.0	73.3	27.9	72.1	0.847	-7
24 Barbados	16	78.3	73.3	96.8	98.0	79.1	73.7	39.6 [e]	60.4 [e]	0.889	8
25 Hong Kong, China	33	81.8	76.1	88.2	96.0	69.9	61.9	25.6	74.4	0.836	-8
26 Luxembourg	32	79.3	72.7	99.0	99.0	59.0 [d]	57.0 [d]	28.7	71.3	0.836	-6
27 Malta	44	78.8	74.3	92.0 [g]	91.0 [g]	75.0 [d]	79.0 [d]	21.1 [e]	78.9 [e]	0.788	-17
28 Singapore	29	79.3	75.0	86.3	95.9	66.6	57.6	31.9	68.1	0.848	-1
29 Antigua and Barbuda	..	..	..	..	..	..	..	..	..	..	..
30 Korea, Rep. of	37	75.4	68.1	96.7	99.3	78.4	65.9	29.2	70.8	0.826	-8
31 Chile	46	78.0	72.2	95.0	95.4	72.1	64.7	22.0 [h]	78.0 [h]	0.783	-16
32 Bahamas	21	76.7	70.2	98.0	98.5	76.2	65.6	39.5 [e]	60.5 [e]	0.876	10
33 Portugal	28	78.5	71.2	87.0 [f]	92.5 [f]	84.0 [d]	77.0 [d]	34.2	65.8	0.852	4
34 Costa Rica	39	79.0	74.3	95.0	94.7	68.3	59.0	26.9	73.1	0.818	-6
35 Brunei Darussalam	36	77.8	72.9	83.4	92.6	74.1	72.0	27.7 [e]	72.3 [e]	0.834	-2
36 Argentina	48	76.2	69.1	96.2	96.2	80.6	68.7	22.1 [h]	77.9 [h]	0.777	-13
37 Slovenia	24	77.6	68.7	96.0	96.0	76.0 [d]	72.0 [d]	39.3 [e]	60.7 [e]	0.867	12
38 Uruguay	31	75.9	69.5	97.7	96.9	79.6	65.1	33.7 [h]	66.3 [h]	0.841	6
39 Czech Rep.	25	75.4	69.3	99.0	99.0	70.0 [d]	69.0 [d]	39.0	61.0	0.864	13
40 Trinidad and Tobago	38	75.7	71.0	97.0	98.8	70.3	59.2	26.8 [e]	73.2 [e]	0.823	1
41 Dominica	..	..	..	..	..	..	..	..	..	..	..
42 Slovakia	26	75.6	66.5	99.0	99.0	73.0 [d]	71.0 [d]	40.7 [e]	59.3 [e]	0.861	14
43 Bahrain	60	74.7	70.4	79.4	89.1	85.9	78.1	15.0 [e]	85.0 [e]	0.746	-19
44 Fiji	52	74.3	70.1	89.3	93.8	77.8	74.9	22.0 [e]	78.0 [e]	0.770	-10
45 Panama	42	75.6	71.4	90.2	91.4	73.1	63.4	27.8 [e]	72.2 [e]	0.804	1
46 Venezuela	43	75.3	69.5	90.3	91.8	68.4	58.0	27.1 [e]	72.9 [e]	0.790	1
47 Hungary	34	73.8	64.3	99.0	99.0	68.0 [d]	66.0 [d]	38.5	61.5	0.834	11
48 United Arab Emirates	66	75.9	73.5	79.8	78.9	72.1	66.1	10.2 [e]	89.8 [e]	0.718	-20
49 Mexico	49	75.1	69.2	87.4	91.8	66.1	64.0	25.7 [e]	74.3 [e]	0.774	-2
50 Saint Kitts and Nevis	..	..	..	..	..	..	..	..	..	..	..
51 Grenada	..	..	..	..	..	..	..	..	..	..	..
52 Poland	35	75.7	66.6	99.0	99.0	80.0 [d]	79.0 [d]	39.0 [e]	61.0 [e]	0.834	13
53 Colombia	41	73.1	67.7	91.4	91.2	70.7	62.7	33.5 [h]	66.5 [h]	0.810	8
54 Kuwait	50	77.7	73.7	74.9	82.2	57.9	52.6	25.3 [e]	74.7 [e]	0.773	0
55 Saint Vincent	..	..	..	..	..	..	..	..	..	..	..
56 Seychelles	..	..	..	..	..	..	..	..	..	..	..
57 Qatar	67	74.8	69.4	79.9	79.2	72.8	65.2	10.0 [e]	90.0 [e]	0.714	-16
58 Saint Lucia	..	..	..	..	..	..	..	..	..	..	..
59 Thailand	40	72.3	66.9	91.6	96.0	55.5	49.4	36.7	63.3	0.812	12
60 Malaysia	45	73.7	69.3	78.1	89.1	62.0	60.0	30.4	69.6	0.785	8
61 Mauritius	54	74.5	67.7	78.8	87.1	61.1	58.2	25.6 [e]	74.4 [e]	0.753	0
62 Brazil	56	70.7	62.8	83.2	83.3	71.8	69.1	29.3	70.7	0.751	-1
63 Belize	72	75.6	72.9	70.0 [g]	70.0 [g]	74.1	72.9	18.5 [e]	81.5 [e]	0.689	-16
64 Libyan Arab Jamahiriya	79	66.3	62.8	63.0	87.9	89.0	85.5	16.3	83.7	0.664	-22

HDI rank		Gender-related development index (GDI) rank	Life expectancy at birth (years) 1995		Adult literacy rate (%) 1995		Combined first-, second- and third-level gross enrolment ratio (%) 1995		Share of earned income (%) 1995[a]		GDI value 1995	HDI rank minus GDI rank[b]
			Female	Male	Female	Male	Female	Male	Female	Male		
Medium human development		–	69.7	65.4	76.9	89.5	63.7	64.9	36.4	63.6	0.656	–
65	Suriname	63	73.4	68.5	91.0	95.1	*71.0*	*71.0*	26.1[e]	73.9[e]	0.735	-5
66	Lebanon	68	71.2	67.4	90.3	94.7	75.1	66.1	22.7[e]	77.3[e]	0.707	-9
67	Bulgaria	47	74.9	67.7	98.0[g]	99.0[g]	69.0[d]	64.0[d]	41.1[e]	58.9[e]	0.782	13
68	Belarus	51	74.6	64.0	97.9	97.9	81.0[d]	79.0[d]	41.5[e]	58.5[e]	0.771	10
69	Turkey	55	70.9	66.1	72.4	91.7	53.7	59.9	35.5	64.5	0.753	7
70	Saudi Arabia	102	72.5	69.3	50.3	71.5	54.4	55.1	10.0[e]	90.0[e]	0.589	-39
71	Oman	104	72.7	68.4	46.0[g]	71.0[g]	58.1	60.1	10.6[e]	89.4[e]	0.580	-40
72	Russian Federation	53	72.1	59.2	99.0[g]	99.0[g]	82.0[d]	75.0[d]	41.3[e]	58.7[e]	0.757	12
73	Ecuador	78	72.2	67.0	88.2	92.0	68.9	64.3	18.6[h]	81.4[h]	0.667	-12
74	Romania	57	73.4	66.0	97.0[g]	99.0[g]	62.0[d]	62.0[d]	37.5[e]	62.5[e]	0.751	10
75	Korea, Dem. People's Rep. of	58	74.5	68.4	95.0	95.0	*75.0*	*75.0*	36.6	63.4	0.749	10
76	Croatia	61	76.0	67.4	98.0[g]	98.0[g]	68.0[d]	67.0[d]	36.6[e]	63.4[e]	0.741	8
77	Estonia	59	75.0	63.4	*99.0*	*99.0*	74.0[d]	69.0[d]	41.9[e]	58.1[e]	0.747	11
78	Iran, Islamic Rep. of	92	69.1	67.9	59.3	77.7	62.6	67.0	18.9[e]	81.1[e]	0.643	-21
79	Lithuania	62	75.9	64.4	99.0[g]	99.0[g]	72.0[d]	68.0[d]	40.9	59.1	0.738	10
80	Macedonia, FYR	64	74.1	69.7	*94.0*	*94.0*	61.0[d]	60.0[d]	34.0[e]	66.0[e]	0.728	9
81	Syrian Arab Rep.	94	70.3	66.0	55.8	85.7	57.8	61.2	19.8[e]	80.2[e]	0.638	-20
82	Algeria	96	69.4	66.8	49.1	73.9	62.0	66.7	19.1[e]	80.9[e]	0.627	-21
83	Tunisia	76	69.8	67.7	54.6	78.6	66.4	67.6	24.7[e]	75.3[e]	0.670	0
84	Jamaica	65	76.3	71.9	89.1	80.8	68.9	63.4	39.2[e]	60.8[e]	0.724	12
85	Cuba	69	77.6	73.9	95.3	96.2	67.3	62.1	31.5[e]	68.5[e]	0.705	9
86	Peru	80	70.2	65.3	83.0	94.5	76.1	72.0	23.8[e]	76.2[e]	0.664	-1
87	Jordan	90	70.8	67.0	79.4	93.4	*66.0*	*66.0*	19.1	80.9	0.647	-10
88	Dominican Rep.	81	72.4	68.3	82.2	82.0	74.0	63.6	24.0[e]	76.0[e]	0.662	0
89	South Africa	74	67.2	61.2	81.7	81.9	82.9	75.4	30.9[e]	69.1[e]	0.680	8
90	Sri Lanka	70	74.8	70.3	87.2	93.4	67.9	64.7	35.5	64.5	0.700	13
91	Paraguay	89	71.4	66.8	90.6	93.5	63.0	61.1	23.2	76.8	0.651	-5
92	Latvia	71	74.2	61.8	*99.0*	*99.0*	69.0[d]	66.0[d]	44.0	56.0	0.697	14
93	Kazakhstan	73	72.3	62.6	*99.0*	*99.0*	75.0[d]	71.0[d]	39.3[e]	60.7[e]	0.685	13
94	Samoa (Western)	..	..	..	..	..	..	..	..	..	..	..
95	Maldives	77	62.0	64.6	93.0	93.3	71.0	71.0	35.3[e]	64.7[e]	0.668	10
96	Indonesia	88	65.8	62.2	78.0	89.6	59.1	61.3	33.0[e]	67.0[e]	0.651	0
97	Botswana	85	53.1	50.1	59.9	80.5	71.6	69.0	38.9[e]	61.1[e]	0.657	4
98	Philippines	82	69.3	65.6	94.3	95.0	81.8	70.9	35.0	65.0	0.661	8
99	Armenia	75	74.6	67.2	*98.8*	*98.8*	83.0[d]	74.0[d]	40.9[e]	59.1[e]	0.670	16
100	Guyana	95	67.1	60.3	97.5	98.7	65.8	58.8	26.9[e]	73.1[e]	0.630	-3
101	Mongolia	84	66.2	63.4	77.2	88.6	59.3	43.8	39.7[e]	60.4[e]	0.658	9
102	Ukraine	83	73.8	63.1	98.0[g]	98.0[g]	78.0[d]	75.0[d]	42.4	57.6	0.660	11
103	Turkmenistan	87	68.3	61.5	97.0[g]	99.0[g]	90.0[d]	90.0[d]	38.3[e]	61.7[e]	0.652	8
104	Uzbekistan	86	70.7	64.3	99.0[g]	99.0[g]	71.0[d]	75.0[d]	39.1[e]	60.9[e]	0.653	10
105	Albania	91	73.8	67.8	*85.0*	*85.0*	60.0[d]	59.0[d]	34.1[e]	65.9[e]	0.644	6
106	China	93	71.3	67.3	72.7	89.9	61.5	64.1	38.1[e]	61.9[e]	0.641	5
107	Namibia	99	57.0	54.6	74.0[g]	78.0[g]	84.9	78.7	34.0[e]	66.0[e]	0.620	0
108	Georgia	98	77.2	68.9	99.0[g]	98.0[g]	69.0[d]	68.0[d]	39.3[e]	60.7[e]	0.626	2
109	Kyrgyzstan	97	72.3	63.6	95.0[g]	99.0[g]	74.0[d]	71.0[d]	39.6	60.4	0.627	4
110	Azerbaijan	100	74.9	67.0	*96.3*	*96.3*	71.0[d]	74.0[d]	36.8[e]	63.2[e]	0.617	2
111	Guatemala	113	68.7	63.7	57.2	72.8	41.7	46.5	21.3[e]	78.7[e]	0.549	-10
112	Egypt	111	66.1	63.6	38.8	63.6	63.4	68.9	25.0	75.0	0.555	-7
113	Moldova, Rep. of	101	71.9	63.5	99.5[f]	98.4[f]	68.0[d]	66.0[d]	41.4[e]	58.6[e]	0.605	4
114	El Salvador	103	72.1	65.9	69.8	73.5	58.1	52.2	33.6	66.4	0.583	3
115	Swaziland	105	61.1	56.5	75.6	78.0	75.4	77.7	32.6	67.4	0.573	2
116	Bolivia	110	62.1	58.9	76.0	90.5	63.5	65.8	26.8[h]	73.2[h]	0.557	-2
117	Cape Verde	107	66.5	64.5	63.8	81.4	64.0	64.0	32.3[e]	67.7[e]	0.565	2
118	Tajikistan	106	70.1	65.9	99.0[g]	99.0[g]	67.0[d]	70.0[d]	36.6[e]	63.4[e]	0.571	4
119	Honduras	114	71.2	66.5	72.7	72.6	61.3	56.2	24.4[e]	75.6[e]	0.544	-3
120	Gabon	112	56.2	52.9	53.3	73.7	60.0	60.0	37.1[e]	62.9[e]	0.551	0
122	São Tomé and Principe	..	..	..	..	..	..	..	..	..	..	..
122	Viet Nam	108	68.5	64.0	91.2	96.5	55.8	57.7	42.0[e]	58.0[e]	0.559	5
123	Solomon Islands	109	73.3	69.1	62.0[g]	62.0[g]	47.0	47.0	39.4[e]	60.6[e]	0.557	5
124	Vanuatu	..	..	..	..	..	..	..	..	..	..	..
125	Morocco	116	67.4	63.9	31.0	56.6	40.6	50.7	27.8[e]	72.2[e]	0.511	-1
126	Nicaragua	115	69.9	65.2	66.6	64.7	65.7	59.7	28.3[e]	71.7[e]	0.526	1
127	Iraq	127	59.7	57.3	45.0	70.7	45.4	55.1	13.9[e]	86.1[e]	0.443	-10
128	Congo	117	53.7	48.7	67.2	83.2	61.2	72.0	36.2[e]	63.8[e]	0.503	1
129	Papua New Guinea	119	57.7	56.2	62.7	81.0	33.9	39.4	34.9[e]	65.1[e]	0.494	0
130	Zimbabwe	118	49.9	47.9	79.9	90.4	65.3	69.7	37.6[e]	62.4[e]	0.497	2

HDI rank	Gender-related development index (GDI) rank	Life expectancy at birth (years) 1995		Adult literacy rate (%) 1995		Combined first-, second- and third-level gross enrolment ratio (%) 1995		Share of earned income (%) 1995[a]		GDI value 1995	HDI rank minus GDI rank[b]
		Female	Male	Female	Male	Female	Male	Female	Male		
Low human development	–	57.5	55.9	38.3	63.0	39.5	52.2	28.6	71.4	0.388	–
131 Myanmar	120	60.6	57.3	77.7	88.7	47.5	46.4	42.3	57.7	0.478	1
132 Cameroon	124	56.7	53.9	52.1	75.1	41.0	48.3	30.4 [e]	69.6 [e]	0.455	-2
133 Ghana	121	58.9	55.2	53.6	75.9	38.1	48.6	43.3 [e]	56.7 [e]	0.466	2
134 Lesotho	123	59.5	57.0	62.3	81.1	61.0	51.3	30.5 [h]	69.5 [h]	0.457	1
135 Equatorial Guinea	126	50.6	47.4	68.1	89.6	64.0	64.0	28.9 [e]	71.1 [e]	0.446	-1
136 Lao People's Dem. Rep.	125	53.8	50.8	44.4	69.4	41.7	57.5	39.6 [e]	60.4 [e]	0.451	1
137 Kenya	122	55.1	52.5	70.0	86.3	50.9	51.8	41.8	58.2	0.459	5
138 Pakistan	131	63.9	61.8	24.4	50.0	27.0	53.1	20.6 [e]	79.4 [e]	0.399	-3
139 India	128	61.8	61.4	37.7	65.5	46.5	60.1	25.4 [e]	74.6 [e]	0.424	1
140 Cambodia	129	54.2	51.4	53.0 [g]	80.0 [g]	54.0	69.5	45.2 [e]	54.8 [e]	0.415	1
141 Comoros	130	57.0	56.0	50.4	64.2	35.6	41.8	35.0 [e]	65.0 [e]	0.402	1
142 Nigeria	133	53.0	49.8	47.3	67.3	43.7	53.9	30.0 [e]	70.0 [e]	0.375	-1
143 Dem. Rep. of the Congo	132	54.0	50.7	67.7	86.6	32.3	48.4	36.4 [e]	63.7 [e]	0.376	1
144 Togo	136	52.0	49.0	37.0	67.0	45.4	72.8	32.3 [e]	67.7 [e]	0.358	-2
145 Benin	135	56.9	51.9	25.8	48.7	26.3	48.1	41.8 [e]	58.2 [e]	0.364	0
146 Zambia	134	43.4	41.9	71.3	85.6	48.5	55.0	39.3	60.7	0.372	2
147 Bangladesh	140	57.0	56.9	26.1	49.4	30.9	39.6	23.1	76.9	0.342	-3
148 Côte d'Ivoire	141	53.1	50.7	30.0	49.9	30.1	43.6	25.8 [e]	74.2 [e]	0.340	-3
149 Mauritania	138	54.1	50.9	26.3	49.6	33.4	41.4	36.7 [e]	63.3 [e]	0.346	1
150 Tanzania, U. Rep. of	137	52.0	49.2	56.8	79.4	32.1	33.4	47.3	52.7	0.354	3
151 Yemen	143	57.2	56.2	39.0 [g]	39.0 [g]	26.9	67.7	21.3 [e]	78.7 [e]	0.336	-2
152 Nepal	148	55.6	56.3	14.0	40.9	42.6	66.6	33.4 [e]	66.6 [e]	0.327	-6
153 Madagascar	139	59.1	56.1	45.8 [i]	45.8 [i]	30.6	30.7	37.5 [e]	62.5 [e]	0.345	4
154 Central African Rep.	142	50.9	46.0	52.4	68.5	20.7	34.0	38.8	61.2	0.340	2
155 Bhutan	147	53.7	50.4	28.1	56.2	*31.0*	*31.0*	32.3 [e]	67.7 [e]	0.330	-2
156 Angola	145	49.1	45.9	29.0 [g]	56.0 [g]	27.5	31.8	39.2 [e]	60.8 [e]	0.331	1
157 Sudan	151	53.6	50.8	34.6	57.7	28.8	33.1	22.4 [e]	77.6 [e]	0.318	-4
158 Senegal	149	51.3	49.3	23.2	43.1	27.9	36.5	35.1 [e]	64.9 [e]	0.326	-1
159 Haiti	144	56.3	52.9	42.2	48.1	28.0	29.6	36.0 [e]	64.0 [e]	0.335	5
160 Uganda	146	41.4	39.6	50.2	73.7	34.2	41.9	40.6 [e]	59.4 [e]	0.331	4
161 Malawi	150	41.4	40.5	41.8	72.0	71.4	79.7	42.0 [e]	58.0 [e]	0.325	1
162 Djibouti	..	..	..	..	..	..	..	..	..	..	..
163 Chad	152	48.9	45.7	34.7	62.1	16.7	37.2	37.2 [h]	62.8 [h]	0.301	0
164 Guinea-Bissau	153	44.9	41.9	42.5	68.0	29.0	29.0	33.0 [e]	67.0 [e]	0.284	0
165 Gambia	154	47.6	44.4	24.9	52.8	34.0	42.6	37.5 [e]	62.5 [e]	0.277	0
166 Mozambique	156	47.8	44.8	23.3	57.7	20.5	29.0	41.9 [e]	58.1 [e]	0.264	-1
167 Guinea	157	46.0	45.0	21.9	49.9	16.2	32.4	40.2 [e]	59.8 [e]	0.258	-1
168 Eritrea	155	51.8	48.7	*25.0*	*25.0*	25.1	31.8	34.3	65.7	0.269	2
169 Ethiopia	158	50.3	47.2	25.3	45.5	15.1	24.1	33.3 [e]	66.7 [e]	0.241	0
170 Burundi	159	46.1	42.9	22.5	49.3	20.1	25.1	42.3 [e]	57.7 [e]	0.230	0
171 Mali	160	48.7	45.4	23.1	39.4	13.9	22.3	39.1 [e]	60.9 [e]	0.229	0
172 Burkina Faso	161	47.4	45.3	9.2	29.5	14.9	23.5	39.6 [e]	60.4 [e]	0.205	0
173 Niger	162	49.2	45.9	6.7	20.9	10.7	18.6	37.1 [e]	62.9 [e]	0.196	0
174 Sierra Leone	163	36.3	33.3	18.2	45.4	23.7	35.7	29.2 [e]	70.8 [e]	0.165	0
All developing countries	–	63.6	60.7	61.7	78.8	53.0	58.9	32.4	67.6	0.564	–
Least developed countries		52.3	50.0	39.3	59.2	30.9	40.3	34.3	65.7	0.332	–
Industrial countries	–	77.9	70.4	98.5	98.8	84.0	81.6	38.0	62.0	0.888	–
World	–	65.3	61.9	71.4	83.7	58.0	62.5	33.7	66.3	0.736	–

Note: Figures in italics are Human Development Report Office estimates.
a. Data refer to 1995 or latest available year.
b. The HDI ranks used in this column are those recalculated for the universe of 163 countries. See table 1.9 in chapter 1. A positive figure indicates that the GDI rank is better than the HDI rank, a negative the opposite.
c. Capped at 100.
d. Carried over from UNDP 1997a.
e. No wage data available. An estimate of 75%, the mean for all countries with wage data available, was used for the ratio of the female non-agricultural wage to the male non-agricultural wage.
f. UNESCO 1998.
g. UNICEF 1998b.
h. Wage data based on Psacharopolous and Tzannatos 1992.
i. Human Development Report Office estimate based on national sources.
Source: Columns 2 and 3: Human Development Report Office calculations based on data from UN 1996d; columns 4 and 5: UNESCO 1997a; columns 6 and 7: UNESCO 1997b; columns 8 and 9: calculations based on estimates from the following: for Real GDP per capita (PPP$), calculations based on World Bank 1997a; Summers and Heston 1991; OECD 1997h; as well as HDRO estimates as indicated in Table 1. For share of economically active population, ILO 1996. For female wages as a percentage of male wages, ILO 1997b; UN 1995b; Psacharopolous and Tzannatos 1992.

HDI rank	Gender empowerment measure (GEM) rank	Seats in parliament held by women (%)[a]	Female administrators and managers (%)[b]	Female professional and technical workers (%)[b]	Women's share of earned income (%)[b,c]	GEM value
High human development	–	14.1	..	..	35	..
1 Canada	7	21.2	42.2	56.1	38 [d]	0.720
2 France	31	9.0	9.4 [e]	41.4 [e]	39	0.489
3 Norway	2	36.4	31.5 [f]	61.9 [f]	42	0.790
4 USA	11	11.2	42.7	52.6	40	0.675
5 Iceland	6	25.4	27.7 [f]	53.5 [f]	42	0.723
6 Finland	5	33.5	25.3	62.5	42	0.725
7 Netherlands	9	28.4	20.3 [f]	44.0 [f]	34 [d]	0.689
8 Japan	38	7.7	8.9	43.3	34	0.472
9 New Zealand	4	29.2	34.0	49.1	39	0.725
10 Sweden	1	40.4	38.9	64.2	45	0.790
11 Spain	16	19.9	31.9 [f]	43.0 [f]	30 [d]	0.617
12 Belgium	19	15.8	18.8	50.5	34	0.600
13 Austria	10	24.7	23.9 [f]	46.1 [f]	34 [d]	0.686
14 United Kingdom	20	11.6	32.9 [f]	44.2 [f]	38	0.593
15 Australia	12	20.5	43.3	25.5	40	0.664
16 Switzerland	13	20.3	28.3	24.9	32	0.654
17 Ireland	21	13.7	22.6 [f]	45.0 [f]	27	0.554
18 Denmark	3	33.0	19.2	46.8	42	0.739
19 Germany	8	25.5	25.8 [f]	49.0 [f]	35	0.694
20 Greece	51	6.3	22.0 [f]	44.2 [f]	32	0.438
21 Italy	26	10.0	53.8	17.8	31 [d]	0.521
22 Israel	32	7.5	19.5 [f]	54.0 [f]	33 [d]	0.484
23 Cyprus	66	5.4	10.2 [e]	40.8 [e]	28	0.379
24 Barbados	18	18.4	38.7	51.2	40 [d]	0.607
25 Hong Kong, China	..	..	..	..	..	..
26 Luxembourg	14	20.0	8.6 [e]	37.7 [e]	29	0.649
27 Malta	..	..	..	..	..	..
28 Singapore	42	4.8	15.4 [f]	36.5 [f]	32	0.467
29 Antigua and Barbuda	..	..	..	..	..	..
30 Korea, Rep. of	83	3.0	4.4 [f]	31.9 [f]	29	0.292
31 Chile	61	7.2	20.1	53.9	22 [g]	0.416
32 Bahamas	15	19.6	34.7 [f]	51.4 [f]	40 [d]	0.649
33 Portugal	22	13.0	31.0 [f]	51.5 [f]	34	0.547
34 Costa Rica	28	15.8	23.4	45.4	27	0.503
35 Brunei Darussalam	..	..	..	..	..	..
36 Argentina	..	..	..	..	..	..
37 Slovenia	36	7.8	28.2	52.9	39 [d]	0.475
38 Uruguay	59	6.9	28.2	63.7	34 [g]	0.422
39 Czech Rep.	24	13.9	26.7 [f]	55.4 [f]	39	0.527
40 Trinidad and Tobago	17	19.4	39.7 [f]	51.7 [f]	27 [d]	0.608
41 Dominica	..	..	..	..	..	..
42 Slovakia	27	14.7	27.4 [f]	57.5 [f]	41 [d]	0.516
43 Bahrain	..	..	..	..	..	..
44 Fiji	78	5.8	9.6	44.7	22 [d]	0.332
45 Panama	44	9.7	27.6	49.2	28 [d]	0.460
46 Venezuela	62	6.3	22.9	57.1	27 [d]	0.414
47 Hungary	30	11.4	33.8 [f]	59.8 [f]	39	0.491
48 United Arab Emirates	92	0	1.6 [e]	25.1 [e]	10 [d]	0.247
49 Mexico	37	14.2 [h]	19.8	45.2	26 [d]	0.474
50 Saint Kitts and Nevis	..	..	..	..	..	..
51 Grenada	..	..	..	..	..	..
52 Poland	29	12.7	34.7 [f]	62.5 [f]	39 [d]	0.494
53 Colombia	41	9.8	31.0	44.0	33 [g]	0.470
54 Kuwait	75	0	5.2 [e]	36.8 [e]	25 [d]	0.345
55 Saint Vincent	..	..	..	..	..	..
56 Seychelles	..	..	..	..	..	..
57 Qatar	..	..	..	..	..	..
58 Saint Lucia	..	..	..	..	..	..
59 Thailand	60	6.6	21.8	52.4	37	0.421
60 Malaysia	45	10.3	18.8	43.6	30	0.458
61 Mauritius	49	7.6	22.6 [f]	38.4 [f]	26 [d]	0.451
62 Brazil	68	6.7	17.3	62.6	29	0.374
63 Belize	40	10.8	36.6	38.8	18 [d]	0.471
64 Libyan Arab Jamahiriya	..	..	..	..	..	..

HDI rank	Gender empowerment measure (GEM) rank	Seats in parliament held by women (%)[a]	Female administrators and managers (%)[b]	Female professional and technical workers (%)[b]	Women's share of earned income (%)[b,c]	GEM value
Medium human development	–	..	..	..	36	..
65 Suriname	53	15.7	12.1	61.8	26 [d]	0.434
66 Lebanon	..	..	..	..	..	..
67 Bulgaria	43	10.8	28.9 [e]	57.0 [e]	41 [d]	0.462
68 Belarus	..	..	..	..	..	..
69 Turkey	85	2.4	10.1	32.6	36	0.281
70 Saudi Arabia	..	..	..	..	..	..
71 Oman	..	..	..	..	..	..
72 Russian Federation	..	..	..	..	..	..
73 Ecuador	69	3.7	27.5	46.6	19 [g]	0.369
74 Romania	64	5.6	28.2 [f]	54.5 [f]	37 [d]	0.402
75 Korea, Dem. People's Rep. of	..	..	..	..	..	..
76 Croatia	..	..	..	..	..	..
77 Estonia	47	10.9	37.4 [f]	67.5 [f]	42 [d]	0.458
78 Iran, Islamic Rep. of	87	4.9	3.5 [e]	32.6 [e]	19 [d]	0.261
79 Lithuania	..	..	..	..	..	..
80 Macedonia, FYR	..	..	..	..	..	..
81 Syrian Arab Rep.	79	9.6	2.9	37.0	20 [d]	0.319
82 Algeria	93	3.2	5.9 [e]	27.6 [e]	19 [d]	0.241
83 Tunisia	74	6.7	12.7	35.6	25 [d]	0.345
84 Jamaica	..	..	..	..	..	..
85 Cuba	25	22.8	18.5 [e]	47.8 [e]	31 [d]	0.523
86 Peru	54	10.8	23.8 [f]	41.3 [f]	24 [d]	0.433
87 Jordan	97	1.7	4.6 [f]	28.7 [f]	19	0.211
88 Dominican Rep.	58	10.0	21.2 [e]	49.5 [e]	24 [d]	0.424
89 South Africa	23	23.7	17.4 [e]	46.7 [e]	31 [d]	0.531
90 Sri Lanka	84	5.3	16.2	19.4	36	0.286
91 Paraguay	67	5.6	22.6	54.1	23	0.374
92 Latvia	52	9.0	39.2 [f]	66.7 [f]	44	0.436
93 Kazakhstan	..	..	..	..	..	..
94 Samoa (Western)	..	..	..	..	..	..
95 Maldives	76	6.3	14.0 [e]	34.6 [e]	35 [d]	0.341
96 Indonesia	70	11.4	6.6 [e]	40.8 [e]	33 [d]	0.365
97 Botswana	48	8.5	36.1 [e]	61.4 [e]	39 [d]	0.457
98 Philippines	46	11.6	32.8	64.1	35	0.458
99 Armenia	..	..	..	..	..	..
100 Guyana	39	20.0	12.8 [e]	47.5 [e]	27 [d]	0.472
101 Mongolia	..	..	..	..	..	..
102 Ukraine	..	..	..	..	..	..
103 Turkmenistan	..	..	..	..	..	..
104 Uzbekistan	..	..	..	..	..	..
105 Albania	..	..	..	..	..	..
106 China	33	21.0 [i]	11.6 [e]	45.1 [e]	38 [d]	0.483
107 Namibia	..	..	..	..	..	..
108 Georgia	73	6.9	18.3	41.8	39 [d]	0.350
109 Kyrgyzstan	..	..	..	..	..	..
110 Azerbaijan	..	..	..	..	..	..
111 Guatemala	35	12.5	32.4 [e]	45.2 [e]	21 [d]	0.479
112 Egypt	88	2.0	11.5	29.5	25	0.258
113 Moldova, Rep. of	..	..	..	..	..	..
114 El Salvador	34	15.5	25.7 [f]	44.1 [f]	34	0.480
115 Swaziland	63	8.5	25.7	60.3	33	0.406
116 Bolivia	65	6.4 [i]	28.3	42.2	27 [g]	0.393
117 Cape Verde	57	11.1	23.3 [e]	48.4 [e]	32 [d]	0.424
118 Tajikistan	..	..	..	..	..	..
119 Honduras	..	..	..	..	..	..
120 Gabon	..	..	..	..	..	..
122 São Tomé and Principe	..	..	..	..	..	..
122 Viet Nam	..	..	..	..	..	..
123 Solomon Islands	..	..	..	..	..	..
124 Vanuatu	..	..	..	..	..	..
125 Morocco	82	0.7	25.6 [e]	31.3 [e]	28 [d]	0.302
126 Nicaragua	..	..	..	..	..	..
127 Iraq	..	..	..	..	..	..
128 Congo	..	..	..	..	..	..
129 Papua New Guinea	91	1.8	11.6 [e]	29.5 [e]	35 [d]	0.254
130 Zimbabwe	56	14.7	15.4 [e]	40.0 [e]	38 [d]	0.428

HDI rank	Gender empowerment measure (GEM) rank	Seats in parliament held by women (%)[a]	Female administrators and managers (%)[b]	Female professional and technical workers (%)[b]	Women's share of earned income (%)[b,c]	GEM value
Low human development	–	7.9	..	..	25	..
131 Myanmar	..	..	..	..	..	..
132 Cameroon	86	5.6	10.1 [e]	24.4 [e]	30 [d]	0.268
133 Ghana	..	..	..	..	..	..
134 Lesotho	50	11.2	33.4 [e]	56.6 [e]	30 [g]	0.451
135 Equatorial Guinea	90	8.8	1.6 [e]	26.8 [e]	29	0.256
136 Lao People's Dem. Rep.	..	..	..	..	..	..
137 Kenya	..	..	..	..	..	..
138 Pakistan	100	2.6	3.9	19.5	21 [d]	0.179
139 India	95	7.3	2.3 [e]	20.5 [e]	25 [d]	0.228
140 Cambodia	..	..	..	..	..	..
141 Comoros	..	..	..	..	..	..
142 Nigeria	..	..	..	..	..	..
143 Dem. Rep. of the Congo	..	..	..	..	..	..
144 Togo	99	1.2	7.9 [e]	21.2 [e]	32 [d]	0.183
145 Benin	..	..	..	..	..	..
146 Zambia	81	9.7	6.1 [e]	31.9 [e]	39	0.304
147 Bangladesh	80	9.1	4.9	34.7	23	0.305
148 Côte d'Ivoire	..	..	..	..	..	..
149 Mauritania	101	0.7	7.7 [e]	20.7 [e]	37 [d]	0.177
150 Tanzania, U. Rep. of	..	..	..	..	..	..
151 Yemen	..	..	..	..	..	..
152 Nepal	..	..	..	..	..	..
153 Madagascar	..	..	..	..	..	..
154 Central African Rep.	98	3.5	9.0 [e]	18.9 [e]	39	0.205
155 Bhutan	..	..	..	..	..	..
156 Angola	..	..	..	..	..	..
157 Sudan	96	5.3	2.4 [e]	28.8 [e]	22 [d]	0.225
158 Senegal	..	..	..	..	..	..
159 Haiti	71	3.6 [g]	32.6 [e]	39.3 [e]	36 [d]	0.356
160 Uganda	..	..	..	..	..	..
161 Malawi	89	5.6	4.8 [e]	34.7 [e]	42 [d]	0.256
162 Djibouti	..	..	..	..	..	..
163 Chad	..	..	..	..	..	..
164 Guinea-Bissau	..	..	..	..	..	..
165 Gambia	94	2.0	15.5	23.7	38 [d]	0.239
166 Mozambique	55	25.2	11.3 [e]	20.4 [e]	42 [d]	0.430
167 Guinea	..	..	..	..	..	..
168 Eritrea	..	..	..	..	..	..
169 Ethiopia	..	..	..	..	..	..
170 Burundi	..	..	..	..	..	..
171 Mali	72	12.2	19.7 [e]	19.0 [e]	39 [d]	0.351
172 Burkina Faso	77	10.8	13.5 [e]	25.8 [e]	40 [d]	0.339
173 Niger	102	1.2	8.5	8.1	37 [d]	0.121
174 Sierra Leone	..	..	..	..	..	..
All developing countries	–	8.6	..	..	32	..
Least developed countries	–	..	..	..	..	..
Industrial countries	–	15.3	..	..	37	..
World	–	11.8	..	..	33	..

a. Data are as of 15 December 1997. A value of 0 was converted to 0.001 for purposes of calculation.
b. Data refer to latest available year.
c. The manufacturing wage was used for the Central African Rep., Finland, Greece, Ireland, Norway and Sweden.
d. No wage data available. An estimate of 75%, the mean for all countries with wage data available, was used for the ratio of the female non-agricultural wage to the male non-agricultural wage.
e. Carried over from UNDP 1997a.
f. Refers to International Standard Classification of Occupations (ISCO) 1988, which is not strictly comparable with the ISCO-1968 classification. See the selected definitions.
g. Wage data based on Psacharopolous and Tzannatos 1992.
h. Does not include upper house or senate.
i. Data are as of 1 January 1997.
Source: Column 2: IPU 1997a; *columns 3 and 4:* ILO 1997b; UN 1995b; *column 5:* Human Development Report Office calculations based on estimates from the following: for Real GDP per capita (PPP$), calculations based on World Bank data 1997a; Summers and Heston; 1991; OECD 1997h; as well as Human Development Report Office estimates as indicated in Table 1. For share of economically active population, ILO 1996. For female wages as a percentage of male wages, ILO 1997b; UN 1995b; Psacharopolous and Tzannatos 1992.

HDI rank	Human development index (HDI) value 1995	Gender-related development index (GDI) value 1995	Gender empowerment measure (GEM) value 1995	HDI value as % of highest in region 1995	GDI value as % of highest in region 1995	GEM value as % of highest in region 1995
Sub-Saharan Africa	0.378 [a]	0.354 [a]	0.339 [a]	–	–	–
56 Seychelles	0.845 [b]	..	..	100	..	..
61 Mauritius	0.833	0.753 [b]	0.451	99	100	85
89 South Africa	0.717	0.680	0.531 [b]	85	90	100
97 Botswana	0.678	0.657	0.457	80	87	86
107 Namibia	0.644	0.620	..	76	82	..
115 Swaziland	0.597	0.573	0.406	71	76	76
117 Cape Verde	0.591	0.565	0.424	70	75	80
120 Gabon	0.568	0.551	..	67	73	..
121 São Tomé and Principe	0.563	..	..	67	..	..
128 Congo	0.519	0.503	..	61	67	..
130 Zimbabwe	0.507	0.497	0.428	60	66	81
132 Cameroon	0.481	0.455	0.268	57	60	50
133 Ghana	0.473	0.466	..	56	62	..
134 Lesotho	0.469	0.457	0.451	56	61	85
135 Equatorial Guinea	0.465	0.446	0.256	55	59	48
137 Kenya	0.463	0.459	..	55	61	..
141 Comoros	0.411	0.402	..	49	53	..
142 Nigeria	0.391	0.375	..	46	50	..
143 Dem. Rep. of the Congo	0.383	0.376	..	45	50	..
144 Togo	0.380	0.358	0.183	45	48	34
145 Benin	0.378	0.364	..	45	48	..
146 Zambia	0.378	0.372	0.304	45	49	57
148 Côte d'Ivoire	0.368	0.340	..	44	45	..
149 Mauritania	0.361	0.346	0.177	43	46	33
150 Tanzania, U. Rep. of	0.358	0.354	..	42	47	..
153 Madagascar	0.348	0.345	..	41	46	..
154 Central African Rep.	0.347	0.340	0.205	41	45	39
156 Angola	0.344	0.331	..	41	44	..
158 Senegal	0.342	0.326	..	41	43	..
160 Uganda	0.340	0.331	..	40	44	..
161 Malawi	0.334	0.325	0.256	40	43	48
163 Chad	0.318	0.301	..	38	40	..
164 Guinea-Bissau	0.295	0.284	..	35	38	..
165 Gambia	0.291	0.277	0.239	34	37	45
166 Mozambique	0.281	0.264	0.430	33	35	81
167 Guinea	0.277	0.258	..	33	34	..
168 Eritrea	0.275	0.269	..	33	36	..
169 Ethiopia	0.252	0.241	..	30	32	..
170 Burundi	0.241	0.230	..	29	30	..
171 Mali	0.236	0.229	0.351	28	30	66
172 Burkina Faso	0.219	0.205	0.339	26	27	64
173 Niger	0.207	0.196	0.121	25	26	23
174 Sierra Leone	0.185	0.165	..	22	22	..
East Asia	0.766 [a]	0.749 [a]	0.388 [a]	–	–	–
25 Hong Kong, China	0.909 [b]	0.836 [b]	..	100	100	..
30 Korea, Rep. of	0.894	0.826	0.292	98	99	60
75 Korea, Dem. Rep. of	0.766	0.749	..	84	90	..
101 Mongolia	0.669	0.658	..	74	79	..
106 China	0.650	0.641	0.483 [b]	72	77	100
South Asia	0.452 [a]	0.412 [a]	0.273 [a]	–	–	–
78 Iran, Islamic Rep. of	0.758 [b]	0.643	0.261	100	92	77
90 Sri Lanka	0.716	0.700 [b]	0.286	94	100	84
95 Maldives	0.683	0.668	0.341 [b]	90	95	100
138 Pakistan	0.453	0.399	0.179	60	57	53
139 India	0.451	0.424	0.228	59	61	67
147 Bangladesh	0.371	0.342	0.305	49	49	89
152 Nepal	0.351	0.327	..	46	47	..
155 Bhutan	0.347	0.330	..	46	47	..
South-East Asia and the Pacific	0.677 [a]	0.651 [a]	0.421 [a]	–	–	–
28 Singapore	0.896 [b]	0.848 [b]	0.467 [b]	100	100	100
35 Brunei Darussalam	0.889	0.834	..	99	98	..
44 Fiji	0.869	0.770	0.332	97	91	71
59 Thailand	0.838	0.812	0.421	94	96	90
60 Malaysia	0.834	0.785	0.458	93	93	98
94 Samoa (Western)	0.694	..	..	77	..	..
96 Indonesia	0.679	0.651	0.365	76	77	78
98 Philippines	0.677	0.661	0.458	76	78	98
122 Viet Nam	0.560	0.559	..	63	66	..
123 Solomon Islands	0.560	0.557	..	63	66	..

HDI rank	Human development index (HDI) value 1995	Gender-related development index (GDI) value 1995	Gender empowerment measure (GEM) value 1995	HDI value as % of highest in region 1995	GDI value as % of highest in region 1995	GEM value as % of highest in region 1995
124 Vanuatu	0.559	..		62	..	
129 Papua New Guinea	0.507	0.494	0.254	57	58	54
131 Myanmar	0.481	0.478	..	54	56	..
136 Lao People's Dem. Rep.	0.465	0.451	..	52	53	..
140 Cambodia	0.422	0.415	..	47	49	..
Arab States	0.747 [a]	0.638 [a]	0.258 [a]	–	–	–
43 Bahrain	**0.872** [b]	0.746	..	100	97	
48 United Arab Emirates	0.855	0.718	0.247	98	93	72
54 Kuwait	0.848	**0.773** [b]	0.345	97	100	100
57 Qatar	0.840	0.714	..	96	92	..
64 Libyan Arab Jamahiriya	0.806	0.664	..	92	86	
66 Lebanon	0.796	0.707	..	91	91	
70 Saudi Arabia	0.778	0.589	..	89	76	..
71 Oman	0.771	0.580	..	88	75	..
81 Syrian Arab Rep.	0.749	0.638	0.319	86	83	93
82 Algeria	0.746	0.627	0.241	86	81	70
83 Tunisia	0.744	0.670	**0.345** [b]	85	87	100
87 Jordan	0.729	0.647	0.211	84	84	61
112 Egypt	0.612	0.555	0.258	70	72	75
125 Morocco	0.557	0.511	0.302	64	66	88
127 Iraq	0.538	0.443		62	57	
151 Yemen	0.356	0.336	..	41	43	..
157 Sudan	0.343	0.318	0.225	39	41	65
162 Djibouti	0.324	..	..	37	..	..
Latin America and the Caribbean	0.839 [a]	0.724 [a]	0.460 [a]	–	–	–
24 Barbados	**0.909** [b]	**0.889** [b]	0.607	100	100	94
29 Antigua and Barbuda	0.895	..	..	98	..	..
31 Chile	0.893	0.783	0.416	98	88	64
32 Bahamas	0.893	0.876	**0.649** [b]	98	99	100
34 Costa Rica	0.889	0.818	0.503	98	92	78
36 Argentina	0.888	0.777	..	98	87	..
38 Uruguay	0.885	0.841	0.422	97	95	65
40 Trinidad and Tobago	0.880	0.823	0.608	97	93	94
41 Dominica	0.879	..	..	97	..	
45 Panama	0.868	0.804	0.460	95	90	71
46 Venezuela	0.860	0.790	0.414	95	89	64
49 Mexico	0.855	0.774	0.474	94	87	73
50 St. Kitts and Nevis	0.854	..	..	94	..	..
51 Grenada	0.851	..	..	94	..	..
53 Colombia	0.850	0.810	0.470	93	91	72
55 Saint Vincent	0.845	..	..	93	..	..
58 Saint Lucia	0.839	..	..	92	..	
62 Brazil	0.809	0.751	0.374	89	85	58
63 Belize	0.807	0.689	0.471	89	78	73
65 Suriname	0.796	0.735	0.434	88	83	67
73 Ecuador	0.767	0.667	0.369	84	75	57
84 Jamaica	0.735	0.724	..	81	81	..
85 Cuba	0.729	0.705	0.523	80	79	81
86 Peru	0.729	0.664	0.433	80	75	67
88 Dominican Rep.	0.720	0.662	0.424	79	74	65
91 Paraguay	0.707	0.651	0.374	78	73	58
100 Guyana	0.670	0.630	0.472	74	71	73
111 Guatemala	0.615	0.549	0.479	68	62	74
114 El Salvador	0.604	0.583	0.480	66	66	74
116 Bolivia	0.593	0.557	0.393	65	63	61
119 Honduras	0.573	0.544	..	63	61	..
126 Nicaragua	0.547	0.526	..	60	59	..
159 Haiti	0.340	0.335	0.356	37	38	55
All developing countries	0.630 [a]	0.565 [a]	0.374 [a]	–	–	–
Eastern Europe and CIS	0.750 [a]	0.738 [a]	0.460 [a]	–	–	–
23 Cyprus	**0.913** [b]	0.847	0.379	100	98	72
37 Slovenia	0.887	**0.867** [b]	0.475	97	100	90
39 Czech Rep.	0.884	0.864	**0.527** [b]	97	100	100
42 Slovakia	0.875	0.861	0.516	96	99	98
47 Hungary	0.857	0.834	0.491	94	96	93
52 Poland	0.851	0.834	0.494	93	96	94
67 Bulgaria	0.789	0.782	0.462	86	90	88
68 Belarus	0.783	0.771	..	86	89	..
69 Turkey	0.782	0.753	0.281	86	87	53
72 Russian Federation	0.769	0.757	..	84	87	..

HDI rank	Human development index (HDI) value 1995	Gender-related development index (GDI) value 1995	Gender empowerment measure (GEM) value 1995	HDI value as % of highest in region 1995	GDI value as % of highest in region 1995	GEM value as % of highest in region 1995
74 Romania	0.767	0.751	0.402	84	87	76
76 Croatia	0.759	0.741	..	83	85	..
77 Estonia	0.758	0.747	0.458	83	86	87
79 Lithuania	0.750	0.738	..	82	85	..
80 Macedonia, FYR	0.749	0.728	..	82	84	..
92 Latvia	0.704	0.697	0.436	77	80	83
93 Kazakhstan	0.695	0.685	..	76	79	..
99 Armenia	0.674	0.670	..	74	77	..
102 Ukraine	0.665	0.660	..	73	76	..
103 Turkmenistan	0.660	0.652	..	72	75	..
104 Uzbekistan	0.659	0.653	..	72	75	..
105 Albania	0.656	0.644	..	72	74	..
108 Georgia	0.633	0.626	0.350	69	72	67
109 Kyrgyzstan	0.633	0.627	..	69	72	..
110 Azerbaijan	0.623	0.617	..	68	71	..
113 Moldova, Rep. of	0.610	0.605	..	67	70	..
118 Tajikistan	0.575	0.571	..	63	66	..
Industrial countries[c]	0.933[a]	0.902[a]	0.659[a]	—	—	—
1 Canada	**0.960**[b]	**0.940**[b]	0.720	100	100	91
2 France	0.946	0.925	0.489	99	98	62
3 Norway	0.943	0.935	0.790	98	100	100
4 USA	0.943	0.927	0.675	98	99	85
5 Iceland	0.942	0.932	0.723	98	99	92
6 Finland	0.942	0.929	0.725	98	99	92
7 Netherlands	0.941	0.905	0.689	98	96	87
8 Japan	0.940	0.902	0.472	98	96	60
9 New Zealand	0.939	0.920	0.725	98	98	92
10 Sweden	0.936	0.932	**0.790**[b]	97	99	100
11 Spain	0.935	0.877	0.617	97	93	78
12 Belgium	0.933	0.893	0.600	97	95	76
13 Austria	0.933	0.891	0.686	97	95	87
14 United Kingdom	0.932	0.907	0.593	97	97	75
15 Australia	0.932	0.918	0.664	97	98	84
16 Switzerland	0.930	0.887	0.654	97	94	83
17 Ireland	0.930	0.859	0.554	97	91	70
18 Denmark	0.928	0.917	0.739	97	98	94
19 Germany	0.925	0.888	0.694	96	95	88
20 Greece	0.924	0.876	0.438	96	93	55
21 Italy	0.922	0.868	0.521	96	92	66
22 Israel	0.913	0.873	0.484	95	93	61
26 Luxembourg	0.900	0.836	0.649	94	89	82
27 Malta	0.899	0.788	..	94	84	..
33 Portugal	0.892	0.852	0.547	93	91	69
World	0.724[a]	0.661[a]	0.437[a]	—	—	—

Note: The highest value in a region or country group is determined on the basis of the fourth decimal place, not shown here.
a. Indicates the median value achieved in the region or country group.
b. Indicates the highest value achieved in the region or country group.
c. Excluding Eastern Europe and CIS.
Source: Human Development Report Office.

5 Trends in human development and per capita income

HDI rank	Human development index (HDI) value					GDP per capita (1987 US$)				
	1960	1970	1980	1992	1995	1960	1970	1980	1990	1995
High human development	..	..	..	..	0.897	5,496	7,945	9,414	11,065	11,621
1 Canada	0.865	0.887	0.911	0.932	0.960	7,261	10,092	13,508	15,895	16,139
2 France	0.853	0.871	0.895	0.927	0.946	7,219	11,166	14,564	17,485	18,069
3 Norway	0.865	0.878	0.901	0.928	0.943	7,895	11,926	17,856	21,914	25,390
4 USA	0.865	0.881	0.905	0.925	0.943	10,707	14,001	16,389	19,426	20,716
5 Iceland	0.853	0.863	0.890	0.914	0.942	6,624	11,095	18,339	21,505	21,331
6 Finland	0.811	0.855	0.880	0.911	0.942	7,351	11,376	15,140	19,576	18,460
7 Netherlands	0.855	0.867	0.888	0.923	0.941	7,943	11,279	13,855	16,283	17,325
8 Japan	0.686	0.875	0.906	0.929	0.940	4,706	11,892	16,384	22,928	24,104
9 New Zealand	0.852	0.861	0.877	0.907	0.939	7,444	8,849	9,956	11,025	12,007
10 Sweden	0.867	0.881	0.899	0.928	0.936	9,873	14,389	16,903	20,018	19,521
11 Spain	0.636	0.820	0.851	0.888	0.935	2,828	5,207	6,657	8,618	9,141
12 Belgium	0.826	0.851	0.873	0.916	0.933	6,363	9,770	13,170	15,679	16,428
13 Austria	0.797	0.857	0.880	0.917	0.933	6,727	10,101	14,160	17,090	18,109
14 United Kingdom	0.857	0.873	0.892	0.919	0.932	6,795	8,463	10,161	12,899	13,445
15 Australia	0.850	0.862	0.890	0.926	0.932	6,989	9,708	11,386	13,072	14,440
16 Switzerland	0.853	0.872	0.897	0.931	0.930	15,779	21,412	24,037	27,820	26,721
17 Ireland	0.710	0.829	0.862	0.892	0.930	3,904	5,656	7,791	10,656	13,134
18 Denmark	0.857	0.879	0.888	0.912	0.928	9,835	14,049	16,858	20,511	22,247
19 Germany	0.841	0.856	0.881	0.918	0.925	..	..	..	..	..
20 Greece	0.573	0.723	0.839	0.874	0.924	1,570	3,228	4,568	4,794	5,020
21 Italy	0.755	0.831	0.857	0.891	0.922	5,296	8,562	11,821	14,642	15,392
22 Israel	0.719	0.827	0.862	0.900	0.913	3,537	5,737	7,653	9,126	10,551
23 Cyprus	0.579	0.733	0.844	0.873	0.913	..	..	4,164	6,826	..
24 Barbados	0.678	0.824	0.856	0.894	0.909	2,290	4,252	5,453	6,022	5,736
25 Hong Kong, China	0.561	0.737	0.830	0.875	0.909	1,631	3,128	5,939	9,897	11,911
26 Luxembourg	0.826	0.843	0.869	0.908	0.900	9,704	12,942	15,606	21,187	21,851
27 Malta	0.517	0.615	0.802	0.843	0.899	989	1,535	3,713	5,593	..
28 Singapore	0.519	0.682	0.780	0.836	0.896	1,510	3,067	5,907	9,877	13,451
29 Antigua and Barbuda	..	..	..	..	0.895	..	..	2,982	5,250	..
30 Korea, Rep. of	0.398	0.523	0.666	0.859	0.894	520	967	1,953	4,132	5,663
31 Chile	0.584	0.682	0.753	0.848	0.893	1,162	1,397	1,580	1,912	2,532
32 Bahamas	..	..	..	..	0.893	6,770	9,568	10,265	11,227	10,110
33 Portugal	0.460	0.588	0.736	0.838	0.892	1,402	2,533	3,728	4,930	5,175
34 Costa Rica	0.550	0.647	0.746	0.848	0.889	1,053	1,351	1,767	1,692	1,899
35 Brunei Darussalam	..	..	..	..	0.889	..	..	17,052	11,193	10,908
36 Argentina	0.667	0.748	0.790	0.853	0.888	2,701	3,533	3,996	3,150	3,793
37 Slovenia	..	..	..	..	0.887	..	..	..	..	..
38 Uruguay	0.737	0.762	0.830	0.859	0.885	1,937	2,022	2,590	2,417	2,786
39 Czech Rep.	..	..	..	..	0.884	..	..	..	3,680	3,164
40 Trinidad and Tobago	0.737	0.789	0.816	0.855	0.880	2,442	3,183	5,218	3,759	3,858
41 Dominica	..	..	..	..	0.879	1,192	1,337	1,139	1,987	..
42 Slovakia	..	..	..	..	0.875	..	..	..	3,622	3,054
43 Bahrain	..	..	..	..	0.872	..	..	10,037	7,240	8,080
44 Fiji	..	..	..	..	0.869	1,116	1,404	1,864	1,948	2,110
45 Panama	0.485	0.592	0.687	0.816	0.868	1,068	1,681	2,248	1,951	2,434
46 Venezuela	0.600	0.728	0.784	0.820	0.860	2,815	3,298	3,067	2,560	2,648
47 Hungary	0.625	0.705	0.838	0.863	0.857	742	1,350	2,059	2,456	2,334
48 United Arab Emirates	0.515	0.601	0.719	0.771	0.855	..	..	29,887	16,858	..
49 Mexico	0.517	0.642	0.758	0.804	0.855	938	1,363	1,949	1,839	1,724
50 Saint Kitts and Nevis	..	..	..	..	0.854	..	..	1,767	3,082	3,736
51 Grenada	..	..	..	..	0.851	..	..	..	1,938	2,101
52 Poland	..	..	..	..	0.851	..	..	1,682	1,559	1,701
53 Colombia	0.469	0.554	0.656	0.813	0.850	639	773	1,040	1,213	1,377
54 Kuwait	..	..	..	..	0.848	..	35,866	18,431	..	17,016
55 Saint Vincent	..	..	..	..	0.845	743	788	940	1,627	1,813
56 Seychelles	..	..	..	..	0.845	1,803	2,032	3,533	4,529	..
57 Qatar	..	..	..	..	0.840	..	..	..	..	..
58 Saint Lucia	..	..	..	..	0.839	..	..	..	2,449	2,792
59 Thailand	0.373	0.465	0.551	0.798	0.838	300	487	718	1,291	1,843
60 Malaysia	0.330	0.471	0.687	0.794	0.834	708	1,001	1,688	2,301	3,108
61 Mauritius	0.486	0.524	0.626	0.778	0.833	815	..	1,297	2,129	2,516
62 Brazil	0.394	0.507	0.673	0.756	0.809	823	1,145	2,049	1,952	2,051
63 Belize	..	..	..	..	0.807	750	966	1,598	1,991	2,113
64 Libyan Arab Jamahiriya	..	..	..	..	0.806	3,275	17,025	13,219	..	..

HDI rank	Human development index (HDI) value					GDP per capita (1987 US$)				
	1960	1970	1980	1992	1995	1960	1970	1980	1990	1995
Medium human development	..	..	..	..	0.670	249	480	818	911	900
65 Suriname	..	..	..	..	0.796	..	1,021	1,220	1,955	2,101
66 Lebanon	..	..	..	..	0.796	..	..	..	..	..
67 Bulgaria	..	..	..	..	0.789	..	..	2,344	3,176	2,605
68 Belarus	..	..	..	..	0.783	..	..	..	2,724	1,712
69 Turkey	0.333	0.441	0.549	0.739	0.782	753	1,125	1,323	1,731	1,865
70 Saudi Arabia	0.448	0.511	0.629	0.742	0.778	..	6,625	10,225	5,434	5,008
71 Oman	..	..	..	..	0.771	750	3,367	3,587	5,653	5,603
72 Russian Federation	..	..	..	..	0.769	..	1,700	3,204	3,193	1,988
73 Ecuador	0.422	0.485	0.613	0.718	0.767	..	668	1,226	1,170	1,241
74 Romania	..	..	..	..	0.767	..	..	1,511	1,452	1,358
75 Korea, Dem. People's Rep. of	..	..	..	..	0.766	..	..	..	..	..
76 Croatia	..	..	..	..	0.759	..	..	..	..	..
77 Estonia	..	..	..	..	0.758	..	..	3,354	3,693	2,530
78 Iran, Islamic Rep. of	0.306	0.406	0.497	0.672	0.758	..	..	2,980	2,667	2,902
79 Lithuania	..	..	..	..	0.750	..	..	..	2,684	1,683
80 Macedonia, FYR	..	..	..	..	0.749	..	..	..	..	..
81 Syrian Arab Rep.	0.318	0.419	0.658	0.727	0.749	..	636	1,168	1,040	1,267
82 Algeria	0.264	0.323	0.476	0.553	0.746	1,988	2,096	2,683	2,624	2,389
83 Tunisia	0.258	0.340	0.499	0.690	0.744	..	718	1,177	1,309	1,436
84 Jamaica	0.529	0.662	0.654	0.749	0.735	1,154	1,555	1,289	1,462	1,578
85 Cuba	..	..	..	..	0.729	..	..	..	..	..
86 Peru	0.420	0.528	0.590	0.642	0.729	964	1,080	1,171	885	1,033
87 Jordan	0.296	0.405	0.553	0.628	0.729	..	..	..	1,558	..
88 Dominican Rep.	0.385	0.455	0.541	0.638	0.720	386	494	744	773	838
89 South Africa	0.464	0.591	0.629	0.650	0.717	1,808	2,396	2,593	2,342	2,165
90 Sri Lanka	0.475	0.506	0.552	0.665	0.716	204	247	328	438	512
91 Paraguay	0.474	0.511	0.602	0.679	0.707	525	604	1,047	1,028	1,049
92 Latvia	..	..	..	..	0.704	1,020	1,777	2,689	3,530	1,912
93 Kazakhstan	..	..	..	..	0.695	793	..	..	1,741	961
94 Samoa (Western)	..	..	..	..	0.694	..	..	655	626	..
95 Maldives	..	..	..	..	0.683	..	..	..	585	693
96 Indonesia	0.223	0.306	0.418	0.586	0.679	190	211	349	537	720
97 Botswana	0.207	0.284	0.414	0.670	0.678	238	310	902	1,674	1,857
98 Philippines	0.419	0.489	0.557	0.621	0.677	418	495	679	628	630
99 Armenia	..	..	..	..	0.674	2,043	887	1,483	1,759	587
100 Guyana	..	..	..	..	0.670	475	571	586	394	541
101 Mongolia	..	..	..	..	0.669	..	..	1,360	1,691	1,294
102 Ukraine	..	..	..	..	0.665	..	..	..	2,072	999
103 Turkmenistan	..	..	..	..	0.660	..	..	..	..	..
104 Uzbekistan	..	..	..	..	0.659	..	..	..	803	592
105 Albania	..	..	..	..	0.656	..	..	698	908	887
106 China	0.248	0.372	0.475	0.644	0.650	75	92	138	285	481
107 Namibia	..	..	..	..	0.644	..	..	1,792	1,475	1,577
108 Georgia	..	..	..	..	0.633	715	1,181	1,966	1,760	433
109 Kyrgyzstan	..	..	..	..	0.633	..	..	..	1,072	501
110 Azerbaijan	..	..	..	..	0.623	..	..	..	1,020	355
111 Guatemala	0.311	0.392	0.477	0.564	0.615	616	795	1,045	858	898
112 Egypt	0.210	0.269	0.360	0.551	0.612	237	338	590	745	726
113 Moldova, Rep. of	..	..	..	..	0.610	..	..	..	..	..
114 El Salvador	0.339	0.422	0.454	0.543	0.604	769	995	985	851	1,024
115 Swaziland	..	..	..	..	0.597	310	610	725	821	800
116 Bolivia	0.308	0.369	0.442	0.530	0.593	610	754	876	737	790
117 Cape Verde	..	..	..	..	0.591	..	298	414	604	..
118 Tajikistan	..	..	..	..	0.575	384	..	..	718	255
119 Honduras	0.280	0.350	0.435	0.524	0.573	691	793	974	886	904
120 Gabon	0.259	0.378	0.468	0.525	0.568	2,307	3,594	5,470	4,543	3,640
121 São Tomé and Principe	..	..	..	..	0.563	..	517	714	502	481
122 Viet Nam	..	..	..	..	0.560	..	..	..	610	816
123 Solomon Islands	..	..	..	..	0.560	..	396	423	585	658
124 Vanuatu	..	..	..	..	0.559	..	..	820	913	..
125 Morocco	0.198	0.282	0.383	0.549	0.557	484	575	782	916	871
126 Nicaragua	0.344	0.462	0.534	0.583	0.547	1,295	1,809	1,376	896	816
127 Iraq	0.348	0.452	0.581	0.614	0.538	3,420	4,437	6,600	1,621	..
128 Congo	0.241	0.307	0.368	0.461	0.519	511	601	902	1,066	906
129 Papua New Guinea	0.208	0.325	0.348	0.408	0.507	570	877	881	803	1,059
130 Zimbabwe	0.284	0.326	0.386	0.474	0.507	460	614	607	656	604

	Human development index (HDI) value					GDP per capita (1987 US$)				
HDI rank	1960	1970	1980	1992	1995	1960	1970	1980	1990	1995
Low human development	..	..	..	..	0.409	227	268	288	348	376
131 Myanmar	0.243	0.318	0.356	0.406	0.481	195	..	..	903	..
132 Cameroon	0.191	0.253	0.332	0.447	0.481	601	652	890	389	727
133 Ghana	0.233	0.283	0.323	0.382	0.473	497	517	433	389	420
134 Lesotho	0.245	0.307	0.404	0.476	0.469	128	131	236	276	354
135 Equatorial Guinea	..	..	..	..	0.465	..	..	..	357	451
136 Lao People's Dem. Rep.	..	..	..	..	0.465	..	..	..	310	363
137 Kenya	0.192	0.254	0.340	0.434	0.463	218	246	372	395	375
138 Pakistan	0.183	0.244	0.287	0.393	0.453	135	223	259	350	381
139 India	0.206	0.254	0.296	0.382	0.451	206	245	262	374	425
140 Cambodia	..	..	..	..	0.422	..	..	..	111	133
141 Comoros	..	..	..	..	0.411	..	..	458	474	415
142 Nigeria	0.184	0.230	0.297	0.348	0.391	329	361	426	359	355
143 Dem. Rep. of the Congo	0.179	0.235	0.286	0.341	0.383	288	309	241	197	..
144 Togo	0.123	0.183	0.255	0.311	0.380	244	400	472	391	327
145 Benin	0.130	0.162	0.197	0.261	0.378	320	361	359	346	..
146 Zambia	0.258	0.315	0.342	0.352	0.378	412	440	375	305	257
147 Bangladesh	0.166	0.199	0.234	0.309	0.371	146	162	144	179	202
148 Côte d'Ivoire	0.168	0.243	0.330	0.370	0.368	500	971	1,186	810	732
149 Mauritania	..	..	..	..	0.361	359	581	523	472	503
150 Tanzania, U. Rep. of	0.162	0.211	0.282	0.306	0.358	123	..	..	152	155
151 Yemen	0.092	0.138	0.253	0.323	0.356	..	..	..	182	206
152 Nepal	0.128	0.162	0.209	0.289	0.351	148	156	148	182	206
153 Madagascar	0.237	0.291	0.344	0.396	0.348	340	353	302	237	199
154 Central African Rep.	0.160	0.196	0.226	0.249	0.347	426	445	412	378	357
155 Bhutan	..	..	..	..	0.347	..	..	313	518	571
156 Angola	0.139	0.195	0.212	0.271	0.344	..	..	..	846	641
157 Sudan	0.160	0.188	0.229	0.276	0.343	814	729	784	684	..
158 Senegal	0.146	0.176	0.233	0.322	0.342	713	723	663	673	661
159 Haiti	0.174	0.218	0.295	0.354	0.340	386	333	428	340	231
160 Uganda	0.185	0.213	0.215	0.272	0.340	..	..	..	470	557
161 Malawi	0.144	0.176	0.216	0.260	0.334	102	127	172	154	146
162 Djibouti	..	..	..	..	0.324	..	..	..	..	..
163 Chad	0.112	0.135	0.151	0.212	0.318	213	198	128	177	178
164 Guinea-Bissau	0.091	0.125	0.148	0.224	0.295	..	202	144	202	214
165 Gambia	0.068	0.107	0.148	0.215	0.291	189	240	289	296	274
166 Mozambique	0.169	0.248	0.247	0.252	0.281	..	..	129	111	133
167 Guinea	0.083	0.111	0.148	0.191	0.277	..	..	..	386	404
168 Eritrea	..	..	..	..	0.275	..	..	..	..	..
169 Ethiopia	..	..	..	..	0.252	..	..	..	153	154
170 Burundi	0.131	0.157	0.219	0.276	0.241	125	161	195	227	182
171 Mali	0.083	0.102	0.146	0.214	0.236	217	225	279	260	256
172 Burkina Faso	0.086	0.116	0.151	0.203	0.219	173	198	232	253	258
173 Niger	0.090	0.134	0.163	0.209	0.207	556	554	461	310	275
174 Sierra Leone	0.095	0.155	0.177	0.209	0.185	119	222	222	232	171
All developing countries	..	..	..	..	0.586	330	474	685	736	867
Least developed countries	..	..	..	..	0.344	245	272	257	254	233
Industrial countries	..	..	..	..	0.911	7,097	9,344	11,169	12,310	12,764
World	..	..	..	..	0.772	1,951	2,660	3,116	3,298	3,417

Note: HDI values for 1960-92 are not strictly comparable with HDI values for 1995. There is a break in the data series reported in this table. Data for 1960-69 are from World Bank, World Data 1995, CD-ROM. Data for 1970-95 are from World Bank 1997d.
Source: Columns 1-5: Human Development Report Office; *columns 7-10:* World Bank 1997d.

HDI rank	Reduction in shortfall (1-HDI) in human development index (HDI) value (%)			GDP per capita (1987 US$)							Average annual rate of change (%)
	1960-70	1970-80	1980-92	1960[a]	Lowest value during 1960-95[a]	Year	Highest value during 1960-95[a]	Year	1995[a]		1960-95[a]
High human development	..	..	..	..	..	..	..	..	..		..
1 Canada	16.0	21.4	23.7	7,261	7,261	1960	16,159	1989	16,139		2.3
2 France	12.5	18.2	30.6	7,219	7,219	1960	18,069	1995	18,069		2.7
3 Norway	9.6	18.6	27.5	7,895	7,895	1960	25,390	1995	25,390		3.4
4 USA	11.5	20.8	20.7	10,707	10,707	1960	20,716	1995	20,716		1.9
5 Iceland	6.9	19.6	22.0	6,624	4,743	1961	21,978	1987	21,331		3.4
6 Finland	23.4	17.3	25.6	7,351	7,351	1960	19,672	1989	18,460		2.7
7 Netherlands	8.1	15.6	31.5	7,943	7,858	1961	17,325	1995	17,325		2.3
8 Japan	60.4	24.8	24.1	4,706	4,706	1960	24,104	1995	24,104		4.8
9 New Zealand	6.1	11.5	24.2	7,444	7,444	1960	12,007	1995	12,007		1.4
10 Sweden	11.0	14.7	28.9	9,873	9,873	1960	20,018	1990	19,521		2.0
11 Spain	50.6	17.4	24.6	2,828	2,828	1960	9,141	1995	9,141		3.4
12 Belgium	14.6	14.4	34.0	6,363	6,363	1960	16,428	1995	16,428		2.7
13 Austria	29.6	15.8	30.9	6,727	6,727	1960	18,109	1995	18,109		2.9
14 United Kingdom	11.1	14.7	25.2	6,795	6,795	1960	13,445	1995	13,445		2.0
15 Australia	7.9	20.8	32.4	6,989	6,989	1960	14,440	1995	14,440		2.1
16 Switzerland	12.7	19.8	32.9	15,779	15,779	1960	27,820	1990	26,721		1.5
17 Ireland	41.2	19.0	21.9	3,904	3,904	1960	13,134	1995	13,134		3.5
18 Denmark	15.0	8.1	21.2	9,835	9,835	1960	22,247	1995	22,247		2.4
19 Germany	9.4	17.7	30.8	..	..	..	..	..	..		..
20 Greece	35.1	41.8	21.9	1,570	1,570	1960	5,020	1995	5,020		3.4
21 Italy	30.8	15.8	23.5	5,296	5,296	1960	15,392	1995	15,392		3.1
22 Israel	38.5	20.2	27.6	3,537	3,537	1960	10,551	1995	10,551		3.2
23 Cyprus	36.5	41.7	18.5	2,390[b]	2,390	1975	7,542	1994	7,542[c]		6 2
24 Barbados	45.3	18.3	26.2	2,290	2,290	1960	6,372	1989	5,736		2.7
25 Hong Kong, China	40.1	35.2	26.6	1,631	1,631	1960	11,911	1995	11,911		5.8
26 Luxembourg	9.9	16.2	30.0	9,704	9,704	1960	21,851	1995	21,851		2.3
27 Malta	20.3	48.5	20.7	989	950	1962	6,240	1993	6,240[d]		5.7
28 Singapore	34.0	30.8	25.4	1,510	1,510	1960	13,451	1995	13,451		6.4
29 Antigua and Barbuda	..	..	..	2,982[e]	2,982	1980	5,879	1994	5,879[c]		5.0
30 Korea, Rep. of	20.9	30.0	57.8	520	520	1960	5,663	1995	5,663		7.1
31 Chile	23.6	22.3	38.5	1,162	1,162	1960	2,532	1995	2,532		2.3
32 Bahamas	..	..	..	6,770	6,477	1975	11,362	1989	10,110		1.2
33 Portugal	23.8	35.9	38.6	1,402	1,402	1960	5,175	1995	5,175		3.8
34 Costa Rica	21.4	28.2	40.1	1,053	1,004	1961	1,904	1994	1,899		1.7
35 Brunei Darussalam	..	..	..	13,275[f]	10,846	1993	19,148	1979	10,908		-0.9
36 Argentina	24.5	16.4	30.1	2,701	2,607	1963	4,032	1994	3,793		1.0
37 Slovenia	..	..	..	..	..	..	..	..	..		..
38 Uruguay	9.7	28.4	17.1	1,937	1,864	1967	2,867	1994	2,786		1.0
39 Czech Rep.	..	..	..	3,395[g]	2,937	1993	3,726	1989	3,164		-0.6
40 Trinidad and Tobago	19.7	13.1	21.0	2,442	2,442	1960	5,356	1981	3,858		1.3
41 Dominica	..	..	..	1,192	970	1979	2,147	1994	2,147[c]		1.7
42 Slovakia	..	..	..	3,340[g]	2,741	1993	3,714	1989	3,054		-0.8
43 Bahrain	..	..	..	10,037[e]	6,921	1987	10,037	1980	8,080		-1.4
44 Fiji	..	..	..	1,116	1,075	1966	2,110	1995	2,110		1.8
45 Panama	20.8	23.4	41.2	1,068	1,068	1960	2,434	1995	2,434		2.4
46 Venezuela	32.0	20.5	16.7	2,815	2,459	1989	3,409	1977	2,648		-0.2
47 Hungary	21.2	45.2	15.3	742	742	1960	2,511	1989	2,334		3.3
48 United Arab Emirates	17.8	29.6	18.4	34,429[f]	14,588	1988	34,429	1973	16,858[h]		-4.1
49 Mexico	25.8	32.5	18.9	938	938	1960	2,070	1981	1,724		1.8
50 Saint Kitts and Nevis	..	..	..	1,427[i]	1,427	1977	3,736	1995	3,736		5.5
51 Grenada	..	..	..	1,498[j]	1,498	1985	2,101	1995	2,101		3.4
52 Poland	..	..	..	1,682[e]	1,416	1982	1,756	1989	1,701		0.1
53 Colombia	16.1	22.9	45.6	639	639	1960	1,377	1995	1,377		2.2
54 Kuwait	..	..	..	35,866[k]	10,578	1988	36,201	1971	17,016		-2.9
55 Saint Vincent	..	..	..	743	671	1967	1,813	1995	1,813		2.6
56 Seychelles	..	..	..	1,803	1,677	1961	5,046	1993	4,965[c]		3.0
57 Qatar	..	..	..	..	..	..	..	..	..		..
58 Saint Lucia	..	..	..	1,737[j]	1,737	1985	2,792	1995	2,792		4.9
59 Thailand	14.6	16.0	55.1	300	300	1960	1,843	1995	1,843		5.3
60 Malaysia	21.0	40.9	34.1	708	708	1960	3,108	1995	3,108		4.3
61 Mauritius	7.3	21.4	40.7	1,343[l]	1,297	1980	2,516	1995	2,516		3.4
62 Brazil	18.7	33.7	25.3	823	823	1960	2,092	1987	2,051		2.6
63 Belize	..	..	..	750	750	1960	2,130	1992	2,113		3.0
64 Libyan Arab Jamahiriya	..	..	..	3,275	3,275	1960	17,025	1970	5,344[m]		1.7

6 Trends in human development and economic growth (continued)

	Reduction in shortfall (1-HDI) in human development index (HDI) value (%)			GDP per capita (1987 US$)						
HDI rank	1960-70	1970-80	1980-92	1960[a]	Lowest value during 1960-95[a]	Year	Highest value during 1960-95[a]	Year	1995[a]	Average annual rate of change (%) 1960-95[a]
Medium human development	..	..	..	..	..		..		..	..
65 Suriname	..	..	..	1,021[k]	1,021	1970	2,690	1987	2,101	2.9
66 Lebanon	..	..	..	..	..		..		..	..
67 Bulgaria	..	..	..	2,344[e]	2,344	1980	3,510	1988	2,605	0.7
68 Belarus	..	..	..	2,460[n]	1,712	1995	2,778	1989	1,712	-4.4
69 Turkey	16.2	19.3	42.1	753	745	1961	1,893	1993	1,865	2.6
70 Saudi Arabia	11.3	24.1	30.5	3,930[o]	3,930	1962	10,225	1980	5,008	0.7
71 Oman	..	..	..	750	740	1961	5,733	1985	5,603	5.9
72 Russian Federation	..	..	..	1,700[k]	1,700	1970	3,328	1989	1,988	0.6
73 Ecuador	11.0	24.8	27.2	626[p]	622	1966	1,241	1995	1,241	2.3
74 Romania	..	..	..	1,105[b]	1,105	1975	1,756	1986	1,358	1.0
75 Korea, Dem. People's Rep. of	..	..	..	..	..		..		..	..
76 Croatia	..	..	..	..	..		..		..	..
77 Estonia	..	..	..	3,354[e]	2,448	1994	4,014	1989	2,530	-1.9
78 Iran, Islamic Rep. of	14.3	15.4	34.8	4,302	2,504	1988	4,976	1976	2,902	-1.9
79 Lithuania	..	..	..	2,482[n]	1,613	1993	2,799	1989	1,683	-4.7
80 Macedonia, FYR	..	..	..	..	..		..		..	..
81 Syrian Arab Rep.	14.7	41.1	20.3	641[r]	554	1966	1,267	1995	1,267	2.2
82 Algeria	8.0	22.6	14.7	1,988	1,327	1962	2,966	1985	2,389	0.5
83 Tunisia	11.0	24.1	38.2	547[s]	547	1961	1,436	1995	1,436	2.9
84 Jamaica	28.1	-2.3	27.5	1,154	1,133	1962	1,851	1972	1,578	0.9
85 Cuba	..	..	..	..	..		..		..	..
86 Peru	18.7	13.0	12.7	964	859	1992	1,228	1981	1,033	0.2
87 Jordan	15.5	24.8	16.9	2,245[t]	1,420	1991	2,293	1987	1,629[c]	-2.9
88 Dominican Rep.	11.3	15.8	21.1	386	365	1961	838	1995	838	2.2
89 South Africa	23.8	9.2	5.7	1,808	1,808	1960	2,663	1981	2,165	0.5
90 Sri Lanka	5.8	9.3	25.3	204	204	1960	512	1995	512	2.7
91 Paraguay	7.0	18.7	19.3	525	525	1960	1,100	1981	1,049	2.0
92 Latvia	..	..	..	1,020	1,020	1960	3,559	1989	1,912	1.8
93 Kazakhstan	..	..	..	1,844[n]	961	1995	1,882	1988	961	-7.8
94 Samoa (Western)	..	..	..	638[u]	585	1982	703	1979	596[v]	-0.5
95 Maldives	..	..	..	421[j]	421	1985	693	1995	693	5.1
96 Indonesia	10.6	16.1	28.9	190	187	1967	720	1995	720	3.9
97 Botswana	9.7	18.1	43.7	238	223	1965	1,857	1995	1,857	6.1
98 Philippines	12.0	13.3	14.4	418	418	1960	691	1982	630	1.2
99 Armenia	..	..	..	887[k]	520	1993	1,962	1989	587	-1.6
100 Guyana	..	..	..	475	394	1990	633	1976	541	0.4
101 Mongolia	..	..	..	1,360[e]	1,240	1993	1,778	1989	1,294	-0.3
102 Ukraine	..	..	..	2,045[n]	999	1995	2,158	1989	999	-8.6
103 Turkmenistan	..	..	..	..	..		..		..	..
104 Uzbekistan	..	..	..	755[n]	592	1995	808	1989	592	-3.0
105 Albania	..	..	..	698[e]	679	1992	908	1990	887	1.6
106 China	16.4	16.4	32.2	75	46	1962	481	1995	481	5.5
107 Namibia	..	..	..	1,792[e]	1,475	1990	1,792	1980	1,577	-0.8
108 Georgia	..	..	..	715	433	1995	2,343	1985	433	-1.4
109 Kyrgyzstan	..	..	..	900[w]	501	1995	1,072	1990	501	-6.3
110 Azerbaijan	..	..	..	1,278[n]	355	1995	1,278	1987	355	-14.8
111 Guatemala	11.7	14.0	16.6	616	616	1960	1,045	1980	898	1.1
112 Egypt	7.4	12.4	29.9	237	237	1960	745	1990	726	3.2
113 Moldova, Rep. of	..	..	..	..	..		..		..	..
114 El Salvador	12.6	5.6	16.3	769	769	1960	1,172	1978	1,024	0.8
115 Swaziland	..	..	..	310	310	1960	826	1987	800	2.8
116 Bolivia	8.9	11.5	15.8	610	610	1960	925	1978	790	0.7
117 Cape Verde	..	..	..	298[k]	247	1974	654	1994	654[c]	3.3
118 Tajikistan	..	..	..	789[w]	255	1995	813	1988	255	-11.8
119 Honduras	9.8	13.0	15.8	691	680	1961	1,004	1979	904	0.8
120 Gabon	16.1	14.5	10.7	2,307	2,307	1960	9,017	1976	3,640	1.3
122 São Tomé and Principe	..	..	..	517[k]	481	1995	714	1980	481	-0.3
122 Viet Nam	..	..	..	534[g]	534	1984	816	1995	816	3.9
123 Solomon Islands	..	..	..	416[x]	273	1972	658	1995	658	1.6
124 Vanuatu	..	..	..	947[y]	789	1992	967	1984	820[c]	-1.0
125 Morocco	10.6	14.1	26.9	484	463	1961	956	1991	871	1.7
126 Nicaragua	18.0	13.4	10.5	1,295	806	1994	2,120	1977	816	-1.3
127 Iraq	15.9	23.5	8.0	3,420	784	1991	8,313	1979	784[z]	-4.6
128 Congo	8.7	8.8	14.7	511	511	1960	1,326	1984	906	1.6
129 Papua New Guinea	14.8	3.3	9.2	570	570	1960	1,120	1994	1,059	1.8
130 Zimbabwe	5.8	8.9	14.3	460	460	1960	705	1974	604	0.8

HDI rank	Reduction in shortfall (1-HDI) in human development index (HDI) value (%)			GDP per capita (1987 US$)						
	1960-70	1970-80	1980-92	1960[a]	Lowest value during 1960-95[a]	Year	Highest value during 1960-95[a]	Year	1995[a]	Average annual rate of change (%) 1960-95[a]
Low human development	..	..	..	..	..	..	..	..	..	..
131 Myanmar	10.0	5.5	7.8	..	..	..	..	..	..	..
132 Cameroon	7.6	10.6	17.2	601	543	1967	1,238	1986	727	0.5
133 Ghana	6.5	5.7	8.7	497	344	1983	529	1971	420	-0.5
134 Lesotho	8.2	14.1	12.0	97	97	1960	354	1995	354	3.8
135 Equatorial Guinea	..	..	..	346[w]	346	1986	451	1995	451	3.0
136 Lao People's Dem. Rep.	..	..	..	287[g]	271	1988	363	1995	363	2.2
137 Kenya	7.7	11.5	14.2	218	195	1961	395	1990	375	1.6
138 Pakistan	7.4	5.7	14.8	135	135	1960	381	1995	381	3.0
139 India	5.9	5.7	12.2	206	206	1960	425	1995	425	2.1
140 Cambodia	..	..	..	104[n]	104	1987	133	1995	133	3.0
141 Comoros	..	..	..	458[e]	415	1995	502	1984	415	-0.7
142 Nigeria	5.7	8.7	7.2	329	256	1967	446	1977	355	0.2
143 Dem. Rep. of the Congo	6.8	6.7	7.7	288	153	1995	332	1974	153[v]	-2.0
144 Togo	6.9	8.7	7.5	244	244	1960	472	1980	327	0.8
145 Benin	3.8	4.2	7.9	320	309	1962	385	1985	362[c]	0.4
146 Zambia	7.7	3.9	1.6	412	257	1995	463	1974	257	-1.3
147 Bangladesh	4.0	4.4	9.7	146	127	1973	202	1995	202	0.9
148 Côte d'Ivoire	9.0	11.5	6.0	500	500	1960	1,353	1979	732	1.1
149 Mauritania	..	..	..	359	354	1963	581	1970	503	1.0
150 Tanzania, U. Rep. of	5.8	9.0	3.4	147[t]	146	1984	155	1995	155	0.4
151 Yemen	5.0	13.4	9.3	..	..	..	..	..	..	..
152 Nepal	3.9	5.6	10.1	148	147	1973	206	1995	206	0.9
153 Madagascar	7.0	7.5	8.0	340	199	1995	361	1971	199	-1.5
154 Central African Rep.	4.3	3.7	3.0	426	333	1993	466	1977	357	-0.5
155 Bhutan	..	..	..	313[e]	313	1980	571	1995	571	4.1
156 Angola	6.5	2.1	7.5	832[j]	596	1993	898	1988	641	-2.6
157 Sudan	3.4	5.0	6.1	814	645	1973	965	1977	800[c]	-0.1
158 Senegal	3.5	6.9	11.6	713	615	1994	752	1976	661	-0.2
159 Haiti	5.4	9.8	8.4	386	226	1994	428	1980	231	-1.5
160 Uganda	3.5	0.2	7.3	460[t]	419	1986	557	1995	557	1.6
161 Malawi	3.8	4.9	5.6	102	102	1960	176	1979	146	1.0
162 Djibouti	..	..	..	..	..	..	..	..	..	..
163 Chad	2.6	1.9	7.2	198[k]	127	1981	198	1970	178	-0.4
164 Guinea-Bissau	3.7	2.6	9.0	202[k]	144	1980	216	1994	214	0.2
165 Gambia	4.2	4.6	7.9	189	189	1960	339	1982	274	1.1
166 Mozambique	9.4	-0.1	0.7	129[e]	86	1986	133	1981	133	0.2
167 Guinea	3.0	4.3	5.0	365[w]	365	1986	404	1995	404	1.1
168 Eritrea	..	..	..	..	..	..	..	..	..	..
169 Ethiopia	..	..	..	179[t]	132	1992	179	1983	154	-1.2
170 Burundi	3.0	7.3	7.3	125	106	1961	233	1991	182	1.1
171 Mali	2.0	5.0	7.9	217	212	1962	288	1979	256	0.5
172 Burkina Faso	3.2	4.0	6.1	173	173	1960	269	1991	258	1.2
173 Niger	4.8	3.4	5.5	556	274	1993	573	1971	275	-2.0
174 Sierra Leone	6.6	2.6	3.8	119	119	1960	253	1983	171	1.0
All developing countries	..	..	..	..	..	..	..	..	..	..
Least developed countries	..	..	..	..	..	..	..	..	..	..
Industrial countries	..	..	..	..	..	..	..	..	..	..
World	..	..	..	..	..	..	..	..	..	..

Note: There is a break in the data series reported in this table. Data for 1960-69 are from World Bank, World Data 1995, CD-ROM. Data for 1970-95 are from World Bank 1997d.
a. The earliest year for which data are given is 1960 and the latest year 1995, unless otherwise specified.
b. 1975.
c. 1994.
d. 1993.
e. 1980.
f. 1973.
g. 1984.
h. 1990.
i. 1977.
j. 1985.
k. 1970.
l. 1976.
m. 1989.
n. 1987.
o. 1962.
p. 1965.
q. 1974.
r. 1963.
s. 1961.
t. 1983.
u. 1978.
v. 1992.
w. 1986.
x. 1967.
y. 1979.
z. 1991.
Source: Columns 1-3: Human Development Report Office calculations; *columns 4-9:* World Bank 1995b;. 1997d; *column 10:* calculated on the basis of data from: World Bank 1995b; 1997d.

HDI rank	Human poverty index (HPI-1) value (%) 1995	People not expected to survive to age 40 (as % of total population) 1995	Adult illiteracy rate (%) 1995	Population without access to Safe water (%) 1990-96	Health services (%) 1990-95	Sanitation (%) 1990-96	Under-weight children under age five (%) 1990-97	Children not reaching grade 5 (%) 1995	Refugees by country of asylum (thousands) 1996	Real GDP per capita (PPP$) Poorest 20% 1980-94	Richest 20% 1980-94	Population below income poverty line (%) $1 a day (1985 PPP$) 1989-94	National poverty line 1989-94
High human development	..	8	10.5	18	..	22	12	21	209.3 T	1,237	19,706	17.0	21.6
23 Cyprus	..	3	..	..	..	..	..	0	0	..	..	..	..
24 Barbados	..	3	2.6	0	..	0	5 a	..	0	..	..	..	..
25 Hong Kong, China	..	2	7.8	..	..	..	..	0	6.9	5,821	50,666	..	..
28 Singapore	6.5	2	8.9	0	0 a	..	14 a	..	0	4,934	47,311	..	..
29 Antigua and Barbuda	..	..	..	..	..	4	10 a	..	..	..	..	..	12.0
30 Korea, Rep. of	..	4	2.0	7	0	0	..	0	0	..	..	..	..
31 Chile	4.1	4	4.8	5	3 a	..	1	8	0.3	1,558	27,145	15.0	..
32 Bahamas	..	6	1.8	..	..	..	..	22	0	..	..	..	..
34 Costa Rica	6.6	4	5.2	4	20 a	16	2	11	23.2	1,136	14,399	18.9	11.0
35 Brunei Darussalam	..	3	11.8	..	..	..	..	5	..	..	..	..	..
36 Argentina	..	6	3.8	29	29 a	32	..	..	10.4	..	..	..	26.0
38 Uruguay	4.1	5	2.7	5 a	0 b	..	7 a	6	0.1	..	..	..	21.0
40 Trinidad and Tobago	3.3	4	2.1	3	0	21	7 a	5	..	..	..	..	21.0
41 Dominica	..	..	..	4	..	20	5 a	16	6	..	..	..	33.0
43 Bahrain	..	5	14.8	..	..	..	..	6	..	..	..	..	..
44 Fiji	..	5	8.4	0	..	8	..	13	0	..	..	..	..
45 Panama	11.1	6	9.2	7	30	17	7	..	0.9	589	17,611	25.6	..
46 Venezuela	..	6	8.9	21	..	41	6 a	22	1.6	1,505	24,411	11.8	31.0
48 United Arab Emirates	14.5	3	20.8	5	1	23	6 c	2	0.5	..	..	..	..
49 Mexico	10.7	8	10.4	17	7	28	14 a	16	34.6	1,437	19,383	14.9	34.0
50 Saint Kitts and Nevis	..	..	..	0	..	0	..	..	..	..	..	..	15.0
51 Grenada	..	..	..	..	..	..	..	..	..	..	..	..	20.0
53 Colombia	11.1	9	8.7	15	19	15	8	42	0.2	1,042	16,154	7.4	19.0
54 Kuwait	..	3	21.4	..	0 a	..	6 a	1	3.8	..	..	..	..
55 Saint Vincent	..	..	..	11	..	2	..	..	..	..	..	..	17.0
56 Seychelles	..	..	..	..	..	..	6 a	3	..	..	..	..	..
57 Qatar	..	5	20.6	..	..	..	..	5	..	..	..	..	..
58 Saint Lucia	..	..	..	..	..	..	..	5	..	..	..	..	25.0
59 Thailand	11.9	10	6.2	11	10 a	4	26 a	..	108.0	1,778	16,732	0.1	13.0
60 Malaysia	..	5	16.5	22	..	6	23	6	0.2	1,923	22,447	5.6	16.0
61 Mauritius	12.1	4	17.1	2	0 a	0	16	1	..	..	..	..	11.0
62 Brazil	..	11	16.7	24	..	30	6	29	2.2	578	18,563	28.7	17.0
63 Belize	..	6	..	11	..	43	..	30	8.5	..	..	..	35.0
64 Libyan Arab Jamahiriya	17.4	13	23.8	3	5	2	5	..	7.7	..	..	..	..
Medium human development	..	9	19.6	31	13	61	19	11	2,781.8 T	848	5,750	25.9	15.0
Excluding China	..	12	21.4	29	13	37	23	15	2,491.7 T	1,108	7,068	..	..
65 Suriname	..	6	7.0	..	..	..	..	..	..	..	..	..	..
66 Lebanon	..	7	7.6	6	5	37	..	..	2.4	..	..	..	..
69 Turkey	..	10	17.7	51	..	38	10	11	8.2	..	..	..	..
70 Saudi Arabia	..	6	37.2	5 a	3 a	14 a	..	6	9.9	..	..	..	..
71 Oman	28.9	6	41.0 d	18	4	22	23	4	..	..	..	..	..
73 Ecuador	15.3	11	9.9	32	12 a	24	17 a	23	0.2	1,188	11,572	30.4	35.0
75 Korea, Dem. People's Rep. of	..	5	..	19	..	..	..	..	..	..	..	..	..
78 Iran, Islamic Rep. of	22.2	10	31.0 d	10	12	19	16	10	2,030.4	..	..	..	..
81 Syrian Arab Rep.	20.9	8	29.2	14	10	33	13	9	27.8	..	..	..	..
82 Algeria	27.1	9	38.4	22	2	9	13	5	190.3	1,922	12,839	1.6 a	..
83 Tunisia	23.3	8	33.3	2	10 a	20	9	8	0.2	1,460	11,459	3.9	14.0
84 Jamaica	11.8	5	15.0	14	10 a	11	10	..	0	922	7,553	4.7	32.0
85 Cuba	..	4	4.3	7	0	34	..	6	1.7	..	..	..	..
86 Peru	23.1	12	11.3	33	56	28	8	..	0.7	813	8,366	49.4	32.0
87 Jordan	10.0	8	13.4	2	3 a	23	9	2	0.9	1,292	10,972	2.5	15.0
88 Dominican Rep.	17.4	9	17.9	35	22	22	6	42	0.6	775	10,277	19.9	21.0
89 South Africa	..	13	18.2	1	..	47	9	35	22.6	516	9,897	23.7	..
90 Sri Lanka	20.6	6	9.8	43	7 a	37	38	2	0	1,348	5,954	4.0	22.0
91 Paraguay	19.1	9	7.9	40	37 a	59	4	29	0.1	..	..	..	22.0
94 Samoa (Western)	..	10	..	18	..	6	..	..	..	..	..	..	..
95 Maldives	..	13	6.8	4	..	34	39	7	..	..	..	..	..
96 Indonesia	20.2	13	16.2	38	7	49	34	10	0.1	1,422	6,654	14.5	8.0
97 Botswana	27.0	31	30.2	7 a	11 a	45	15 a	11	0.2	..	..	34.7 a	..
98 Philippines	17.7	9	5.4	16	29	25	30	30	2.3	842	6,190	27.5 a	41.0
100 Guyana	..	14	1.9	39	..	19	18	..	..	..	..	..	43.0
101 Mongolia	14.0	11	17.1	20 c	5 a	14	12	..	..	..	..	..	36.0
106 China	17.1	7	18.5	33	12	76	16	8	290.1	722	5,114	29.4	11.0
107 Namibia	30.0	26	24.0 d	43	41	66	26	18	2.2	..	..	..	..
111 Guatemala	29.3	14	35.0	23	43	17	27	..	1.6	357	10,710	53.0	58.0
112 Egypt	34.0	13	48.6	13	1	12	15	2	6.0	1,653	7,809	7.6	..

HDI rank	Human poverty index (HPI-1) value (%) 1995	People not expected to survive to age 40 (as % of total population) 1995	Adult illiteracy rate (%) 1995	Population without access to Safe water (%) 1990-96	Health services (%) 1990-95	Sanitation (%) 1990-96	Under-weight children under age five (%) 1990-97	Children not reaching grade 5 (%) 1995	Refugees by country of asylum (thousands) 1996	Real GDP per capita (PPP$) Poorest 20% 1980-94	Richest 20% 1980-94	Population below income poverty line (%) $1 a day (1985 PPP$) 1989-94	National poverty line 1989-94
114 El Salvador	27.8	12	28.5	31	60	19	11	42	0.2	..	..	..	38.0
115 Swaziland	..	21	23.3	40	..	30	10 a	22	0.6	..	..	..	..
116 Bolivia	21.6	18	16.9	37	33	42	11	..	0.7	703	6,049	7.1	..
117 Cape Verde	..	13	28.4	49	..	76	19 a	..	..	..	..	..	44.0
119 Honduras	21.8	12	27.3	13	31	13	18	40	0.1	399	6,027	46.5	53.0
120 Gabon	..	26	36.8	32 a	..	..	..	..	0.8	..	..	..	..
121 São Tomé and Principe	..	..	..	18	..	65	17 a	..	..	..	..	..	46.0
122 Viet Nam	26.1	11	6.3	57	10	79	45	..	34.4	406	2,288	..	51.0
123 Solomon Islands	..	6	..	39	..	89	..	19	2.0	..	..	..	..
124 Vanuatu	..	10	..	13 a	..	9 a	20	39	..	..	..	..	..
125 Morocco	40.2	12	56.3	35	30 a	42	9	22	0.1	1,079	7,570	1.1	13.0
126 Nicaragua	26.2	12	34.3	39	17 a	69	12	46	0.6	479	6,293	43.8	50.0
127 Iraq	30.1	17	42.0	22	7 a	30	12	..	113.0	..	..	..	..
128 Congo	31.5	32	25.1	66	17 a	31	24 a	46	20.5	..	..	..	..
129 Papua New Guinea	29.8	19	27.8	72	4 a	78	35 a	41	10.2	..	..	..	..
130 Zimbabwe	25.2	34	14.9	21	15	48	16	24	0.6	420	6,542	41.0	26.0
Low human development	..	22	49.0	29	30	65	45	36	5,565.3 T	531	2,884	43.8	..
Excluding India	..	27	50.3	41	48	58	37	32	5,332.0 T				
131 Myanmar	27.5	19	16.9	40	40	57	31	..	..	..	..	..	..
132 Cameroon	30.9	26	36.6	50	20	50	14	..	46.4	..	..	..	..
133 Ghana	31.8	23	35.5	35	40	45	27	..	35.6	790	4,220	..	31.0
134 Lesotho	25.7	23	28.7	38	20 a	62	16	21	..	137	2,945	50.4	26.0
135 Equatorial Guinea	..	34	21.5	5	..	46	..	..	..	..	..	..	..
136 Lao People's Dem. Rep.	39.4	28	43.4	56	33 a	82	40	47	..	700	2,931	..	46.0
137 Kenya	27.1	27	21.9	47	23	23	23	32	223.6	238	4,347	50.2	37.0
138 Pakistan	46.0	15	62.2	26	45 a	53	38	..	1,202.7	907	4,288	11.6	34.0
139 India	35.9	16	48.0	19	15	71	53	38	233.4	527	2,641	52.5	..
140 Cambodia	39.9	27	35.0 d	64	47 a	86	40	50	0	..	..	..	..
141 Comoros	..	22	42.7	47	..	77	26	22	..	..	..	..	..
142 Nigeria	40.5	31	42.9	50	49	43	36	20	8.5	308	3,796	28.9	21.0
143 Dem. Rep. of the Congo	41.1	30	22.7	58	74 a	82	34	36	676.0	..	..	..	..
144 Togo	39.8	33	48.3	45	39 a	59	19	29	12.6	..	..	..	17.3
145 Benin	..	27	63.0	50	82 a	80	..	39	6.0	..	..	..	33.0
146 Zambia	36.9	42	21.8	73	25 a	36	24	16	131.1	216	2,797	84.6	86.0
147 Bangladesh	46.5	21	61.9	3	55	52	56	..	30.7	606	2,445	28.5	48.0
148 Côte d'Ivoire	46.4	32	59.9	18 e	70 a	61	24	27	327.7	551	3,572	17.7 a	..
149 Mauritania	45.9	29	62.3	26	37	68	23	37	15.9	290	3,743	31.4 a	57.0
150 Tanzania, U. Rep. of	39.8	31	32.2	62	58	14	27	17	498.7	217	1,430	16.4	50.0
151 Yemen	48.9	22	62.0 e	39	62	76	39	..	53.5	..	..	..	..
152 Nepal	..	22	72.5	37	..	82	47	48	126.8	455	1,975	53.1 a	..
153 Madagascar	47.7	21	54.2 b	66	62	59	34	72	..	203	1,750	72.3	59.0
154 Central African Rep.	40.7	35	40.0	62	48	73	27	..	36.6	..	..	..	..
155 Bhutan	44.9	28	57.8	42	35 a	30	38 a	18	..	..	..	..	..
156 Angola	..	38	..	68	..	84	..	..	9.4	..	..	..	..
157 Sudan	42.5	27	53.9	50	30	78	34	6	393.9	..	..	..	..
158 Senegal	48.6	32	66.9	37	10	61	22	19	65.0	299	5,010	54.0	..
159 Haiti	44.5	25	55.0	63	40	75	28	..	..	..	..	..	..
160 Uganda	42.1	44	38.2	54	51	43	26	..	264.3	309	2,189	50.0	55.0
161 Malawi	47.7	46	43.6	63	65	94	30	..	1.3	..	..	42.1	..
162 Djibouti	..	33	53.8	10	..	45	23	6	25.1	..	..	..	..
163 Chad	..	37	51.9	76	70	79	..	72	0.1	..	..	..	..
164 Guinea-Bissau	42.9	42	45.1	41	60	70	23 a	..	15.4	90	2,533	87.0	49.0
165 Gambia	..	38	61.4	52	7	63	..	..	6.9	..	..	..	64.0
166 Mozambique	48.5	38	59.9	37	61 a	46	27	53	0.2	..	..	..	..
167 Guinea	49.1	38	64.1	54	20	69	26	20	663.9	270	4,518	26.3	..
168 Eritrea	..	33	..	78	..	..	44	21	2.1	..	..	..	..
169 Ethiopia	55.5	34	64.5	75	54	81	48	49	390.5	..	..	33.8 a	..
170 Burundi	49.5	37	64.7	48	20	49	37	..	1.0	..	..	..	..
171 Mali	52.8	36	69.0	34	60	94	27	28	18.2	..	..	..	..
172 Burkina Faso	58.2	38	80.8	22 f	10	63	30	21	2.8	..	..	..	..
173 Niger	62.1	36	86.4	52	1	83	36	23	25.8	296	1,742	61.5	..
174 Sierra Leone	58.2	50	68.6	66	62	89	29	..	13.5	..	..	..	75.0
All developing countries	..	14	29.6	29	20	58	30	22	8,556.4 T	768	6,195	32.2	..
Least developed countries	..	29	50.8	43	51	64	39 d	36	3,424.4 T	..	..	..	..
Industrial countries	..	5	1.4	..	..	..	..	1	3,889.8 T	4,811	32,273	..	..
World	..	13	22.4	..	..	..	30 d	21	12,446.2 T	1,759	12,584	..	..

a. Data refer to a year or period other than that specified in the column heading, differ from the standard definition or refer to only part of the country.
b. Human Development Report Office estimate based on national sources.
c. Carried over from UNDP 1997a.
d. UNICEF 1998b.
e. World Bank 1997d.
f. WHO, WSSCC and UNICEF 1996.
Source: Column 1: Human Development Report Office calculations; *column 2:* UN 1996d; *column 3:* calculated on the basis of: UNESCO 1997a; *columns 4, 6 and 7:* UNICEF 1998b; *column 5:* UNICEF 1997; *column 8:* UNESCO 1998; *column 9:* UNHCR 1996; *columns 10 and 11:* UNDP 1996a; *columns 12 and 13:* UNDP 1997a.

8 Trends in human development

HDI rank	Life expectancy at birth (years)		Infant mortality rate (per 1,000 live births)		Population with access to safe water (%)		Underweight children under age five (%)		Adult literacy rate (%)		Gross enrolment ratio for all levels (% age 6-23)		Real GDP per capita (PPP$)	
	1960	1995	1960	1996	1975-80	1990-96	1975	1990-97	1970	1995	1980	1995	1960	1995
High human development	55.9	70.1	98	29	59	82	21	12	76	90	58	70	1,944	7,835
23 Cyprus	68.6	77.2	30	9	..	..	..	..	..	..	..	..	2,039	13,379 [a,b]
24 Barbados	64.2	76.0	74	11	..	..	..	..	92	97	67	76	2,323	22,950
25 Hong Kong, China	66.2	79.0	..	..	..	..	..	..	79	92	59	72	2,409	22,604
28 Singapore	64.5	77.1	36	4	..	..	..	..	74	91	53	72	..	..
29 Antigua and Barbuda	..	..	..	..	..	..	..	..	..	..	..	..	..	..
30 Korea, Rep. of	53.9	71.7	85	6	66	93	..	..	87	98	66	82	690	11,594
31 Chile	57.1	75.1	114	11	..	..	2	1	88	95	65	72	3,130	9,930
32 Bahamas	63.2	73.2	50	19	..	..	..	..	95	98	70	75	..	..
34 Costa Rica	61.6	76.6	85	13	72	96	10	2	88	95	55	68	2,160	5,969
35 Brunei Darussalam	62.2	75.1	63	9	..	..	..	..	57	88	64	70	..	..
36 Argentina	64.9	72.6	60	22	..	..	..	..	93	96	65	77	3,381	8,498
38 Uruguay	67.7	72.7	50	20	..	..	6	7 [c]	93	97	63	75	4,401	6,854
40 Trinidad and Tobago	63.4	73.1	56	15	93	97	14	7 [c]	92	98	59	67	4,754	9,437
41 Dominica	..	..	..	..	..	..	..	..	..	..	..	..	..	..
43 Bahrain	55.5	72.2	130	18	..	..	..	..	53	85	58	85	..	..
44 Fiji	59.0	72.1	71	20	..	..	..	..	74	92	63	79	2,354	6,159
45 Panama	60.7	73.4	69	18	77	93	14	7	79	91	66	70	1,533	6,258
46 Venezuela	59.5	72.3	81	24	79	79	14	6 [c]	76	91	58	68	3,899	8,090
48 United Arab Emirates	53.0	74.4	145	15	..	..	..	..	54	79	44	82	..	..
49 Mexico	56.9	72.1	95	27	62	83	19	14 [c]	75	90	68	66	2,870	6,769
50 Saint Kitts and Nevis	..	..	..	..	..	..	..	..	..	..	..	..	..	..
51 Grenada	..	..	..	..	..	..	..	..	..	..	..	..	..	..
53 Colombia	56.5	70.3	99	26	64	85	19	8	81	91	53	70	1,874	6,347
54 Kuwait	59.5	75.4	89	13	..	..	..	..	57	79	..	..	..	..
55 Saint Vincent	..	..	..	..	..	..	..	..	..	..	..	..	..	..
56 Seychelles	..	..	..	..	..	..	..	..	..	..	..	..	..	..
57 Qatar	53.1	71.1	145	17	..	..	..	..	58	79	60	73	..	..
58 Saint Lucia	..	..	..	..	..	..	..	..	..	..	..	..	..	..
59 Thailand	52.3	69.5	103	31	25	89	36	26 [c]	78	94	49	53	985	7,742
60 Malaysia	53.9	71.4	72	11	..	..	31	23	57	84	54	62	1,783	9,572
61 Mauritius	59.2	70.9	70	20	99	98	32	16	65	83	48	61	2,113	13,294
62 Brazil	54.7	66.6	116	44	62	76	18	6	68	83	54	72	1,404	5,928
63 Belize	61.4	74.2	74	36	..	..	..	..	..	..	..	..	..	..
64 Libyan Arab Jamahiriya	46.7	64.3	160	50	87	97	..	..	36	76	..	..	..	..
Medium human development	47.1	67.5	145	40	..	..	30	19	53	81	51	64	864	3,355
Excluding China	47.1	66.0	139	43	..	..	36	23	57	79	52	65	1,172	3,945
65 Suriname	60.1	70.9	70	25	..	..	..	..	82	93	..	..	2,234	4,862
66 Lebanon	59.6	69.3	68	33	..	..	..	..	80	92	67	75	..	..
69 Turkey	50.1	68.5	190	41	68	49	15	10	57	82	44	63	1,669	5,516
70 Saudi Arabia	44.4	70.7	170	25	64	95 [c]	..	..	..	..	36	56	..	..
71 Oman	40.1	70.3	214	15	..	..	..	..	..	..	28	60	2,040	9,383
73 Ecuador	53.1	69.5	124	31	36	68	20	17 [c]	75	90	69	72	1,461	4,602
75 Korea, Dem. People's Rep. of	54.0	71.6	86	23	..	..	..	..	..	..	46	68	..	..
78 Iran, Islamic Rep. of	49.5	68.5	169	33	51	90	43	16	..	..	60	64	1,985	5,480
81 Syrian Arab Rep.	49.8	68.1	135	28	..	..	20	13	41	71	60	64	..	..
82 Algeria	47.0	68.1	168	34	77	78	23	13	25	62	52	66	1,676	5,618
83 Tunisia	48.3	68.7	159	28	35	98	17	9	28	67	50	67	1,394	5,261
84 Jamaica	62.7	74.1	63	10	86	86	14	10	70	85	67	65	1,829	3,801
85 Cuba	63.8	75.7	65	10	..	..	..	..	82	96	72	63	..	..
86 Peru	47.7	67.7	142	45	..	..	17	8	71	89	65	79	2,130	3,940
87 Jordan	46.9	68.9	135	21	..	..	18	9	54	87	..	..	1,328	4,187
88 Dominican Rep.	51.8	70.3	125	45	55	65	17	6	68	82	60	68	1,227	3,923
89 South Africa	49.0	64.1	89	50	..	..	..	..	70	82	..	..	2,984	4,334
90 Sri Lanka	62.0	72.5	71	17	19	57	58	38	80	90	58	66	1,389	3,408
91 Paraguay	63.9	69.1	66	28	13	60	9	4	81	92	49	62	1,220	3,583
94 Samoa (Western)	49.8	68.4	134	42	..	..	..	..	..	..	..	..	..	..
95 Maldives	43.6	63.3	160	54	..	..	..	..	87	93	..	..	..	..
96 Indonesia	41.2	64.0	139	47	11	62	51	34	56	84	51	62	490	3,971
97 Botswana	46.5	51.7	116	40	..	..	..	..	44	70	51	71	474	5,611
98 Philippines	52.8	67.4	79	32	..	..	39	30	84	95	61	78	1,183	2,762
100 Guyana	56.1	63.5	100	60	..	..	..	..	91	98	61	67	1,630	3,205
101 Mongolia	46.8	64.8	128	55	..	..	..	..	63	83	60	52	..	..
106 China	47.1	69.2	150	38	..	..	26	16	52	82	50	58	723	2,935
107 Namibia	42.5	55.8	146	60	..	..	..	..	..	..	..	..	..	..
111 Guatemala	45.6	66.1	125	43	39	77	30	27	44	65	35	46	1,667	3,682
112 Egypt	46.1	64.8	179	57	75	87	17	15	32	51	51	69	557	3,829

HDI rank	Life expectancy at birth (years)		Infant mortality rate (per 1,000 live births)		Population with access to safe water (%)		Underweight children under age five (%)		Adult literacy rate (%)		Gross enrolment ratio for all levels (% age 6-23)		Real GDP per capita (PPP$)	
	1960	1995	1960	1996	1975-80	1990-96	1975	1990-97	1970	1995	1980	1995	1960	1995
114 El Salvador	50.5	69.4	130	34	53	69	22	11	56	72	47	55	1,305	2,610
115 Swaziland	40.2	58.8	157	68	..	..	..	..	49	77	59	72	1,182	2,954
116 Bolivia	42.7	60.5	167	71	34	63	17	11	58	83	54	66	1,142	2,617
117 Cape Verde	52.0	65.7	110	54	..	..	..	..	36	72	45	64	..	..
119 Honduras	46.3	68.8	145	29	41	87	23	18	54	73	47	60	901	1,977
120 Gabon	40.8	54.5	171	87	..	..	..	..	26	63	..	..	1,373	3,766 a
121 São Tomé and Principe	..	..	..	..	..	..	..	..	..	..	..	..	..	..
122 Viet Nam	44.2	66.4	147	33	..	..	55	45	73	94	52	55	..	..
123 Solomon Islands	50.3	71.1	120	24	..	..	..	..	..	..	..	..	..	..
124 Vanuatu	46.5	66.3	141	41	..	..	..	..	..	..	..	..	..	..
125 Morocco	46.7	65.7	163	64	..	..	19	9	21	44	38	46	854	3,477
126 Nicaragua	47.0	67.5	141	44	46	61	20	12	57	66	53	62	1,756	1,837 a
127 Iraq	48.5	58.5	139	94	66	78	19	12	30	58	67	53	..	..
128 Congo	41.7	51.2	140	81	38	34	43	24 c	34	75	..	..	1,092	2,554
129 Papua New Guinea	40.6	56.8	165	79	20	28	39	35 c	47	72	28	38	1,136	2,500
130 Zimbabwe	45.3	48.9	109	49	..	..	25	16	66	85	41	68	937	2,135
Low human development	42.2	56.7	167	90	..	..	60	45	31	51	37	47	656	1,362
Excluding India	40.0	53.2	169	102	..	..	44	37	27	49	34	39	716	1,296
131 Myanmar	43.7	58.9	158	105	17	60	41	31	72	83	39	48	341	1,130 a,b
132 Cameroon	39.2	55.3	163	63	..	..	19	14	32	63	48	46	736	2,355
133 Ghana	45.0	57.0	132	70	35	65	35	27	31	65	48	44	1,049	2,032
134 Lesotho	42.9	58.1	149	96	17	62	20	16	47	71	52	56	346	1,290
135 Equatorial Guinea	36.8	49.0	188	111	..	..	..	..	46	79	57	64	..	..
136 Lao People's Dem. Rep.	40.4	52.2	155	102	..	..	..	..	32	57	44	50	..	..
137 Kenya	44.7	53.8	124	61	17	53	25	23	43	78	62	55	635	1,438
138 Pakistan	43.6	62.8	163	95	25	74	47	38	20	38	19	38	820	2,209
139 India	44.0	61.6	165	73	..	..	71	53	34	52	40	56	617	1,422
140 Cambodia	42.4	52.9	146	108	..	..	..	..	..	..	..	..	..	..
141 Comoros	42.5	56.5	165	83	..	..	..	..	42	57	45	39	..	..
142 Nigeria	39.5	51.4	189	114	..	..	30	36	21	57	50	50	1,133	1,270
143 Dem. Rep. of the Congo	41.3	52.4	153	128	19	42	..	..	44	77	46	38	..	..
144 Togo	39.3	50.5	182	78	16	55	25	19	23	52	61	50	411	1,167
145 Benin	36.9	54.4	179	84	34	50	..	..	10	37	34	35	1,075	1,800
146 Zambia	41.6	42.7	135	112	42	27	17	24	48	78	46	48	1,172	986
147 Bangladesh	39.6	56.9	156	83	..	..	84	56	25	38	30	39	621	1,382
148 Côte d'Ivoire	39.2	51.8	165	90	..	..	18	24	16	40	39	39	1,021	1,731
149 Mauritania	38.5	52.5	177	124	..	..	39	23	27	38	19	36	930	1,622
150 Tanzania, U. Rep. of	40.5	50.6	147	93	39	38	25	27	37	68	44	34	272	636
151 Yemen	35.9	56.7	224	78	..	..	33	39	..	..	..	..	..	..
152 Nepal	38.3	55.9	195	82	8	63	..	..	14	28	28	55	584	1,145
153 Madagascar	40.7	57.6	178	100	..	..	30	34	..	..	60	33	1,013	673
154 Central African Rep.	38.5	48.4	174	103	..	..	..	..	13	60	33	37	806	1,092
155 Bhutan	37.3	52.0	203	90	..	..	..	..	20	42	..	..	..	..
156 Angola	33.0	47.4	208	170	17	32	..	..	..	..	54	31	..	..
157 Sudan	39.2	52.2	160	73	..	..	..	..	21	46	25	31	..	..
158 Senegal	37.2	50.3	172	74	36	63	19	22	15	33	24	31	1,136	1,815
159 Haiti	42.1	54.6	182	94	12	37	26	28	24	45	..	..	921	917
160 Uganda	43.0	40.5	133	88	35	46	28	26	37	62	25	34	371	1,483
161 Malawi	37.8	41.0	206	137	51	37	19	30	38	56	33	67	423	773
162 Djibouti	36.0	49.2	186	112	..	..	..	..	23	46	19	20	..	..
163 Chad	34.8	47.2	195	92	..	..	..	..	24	48	16	25	785	1,172
164 Guinea-Bissau	34.0	43.4	200	132	10	59	..	..	30	55	27	29	..	..
165 Gambia	32.3	46.0	213	78	..	..	..	..	17	39	23	34	411	948
166 Mozambique	37.3	46.3	190	133	..	..	..	..	16	40	29	25	1,368	959
167 Guinea	33.6	45.5	203	130	14	46	..	..	16	36	21	24	..	..
168 Eritrea	39.1	50.2	166	78	..	..	..	..	..	..	..	..	..	..
169 Ethiopia	35.9	48.7	187	113	8	25	45	48	16	36	16	18	262	455
170 Burundi	41.3	44.5	153	106	29	52	27	37	18	35	11	31	473	637
171 Mali	34.8	47.0	209	134	..	..	36	27	7	31	..	..	541	565
172 Burkina Faso	36.1	46.3	186	82	25	22 d	34	30	8	19	8	20	290	784
173 Niger	35.3	47.5	191	191	..	..	50	36	6	14	12	15	604	765
174 Sierra Leone	31.5	34.7	219	164	14	34	22	29	13	31	30	28	871	625
All developing countries	46.0	62.2	149	65	..	71	40	30	48	70	46	57	915	3,068
Least developed countries	39.1	51.2	170	109 e	..	57	..	39 e	30	49	32	36	562	1,008
Industrial countries	68.6	74.2	39	13	..	..	..	..	..	99	..	83	..	16,337
World	50.2	63.6	129	60 e	..	..	..	30 e	..	78	..	62	..	5,990

Note: Aggregates differ from those in other tables due to lack of trend data.
a. Preliminary update of the Penn World Tables using an expanded set of international comparisons, as described in Summers and Heston 1991.
b. Provisional.
c. Data refer to a year or period other than that specified in the column heading, differ from the standard definition or refer to only part of the country.
d. WHO, WSSCC and UNICEF 1996.
e. UNICEF 1998b.
Source: Columns 1 and 2: UN 1996d; *columns 3-8:* UNICEF 1998b; *columns 9-12:* UNESCO 1997a; *column 13:* Summers and Heston; 1991; *column 14:* calculations based on World Bank 1997a.

Index: North=100 (see note)

HDI rank	Life expectancy at birth		Adult literacy		Daily calorie supply per capita		Access to safe water		Under-five mortality	
	1960	1995	1970	1995	1970	1995	1975-80	1990-96	1960	1996
High human development	81	95	77	91	84	91	59	84	34	45
23 Cyprus	100	100+	..	..	100+	100+	..	..	100+	100+
24 Barbados	94	100+	93	99	93	100	..	..	54	100+
25 Hong Kong, China	97	100+	80	94	91	100+	..	..	..	..
28 Singapore	94	100+	75	92	..	..	..	..	100+	72
29 Antigua and Barbuda	..	..	..	..	83	73	..	..	..	72
30 Korea, Rep. of	79	97	88	99	93	100	67	94	39	100+
31 Chile	83	100+	89	97	87	86	..	..	36	100+
32 Bahamas	92	99	96	100	85	78	..	..	72	69
34 Costa Rica	90	100+	89	96	79	90	73	97	44	100+
35 Brunei Darussalam	91	100+	58	89	77	89	..	..	56	100+
36 Argentina	95	98	94	98	100+	98	..	..	68	63
38 Uruguay	99	98	93	99	100+	89	..	..	88	72
40 Trinidad and Tobago	92	99	93	99	82	81	94	98	67	93
41 Dominica	..	..	..	..	67	94	..	..	..	79
43 Bahrain	81	97	54	86	..	..	..	..	24	72
44 Fiji	86	97	74	93	79	96	..	..	51	66
45 Panama	88	99	80	92	74	78	78	94	47	79
46 Venezuela	87	98	77	92	..	..	80	80	70	56
48 United Arab Emirates	77	100	55	80	100+	100+	..	..	20	88
49 Mexico	83	97	76	91	89	99	63	84	33	49
50 Saint Kitts and Nevis	..	..	..	..	58	68	..	..	..	42
51 Grenada	..	..	..	..	72	83	..	..	..	51
53 Colombia	82	95	82	93	68	87	65	86	38	51
54 Kuwait	87	100+	58	80	..	..	..	..	38	100+
55 Saint Vincent	..	..	..	..	76	76	..	..	..	69
56 Seychelles	..	..	..	..	61	73	..	..	..	83
57 Qatar	77	96	58	81	..	..	..	..	21	75
58 Saint Lucia	..	..	..	..	65	87	..	..	..	72
59 Thailand	76	94	79	95	71	71	25	90	33	42
60 Malaysia	79	96	58	85	83	88	..	..	47	100+
61 Mauritius	86	96	66	84	77	91	100	100	58	69
62 Brazil	80	90	69	84	79	89	63	74	28	30
63 Belize	90	100	..	..	75	88	..	..	47	36
64 Libyan Arab Jamahiriya	68	87	37	77	81	99	88	98	18	26
Medium human development	69	91	54	82	68	86	..	..	24	30
Excluding China	69	89	57	80	72	87	..	..	24	27
65 Suriname	88	96	83	94	72	80	..	..	51	51
66 Lebanon	87	93	81	94	77	100+	..	..	58	40
69 Turkey	73	92	57	83	99	100+	69	81	22	34
70 Saudi Arabia	65	95	36	64	62	87	65	96	17	53
71 Oman	58	95	..	..	..	..	..	..	18	88
73 Ecuador	77	94	76	91	72	77	36	69	27	40
75 Korea, Dem. People's Rep. of	79	97	..	..	83	72	..	..	41	53
78 Iran, Islamic Rep. of	72	92	..	..	66	93	52	91	21	43
81 Syrian Arab Rep.	73	92	42	72	77	100+	..	..	24	47
82 Algeria	69	92	25	62	60	96	78	79	19	41
83 Tunisia	71	93	29	68	74	100+	35	99	19	45
84 Jamaica	91	100	70	86	82	83	87	87	65	100+
85 Cuba	93	100+	83	97	87	72	..	..	91	100+
86 Peru	70	91	72	90	73	68	..	..	21	27
87 Jordan	68	93	54	88	80	86	..	..	35	63
88 Dominican Rep.	75	95	69	83	66	73	56	66	33	28
89 South Africa	71	86	71	83	93	91	..	..	39	24
90 Sri Lanka	90	98	81	91	74	73	19	58	38	83
91 Paraguay	93	93	82	93	86	81	13	42	54	47
94 Samoa (Western)	73	92	..	..	..	..	..	..	23	30
95 Maldives	64	85	88	95	47	70	..	..	19	21
96 Indonesia	60	86	57	85	62	85	11	63	23	22
97 Botswana	68	70	44	71	70	68	..	..	29	32
98 Philippines	77	91	85	96	55	73	..	..	46	42
100 Guyana	82	86	92	99	74	76	..	..	39	19
101 Mongolia	68	87	64	84	76	60	..	..	27	22
106 China	69	93	52	83	66	86	..	..	23	34
107 Namibia	62	75	..	..	71	66	..	..	24	21
111 Guatemala	67	89	44	66	70	73	39	65	24	28
112 Egypt	67	87	33	52	78	100+	76	80	17	20

		Life expectancy at birth		Adult literacy		Daily calorie supply per capita		Access to safe water		Under-five mortality	
	Index: North=100 (see note)										
HDI rank		1960	1995	1970	1995	1970	1995	1975-80	1990-96	1960	1996
114	El Salvador	74	94	57	73	61	81	54	70	23	40
115	Swaziland	59	79	49	78	78	84	..	..	21	16
116	Bolivia	62	82	59	84	66	69	34	67	19	16
117	Cape Verde	76	89	36	73	49	95	..	..	30	22
119	Honduras	67	92	55	74	72	75	41	88	24	45
120	Gabon	59	73	26	64	70	77	..	..	17	11
121	São Tomé and Principe	..	..	..	..	..	..	..	..	..	20
122	Viet Nam	64	90	74	95	70	77	..	..	22	36
123	Solomon Islands	73	96	..	..	71	66	..	..	27	55
124	Vanuatu	68	89	..	..	80	79	..	..	22	30
125	Morocco	68	89	21	44	80	99	..	..	22	21
126	Nicaragua	69	91	58	67	80	73	46	54	23	28
127	Iraq	71	79	30	59	75	72	67	79	29	13
128	Congo	61	69	35	76	66	66	38	34	22	15
129	Papua New Guinea	59	77	48	73	64	72	20	28	24	14
130	Zimbabwe	66	66	67	86	74	62			27	22
Low human development		61	76	31	52	70	73	..	..	20	11
Excluding India		58	72	28	50	71	71	22	55	19	10
131	Myanmar	64	79	72	84	66	86	17	61	21	11
132	Cameroon	57	75	33	64	76	70	..	..	19	16
133	Ghana	66	77	31	65	70	82	35	66	23	14
134	Lesotho	63	78	47	72	66	62	17	57	24	11
135	Equatorial Guinea	54	66	47	80	..	..	..	..	16	9
136	Lao People's Dem. Rep.	59	70	32	57	71	67	..	..	21	12
137	Kenya	65	73	44	79	72	63	17	54	24	18
138	Pakistan	64	85	21	38.	73	78	25	75	22	12
139	India	64	83	34	53	69	75	..	..	21	14
140	Cambodia	62	71	..	..	68	63	..	..	23	9
141	Comoros	62	76	42	58	61	57	..	..	20	13
142	Nigeria	58	69	21	58	75	79	..	..	24	8
143	Dem. Rep. of the Congo	60	71	44	78	72	59	19	42	16	8
144	Togo	57	68	23	52	75	55	16	64	18	13
145	Benin	54	73	11	38	65	76	34	51	16	11
146	Zambia	61	58	48	79	71	61	42	27	23	8
147	Bangladesh	58	77	25	39	72	63	..	..	20	14
148	Côte d'Ivoire	57	70	16	41	80	79	..	..	16	11
149	Mauritania	56	71	27	38	62	81	..	..	15	9
150	Tanzania, U. Rep. of	59	68	38	69	58	63	39	38	20	11
151	Yemen	52	76	..	..	58	64	..	..	14	15
152	Nepal	56	75	14	28	64	75	8	64	16	14
153	Madagascar	59	78	..	..	80	63	..	..	13	10
154	Central African Rep.	56	65	13	61	79	59	..	..	14	10
155	Bhutan	54	70	20	43	..	..	..	..	16	12
156	Angola	48	64	..	..	69	60	17	32	14	5
157	Sudan	57	70	21	47	72	73	..	..	23	14
158	Senegal	54	68	16	34	84	75	36	53	16	12
159	Haiti	61	74	24	46	..	..	12	28	19	12
160	Uganda	63	55	37	63	76	71	35	38	22	11
161	Malawi	55	55	39	57	78	64	52	37	13	7
162	Djibouti	52	66	24	47	61	58	..	..	17	10
163	Chad	51	64	24	49	72	61	..	..	15	11
164	Guinea-Bissau	50	59	30	56	66	77	10	60	15	7
165	Gambia	47	62	17	39	70	67	..	..	13	15
166	Mozambique	54	62	16	41	63	53	..	..	18	7
167	Guinea	49	61	16	36	73	68	14	56	13	8
168	Eritrea	57	68	..	..	..	..	..	..	20	13
169	Ethiopia	52	66	17	36	..	..	8	25	18	9
170	Burundi	60	60	18	36	69	55	29	60	19	9
171	Mali	51	63	7	31	69	68	..	..	10	7
172	Burkina Faso	53	62	8	19	58	71	25	79	15	10
173	Niger	51	64	6	14	66	68	..	..	15	5
174	Sierra Leone	46	47	13	32	80	63	14	34	13	6
All developing countries		67	84	48	71	71	82	..	..	23	17
Least developed countries		57	69	30	50	69	67	..	..	18	10
Industrial countries		100	100	100	100	100	100	100	100	100	100
World		..	..	..	..	..	..	..	..	..	..

Note: North refers to the industrial countries. All figures are expressed in relation to the North average, which is indexed to equal 100. The smaller the figure the bigger the gap, and the closer the figure to 100 the smaller the gap, and a figure of 100+ indicates that the country exceeds the North average for that indicator.
Source: Columns 1 and 2: UN 1996d; columns 3 and 4: UNESCO 1997a; columns 5 and 6: FAO 1997a; columns 7-10: UNICEF 1998b.

HDI rank	Female net enrolment				Female tertiary students		Female tertiary natural and applied science students (as % of female students) 1995
	Primary		Secondary		Per 100,000 women 1995	Index (1985=100) 1995	
	Ratio (%) 1995	Index (1985=100) 1995	Ratio (%) 1995	Index (1985=100) 1995			
High human development	..	..	..	..	1,897	..	29
23 Cyprus	96	98	94	109	..	..	28
24 Barbados	..	..	..	..	2,965	..	44
25 Hong Kong, China	92	96	73	107	1,701	..	19
28 Singapore	..	..	..	..	2,249	201	..
29 Antigua and Barbuda	..	..	..	..	..	..	..
30 Korea, Rep. of	99	104	96	114	3,507	164	16
31 Chile	85	..	57	..	2,181	155	29
32 Bahamas	..	..	..	..	3,136	..	..
34 Costa Rica	..	..	..	..	2,677	..	..
35 Brunei Darussalam	91	117	71	129	640	..	36
36 Argentina	..	..	..	..	3,726	..	36
38 Uruguay	95	109	..	..	2,669	..	..
40 Trinidad and Tobago	94	102	..	..	610	142	34
41 Dominica	..	..	..	..	..	..	28
43 Bahrain	100	102	87	113	1,922	..	42
44 Fiji	100	103	..	..	959	..	..
45 Panama	..	..	..	..	3,498	117	36
46 Venezuela	..	..	24	133	2,645	..	..
48 United Arab Emirates	82	106	75	..	1,011	118	..
49 Mexico	..	..	..	..	1,444	124	26
50 Saint Kitts and Nevis	..	..	..	..	..	..	..
51 Grenada	..	..	..	..	..	..	..
53 Colombia	..	..	53	..	1,654	129	32
54 Kuwait	65	76	..	..	2,590	151	43
55 Saint Vincent	..	..	..	..	..	..	..
56 Seychelles	..	..	..	..	..	..	33
57 Qatar	80	85	71	103	3,243	115	44
58 Saint Lucia	..	..	..	..	..	..	..
59 Thailand	..	..	..	..	2,202	..	23
60 Malaysia	92	..	..	..	862	..	..
61 Mauritius	96	96	..	..	537	..	..
62 Brazil	..	..	..	..	1,200	..	34
63 Belize	98	115	..	..	133	..	..
64 Libyan Arab Jamahiriya	96	..	..	..	1,930	..	..
Medium human development	95	..	..	..	683	175	..
Excluding China	90	..	..	..	1,234	..	27
65 Suriname	..	..	..	..	1,418	..	..
66 Lebanon	..	..	..	..	2,605	..	37
69 Turkey	94	..	41	..	1,537	247	28
70 Saudi Arabia	61	145	41	186	1,508	188	..
71 Oman	70	111	55	..	441	..	..
73 Ecuador	92	..	..	..	1,705	..	..
75 Korea, Dem. People's Rep. of	..	..	..	..	..	..	..
78 Iran, Islamic Rep. of	..	..	..	..	1,144	522	20
81 Syrian Arab Rep.	87	95	37	88	1,289	105	30
82 Algeria	91	117	53	139	1,000	197	35
83 Tunisia	95	109	..	..	1,110	271	28
84 Jamaica	100	105	68	113	658	..	..
85 Cuba	99	109	..	..	1,336	53	35
86 Peru	90	..	52	..	2,593	..	..
87 Jordan	89	..	..	..	..	..	35
88 Dominican Rep.	83	120	26	..	2,080	..	..
89 South Africa	96	..	57	..	1,590	..	38
90 Sri Lanka	..	..	..	..	388	129	..
91 Paraguay	89	100	34	..	1,069	..	42
94 Samoa (Western)	99	..	48	..	509	..	26
95 Maldives	..	..	..	..	..	..	..
96 Indonesia	95	100	39	..	812	..	23
97 Botswana	99	105	48	192	392	250	26
98 Philippines	..	..	..	..	3,223	..	27
100 Guyana	89	..	..	..	804	289	24
101 Mongolia	81	..	65	..	2,190	..	53
106 China	98	..	..	..	318	160	..
107 Namibia	..	..	..	..	894	..	31
111 Guatemala	..	..	..	..	358	..	..
112 Egypt	..	..	..	..	1,336	128	27

		Female net enrolment				Female tertiary students		Female tertiary natural and applied science students (as % of female students) 1995
		Primary		Secondary				
HDI rank		Ratio (%) 1995	Index (1985=100) 1995	Ratio (%) 1995	Index (1985=100) 1995	Per 100,000 women 1995	Index (1985=100) 1995	
114	El Salvador	80	..	22	..	2,013	155	28
115	Swaziland	96	120	..	..	493	..	16
116	Bolivia	..	..	..	..	1,449	..	..
117	Cape Verde	100	105	22	244	..	..	..
119	Honduras	91	97	..	..	952	144	26
120	Gabon	..	..	..	..	288	..	..
121	São Tomé and Principe	..	..	..	..	..	..	..
122	Viet Nam	..	..	..	..	246	..	..
123	Solomon Islands	..	..	..	..	..	..	31
124	Vanuatu	..	..	..	..	..	..	..
125	Morocco	62	129	..	..	944	161	28
126	Nicaragua	85	108	..	..	1,064	104	..
127	Iraq	..	..	..	..	861	..	..
128	Congo	..	..	..	..	271	..	..
129	Papua New Guinea	..	..	..	..	209	294	..
130	Zimbabwe	..	..	..	..	369	..	14
Low human development		..	..	..	..	318	..	..
Excluding India		..	..	..	..	178	..	..
131	Myanmar	..	..	..	..	715	140	61
132	Cameroon	..	..	..	..	88	..	..
133	Ghana	..	..	..	..	54	..	..
134	Lesotho	71	88	21	117	255	218	21
135	Equatorial Guinea	..	..	..	..	..	..	..
136	Lao People's Dem. Rep.	61	..	15	..	79	74	11
137	Kenya	..	..	..	..	90	..	..
138	Pakistan	..	..	..	..	238	..	..
139	India	..	..	..	..	445	124	..
140	Cambodia	..	..	..	..	35	..	..
141	Comoros	48	..	..	..	33	..	..
142	Nigeria	..	..	..	..	203	..	..
143	Dem. Rep. of the Congo	50	..	18	..	63	..	..
144	Togo	72	..	..	..	89	189	5
145	Benin	43	119	..	..	75	107	11
146	Zambia	75	88	14	..	141	243	..
147	Bangladesh	..	..	..	..	188	..	..
148	Côte d'Ivoire	..	..	..	..	209	243	10
149	Mauritania	55	..	..	..	164	..	15
150	Tanzania, U. Rep. of	48	86	..	..	14	233	9
151	Yemen	..	..	..	..	173	..	..
152	Nepal	..	..	..	..	231	..	..
153	Madagascar	..	..	..	..	294	108	31
154	Central African Rep.	..	..	..	..	35	..	..
155	Bhutan	..	..	..	..	..	..	..
156	Angola	..	..	..	..	19	..	..
157	Sudan	..	..	..	..	341	..	..
158	Senegal	48	123	..	..	142	..	..
159	Haiti	..	..	..	..	80	..	..
160	Uganda	..	..	..	..	99	309	17
161	Malawi	100	244	2	..	50	..	15
162	Djibouti	28	108	..	..	20	..	..
163	Chad	..	..	..	..	11	..	3
164	Guinea-Bissau	..	..	..	..	..	..	..
165	Gambia	..	..	..	..	109	..	..
166	Mozambique	35	74	5	..	21	..	21
167	Guinea	..	..	..	..	10	..	..
168	Eritrea	30	..	14	..	27	..	..
169	Ethiopia	19	..	..	..	24	100	11
170	Burundi	48	137	4	200	41	146	..
171	Mali	19	146	..	..	20	..	..
172	Burkina Faso	24	141	5	250	43	179	8
173	Niger	..	..	..	..	17	..	..
174	Sierra Leone	..	..	..	..	41	..	31
All developing countries		..	..	..	..	679	..	..
Least developed countries		..	..	..	..	168	..	..
Industrial countries		98	..	90	..	3,717	123	27
World		..	..	..	..	1,369	..	..

Source: Columns 1, 3, 5 and 7: UNESCO 1998; *columns 2, 4 and 6:* calculated on the basis of data from UNESCO 1998.

Women's participation in economic and political life

HDI rank	Female administrators and managers (%) 1992-96	Female professional and technical workers (%) 1992-96	Female sales and service workers (%) 1992-96	Female clerical workers (%) 1992-96	Women in government			Female unpaid family workers (as % of total) 1990	Female economic activity rate (as % of male rate) 1995
					Total[a] (%) 1995	At ministerial level[a] (%) 1995	At sub-ministerial level[a] (%) 1995		
High human development	..	..	..	..	9	6	10	49	57
23 Cyprus	10 [b]	41 [b]	45 [b,c]	50 [b,d]	5	8	3	83	62
24 Barbados	39	51	58	80	23	33	24	67	88
25 Hong Kong, China	20	38	39	71	..	..	..	77	58
28 Singapore	15 [e]	37 [e]	43 [e]	77 [e]	5	0	7	77	64
29 Antigua and Barbuda	..	..	..	..	30	0	47	..	..
30 Korea, Rep. of	4 [e]	32 [e]	60 [e]	52 [e]	2	3	1	87	68
31 Chile	20	54	58	47	12	16	10	42	47
32 Bahamas	35 [e]	51 [e]	59 [e]	79 [e]	34	20	38	72	87
34 Costa Rica	23	45	48	49	21	15	24	34	42
35 Brunei Darussalam	11 [b]	35 [b]	40 [b,c]	52 [b,d]	2	0	3	55	51
36 Argentina	..	..	..	..	3	0	4	..	45
38 Uruguay	28	64	59	54	3	0	5	40	68
40 Trinidad and Tobago	40 [e]	52 [e]	49 [e]	72 [e]	14	20	10	54	49
41 Dominica	36 [b]	57 [b]	69 [b,c]	..	31	8	39	50	..
43 Bahrain	6	26	8	23	0	0	0	8	24
44 Fiji	10	45	28	45	10	9	11	20	38
45 Panama	28	49	50	73	11	11	11	15	51
46 Venezuela	23	57	47	60	6	4	9	34	50
48 United Arab Emirates	2 [b]	25 [b]	25 [b,c]	8 [b,d]	0	0	0	9	15
49 Mexico	20	45	43	60	7	14	4	11	46
50 Saint Kitts and Nevis	..	..	..	..	21	10	28	..	..
51 Grenada	32 [b]	53 [b]	58 [b,c]	64 [b,d]	19	10	24	74	60
53 Colombia	31	44	55	59	25	11	29	4	45
54 Kuwait	5 [b]	37 [b]	46 [b,c]	19 [b,d]	6	0	9	42	..
55 Saint Vincent	..	..	..	..	25	10	50	..	..
56 Seychelles	29 [b]	58 [b]	59 [b,c]	59 [b,d]	21	31	19	60	..
57 Qatar	..	..	..	..	2	0	3	4	15
58 Saint Lucia	..	..	..	..	5	8	0	..	..
59 Thailand	22	52	59	52	4	4	5	64	87
60 Malaysia	19	44	40	54	6	8	5	64	58
61 Mauritius	23 [e]	38 [e]	28 [e]	49 [e]	7	4	8	48	..
62 Brazil	17	63	64	41	13	4	15	46	54
63 Belize	37	39	56	71	10	0	14	..	30
64 Libyan Arab Jamahiriya	..	..	..	..	0	0	0	..	26
Medium human development	..	..	..	..	5	6	4	..	73
Excluding China	..	..	..	..	6	4	6	54	57
65 Suriname	12	62	51	57	14	0	21	42	47
66 Lebanon	..	..	..	..	0	0	0	..	39
69 Turkey	10	33	11	35	5	3	6	69	57
70 Saudi Arabia	..	..	..	..	0	0	0	..	15
71 Oman	..	..	..	..	4	0	4	..	16
73 Ecuador	28	47	54	57	10	7	10	27	36
75 Korea, Dem. People's Rep. of	..	..	..	..	1	1	1	69	77
78 Iran, Islamic Rep. of	4 [b]	33 [b]	7 [b,c]	5 [b,d]	0	0	1	43	32
81 Syrian Arab Rep.	3	37	3	16	4	7	2	5	35
82 Algeria	6 [b]	28 [b]	19 [b,c]	11 [b,d]	2	0	3	6	32
83 Tunisia	13	36	17	33	5	3	7	49	44
84 Jamaica	..	59	69	62	13	6	16	..	86
85 Cuba	19 [b]	48 [b]	..	..	8	4	10	5	61
86 Peru	24 [e]	41 [e]	62 [e]	48 [e]	10	6	11	..	42
87 Jordan	5 [e]	29 [e]	6 [e]	26 [e]	2	3	0	4	27
88 Dominican Rep.	21 [b]	50 [b]	..	..	12	3	16	43	41
89 South Africa	17 [b]	47 [b]	..	66	7	9	6	..	60
90 Sri Lanka	16	19	..	44	9	13	8	56	55
91 Paraguay	23	54	65	47	3	0	4	..	41
94 Samoa (Western)	12 [b]	47 [b]	54 [b,c]	53 [b,c]	7	7	7	8	..
95 Maldives	14 [b]	35	12 [b,c]	25 [b,d]	10	5	11	29	73
96 Indonesia	7 [b]	41 [b]	58 [b,c]	44 [b,d]	2	4	1	66	66
97 Botswana	36 [b]	61 [b]	70 [b,c]	60 [b,d]	11	0	15	35	85
98 Philippines	33	64	63	57	24	8	26	53	59
100 Guyana	13 [b]	48 [b]	..	..	16	11	21	..	49
101 Mongolia	..	..	..	..	5	0	9	..	88
106 China	12 [b]	45 [b]	52 [b,c]	39 [b,d]	4	6	4	69	82
107 Namibia	21 [b]	41 [b]	..	..	7	10	6	..	68
111 Guatemala	32 [b]	45 [b]	72 [b,c]	54 [b,d]	18	19	18	21	36
112 Egypt	12	30	10	35	2	3	2	62	40

HDI rank	Female administrators and managers (%) 1992-96	Female professional and technical workers (%) 1992-96	Female sales and service workers (%) 1992-96	Female clerical workers (%) 1992-96	Women in government			Female unpaid family workers (as % of total) 1990	Female economic activity rate (as % of male rate) 1995
					Total[a] (%) 1995	At ministerial level[a] (%) 1995	At sub-ministerial level[a] (%) 1995		
114 El Salvador	26 [e]	44 [e]	69 [e]	59 [e]	18	6	25	58	52
115 Swaziland	26	60	..	42	7	0	13	59	60
116 Bolivia	28	42	67	57	9	0	10	79	60
117 Cape Verde	23 [b]	48 [b]	57 [b,c]	63 [b,d]	12	13	10	54	64
119 Honduras	53	45	4	55	17	11	21	..	42
120 Gabon	..	..	..	..	6	3	11	..	80
121 São Tomé and Principe	..	..	..	..	4	0	11	54	..
122 Viet Nam	..	..	..	..	4	7	2	..	97
123 Solomon Islands	3 [b]	27 [b]	40 [b,c]	27 [b,d]	0	0	0	..	88
124 Vanuatu	13 [b]	35 [b]	..	..	0	0	0	..	..
125 Morocco	26 [b]	31 [b]	17	28	1	0	2	31	53
126 Nicaragua	..	..	..	..	11	11	10	..	51
127 Iraq	13 [b]	44 [b]	16 [b,c]	7 [b,d]	0	0	0	50	22
128 Congo	6 [b]	29 [b]	..	..	4	6	0	65	77
129 Papua New Guinea	12 [b]	30 [b]	..	..	2	0	3	..	72
130 Zimbabwe	15 [b]	40 [b]	30 [b,c]	34 [b,d]	11	3	19	..	80
Low human development	..	..	..	..	5	5	5	..	56
Excluding India	..	..	..	..	4	5	4	42	68
131 Myanmar	..	..	..	..	0	0	0	..	77
132 Cameroon	10 [b]	24 [b]	31 [b,c]	37 [b,d]	5	3	7	70	60
133 Ghana	9 [b]	36 [b]	68 [b,c]	59 [b,d]	11	11	10	63	103
134 Lesotho	33 [b]	57 [b]	..	..	14	7	16	39	58
135 Equatorial Guinea	2 [b]	27 [b]	..	..	3	4	0	74	55
136 Lao People's Dem. Rep.	..	..	..	..	3	0	4	..	89
137 Kenya	..	..	..	..	5	0	6	..	85
138 Pakistan	4	20	5	2	2	4	1	33	36
139 India	2 [b]	21 [b]	..	..	6	4	6	..	46
140 Cambodia	..	..	..	..	5	0	7	..	109
141 Comoros	..	..	..	..	3	7	0	..	74
142 Nigeria	6 [b]	26 [b]	11 [b,c]	58 [b,d]	4	4	4	46	56
143 Dem. Rep. of the Congo	9 [b]	17 [b]	..	..	2	3	0	..	77
144 Togo	8 [b]	21 [b]	..	..	3	4	0	54	67
145 Benin	..	..	..	..	10	15	5	40	93
146 Zambia	6 [b]	32 [b]	22 [b]	58 [b]	9	7	9	54	83
147 Bangladesh	5	35	..	..	3	5	3	6	73
148 Côte d'Ivoire	..	..	..	..	3	8	0	62	49
149 Mauritania	8 [b]	21 [b]	45 [b,c]	25 [b,d]	5	4	5	38	..
150 Tanzania, U. Rep. of	..	..	..	..	9	16	5	..	98
151 Yemen	..	..	..	..	0	0	0	69	39
152 Nepal	..	..	..	..	0	0	0	55	68
153 Madagascar	..	..	..	..	0	0	0	..	81
154 Central African Rep.	9 [b]	19 [b]	12 [b,c]	59 [b,d]	5	5	5	55	88
155 Bhutan	..	..	..	..	5	13	0	..	66
156 Angola	..	..	..	..	6	7	6	..	87
157 Sudan	2 [b]	29 [b]	..	..	1	0	1	..	40
158 Senegal	..	..	..	..	2	4	0	..	74
159 Haiti	33 [b]	39 [b]	88 [b,c]	65 [b,d]	14	17	11	37	76
160 Uganda	..	..	..	..	10	13	8	74	91
161 Malawi	5 [b]	35 [b]	28 [b,c]	33 [b,d]	6	5	7	58	96
162 Djibouti	2 [b]	20 [b]	..	..	1	0	2	22	..
163 Chad	..	..	..	..	3	5	0	..	80
164 Guinea-Bissau	..	..	..	..	12	8	16	4	67
165 Gambia	16	24	14	28	7	22	2	64	81
166 Mozambique	11 [b]	20 [b]	..	..	13	4	15	82	94
167 Guinea	..	..	..	..	5	15	0	60	90
168 Eritrea	17	30	43	48	..	..	..	..	90
169 Ethiopia	11 [b]	24 [b]	..	..	11	12	10	67	69
170 Burundi	13 [b]	30 [b]	..	..	4	8	0	60	97
171 Mali	20 [b]	19 [b]	41 [b,c]	57 [b,d]	7	10	0	53	87
172 Burkina Faso	14 [b]	26 [b]	22 [b,c]	63 [b,d]	10	11	9	66	87
173 Niger	9	8	0	30	9	10	9	24	79
174 Sierra Leone	8 [b]	32 [b]	15 [b,c]	66 [b,d]	5	4	5	74	57
All developing countries	..	..	..	..	5	5	5	48	64
Least developed countries	..	..	..	..	5	6	4	41	76
Industrial countries	37	50	55	69	13	11	13	75	79
World	..	..	..	..	7	7	7	58	68

a. Including elected heads of state and governors of central banks. For countries for which the value is zero, no women ministers were reported by the United Nations Division for the Advancement of Women; this information could not be reconfirmed by the Human Development Report Office.
b. Carried over from UNDP 1997a.
c. Excludes sales workers.
d. Includes sales workers.
e. Refers to the International Standard Classification of Occupations (ISCO) 1988, which is not strictly comparable with the ISCO-1968 classification. See the selected definitions.
Source: Columns 1-4 and 9: calculated on the basis of data from ILO 1997b; columns 5-7: calculated by the United Nations Division for the Advancement of Women based on data from Keesing's Worldwide 1995; column 8: UN 1995b.

12 Child survival and development

HDI rank	Infant mortality rate (per 1,000 live births) 1996	Under-five mortality rate (per 1,000 live births) 1996	Pregnant women aged 15-49 with anaemia (%) 1975-91	Births attended by trained health personnel (%) 1990-96	Low-birth-weight infants (%) 1990-94	Maternal mortality rate (per 100,000 live births) 1990	Mothers exclusively breast-feeding at three months (%) 1990-96	Oral rehydration therapy use rate (%) 1990-97	Under-weight children under age five (%) 1990-97
High human development	**29**	**35**	**..**	**85**	**9**	**148**	**34**	**..**	**12**
23 Cyprus	9	10	..	100	..	..	..	..	..
24 Barbados	11	12	29	98	10	..	..	..	5[a]
25 Hong Kong, China	..	..	..	..	..	7	..	..	..
28 Singapore	4	4	57	100	7	10	..	..	..
29 Antigua and Barbuda	18	22	..	90	8	..	..	..	10
30 Korea, Rep. of	6	7	..	98	9	130	..	..	..
31 Chile	11	13	32	98	5	65	77	..	1
32 Bahamas	19	23	12	100	..	..	..	..	2
34 Costa Rica	13	15	..	93	7	60	35	31	..
35 Brunei Darussalam	9	11	..	98	..	..	..	..	..
36 Argentina	22	25	..	97	7	100	..	..	7[a]
38 Uruguay	20	22	..	96	8	85	..	..	7[a]
40 Trinidad and Tobago	15	17	..	98	10	90	10[a]	..	5[a]
41 Dominica	17	20	28	96	10	..	..	..	..
43 Bahrain	18	22	..	97	6	..	..	5	..
44 Fiji	20	24	40	96	12	..	..	..	7
45 Panama	18	20	..	86	9	55	32	94	6[a]
46 Venezuela	24	28	52	69	9	120	..	..	..
48 United Arab Emirates	15	18	..	96	6	26	..	..	14[a]
49 Mexico	27	32	..	77	8	110	38[a]	81	..
50 Saint Kitts and Nevis	31	38	57	100	9	..	..	..	..
51 Grenada	25	31	63	81	9	..	..	..	..
53 Colombia	26	31	8	85	9	100	16	53	8
54 Kuwait	13	14	..	99	7	29	..	..	6[a]
55 Saint Vincent	19	23	20	73	8	..	..	..	..
56 Seychelles	15	19	..	99	10	..	..	..	6[a]
57 Qatar	17	21	..	97	..	..	..	71	..
58 Saint Lucia	18	22	22	99	8	..	..	..	..
59 Thailand	31	38	48	71	13	200	4[a]	95	26[a]
60 Malaysia	11	13	36	94	8	80	..	..	23
61 Mauritius	20	23	..	97	13	120	16	..	16
62 Brazil	44	52	..	88	11	220	42	54	6
63 Belize	36	44	65	77	10	..	24	..	5
64 Libyan Arab Jamahiriya	50	61	..	76	..	220	..	49	..
Medium human development	**40**	**52**	**..**	**75**	**11**	**210**	**53**	**81**	**19**
Excluding China	**43**	**56**	**..**	**62**	**12**	**311**	**41**	**75**	**23**
65 Suriname	25	31	..	91	13	..	..	82	..
66 Lebanon	33	40	..	45	10	300	..	..	..
69 Turkey	41	47	..	76	8	180	14	100	10
70 Saudi Arabia	25	30	23	82	7	130	..	58	..
71 Oman	15	18	..	87	8	190	28	85	23
73 Ecuador	31	40	..	64	13	150	29	64	17[a]
75 Korea, Dem. People's Rep. of	23	30	..	100	..	70	..	..	16
78 Iran, Islamic Rep. of	33	37	..	77	9	120	53	37	16
81 Syrian Arab Rep.	28	34	..	67	11	180	..	27	13
82 Algeria	34	39	..	77	9	160	48	98	13
83 Tunisia	28	35	38	69	8	170	12	41	9
84 Jamaica	10	11	62	82	10	120	..	..	10
85 Cuba	10	10	..	90	8	95	..	..	..
86 Peru	45	58	..	56	11	280	63	55	8
87 Jordan	21	25	..	87	7	150	32	41	9
88 Dominican Rep.	45	56	..	96	11	110	25	39	6
89 South Africa	50	66	..	82	..	230	..	..	9
90 Sri Lanka	17	19	..	94	25	140	24	34	38
91 Paraguay	28	34	..	66	5	160	7	33	4
94 Samoa (Western)	42	53	..	95	6	..	..	..	..
95 Maldives	54	76	..	90	20	..	8	..	39
96 Indonesia	47	71	74	36	14	650	47	97	34
97 Botswana	40	50	..	78	8	250	41[a]	..	15
98 Philippines	32	38	48	53	15	280	33	87	30
100 Guyana	60	83	58	90	19	..	..	..	18
101 Mongolia	55	71	..	99	6	65	..	85	12
106 China	38	47	..	84	9	95	64	66	16
107 Namibia	60	77	..	68	16	370	22	66	26
111 Guatemala	43	56	..	35	15	200	50	22	27
112 Egypt	57	78	75	46	10	170	53	95	15

HDI rank	Infant mortality rate (per 1,000 live births) 1996	Under-five mortality rate (per 1,000 live births) 1996	Pregnant women aged 15-49 with anaemia (%) 1975-91	Births attended by trained health personnel (%) 1990-96	Low-birth-weight infants (%) 1990-94	Maternal mortality rate (per 100,000 live births) 1990	Mothers exclusively breast-feeding at three months (%) 1990-96	Oral rehydration therapy use rate (%) 1990-97	Under-weight children under age five (%) 1990-97
114 El Salvador	34	40	14	87	11	300	20	69	11
115 Swaziland	68	97	..	55	10	..	37	99	10 a
116 Bolivia	71	102	..	47	12	650	53	41	11
117 Cape Verde	54	73	48	30	11	..	..	..	19 a
119 Honduras	29	35	..	88	9	220	11	32	18
120 Gabon	87	145	..	80	..	500	57	25	..
121 São Tomé and Principe	62	80	..	86	7	..	..	74	17 a
122 Viet Nam	33	44	..	95	17	160	..	..	45
123 Solomon Islands	24	29	30	87	20	..	..	..	..
124 Vanuatu	41	53	87	86	7	..	..	..	20 a
125 Morocco	64	74	..	40	9	610	31	29	9
126 Nicaragua	44	57	..	61	15	160	11	54	12
127 Iraq	94	122	..	54	15	310	..	..	12
128 Congo	81	108	..	..	16	890	43 a	41	24 a
129 Papua New Guinea	79	112	..	20	23	930	..	..	35 a
130 Zimbabwe	49	73	..	69	14	570	16	60	16
Low human development	90	140	..	32	26	766	40	75	45
Excluding India	102	159	..	30	21	904	31	86	37
131 Myanmar	105	150	60	57	16	580	30	96	31
132 Cameroon	63	102	..	64	13	550	7	43	14
133 Ghana	70	110	..	44	7	740	19	93	27
134 Lesotho	96	139	..	40	11	610	54	84	16
135 Equatorial Guinea	111	173	..	58	..	..	..	..	..
136 Lao People's Dem. Rep.	102	128	..	..	18	650	36	..	40
137 Kenya	61	90	40	45	16	650	17	76	23
138 Pakistan	95	136	..	19	25	340	16	97	38
139 India	73	111	88	34	33	570	51	67	53
140 Cambodia	108	170	..	47	..	900	..	..	40
141 Comoros	83	122	..	52	8	..	5	32	26
142 Nigeria	114	191	65	31	16	1,000	2	86	36
143 Dem. Rep. of the Congo	128	207	..	..	15	870	32	90	34
144 Togo	78	125	47	54	20	640	..	94	19
145 Benin	84	140	46	45	..	990	..	60	..
146 Zambia	112	202	..	51	13	940	13	99	24
147 Bangladesh	83	112	58	14	50	850	51	96	56
148 Côte d'Ivoire	90	150	34	45	14	810	62	73	24
149 Mauritania	124	183	24	40	11	930	60	51	23
150 Tanzania, U. Rep. of	93	144	..	53	14	770	40	91	27
151 Yemen	78	105	..	16	19	1,400	..	92	39
152 Nepal	82	116	..	9	..	1,500	83	29	47
153 Madagascar	100	164	..	57	17	490	47	85	34
154 Central African Rep.	103	164	..	46	15	700	23	100	27
155 Bhutan	90	127	30	15	..	1,600	..	85	38 a
156 Angola	170	292	..	15	19	1,500	3	..	..
157 Sudan	73	116	50	69	15	660	14 a	35	34
158 Senegal	74	127	53	46	11	1,200	9	84	22
159 Haiti	94	134	..	21	15	1,000	3	31	28
160 Uganda	88	141	..	38	..	1,200	70	49	26
161 Malawi	137	217	..	55	20	560	11	78	30
162 Djibouti	112	157	..	79	11	..	..	..	23
163 Chad	92	149	..	15	..	1,500	..	..	..
164 Guinea-Bissau	132	223	..	27	20	910	..	..	23 a
165 Gambia	78	107	..	44	..	1,100	..	..	..
166 Mozambique	133	214	58	25	20	1,500	..	83	27
167 Guinea	130	210	..	31	21	1,600	52	31	26
168 Eritrea	78	120	..	21	13	1,400	66	38	44
169 Ethiopia	113	177	..	14	16	1,400	74	95	48
170 Burundi	106	176	..	19	..	1,300	89 a	..	37
171 Mali	134	220	50	24	17	1,200	42	29	27
172 Burkina Faso	82	158	55	42	21	930	12	100	30
173 Niger	191	320	57	15	15	1,200	..	85	36
174 Sierra Leone	164	284	45	25	11	1,800	..	..	29
All developing countries	65	95	..	58	18	488	45	76 b	30
Least developed countries	109 b	171 b	..	29 b	22	1,100 b	46	80 b	39 b
Industrial countries	13	16	..	99	7	30	..	..	..
World	60 b	88 b	..	57 b	17	430 b	..	..	30 b

a. Data refer to a year or period other than that specified in the column heading, differ from the standard definition or refer to only part of the country.
b. UNICEF 1998b.
Source: Columns 1 and 2 and 4-9: UNICEF 1998b; column 3: UN 1994d.

HDI rank	One-year-olds fully immunized against — Tuberculosis (%) 1995-96	Measles (%) 1995-96	AIDS cases (per 100,000 people)[a] 1996	Tuberculosis cases (per 100,000 people) 1995	Malaria cases (per 100,000 people) 1994	Cigarette consumption per adult (1970-72=100) 1990-92	Doctors (per 100,000 people)[b] 1993	Nurses (per 100,000 people)[b] 1993	People with disabilities (as % of total population)[c] 1985-92	Public expenditure on health — As % of GNP 1960	As % of GDP 1990
High human development	**95**	**81**	**8.6**	**46.0**	**187**	**100**	**122**	**84**	**..**	**1.2**	**2.2**
23 Cyprus	..	90	0.5	4.8	..	..	231	425	2.3	0.6	..
24 Barbados	..	100	49.4	7.7	..	..	113	323	..	3.0	..
25 Hong Kong, China	..	..	1.2	..	..	111	..	..	0.8	..	1.1
28 Singapore	97	88	3.2	56.8	8	64	147	416	0.4	1.0	1.1
29 Antigua and Barbuda	..	100	19.7	..	..	..	76	233	..	..	..
30 Korea, Rep. of	93	92	0.1	73.9	(.)	127	127	232	..	0.2	2.7
31 Chile	96	96	2.2	..	..	86	108	42	..	2.0	3.4
32 Bahamas	..	92	133.6	20.4	..	..	141	258	..	..	..
34 Costa Rica	91	86	5.5	9.4	133	72	126	95	..	3.0	..
35 Brunei Darussalam	100	100	0.7	..	13	..	..	..	..	..	..
36 Argentina	100	100	5.9	38.6	3	89	268	54	..	1.3	2.5
38 Uruguay	98	85	4.9	19.6	..	104	309	61	..	2.6	2.5
40 Trinidad and Tobago	..	88	31.2	13.8	2	124	90	168	1.1	1.7	..
41 Dominica	100	100	19.7	11.3	..	..	46	263	..	..	..
43 Bahrain	..	95	0.9	20.7	..	..	11	289	1.0	..	..
44 Fiji	100	94	..	25.9	..	138	38	215	0.9	..	..
45 Panama	100	92	9.1	50.0	26	83	119	98	1.4	3.0	..
46 Venezuela	90	64	2.8	25.4	64	93	194	77	3.8	2.6	2.0
48 United Arab Emirates	98	90	..	..	..	..	168	321	..	..	..
49 Mexico	97	75	4.4	12.4	14	61	107	40	..	1.9	1.6
50 Saint Kitts and Nevis	..	100	9.7	9.8	..	..	89	590	..	..	..
51 Grenada	..	85	19.6	2.2	..	..	50	239	..	..	..
53 Colombia	98	95	2.9	27.7	362	93	105	49	1.2	0.4	1.8
54 Kuwait	..	99	0.3	19.9	50	..	178	468	0.4	..	..
55 Saint Vincent	100	100	0.5	21.4	..	..	46	187	..	..	..
56 Seychelles	100	98	2.7	12.3	..	..	104	417	..	..	..
57 Qatar	98	86	0.4	55.5	74	..	143	354	0.2	..	..
58 Saint Lucia	89	95	16.8	8.5	..	..	35	177	..	..	..
59 Thailand	98	85	30.2	78.0	177	130	24	99	0.7	0.4	1.1
60 Malaysia	97	81	1.5	59.5	299	116	43	160	..	1.1	1.3
61 Mauritius	87	61	..	13.7	3	140	85	241	2.6	1.5	..
62 Brazil	90	74	10.0	55.4	360	113	134	41	1.8	0.6	2.8
63 Belize	90	81	17.2	28.6	4,787	..	47	76	6.6	..	..
64 Libyan Arab Jamahiriya	99	92	..	26.6	1	..	137	366	..	1.3	..
Medium human development	**94**	**91**	**..**	**52.0**	**201**	**206**	**99**	**100**	**3.9**	**0.9**	**2.1**
Excluding China	**90**	**85**	**2.3**	**86.9**	**634**	**130**	**71**	**122**	**1.8**	**0.8**	**2.1**
65 Suriname	..	78	14.6	..	1,115	161	40	227	..	..	..
66 Lebanon	..	85	0.2	32.7	..	..	191	122	..	0.8	1.5
69 Turkey	69	84	0.1	37.8	7	108	103	151	1.4	0.6	3.1
70 Saudi Arabia	91	92	0.5	..	56	175	166	348	..	..	..
71 Oman	96	98	0.5	10.2	341	..	120	290	..	..	..
73 Ecuador	100	79	0.6	68.9	267	134	111	34	..	0.4	..
75 Korea, Dem. People's Rep. of	60	60	..	..	..	91	..	..	..	0.5	..
78 Iran, Islamic Rep. of	90	95	0.1	29.3	77	102	..	..	..	0.8	1.5
81 Syrian Arab Rep.	100	95	0.1	31.0	4	211	109	212	1.0	0.4	0.4
82 Algeria	94	68	0.2	..	1	168	83	..	..	1.2	5.4
83 Tunisia	86	86	0.6	26.5	..	127	67	283	0.9	1.6	3.3
84 Jamaica	98	99	21.4	4.4	(.)	61	57	69	..	2.0	..
85 Cuba	99	94	0.9	14.7	(.)	85	518	752	1.7	3.0	..
86 Peru	93	71	4.1	192.6	528	85	73	49	0.2	1.1	1.9
87 Jordan	..	98	0.1	9.4	..	165	158	224	0.5	0.6	1.8
88 Dominican Rep.	98	78	4.6	51.8	22	111	77	20	..	1.3	2.1
89 South Africa	95	76	1.7	209.6	25	128	59	175	..	0.5	3.2
90 Sri Lanka	88	86	0.1	33.2	1,540	93	23	112	0.4	2.0	1.8
91 Paraguay	89	81	1.0	36.7	12	92	67	10	..	0.5	1.2
94 Samoa (Western)	98	96	1.2	30.9	..	..	38	186	..	..	..
95 Maldives	98	94	0.8	90.9	7	..	19	13	..	..	..
96 Indonesia	99	92	(.)	16.2	..	103	12	67	1.1	0.3	0.7
97 Botswana	67	82	98.7	390.0	2,089	..	..	..	4.0	1.5	..
98 Philippines	82	72	0.1	347.1	345	88	11	43	1.1	0.4	1.0
100 Guyana	88	91	17.1	35.7	4,819	341	33	88	3.9	..	..
101 Mongolia	92	88	..	122.2	..	..	268	452	..	..	..
106 China	97	97	..	29.3	6	260	115	88	4.9	1.3	2.1
107 Namibia	79	61	165.5	100.3	27,209	..	23	81	..	0.6	2.1
111 Guatemala	76	69	7.6	31.7	214	..	90	30	3.8	0.6	2.1
112 Egypt	91	85	(.)	37.8	..	166	202	222	1.6	0.6	1.0

HDI rank	Tuberculosis (%) 1995-96	Measles (%) 1995-96	AIDS cases (per 100,000 people)[a] 1996	Tuberculosis cases (per 100,000 people) 1995	Malaria cases (per 100,000 people) 1994	Cigarette consumption per adult (1970-72=100) 1990-92	Doctors (per 100,000 people)[b] 1993	Nurses (per 100,000 people)[b] 1993	People with disabilities (as % of total population)[c] 1985-92	Public expenditure on health As % of GNP 1960	As % of GDP 1990
114 El Salvador	100	97	7.1	42.8	51	80	91	38	..	0.9	2.6
115 Swaziland	68	59	28.3	239.8	..	..	..	..	..	..	..
116 Bolivia	90	87	0.4	129.7	480	108	51	25	2.6	0.4	2.4
117 Cape Verde	80	66	8.9	78.5	6	..	29	57	4.3	..	..
119 Honduras	100	91	13.7	88.2	949	..	22	17	..	1.0	2.9
120 Gabon	54	38	23.4	103.6	..	..	19	56	..	0.5	..
121 São Tomé and Principe	85	57	3.0	..	..	..	32	..	..	..	..
122 Viet Nam	95	96	0.5	75.5	1,189	..	..	..	5.7	..	1.1
123 Solomon Islands	71	67	..	93.1	35,980	56	..	141	..	..	..
124 Vanuatu	72	61	..	46.8	2,285	..	..	..	..	..	..
125 Morocco	96	93	0.2	112.5	1	135	34	94	1.6	1.0	0.9
126 Nicaragua	93	78	0.6	68.9	1,035	106	82	56	..	0.4	6.7
127 Iraq	99	97	0.1	134.1	500	79	51	64	0.9	1.0	..
128 Congo	50	42	..	139.4	1,428	102	27	49	..	1.6	..
129 Papua New Guinea	78	44	1.6	187.0	14,974	..	18	97	..	..	2.8
130 Zimbabwe	74	77	79.3	275.5	2,964	61	14	164	..	1.2	3.2
Low human development	84	69	2.5	93.6	2,152	133	36	..	1.0	0.6	1.5
Excluding India	76	60	5.9	52.7	5,683	137	21	45	..	0.7	1.7
131 Myanmar	92	86	1.5	40.4	1,582	167	28	43	0.4	0.7	1.0
132 Cameroon	54	46	10.9	..	1,065	274	7	..	..	1.0	1.0
133 Ghana	65	53	6.5	23.8	..	61	4	..	..	1.1	1.7
134 Lesotho	55	82	16.4	239.1	..	..	5	33	..	1.0	..
135 Equatorial Guinea	99	61	18.1	76.5	3,812	..	21	34	..	..	..
136 Lao People's Dem. Rep.	62	62	0.3	25.1	1,111	118	..	..	..	0.5	1.0
137 Kenya	56	38	22.4	103.7	23,068	119	15	23	..	1.5	2.7
138 Pakistan	93	78	(.)	7.1	82	102	52	32	4.9	0.3	1.8
139 India	96	81	0.1	130.8	243	236	48	..	0.2	0.5	1.3
140 Cambodia	90	72	2.9	145.6	870	130	58	136	..	..	..
141 Comoros	89	48	..	21.1	..	..	10	33	..	..	3.3
142 Nigeria	49	45	0.3	12.0	..	128	21	142	..	0.3	1.2
143 Dem. Rep. of the Congo	51	41	..	88.1	..	123	..	..	..	..	0.8
144 Togo	63	39	35.8	37.2	8,274	88	6	31	..	1.3	2.5
145 Benin	90	74	9.0	44.4	10,398	102	6	33	..	1.5	2.8
146 Zambia	100	93	46.9	157.7	44,498	86	..	..	1.6	1.0	2.2
147 Bangladesh	88	59	..	36.0	143	194	18	5	0.8	..	1.4
148 Côte d'Ivoire	68	65	40.7	87.5	..	89	..	..	..	1.5	1.7
149 Mauritania	93	53	0.6	169.3	..	..	11	27	..	0.5	..
150 Tanzania, U. Rep. of	96	81	..	132.7	27,343	97	4	46	..	0.5	3.2
151 Yemen	59	51	0.4	96.0	260	172	26	51	..	..	1.5
152 Nepal	73	45	0.2	92.3	45	341	5	5	3.0	0.2	2.2
153 Madagascar	87	68	(.)	79.5	..	170	24	55	..	1.4	1.3
154 Central African Rep.	94	46	61.1	102.0	2,562	..	6	45	..	1.3	2.6
155 Bhutan	98	86	..	73.4	2,238	..	20	6	..	..	..
156 Angola	74	65	1.0	73.8	6,377	100	..	..	..	..	..
157 Sudan	96	75	0.8	41.5	..	88	10	70	5.3	1.0	0.5
158 Senegal	80	60	1.7	91.0	..	244	7	35	..	1.5	2.3
159 Haiti	68	31	..	..	331	..	16	13	..	1.0	3.2
160 Uganda	96	66	13.8	129.4	..	100	4	28	..	0.7	1.6
161 Malawi	95	89	36.6	198.0	49,410	165	2	6	2.9	0.2	2.9
162 Djibouti	58	47	60.8	..	1,050	..	20	..	..	..	..
163 Chad	40	28	19.0	50.3	..	..	2	6	..	0.5	4.7
164 Guinea-Bissau	72	53	3.4	163.5	..	93	18	45	..	..	..
165 Gambia	99	89	6.8	92.1	..	..	2	25	..	..	..
166 Mozambique	83	67	12.6	103.6	..	124	..	..	..	..	4.4
167 Guinea	59	49	13.4	47.2	8,567	..	15	3	..	1.0	2.3
168 Eritrea	52	38	24.7	676.5	..	..	2	..	..	..	..
169 Ethiopia	87	54	1.5	25.5	..	150	4	8	3.8	0.7	2.3
170 Burundi	77	50	8.8	..	14,022	..	6	17	..	0.8	1.7
171 Mali	70	35	5.3	28.6	..	..	4	9	2.8	1.0	2.8
172 Burkina Faso	61	54	9.2	14.0	4,637	..	..	..	..	0.6	7.0
173 Niger	63	59	6.9	21.6	9,238	155	3	17	..	0.2	3.4
174 Sierra Leone	77	79	0.9	46.6	..	176	..	..	..	..	1.7
All developing countries	89	79	3.5	68.6	954	160	76	85	2.6	1.0	2.0
Least developed countries	80	60	7.4	69.9	6,765	156	14	26	..	..	1.9
Industrial countries	92	86	5.0	27.6	..	90	287	780	..	..	..
World	89	79	3.9	59.7	..	115	122	241	..	..	..

a. The number of reported cases in adults and children.
b. Data refer to 1993 or a year around 1993.
c. See the selected definitions.
Source: Columns 1 and 2: UNICEF 1998b; *column 3:* UNAIDS and WHO 1997; *columns 4 and 5:* WHO 1997d; *column 6:* WHO 1997c; *columns 7 and 8:* WHO 1997d; *column 9:* UN 1993; *columns 10 and 11:* UN 1993; World Bank 1993.

HDI rank	Daily per capita supply of calories		Per capita supply of cereals[a]		Daily per capita supply of fat[a]		Daily per capita supply of protein[a]		Food production per capita index (1980=100)	Food imports (as % of merchandise imports)	Food aid in cereals (thousands of metric tons)	Food consumption (as % of total household consumption)
	1970	1995	Total (kg) 1994/95	Change (%) 1970-95	Total (grams) 1994/95	Change (%) 1970-95	Total (grams) 1994/95	Change (%) 1970-95	1996	1993	1994-95[b]	1980-85
High human development	2,536	2,858	132	-4	80	55	74	14	114	7	108 T	..
23 Cyprus	3,102	3,676	114	-9	179	49	106	22	106	18	..	..
24 Barbados	2,805	3,155	108	1	110	28	88	11	87	20	..	..
25 Hong Kong, China	2,743	3,187	116	-19	142	46	106	25	58	6	..	..
28 Singapore	..	..	..	..	..	..	..	..	17	6	..	..
29 Antigua and Barbuda	2,489	2,300	85	-9	93	12	87	36	92	..	..	..
30 Korea, Rep. of	2,793	3,159	165	-24	81	224	85	18	135	6	..	35
31 Chile	2,619	2,713	137	-12	79	34	80	16	143	6	2	29
32 Bahamas	2,575	2,458	..	..	82	-4	79	1	78	..	..	..
34 Costa Rica	2,391	2,855	111	5	79	39	69	19	112	8[c]	2	33
35 Brunei Darussalam	2,331	2,818	141	8	86	100	86	59	90	..	..	..
36 Argentina	3,340	3,097	127	-5	115	5	97	-5	108	5	..	35
38 Uruguay	3,041	2,813	112	-15	110	-2	91	..	144	8	..	31
40 Trinidad and Tobago	2,464	2,550	112	-15	71	15	58	-9	84	15	7	19
41 Dominica	2,012	2,982	106	36	82	74	81	62	165	..	..	..
43 Bahrain	..	..	..	..	..	..	..	..	50	..	..	..
44 Fiji	2,380	3,015	145	36	112	78	75	39	105	..	..	..
45 Panama	2,236	2,462	128	8	69	35	66	12	90	10	..	38
46 Venezuela	..	..	..	..	69	30	..	..	102	11	..	23
48 United Arab Emirates	3,196	3,329	125	-21	107	39	103	20	172	..	..	..
49 Mexico	2,698	3,116	178	7	86	48	84	20	101	8	44	35[c,d]
50 Saint Kitts and Nevis	1,762	2,156	82	12	77	40	64	60	66	..	..	..
51 Grenada	2,185	2,630	95	6	91	36	73	24	76	..	..	..
53 Colombia	2,042	2,749	98	31	67	60	64	33	109	8	15	29
54 Kuwait	..	..	..	..	106	51	..	..	103	13[c]	..	..
55 Saint Vincent	2,295	2,397	98	..	68	13	63	17	108	..	..	..
56 Seychelles	1,826	2,311	107	-11	74	106	77	57	97	..	..	..
57 Qatar	..	..	..	..	..	..	..	..	145	..	..	..
58 Saint Lucia	1,954	2,757	119	53	74	28	87	67	123	..	3	..
59 Thailand	2,148	2,247	129	-18	45	55	52	2	106	5[c]	3	30
60 Malaysia	2,518	2,765	127	-19	86	54	65	27	149	17[c]	0	23[c]
61 Mauritius	2,322	2,886	167	11	87	74	79	58	120	13[c]	..	24
62 Brazil	2,398	2,824	105	8	80	70	70	15	127	10	33	35
63 Belize	2,265	2,776	102	-6	77	22	64	10	124	18	..	..
64 Libyan Arab Jamahiriya	2,439	3,117	193	30	114	52	72	20	..	..	..	..
Medium human development	2,058	2,718	184	19	64	117	70	39	169	7	..	..
Excluding China	2,158	2,732	183	24	60	47	69	26	116	..	1,966 T	..
65 Suriname	2,177	2,521	150	11	47	7	63	13	79	..	17	..
66 Lebanon	2,330	3,269	137	5	107	67	82	39	164	..	7	..
69 Turkey	2,991	3,577	231	13	95	28	103	14	101	6	..	40
70 Saudi Arabia	1,872	2,736	168	29	68	106	73	52	134	..	..	..
71 Oman	..	..	..	..	..	..	..	..	71	19	..	..
73 Ecuador	2,175	2,420	93	18	89	78	50	-2	118	5	32	30
75 Korea, Dem. People's Rep. of	2,498	2,282	159	-16	41	32	76	1	..	..	..	..
78 Iran, Islamic Rep. of	1,994	2,945	210	36	64	49	77	40	131	..	..	37
81 Syrian Arab Rep.	2,317	3,295	234	44	91	49	86	34	85	19[c]	59	..
82 Algeria	1,798	3,035	234	59	74	106	82	74	116	29[c]	23	..
83 Tunisia	2,221	3,173	205	19	95	67	83	36	124	8	22	37
84 Jamaica	2,483	2,615	98	-14	63	3	67	..	118	14[c]	46	36
85 Cuba	2,619	2,277	105	-17	55	-20	54	-22	66	..	3	..
86 Peru	2,207	2,147	106	5	52	37	59	..	124	20	348	35
87 Jordan	2,415	2,726	158	-6	84	40	73	11	113	20	111	35
88 Dominican Rep.	1,988	2,308	91	57	68	39	52	18	91	..	2	46
89 South Africa	2,807	2,865	184	2	77	12	72	-3	79	6	..	34
90 Sri Lanka	2,229	2,302	148	7	50	2	50	14	87	16[c]	342	43
91 Paraguay	2,591	2,552	78	-17	77	26	76	4	124	11	1	30
94 Samoa (Western)	..	..	..	..	..	..	..	..	83	..	..	..
95 Maldives	1,428	2,211	122	33	50	35	87	61	84	..	3	..
96 Indonesia	1,859	2,699	187	51	55	90	63	62	146	7	15	48
97 Botswana	2,101	2,140	135	-9	48	9	69	-9	95	..	7	25
98 Philippines	1,670	2,319	139	25	47	42	57	30	94	8	44	51
100 Guyana	2,224	2,388	145	23	45	-8	64	12	125	..	30	..
101 Mongolia	2,279	1,895	121	-15	66	-22	64	-22	63	..	12	..
106 China	2,000	2,708	184	17	67	191	71	48	215	..	..	61[c,d]
107 Namibia	2,149	2,093	126	25	35	-20	59	16	64	..	..	..
111 Guatemala	2,100	2,298	148	6	41	8	58	4	103	11[c]	144	36
112 Egypt	2,352	3,315	250	44	61	30	88	38	121	24	179	49

HDI rank	Daily per capita supply of calories		Per capita supply of cereals[a]		Daily per capita supply of fat[a]		Daily per capita supply of protein[a]		Food production per capita index (1980=100)	Food imports (as % of merchandise imports)	Food aid in cereals (thousands of metric tons)	Food consumption (as % of total household consumption)
	1970	1995	Total (kg) 1994/95	Change (%) 1970-95	Total (grams) 1994/95	Change (%) 1970-95	Total (grams) 1994/95	Change (%) 1970-95	1996	1993	1994-95[b]	1980-85
114 El Salvador	1,827	2,571	161	38	53	39	64	36	92	15[c]	7	33
115 Swaziland	2,346	2,660	153	5	48	12	63	-3	76	..	1	..
116 Bolivia	2,000	2,189	121	25	52	21	57	14	122	9	175	33[c]
117 Cape Verde	1,475	3,003	180	68	95	188	67	72	114	11[c]	65	..
119 Honduras	2,177	2,358	127	-3	59	44	54	-2	73	..	73	39
120 Gabon	2,118	2,443	80	105	52	33	71	16	84	..	..	..
121 São Tomé and Principe	..	..	..	..	71	8	..	..	75	..	6	..
122 Viet Nam	2,122	2,438	178	2	33	50	56	10	149	..	64	..
123 Solomon Islands	2,150	2,085	83	98	41	-7	44	-21	65	..	..	..
124 Vanuatu	2,412	2,499	55	-8	100	11	55	-18	82	..	..	..
125 Morocco	2,404	3,140	261	20	64	49	84	29	143	17	13	38
126 Nicaragua	2,411	2,308	129	1	53	15	54	-25	78	23[c]	33	..
127 Iraq	2,254	2,266	140	-12	75	74	48	-21	72	..	68	..
128 Congo	1,996	2,083	58	115	53	23	45	25	91	..	12	37
129 Papua New Guinea	1,920	2,273	72	112	53	61	49	23	86	..	..	..
130 Zimbabwe	2,222	1,961	154	-16	49	-4	46	-26	85	18[c]	4	40
Low human development	2,107	2,315	152	10	43	38	56	10	116	..	3,859 T	..
Excluding India	2,146	2,237	140	9	45	36	53	2	104	..	3,595 T	..
131 Myanmar	1,997	2,728	220	35	47	42	68	31	125	..	5	..
132 Cameroon	2,280	2,199	106	1	44	-6	52	-15	91	16[c]	2	24
133 Ghana	2,121	2,574	94	32	38	-10	53	2	122	..	101	50[c]
134 Lesotho	1,986	1,965	185	-7	32	33	58	-5	89	..	15	..
135 Equatorial Guinea	..	..	..	..	..	..	..	..	59	..	3	..
136 Lao People's Dem. Rep.	2,154	2,105	180	-13	25	9	55	-2	99	..	10	..
137 Kenya	2,180	1,980	129	-9	46	35	53	-17	91	8[c]	102	38
138 Pakistan	2,198	2,471	154	3	67	97	62	15	122	14	103	37
139 India	2,078	2,382	162	11	42	40	59	16	127	..	264	52
140 Cambodia	2,059	1,996	170	-9	25	32	44	-8	132	..	64	..
141 Comoros	1,848	1,794	86	16	38	-5	44	26	79	..	10	..
142 Nigeria	2,254	2,497	126	13	60	13	54	8	143	..	..	48
143 Dem. Rep. of the Congo	2,158	1,870	35	..	31	-9	31	-16	84	..	83	..
144 Togo	2,261	1,736	109	-3	42	24	45	-12	108	23[c]	8	..
145 Benin	1,964	2,386	101	28	43	..	57	19	131	..	15	37
146 Zambia	2,140	1,915	159	-9	30	-27	51	-20	97	..	11	36
147 Bangladesh	2,177	2,001	173	..	22	47	44	-2	98	15[c]	888	59
148 Côte d'Ivoire	2,428	2,494	114	23	42	..	50	-6	105	..	56	39
149 Mauritania	1,868	2,568	168	63	66	27	75	1	82	..	22	..
150 Tanzania, U. Rep. of	1,749	2,003	107	67	31	15	49	17	80	..	118	64
151 Yemen	1,763	2,013	165	8	40	38	55	8	77	..	..	..
152 Nepal	1,933	2,367	198	13	33	27	60	-31	112	..	21	57
153 Madagascar	2,406	1,996	113	-22	28	-15	47	-23	74	11[c]	26	59
154 Central African Rep.	2,378	1,877	48	4	64	14	42	20	99	4[c]	1	..
155 Bhutan	..	..	..	..	..	..	..	..	91	..	4	..
156 Angola	2,071	1,904	61	-18	37	6	43	-7	90	..	..	..
157 Sudan	2,167	2,310	158	16	67	..	72	18	87	..	132	60[c]
158 Senegal	2,546	2,365	165	-8	72	7	66	2	112	29[c]	16	49
159 Haiti	..	..	..	..	..	..	..	..	64	..	117	..
160 Uganda	2,294	2,249	58	-9	31	-14	52	-9	99	..	62	..
161 Malawi	2,340	2,026	158	-17	27	-40	55	-26	78	..	204	30
162 Djibouti	1,842	1,827	110	-3	45	22	39	-7	70	..	23	..
163 Chad	2,183	1,917	125	-20	49	2	53	-17	84	..	14	..
164 Guinea-Bissau	1,989	2,423	162	38	61	2	48	12	118	..	2	..
165 Gambia	2,108	2,122	134	-18	49	-6	45	-20	56	..	2	..
166 Mozambique	1,886	1,675	81	17	31	7	32	-9	83	..	320	..
167 Guinea	2,212	2,150	113	18	47	-16	45	-6	79	..	29	..
168 Eritrea	..	..	..	..	..	..	..	..	..	..	140	..
169 Ethiopia	..	..	..	..	..	..	..	..	..	6[c]	720	49
170 Burundi	2,094	1,741	37	-8	13	-13	55	-25	81	..	48	..
171 Mali	2,095	2,137	184	13	47	..	58	-2	90	..	17	57
172 Burkina Faso	1,762	2,248	215	34	49	63	69	28	135	..	19	..
173 Niger	1,992	2,135	221	-4	31	..	61	9	70	..	32	..
174 Sierra Leone	2,419	1,992	114	-12	56	-13	45	-2	85	..	30	56
All developing countries	2,131	2,572	165	14	58	77	65	25	139	..	5,935 T	..
Least developed countries	2,090	2,103	143	12	35	16	50	-1	94	..	3,290 T	..
Industrial countries	3,016	3,157	130	1	117	20	99	11	103	..	..	..
World	2,337	2,702	157	11	71	48	73	20	132	..	..	..

a. Amounts of cereals, fat and protein available for human consumption. Per capita supplies represent the average supply available for the population as a whole and do not necessarily indicate what is actually consumed by individuals.
b. The time reference for food aid is the crop year, July to June.
c. Data refer to a year or period other than that specified in the column heading.
d. Includes beverages and tobacco.
Source: Columns 1, 2 and 9: FAO 1997a; columns 3-8: FAO 1998; columns 10 and 11: World Bank 1997d; column 12: World Bank 1993.

Education imbalances

HDI rank	Gross enrolment ratio				Tertiary natural and applied science enrolment (as % of total tertiary) 1995	R & D scientists and technicians (per 1,000 people) 1990-96	Public expenditure on				
	Primary		Secondary				Education (as % of GNP)		Education (as % of total government expenditure) 1993-95	Primary and secondary education (as % of all levels) 1990-95	Higher education (as % of all levels) 1990-95
	Total (%) 1995	Female as % of male 1995	Total (%) 1995	Female as % of male 1995			1985	1995			
High human development	**107**	**99**	**59**	**109**	**30**	**0.6**	**4.1**	**4.1**	**18.4**	**70**	**18**
23 Cyprus	100	100	97	103	19	0.4	3.7	4.4	13.2	83	7
24 Barbados	..	..	..	..	19	..	6.1	7.2	19.0	75	19
25 Hong Kong, China	96	102	75	105	36	0.2	2.8	2.8	17.0	56	37
28 Singapore	..	..	..	..	..	2.6	4.4	3.0	23.4	60	35
29 Antigua and Barbuda	..	..	..	..	..	..	2.7	..	..	..	..
30 Korea, Rep. of	101	101	101	100	39	2.9	4.5	3.7	17.4	79	8
31 Chile	99	98	69	111	42	..	4.4	2.9	14.0	70	18
32 Bahamas	94	99	90	103	..	..	4.0	..	16.3	..	..
34 Costa Rica	107	99	50	108	18	..	4.5	4.5	19.9	62	31
35 Brunei Darussalam	110	95	78	108	6	..	2.1	..	..	45	1
36 Argentina	113	99	77	111	30	0.8	..	4.5	15.0	72	17
38 Uruguay	111	98	82	120	..	0.7	2.8	2.8	13.3	57	27
40 Trinidad and Tobago	96	112	72	120	45	..	6.1	4.5	..	73	13
41 Dominica	..	..	..	..	58	..	5.9	..	10.6	86	3
43 Bahrain	108	102	99	103	39	..	4.1	4.8	12.8	73	..
44 Fiji	128	99	64	102	..	0.2	6.0	5.4	18.6	88	9
45 Panama	106	..	68	..	26	..	4.6	5.2	20.9	51	25
46 Venezuela	94	103	35	141	..	0.2	5.1	5.2	22.4	26	35
48 United Arab Emirates	94	96	80	111	..	..	1.7	1.8	16.3	..	..
49 Mexico	115	97	58	102	33	0.3	3.9	5.3	26.0	72	19
50 Saint Kitts and Nevis	..	..	..	..	..	..	5.8	3.3	9.8	77	12
51 Grenada	..	..	..	..	..	..	..	..	..	..	..
53 Colombia	114	99	67	116	31	..	2.9	3.5	12.9	72	17
54 Kuwait	73	99	64	100	23	..	4.9	5.6	11.0	57	16
55 Saint Vincent	..	..	..	..	..	..	5.8	..	13.8	96	..
56 Seychelles	..	..	..	..	45	..	10.7	7.5	16.3	60	13
57 Qatar	89	95	83	101	..	0.5	4.1	3.4	..	..	..
58 Saint Lucia	..	..	..	..	..	..	5.5	9.9	22.2	69	13
59 Thailand	87	..	55	..	19	0.2	3.8	4.2	20.1	73	17
60 Malaysia	91	101	57	107	..	0.2	6.6	5.3	15.5	76	17
61 Mauritius	107	99	62	107	..	0.5	3.8	4.3	17.3	74	17
62 Brazil	112	..	45	..	22	0.2	3.8	..	..	56	26
63 Belize	121	95	49	111	..	..	..	6.1	21.3	82	8
64 Libyan Arab Jamahiriya	106	97	97	..	..	..	7.1	..	19.8	..	..
Medium human development	**113**	**96**	**63**	**88**	**33**	**0.5**	**4.3**	**3.6**	**14.9**	**73**	**19**
Excluding China	**108**	**94**	**58**	**88**	**30**	**..**	**4.7**	**4.6**	**17.2**	**77**	**21**
65 Suriname	..	..	..	..	..	..	9.4	3.5	..	75	8
66 Lebanon	109	97	81	109	17	..	..	2.0	12.5	..	..
69 Turkey	105	95	56	67	21	0.3	1.8	3.4	..	68	32
70 Saudi Arabia	78	96	58	87	..	..	6.7	5.5	17.8	82	18
71 Oman	80	95	66	94	..	..	4.0	4.6	16.3	93	6
73 Ecuador	109	99	50	100	..	0.3	3.7	3.4	17.5	60	22
75 Korea, Dem. People's Rep. of	..	..	..	..	..	..	..	..	..	..	..
78 Iran, Islamic Rep. of	99	93	69	82	37	0.7	3.6	4.0	17.8	63	23
81 Syrian Arab Rep.	101	90	44	85	29	..	6.1	..	17.3	96	..
82 Algeria	107	89	62	89	52	..	8.5	..	17.6	95	..
83 Tunisia	116	94	61	94	24	0.4	5.8	6.8	17.4	79	19
84 Jamaica	109	99	66	113	..	(.)	5.7	8.2	7.7	66	23
85 Cuba	105	96	80	105	23	2.7	6.3	..	10.2	58	16
86 Peru	123	97	70	93	..	0.8	2.9	3.8	..	..	..
87 Jordan	94	101	..	..	28	0.1	5.5	6.3	16.6	58	34
88 Dominican Rep.	103	101	41	138	..	..	1.8	1.9	13.2	67	9
89 South Africa	117	97	82	116	57	1.2	6.0	6.8	20.5	82	15
90 Sri Lanka	113	98	75	110	..	0.2	2.6	3.1	8.1	73	12
91 Paraguay	109	97	38	103	25	..	1.5	2.9	16.9	68	18
94 Samoa (Western)	116	98	47	114	14	..	..	..	10.7	..	..
95 Maldives	134	97	49	100	..	..	4.4	8.4	13.6	99	..
96 Indonesia	114	96	48	85	28	..	..	..	..	79	18
97 Botswana	115	103	56	107	24	..	6.8	9.6	20.5	80	12
98 Philippines	116	..	79	..	31	0.2	1.4	2.2	10.1	..	..
100 Guyana	94	98	76	125	43	..	9.8	4.1	8.1	71	8
101 Mongolia	88	103	59	136	24	1.1	7.8	5.6	..	64	18
106 China	118	98	67	89	37	0.6	2.5	2.3	12.2	67	17
107 Namibia	133	102	62	118	5	..	..	9.4	21.3	81	7
111 Guatemala	84	87	25	92	..	0.2	1.8	1.7	18.2	67	16
112 Egypt	100	87	74	85	15	0.7	6.3	5.6	13.8	64	36

HDI rank	Gross enrolment ratio Primary Total (%) 1995	Gross enrolment ratio Primary Female as % of male 1995	Gross enrolment ratio Secondary Total (%) 1995	Gross enrolment ratio Secondary Female as % of male 1995	Tertiary natural and applied science enrolment (as % of total tertiary) 1995	R & D scientists and technicians (per 1,000 people) 1990-96	Public expenditure on Education (as % of GNP) 1985	Public expenditure on Education (as % of GNP) 1995	Education (as % of total government expenditure) 1993-95	Primary and secondary education (as % of all levels) 1990-95	Higher education (as % of all levels) 1990-95
114 El Salvador	88	101	32	113	25	0.3	3.1	2.2	31.0	68	7
115 Swaziland	122	95	52	96	22	..	5.9	8.1	21.7	63	28
116 Bolivia	..	..	..	..	..	0.4	2.1	6.6	8.2	50	29
117 Cape Verde	131	98	27	93	..	..	3.6	..	19.9	72	3
119 Honduras	112	101	32	..	26	..	4.2	3.9	16.5	74	17
120 Gabon	..	..	..	..	..	0.2	4.5	..	..	100	..
121 São Tomé and Principe	..	..	..	..	..	..	4.6	..	..	..	..
122 Viet Nam	114	..	47	..	..	0.3	..	2.7	7.4	..	..
123 Solomon Islands	97	87	17	67	29	..	4.7	..	7.9	86	14
124 Vanuatu	106	102	20	78	..	..	..	4.9	..	91	6
125 Morocco	83	76	39	75	29	..	6.3	5.6	22.6	84	16
126 Nicaragua	110	103	47	116	..	0.3	6.8	..	12.2	78	..
127 Iraq	..	..	..	..	..	..	4.0	..	..	77	21
128 Congo	114	92	53	73	11	..	5.1	5.9	14.7	62	28
129 Papua New Guinea	80	85	14	65	..	..	..	..	..	..	..
130 Zimbabwe	116	97	44	80	23	..	9.1	8.5	..	78	17
Low human development	88	77	34	68	..	..	3.2	..	12.6	..	..
Excluding India	75	72	17	72	..	..	..	..	14.6	..	..
131 Myanmar	103	97	30	103	36	..	..	1.3	14.4	88	12
132 Cameroon	88	90	27	69	..	..	3.1	..	16.1	87	13
133 Ghana	..	..	..	..	..	..	2.6	..	24.3	64	11
134 Lesotho	99	114	28	155	25	..	4.3	5.9	12.2	82	17
135 Equatorial Guinea	..	..	..	..	..	..	..	1.8	5.6	..	..
136 Lao People's Dem. Rep.	107	74	25	61	45	..	..	2.4	..	83	4
137 Kenya	85	100	24	85	..	..	6.4	7.4	16.1	82	14
138 Pakistan	74	45	0	..	..	0.1	2.5	..	..	67	18
139 India	100	82	49	64	..	0.3	3.4	3.5	12.1	65	14
140 Cambodia	122	81	27	59	..	..	..	..	..	..	..
141 Comoros	78	84	19	81	..	..	4.1	3.9	..	72	17
142 Nigeria	89	79	30	85	41	0.1	..	..	..	..	..
143 Dem. Rep. of the Congo	72	69	26	59	..	..	1.0	..	..	..	..
144 Togo	118	69	27	34	16	..	5.0	5.6	18.7	66	27
145 Benin	72	57	16	43	19	0.2	..	3.1	15.2	79	19
146 Zambia	89	93	28	62	..	..	4.7	1.8	..	60	23
147 Bangladesh	..	..	..	..	..	..	1.9	2.3	8.7	88	8
148 Côte d'Ivoire	69	73	23	50	26	..	..	..	..	99	..
149 Mauritania	78	85	15	58	8	..	..	5.0	16.1	76	20
150 Tanzania, U. Rep. of	67	97	5	83	39	..	4.4	..	11.4	74	17
151 Yemen	79	40	23	22	..	..	..	7.5	20.8	..	..
152 Nepal	110	69	37	51	17	..	2.6	2.9	13.2	62	28
153 Madagascar	72	96	14	100	23	(.)	2.9	..	13.6	82	..
154 Central African Rep.	..	..	..	..	..	0.1	2.8	..	20.9	71	24
155 Bhutan	..	..	..	..	..	..	..	..	..	..	..
156 Angola	..	..	..	..	..	..	5.1	..	10.7	96	4
157 Sudan	54	81	13	86	..	..	..	..	..	..	..
158 Senegal	65	79	16	60	..	..	..	3.6	33.1	69	24
159 Haiti	..	..	..	..	..	..	1.2	..	20.0	72	9
160 Uganda	73	85	12	60	13	..	3.5	..	15.0	..	..
161 Malawi	135	90	6	57	18	..	3.5	5.7	15.0	76	17
162 Djibouti	38	75	13	73	..	..	2.7	..	11.1	75	14
163 Chad	55	49	9	27	14	..	..	2.2	..	61	8
164 Guinea-Bissau	64	58	..	..	..	..	3.2	..	..	..	..
165 Gambia	73	86	22	54	..	..	3.2	5.5	16.0	70	11
166 Mozambique	60	71	7	56	50	..	4.2	..	12.0	66	10
167 Guinea	48	54	12	33	..	..	..	..	..	64	18
168 Eritrea	57	81	19	73	..	..	..	..	..	..	..
169 Ethiopia	31	62	11	83	36	..	3.0	4.7	13.0	81	11
170 Burundi	70	82	7	63	..	0.1	2.5	2.8	..	72	28
171 Mali	32	64	9	50	..	..	3.7	2.2	13.2	67	18
172 Burkina Faso	38	65	8	55	18	..	..	3.6	11.1	68	32
173 Niger	29	61	7	44	..	..	..	..	10.8	77	..
174 Sierra Leone	..	..	..	..	30	..	..	1.9	..	53	35
All developing countries	101	87	50	81	..	0.4	4.1	3.8	..	..	..
Least developed countries	70	76	17	69	..	..	..	..	..	..	..
Industrial countries	101	99	99	102	33	3.8	5.1	5.2	..	..	..
World	101	89	58	85	..	1.3	4.9	4.9	..	..	..

Source: Columns: 1-5, 7 and 8: UNESCO 1998; columns 6, 9-11: UNESCO 1997d.

16 Profile of people in work

HDI rank		Labour force (as % of total population) 1995	Women's share of adult labour force (% age 15 and above)		Percentage of labour force in						Real earnings per employee annual growth rate (%)	
					Agriculture		Industry		Services			
		1995	1970	1995	1970	1990	1970	1990	1970	1990	1970-80	1980-92
High human development		45	28	37	47	28	21	24	33	48	..	..
23	Cyprus	48	33	38	38	14	28	30	34	56	..	..
24	Barbados	52	41	47	17	7	41	23	42	70	..	..
25	Hong Kong, China	52	34	37	4	1	55	37	41	62	..	4.8
28	Singapore	51	26	39	3	0	30	36	66	64	3.0	5.1
29	Antigua and Barbuda	..	..	..	..	..	..	..	..	..	..	..
30	Korea, Rep. of	49	33	40	49	18	20	35	31	47	10.0	8.4
31	Chile	40	22	32	24	19	29	25	47	56	8.1	-0.3
32	Bahamas	52	41	47	8	5	21	15	71	79	..	..
34	Costa Rica	39	18	30	43	26	20	27	37	47	..	..
35	Brunei Darussalam	43	18	34	12	2	34	24	55	74	..	..
36	Argentina	39	25	31	16	12	34	32	50	55	-2.1	-2.2
38	Uruguay	45	26	41	19	14	29	27	52	59	..	-2.3
40	Trinidad and Tobago	42	29	33	..	..	..	..	..	..	..	..
41	Dominica	..	..	..	..	..	..	..	..	..	..	..
43	Bahrain	44	5	19	7	2	38	30	54	68	..	..
44	Fiji	37	11	27	52	46	17	15	32	39	0.2	2.0
45	Panama	41	25	34	42	26	18	16	41	58	4.9	-5.4
46	Venezuela	39	21	33	26	12	25	27	49	61	..	..
48	United Arab Emirates	50	4	13	9	8	39	27	52	65	..	..
49	Mexico	39	19	32	44	28	24	24	32	48	..	..
50	Saint Kitts and Nevis	..	..	..	..	..	..	..	..	..	..	..
51	Grenada	..	..	..	..	..	..	..	..	..	-0.2	1.0
53	Colombia	42	23	37	45	27	19	23	36	50	7.0	-1.6
54	Kuwait	37	8	31	2	1	34	25	64	74	..	..
55	Saint Vincent	..	..	..	..	..	..	..	..	..	..	..
56	Seychelles	..	..	..	..	..	..	..	..	..	..	..
57	Qatar	57	4	13	10	3	26	32	64	65	..	..
58	Saint Lucia	..	..	..	..	..	..	..	..	..	..	..
59	Thailand	59	48	46	80	64	6	14	14	22	2.0	2.3
60	Malaysia	40	30	37	54	27	14	23	32	50	..	..
61	Mauritius	42	20	31	34	17	25	43	41	40	1.8	0.4
62	Brazil	46	23	35	47	23	20	23	33	54	5.0	-2.4
63	Belize	33	20	23	40	34	20	19	40	48	..	..
64	Libyan Arab Jamahiriya	29	16	21	37	11	22	23	41	66	..	..
Medium human development		52	38	43	73	64	11	16	15	19	..	..
	Excluding China	41	31	37	61	47	15	19	25	35	..	..
65	Suriname	36	22	32	27	21	22	18	51	61	..	..
66	Lebanon	33	18	28	20	7	25	31	55	62	..	..
69	Turkey	46	37	36	71	54	12	18	17	28	6.1	3.0
70	Saudi Arabia	33	5	13	..	..	..	..	..	..	..	..
71	Oman	27	6	14	57	45	18	24	25	32	..	..
73	Ecuador	37	18	26	51	33	20	19	28	48	3.3	-0.7
75	Korea, Dem. People's Rep. of	53	45	44	55	38	25	32	21	30	..	..
78	Iran, Islamic Rep. of	30	18	24	48	32	27	25	25	43	..	-6.8
81	Syrian Arab Rep.	30	21	25	56	33	18	24	25	43	..	..
82	Algeria	31	19	24	55	26	18	31	27	43	-1.3	..
83	Tunisia	37	24	30	49	28	22	33	28	39	..	..
84	Jamaica	51	43	46	33	25	18	23	49	52	-0.2	-1.5
85	Cuba	48	20	38	30	18	26	30	43	51	..	..
86	Peru	36	22	29	48	36	18	18	34	47	..	-3.3
87	Jordan	28	14	21	33	15	24	23	43	61	..	..
88	Dominican Rep.	42	21	30	48	25	14	29	38	46	-1.1	..
89	South Africa	39	33	37	31	14	30	32	39	55	2.7	0.2
90	Sri Lanka	42	25	36	55	49	14	21	30	31	..	1.4
91	Paraguay	37	26	29	50	39	19	22	31	39	..	..
94	Samoa (Western)	..	..	..	..	..	..	..	..	..	..	..
95	Maldives	41	36	43	66	32	20	31	14	37	5.2	4.3
96	Indonesia	46	30	40	66	55	10	14	23	31	..	..
97	Botswana	44	55	46	82	46	5	20	13	33	..	..
98	Philippines	41	33	37	58	46	15	15	27	39	-3.7	5.2
100	Guyana	42	20	33	32	22	29	25	40	53	..	..
101	Mongolia	48	46	47	48	32	21	23	31	45	..	..
106	China	60	41	45	78	72	10	15	12	13	..	..
107	Namibia	41	39	41	64	49	15	15	21	36	..	..
111	Guatemala	36	19	27	61	52	17	17	22	30	-3.2	-1.6
112	Egypt	36	24	29	61	40	13	22	26	38	4.1	-3.6

HDI rank	Labour force (as % of total population) 1995	Women's share of adult labour force (% age 15 and above)		Percentage of labour force in						Real earnings per employee annual growth rate (%)	
				Agriculture		Industry		Services			
	1995	1970	1995	1970	1990	1970	1990	1970	1990	1970-80	1980-92
114 El Salvador	41	21	35	57	36	14	21	29	43	2.4	..
115 Swaziland	36	34	37	65	39	13	22	22	38	..	..
116 Bolivia	40	30	37	55	47	20	18	25	36	1.7	-0.8
117 Cape Verde	39	28	39	47	31	27	30	27	40	..	..
119 Honduras	36	23	30	67	41	11	20	21	39	..	..
120 Gabon	47	45	44	79	52	9	16	12	33	..	..
121 São Tomé and Principe	..	..	..	..	..	..	..	..	..	..	..
122 Viet Nam	51	48	49	77	71	7	14	15	15	..	..
123 Solomon Islands	51	45	46	82	77	5	7	14	16	..	..
124 Vanuatu	..	..	..	..	..	..	..	..	..	..	..
125 Morocco	39	29	34	65	45	14	25	21	31	..	-2.5
126 Nicaragua	38	24	34	51	29	18	26	31	45	-2.0	..
127 Iraq	27	16	18	53	16	20	18	28	66	..	..
128 Congo	41	41	43	66	49	11	15	23	37	..	..
129 Papua New Guinea	49	41	42	..	..	..	..	..	..	2.9	..
130 Zimbabwe	46	44	45	77	68	11	8	12	24	1.6	0.1
Low human development	44	36	38	76	66	10	13	14	21	..	..
Excluding India	44	40	44	80	69	7	10	13	21	..	..
131 Myanmar	52	44	43	78	73	7	10	15	17	..	..
132 Cameroon	40	37	37	85	70	5	9	10	21	..	..
133 Ghana	47	50	50	60	59	15	13	25	28	-14.8	..
134 Lesotho	41	40	37	43	40	36	28	21	32	..	..
135 Equatorial Guinea	42	36	35	..	..	..	..	..	..	..	..
136 Lao People's Dem. Rep.	48	45	47	81	78	5	6	14	16	..	..
137 Kenya	50	45	46	86	80	5	7	9	13	-3.4	-2.1
138 Pakistan	36	21	26	65	52	16	19	19	30	3.4	..
139 India	43	33	31	73	64	12	16	16	20	0.4	2.5
140 Cambodia	52	49	52	79	74	4	8	17	19	..	..
141 Comoros	45	44	42	83	77	7	9	10	13	..	..
142 Nigeria	40	37	36	71	43	11	7	19	50	-0.8	..
143 Dem. Rep. of the Congo	42	45	43	75	68	11	13	14	19	..	..
144 Togo	41	39	39	74	66	9	10	17	24	..	..
145 Benin	45	49	49	81	64	5	8	14	28	..	..
146 Zambia	41	44	45	79	75	7	8	14	17	-3.2	3.8
147 Bangladesh	50	40	42	84	65	7	16	10	18	-3.0	-0.7
148 Côte d'Ivoire	39	32	32	76	60	6	10	19	30	-0.9	..
149 Mauritania	46	46	44	84	55	3	10	12	34	..	..
150 Tanzania, U. Rep. of	51	51	49	90	84	3	5	7	11	..	..
151 Yemen	32	25	27	78	61	7	17	15	22	..	..
152 Nepal	46	39	40	94	94	1	0	4	6	..	..
153 Madagascar	47	45	44	84	78	5	7	11	15	-0.8	..
154 Central African Rep.	49	49	47	89	80	2	3	8	16	..	..
155 Bhutan	49	39	39	95	94	2	1	4	5	..	..
156 Angola	46	47	46	78	75	7	8	15	17	..	..
157 Sudan	39	26	28	79	69	5	8	16	22	..	..
158 Senegal	45	41	42	83	77	6	8	12	16	..	..
159 Haiti	44	46	43	74	68	7	9	18	23	..	..
160 Uganda	50	48	48	90	85	3	5	7	11	..	..
161 Malawi	48	50	49	91	87	4	5	5	8	..	..
162 Djibouti	..	..	..	..	..	..	..	..	..	..	..
163 Chad	48	42	44	92	83	2	4	5	13	..	..
164 Guinea-Bissau	47	39	40	89	85	1	2	9	13	..	..
165 Gambia	51	44	44	87	82	5	8	8	11	..	..
166 Mozambique	52	50	49	86	83	6	8	8	9	..	..
167 Guinea	48	48	47	92	87	1	2	7	11	..	..
168 Eritrea	50	47	47	86	80	4	5	10	15	..	..
169 Ethiopia	44	42	40	91	86	2	2	7	12	..	..
170 Burundi	53	51	49	94	92	2	3	4	6	-7.5	..
171 Mali	49	46	46	93	86	1	2	6	12	..	..
172 Burkina Faso	50	49	47	92	92	3	2	5	6	..	..
173 Niger	48	45	44	93	90	2	4	5	6	..	..
174 Sierra Leone	37	35	35	76	67	12	15	12	17	..	..
All developing countries	48	37	41	72	61	12	16	17	23	..	..
Least developed countries	47	43	48	85	76	5	9	10	15	..	..
Industrial countries	49	40	44	18	10	38	33	45	57	..	..
World	48	38	41	56	49	19	20	25	31	..	..

Note: Percentage shares of labour force in agriculture, industry and services may not necessarily add to 100 because of rounding.
Source: Columns 1-9: ILO 1996; *columns 10 and 11:* World Bank 1995c.

Access to information and communications

HDI rank	Radios (per 1,000 people) 1995	Televisions (per 1,000 people) 1995	Printing and writing paper consumed (metric tons per 1,000 people) 1995	Post offices (per 100,000 people) 1991	Main telephone lines (per 1,000 people) 1995	Public pay phones (per 1,000 people) 1995	International telephone calls (minutes per person) 1995	Fax machines (per 1,000 people) 1995	Cellular mobile telephone subscribers (per 1,000 people) 1995	Internet users (per 1,000 people) 1995	Personal computers (per 1,000 people) 1995
High human development	442	253	18.5	..	133	2.6	13.0	..	16.6	2.6	30.0
23 Cyprus	309	143	34.0	..	474	2.7	160.3	..	60.7	4.1	40.9
24 Barbados	900	287	14.0	..	345	2.0	122.6	6.8	17.7	0.1	57.5
25 Hong Kong, China	668	359	98.4	..	533	0.8	274.8	46.3	129.7	48.5	130.0
28 Singapore	601	362	98.0	24.2	479	10.4	258.8	..	102.5	30.1	180.8
29 Antigua and Barbuda	439	409	3.4	17.3	..	3.1	..	..	..	22.7	..
30 Korea, Rep. of	1,024	321	51.3	7.7	415	6.9	12.4	..	36.6	6.5	108.3
31 Chile	348	280	16.1	8.4	132	1.3	9.5	..	13.8	7.0	37.8
32 Bahamas	735	233	6.9	..	..	2.8	..	..	..	9.7	..
34 Costa Rica	263	220	5.4	..	164	2.2	15.5	..	5.5	4.3	..
35 Brunei Darussalam	273	609	2.1	4.6	240	1.0	108.0	7.0	126.3	2.9	..
36 Argentina	676	347	18.4	..	160	2.0	4.4	1.5	9.9	1.4	24.6
38 Uruguay	609	305	13.6	..	196	1.8	16.2	3.5	12.6	2.5	22.0
40 Trinidad and Tobago	505	318	10.6	19.6	160	1.4	44.9	1.6	4.3	1.5	19.2
41 Dominica	634	141	0.9	..	251	3.8	..	..	..	5.3	..
43 Bahrain	575	439	7.6	..	242	1.7	152.6	10.8	47.5	1.7	50.3
44 Fiji	612	89	10.8	..	83	0.7	19.3	3.8	2.8	0.1	..
45 Panama	228	229	2.1	..	114	1.2	14.9	..	..	0.6	..
46 Venezuela	458	180	11.3	..	111	2.6	5.8	..	18.0	0.5	16.7
48 United Arab Emirates	271	263	38.4	10.0	283	5.1	211.8	10.5	54.3	1.1	48.4
49 Mexico	263	192	12.1	..	96	2.7	10.3	..	7.0	1.5	26.1
50 Saint Kitts and Nevis	668	..	3.9	18.2	351	..	196.1	..	4.4	..	..
51 Grenada	598	158	0.8	..	255	2.3	81.6	..	..	..	..
53 Colombia	564	188	9.1	..	100	1.1	3.3	2.6	7.1	0.7	16.2
54 Kuwait	473	373	6.7	..	226	0.3	74.5	20.7	69.6	2.1	56.2
55 Saint Vincent	670	234	0.5	..	164	1.4	..	6.6	..	1.3	..
56 Seychelles	548	184	3.5	7.1	178	3.0	28.6	..	4.3	..	..
57 Qatar	438	457	2.2	..	223	1.1	137.6	17.1	33.5	1.8	..
58 Saint Lucia	765	301	7.5	..	184	2.5	76.4	..	6.0	2.7	..
59 Thailand	189	227	13.1	7.3	59	0.8	3.7	..	18.3	0.7	13.6
60 Malaysia	432	231	32.6	12.4	166	4.9	18.3	..	49.9	2.0	37.3
61 Mauritius	367	192	11.1	9.4	131	0.8	17.7	17.7	10.4	..	31.9
62 Brazil	399	278	13.0	7.9	75	2.3	1.8	..	8.0	1.2	13.0
63 Belize	587	167	1.4	..	134	0.9	27.1	..	5.7	(.)	27.8
64 Libyan Arab Jamahiriya	231	138	0.5	..	59	0.1	8.6	..	..	..	..
Medium human development	194	203	5.2	..	41	0.6	2.2	0.3	3.0	0.3	3.5
Excluding China	207	141	4.8	..	51	0.5	3.9	..	3.0	0.9	6.3
65 Suriname	679	195	0.9	..	130	0.4	13.5	1.7	9.0	1.2	..
66 Lebanon	891	268	4.1	..	82	(.)	8.5	..	30.0	0.6	12.5
69 Turkey	164	240	10.1	..	212	0.9	6.1	1.6	7.0	0.8	12.5
70 Saudi Arabia	291	269	4.6	..	96	0.9	30.0	..	0.9	0.1	..
71 Oman	580	61	1.0	..	79	1.6	25.2	..	3.7	..	12.7
73 Ecuador	332	148	5.1	4.9	65	0.4	3.2	..	4.3	0.4	3.9
75 Korea, Dem. People's Rep. of	136	115	0.1	..	46	0.1	..	..	..	..	..
78 Iran, Islamic Rep. of	228	134	3.7	..	76	0.8	3.1	..	0.4	(.)	..
81 Syrian Arab Rep.	264	89	2.7	..	63	0.1	4.1	0.3	..	..	0.1
82 Algeria	238	71	2.8	10.6	42	0.2	2.8	0.2	..	(.)	3.0
83 Tunisia	200	156	6.4	..	58	0.8	8.7	2.8	0.4	0.1	6.7
84 Jamaica	438	306	8.0	..	116	0.7	21.8	..	17.9	0.6	..
85 Cuba	351	200	2.0	..	32	0.6	1.0	..	0.2	(.)	..
86 Peru	259	100	4.3	..	47	1.0	2.7	0.6	3.1	0.3	6.0
87 Jordan	251	175	7.4	..	73	0.1	16.5	7.4	2.6	0.2	8.0
88 Dominican Rep.	176	87	2.1	..	73	0.6	..	..	4.2	0.2	..
89 South Africa	316	101	16.6	..	95	1.7	7.4	..	12.9	11.1	26.5
90 Sri Lanka	206	66	4.8	23.0	11	0.1	1.5	..	2.9	(.)	1.1
91 Paraguay	180	144	6.7	7.2	34	0.3	4.2	..	3.2	..	..
94 Samoa (Western)	485	38	0.6	..	..	..	..	..	..	..	..
95 Maldives	118	40	4.0	..	57	0.7	12.6	14.3	..	..	12.3
96 Indonesia	149	147	5.5	5.4	17	0.6	1.1	0.4	1.1	0.1	3.8
97 Botswana	131	24	..	12.8	41	0.4	20.4	2.2	..	..	..
98 Philippines	147	126	5.3	4.0	21	0.1	2.6	..	7.3	0.3	8.6
100 Guyana	494	42	1.6	..	53	0.3	24.4	..	1.5	..	..
101 Mongolia	134	59	0.2	..	33	(.)	0.8	0.9	..	..	..
106 China	185	247	5.5	..	34	0.7	1.1	0.2	3.0	(.)	2.1
107 Namibia	140	29	..	..	51	0.7	31.5	..	2.3	0.1	..
111 Guatemala	71	122	3.8	6.5	27	0.4	3.4	..	2.8	(.)	2.8
112 Egypt	312	126	3.2	12.4	46	0.1	1.7	..	0.1	0.3	..

HDI rank	Radios (per 1,000 people) 1995	Televisions (per 1,000 people) 1995	Printing and writing paper consumed (metric tons per 1,000 people) 1995	Post offices (per 100,000 people) 1991	Main telephone lines (per 1,000 people) 1995	Public pay phones (per 1,000 people) 1995	International telephone calls (minutes per person) 1995	Fax machines (per 1,000 people) 1995	Cellular mobile telephone subscribers (per 1,000 people) 1995	Internet users (per 1,000 people) 1995	Personal computers (per 1,000 people) 1995
114 El Salvador	459	241	4.2	5.2	53	1.1	11.9	..	2.5	..	..
115 Swaziland	163	96	..	8.3	21	0.5	26.6	..	..	(.)	..
116 Bolivia	672	202	1.9	2.8	47	(.)	3.1	..	1.0	0.1	..
117 Cape Verde	179	3	0.3	16.8	55	0.5	10.0	1.3	..	..	..
119 Honduras	409	80	2.8	..	29	0.2	6.1	..	..	..	..
120 Gabon	181	76	0.3	8.5	24	0.1	12.1	0.3	3.0	..	4.5
121 São Tomé and Principe	271	..	(.)	9.1	19	0.3	4.2	1.3	..	..	..
122 Viet Nam	106	163	1.3	..	11	(.)	0.5	0.2	0.3	..	0.4
123 Solomon Islands	122	16	(.)	..	17	0.3	7.1	2.1	0.7	0.2	..
124 Vanuatu	296	10	0.3	..	25	0.3	16.3	3.3	0.7	..	..
125 Morocco	226	145	2.5	..	43	0.7	4.9	..	1.1	0.1	1.7
126 Nicaragua	280	170	0.6	..	23	0.1	7.1	..	1.1	0.3	..
127 Iraq	224	74	0.4	..	33	..	..	..	..	..	..
128 Congo	116	17	0.1	..	8	(.)	..	..	..	..	..
129 Papua New Guinea	77	166	0.9	..	10	0.1	5.6	..	..	..	..
130 Zimbabwe	89	27	1.8	2.8	14	0.2	5.1	..	..	0.1	3.0
Low human development	102	47	1.3	13.7	9	0.2	0.5	..	0.1	..	..
Excluding India	123	32	0.6	..	6	(.)	0.6	0.4	0.2	..	..
131 Myanmar	89	76	0.4	..	4	(.)	0.3	..	..	..	..
132 Cameroon	152	75	0.3	..	5	(.)	1.8	..	0.2	..	..
133 Ghana	231	16	0.3	6.5	4	(.)	1.0	..	0.4	(.)	1.2
134 Lesotho	37	7	..	..	9	0.1	..	0.3	..	..	..
135 Equatorial Guinea	425	92	..	..	6	(.)	2.0	0.3	..	..	..
136 Lao People's Dem. Rep.	129	7	0.1	4.9	4	..	1.0	..	0.3	..	..
137 Kenya	96	18	1.5	..	9	0.2	0.8	0.1	0.1	(.)	0.7
138 Pakistan	92	22	1.7	11.5	16	0.1	0.5	1.2	0.3	(.)	1.2
139 India	81	61	1.9	17.6	13	0.3	0.4	..	0.1	(.)	1.2
140 Cambodia	112	8	0.1	..	1	(.)	0.5	0.1	1.5	..	..
141 Comoros	137	5	0.7	..	9	0.1	1.9	..	..	..	..
142 Nigeria	197	38	0.3	4.0	4	(.)	0.9	..	0.1	..	..
143 Dem. Rep. of the Congo	98	41	(.)	1.3	1	(.)	..	0.1	0.2	..	..
144 Togo	215	12	0.5	..	5	(.)	2.1	2.4	..	..	..
145 Benin	92	73	0.1	3.9	5	0.1	1.0	0.2	0.2	..	..
146 Zambia	99	64	0.5	..	8	0.1	1.3	0.1	0.2	0.1	..
147 Bangladesh	47	7	1.2	..	2	(.)	0.2	(.)	..	..	..
148 Côte d'Ivoire	153	59	0.8	3.0	8	(.)	2.3	..	..	(.)	..
149 Mauritania	150	58	0.1	..	4	0.1	2.2	0.1	..	..	..
150 Tanzania, U. Rep. of	276	16	0.5	3.7	3	(.)	0.2	..	0.1	..	..
151 Yemen	43	267	(.)	..	12	(.)	1.5	0.1	0.6	..	..
152 Nepal	36	3	0.1	..	4	(.)	0.7	..	..	(.)	..
153 Madagascar	192	24	0.4	8.0	2	(.)	0.3	..	..	..	..
154 Central African Rep.	75	5	0.1	..	2	(.)	0.7	0.1	..	..	..
155 Bhutan	17	..	(.)	5.5	9	(.)	0.7	..	..	..	..
156 Angola	34	51	0.2	0.7	6	(.)	1.7	..	0.2	..	..
157 Sudan	270	86	0.1	..	3	(.)	0.3	0.2	..	..	..
158 Senegal	120	37	0.2	1.9	10	0.5	2.4	..	..	(.)	7.2
159 Haiti	53	5	0.2	2.0	8	(.)	..	..	..	..	..
160 Uganda	117	26	0.2	..	2	(.)	0.3	0.1	0.1	(.)	0.5
161 Malawi	256	..	0.1	..	4	0.1	0.8	0.1	..	..	..
162 Djibouti	80	73	(.)	..	13	0.1	7.0	0.2	..	0.2	..
163 Chad	248	2	0.1	0.6	1	(.)	0.3	(.)	..	..	..
164 Guinea-Bissau	42	..	(.)	..	9	..	2.1	0.5	..	..	..
165 Gambia	164	..	(.)	..	17	0.2	4.3	0.9	1.3	..	..
166 Mozambique	38	3	(.)	1.6	3	(.)	0.9	..	..	..	..
167 Guinea	44	76	(.)	..	2	(.)	0.5	(.)	0.1	(.)	0.2
168 Eritrea	98	6	..	5	(.)	0.3	0.2	..	..	..	..
169 Ethiopia	193	4	0.1	..	3	(.)	0.2	(.)	..	(.)	..
170 Burundi	68	7	0.1	0.6	3	(.)	0.4	..	..	..	..
171 Mali	46	12	(.)	..	2	(.)	0.7	..	..	..	..
172 Burkina Faso	28	6	(.)	..	3	(.)	0.6	..	..	..	..
173 Niger	68	23	(.)	0.8	2	(.)	0.4	(.)	..	..	..
174 Sierra Leone	250	16	0.1	2.0	4	(.)	0.5	0.2	..	..	..
All developing countries	185	145	5.2	..	39	0.7	2.8	..	3.6	0.5	6.5
Least developed countries	113	32	0.4	..	3	(.)	0.5	0.1	..	..	..
Industrial countries	1,005	524	78.2	..	414	3.7	41.6	23.2	61.1	17.9	156.3
World	364 a	228	20.9	..	122 b	1.4	10.9	..	16.8 b	4.8 b	43.6 b

a. UNESCO 1998.
b. ITU 1997a.
Source: Column 1: UNESCO 1998; *column 2:* ITU 1997b; *column 3:* UNESCO 1997d; *column 4:* UNDP 1994; *columns 5-7 and 9-11:* ITU 1997a; *column 8:* calculated on the basis of estimates from: ITU 1997b.

	ELECTIONS					POLITICAL PARTIES		WOMEN'S PARTICIPATION		
	Lower or single house		Upper house or senate		Voter turnout at last elections for lower or single house (%)	Parties represented in		Year women received right		Year first woman elected (E) or nominated (N) to national parliament
HDI rank	Date of last elections	Members elected (E) or appointed (A)	Date of last elections	Members elected (E) or appointed (A)		Lower or single house	Upper house or senate	To vote[a]	To stand for election[a]	
High human development										
23 Cyprus	05 1996	E	..	..	93	5	..	1960	1960	1963 E
24 Barbados	09 1994	E	09 1994	A	60	3 [b]	2 [b]	1950	1950	1966 N
28 Singapore	01 1997	E+A	..	..	41	3	..	1947	1947	1963 E
29 Antigua and Barbuda	03 1994	E	03 1994	A	62	3	3 [b]	1951	1951	1984 N
30 Korea, Rep. of	04 1996	E	..	..	64	4 [b]	..	1948	1948	1948 E
31 Chile	12 1997	E	12 1997	E+A	86	8 [b]	6 [b]	1949	1949	1951 E
32 Bahamas	03 1997	E	03 1997	A	68	2	2	1964	1964	1977 N
34 Costa Rica	02 1998	E	..	..	71	6	..	1949	1949	1953 E
35 Brunei Darussalam	_ c	_ c	_ c	_ c	_ c	_ c	_ c	_ d	_ d	_ d
36 Argentina	10 1997	E	12 1995	E	78	6 [b]	4 [b]	1947	1947	1951 E
38 Uruguay	11 1994	E	11 1994	E	91	3 [b]	3 [b]	1932	1932	1942 E
40 Trinidad and Tobago	11 1995	E	11 1995	A	63	3	2 [b]	1946	1946	1962 E
41 Dominica	06 1995	E+A	..	..	75	3	..	1951	1951	1980 E
43 Bahrain	12 1973[e]	E	_ e	_ e	_ e	_ e	_ e	_ d	_ d	_ d
44 Fiji	02 1994	E	02 1994	A	75 [f]	6 [b]	..	1963	1963	1970 N
45 Panama	05 1994	E	..	..	74	4 [b]	..	1946	1946	1946 E
46 Venezuela	12 1993	E	12 1993	E	60	5 [b]	5 [b]	1946	1946	1948 E
48 United Arab Emirates	11 1995	A	..	..	–	..	..	_ d	_ d	_ d
49 Mexico	07 1997	E	..	E	58	5 [b]	5 [b]	1947	1953	1952 N
50 Saint Kitts and Nevis	07 1995	E+A	..	..	68 [f]	4	..	1951	1951	1984 E
51 Grenada	06 1995	E	06 1995	A	62 [f]	3	†	1951	1951	1976 E
53 Colombia	03 1998	E	03 1994	E	36 [f]	2 [b]	5 [b]	1954	1954	1954 N
54 Kuwait	10 1996	E	..	..	80	0	..	_ d	_ d	_ d
55 Saint Vincent	02 1994	E+A	..	..	66	3	..	1951	1951	1979 E
56 Seychelles	07 1993	E	..	..	87	3	..	1948	1948	1976 E
57 Qatar	_ c	_ c	_ c	_ c	_ c	_ c	_ c	_ d	_ d	_ d
58 Saint Lucia	05 1997	E	05 1997	A	66	2	2 [b]	1924	1924	1979 N
59 Thailand	11 1996	E	03 1996	A	62	11	9 [b]	1932	1932	1948 N
60 Malaysia	04 1995	E	04 1995	E+A	72	9 [b]	†	1957	1957	1959 E
61 Mauritius	12 1995	E+A	..	..	80	5	..	1956	1956	1976 E
62 Brazil	10 1994	E	10 1994	E	82	11 [b]	8 [b]	1934	1934	1933 E
63 Belize	06 1993	E	06 1993	A	75 [f]	2	2 [b]	1954	1954	1984 E
64 Libyan Arab Jamahiriya	1997 [g]	E	..	..	..	1	..	1964	1964	†
Medium human development										
65 Suriname	05 1996	E	..	..	67 [f]	5	..	1948	1948	1975 E
66 Lebanon	08 1996	E	..	..	44	10 [b]	..	1952	1952	1991 N
69 Turkey	12 1995	E	..	..	85	5	..	1930	1934	1935 N
70 Saudi Arabia	_ c	_ c	_ c	_ c	_ c	_ c	_ c	_ d	_ d	_ d
71 Oman	_ c	_ c	_ c	_ c	_ c	_ c	_ c	_ d	_ d	_ d
73 Ecuador	05 1996	E	..	..	68 [f]	8 [b]	..	1929	1929	1956 E
75 Korea, Dem. People's Rep. of	04 1990	E	..	..	..	1	..	1946	1946	1948 E
78 Iran, Islamic Rep. of	03 1996	E	..	..	77	2 [b]	..	1963	1963	1963 E
81 Syrian Arab Rep.	08 1994	E	..	..	61	6 [b]	..	1953	1953	1973 E
82 Algeria	06 1997	E	12 1997	E	66	10 [b]	4	1962	1962	1962 N
83 Tunisia	03 1994	E	..	..	95	5	..	1959	1959	1959 E
84 Jamaica	12 1997	E	01 1998	A	60	2	..	1944	1944	1944 E
85 Cuba	01 1998	E	..	..	98	1	..	1934	1934	1940 E
86 Peru	04 1995	E	..	..	63 [f]	13	..	1955	1955	1956 E
87 Jordan	11 1997	E	11 1997	A	47	..	..	1974	1974	1989 N
88 Dominican Rep.	05 1994	E	05 1994	E	42 [f]	3	5	1942	1942	1942 E
89 South Africa	04 1994	E	04 1994	E	87	7	5	1930	1930	1933 E
90 Sri Lanka	08 1994	E	..	..	76	7 [b]	..	1931	1931	1947 E
91 Paraguay	05 1993	E	05 1993	E	66	3	3	1961	1961	1963 E
94 Samoa (Western)	04 1996	E	..	..	86	2 [b]	..	1990	1990	1976 N
95 Maldives	12 1994	E+A	..	..	75	..	..	1932	1932	1979 E
96 Indonesia	05 1997	E+A	..	..	89	3	..	1945	1945	1950 N
97 Botswana	10 1994	E	..	..	77	2	..	1965	1965	1979 E
98 Philippines	01 1998	E+A	05 1995	E	67	5 [b]	†	1937	1937	1941 E
100 Guyana	12 1997	E	..	..	98	4	..	1953	1945	1968 E
101 Mongolia	06 1996	E	..	..	88	4 [b]	..	1924	1924	1951 E
106 China	1997-98	E	..	..	†	1	..	1949	1949	1954 E
107 Namibia	12 1994	E	01 1992	E	75	5	..	1989	1989	1989 E
111 Guatemala	11 1995	E	..	..	†	7	..	1946	1946	1956 E
112 Egypt	11 1995	E+A	..	..	48	6 [b]	..	1956	1956	1957 E

	ELECTIONS					POLITICAL PARTIES		WOMEN'S PARTICIPATION		
	Lower or single house		Upper house or senate		Voter turnout at last elections for lower or single house (%)	Parties represented in		Year women received right		Year first woman elected (E) or nominated (N) to national parliament
HDI rank	Date of last elections	Members elected (E) or appointed (A)	Date of last elections	Members elected (E) or appointed (A)		Lower or single house	Upper house or senate	To vote[a]	To stand for election[a]	
114 El Salvador	03 1997	E	..	..	89	9	..	1939	1961	1961 E
115 Swaziland	09 1993	E+A	09 1993	E+A	†		..	1968	1968	1972 E
116 Bolivia	06 1997	E	06 1997	E	70	7	5	1952	1952	1966 E
117 Cape Verde	12 1995	E	..	..	77	3	..	1975	1975	1975 E
119 Honduras	11 1997	E	..	..	73 f	5	..	1955	1955	1957 E
120 Gabon	12 1996	E	01 1997	E	†	5 b	6 b	1956	1956	1961 E
121 São Tomé and Principe	10 1994	E	..	..	52	3 b	..	1975	1975	1975 E
122 Viet Nam	07 1997	E	..	..	100	1 b	..	1946	1946	1976 E
123 Solomon Islands	08 1997	E	..	..	64 f	2	..	†	†	1993 E
124 Vanuatu	03 1998	E	..	..	75	5 b	..	1975	1975	1987 E
125 Morocco	11 1997	E	12 1997	E	58	15	13	1963	1963	1993 E
126 Nicaragua	10 1996	E	..	..	77	4 b	..	1955	1955	1972 E
127 Iraq	03 1996	E	..	..	94	4 b	..	1980	1980	1980 E
128 Congo	01 1998 h	A	–	–	–	–	–	1963	1963	1963 E
129 Papua New Guinea	06 1997	E	..	..	81	9 b	..	1964	1963 †	1977 E
130 Zimbabwe	04 1995	E+A	..	..	57	2	..	1957	1978	1980 E
Low human development										
131 Myanmar	04 1990 i	E	–	–	76	–	–	1935	1946	1947 E
132 Cameroon	05 1997	E	..	..	76	4 b	..	1946	1946	1960 E
133 Ghana	12 1996	E	..	..	65	4	..	1954	1954	1960 N j
134 Lesotho	03 1993	E	05 1993	A	72	1	..	1965	1965	1965 N
135 Equatorial Guinea	11 1993	E	..	..	†	4	..	1963	1963	1968 E
136 Lao People's Dem. Rep.	12 1997	E	..	..	99	1 b	..	1958	1958	1958 E
137 Kenya	12 1997	E+A	..	..	65	10	..	1963	1963	1969 E
138 Pakistan	02 1997	E	03 1997	E	35	4 b	8 b	1947	1947	1973 E
139 India	02 1998	E+A	04 1996	E+A	†	13 b	8 b	1950	1950	1952 E
140 Cambodia	05 1993	E	..	..	87	4	..	1955	1955	1958 E
141 Comoros	12 1996	E	..	..	20	2 b	..	1956	1956	1993 E
142 Nigeria	07 1992 k	E	–	–	–	–	–	1958 j	1958 j	†
143 Dem. Rep. of the Congo	10 1993 l	E	..	..	..	..	..	1967	1970	1970 E
144 Togo	02 1994	E	..	..	65	5	..	1945	1945	1961 E
145 Benin	03 1995	E	..	..	76 f	6 b	..	1956	1956	1979 E
146 Zambia	11 1996	E+A	..	..	40	4 b	..	1962	1962	1964 E
147 Bangladesh	06 1996	E	..	..	74	4 b	..	1972	1972	1973 E
148 Côte d'Ivoire	11 1995	E	..	..	71	2	..	1952	1952	1965 E
149 Mauritania	10 1996	E	04 1996	E	..	3 b	3	1961	1961	1975 E
150 Tanzania, U. Rep. of	10 1995	E+A	..	..	..	5	..	1959	1959	†
151 Yemen	04 1997	E	..	..	61	4 b	..	1967 m / 1970 n	1967 m / 1970 n	1990 E j
152 Nepal	11 1994	E	06 1995	E+A	62	5 b	4	1951	1951	1952 N
153 Madagascar	06 1993	E	..	..	60	16 b	..	1959	1959	1965 E
154 Central African Rep.	08 1993	E	..	..	56	12 b	..	1986	1986	1987 E
155 Bhutan	1997 g	E+A	..	..	..	..	..	1953	1953	1975 E
156 Angola	09 1992	E	..	..	91	11	..	1975	1975	1980 E
157 Sudan	03 1996	E	..	..	..	..	..	1964	1964	1964 E
158 Senegal	05 1993	E	..	..	41	6	..	1945	1945	1963 E
159 Haiti	06 1995	E	04 1997	E	31	6 b	†	1950	1950	1961 E
160 Uganda	06 1996	E	..	..	..	..	..	1962	1962	1962 N
161 Malawi	05 1994	E	..	..	80	3	..	1961	1961	1964 E
162 Djibouti	12 1997	E	..	..	57	1	..	1946	1986	– o
163 Chad	01 1997	E	..	..	49	10	..	1958	1958	1962 E
164 Guinea-Bissau	07 1994	E	..	..	45 f	5	..	1977	1977	1972 N
165 Gambia	01 1997	E+A	..	..	69	4 b	..	1960	1960	1982 E j
166 Mozambique	10 1994	E	..	..	88	3	..	1975	1975	1977 E
167 Guinea	06 1995	E	..	..	62	5 b	..	1958	1958	1963 E
168 Eritrea	02 1994	E	..	..	..	†	..	1955 j	1955 j	1994 E
169 Ethiopia	05 1995	E	05 1995	E	85 f	2 b	†	1955	1955	1957 E
170 Burundi	06 1993	E	..	..	..	..	..	1961	1961	1982 E
171 Mali	07 1997	E	..	..	22	8	..	1956	1956	1964 E
172 Burkina Faso	05 1997	E	12 1995	E+A	45	4	..	1958	1958	1978 E
173 Niger	11 1996	E	..	..	39	4 b	..	1948	1948	1989 E
174 Sierra Leone	02 1996 p	–	–	–	–	–	–	1961	1961	†

† No information or confirmation available.
a. Refers to year in which right to election or representation on a universal and equal basis was recognized. In some countries confirmation and constitutional rights came later.
b. There are also independent and other parties not sufficiently represented to constitute a parliamentary group.
c. The country has never had a parliament.
d. Women's right to vote and stand for election has not been recognized.
e. Bahrain's first legislature dissolved by decree of the emir on 26 August 1975.
f. Average turnout in the 1990s. No official data are available. The figures are from IDEA 1997.
g. Data valid as of 1997.
h. Transitional appointed unicameral parliament created by decree.
i. The parliament elected in 1990 has never been convened nor authorized to sit, and many of its members were detained or forced into exile.
j. Exact information on election or nomination is not available.
k. Bicameral parliament dissolved following a military coup in November 1993.
l. Transitional unicameral parliament dissolved following change in government in May 1997.
m. Refers to the former People's Democratic Rep. of Yemen.
n. Refers to the former Arab Rep. of Yemen.
o. The country has not yet elected or nominated a woman to the national parliament.
p. Unicameral parliament dissolved following a military coup on 25 April 1997.

19 Military expenditure and resource use imbalances

		Defence expenditure					Military expenditure (as % of combined education and health expenditure)		Imports of conventional weapons (1990 prices)[a]		Total armed forces	
		US$ millions (1995 prices)		As % of GDP		Per capita (US$; 1995 prices)				US$ millions	Index (1991=100)	Thous-ands	Index (1985=100)
HDI rank		1985	1996	1985	1996	1985	1996	1960	1990-91	1996	1996	1996	1996
High human development		37,192 T	57,518 T	2.9	2.6	87	112	67	38	5,228 T	..	2,125.0 T	111
23	Cyprus	119	420	3.6	5.2	179	500	..	17	195	..	10.0	100
24	Barbados	16	14	0.9	0.7	71	50	..	5	..	..	0.6	60
25	Hong Kong, China	..	..	..	..	..	..	..	10	..	..	..	..
28	Singapore	1,622	3,959	6.7	5.5	634	1,325	11	129	104	33	53.9	98
29	Antigua and Barbuda	3	3	0.5	0.8	39	46	..	..	..	..	0.2	200
30	Korea, Rep. of	8,592	15,168	5.1	3.3	209	336	273	60	1,727	437	660.0	110
31	Chile	1,696	1,990	7.8	3.5	140	138	60	68	124	146	89.7	89
32	Bahamas	13	21	0.5	0.6	56	80	..	..	..	..	0.9	180
34	Costa Rica	40	50	0.7	0.6	15	14	17	5	..	..	..	..
35	Brunei Darussalam	280	330	6.0	6.5	1,250	1,091	..	125	..	..	5.0	122
36	Argentina	4,945	3,732	3.8	1.5	162	108	62	51	45	..	72.5	67
38	Uruguay	326	270	3.5	2.3	108	85	40	38	..	..	25.6	80
40	Trinidad and Tobago	100	71	1.4	1.1	84	54	..	9	..	..	2.1	100
41	Dominica	..	..	..	..	..	..	..	..	..	..	..	..
43	Bahrain	206	279	3.5	5.5	494	476	..	41	..	..	11.0	393
44	Fiji	19	47	1.2	2.6	27	60	..	37	..	..	3.6	133
45	Panama	123	109	2.0	1.4	56	40	2	34	..	..	..	..
46	Venezuela	1,125	903	2.1	1.2	65	40	40	33	..	..	46.0	94
48	United Arab Emirates	2,790	2,028	7.6	5.2	1,993	830	..	44	271	213	64.5	150
49	Mexico	1,695	2,582	0.7	0.8	22	28	23	5	18	..	175.0	136
50	Saint Kitts and Nevis	..	..	..	..	..	..	..	..	..	..	..	..
51	Grenada	..	..	..	..	..	..	..	..	..	..	..	..
53	Colombia	579	1,846	1.6	2.6	20	52	57	57	..	..	146.3	221
54	Kuwait	2,453	3,505	9.1	12.9	1,434	2,218	..	88	1,363	221	15.3	128
55	Saint Vincent	..	..	..	..	..	..	..	..	..	..	..	..
56	Seychelles	11	10	2.1	3.1	168	144	..	..	..	..	0.3	25
57	Qatar	410	740	6.0	10.2	1,301	1,334	..	192	393	..	11.8	197
58	Saint Lucia	..	..	..	..	..	..	..	..	..	..	..	..
59	Thailand	2,559	4,212	5.0	2.5	49	69	96	71	355	56	254.0	108
60	Malaysia	2,409	3,542	5.6	4.2	155	148	48	38	143	..	114.5	104
61	Mauritius	3	60	0.3	2.3	3	52	4	4	..	..	1.3	130
62	Brazil	3,209	10,341	0.8	2.1	24	63	72	23	490	297	295.0	107
63	Belize	5	14	1.4	2.5	33	64	..	..	..	..	1.1	183
64	Libyan Arab Jamahiriya	1,844	1,272	6.2	5.1	490	227	29	71	..	..	65.0	89
Medium human development		129,186 T	93,209 T	12.4	4.9	73	44	159	84	7,411 T	152	8,783.0 T	90
Excluding China		102,079 T	58,525 T	13.7	4.4	148	67	..	74	5,454 T	..	5,848.0 T	100
65	Suriname	11	14	2.4	3.5	29	33	..	27	..	..	1.8	90
66	Lebanon	273	474	9.0	4.4	102	116	..	..	..	..	48.9	281
69	Turkey	3,134	6,856	4.5	3.9	62	110	153	87	1,066	112	525.0	83
70	Saudi Arabia	24,530	16,999	19.6	12.8	2,125	1,030	150	151	1,611	121	162.5	260
71	Oman	2,946	1,876	20.8	15.6	1,841	955	..	293	478	..	43.5	1,740
73	Ecuador	388	528	1.8	3.4	41	44	104	26	..	..	57.1	134
75	Korea, Dem. People's Rep. of	5,675	5,330	23.0	27.2	278	243	..	..	..	..	1,054.0	126
78	Iran, Islamic Rep. of	19,423	3,301	36.0	5.0	435	49	141	38	437	250	513.0	168
81	Syrian Arab Rep.	4,756	1,553	16.4	4.8	453	105	329	373	21	15	421.0	105
82	Algeria	1,301	1,764	1.7	4.0	59	62	31	11	..	..	123.7	73
83	Tunisia	569	390	5.0	2.0	80	42	45	31	..	..	35.0	100
84	Jamaica	27	28	0.9	0.6	12	11	..	8	..	..	3.3	157
85	Cuba	2,181	686	9.6	5.4	216	62	64	125	..	..	100.0	62
86	Peru	875	1,061	4.5	1.9	47	44	59	39	204	..	125.0	98
87	Jordan	822	390	15.9	5.6	235	85	464	138	..	..	98.7	140
88	Dominican Rep.	70	101	1.1	1.1	11	13	147	22	..	..	24.5	110
89	South Africa	3,922	2,506	2.7	1.8	117	58	26	41	39	..	137.9	130
90	Sri Lanka	311	867	3.8	6.5	20	47	17	107	..	..	115.0	532
91	Paraguay	82	110	1.3	1.3	22	22	94	42	..	..	20.2	140
94	Samoa (Western)	..	..	..	..	..	..	..	..	..	..	..	..
95	Maldives	..	..	..	..	..	..	..	..	..	..	..	..
96	Indonesia	3,197	4,599	2.8	2.1	20	23	207	49	537	226	299.2	108
97	Botswana	51	224	1.1	6.7	47	147	..	22	..	..	7.5	188
98	Philippines	647	1,457	1.4	2.0	12	21	44	41	31	..	107.5	94
100	Guyana	43	7	6.8	1.0	54	9	..	21	..	..	1.6	24
101	Mongolia	47	14	9.0	1.7	24	6	..	..	..	..	21.0	64
106	China	27,107	34,684	7.9	5.7	26	29	387	114	1,957	1,296	2,935.0	75
107	Namibia	..	71	..	3.0	..	42	..	23	..	..	8.1	..
111	Guatemala	160	154	1.8	1.4	20	14	45	31	..	..	44.2	139
112	Egypt	3,527	2,629	7.2	4.5	73	43	117	52	803	65	440.0	99

HDI rank	Defence expenditure US$ millions (1995 prices) 1985	1996	As % of GDP 1985	1996	Per capita (US$; 1995 prices) 1985	1996	Military expenditure (as % of combined education and health expenditure) 1960	1990-91	Imports of conventional weapons (1990 prices)[a] US$ millions 1996	Index (1991=100) 1996	Total armed forces Thous- ands 1996	Index (1985 =100) 1996
114 El Salvador	344	122	4.4	1.5	72	21	34	66	..	..	28.4	68
115 Swaziland	..	..	..	..	..	..	..	11	..	..	..	..
116 Bolivia	173	152	2.0	2.1	27	18	105	57	..	..	33.5	121
117 Cape Verde	5	4	0.9	1.7	15	9	..	..	..	..	1.1	14
119 Honduras	98	57	2.1	1.3	22	9	38	92	..	..	18.8	113
120 Gabon	108	109	1.8	2.0	108	81	..	51	..	..	4.7	196
121 São Tomé and Principe	..	..	..	..	..	..	..	..	..	..	..	..
122 Viet Nam	3,277	930	19.4	4.0	53	12	..	..	118	..	572.0	56
123 Solomon Islands	..	..	..	..	..	..	..	..	..	..	..	..
124 Vanuatu	..	..	..	..	..	..	..	..	..	..	..	..
125 Morocco	875	1,539	5.4	4.3	40	54	49	72	109	122	194.0	130
126 Nicaragua	301	36	17.4	1.5	92	8	100	97	..	..	17.0	27
127 Iraq	17,573	1,224	25.9	8.3	1,105	56	128	271	..	..	382.5	74
128 Congo	76	54	1.9	1.9	41	19	7	37	..	..	10.0	115
129 Papua New Guinea	49	77	1.5	1.5	14	17	..	41	..	..	3.7	116
130 Zimbabwe	232	232	3.1	3.9	28	20	..	66	..	..	43.0	105
Low human development	19,137T	21,217T	3.3	3.0	14	12	76	66	..	..	3,197.0T	108
Excluding India	10,584T	11,059T	3.7	3.2	16	12	..	67	..	..	2,052.0T	120
131 Myanmar	1,200	1,929	5.1	7.6	32	40	241	222	..	..	321.0	173
132 Cameroon	217	218	1.4	2.4	21	16	63	48	..	..	13.1	180
133 Ghana	86	118	1.0	1.4	7	7	22	12	..	..	7.0	46
134 Lesotho	63	31	4.6	5.0	41	15	..	48	..	..	2.0	100
135 Equatorial Guinea	4	2	2.0	1.0	11	5	..	..	..	..	1.3	59
136 Lao People's Dem. Rep.	75	76	7.8	4.1	21	15	..	..	..	..	37.0	69
137 Kenya	350	207	3.1	2.2	17	7	8	24	..	..	24.2	177
138 Pakistan	2,835	3,579	6.9	5.7	29	27	393	125	..	..	587.0	122
139 India	8,553	10,158	3.0	2.8	11	11	68	65	1,317	88	1,145.0	91
140 Cambodia	..	177	..	5.7	..	18	..	..	..	..	87.7	251
141 Comoros	..	..	..	..	..	..	..	..	..	..	..	..
142 Nigeria	1,475	1,521	1.7	3.5	16	15	11	33	..	..	77.1	82
143 Dem. Rep. of the Congo	111	166	1.5	2.8	4	4	..	71	..	..	28.1	59
144 Togo	26	27	1.3	2.5	9	6	..	39	..	..	7.0	194
145 Benin	29	26	1.1	1.4	7	5	28	..	..	..	4.8	107
146 Zambia	55	58	1.1	1.8	8	6	42	63	..	..	21.6	133
147 Bangladesh	341	517	1.4	1.7	3	4	..	41	..	..	117.5	129
148 Côte d'Ivoire	104	92	0.8	0.9	10	6	8	14	..	..	8.4	64
149 Mauritania	71	31	6.5	2.9	42	13	..	40	..	..	15.7	185
150 Tanzania, U. Rep. of	191	83	4.4	2.5	9	3	4	77	..	..	34.6	86
151 Yemen	668	354	9.9	3.7	66	24	..	197	..	..	42.0	66
152 Nepal	49	39	1.5	0.9	3	2	67	35	..	..	43.0	172
153 Madagascar	74	36	2.0	0.8	7	3	8	37	..	..	21.0	100
154 Central African Rep.	24	29	1.4	2.4	9	8	..	33	..	..	2.7	117
155 Bhutan	..	..	..	..	..	..	..	..	..	..	..	..
156 Angola	883	441	15.1	6.4	101	40	..	208	..	..	97.0	196
157 Sudan	146	397	3.2	4.3	7	13	52	44	..	..	89.0	157
158 Senegal	86	73	1.1	1.7	13	8	13	33	..	..	13.4	133
159 Haiti	42	62	1.5	3.5	7	9	100	30	..	..	..	..
160 Uganda	72	150	1.8	2.4	5	8	..	18	..	..	50.0	250
161 Malawi	29	23	1.0	1.2	4	2	..	24	..	..	9.8	185
162 Djibouti	44	20	7.9	5.2	102	31	..	..	..	..	8.4	280
163 Chad	51	38	2.9	2.7	10	6	..	74	..	..	25.4	208
164 Guinea-Bissau	15	8	5.7	2.9	17	7	..	..	..	..	7.3	85
165 Gambia	3	14	1.5	3.9	4	13	..	11	..	..	0.8	160
166 Mozambique	326	61	8.5	3.7	24	3	..	121	..	..	11.0	70
167 Guinea	71	55	1.8	1.9	12	8	52	37	..	..	9.7	98
168 Eritrea	..	59	..	7.5	..	16	..	..	..	..	55.0	..
169 Ethiopia	610	122	17.9	2.0	14	2	107	190	..	..	120.0	55
170 Burundi	48	49	3.0	4.1	10	7	..	42	..	..	18.5	356
171 Mali	41	40	1.4	1.8	5	4	57	53	..	..	7.4	151
172 Burkina Faso	46	65	1.1	2.4	6	6	29	30	..	..	5.8	145
173 Niger	16	21	0.5	0.9	3	2	43	11	..	..	5.3	241
174 Sierra Leone	7	45	1.0	5.9	2	9	..	23	..	..	14.2	458
All developing countries	185,515T	171,934T	7.1	3.7	51	39	102	63	..	..	14,105.0T	96
Least developed countries	5,436T	5,348T	4.3	2.5	13	10	..	72	..	..	1,323.0T	123
Industrial countries	628,981T	609,149T	4.2	2.7	728	493	110	33	..	..	7,047.0T	78
World	814,496T	781,093T	4.7	2.9	182	137	109	38	..	..	21,152.0T	91

a. Figures are trend indicator values.
Source: Columns 1-6, 9 and 11: IISS 1997; *columns 7 and 8:* UNDP 1997a; *columns 10 and 12:* calculated on the basis of data from: IISS 1997.

HDI rank	Total external debt US$ billions 1995	Total external debt As % of GNP 1995	Debt service ratio 1980	Debt service ratio 1995	ODA US$ millions 1995	ODA As % of GNP 1995	ODA Per capita (US$)	Net foreign direct investment (as % of GNP) 1993-95	Trade (as % of GDP) 1993-95	Export-import ratio (exports as % of imports) 1995	Terms of trade (1987=100) 1995	Current account balance before official transfers (US$ millions) 1995
High human development	610 T	36	34	20	1,871 T	0.1	5	1.4	64	96	94	-29,915 T
23 Cyprus	..	..	..	..	30	..	41	..	99	..	..	..
24 Barbados	0.6	..	..	..	5	0.3	19	0.7	96	..	..	..
25 Hong Kong, China	..	..	..	..	13	(.)	2	..	297	100	87	..
28 Singapore	..	..	..	..	..	..	..	6.0	..	111	89	15,093
29 Antigua and Barbuda	..	..	..	..	12	2.6	184	5.6	218	..	..	..
30 Korea, Rep. of	..	..	..	..	-147	(.)	-3	-0.2	67	95	102	-8,251
31 Chile	25.6	43	43	26	203	0.3	14	2.6	55	99	94	157
32 Bahamas	..	..	..	..	..	..	..	..	..	..	..	..
34 Costa Rica	3.8	43	29	16	-7	-0.1	-2	4.3	81	93	92	-143
35 Brunei Darussalam	..	..	..	..	..	..	..	..	..	..	..	..
36 Argentina	89.8	33	37	35	277	0.1	8	0.5	16	91	120	-2,390
38 Uruguay	5.3	32	19	24	51	0.3	16	0.7	41	90	112	-358
40 Trinidad and Tobago	2.6	54	7	15	17	0.4	13	6.3	68	112	86	294
41 Dominica	0.1	..	..	..	43	19.8	589	5.5	109	..	..	..
43 Bahrain	..	..	..	..	5	0.1	9	-0.6	191	..	..	..
44 Fiji	0.3	..	..	..	45	2.4	58	3.5	104	..	..	..
45 Panama	7.2	101	6	4	90	1.3	34	3.1	79	100	86	-141
46 Venezuela	35.8	49	27	22	44	0.1	2	1.2	49	111	82	2,255
48 United Arab Emirates	..	..	..	..	..	..	..	..	139	..	93	..
49 Mexico	165.7	70	44	24	..	..	..	2.9	48	95	92	-654
50 Saint Kitts and Nevis	0.1	..	..	..	7	3.2	171	9.6	..	..	..	..
51 Grenada	0.1	..	..	..	11	4.1	121	9.0	47	..	..	..
53 Colombia	20.8	28	16	25	251	0.3	7	3.4	35	76	80	-4,116
54 Kuwait	..	..	..	..	..	..	..	0.3	104	146	88	4,198
55 Saint Vincent	0.2	..	1	7	27	11.0	243	12.6	..	..	..	..
56 Seychelles	0.2	..	..	..	19	3.7	259	10.6	129	..	..	..
57 Qatar	..	..	..	..	..	..	..	..	..	..	..	..
58 Saint Lucia	0.1	..	..	..	39	7.4	247	12.0	141	..	..	..
59 Thailand	56.8	25	19	10	832	0.5	14	1.3	90	84	100	-13,554
60 Malaysia	34.4	43	6	8	-452	-0.6	-22	7.2	194	91	92	-4,147
61 Mauritius	1.8	46	9	9	20	0.5	18	0.4	120	95	103	-22
62 Brazil	159.1	24	63	38	408	0.1	3	0.7	16	72	101	-18,136
63 Belize	0.3	..	..	..	18	3.2	83	3.8	109	..	..	..
64 Libyan Arab Jamahiriya	..	..	..	..	10	..	2	..	..	..	..	..
Medium human development	633 T	41	..	18	17,392 T	0.9	9	2.7	51	91	99	-43,697 T
Excluding China	515 T	62	20	24	14,775 T	1.3	18	1.1	58	88	96	-45,315 T
65 Suriname	..	..	..	..	111	31.3	271	4.2	11	22	95	-5,092
66 Lebanon	3.0	26	..	13	233	2.0	58	0.3	70	22	95	-5,092
69 Turkey	73.6	44	28	28	233	0.1	4	0.5	45	85	109	-2,339
70 Saudi Arabia	..	..	..	..	29	(.)	2	-1.5	70	121	92	-8,108
71 Oman	3.1	30	6	8	62	0.6	28	1.4	89	113	77	-979
73 Ecuador	14.0	84	34	27	..	..	..	2.8	56	83	71	-822
75 Korea, Dem. People's Rep. of	..	..	..	..	43	..	2	..	..	..	..	..
78 Iran, Islamic Rep. of	21.9	..	7	..	171	..	3	..	..	..	..	..
81 Syrian Arab Rep.	21.3	135	11	5	225	1.4	16	0.4	..	93	78	440
82 Algeria	32.6	83	27	39	309	0.8	11	(.)	57	88	83	-2,310
83 Tunisia	9.9	57	15	17	126	0.7	14	1.5	93	84	91	-737
84 Jamaica	4.3	135	19	18	60	1.7	24	5.3	145	81	105	-245
85 Cuba	..	..	..	..	68	..	6	..	..	..	..	..
86 Peru	30.8	54	45	15	410	0.7	17	3.3	30	61	83	-4,223
87 Jordan	7.9	126	8	13	514	7.9	122	0.1	121	69	128	-476
88 Dominican Rep.	4.3	37	25	8	106	0.9	14	2.3	55	84	123	-125
89 South Africa	..	..	..	..	361	0.3	9	(.)	44	90	111	-3,500
90 Sri Lanka	8.2	64	12	7	494	3.9	27	0.5	83	80	88	-546
91 Paraguay	2.3	29	19	..	97	1.1	20	2.6	82	..	100	-1,473
94 Samoa (Western)	0.2	..	..	..	..	..	..	..	..	..	..	..
95 Maldives	0.2	..	..	..	33	13.2	130	3.6	..	..	..	..
96 Indonesia	107.8	57	..	31	1,121	0.6	6	2.3	53	87	79	-7,023
97 Botswana	0.7	16	2	3	81	1.9	56	1.6	101	115	152	342
98 Philippines	39.4	52	27	16	883	1.2	13	1.9	80	92	114	-1,980
100 Guyana	2.1	..	..	..	144	27.0	172	0.5	159	..	..	..
101 Mongolia	0.5	62	..	9	203	21.5	82	1.2	..	93	..	39
106 China	118.1	17	..	10	2,617	0.4	2	5.2	40	100	105	1,618
107 Namibia	..	..	..	..	189	5.4	122	1.5	110	91	..	50
111 Guatemala	3.3	22	8	11	216	1.5	20	0.5	47	73	93	-572
112 Egypt	34.1	73	13	15	2,212	3.7	38	1.3	54	65	95	-956

HDI rank	Total external debt US$ billions 1995	Total external debt As % of GNP 1995	Debt service ratio (debt service as % of exports of goods and services) 1980	Debt service ratio 1995	Total net official development assistance (ODA) received, 1996 (net disbursements) US$ millions 1995	ODA As % of GNP	ODA Per capita (US$)	Net foreign direct investment (as % of GNP) 1993-95	Trade (as % of GDP) 1993-95	Export-import ratio (exports as % of imports) 1995	Terms of trade (1987=100) 1995	Current account balance before official transfers (US$ millions) 1995
114 El Salvador	2.6	27	7	9	317	3.3	56	0.4	55	59	89	-70
115 Swaziland	0.3	..	..	..	31	2.8	34	5.5	186	..	..	..
116 Bolivia	5.3	91	35	29	850	14.6	115	2.6	48	72	67	-218
117 Cape Verde	0.2	..	..	..	120	29.0	316	0.6	75	..	..	..
119 Honduras	4.6	125	21	31	367	9.5	62	1.4	80	79	77	-201
120 Gabon	4.5	122	18	16	127	2.9	118	-1.4	101	116	90	378
121 São Tomé and Principe	0.3	..	..	..	47	127.0	364	..	108	..	..	..
122 Viet Nam	26.5	130	..	5	927	4.6	13	7.0	83	75	..	-2,021
123 Solomon Islands	0.2	..	..	..	43	12.3	115	4.9	..	..	..	..
124 Vanuatu	0.1	..	..	..	31	14.6	183	16.0	..	..	..	..
125 Morocco	22.2	71	33	32	651	2.1	25	0.9	62	71	90	-1,521
126 Nicaragua	9.3	590	22	39	954	60.6	218	4.4	76	46	95	-706
127 Iraq	..	..	..	..	387	..	19	..	..	..	..	..
128 Congo	6.0	366	11	14	430	25.3	163	0.1	128	69	93	-570
129 Papua New Guinea	2.4	53	14	21	385	8.0	89	9.9	106	125	90	674
130 Zimbabwe	4.9	79	4	..	374	6.0	34	0.7	74	84	84	-425
Low human development	339 T	57	11	26	18,930 T	3.3	11	0.7	39	56	110	-14,555 T
Excluding India	246 T	95	12	23	16,994 T	7.3	20	1.1	56	48	90	-8,825 T
131 Myanmar	5.8	..	25	..	56	..	1	..	..	..	..	..
132 Cameroon	9.4	124	15	20	413	5.7	31	1.4	46	92	79	-171
133 Ghana	5.9	95	13	23	654	10.8	38	3.7	59	70	64	-414
134 Lesotho	0.7	45	2	6	107	8.6	54	1.6	138	65	..	108
135 Equatorial Guinea	0.3	..	..	..	31	20.5	78	0.7	113	..	..	..
136 Lao People's Dem. Rep.	2.2	125	..	6	339	19.2	69	5.1	53	67	..	-224
137 Kenya	7.4	98	21	26	606	6.9	23	0.4	72	77	98	-400
138 Pakistan	30.2	50	18	..	877	1.4	7	0.7	36	66	114	-1,965
139 India	93.8	28	9	28	1,936	0.6	2	0.4	27	75	150	-5,830
140 Cambodia	2.0	74	..	1	453	15.4	45	5.5	36	68	..	-186
141 Comoros	0.2	..	..	..	40	17.1	80	0.9	64	..	..	..
142 Nigeria	35.0	141	4	12	192	0.8	2	1.7	81	20	86	-510
143 Dem. Rep. of the Congo	13.1	..	..	..	167	3.2	4	(.)	..	..	..	..
144 Togo	1.5	121	9	6	166	13.3	41	..	65	79	90	-57
145 Benin	1.7	82	6	8	293	14.9	54	0.3	64	64	110	36
146 Zambia	6.9	191	25	174	614	19.4	68	1.7	71	89	85	..
147 Bangladesh	16.4	56	24	13	1,255	4.5	10	(.)	37	64	94	-1,029
148 Côte d'Ivoire	19.0	252	39	23	968	10.7	69	0.2	76	101	81	-269
149 Mauritania	2.5	243	17	21	274	27.0	120	0.3	104	84	106	-27
150 Tanzania, U. Rep. of	7.3	207	21	17	894	23.2	30	4.3	96	56	83	-629
151 Yemen	6.2	155	..	3	260	6.5	17	0.5	88	70	84	146
152 Nepal	2.4	53	3	8	401	8.9	19	0.2	60	70	85	-375
153 Madagascar	4.3	142	20	9	364	12.0	27	0.3	54	65	82	-276
154 Central African Rep.	0.9	..	5	7	167	15.0	51	0.3	46	73	91	-25
155 Bhutan	0.1	..	..	..	62	23.5	89	..	85	..	..	..
156 Angola	11.5	275	..	13	544	19.4	51	9.6	132	78	86	-769
157 Sudan	17.6	..	26	..	230	..	9	..	..	..	..	..
158 Senegal	3.9	82	29	19	582	12.4	69	(.)	69	79	107	3
159 Haiti	0.8	40	6	45	375	17.9	52	0.1	17	27	52	-67
160 Uganda	3.6	64	17	21	684	12.0	36	2.2	33	45	58	-428
161 Malawi	2.1	167	28	26	501	35.3	51	0.1	69	45	87	-450
162 Djibouti	0.3	..	..	..	97	..	153	0.8	101	..	..	..
163 Chad	0.9	81	8	6	305	30.0	47	0.6	46	51	103	-38
164 Guinea-Bissau	0.9	354	..	67	180	72.9	168	0.4	48	25	92	-41
165 Gambia	0.4	..	6	14	38	10.7	34	2.6	104	75	111	-8
166 Mozambique	5.8	444	..	35	923	72.2	57	2.8	102	36	124	..
167 Guinea	3.2	91	..	25	295	8.3	45	1.0	46	66	91	-197
168 Eritrea	..	..	..	..	157	22.8	44	..	..	..	..	..
169 Ethiopia	5.2	100	7	14	849	14.6	15	0.1	39	59	74	-93
170 Burundi	1.2	110	..	28	204	19.4	33	0.2	43	47	52	-6
171 Mali	3.1	132	5	13	505	21.0	52	(.)	38	55	103	-164
172 Burkina Faso	1.3	55	6	11	418	17.9	40	..	45	55	103	15
173 Niger	1.6	91	22	20	259	14.1	29	0.1	30	59	101	-126
174 Sierra Leone	1.2	160	23	60	195	24.1	46	0.1	40	37	89	-89
All developing countries	1,583 T	41	24	19	58,480 T a,b	0.9	9 c	1.8	56	91	97	-88,167 T
Least developed countries	136 T a	113 a	..	..	14,235 T a	14.2 c	25 c	1.3	54	64	89	-4,999 T
Industrial countries	..	..	..	..	..	..	..	-0.5	39	102	103	473 T
World	..	..	..	..	..	..	..	-0.1	42	–	–	–

a. World Bank 1997b.
b. Total net ODA to countries and territories on Part I of the OECD Development Assistance Committee (DAC) List of Aid Recipients.
c. OECD 1998.
Source: Columns 1-4, 8-10 and 12: World Bank 1997d; columns 5-7: OECD 1998; column 11: World Bank 1997d.

Growing urbanization

HDI rank	Urban population (as % of total)			Urban population annual growth rate (%)		Population in cities of more than 750,000		Largest city	Population (thousands)	
	1970	1995	2015	1970-1995	1995-2015	As % of total population 1995	As % of urban population 1995	City	1995	2015
High human development	**53**	**71**	**79**	**3.3**	**1.7**	**35**	**49**	–	**–**	**–**
23 Cyprus	41	54	65	1.9	1.8	..	..	..	..	..
24 Barbados	37	47	58	1.3	1.5	..	..	..	..	..
25 Hong Kong, China	88	95	97	2.1	0.4	95	100	Hong Kong	5,817	6,325
28 Singapore	100	100	100	1.9	0.9	100	100	Singapore	3,327	4,009
29 Antigua and Barbuda	33	36	43	0.9	1.6	..	..	..	..	..
30 Korea, Rep. of	41	81	92	4.2	1.3	58	71	Seoul	11,609	12,980
31 Chile	75	84	87	2.1	1.3	34	41	Santiago	4,891	6,066
32 Bahamas	72	86	91	2.8	1.6	..	..	..	..	..
34 Costa Rica	40	49	60	3.7	2.8	27	55	San José	920	1,526
35 Brunei Darussalam	62	69	79	3.8	2.3	..	..	..	..	..
36 Argentina	78	88	92	2.0	1.3	43	49	Buenos Aires	11,802	13,856
38 Uruguay	82	90	93	0.9	0.7	42	46	Montevideo	1,325	1,433
40 Trinidad and Tobago	63	72	79	1.7	1.5	..	..	..	..	..
41 Dominica	47	69	75	1.6	0.8	..	..	..	..	..
43 Bahrain	79	90	95	4.4	1.9	..	..	..	..	..
44 Fiji	35	41	51	2.3	2.6	..	..	..	..	..
45 Panama	48	56	65	2.9	2.2	37	66	Panama City	967	1,428
46 Venezuela	72	86	90	3.6	2.0	36	42	Caracas	3,007	2,447
48 United Arab Emirates	57	84	89	11.3	1.9	36	43	Abu Dhabi	799	1,161
49 Mexico	59	73	78	3.3	1.7	33	45	Mexico City	16,562	19,180
50 Saint Kitts and Nevis	34	34	40	-0.5	1.0	..	..	..	..	..
51 Grenada	32	36	48	0.4	2.0	..	..	..	..	..
53 Colombia	57	73	80	3.1	1.9	37	51	Bogotá	6,079	8,394
54 Kuwait	78	97	98	4.3	2.2	64	66	Kuwait City	1,090	1,488
55 Saint Vincent	15	48	68	5.9	2.6	..	..	..	..	..
56 Seychelles	26	55	67	4.3	2.0	..	..	..	..	..
57 Qatar	80	91	94	7.2	1.6	..	..	..	..	..
58 Saint Lucia	41	37	44	1.0	2.0	..	..	..	..	..
59 Thailand	13	20	29	3.6	2.6	11	56	Bangkok	6,547	9,844
60 Malaysia	34	54	66	4.5	2.7	6	11	Kuala Lumpur	1,236	1,878
61 Mauritius	42	41	49	1.1	1.9	..	..	..	..	..
62 Brazil	56	78	87	3.4	1.6	34	44	São Paulo	16,533	20,320
63 Belize	51	47	51	1.8	2.6	..	..	..	..	..
64 Libyan Arab Jamahiriya	45	85	90	6.8	3.4	46	54	Tripoli	1,682	3,137
Medium human development	**23**	**38**	**53**	**3.9**	**2.8**	**15**	**38**	–	**–**	**–**
Excluding China	**33**	**48**	**61**	**4.0**	**2.8**	**18**	**37**	–	**–**	**–**
65 Suriname	46	49	61	0.8	2.3	..	..	..	..	..
66 Lebanon	59	88	93	2.4	1.7	61	69	Beirut	1,826	2,481
69 Turkey	38	69	85	4.6	2.3	26	37	Istanbul	7,911	12,328
70 Saudi Arabia	49	83	90	7.0	3.5	27	32	Riyadh	2,619	5,230
71 Oman	12	76	93	12.8	5.0	..	..	..	..	..
73 Ecuador	40	59	71	4.3	2.6	27	46	Guayaquil	1,831	2,959
75 Korea, Dem. People's Rep. of	54	61	69	2.3	1.7	11	18	Pyongyang	2,484	3,289
78 Iran, Islamic Rep. of	42	59	69	5.0	3.2	22	37	Teheran	6,836	10,309
81 Syrian Arab Rep.	43	52	62	4.1	3.3	27	52	Damascus	2,036	3,500
82 Algeria	40	56	68	4.3	3.0	13	24	Algiers	3,705	6,352
83 Tunisia	45	62	74	3.6	2.4	19	31	Tunis	1,722	2,500
84 Jamaica	42	54	64	2.2	1.9	..	..	..	..	..
85 Cuba	60	76	83	2.0	0.7	20	27	Havana	2,221	2,422
86 Peru	57	71	78	3.2	2.0	28	40	Lima	6,667	9,388
87 Jordan	51	71	80	4.9	3.5	22	31	Amman	1,183	2,284
88 Dominican Rep.	40	62	73	4.1	2.2	57	92	Santo Domingo	3,166	4,663
89 South Africa	48	49	56	2.6	2.7	30	60	Cape Town	2,727	4,371
90 Sri Lanka	22	22	32	1.5	3.0	..	..	..	..	..
91 Paraguay	37	52	65	4.4	3.5	22	43	Asunción	1,081	1,959
94 Samoa (Western)	20	21	27	0.8	2.7	..	..	..	..	..
95 Maldives	13	27	36	6.0	4.8	..	..	..	..	..
96 Indonesia	17	35	52	5.0	3.2	9	26	Jakarta	8,621	13,923
97 Botswana	9	60	89	11.8	4.1	..	..	..	..	..
98 Philippines	33	54	68	4.4	2.9	15	28	Metro Manila	9,286	14,657
100 Guyana	30	35	48	1.4	2.6	..	..	..	..	..
101 Mongolia	45	61	71	4.0	2.7	..	..	..	..	..
106 China	17	30	46	3.8	2.9	12	40	Shanghai	13,584	17,969
107 Namibia	19	36	53	5.4	4.4	..	..	..	..	..
111 Guatemala	36	39	48	3.2	3.7	21	53	Guatemala City	2,205	4,467
112 Egypt	42	45	54	2.5	2.5	23	52	Cairo	9,690	14,418

HDI rank	Urban population (as % of total)			Urban population annual growth rate (%)		Population in cities of more than 750,000		Largest city	Population (thousands)	
	1970	1995	2015	1970-1995	1995-2015	As % of total population 1995	As % of urban population 1995	City	1995	2015
114 El Salvador	39	45	54	2.4	2.7	21	48	San Salvador	1,214	2,056
115 Swaziland	10	31	47	7.8	4.7	..	..	..	..	..
116 Bolivia	41	61	74	3.9	3.1	28	47	La Paz	1,250	2,125
117 Cape Verde	20	54	73	5.7	3.7	..	..	..	..	..
119 Honduras	29	44	56	4.9	3.7	18	40	Tegucigalpa	995	2,016
120 Gabon	25	50	66	6.0	3.9	..	..	..	..	..
121 São Tomé and Principe	23	43	56	5.0	3.2	..	..	..	..	..
122 Viet Nam	18	19	24	2.5	2.6	6	33	Ho Chi Minh City	3,521	4,797
123 Solomon Islands	9	17	29	6.3	5.7	..	..	..	..	..
124 Vanuatu	13	19	27	4.4	4.3	..	..	..	..	..
125 Morocco	35	52	64	3.9	2.6	17	32	Casablanca	3,101	4,835
126 Nicaragua	47	62	71	4.0	3.0	27	44	Managua	1,124	1,912
127 Iraq	56	75	82	4.3	3.2	35	46	Baghdad	4,336	6,866
128 Congo	33	58	70	5.3	3.7	39	66	Brazzaville	1,004	2,064
129 Papua New Guinea	10	16	24	4.4	4.1	..	..	..	..	..
130 Zimbabwe	17	32	46	5.7	3.9	13	40	Harare	1,410	3,164
Low human development	18	27	39	4.1	3.7	11	40	–	–	–
Excluding India	16	28	41	5.0	4.4	12	40	–	–	–
131 Myanmar	23	26	37	2.6	3.3	9	33	Yangon	3,873	6,775
132 Cameroon	20	45	59	6.1	4.1	18	41	Douala	1,320	2,894
133 Ghana	29	36	48	3.7	4.2	10	27	Accra	1,673	3,469
134 Lesotho	9	24	39	6.9	5.0	..	..	..	..	..
135 Equatorial Guinea	27	42	61	3.1	4.4	..	..	..	..	..
136 Lao People's Dem. Rep.	10	21	33	5.6	5.1	..	..	..	..	..
137 Kenya	10	29	45	7.8	4.6	7	23	Nairobi	1,810	4,228
138 Pakistan	25	34	47	4.3	4.1	18	52	Karachi	9,733	19,377
139 India	20	27	36	3.3	2.8	11	41	Mumbai	15,138	26,218
140 Cambodia	12	20	33	3.8	4.4	..	..	..	..	..
141 Comoros	19	30	43	5.2	4.6	..	..	..	..	..
142 Nigeria	20	40	55	5.7	4.5	11	27	Lagos	10,287	24,640
143 Dem. Rep. of the Congo	30	29	39	3.1	4.6	11	39	Kinshasa	4,241	9,430
144 Togo	13	31	43	6.4	4.4	..	..	..	..	..
145 Benin	17	38	53	6.3	4.6	..	..	..	..	..
146 Zambia	30	43	52	4.1	3.4	16	38	Lusaka	1,317	2,923
147 Bangladesh	8	18	31	6.0	4.3	10	56	Dhaka	8,545	19,486
148 Côte d'Ivoire	27	43	56	5.6	3.4	20	47	Abidjan	2,793	5,259
149 Mauritania	14	51	69	8.1	3.9	..	..	..	..	..
150 Tanzania, U. Rep. of	7	24	38	8.6	5.0	9	37	Dar-es-Salaam	1,747	3,789
151 Yemen	13	34	49	7.4	5.5	..	..	..	..	..
152 Nepal	4	10	18	6.6	5.3	..	..	..	..	..
153 Madagascar	14	26	39	5.8	5.1	6	22	Antananarivo	876	2,218
154 Central African Rep.	30	39	50	3.4	3.4	..	..	..	..	..
155 Bhutan	3	6	12	5.0	6.0	..	..	..	..	..
156 Angola	15	31	44	5.7	4.9	19	62	Luanda	2,081	4,969
157 Sudan	16	31	49	5.4	4.4	8	27	Khartoum	2,249	4,667
158 Senegal	33	44	57	3.9	3.9	21	47	Dakar	1,708	3,489
159 Haiti	20	32	45	3.8	3.7	21	65	Port-au-Prince	1,461	2,973
160 Uganda	8	13	21	4.7	5.5	5	39	Kampala	954	2,548
161 Malawi	6	13	23	6.4	5.3	..	..	..	..	..
162 Djibouti	62	82	86	7.0	2.6	..	..	..	..	..
163 Chad	12	22	31	4.9	4.2	13	59	Ndjamena	826	1,883
164 Guinea-Bissau	15	22	32	4.4	4.0	..	..	..	..	..
165 Gambia	15	29	43	6.3	4.0	..	..	..	..	..
166 Mozambique	6	34	52	10.0	4.7	13	38	Maputo	2,212	5,306
167 Guinea	14	29	43	5.7	4.5	21	73	Conakry	1,558	3,527
168 Eritrea	11	17	26	4.0	4.9	..	..	..	..	..
169 Ethiopia	9	15	26	5.2	5.8	4	28	Addis Ababa	2,431	6,578
170 Burundi	2	8	15	7.0	6.0	..	..	..	..	..
171 Mali	14	27	40	5.4	5.0	9	32	Bamako	919	2,249
172 Burkina Faso	6	16	27	6.9	5.7	8	50	Ouagadougou	824	2,546
173 Niger	9	18	29	6.4	5.6	..	..	..	..	..
174 Sierra Leone	18	33	47	4.5	4.2	..	..	..	..	..
All developing countries	25	37	49	3.8	2.9	16	41	–	–	–
Least developed countries	13	23	35	5.1	4.6	10	41	–	–	–
Industrial countries	67	74	79	1.1	0.6	30	40	–	–	–
World	37	45	55	2.6	2.2	19	41	–	–	–

Source: Columns 1, 3, 8 and 10: UN 1996e; *columns 2, 4-7 and 9:* calculated on the basis of data from UN 1996e.

22 Population trends

HDI rank	Estimated population (millions)			Annual population growth rate (%)		Population doubling date (at current growth rate)	Crude birth rate	Crude death rate	Dependency ratio (%)	Total fertility rate	Contraceptive prevalence rate, any method (%)
	1970	1995	2015	1970-1995	1995-2015	1995	1995	1995	1995	1995	1990-95
High human development	**310.1 T**	**514.8 T**	**650.6 T**	**2.1**	**1.2**	**2044**	**21.5**	**6.3**	**57.8**	**2.5**	**69**
23 Cyprus	0.6	0.7	0.9	0.8	0.9	2050	16.8	7.7	57.2	2.4	..
24 Barbados	0.2	0.3	0.3	0.4	0.4	2298	14.8	9.0	53.2	1.7	55
25 Hong Kong, China	3.9	6.1	6.5	1.8	0.3	2081	11.3	5.9	41.5	1.3	86
28 Singapore	2.1	3.3	4.0	1.9	0.9	2041	17.0	5.0	40.2	1.8	74
29 Antigua and Barbuda	0.1	0.1	0.1	0.6	0.7	2111	..	..	..	..	53
30 Korea, Rep. of	31.9	44.9	51.1	1.4	0.7	2075	15.3	6.3	40.7	1.7	79
31 Chile	9.5	14.2	17.9	1.6	1.2	2045	20.8	5.6	56.4	2.5	..
32 Bahamas	0.2	0.3	0.4	2.0	1.3	2038	18.2	5.2	50.3	2.0	62
34 Costa Rica	1.7	3.4	4.9	2.8	1.8	2028	25.2	3.8	65.7	3.1	75
35 Brunei Darussalam	0.1	0.3	0.4	3.3	1.6	2027	23.7	3.1	57.0	2.9	..
36 Argentina	24.0	34.8 T	43.5	1.5	1.1	2049	20.4	8.1	62.1	2.7	..
38 Uruguay	2.8	3.2	3.5	0.5	0.5	2122	16.9	10.3	57.9	2.3	..
40 Trinidad and Tobago	1.0	1.3	1.6	1.1	1.0	2079	17.3	6.1	58.4	2.2	53
41 Dominica	0.1	0.1	0.1	0.1	0.3	..	..	..	..	..	50
43 Bahrain	0.2	0.6	0.8	3.8	1.6	2028	23.3	3.7	51.8	3.2	53
44 Fiji	0.5	0.8	1.1	1.7	1.5	2039	23.2	4.6	62.3	2.9	41
45 Panama	1.5	2.6	3.5	2.3	1.4	2037	23.7	5.2	62.9	2.8	64
46 Venezuela	10.7	21.8	30.9	2.9	1.8	2029	26.1	4.7	67.5	3.1	49
48 United Arab Emirates	0.2	2.2	3.0	9.6	1.6	2029	19.9	2.8	47.4	3.6	..
49 Mexico	50.6	91.1	119.2	2.4	1.4	2037	25.8	5.1	66.1	2.9	53
50 Saint Kitts and Nevis	(.)	(.)	(.)	-0.5	0.2	..	..	..	..	..	41
51 Grenada	0.1	0.1	0.1	-0.1	0.6	2156	..	..	..	..	54
53 Colombia	21.4	35.8	47.6	2.1	1.4	2036	24.7	5.7	63.1	2.8	72
54 Kuwait	0.7	1.7	2.6	3.3	2.1	2018	22.7	2.2	67.3	2.9	35
55 Saint Vincent	0.1	0.1	0.1	1.0	0.9	2074	..	..	..	..	58
56 Seychelles	0.1	0.1	0.1	1.3	0.9	2059	..	..	..	..	..
57 Qatar	0.1	0.5	0.7	6.6	1.5	2033	19.0	3.5	39.9	3.9	32
58 Saint Lucia	0.1	0.1	0.2	1.4	1.2	2045	..	..	..	..	47
59 Thailand	35.7	58.2	66.3	2.0	0.7	2086	17.4	6.4	49.0	1.8	74
60 Malaysia	10.9	20.1	28.0	2.5	1.7	2029	27.0	5.0	72.0	3.4	48
61 Mauritius	0.8	1.1	1.4	1.2	1.0	2059	20.1	6.6	50.5	2.3	75
62 Brazil	96.0	159.0	199.6	2.0	1.1	2050	20.6	7.2	57.3	2.3	77
63 Belize	0.1	0.2	0.3	2.2	2.1	2022	32.7	4.5	86.0	3.9	47
64 Libyan Arab Jamahiriya	2.0	5.4	10.1	4.1	3.2	2015	40.9	7.5	92.4	6.2	40
Medium human development	**1,309.0 T**	**2,081.6 T**	**2,613.3 T**	**1.9**	**1.1**	**2047**	**21.6**	**7.2**	**56.0**	**2.5**	**72**
Excluding China	**478.4 T**	**861.4 T**	**1,204.2 T**	**2.4**	**1.7**	**2033**	**27.8**	**7.2**	**69.0**	**3.5**	**54**
65 Suriname	0.4	0.4	0.5	0.6	1.2	2055	23.6	5.6	66.2	2.5	..
66 Lebanon	2.5	3.0	4.0	0.8	1.4	2033	25.6	6.8	65.6	2.9	53
69 Turkey	35.3	60.8	78.6	2.2	1.3	2039	22.5	6.7	57.0	2.6	63
70 Saudi Arabia	5.7	18.3	33.5	4.7	3.1	2015	34.7	4.4	79.4	6.1	..
71 Oman	0.7	2.2	4.8	4.6	3.9	2011	43.9	4.5	98.1	7.2	9
73 Ecuador	6.0	11.5	15.9	2.6	1.7	2030	26.9	6.1	68.8	3.3	57
75 Korea, Dem. People's Rep. of	14.3	22.1	27.7	1.8	1.1	2038	21.6	5.5	45.6	2.1	62
78 Iran, Islamic Rep. of	28.4	68.4	109.5	3.6	2.4	2026	35.9	6.4	93.3	5.0	65
81 Syrian Arab Rep.	6.3	14.2	22.7	3.3	2.4	2022	31.8	5.2	91.6	4.4	36
82 Algeria	13.7	28.1	41.6	2.9	2.0	2024	30.0	6.1	74.7	4.1	52
83 Tunisia	5.1	9.0	12.1	2.3	1.5	2033	24.8	6.1	64.9	3.1	60
84 Jamaica	1.9	2.5	3.0	1.1	1.1	2068	22.9	6.0	61.6	2.5	62
85 Cuba	8.5	11.0	11.6	1.0	0.3	2157	14.0	6.9	45.6	1.6	70
86 Peru	13.2	23.5	31.9	2.3	1.5	2034	26.2	6.7	67.4	3.2	64
87 Jordan	2.3	5.4	9.6	3.5	2.9	2016	38.2	5.1	85.3	5.4	35
88 Dominican Rep.	4.4	7.8	10.3	2.3	1.4	2037	25.6	5.4	64.3	3.0	64
89 South Africa	22.5	41.5	61.8	2.5	2.0	2026	30.4	8.4	71.5	4.0	50
90 Sri Lanka	12.5	17.9	22.1	1.5	1.1	2066	18.2	5.9	55.5	2.2	66
91 Paraguay	2.3	4.8	7.8	2.9	2.4	2021	32.7	5.7	82.4	4.4	56
94 Samoa (Western)	0.1	0.2	0.2	0.5	1.6	2060	26.8	6.1	74.5	4.0	..
95 Maldives	0.1	0.3	0.5	3.0	3.2	2015	41.7	8.0	100.8	6.8	..
96 Indonesia	120.3	197.5	251.8	2.0	1.2	2042	23.9	8.0	59.4	2.8	55
97 Botswana	0.6	1.5	2.2	3.3	2.1	2026	36.1	12.0	84.6	4.7	33
98 Philippines	37.5	67.8	94.9	2.4	1.7	2029	29.8	6.1	72.1	3.8	40
100 Guyana	0.7	0.8	1.0	0.6	1.0	2062	23.6	7.7	57.2	2.4	31
101 Mongolia	1.3	2.5	3.6	2.7	1.9	2027	28.4	7.3	74.6	3.4	61
106 China	830.7	1,220.2	1,409.1	1.6	0.7	2072	17.3	7.2	48.0	1.9	83
107 Namibia	0.8	1.5	2.5	2.7	2.4	2023	36.7	11.9	85.3	5.1	29
111 Guatemala	5.2	10.6	17.8	2.9	2.6	2019	37.5	7.2	91.6	5.1	31
112 Egypt	35.3	62.1	85.4	2.3	1.6	2032	27.4	7.6	73.1	3.6	47

HDI rank	Estimated population (millions)			Annual population growth rate (%)		Population doubling date (at current growth rate) 1995	Crude birth rate 1995	Crude death rate 1995	Dependency ratio (%) 1995	Total fertility rate 1995	Contraceptive prevalence rate, any method (%) 1990-95
	1970	1995	2015	1970-1995	1995-2015						
114 El Salvador	3.6	5.7	8.1	1.8	1.8	2026	28.9	6.1	71.3	3.3	53
115 Swaziland	0.4	0.9	1.4	2.9	2.5	2020	37.8	10.0	84.3	4.7	20
116 Bolivia	4.2	7.4	11.2	2.3	2.1	2024	34.5	9.7	79.8	4.6	45
117 Cape Verde	0.3	0.4	0.6	1.5	2.1	2022	32.8	7.8	84.8	3.7	..
119 Honduras	2.6	5.7	9.0	3.2	2.4	2020	35.3	5.8	88.4	4.6	47
120 Gabon	0.5	1.1	1.7	3.1	2.4	2020	36.5	14.8	78.6	5.2	..
121 São Tomé and Principe	0.1	0.1	0.2	2.4	1.8	2032	..	..	..	..	..
122 Viet Nam	42.7	73.8	98.1	2.2	1.4	2034	27.0	7.5	72.0	3.2	65
123 Solomon Islands	0.2	0.4	0.7	3.5	3.0	2016	36.8	4.2	90.0	5.2	..
124 Vanuatu	0.1	0.2	0.3	2.7	2.5	2022	34.0	6.7	88.9	4.5	..
125 Morocco	15.3	26.5	35.6	2.2	1.5	2034	27.1	7.2	68.1	3.4	50
126 Nicaragua	2.1	4.1	6.5	2.8	2.3	2021	34.7	6.1	87.3	4.1	49
127 Iraq	9.4	20.1	34.2	3.1	2.7	2019	37.4	9.5	84.5	5.5	14
128 Congo	1.3	2.6	4.5	2.9	2.8	2019	43.6	14.7	96.0	6.1	..
129 Papua New Guinea	2.4	4.3	6.5	2.3	2.1	2025	32.9	10.3	73.8	4.9	..
130 Zimbabwe	5.3	11.2	16.8	3.1	2.1	2028	38.8	14.1	88.9	4.9	48
Low human development	996.9 T	1,797.7 T	2,628.2 T	2.4	1.9	2028	32.7	11.2	76.1	4.3	31
Excluding India	442.0 T	868.7 T	1,416.6 T	2.7	2.5	2022	39.6	13.1	89.1	5.4	19
131 Myanmar	27.1	45.1	61.1	2.1	1.5	2033	28.0	10.3	66.1	3.5	17
132 Cameroon	6.6	13.2	22.5	2.8	2.7	2020	39.9	12.4	91.7	5.5	16
133 Ghana	8.6	17.3	29.4	2.8	2.7	2019	39.3	11.0	91.6	5.5	20
134 Lesotho	1.1	2.0	3.3	2.6	2.4	2023	36.2	11.0	85.5	5.0	23
135 Equatorial Guinea	0.3	0.4	0.6	1.3	2.4	2023	42.1	17.1	89.6	5.7	..
136 Lao People's Dem. Rep.	2.7	4.9	8.4	2.4	2.4	2017	44.7	14.4	91.5	6.7	19
137 Kenya	11.5	27.1	43.2	3.5	2.4	2026	37.3	11.5	95.9	5.1	33
138 Pakistan	65.7	136.3	224.5	3.0	2.5	2020	37.8	8.5	84.4	5.3	18
139 India	554.9	929.0	1,211.7	2.1	1.3	2038	26.3	9.4	65.5	3.2	41
140 Cambodia	6.9	10.0	14.7	1.5	1.9	2026	36.0	13.1	83.5	4.7	..
141 Comoros	0.3	0.6	1.1	3.3	2.9	2017	42.0	10.9	96.5	5.8	21
142 Nigeria	55.1	111.7	190.9	2.9	2.7	2019	43.8	14.7	93.6	6.2	6
143 Dem. Rep. of the Congo	20.3	45.5	80.9	3.3	2.9	2021	46.5	14.0	100.0	6.5	8
144 Togo	2.0	4.1	6.9	2.9	2.7	2020	43.2	14.9	96.2	6.3	12
145 Benin	2.7	5.4	9.6	2.8	2.9	2019	43.6	13.0	105.8	6.1	16
146 Zambia	4.2	8.1	13.2	2.7	2.5	2023	43.3	17.9	101.9	5.7	25
147 Bangladesh	66.7	118.2	162.7	2.3	1.6	2037	26.8	10.4	81.3	3.3	49
148 Côte d'Ivoire	5.5	13.7	21.0	3.7	2.2	2029	38.1	13.5	90.8	5.4	11
149 Mauritania	1.2	2.3	3.7	2.5	2.4	2022	39.0	13.7	86.2	5.2	3
150 Tanzania, U. Rep. of	13.7	30.0	49.9	3.2	2.6	2025	42.2	14.0	94.2	5.7	18
151 Yemen	6.3	15.0	29.8	3.5	3.5	2013	48.2	11.2	99.8	7.6	7
152 Nepal	11.3	21.5	34.1	2.6	2.4	2022	38.0	12.0	87.6	5.2	29
153 Madagascar	6.9	14.9	27.0	3.1	3.0	2017	42.4	10.6	97.7	5.9	17
154 Central African Rep.	1.8	3.3	5.0	2.3	2.1	2027	38.4	16.7	85.8	5.1	15
155 Bhutan	1.0	1.8	2.9	2.1	2.6	2020	41.4	14.4	84.5	5.9	..
156 Angola	5.6	10.8	19.8	2.7	3.1	2015	49.3	18.9	102.3	6.9	..
157 Sudan	13.9	26.7	40.4	2.7	2.1	2026	34.2	12.7	78.9	4.8	8
158 Senegal	4.2	8.3	13.8	2.8	2.6	2021	42.0	15.2	90.4	5.8	13
159 Haiti	4.5	7.1	10.4	1.8	1.9	2032	34.7	12.9	79.5	4.7	18
160 Uganda	9.8	19.7	34.8	2.8	2.9	2021	51.0	21.4	103.9	7.1	15
161 Malawi	4.5	9.7	16.1	3.1	2.6	2022	49.2	22.4	98.2	6.9	22
162 Djibouti	0.1	0.6	1.0	5.8	2.3	2020	38.8	15.6	78.8	5.6	..
163 Chad	3.7	6.3	10.3	2.2	2.5	2020	42.5	17.9	89.5	5.7	..
164 Guinea-Bissau	0.5	1.1	1.6	2.9	2.0	2030	41.4	21.2	85.4	5.6	..
165 Gambia	0.5	1.1	1.7	3.6	2.1	2025	41.6	18.3	78.5	5.4	12
166 Mozambique	9.4	17.3	28.3	2.5	2.5	2022	43.9	18.1	92.8	6.3	..
167 Guinea	3.9	7.3	11.9	2.6	2.5	2046	49.4	19.4	98.7	6.8	2
168 Eritrea	1.8	3.2	5.4	2.2	2.7	2013	41.4	15.2	88.7	5.6	5
169 Ethiopia	28.8	56.4	103.6	2.7	3.1	2016	48.6	17.1	96.0	7.0	4
170 Burundi	3.5	6.1	10.0	2.2	2.6	2019	44.2	18.3	98.2	6.5	9
171 Mali	5.5	10.8	19.2	2.8	2.9	2017	49.1	18.1	99.9	6.9	7
172 Burkina Faso	5.4	10.5	18.3	2.7	2.8	2019	46.8	17.9	100.7	6.8	8
173 Niger	4.2	9.2	17.1	3.2	3.2	2015	51.4	18.0	103.4	7.3	4
174 Sierra Leone	2.7	4.2	6.7	1.9	2.4	2018	47.8	27.7	89.0	6.3	..
All developing countries	2,616.1 T	4,394.0 T	5,892.2 T	2.1	1.5	2037	26.1	8.7	63.9	3.2	56
Least developed countries	285.7 T	542.5 T	873.7 T	2.6	2.4	2022	39.2	14.1	88.8	5.3	22
Industrial countries	1,043.5 T	1,233.1 T	1,294.7 T	0.7	0.2	2223	12.6	10.1	50.5	1.7	70
World	3,659.6 T	5,627.1 T	7,186.9 T	1.7	1.2	2046	23.2	9.0	60.8	2.9	58

Source: Columns 1-3 and 7, 8 and 10: UN 1996d; columns 4-6 and 9: calculated on the basis of data from UN 1996d; column 11: UN 1997f.

23 Energy use

		Electricity consumption				Traditional fuel consumption (as % of total consumption)		House-hold energy from fuel-wood[a] (%)	Commercial energy use (oil equivalent)						Net commercial energy imports (as % of energy consumption)	
		Total (millions of kilowatt-hours)	Index (1980=100)	Per capita (kilowatt-hours)					Total (1,000 metric tons)		Per capita (kg)		GDP output per kilogram (US$)[b]			
HDI rank		1995	1995	1980	1995	1980	1995	1990	1980	1994	1980	1994	1980	1994	1980	1994
High human development		1,172,392 T	268	1,112	2,278	19	12	..	386,950 T	721,742 T	982	1,422	2.3	2.0	-85	-45
23	Cyprus	2,473	239	1,692	3,319	(.)	..	..	938	1,961	1,535	2,701	2.7	2.8	100	100
24	Barbados	613	185	1,333	2,349	17	..	..	396	363	1,590	1,375	3.4	4.2	86	69
25	Hong Kong, China	33,979	275	2,449	5,549	1	..	..	5,628	13,243	1,117	2,185	5.3	5.3	100	100
28	Singapore	22,057	322	2,836	6,630		..	..	6,049	23,743	2,651	8,103	2.2	1.6	100	100
29	Antigua and Barbuda	98	163	984	1,485	..	..	..	106	131	1,738	2,017	1.7	2.9	100	100
30	Korea, Rep. of	205,102	512	1,051	4,567	6	1	..	41,426	132,538	1,087	2,982	1.8	1.8	77	86
31	Chile	29,906	255	1,054	2,105	14	13	..	7,743	14,155	695	1,012	2.3	2.3	50	68
32	Bahamas	1,028	121	4,062	3,685	..	..	..	1,764	1,867	8,400	6,864	1.2	1.5	100	100
34	Costa Rica	4,868	221	964	1,422	33	11	..	1,292	1,843	566	558	3.1	3.4	86	67
35	Brunei Darussalam	1,560	333	2,430	5,324	5	..	..	330	3,045	1,710	10,839	10.0	1.0	-5,557	-515
36	Argentina	69,291	175	1,413	1,993	7	4	43	39,669	51,405	1,411	1,504	2.8	2.7	8	-18
38	Uruguay	7,536	222	1,163	2,365	20	25	..	2,208	1,971	758	624	3.4	4.6	89	67
40	Trinidad and Tobago	4,229	206	1,900	3,286	2	1	..	3,863	6,935	3,570	5,436	1.5	0.7	-240	-87
41	Dominica	37	336	149	521	..	..	..	12	21	164	290	7.0	7.4	83	71
43	Bahrain	4,750	286	4,784	8,528	..	..	..	3,169	5,719	9,488	10,268	1.1	0.8	-62	-26
44	Fiji	544	175	489	694	32	52	..	334	404	527	527	3.5	3.9	100	76
45	Panama	3,606	199	930	1,371	27	18	..	1,376	1,597	703	618	3.2	3.9	97	87
46	Venezuela	74,752	208	2,379	3,422	1	1	..	35,011	46,300	2,354	2,186	1.3	1.2	-280	-269
48	United Arab Emirates	19,070	303	6,204	8,629	..	..	..	8,558	25,137	8,205	10,531	3.6	..	-996	-454
49	Mexico	150,039	222	999	1,646	4	4	23	97,434	140,840	1,464	1,561	1.3	1.2	-49	-48
50	Saint Kitts and Nevis	86	..	..	2,098	..	..	..	..	20	..	486	..	7.3	..	100
51	Grenada	71	284	281	772	..	..	..	17	27	191	293	6.5	6.9	100	100
53	Colombia	45,619	221	778	1,274	21	22	60	13,972	22,470	501	622	2.1	2.1	7	-99
54	Kuwait	24,126	256	6,849	14,267	..	..	..	9,500	13,968	6,909	8,622	2.7	2.0	-739	-693
55	Saint Vincent	65	241	276	580	..	..	..	17	22	174	199	5.4	8.8	76	73
56	Seychelles	128	256	794	1,753	..	..	..	70	122	1,110	1,691	3.2	2.9	100	100
57	Qatar	5,738	236	10,616	10,471	(.)	..	..	4,738	7,684	20,690	12,597	..	..	-488	-267
58	Saint Lucia	113	195	504	796	..	..	..	39	53	315	338	..	7.9	100	100
59	Thailand	84,280	531	340	1,447	48	33	77	12,093	44,395	259	769	2.8	2.2	96	61
60	Malaysia	46,609	458	740	2,314	14	6	..	9,522	33,410	692	1,699	2.4	1.7	-58	-71
61	Mauritius	1,120	240	482	1,003	44	38	60	339	431	351	387	3.7	6.3	94	92
62	Brazil	310,751	223	1,145	1,954	41	31	32	72,141	112,795	595	718	3.5	2.8	65	39
63	Belize	148	274	370	695	53	40	..	74	88	507	417	3.2	5.1	100	100
64	Libyan Arab Jamahiriya	18,000	372	1,588	3,329	2	1	..	7,122	13,039	2,340	2,499	5.7	..	-1,255	-473
Medium human development		1,852,216 T	288	400	891	13	9	..	753,393 T	1,416,345 T	468	690	1.2	1.2	-107	-54
	Excluding China	846,690 T	248	560	987	19	12	..	340,263 T	625,305 T	556	741	2.4	1.8	-231	-121
65	Suriname	1,614	102	4,442	3,780	1	..	..	1,002	784	2,813	1,926	0.4	1.1	77	70
66	Lebanon	5,573	198	1,056	1,852	4	3	32	2,376	3,790	840	964	..	..	97	98
69	Turkey	81,038	329	554	1,332	18	4	48	31,314	57,580	705	957	1.9	1.9	45	53
70	Saudi Arabia	99,833	528	1,969	5,469	..	..	..	35,496	83,772	3,787	4,566	2.7	1.1	-1,361	-463
71	Oman	8,258	863	847	3,742	..	..	..	1,346	5,018	1,223	2,392	2.9	2.4	-1,024	-787
73	Ecuador	8,349	248	423	729	26	15	65	4,209	6,345	529	565	2.3	2.2	-156	-231
75	Korea, Dem. People's Rep. of	36,000	103	1,981	1,629	3	1	..	30,932	26,464	1,694	1,129	..	..	9	12
78	Iran, Islamic Rep. of	81,330	363	570	1,190	2	1	..	38,347	94,159	980	1,505	3.0	1.9	-118	-136
81	Syrian Arab Rep.	15,300	406	433	1,077	(.)	..	33	5,343	13,675	614	997	1.9	1.2	-78	-130
82	Algeria	19,441	273	381	692	3	2	29	12,078	24,834	647	906	4.2	2.6	-452	-318
83	Tunisia	7,620	272	434	848	15	14	37	3,083	5,264	483	595	2.4	2.4	-99	9
84	Jamaica	5,829	328	834	2,362	6	8	61	2,169	2,703	1,017	1,083	1.3	1.5	99	100
85	Cuba	11,189	112	1,029	1,021	28	22	25	9,645	10,133	992	923	..	..	97	88
86	Peru	16,759	167	579	712	19	25	76	8,139	8,555	471	367	2.5	2.7	-36	0
87	Jordan	5,616	525	366	1,045	(.)	..	20	1,710	4,306	784	1,067	..	1.5	100	96
88	Dominican Rep.	6,506	196	582	832	30	12	55	2,083	2,591	366	337	2.0	2.5	93	94
89	South Africa	188,975	189	3,025	3,992	4	4	..	60,511	86,995	2,074	2,146	1.3	1.0	-14	-35
90	Sri Lanka	4,800	288	113	268	54	51	85	1,411	1,728	96	97	3.4	5.1	91	80
91	Paraguay	3,692	508	233	765	66	51	68	550	1,402	175	299	6.0	3.5	88	-123
94	Samoa (Western)	65	167	252	394	..	..	..	0	71	0	433	..	..	..	100
95	Maldives	57	1,425	25	224	..	..	..	14	34	89	139	..	4.8	-150	24
96	Indonesia	68,804	483	94	348	52	32	86	25,028	69,740	169	366	2.1	1.9	-275	-120
97	Botswana	..	..	..	..	36	..	57	384	549	426	387	2.1	4.7	32	55
98	Philippines	33,426	186	373	493	36	32	81	13,406	21,199	277	316	2.5	1.9	79	71
100	Guyana	334	81	545	402	23	35	..	599	288	788	350	0.7	1.5	100	100
101	Mongolia	3,010	162	1,119	1,222	14	4	..	1,943	2,550	1,168	1,058	1.2	1.2	39	15
106	China	1,005,526	334	307	839	8	6	80	413,130	791,040	421	664	0.3	0.7	-4	-1
107	Namibia	..	..	..	..	..	..	..	..	..	..	..	..	..	..	..
111	Guatemala	3,229	193	242	304	53	61	73	1,443	2,165	209	210	5.0	4.3	84	74
112	Egypt	48,864	258	433	787	5	4	..	15,176	34,071	371	600	1.6	1.2	-120	-79

HDI rank	Electricity consumption Total (millions of kilowatt-hours) 1995	Index (1980=100) 1995	Per capita (kilowatt-hours) 1980	Per capita (kilowatt-hours) 1995	Traditional fuel consumption (as % of total consumption) 1980	Traditional fuel consumption (as % of total consumption) 1995	Household energy from fuelwood[a] (%) 1990	Commercial energy use Total (1,000 metric tons) 1980	Commercial energy use Total (1,000 metric tons) 1994	Per capita (kg) 1980	Per capita (kg) 1994	GDP output per kilogram (US$)[b] 1980	GDP output per kilogram (US$)[b] 1994	Net commercial energy imports (as % of energy consumption) 1980	Net commercial energy imports (as % of energy consumption) 1994
114 El Salvador	3,370	218	339	595	50	44	71	1,000	2,032	220	370	4.5	2.7	63	70
115 Swaziland	..	..	..	..	..	..	..	191	232	338	264	2.2	3.0	19	22
116 Bolivia	3,030	193	292	409	19	13	81	1,713	2,698	320	373	2.7	2.1	-107	-61
117 Cape Verde	39	244	55	101	..	..	..	105	114	363	307	1.1	2.1	100	100
119 Honduras	2,746	297	259	486	54	50	..	843	1,173	230	204	4.2	4.4	76	82
120 Gabon	940	177	767	874	36	32	..	759	692	1,098	652	5.0	5.5	-1,106	-2,212
121 São Tomé and Principe	15	167	96	113	..	..	..	13	23	139	184	5.2	2.6	85	87
122 Viet Nam	14,867	353	78	201	53	45	88	4,024	7,267	75	101	..	7.5	32	-55
123 Solomon Islands	32	152	93	85	14	60	..	389	58	1,670	159	0.3	3.9	100	100
124 Vanuatu	30	150	171	178	13	..	..	39	46	339	279	2.4	2.9	100	100
125 Morocco	12,724	258	254	480	5	5	67	4,927	8,509	254	327	3.1	2.9	87	95
126 Nicaragua	1,699	160	380	412	48	43	..	756	1,273	270	300	5.1	2.7	83	63
127 Iraq	29,000	254	878	1,443	(.)	(.)	60	12,003	23,864	923	1,213	7.2	..	-1,038	-25
128 Congo	547	336	98	211	56	51	..	262	847	157	331	5.7	2.8	-1,193	-1,013
129 Papua New Guinea	1,790	143	406	416	64	63	..	705	990	228	236	3.9	4.8	89	-150
130 Zimbabwe	10,350	142	1,020	925	34	37	..	2,797	4,722	399	438	1.5	1.4	28	24
Low human development	549,922 T	306	143	307	51	40	..	140,468 T	311,426 T	112	177	2.4	2.0	-46	-17
Excluding India	133,755 T	221	106	155	68	67	..	46,561 T	84,788 T	82	101	3.7	3.0	-184	-116
131 Myanmar	3,780	254	44	84	66	65	89	1,858	2,181	55	49	..	9.1	-4	1
132 Cameroon	2,746	189	168	208	69	80	74	774	1,335	89	103	10.0	6.9	-269	-333
133 Ghana	5,935	122	451	342	68	79	86	1,303	1,542	121	93	3.6	4.5	57	66
134 Lesotho	..	..	..	..	..	..	..	..	..	..	..	..	..	..	..
135 Equatorial Guinea	20	111	83	50	84	67	..	19	31	88	80	..	5.2	95	97
136 Lao People's Dem. Rep.	295	136	68	60	87	90	..	107	182	33	38	..	9.1	-121	-18
137 Kenya	3,919	217	109	144	75	78	79	1,991	2,872	120	110	3.1	3.3	95	83
138 Pakistan	60,155	402	176	441	27	20	72	11,698	32,133	142	254	1.8	1.5	38	40
139 India	416,167	349	173	448	35	23	84	93,907	226,638	137	248	1.9	1.6	21	21
140 Cambodia	194	194	15	19	71	90	..	393	512	60	52	..	2.4	97	96
141 Comoros	16	160	26	26	..	..	..	15	18	45	37	10.2	11.8	100	100
142 Nigeria	14,810	209	98	133	64	68	74	9,879	17,503	139	162	3.1	2.2	-968	-484
143 Dem. Rep of the Congo	4,898	113	161	108	80	..	94	1,487	1,902	55	45	4.4	..	1	1
144 Togo	408	211	74	100	38	70	83	195	183	75	46	6.3	6.9	99	100
145 Benin	269	220	35	50	85	89	84	149	107	43	20	8.3	18.0	93	-194
146 Zambia	6,310	98	1,125	781	55	73	86	1,685	1,296	294	149	1.3	1.8	32	31
147 Bangladesh	11,689	441	30	99	68	49	83	2,809	7,566	32	64	4.5	3.1	60	28
148 Côte d'Ivoire	1,913	109	214	140	53	54	70	1,435	1,406	175	103	6.8	6.8	87	70
149 Mauritania	152	163	60	67	1	..	80	214	229	138	103	3.8	4.8	100	100
150 Tanzania, U. Rep. of	1,738	227	41	58	84	91	89	1,023	975	55	34	..	4.5	92	83
151 Yemen	1,980	..	..	132	..	2	75	1,364	3,044	160	206	..	..	100	-463
152 Nepal	1,075	432	17	50	95	91	84	174	582	12	28	12.5	7.3	91	88
153 Madagascar	611	140	48	41	77	86	84	391	479	45	36	6.7	5.6	90	83
154 Central African Rep.	102	150	29	31	91	89	..	59	93	26	29	16.2	12.1	71	76
155 Bhutan	246	1,118	17	139	100	81	..	..	22	..	33	..	16.9	..	95
156 Angola	1,870	125	214	173	47	69	85	937	931	133	89	..	7.0	-722	-2,576
157 Sudan	1,331	152	47	50	76	83	82	1,150	1,731	62	66	12.7	12.1	94	95
158 Senegal	774	122	115	93	49	55	82	875	803	158	97	4.2	6.3	100	100
159 Haiti	407	129	59	57	82	87	72	240	200	45	29	9.6	7.9	77	93
160 Uganda	677	185	28	34	87	90	86	320	425	25	23	..	22.6	52	58
161 Malawi	803	196	66	83	89	90	89	334	370	54	39	3.2	3.4	70	59
162 Djibouti	184	157	416	306	..	..	..	517	548	1,840	909	..	..	100	100
163 Chad	89	189	10	14	87	98	82	93	100	21	16	6.2	10.9	100	100
164 Guinea-Bissau	43	307	18	40	76	57	..	31	39	38	37	3.8	5.8	100	100
165 Gambia	74	164	70	67	80	79	..	53	60	83	56	3.5	4.9	100	100
166 Mozambique	1,164	26	364	67	73	91	83	1,123	619	93	40	1.4	3.3	-15	74
167 Guinea	543	143	85	74	68	72	87	356	418	80	65	..	6.1	89	86
168 Eritrea	..	..	..	..	..	..	..	..	..	..	..	..	..	..	..
169 Ethiopia	1,265	..	18	22	92	91	86	624	1,193	17	22	..	7.0	91	87
170 Burundi	149	355	10	25	93	94	77	58	143	14	23	13.9	8.3	98	97
171 Mali	290	276	15	27	85	90	81	164	205	25	22	11.2	11.5	87	80
172 Burkina Faso	220	195	16	21	91	87	85	144	160	21	16	11.2	16.0	100	100
173 Niger	370	170	39	40	78	78	71	210	327	38	37	12.1	7.4	93	83
174 Sierra Leone	241	120	62	57	64	86	..	310	323	96	77	2.3	2.4	100	100
All developing countries	3,574,530 T	284	387	814	22	15	..	1,280,811 T	2,449,513 T	393	568	1.7	1.5	-94	-47
Least developed countries	43,741 T	154	76	81	77	84	..	19,166 T	27,540 T	53	53	5.1	5.1	19	-97
Industrial countries	9,300,133 T	147	6,601	7,542	1	3	..	4,919,887 T	5,467,912 T	4,587	4,452	2.3	2.8	24	19
World	12,874,663 T	174	1,566	2,290	7	7	..	6,200,698 T	7,917,425 T	1,431	1,429	2.2	2.4	..	..

a. Data are omitted for countries deriving less than 20% of household energy from fuelwood.
b. Estimated real GDP (at 1987 prices) divided by kilograms of oil equivalent of commercial energy use.
Source: Columns 1-4: UN 1997b; columns 5 and 6: WRI 1998; column 7: UN 1995b; columns 8-15: World Bank 1997d.

24 Profile of environmental degradation

HDI rank	Land area (1,000 ha) 1995	Forest and wood-land (as % of land area) 1995	Internal renewable water resources per capita (cubic metres per year) 1998	Annual fresh water withdrawals — As % of water resources 1987-95	Annual fresh water withdrawals — Per capita (cubic metres) 1987-95	Annual rate of deforestation[a] (%) 1990-95	Annual rate of reforestation (%) 1980-90	CO_2 emissions per capita (metric tons) 1995	Loss of mangroves (%) 1980-90
High human development	1,896,477 T	41.7	18,223	2.6	571	..	..	4.0	..
23 Cyprus	925	..	..	..	..	0	..	7.0	..
24 Barbados	43	..	..	..	..	0	..	3.2	..
25 Hong Kong, China	104	..	..	..	..	..	..	5.1	..
28 Singapore	61	6.6	172	31.7 b	84 b	0	..	19.1	76
29 Antigua and Barbuda	44	..	..	..	..	0	..	..	..
30 Korea, Rep. of	9,873	77.2	1,434	41.7	632	0.2	..	8.3	..
31 Chile	74,880	10.5	31,570	3.6 b	1,625 b	0.4	8	3.1	..
32 Bahamas	1,388	..	..	..	..	2.6	..	6.1	..
34 Costa Rica	5,106	24.4	26,027	1.4 b	780 b	3.0	27	1.5	..
35 Brunei Darussalam	577	..	..	..	..	0.6	..	28.1	17
36 Argentina	273,669	12.4	19,212	4.0 b	1,043 b	0.3	1	3.7	..
38 Uruguay	17,481	4.7	18,215	1.1 b	241 b	(..)	1	1.7	..
40 Trinidad and Tobago	513	31.4	3,869	2.9 b	148 b	1.5	1	13.3	..
41 Dominica	75	..	..	..	..	0	..	..	..
43 Bahrain	68	..	..	..	..	0	..	26.6	0
44 Fiji	1,827	45.7	34,732	0.1	42	0.4	10	1.0	7
45 Panama	7,443	37.6	52,042	0.9 b	755 b	2.1	9	2.6	..
46 Venezuela	88,205	49.9	36,830	0.5 b	382 b	1.1	11	8.2	..
48 United Arab Emirates	8,360	0.7	64	1,405.3	954	0	47	30.9	..
49 Mexico	190,869	29.0	3,729	21.7	915	0.9	7	3.9	..
50 Saint Kitts and Nevis	36	..	..	..	..	0	..	..	..
51 Grenada	(.)	..	..	..	..	0	..	..	..
53 Colombia	103,870	51.0	28,393	0.5	174	0.5	12	1.9	..
54 Kuwait	1,782	0.3	11	2,690.0	307	0	34	28.8	..
55 Saint Vincent	39	..	..	..	..	..	..	..	..
56 Seychelles	45	..	..	..	..	0	..	..	..
57 Qatar	1,100	..	..	..	..	0	..	52.9	..
58 Saint Lucia	62	..	..	..	..	3.6	..	..	..
59 Thailand	51,089	22.8	1,845	29.0	602	2.6	8	3.0	87
60 Malaysia	32,855	47.1	21,259	2.1 b	768 b	2.4	15	5.3	32
61 Mauritius	203	5.9	1,915	16.3 b	410 b	0	2	1.3	..
62 Brazil	845,651	65.2	31,424	0.7	246	0.5	5	1.6	..
63 Belize	2,280	86.1	69,565	0.1	109	3.0	..	1.9	..
64 Libyan Arab Jamahiriya	175,954	0.2	100	766.7	880	0	7	7.3	0
Medium human development	3,096,900 T	19.6	4,357	9.0	488	..	..	2.6	..
Excluding China	2,167,800 T	21.9	7,374	5.8	529	..	..	2.6	..
65 Suriname	15,600	94.4	452,489	0.2	1,192	0.1	4	5.0	..
66 Lebanon	1,023	5.1	1,315	30.8	444	7.8	..	4.4	0
69 Turkey	76,963	11.5	3,074	16.1	544	0	..	2.7	0
70 Saudi Arabia	214,969	0.1	119	709.1	1,003	0.8	..	13.9	..
71 Oman	21,246	..	393	124.2	656	0	..	5.2	..
73 Ecuador	27,684	40.2	25,791	1.8	581	1.6	4	2.0	..
75 Korea, Dem. People's Rep. of	12,041	51.2	2,887	21.1	727	0	7	11.6	..
78 Iran, Islamic Rep. of	162,200	1.0	1,755	54.6	1,079	1.7	10	3.8	..
81 Syrian Arab Rep.	18,378	1.2	456	205.9	1,069	2.2	15	3.2	0
82 Algeria	238,174	0.8	460	32.4	180	1.2	5	3.3	0
83 Tunisia	15,536	3.6	371	87.3	376	0.5	8	1.7	0
84 Jamaica	1,083	16.2	3,269	3.9 b	159 b	7.2	5	3.7	..
85 Cuba	10,982	16.8	3,104	23.5 b	870 b	1.2	8	2.7	..
86 Peru	128,000	52.8	1,613	15.3	300	0.3	7	1.3	..
87 Jordan	8,893	0.5	114	144.7	201	2.5	5	2.5	0
88 Dominican Rep.	4,838	32.7	2,430	14.9	446	1.6	6	1.5	..
89 South Africa	122,104	7.0	1,011	29.7	359	0.2	2	7.4	50
90 Sri Lanka	6,463	27.8	2,341	14.6 b	503 b	1.1	6	0.3	..
91 Paraguay	39,730	29.0	18,001	0.5	112	2.6	15	0.8	0
94 Samoa (Western)	284	..	..	..	..	1.0	..	0.8	..
95 Maldives	30	..	..	..	..	..	..	0.7	..
96 Indonesia	181,157	60.6	12,251	0.7	96	1.0	18	1.5	45
97 Botswana	56,673	24.6	1,870	3.9	84	0.5	..	1.5	0
98 Philippines	29,817	22.7	4,476	9.1 b	686 b	3.5	..	0.9	..
100 Guyana	19,685	94.4	281,542	0.6	1,819	(..)	29	1.1	..
101 Mongolia	156,650	6.0	9,375	2.2	271	0	..	3.4	0
106 China	929,100	14.4	2,231	16.4 b	461 b	0.1	4	2.7	..
107 Namibia	82,329	15.0	3,751	4.0	179	0.3	..	..	0
111 Guatemala	10,843	35.4	10,033	0.6 b	139 b	2.0	10	0.7	..
112 Egypt	99,545	(.)	43	1,967.9	921	0	2	1.5	..

HDI rank	Land area (1,000 ha) 1995	Forest and wood-land (as % of land area) 1995	Internal renewable water resources per capita (cubic metres per year) 1998	Annual fresh water withdrawals		Annual rate of defores-tation[a] (%) 1990-95	Annual rate of refores-tation (%) 1980-90	CO$_2$ emissions per capita (metric tons) 1995	Loss of mangroves (%) 1980-90
				As % of water resources 1987-95	Per capita (cubic metres) 1987-95				
114 El Salvador	2,072	5.1	3,128	5.3[b]	244[b]	3.3	15	0.9	..
115 Swaziland	1,720	8.5	2,836	24.9[b]	1,171[b]	0	..	0.5	0
116 Bolivia	108,438	44.6	37,703	0.4	201	1.2	4	1.4	0
117 Cape Verde	403	..	..	..	..	-24.0	..	0.3	..
119 Honduras	11,189	36.8	9,015	2.8	294	2.3	24	0.7	..
120 Gabon	25,767	69.3	140,171	(.)	70	0.5	5	3.3	50
121 São Tomé and Principe	96	..	..	..	..	0	..	0.6	..
122 Viet Nam	32,549	28.0	4,827	7.7	416	1.0	4	0.4	62
123 Solomon Islands	2,799	85.4	107,194	(.)	0	0.2	2	0.4	..
124 Vanuatu	1,219	..	..	..	..	0.8	..	0.4	..
125 Morocco	44,630	8.6	1,071	36.2	433	0.3	4	1.1	0
126 Nicaragua	12,140	45.8	39,203	0.5[b]	368[b]	2.5	27	0.7	..
127 Iraq	43,737	0.2	1,615	121.6	2,368	0	..	4.9	..
128 Congo	34,150	57.2	78,668	(.)	20	0.2	12	0.5	0
129 Papua New Guinea	45,286	81.6	174,055	(.)	28	0	7	0.6	..
130 Zimbabwe	38,685	22.5	1,182	8.7	136	0.6	2	0.9	..
Low human development	2,501,298 T	22.1	4,404	7.6	484	..	..	0.7	..
Excluding India	2,203,979 T	22.1	7,090	3.8	335	..	..	0.4	..
131 Myanmar	65,755	41.3	22,719	0.4	101	1.4	18	0.1	58
132 Cameroon	43,540	45.0	18,711	0.2	38	0.6	14	0.3	40
133 Ghana	22,754	39.7	1,607	1.0[b]	35[b]	1.3	2	0.2	..
134 Lesotho	3,035	0.2	2,395	1.0	30	0	16	..	0
135 Equatorial Guinea	2,805	63.5	69,767	(.)	15	0.5	..	0.3	60
136 Lao People's Dem. Rep.	23,080	53.9	50,392	0.4	259	1.2	4	0.1	0
137 Kenya	56,914	2.3	696	10.2	87	0.3	1	0.3	70
138 Pakistan	77,088	2.3	1,678	62.7	1,269	2.9	3	0.6	78
139 India	297,319	21.9	1,896	20.5[b]	612[b]	(..)	14	1.0	85
140 Cambodia	17,652	55.7	8,195	0.6	66	1.6	..	(.)	5
141 Comoros	223	..	..	..	..	5.6	..	0.1	..
142 Nigeria	91,077	15.1	1,815	1.6	41	0.9	3	0.8	..
143 Dem. Rep. of the Congo	226,705	48.2	19,001	(.)	10	0.7	10	(.)	50
144 Togo	5,439	22.9	2,594	0.8	28	..	12	0.2	..
145 Benin	11,062	41.8	1,751	1.4	28	1.2	5	0.1	..
146 Zambia	74,339	42.2	9,229	2.1	216	0.8	6	0.3	0
147 Bangladesh	13,017	7.8	10,940	1.7	217	0.8	7	0.2	73
148 Côte d'Ivoire	31,800	17.2	5,265	0.9	67	0.6	7	0.8	..
149 Mauritania	102,522	0.5	163	407.5[b]	923[b]	0	24	1.4	0
150 Tanzania, U. Rep. of	88,359	36.8	2,485	1.5	40	1.0	8	0.1	60
151 Yemen	52,797	(.)	243	..	..	0	..	1.0	..
152 Nepal	14,300	33.7	7,338	1.6	154	1.1	14	0.1	..
153 Madagascar	58,154	26.0	20,614	4.8	1,579	0.8	2	0.1	40
154 Central African Rep.	62,298	48.0	40,413	0.1	26	0.4	48	0.1	0
155 Bhutan	4,700	58.6	49,557	(.)	13	0.3	7	0.1	0
156 Angola	124,670	17.8	15,376	0.3	57	1.0	1	0.4	50
157 Sudan	237,600	17.5	1,227	50.9	666	0.8	6	0.1	0
158 Senegal	19,253	38.3	2,933	5.2	202	0.7	25	0.4	0
159 Haiti	2,756	0.8	1,460	0.4	7	3.4	33	0.1	..
160 Uganda	19,965	30.6	1,829	0.5[b]	20[b]	0.9	..	(.)	0
161 Malawi	9,408	35.5	1,690	5.3	98	1.6	8	0.1	0
162 Djibouti	2,320	..	..	..	..	0	..	(.)	70
163 Chad	125,920	8.8	2,176	1.2	34	0.8	6	..	0
164 Guinea-Bissau	2,812	82.1	14,109	0.1	17	0.4	..	0.2	70
165 Gambia	1,000	9.1	2,513	0.7[b]	30[b]	0.9	..	0.2	..
166 Mozambique	78,409	21.5	5,350	0.6	40	0.7	4	0.1	60
167 Guinea	24,572	25.9	29,454	0.3	142	1.1	5	0.1	60
168 Eritrea	10,100	..	789	..	..	0	..	..	..
169 Ethiopia	110,000	12.3	1,771	2.0	51	0.5	10	0.7	0
170 Burundi	2,568	12.3	546	2.8	20	0.4	19	(.)	0
171 Mali	122,019	9.5	5,071	2.3	162	1.0	27	(.)	0
172 Burkina Faso	27,360	15.6	1,535	2.2	39	0.7	8	(.)	0
173 Niger	126,670	2.0	346	14.3	69	0	10	0.1	0
174 Sierra Leone	7,162	18.3	34,957	0.2	98	3.0	3	0.1	..
All developing countries	7,494,675 T	26.0	5,975	6.3	496	..	..	2.0	..
Least developed countries	1,866,384 T	23.1	9,940	1.4	186	..	..	0.2	..
Industrial countries	5,354,241 T	27.9	10,804	9.5	1,069	..	..	11.4	..
World	12,848,916 T	26.8	6,918[c]	7.3[c]	626[c]	0.3[c]	..	4.1	..

a. Positive numbers indicate loss of forest area; negative numbers indicate gain in forest area.
b. Data refer to an earlier year or period than that specified in the column heading.
c. WRI 1998.
Source: Column 1: FAO 1996a; *column 2:* calculated on the basis of data from FAO 1996a; *columns 3-7:* WRI 1998; *column 8:* calculated on the basis of data from: CDIAC 1998; *column 9:* WRI 1996a.

25

National income accounts

HDI rank	GDP (US$ billions) 1995	Agriculture (as % of GDP) 1995	Industry (as % of GDP) 1995	Services (as % of GDP) 1995	Consumption Private (as % of GDP) 1995	Consumption Government (as % of GDP) 1995	Gross domestic investment (as % of GDP)[a] 1995	Gross domestic savings (as % of GDP)[a] 1995	Tax revenue (as % of GDP) 1995	Central government expenditure (as % of GDP) 1995	Exports (as % of GDP) 1995	Imports (as % of GDP) 1995
High human development	2,482 T	9	36	56	60	12	27	26	..	25	31	32
23 Cyprus	..	..	..	..	..	..	..	..	..	..	..	..
24 Barbados	..	..	..	..	..	..	..	..	..	..	..	..
25 Hong Kong, China	144	0	17[b]	83[b]	59	9	35	33	..	..	147	149
28 Singapore	84	0	36	64	40	9	33	..	..	15	..	..
29 Antigua and Barbuda	..	..	..	..	..	..	..	..	..	..	..	..
30 Korea, Rep. of	455	7[b]	43[b]	50[b]	54	10	37	36	18	18	33	34
31 Chile	67	..	..	..	62	9	27	29	18	20	29	27
32 Bahamas	..	..	..	..	..	..	..	..	..	..	..	..
34 Costa Rica	9	17	24	58	60	17	25	24	22	28	41	42
35 Brunei Darussalam	..	..	..	..	..	..	..	..	..	..	..	..
36 Argentina	281	6	31	63	..	..	18	18	..	..	9	8
38 Uruguay	18	9	26	65	74	13	14	13	28	32	19	20
40 Trinidad and Tobago	5	3	42	54	62	13	14	25	..	..	39	29
41 Dominica	..	..	..	..	..	..	..	..	9	..	..	..
43 Bahrain	..	..	..	..	..	..	..	..	..	..	..	..
44 Fiji	..	..	..	..	70	19	14	12	21	..	51	53
45 Panama	7	11	15	74	64	15	24	22	..	28	39	40
46 Venezuela	75	5	38	56	73	6	16	21	..	19	27	22
48 United Arab Emirates	39	2[b]	57[b]	40[b]	..	..	..	..	..	12	..	..
49 Mexico	250	8	26	67	71	10	15	19	..	14	25	22
50 Saint Kitts and Nevis	..	..	..	..	..	..	..	..	..	..	..	..
51 Grenada	..	..	..	..	58	16	32	25	23	..	20	27
53 Colombia	76	14[b]	32[b]	54[b]	75	9	20	16	..	14	15	20
54 Kuwait	27	0	53	46	49	33	12	18	1	51	55	49
55 Saint Vincent	..	..	..	..	..	..	..	..	25	..	..	..
56 Seychelles	..	..	..	..	..	..	..	..	..	..	..	..
57 Qatar	..	..	..	..	..	..	..	..	..	..	..	..
58 Saint Lucia	..	..	..	..	..	..	..	..	..	..	..	..
59 Thailand	167	11	40	49	54	10	43	36	17	11	42	48
60 Malaysia	85	13	43	44	51	12	41	37	21	23	96	99
61 Mauritius	4	9	33	58	65	12	25	22	18	23	58	62
62 Brazil	688	14	37	49	62	17	22	21	..	39	7	8
63 Belize	..	..	..	..	..	..	..	..	21	..	..	..
64 Libyan Arab Jamahiriya	..	..	..	..	..	..	..	..	..	..	..	..
Medium human development	1,776 T	17	40	43	57	12	32	31	..	..	24	25
Excluding China	1,078 T	15	34	52	66	12	26	22	..	..	26	30
65 Suriname	..	..	..	..	..	..	..	..	..	26	..	..
66 Lebanon	11	7[b]	24[b]	69[b]	..	10	25	20	14	27	20	25
69 Turkey	165	16	31	53	70	..	..	..	..	..	..	..
70 Saudi Arabia	126	..	..	..	..	..	..	..	8	43	..	..
71 Oman	12	..	..	..	..	..	..	..	..	..	..	..
73 Ecuador	18	12	36	52	67	13	19	21	..	16	29	27
75 Korea, Dem. People's Rep. of	..	..	..	..	..	..	..	..	..	..	..	..
78 Iran, Islamic Rep. of	..	..	..	..	53	13	29	34	..	..	21	16
81 Syrian Arab Rep.	17	..	..	..	..	..	..	..	..	27	..	..
82 Algeria	41	13	47	41	56	16	32	29	..	..	27	30
83 Tunisia	18	12	29	59	63	16	24	20	..	..	45	49
84 Jamaica	4	9	38	53	80	9	17	10	..	..	69	76
85 Cuba	..	..	..	..	..	..	..	..	..	..	..	..
86 Peru	57	7	38	55	83	6	17	11	14	19	12	18
87 Jordan	6	8[b]	27[b]	65[b]	..	..	..	..	..	31	..	..
88 Dominican Rep.	11	15	22	64	80	4	20	16	..	17	26	29
89 South Africa	136	5	31	64	61	21	18	18	..	33	22	22
90 Sri Lanka	13	23	25	52	74	12	25	14	18	29	36	47
91 Paraguay	8	24[b]	22[b]	54[b]	..	..	..	..	..	13	..	..
94 Samoa (Western)	..	..	..	..	..	..	..	..	..	..	..	..
95 Maldives	..	..	..	..	..	..	..	..	..	..	..	..
96 Indonesia	198	17	42	41	56	8	38	36	..	16	25	27
97 Botswana	4	5	46	48	45	32	25	23	..	38	49	52
98 Philippines	74	22	32	46	74	11	23	15	..	18	36	44
100 Guyana	..	..	..	..	..	..	..	..	..	..	73	86
101 Mongolia	1	..	..	..	..	..	..	..	20	21	..	..
106 China	698	21	48	31	46	12	40	42	..	..	21	19
107 Namibia	3	14[b]	29[b]	56[b]	..	..	..	..	..	41	..	..
111 Guatemala	14	25[b]	19[b]	56[b]	..	..	..	..	..	9	..	..
112 Egypt	47	20	21	59	81	13	17	6	..	43	21	32

HDI rank	GDP (US$ billions) 1995	Agriculture (as % of GDP) 1995	Industry (as % of GDP) 1995	Services (as % of GDP) 1995	Consumption Private (as % of GDP) 1995	Consumption Government (as % of GDP) 1995	Gross domestic investment (as % of GDP)a 1995	Gross domestic savings (as % of GDP)a 1995	Tax revenue (as % of GDP) 1995	Central government expenditure (as % of GDP) 1995	Exports (as % of GDP) 1995	Imports (as % of GDP) 1995
114 El Salvador	9	14	22	65	86	8	19	6	12	15	21	34
115 Swaziland	..	..	..	..	64	27	17	9	..	..	83	91
116 Bolivia	6	..	..	..	..	..	..	..	12	24	..	..
117 Cape Verde	..	..	..	..	..	..	..	..	..	..	..	..
119 Honduras	4	21	33	46	73	14	23	14	..	..	36	45
120 Gabon	5	..	..	..	42	10	26	48	..	..	61	39
121 São Tomé and Principe	..	..	..	..	..	..	..	..	..	..	..	..
122 Viet Nam	20	28	30	42	77	7	27	16	..	..	36	47
123 Solomon Islands	..	..	..	..	..	..	..	..	..	..	..	..
124 Vanuatu	..	..	..	..	..	..	..	..	..	..	..	..
125 Morocco	32	14	33	53	71	15	21	13	..	..	27	35
126 Nicaragua	2	33 b	20 b	46 b	..	..	..	..	24	30	..	..
127 Iraq	..	..	..	..	..	..	..	..	..	..	..	..
128 Congo	2	10	38	51	64	12	27	23	..	..	62	66
129 Papua New Guinea	5	26	38 b	34 b	48	12	24	39	..	29	61	45
130 Zimbabwe	7	15 b	36 b	48 b	..	..	..	..	..	..	..	..
Low human development	543 T	30	28	42	70	11	22	19	..	..	16	19
Excluding India	219 T	32	26	43	75	12	18	12	..	..	22	28
131 Myanmar	..	..	..	..	..	..	..	..	..	..	..	..
132 Cameroon	8	39	23	38	71	9	15	21	..	16	26	20
133 Ghana	6	46	16	38	77	12	19	10	..	21	25	34
134 Lesotho	1	10	56	34	85	23	87	-9	..	33	21	117
135 Equatorial Guinea	..	..	..	..	..	..	..	..	..	..	..	..
136 Lao People's Dem. Rep.	2	52 b	18 b	30 b	..	..	..	..	..	..	..	..
137 Kenya	9	29	17	54	72	15	19	13	..	27	33	39
138 Pakistan	61	26	24	50	73	12	19	16	15	23	16	19
139 India	324	29	29	41	68	10	25	22	10	16	12	15
140 Cambodia	3	51	14	34	..	..	..	..	..	..	..	..
141 Comoros	..	..	..	..	87	21	17	-8	..	..	19	44
142 Nigeria	27	28	53	18	..	10	..	..	..	..	..	..
143 Dem. Rep. of the Congo	..	..	..	..	..	..	..	..	..	..	..	..
144 Togo	1	38 b	21 b	41 b	80	11	14	9	..	..	31	..
145 Benin	2	34 b	12 b	53 b	..	..	..	..	..	..	..	..
146 Zambia	4	22	40	37	88	9	12	3	13	17	31	40
147 Bangladesh	29	31	18	52	78	14	17	8	..	..	14	22
148 Côte d'Ivoire	10	31	20	50	67	12	13	20	..	..	41	34
149 Mauritania	1	27 b	30 b	43 b	80	9	15	11	..	..	50	54
150 Tanzania, U. Rep. of	4	58	17	24	97	10	31	-7	..	..	30	68
151 Yemen	5	22 b	27 b	51 b	..	..	..	..	..	39	..	..
152 Nepal	4	42	22	36	79	8	23	12	9	..	24	35
153 Madagascar	3	34	13	53	91	7	11	3	8	19	23	31
154 Central African Rep.	1	44 b	13 b	43 b	80	13	15	6	..	..	18	27
155 Bhutan	..	..	..	..	..	..	..	..	6	..	..	..
156 Angola	4	12	59	28	9	47	27	43	..	..	74	58
157 Sudan	..	..	..	..	..	..	..	..	..	..	..	..
158 Senegal	5	20	18	62	79	11	16	10	..	..	32	37
159 Haiti	2	44 b	12 b	44 b	..	..	..	..	..	..	..	..
160 Uganda	6	50	14	36	83	10	16	7	..	..	12	21
161 Malawi	1	42	27	31	76	20	15	4	..	..	29	40
162 Djibouti	..	..	..	..	71	34	12	-5	..	..	42	59
163 Chad	1	44 b	22 b	35 b	..	..	..	..	..	..	..	..
164 Guinea-Bissau	(.)	46	24	30	98	8	16	-5	..	..	13	35
165 Gambia	(.)	28 b	15 b	58 b	..	19	..	..	..	20	53	72
166 Mozambique	1	33 b	12 b	55	..	..	..	..	..	..	..	..
167 Guinea	4	24	31	45	81	8	15	11	..	..	21	25
168 Eritrea	..	..	..	..	95	32	21	-27	..	..	30	77
169 Ethiopia	5	57 b	10 b	33 b	81	12	17	7	..	..	15	25
170 Burundi	1	56	18	26	95	12	11	-7	..	..	12	31
171 Mali	2	46	17	37	79	11	26	10	..	..	22	38
172 Burkina Faso	2	34 b	27 b	39 b	..	..	..	..	..	..	..	..
173 Niger	2	39 b	18 b	44 b	..	..	..	..	..	..	..	..
174 Sierra Leone	1	42	27	31	98	11	6	-9	..	20	13	27
All developing countries	4,801 T	14	36	49	60	12	28	27	..	..	27	28
Least developed countries	93 T	36	21	43	..	..	..	..	..	..	27	28
Industrial countries	22,788 T	3	31	66	60	16	23	24	..	33	20	19
World	27,846 T c	5 c	33 c	63 c	63 c	15 c	23 c	21 c	..	..	21 c	21 c

Note: The percentage shares of agriculture, industry and services may not necessarily add to 100 because of rounding.
a. Includes public and private investment and savings.
b. Data refer to a year other than that specified in the column heading.
c. World Bank 1997e.
Source: Columns 1-8: World Bank 1997e; *columns 9, 11 and 12:* World Bank 1997d; *column 10:* calculated on the basis of data from: World Bank 1997e.

HDI rank		GNP (US$ billions) 1995	GNP per capita (US$) 1995	GNP annual growth rate (%) 1980-95	GNP per capita annual growth rate (%) 1965-80	GNP per capita annual growth rate (%) 1980-95	Average annual rate of inflation (%) 1985-95	Average annual rate of inflation (%) 1995	Exports as % of GDP (% annual growth rate) 1980-94	Tax revenue as % of GDP (% annual growth rate) 1980-92	Overall budget surplus/deficit (as % of GDP) 1980	Overall budget surplus/deficit (as % of GDP) 1995
	High human development	2,393.9T	4,693	3.2	4.8	1.4	275.1	27.6	4.1	-0.5	0.2	..
23	Cyprus	..	..	..	..	..	..	..	1.4	..	..	..
24	Barbados	1.7	6,560	1.6	3.5	1.2	..	0.3	..	..	..	..
25	Hong Kong, China	142.3	22,990	6.2	6.2	4.8	8.7	4.6	7.0	..	..	..
28	Singapore	79.8	26,730	7.9	8.3	6.0	3.9	2.6	2.9	0.3	2.1	14.3
29	Antigua and Barbuda	..	..	..	-1.4	..	..	..	..	..	..	..
30	Korea, Rep. of	435.1	9,700	8.7	7.3	7.5	6.7	5.3	2.3	0.2	-2.2	-0.2
31	Chile	59.2	4,160	4.9	(.)	3.2	17.9	12.3	2.2	-1.8	5.4	1.6
32	Bahamas	3.3	11,940	1.8	1.0	-0.1	..	2.8	..	..	..	..
34	Costa Rica	8.9	2,610	3.4	3.3	0.7	18.4	23.8	4.3	1.4	-7.4	-2.9
35	Brunei Darussalam	7.2	25,160	..	..	..	..	3.6	..	..	..	..
36	Argentina	278.4	8,030	1.0	1.7	-0.4	255.6	4.5	2.5	..	-2.6	-1.1
38	Uruguay	16.5	5,170	..	2.5	-0.6	70.7	41.7	4.1	2.2	0	-2.8
40	Trinidad and Tobago	4.9	3,770	-0.4	3.1	-1.5	6.8	4.2	9.7	..	7.2	..
41	Dominica	0.2	2,990	4.2	-0.8	4.3	..	..	..	..	..	..
43	Bahrain	4.5	7,840	1.2	..	-2.4	..	1.4	..	..	..	..
44	Fiji	1.9	2,440	1.9	4.2	0.6	..	6.3	..	..	..	..
45	Panama	7.2	2,750	2.1	2.8	0.1	1.7	2.7	0.5	0.6	-5.5	4.3
46	Venezuela	65.4	3,020	1.4	2.3	-1.1	37.6	50.1	1.0	-2.1	0	-4.1
48	United Arab Emirates	42.8	17,400	0.3	0.6	-5.3	..	..	..	..	2.1	0.2
49	Mexico	304.6	3,320	1.2	3.6	-0.9	36.7	35.8	4.4	-0.8	-3.0	..
50	Saint Kitts and Nevis	0.2	5,170	4.3	4.0	4.9	..	3.0	..	..	..	..
51	Grenada	0.3	2,980	3.2	0.1	3.0	..	3.6	..	..	..	..
53	Colombia	70.3	1,910	3.5	3.7	1.6	25.2	21.1	2.8	..	-1.8	-0.5
54	Kuwait	28.9	17,390	-0.3	0.6	-1.5	-0.5	5.2	..	..	58.7	..
55	Saint Vincent	0.3	2,280	5.4	0.2	4.5	..	2.4	..	..	..	..
56	Seychelles	0.5	6,620	3.3	4.6	2.3	..	..	..	..	..	..
57	Qatar	7.5	11,600	-1.4	..	-7.9	..	..	..	..	..	..
58	Saint Lucia	0.5	3,370	..	2.7	..	..	3.8	..	..	..	..
59	Thailand	159.6	2,740	7.9	4.4	6.3	5.0	6.5	5.4	1.7	-4.9	1.8
60	Malaysia	78.3	3,890	6.7	4.7	4.0	3.3	5.1	4.2	..	-6.0	0.8
61	Mauritius	3.8	3,380	5.7	3.7	4.6	8.8	4.2	1.6	1.2	-10.3	-1.4
62	Brazil	579.8	3,640	1.4	6.3	-0.4	875.3	72.5	5.7	-1.3	-2.2	..
63	Belize	..	2,630	4.4	3.4	1.7	..	2.7	4.5	..	..	..
64	Libyan Arab Jamahiriya	..	..	..	0.6	..	..	..	..	..	..	..
	Medium human development	1,807.2T	934	4.9	3.8	3.1	29.8	20.5	3.0	..	..	-1.6
	Excluding China	1,062.4T	1,449	3.0	3.2	0.6	39.1	24.8	3.1	..	-3.6	..
65	Suriname	0.4	880	4.4	5.5	3.4	..	271.4	..	..	..	..
66	Lebanon	10.7	2,660	..	0.6	..	..	..	..	..	..	..
69	Turkey	169.5	2,780	4.5	3.6	2.3	64.6	82.5	9.7	0.4	-3.1	-4.1
70	Saudi Arabia	133.5	7,040	0.6	0.6	-4.0	2.8	5.0	..	..	..	..
71	Oman	10.6	4,820	8.6	9.0	3.7	-0.2	3.7	..	-3.0	0.4	-11.2
73	Ecuador	16.0	1,390	2.4	5.4	-0.1	45.5	23.3	3.3	2.7	-1.4	-1.3
75	Korea, Dem. People's Rep. of	..	..	..	0.6	..	..	..	..	..	..	..
78	Iran, Islamic Rep. of	..	..	3.1	2.9	-0.2	..	39.7	6.8	1.0	..	..
81	Syrian Arab Rep.	15.8	1,120	3.4	5.1	0.1	16.0	10.0	..	5.5	-9.7	-3.8
82	Algeria	44.6	1,600	1.8	4.2	-0.9	22.9	28.3	1.2	..	..	..
83	Tunisia	16.4	1,820	3.6	4.7	1.2	6.0	4.8	0.9	-0.4	-2.8	..
84	Jamaica	3.8	1,510	2.6	-0.1	1.4	28.3	22.4	1.0	..	-15.5	..
85	Cuba	..	..	..	0.6	..	..	..	..	..	..	..
86	Peru	55.0	2,310	1.4	0.8	-0.8	398.5	9.8	0.1	-4.9	-2.4	-1.3
87	Jordan	6.4	1,510	..	5.8	..	..	..	..	..	..	1.1
88	Dominican Rep.	11.4	1,460	3.2	3.8	1.1	26.4	7.0	1.8	(.)	-2.6	0
89	South Africa	130.9	3,160	1.3	3.2	-1.0	13.9	10.2	0.8	2.0	-2.3	-6.2
90	Sri Lanka	12.6	700	4.6	2.8	3.2	11.8	8.5	1.3	-0.5	-18.3	-0.1
91	Paraguay	8.2	1,690	2.9	4.1	(.)	24.9	10.2	5.4	-0.5	0.3	1.2
94	Samoa (Western)	0.2	1,120	..	..	..	..	..	..	..	..	..
95	Maldives	0.3	990	..	1.8	..	..	6.7	..	..	..	..
96	Indonesia	190.1	980	6.8	5.2	4.9	8.8	8.7	-1.9	-1.2	-2.3	0.6
97	Botswana	4.4	3,020	8.8	9.9	5.4	11.5	9.2	..	1.1	-0.2	..
98	Philippines	71.9	1,050	2.1	3.2	-0.3	9.8	7.4	2.5	1.6	-1.4	-1.5
100	Guyana	0.5	590	-1.0	0.7	-1.7	..	7.7	0.1	..	..	..
101	Mongolia	0.8	310	..	0.6	..	51.6	29.9	-6.6	..	..	-1.9
106	China	744.9	620	10.1	4.1	8.6	9.3	12.8	2.9	..	..	-1.9
107	Namibia	3.1	2,000	..	0.6	..	10.4	4.7	..	..	..	-4.8
111	Guatemala	14.3	1,340	1.6	3.0	-1.3	18.6	10.0	-2.3	..	-3.4	-1.2
112	Egypt	45.5	790	4.3	2.8	1.9	15.7	8.3	0.5	..	-6.3	2.0

HDI rank	GNP (US$ billions) 1995	GNP per capita (US$) 1995	GNP annual growth rate (%) 1980-95	GNP per capita annual growth rate (%) 1965-80	GNP per capita annual growth rate (%) 1980-95	Average annual rate of inflation (%) 1985-95	Average annual rate of inflation (%) 1995	Exports as % of GDP (% annual growth rate) 1980-94	Tax revenue as % of GDP (% annual growth rate) 1980-92	Overall budget surplus/deficit (as % of GDP) 1980	Overall budget surplus/deficit (as % of GDP) 1995
114 El Salvador	9.1	1,610	1.9	1.5	0.5	14.9	9.8	-0.4	-1.7	-5.7	-0.1
115 Swaziland	1.1	1,170	4.2	3.7	1.0	..	7.1	..	..	..	..
116 Bolivia	5.9	800	1.7	1.7	-0.5	18.4	11.5	2.9	..	..	-3.6
117 Cape Verde	0.4	960	4.8	..	2.9	..	..	-1.1	..	..	..
119 Honduras	3.6	600	2.7	1.1	-0.5	14.3	25.2	-1.8	..	..	-0.2
120 Gabon	3.8	3,490	-1.5	5.6	-4.3	5.0	3.9	2.3	-1.3	6.1	..
121 São Tomé and Principe	(.)	350	-1.6	3.3	-3.7	..	74.5	1.4	..	..	..
122 Viet Nam	17.6	240	..	0.6	..	88.3	19.5	..	..	..	..
123 Solomon Islands	0.3	910	6.7	5.0	3.4	..	9.8	..	..	..	..
124 Vanuatu	0.2	1,200	..	..	..	..	..	..	..	..	..
125 Morocco	29.6	1,110	2.8	2.7	0.7	4.8	6.5	1.5	1.0	-9.7	..
126 Nicaragua	1.7	380	-0.8	-0.7	-3.7	961.6	11.2	1.7	-1.6	-7.2	-4.3
127 Iraq	..	..	..	0.6	..	..	..	..	..	..	..
128 Congo	1.8	680	2.5	2.7	-0.6	2.2	11.0	1.4	..	-5.2	-0.1
129 Papua New Guinea	5.0	1,160	3.4	0.6	1.1	4.5	16.7	2.7	-0.1	-1.9	-4.1
130 Zimbabwe	5.9	540	2.8	1.7	-0.2	20.9	23.4	0.6	3.0	-10.9	..
Low human development	**544.8 T**	**316**	**4.4**	**1.4**	**2.0**	**15.4**	**26.4**	**1.9**	**..**	**-5.8**	**..**
Excluding India	225.1 T	286	2.9	1.2	0.1	25.1	58.8	0.9	..	..	..
131 Myanmar	..	..	..	1.6	..	..	..	4.0	-4.1	..	..
132 Cameroon	8.6	650	1.5	2.4	-1.3	2.0	16.0	4.7	-1.9	0.5	-1.7
133 Ghana	6.7	390	2.8	-0.8	-0.3	28.6	39.9	0.9	..	-4.2	-2.5
134 Lesotho	1.5	770	3.4	6.8	0.9	13.4	7.9	-1.0	4.1	..	..
135 Equatorial Guinea	0.2	380	..	..	..	..	5.8	..	..	..	..
136 Lao People's Dem. Rep.	1.7	350	..	0.6	..	22.6	19.8	..	..	..	..
137 Kenya	7.6	280	3.2	3.1	(.)	13.0	8.0	2.5	1.4	-4.5	-3.2
138 Pakistan	60.0	460	5.8	1.8	2.7	9.2	14.3	3.5	-0.8	-5.7	-4.8
139 India	319.7	340	5.3	1.5	3.2	9.8	8.0	2.4	1.1	-6.5	-5.4
140 Cambodia	2.7	270	..	0.6	..	..	8.9	..	..	..	..
141 Comoros	0.2	470	2.0	0.6	-0.7	..	7.0	9.5	..	..	..
142 Nigeria	28.4	260	2.3	4.2	-0.8	33.0	57.4	-3.2	..	..	..
143 Dem. Rep. of the Congo	5.3	120	-2.7	-1.3	-5.8	..	..	..	..	..	..
144 Togo	1.3	310	0.5	1.7	-2.4	..	8.9	-3.3	..	-2.0	..
145 Benin	2.0	370	3.4	-0.3	0.3	..	..	-4.6	..	..	..
146 Zambia	3.6	400	0.6	-1.2	-2.4	91.5	46.2	-0.4	..	-18.5	-2.9
147 Bangladesh	28.6	240	4.5	-0.3	2.2	6.4	8.8	3.9	..	2.5	..
148 Côte d'Ivoire	9.3	660	0.1	2.8	-3.4	4.0	14.1	0.3	1.1	-10.8	..
149 Mauritania	1.1	460	2.3	-0.1	-0.2	6.9	4.4	0.6	..	..	..
150 Tanzania, U. Rep. of	3.7	120	..	0.8	..	32.3	34.0	..	..	-7.0	..
151 Yemen	4.0	260	..	5.1	..	..	..	..	..	..	-17.3
152 Nepal	4.4	200	4.9	(.)	2.2	11.6	6.7	..	1.7	-3.0	..
153 Madagascar	3.2	230	-0.1	-0.4	-3.0	18.4	46.8	-1.4	-4.7	..	-4.8
154 Central African Rep.	1.1	340	0.8	0.8	-1.5	3.8	11.7	-3.5	..	-3.5	..
155 Bhutan	0.3	420	7.3	0.6	4.8	..	8.3	..	-2.6	..	..
156 Angola	4.4	410	..	0.6	..	169.5	1,184.1	..	..	..	..
157 Sudan	..	..	..	0.8	..	..	..	..	..	..	..
158 Senegal	5.1	600	2.9	-0.5	0.1	3.7	2.3	0.4	..	0.9	..
159 Haiti	1.8	250	-2.1	0.9	-4.0	14.7	23.7	-0.5	..	-4.7	..
160 Uganda	4.7	240	..	-2.2	..	65.7	8.6	..	..	-3.1	..
161 Malawi	1.6	170	2.4	3.2	-0.7	22.1	76.0	-1.7	..	-15.9	..
162 Djibouti	..	..	..	..	..	..	..	..	..	..	..
163 Chad	1.1	180	4.9	-1.9	2.4	3.1	6.6	-4.6	..	..	..
164 Guinea-Bissau	0.3	250	4.6	-2.7	2.7	62.5	45.9	-10.3	..	..	..
165 Gambia	0.4	320	2.5	2.3	-1.2	9.0	4.8	-0.3	..	-4.5	3.5
166 Mozambique	1.4	80	1.1	0.6	-0.8	52.2	44.2	-2.6	..	..	..
167 Guinea	3.6	550	..	1.3	..	..	5.3	..	..	..	..
168 Eritrea	..	..	..	..	..	..	..	..	..	..	..
169 Ethiopia	5.7	100	..	0.4	..	..	13.7	..	..	-3.1	-8.5
170 Burundi	1.0	160	2.6	2.4	-0.2	6.1	12.2	1.3	..	-3.9	..
171 Mali	2.4	250	2.0	2.1	-0.7	4.6	12.5	3.6	..	-4.6	..
172 Burkina Faso	2.4	230	3.5	1.7	0.8	2.6	8.0	-1.5	..	0.2	..
173 Niger	2.0	220	-0.7	-2.5	-3.9	1.3	5.2	-4.1	..	-4.7	..
174 Sierra Leone	0.8	180	-0.3	0.7	-2.0	61.6	32.2	-6.6	-1.3	-12.1	-5.0
All developing countries	**4,744.8 T**	**1,141**	**4.1**	**3.0**	**2.1**	**127.4**	**24.2**	**3.3**	**..**	**..**	**-1.8**
Least developed countries	99.7 T	215	2.1	0.4	-0.4	39.9	102.9	0.7	..	..	..
Industrial countries	**22,332.3 T**	**18,158ᵃ**	**2.2**	**..**	**1.7**	**9.5**	**9.1**	**2.3**	**..**	**..**	**-2.6**
World	**27,077.1 T**	**4,880ᵃ**	**2.6**	**..**	**0.9**	**28.6**	**12.1**	**2.5**	**..**	**..**	**-2.5**

a. World Bank 1997e.
Source: Columns 1-4 and 6-8: World Bank 1997d; *columns 5, 9-11:* World Bank 1997e.

HDI rank	Human poverty index (HPI-2) value (%) 1995	People not expected to survive to age 60 (as % of total population) 1995	People who are functionally illiterate (% age 16-65) 1995[a]	Long-term unemployment[b] (as % of total labour force) 1995	Population below income poverty line (%) EU and OECD standard[c] 1989-94	Population below income poverty line (%) $14.40 a day (1985 PPP$)[d]	Real GDP per capita (PPP$) Poorest 20% 1980-94	Real GDP per capita (PPP$) Richest 20% 1980-94	Maternal mortality rate (per 100,000 live births) 1990	Infant mortality rate (per 1,000 live births) 1996	Under-five mortality rate (per 1,000 live births) 1996
High human development	..	11	..	..	..	..	5,991	39,606	13	7	7
1 Canada	12.0	9	16.6	1.3	11.7	6[f]	5,971	42,110	6	6	7
2 France	11.8	11	16.8[g]	4.9	7.5	12[f]	5,359	40,098	15	5	6
3 Norway	11.3	9	16.8[g]	1.3	6.6	3[f]	6,315	37,379	6	5	6
4 USA	16.5	13	20.7	0.5	19.1	14	5,800	51,705	..	5	5
5 Iceland	..	8							11	4	4
6 Finland	11.8	11	16.8[g]	6.1	6.2	4	5,141	30,682	12	8	8
7 Netherlands	8.2	9	10.5	3.2	6.7	14	7,109	31,992	12	5	6
8 Japan	12.0	8	16.8[g]	0.6	11.8	4	8,987	38,738	18	4	6
9 New Zealand	12.6	10	18.4	1.3	9.2	..	4,264	37,369	25	7	7
10 Sweden	6.8	8	7.5	1.5	6.7	5	7,160	33,026	7	4	4
11 Spain	13.1	10	16.8[g]	13.0	10.4	21	5,669	24,998	7	5	5
12 Belgium	12.4	10	18.4[h]	6.2	5.5	12	7,718	35,172	10	6	7
13 Austria		11		1.1					10	5	6
14 United Kingdom	15.0	9	21.8	3.8	13.5	13	3,963	38,164	9	6	7
15 Australia	12.5	9	17.0	2.6	12.9	8	4,077	39,098	9	6	6
16 Switzerland	..	9	18.9	1.1	..	..	5,907	50,666	10	6	7
17 Ireland	15.2	9	22.6	7.6	11.1	37[f]	..	..	6	5	5
18 Denmark	12.0	12	16.8[g]	2.0	7.5	8	5,454	38,986	9	6	6
19 Germany	10.5	11	14.4	4.0	5.9	12	6,594	37,963	22	5	6
20 Greece		9							10	8	9
21 Italy	11.6	9	16.8[g]	7.6	6.5	2	6,174	37,228	12	6	7
22 Israel	..	9	..	..	..	..	4,539	29,957	7	8	9
26 Luxembourg	..	11	..	0.7	5.4	4[f]	..	..	..	7	7
27 Malta		9							..	10	11
33 Portugal		12		3.7					15	7	7
37 Slovenia	..	15	..	..	..	1[i]			13	6	6
39 Czech Rep.	..	14	..	..	..	1[i]	4,426	15,764	15	6	7
42 Slovakia	..	19	..	..	..	1[i]	3,344	8,823	..	10	11
47 Hungary	..	24	..	..	10.0	2[i]	2,878	11,088	30	11	12
52 Poland	..	20	42.6	..	11.6	13[i]	2,186	8,605	19	12	14
Medium human development	..	27	..	..	..	..	1,214	9,912	69	28	36
67 Bulgaria	..	18	..	..	..	33[i]	1,793	8,489	27	16	19
68 Belarus	..	24	..	..	..	23[i]	2,355	6,981	37	14	18
72 Russian Federation	..	32	..	..	22.1	38[i]	881	12,804	75	20	25
74 Romania	..	21	..	..	..	22[i]	1,714	6,485	130	21	25
76 Croatia		16							..	10	11
77 Estonia	..	23	..	..	..	40[i]	1,191	8,357	41	13	16
79 Lithuania	..	23	..	..	..	46[i]	1,260	6,547	36	14	18
80 Macedonia, FYR		14							..	26	30
92 Latvia	..	25	..	..	..	23[i]	2,405	9,193	40	16	20
93 Kazakhstan	..	26	..	..	..	50[i]	1,391	7,494	80	38	45
99 Armenia	..	26	..	..	..	..			50	25	30
102 Ukraine	..	24	..	..	..	41[i]	1,544	5,753	50	18	24
103 Turkmenistan	..	29	..	..	..	48[i]	1,048	6,694	55	57	78
104 Uzbekistan	..	25	..	..	..	29[i]	..	..	55	46	60
105 Albania		16							65	34	40
108 Georgia	..	17	..	..	..	..			33	23	29
109 Kyrgyzstan	..	25	..	..	..	76[i]			110	39	50
110 Azerbaijan		21							22	34	45
113 Moldova, Rep. of	..	26	..	..	..	65[i]	818	4,918	60	26	32
118 Tajikistan		25							130	56	76
All developing countries	..	27	..	..	..	..	768	6,195	488	65	95
Industrial countries	..	16	..	..	..	..	4,811	32,273	30	13	16
World	..	25	..	..	..	..	1,759	12,584	430[j]	60[j]	88[j]
North America	..	13	..	..	..	..	5,817	50,759	12	8	8
Eastern Europe and CIS	..	26	..	..	..	..	1,505	9,962	62	26	33
Western and Southern Europe	..	10	..	..	..	..	6,157	36,096	14	5	6
OECD	..	13	..	..	..	..	5,598	37,988	49	13	15
European Union	..	10	..	..	..	..	5,781	36,138	13	6	6
Nordic countries	..	10	..	..	..	..	6,182	34,658	8	5	5

a. Based on level 1 prose. Data refer to 1995 or a year around 1995.
b. Unemployment lasting at least 12 months or more.
c. Poverty is measured at 50% of the median adjusted disposable personal income.
d. US poverty line.
e. Data refer to 1990 or a year around 1990.
f. Data refer to a year or period other than that specified in the column heading.
g. The unweighted average for level 1 prose (excluding Poland) was applied.
h. Data refer to Flanders.
i. Income poverty line is $4 (1990 PPP$) a day per person.
j. UNICEF 1998b.
Source: Column 1: Human Development Report Office calculations; *column 2:* UN 1996d; *column 3:* UNESCO 1997c; *column 4:* ILO 1997a; *column 5:* Smeeding 1997; *columns 6-8:* UNDP 1997a; *columns 9-11:* UNICEF 1998b.

HDI rank	Female net enrolment				Female tertiary students		Female tertiary natural and applied science enrolment (as % of female tertiary students) 1995
	Primary		Secondary				
	Ratio (%) 1995	Index (1985=100) 1995	Ratio (%) 1995	Index (1985=100) 1995	Per 100,000 women 1995	Index (1985=100) 1995	
High human development	98	101	91	..	4,046	134	24
1 Canada	94	99	91	102	7,170	105	..
2 France	99	102	93	109	4,033	177	30
3 Norway	99	103	94	107	4,325	184	27
4 USA	97	104	89	97	5,852	112	..
5 Iceland	..	..	..	..	3,187	146	..
6 Finland	99	..	93	..	4,312	175	23
7 Netherlands	99	105	..	..	3,456	153	17
8 Japan	100	100	97	..	2,765	207	13
9 New Zealand	100	100	94	111	5,046	189	31
10 Sweden	100	..	97	..	3,184	146	27
11 Spain	100	100	97	..	4,127	176	..
12 Belgium	98	103	98	109	3,261	145	24
13 Austria	100	..	90	..	2,800	142	26
14 United Kingdom	100	100	93	113	3,409	211	24
15 Australia	98	100	90	114	5,405	241	25
16 Switzerland	100	105	..	..	1,525	144	15
17 Ireland	100	100	87	104	3,537	206	33
18 Denmark	99	101	88	105	3,337	151	28
19 Germany	100	..	88	..	2,223	..	21
20 Greece	..	..	83	102	2,765	157	27
21 Italy	..	..	..	..	3,237	173	33
22 Israel	..	..	..	..	3,703	..	32
26 Luxembourg	..	..	..	..	..	..	..
27 Malta	99	103	83	111	1,690	615	21
33 Portugal	100	100	83	..	3,530	325	38
37 Slovenia	99	..	..	..	2,722	..	29
39 Czech Rep.	98	..	89	..	1,787	..	25
42 Slovakia	..	..	..	..	1,661	..	..
47 Hungary	94	96	76	109	1,796	185	28
52 Poland	96	97	86	113	2,462	186	31
Medium human development	..	..	..	..	2,843	..	34
67 Bulgaria	96	..	..	..	3,574	260	45
68 Belarus	95	..	..	..	3,062	..	..
72 Russian Federation	100	..	..	..	3,106	77	34
74 Romania	92	..	74	..	1,344	216	38
76 Croatia	..	..	..	..	1,811	..	27
77 Estonia	94	..	81	..	2,651	150	25
79 Lithuania	..	..	..	..	2,285	70	..
80 Macedonia, FYR	84	..	51	..	1,504	..	38
92 Latvia	82	..	78	..	1,845	98	28
93 Kazakhstan	..	..	..	..	3,032	..	..
99 Armenia	..	..	..	..	4,820	..	..
102 Ukraine	..	..	..	..	3,109	..	..
103 Turkmenistan	..	..	..	..	1,960	..	..
104 Uzbekistan	..	..	..	..	3,529	..	..
105 Albania	97	..	..	..	983	91	40
108 Georgia	82	..	70	..	2,862	..	40
109 Kyrgyzstan	95	..	..	..	1,145	..	38
110 Azerbaijan	..	..	..	..	1,458	..	..
113 Moldova, Rep. of	..	..	..	..	2,103	..	..
118 Tajikistan	..	..	..	..	1,240	71	13
All developing countries	..	..	..	..	679	..	..
Industrial countries	98	..	90	..	3,717	123	27
World	..	..	..	..	1,369	..	..
North America	97	104	89	97	5,982	111	..
Eastern Europe and CIS	97	..	..	..	2,737	..	33
Western and Southern Europe	100	102	91	..	3,225	174	27
OECD	98	102	86	..	3,691	132	24
European Union	100	101	92	..	3,275	180	27
Nordic countries	99	..	94	..	3,669	161	26

Source: Columns 1, 3, 5 and 7: UNESCO 1998; columns 2, 4 and 6: calculated on the basis of data from: UNESCO 1998.

HDI rank	Female administrators and managers (%) 1992-96	Female professional and technical workers (%) 1992-96	Female sales and service workers (%) 1992-96	Female clerical workers (%) 1992-96	Women in government Total[a] (%) 1995	At ministerial level[a] (%) 1995	At sub-ministerial level[a] (%) 1995	Female unpaid family workers (as % of total) 1990	Female economic activity rate (as % of male rate) 1995
High human development	37	50	55	69	16	14	16	75	75
1 Canada	42	56 [b]	52	80	19	19	19	80	82
2 France	9 [b]	41 [b]	..	..	9	7	9	82	80
3 Norway	32	62	63	77	44	41	46	67	84
4 USA	43	53	55	79	30	21	31	76	82
5 Iceland	28	54	66	81	8	13	6	..	82
6 Finland	25	63	60	74	16	35	10	38	91
7 Netherlands	20	44	70	66	20	26	17	91	66
8 Japan	9	43	45	60	8	7	9	82	69
9 New Zealand	34	49	67	78	17	7	20	66	79
10 Sweden	39 [b]	64 [b]	77 [b,c]	77 [b,d]	33	48	26	67	92
11 Spain	32	43	54	55	10	15	7	62	56
12 Belgium	19	51	59	56	8	11	7	85	67
13 Austria	24	46	68	66	7	21	4	75	67
14 United Kingdom	33	44	66	75	8	9	8	..	76
15 Australia	43	26	46	47	24	13	27	59	74
16 Switzerland	28	25	65	45	7	17	4	..	66
17 Ireland	23	45	49	71	11	18	9	37	50
18 Denmark	19	47	76	72	19	30	17	97	86
19 Germany	26	49	74	68	7	16	5	..	72
20 Greece	22	44	50	55	6	0	10	76	58
21 Italy	54	18	48	34	10	3	12	63	61
22 Israel	20	54	52	73	10	13	9	72	66
26 Luxembourg	9 [b]	38 [b]	72 [b]	48 [b]	8	17	4	84	57
27 Malta	..	..	..	..	2	0	2	..	36
33 Portugal	31	52	60	59	18	9	19	60	77
37 Slovenia	28	53	69	71	..	..	..	62	87
39 Czech Rep.	27	55	68	80	1	0	2	76	91
42 Slovakia	27	58	63	79	13	14	13	66	92
47 Hungary	34	60	54	93	8	5	8	82	80
52 Poland	35	63	67	76	8	6	9	76	85
Medium human development	..	..	..	..	3	3	3	..	91
67 Bulgaria	29 [b]	57 [b]	..	..	9	9	8	..	93
68 Belarus	..	..	..	..	4	8	3	..	95
72 Russian Federation	..	..	..	..	2	3	2	..	94
74 Romania	28	55	72	76	3	0	4	67	80
76 Croatia	..	..	..	..	..	..	..	74	77
77 Estonia	37	68	75	85	10	6	12	..	96
79 Lithuania	..	..	..	..	9	0	12	..	92
80 Macedonia, FYR	..	..	..	..	..	..	..	88	69
92 Latvia	39	67	75	82	16	6	17	..	100
93 Kazakhstan	..	..	..	..	1	3	0	91	86
99 Armenia	..	..	..	..	2	0	3	..	92
102 Ukraine	..	..	..	..	1	0	1	..	94
103 Turkmenistan	..	..	..	..	4	4	4	..	83
104 Uzbekistan	..	..	..	..	3	3	3	..	86
105 Albania	..	..	..	..	12	0	16	..	69
108 Georgia	18	42	41	64	3	0	5	..	86
109 Kyrgyzstan	..	..	..	..	8	4	11	..	87
110 Azerbaijan	..	..	..	..	5	4	6	..	78
113 Moldova, Rep. of	..	..	..	..	4	0	5	..	94
118 Tajikistan	..	..	..	..	4	7	3	..	77
All developing countries	..	..	..	..	5	5	5	48	64
Industrial countries	37	50	55	69	13	11	13	75	79
World	..	..	..	..	7	7	7	58	68
North America	43	53	55	80	29	21	30	76	82
Eastern Europe and CIS	..	..	..	..	4	3	4	..	90
Western and Southern Europe	33	49	59	58	11	13	10	71	69
OECD	36	49	52	67	14	13	14	70	71
European Union	33	48	61	62	10	12	9	71	70
Nordic countries	28	59	66	74	28	40	24	67	89

a. Including elected heads of state and governors of central banks. For countries for which the value is zero, no women ministers were reported by the United Nations Division for the Advancement of Women; this information could not be reconfirmed by the Human Development Report Office.
b. UNDP 1997a.
c. Excludes sales workers.
d. Includes sales workers.
Sources: Columns 1-4 and 9: calculated on the basis of data from ILO 1997b; *columns 5-7:* calculated by the United Nations Division for the Advancement of Women based on data from Keesing's Worldwide 1995. *column 8:* UN 1995b.

HDI rank	Adults who smoke (%) Male 1986-95	Adults who smoke (%) Female 1986-95	Alcohol consumption per capita (litres)a 1995	Likelihood of dying after age 65 of Heart disease (%) Male 1990-93	Heart disease (%) Female 1990-93	Cancer (%) Male 1990-93	Cancer (%) Female 1990-93	AIDS cases (per 100,000 people)b 1996	People with disabilities (as % of total population)c 1985-92	Doctors (per 100,000 people) 1993	Public expenditure on health (as % of total public expenditure) 1989-91	Private expenditure on health (as % of total health expenditure) 1989-91	Total expenditure on health (as % of GDP) 1960	Total expenditure on health (as % of GDP) 1991
High human development	38	23	8.0	27	30	25	17	6.5	9.9	255	13.4	33.6	4.5	9.7
1 Canada	31	29	6.1	..	..	..	..	2.7	15.5	221	14.6	27.8	5.3	9.9
2 France	40	27	11.9	22	24	29	18	6.3	..	280	13.2	26.1	4.3	9.1
3 Norway	36	36	3.9	34	31	22	16	1.2	..	..	13.0	3.4	3.2	8.4
4 USA	28	23	6.6	..	..	..	..	13.8	12.0	245	14.8	56.1	5.3	13.3
5 Iceland	31	28	..	..	..	..	..	1.1	..	..	19.3	13.0	3.4	8.3
6 Finland	27	19	6.4	37	35	21	15	0.4	17.0	269	14.7	19.1	3.8	8.9
7 Netherlands	36	29	7.9	28	29	29	19	2.4	11.5	..	10.4	26.9	4.0	8.7
8 Japan	59	15	6.8	21	26	25	16	0.2	2.3	177	30.7	28.0	3.0	6.8
9 New Zealand	24	22	7.2	35	34	25	18	1.6	13.0	210	..	21.1	4.2	7.7
10 Sweden	22	24	5.7	39	36	21	17	1.5	12.0	299	11.1	22.0	4.7	8.8
11 Spain	48	25	9.6	24	28	24	14	14.3	15.0	400	11.8	17.8	1.6	6.5
12 Belgium	31	19	10.1	..	..	..	..	1.5	..	365	12.2	11.1	3.4	8.1
13 Austria	42	27	10.8	38	40	25	18	1.6	22.7	327	11.2	32.9	4.4	8.5
14 United Kingdom	28	26	7.2	..	..	..	..	2.1	14.2	164	12.2	16.7	3.9	6.6
15 Australia	29	21	7.7	34	37	25	17	3.1	15.6	..	..	15.4	4.8	8.6
16 Switzerland	36	26	9.8	32	35	28	19	4.4	..	301	15.7	31.7	3.3	8.0
17 Ireland	29	28	7.2	35	32	24	19	1.4	3.5	167	12.0	24.2	3.8	8.0
18 Denmark	37	37	10.1	32	31	25	20	3.0	12.0	283	9.0	18.5	3.6	7.0
19 Germany	37	22	11.2	35	36	24	18	1.4	8.4	319	12.3	28.2	4.9	9.1
20 Greece	46	28	7.2	29	31	22	12	2.0	..	387	12.2	23.0	2.6	4.8
21 Italy	38	26	..	26	28	26	17	8.6	2.7	..	14.8	22.5	3.6	8.3
22 Israel	45	30	8.0	34	32	18	16	0.7	..	459	..	..	1.0	4.2
26 Luxembourg	32	26	..	45	50	18	11	2.9	..	213	10.3	8.6	..	6.6
27 Malta	40	18	..	..	..	..	..	1.1	..	250	..	..	..	6.6
33 Portugal	38	15	10.6	18	19	18	12	7.3	11.0	291	9.8	38.3	2.3	6.2
37 Slovenia	35	23	7.7	..	..	..	..	0.4	..	219	..	..	..	..
39 Czech Rep.	43	31	11.7	33	31	23	17	0.2	..	293	..	..	2.9	5.9
42 Slovakia	43	26	10.1	..	..	..	..	..	..	325	..	..	..	..
47 Hungary	40	27	11.0	28	28	22	17	0.5	15.7	337	..	..	2.6	6.0
52 Poland	51	29	6.2	24	20	19	12	0.3	9.9	..	..	..	3.5	5.1
Medium human development	..	..	5.4	36	35	15	8	0.3	..	358	..	..	..	3.4
67 Bulgaria	49	17	5.6	35	35	12	8	0.1	0.4	333	..	..	2.0	5.4
68 Belarus	..	..	..	39	40	15	8	..	..	379	..	..	..	3.2
72 Russian Federation	67	30	5.2	37	36	16	10	(.)	..	380	..	..	..	3.0
74 Romania	..	..	9.0	..	..	..	..	2.4	..	176	..	..	2.0	3.9
76 Croatia	..	..	11.5	..	..	..	..	0.4	..	201	..	..	..	..
77 Estonia	52	24	..	42	45	..	..	0.5	..	312	..	..	..	..
79 Lithuania	52	10	..	..	..	..	..	0.1	..	399	..	..	..	3.6
80 Macedonia, FYR	..	..	..	..	..	..	..	0.1	..	219	..	..	..	..
92 Latvia	67	12	..	40	39	16	10	0.2	..	303	..	..	..	4.4
93 Kazakhstan	..	..	..	..	..	..	..	(.)	..	360	..	..	..	..
99 Armenia	..	..	..	48	52	11	7	0.2	..	312	..	..	..	4.2
102 Ukraine	..	..	3.8	30	30	13	8	0.3	..	429	..	..	..	3.3
103 Turkmenistan	27	1	..	..	..	..	..	..	..	353	..	..	..	5.0
104 Uzbekistan	40	1	..	51	54	9	6	..	..	335	..	..	..	5.9
105 Albania	50	8	..	30	31	10	5	(.)	..	141	..	..	..	4.0
108 Georgia	..	..	..	..	..	..	..	..	..	436	..	..	..	4.5
109 Kyrgyzstan	..	..	..	36	40	16	10	..	..	310	..	..	..	5.0
110 Azerbaijan	..	..	..	..	..	..	..	(.)	..	390	..	..	..	4.3
113 Moldova, Rep. of	..	..	..	..	..	..	..	(.)	..	356	..	..	..	3.9
118 Tajikistan	..	..	..	36	38	10	6	..	..	210	..	..	..	6.0
All developing countries	50	8	..	..	..	..	..	3.5	2.6	76	..	..	..	..
Industrial countries	42	24	7.4	30	31	22	14	5.0	..	287	..	..	..	9.4
World	48	12	..	..	..	..	..	3.9	4.0	122	..	..	..	..
North America	28	23	6.5	..	..	..	..	12.7	12.3	243	14.8	56.1	5.3	13.0
Eastern Europe and CIS	58	26	6.0	35	33	16	10	0.3	..	354	..	..	..	3.7
Western and Southern Europe	39	25	10.2	29	30	25	17	5.4	9.2	321	12.7	24.2	4.1	8.5
OECD	40	22	8.0	27	29	25	16	5.7	9.3	224	13.4	33.6	4.5	9.7
European Union	37	25	9.7	28	30	25	17	5.0	10.2	291	12.6	23.5	4.1	8.2
Nordic countries	29	28	6.5	36	34	22	17	1.5	13.3	287	11.6	16.8	4.0	8.3

a. Litres of 100% alcohol.
b. The number of reported cases in adults and children.
c. See the selected definitions.
Source: Columns 1 and 2: calculated on the basis of data from: WHO 1997c; *column 3:* The Brewers and Licensed Retailers Association 1997. *columns 4-7:* WHO 1994; *column 8:* UNAIDS and WHO 1997; *column 9:* UN 1993; *column 10:* WHO 1997d; *columns 11-14:* World Bank 1993.

		Full-time students per 100 people (age 5-29) 1995	Secondary full-time net enrolment ratio (%)[a] 1995	Tertiary students (per 100,000 people) 1995	Tertiary natural and applied science enrolment (as % of total tertiary) 1995	R & D scientists and technicians (per 1,000 people) 1990-96	Public expenditure on				
							Education (as % of GNP)		Education (as % of total government expenditure) 1993-95	Primary and secondary education (as % of all levels) 1990-95	Higher education (as % of all levels) 1990-95
HDI rank							1985	1995			
High human development		**59**	**84**	**3,976**	**28**	**4**	**5.2**	**5.2**	**12.3**	**71.2**	**20.9**
1	Canada	59	79	6,865	..	4	6.6	7.3	13.7	62.2	34.6
2	France	64	93	3,786	24	5	5.8	5.9	10.8	70.4	16.5
3	Norway	59	90	3,994	19	5	5.9	8.3	15.0	54.2	26.0
4	USA	59	79	5,398	..	4	4.9	5.3	14.1	69.6	23.3
5	Iceland	65	77	2,756	..	4	4.9	5.0	12.0	70.6	20.8
6	Finland	68	90	4,171	37	5	5.4	7.6	11.9	63.0	26.1
7	Netherlands	60	93 [b]	3,769	20	4	6.4	5.3	9.5	62.1	31.0
8	Japan	56	94	3,190	23	7	..	3.8	10.8	78.2	13.5
9	New Zealand	60	77	4,603	20	3	4.7	6.7	17.1	64.4	29.4
10	Sweden	59	96	2,936	29	7	7.7	8.0	11.0	66.4	26.7
11	Spain	61	75	3,992	..	2	3.3	5.0	12.6	75.5	14.7
12	Belgium	62	100 [b]	3,337	25	4	6.2	5.7	10.2	68.0	20.3
13	Austria	56	88	2,983	29	2	5.9	5.5	7.7	70.2	19.4
14	United Kingdom	53	75	3,380	31	3	4.9	5.5	11.4	74.7	23.0
15	Australia	55	94	5,401	29	4	5.6	5.6	13.6	69.3	29.5
16	Switzerland	57	84	2,067	32	..	4.8	5.5	15.6	74.0	20.0
17	Ireland	63	81	3,545	31	2	6.4	6.3	13.2	66.8	23.3
18	Denmark	63	82	3,255	24	5	7.2	8.3	12.6	61.3	22.8
19	Germany	60	94 [b]	2,631	35	4	..	4.7	9.4	73.0	21.8
20	Greece	52	56	2,841	30	1	2.9	3.7	7.0	76.8	22.6
21	Italy	59	..	3,170	28	2	5.0	4.9	8.8	71.3	15.7
22	Israel	..	..	3,598	27	..	7.0	6.6	12.3	65.4	17.2
26	Luxembourg	..	78	..	..	..	3.8		..	76.1	3.3
27	Malta	..	..	1,773	13	(.)	3.4	5.2	11.8	62.9	17.9
33	Portugal	..	73	3,209	30	1	4.0	5.4		73.3	14.9
37	Slovenia	..	..	2,489	18	4	..	5.8	12.6	67.7	16.9
39	Czech Rep.	55	72	1,908	36	2	..	6.1	16.9	70.5	14.7
42	Slovakia	..	..	1,715	..	3	..	5.1	..	48.5	16.7
47	Hungary	52	71	1,777	29	2	5.5	6.6	6.9	62.8	17.8
52	Poland	..	..	2,220	29	2	4.9	4.6	14.0	59.5	16.0
Medium human development		**..**	**..**	**2,756**	**46**	**3**	**..**	**4.8**	**12.2**	**60.2**	**11.8**
67	Bulgaria	..	..	2,942	25	3	5.5	4.2	..	53.7	15.8
68	Belarus	..	..	3,031	35	3	..	5.6	17.1	71.6	11.0
72	Russian Federation	60	..	3,004	49	4	3.2	4.1	9.6	..	..
74	Romania	..	..	1,483	51	2	2.2	3.2	13.6	60.3	15.9
76	Croatia	..	..	1,917	38	3	..	5.3	..	..	..
77	Estonia	..	..	2,670	34	3	..	6.9	25.5	55.0	17.6
79	Lithuania	..	..	2,023	..	1	5.3	6.1	21.8	52.2	18.0
80	Macedonia, FYR	..	..	1,372	41	2	5.5	5.5	18.7	77.7	22.2
92	Latvia	..	..	1,737	34	2	3.4	6.3	16.8	72.7	12.2
93	Kazakhstan	..	..	2,807	42	..	..	4.5	17.6	60.4	12.5
99	Armenia	..	..	4,709	..	..	..	..	20.5	57.7	22.6
102	Ukraine	..	..	2,977	..	4	5.2	7.7	15.7	54.7	10.7
103	Turkmenistan	..	..	1,889	..	..	..	..	19.7	..	..
104	Uzbekistan	..	..	3,392	..	2	..	9.5	24.4	69.9	9.7
105	Albania	..	..	902	24	..	..	3.4		77.8	10.3
108	Georgia	..	..	2,845	48	..	..	5.2	6.9	45.1	18.5
109	Kyrgyzstan	..	..	1,115	28	1	7.9	6.8	23.1	73.1	8.3
110	Azerbaijan	..	..	1,593	38	..	5.7	3.0	17.5	61.1	7.8
113	Moldova, Rep. of	..	..	1,976	34	2	..	6.1	22.9	..	..
118	Tajikistan	..	..	1,870	23	1	..	8.6	16.1	67.6	10.3
All developing countries		**..**	**..**	**832**	**..**	**(.)**	**4.1**	**3.8**	**..**	**..**	**..**
Industrial countries		**59**	**..**	**3,645**	**33**	**4**	**5.1**	**5.2**	**..**	**..**	**..**
World		**..**	**..**	**1,451**	**..**	**1**	**4.9**	**4.9**	**..**	**..**	**..**
North America		59	79	5,544	..	4	5.0	5.5	..	..	..
Eastern Europe and CIS		..	..	2,643	43	3	..	4.9	..	..	..
Western and Southern Europe		61	88	3,264	28	4	5.5	5.8	..	..	..
OECD		56	72	3,717	29	3	5.1	5.1	..	..	..
European Union		59	85	3,299	29	4	5.4	5.7	..	..	..
Nordic countries		62	90	3,463	28	6	6.8	8.0	..	..	..

a. At age 17.
b. Schooling is compulsory at age 17.
Source: Columns 1 and 2: OECD 1997c; *columns 3, 4, 6 and 7:* UNESCO 1998; *columns 5 and 8-10:* UNESCO 1997d.

HDI rank	Labour force (as % of total population) 1995	Women's share of adult labour force (% age 15 and above) 1970	1995	Percentage of labour force in — Agriculture 1990	Industry 1990	Services 1990	Future labour force replacement ratio 1995	Real earnings per employee annual growth rate (%) 1980-92	Labour force unionized[a] Total (%) 1995	Change (%) 1985-95	Weekly hours of work (per person in manufacturing) 1993-96	Expenditure on labour market programmes (as % of GDP) 1995-97
High human development	50	36	43	7	31	63	93	1.3	27	-14	40	1.4
1 Canada	53	32	45	3	25	71	97	0.1	37	2	39	1.9
2 France	45	36	44	5	29	66	96	..	9	-37	39	3.1
3 Norway	51	29	46	6	25	68	96	2.3	58	4	37	2.1
4 USA	51	36	45	3	26	71	108	0.4	14	-22	42	0.5
5 Iceland	56	34	45	11	27	63	117	..	83	6	43	..
6 Finland	51	44	48	8	31	61	92	2.6	79	16	38	5.5
7 Netherlands	47	26	40	5	26	70	86	1.7	26	-11	38	4.8
8 Japan	53	39	41	7	34	59	76	1.9	24	-17	38	0.5
9 New Zealand	49	29	44	10	25	65	113	0.1	24	-55	42	1.9
10 Sweden	54	36	48	4	30	66	95	1.2	91	9	38	4.5
11 Spain	43	24	36	12	33	55	79	1.2	19	62	37	2.8
12 Belgium	41	30	40	3	28	70	87	0.5	52	0	33	4.2
13 Austria	47	38	40	8	38	55	84	2.0	41	-19	35	1.8
14 United Kingdom	50	36	43	2	29	69	96	2.5	33	28	43	1.8
15 Australia	51	31	43	6	26	68	103	0.5	35	-30	39	2.1
16 Switzerland	53	34	40	6	35	60	82	..	23	-22	41	1.9
17 Ireland	40	26	33	14	29	57	120	2.0	49	-13	41	4.3
18 Denmark	56	36	46	6	28	66	83	-0.3	80	2	32	6.6
19 Germany	50	39	42	4	38	58	76	..	29	-18	37	3.8
20 Greece	42	26	37	23	27	50	82	0.8	24	-34	41	0.8
21 Italy	44	28	38	9	31	60	71	5.8	44	-7	..	2.0
22 Israel	42	30	40	4	29	67	152	-1.6	23	-77	42	..
26 Luxembourg	43	27	37	4	27	69	85	..	43	-18	41	0.9
27 Malta	37	21	26	3	35	63	107	..	65	36	..	..
33 Portugal	50	25	43	18	34	48	86	0.5	26	-50	40	2.1
37 Slovenia	50	36	46	6	46	48	85	..	..	40	..	..
39 Czech Rep.	55	46	48	11	45	43	89	..	43	-44	40	0.3
42 Slovakia	53	41	48	12	33	55	109	..	62	-20	36	..
47 Hungary	47	40	44	15	38	47	86	1.7	60	-25	37	1.4
52 Poland	50	45	46	27	36	37	112	-0.8	34	-43	43	2.1
Medium human development	49	49	48	19	39	42	118	..	..	..	..	..
67 Bulgaria	51	44	48	13	48	38	91	..	58	-66	..	..
68 Belarus	52	51	49	20	40	40	108	..	88	-12	..	..
72 Russian Federation	52	51	48	14	42	45	102	..	75	..	30	..
74 Romania	47	44	44	24	47	29	99	..	41	-20	..	..
76 Croatia	47	38	44	16	34	50	92	..	..	..	..	..
77 Estonia	55	51	49	14	41	44	100	..	36	-56	34	..
79 Lithuania	51	49	48	18	41	41	107	..	..	..	34	..
80 Macedonia, FYR	46	30	41	22	40	38	118	..	..	..	..	..
92 Latvia	54	51	50	16	40	44	102	..	..	..	39	..
93 Kazakhstan	48	47	46	22	32	46	148	..	..	..	34	..
99 Armenia	48	46	46	18	43	39	143	..	..	..	..	..
102 Ukraine	50	51	48	20	40	40	99	..	..	..	..	..
103 Turkmenistan	42	46	45	37	23	40	218	..	..	..	..	..
104 Uzbekistan	41	48	46	35	25	40	223	..	..	..	..	..
105 Albania	49	40	41	55	23	22	156	..	..	..	..	..
108 Georgia	49	48	46	26	31	43	119	..	..	..	..	..
109 Kyrgyzstan	42	48	47	32	27	41	203	..	..	..	..	..
110 Azerbaijan	43	45	44	31	29	40	164	..	64	-34	..	..
113 Moldova, Rep. of	49	52	48	33	30	37	132	..	..	..	22	..
118 Tajikistan	37	45	44	41	23	36	244	..	..	..	..	..
All developing countries	48	37	41	61	16	23	176	..	..	..	..	..
Industrial countries	49	40	44	10	33	57	100	..	36	-15	38	..
World	48	38	41	49	20	31	159	..	..	..	..	..
North America	51	36	45	3	26	71	107	0.4	16	-20	41	0.7
Eastern Europe and CIS	50	48	47	19	39	42	116	..	..	..	..	..
Western and Southern Europe	47	33	41	7	33	60	82	2.7	32	-9	38	3.0
OECD	48	35	42	11	30	60	104	1.8	27	-14	40	1.4
European Union	47	34	41	6	32	62	84	2.6	32	-3	39	2.9
Nordic countries	53	37	46	6	29	65	92	1.3	80	8	36	4.7

Note: Percentage shares of labour force in agriculture, industry and services may not necessarily add to 100 because of rounding.
a. Union membership as a percentage of wage and salary earners.
Source: Columns 1-6: ILO 1996; column 7: calculated on the basis of estimates from: UN 1996d; column 8: World Bank 1995c; columns 9 and 10: ILO 1997a; column 11: ILO 1997b; column 12: OECD 1997d.

HDI rank		Un-employed people (thousands) 1996	Total unemploy-ment rate (%) 1996	Unemploy-ment rate (%) Male 1996	Unemploy-ment rate (%) Female 1996	Youth unemployment rate (%) Male (age 15-24) 1996	Youth unemployment rate (%) Female (age 15-24) 1996	Incidence of long-term unemployment (%) 6 months or more Male 1996	6 months or more Female 1996	12 months or more Male 1996	12 months or more Female 1996	Discouraged workers (as % of total labour force) 1993	Involuntary part-time workers (as % of total labour force) 1993	Unemployment benefits expenditure (as % of total government expenditure) 1991
	High human development	37,740 T	8.1	7.3	8.8	16	17	45	42	29	26	1.2	3.6	2.0
1	Canada	1,469	9.7	9.9	9.4	18	15	29	27	15	12	0.9	5.5	8.1
2	France	3,162	12.1	10.4	14.2	22	32	59	64	37	42	0.2	4.8	3.2
3	Norway	109	4.9	4.8	4.9	12	13	32	28	16	12	1.2	..	2.2
4	USA	7,236	5.4	5.4	5.4	13	11	19	16	10	8	0.9	5.0	1.5
5	Iceland	6	3.7	3.4	4.1	9	8	33	28	22	16	..	..	..
6	Finland	408	16.1	15.8	16.5	25	25	59	52	41	31	1.5	2.9	3.6
7	Netherlands	462	6.4	5.2	8.1	11	12	81	82	54	45	0.6	5.6	4.5
8	Japan	2,250	3.4	3.4	3.4	7	7	47	31	24	13	2.2	1.9	0.7
9	New Zealand	110	6.1	6.1	6.1	12	11	40	37	24	21	1.0	6.3	..
10	Sweden	344	8.0	8.4	7.4	17	15	40	36	19	15	2.0	6.2	0.8
11	Spain	2,275	22.2	17.6	29.6	36	49	67	77	50	61	0.2	1.0	7.0
12	Belgium	588	9.5	7.4	12.4	17	24	75	79	59	63	1.5	3.8	5.8
13	Austria	231	5.3	5.3	5.2	7	7	38	48	23	29	..	..	1.8
14	United Kingdom	2,336	8.2	9.7	6.3	18	11	64	48	46	28	0.6	3.2	1.7
15	Australia	783	8.5	8.9	8.0	15	14	51	45	31	25	1.6	6.9	4.0
16	Switzerland	169	3.8	3.5	4.3	5	4	50	54	21	29	..	..	0.4
17	Ireland	279	11.9	11.9	11.9	19	17	79	70	65	51	0.5	3.3	6.3
18	Denmark	246	6.8	5.5	8.4	9	12	44	45	28	25	1.6	4.8	5.5
19	Germany	3,848	9.0	8.1	10.2	8	8	63 [a]	68 [a]	46 [a]	51 [a]	1.5	3.0	
20	Greece	425 [a]	..	..	..	19	38	64 [a]	78 [a]	42 [a]	58 [a]	0.3	3.1	
21	Italy	2,814	12.2	9.6	16.5	30	39	79	83	64	67	2.6	2.3	1.0
22	Israel	144	..	..	..	..	..	..	..	..	..	..	..	..
26	Luxembourg	5	3.3	2.5	4.7	10	8	49	41	30	25	..	..	..
27	Malta	6	..	..	..	..	..	..	..	..	..	..	..	..
33	Portugal	344	7.5	6.6	8.5	15	19	64	69	52	54	0.1	1.8	
37	Slovenia	127	13.9 [b]	..	..	..	..	..	..	..	..	..	..	..
39	Czech Rep.	199	3.9	3.3	4.6	6	8	51	54	31	32	..	..	..
42	Slovakia	232	12.6 [b]	..	..	..	..	..	..	..	..	..	..	..
47	Hungary	4,775	9.8	10.7	8.7	19	16	77	73	57	50	..	..	..
52	Poland	2,360	12.2	..	..	29	..	59	66	35	43	..	..	..
	Medium human development	4,807 T	..	..	..	..	..	..	..	..	..	..	..	..
67	Bulgaria	479	12.5 [b]	..	..	..	..	..	..	..	..	..	..	..
68	Belarus	183	3.8 [b]	..	..	..	..	..	..	..	..	..	..	..
72	Russian Federation	2,327	3.5 [b]	..	..	..	..	..	..	..	..	..	..	..
74	Romania	658	7.8 [b]	..	..	..	..	..	..	..	..	..	..	..
76	Croatia	261	..	..	..	..	..	..	..	..	..	..	..	..
77	Estonia	16 [a]	2.2 [b]	..	..	..	..	..	..	..	..	..	..	..
79	Lithuania	109	7.1 [b]	..	..	..	..	..	..	..	..	..	..	..
80	Macedonia, FYR	238 [c]	..	..	..	..	..	..	..	..	..	..	..	..
92	Latvia	91	7.0 [b]	..	..	..	..	..	..	..	..	..	..	..
93	Kazakhstan	282	3.5 [b]	..	..	..	..	..	..	..	..	..	..	..
99	Armenia	..	9.1 [b]	..	..	..	..	..	..	..	..	..	..	..
102	Ukraine	..	..	..	..	..	..	..	..	..	..	..	..	..
103	Turkmenistan	..	..	..	..	..	..	..	..	..	..	..	..	..
104	Uzbekistan	31	0.4 [b]	..	..	..	..	..	..	..	..	..	..	..
105	Albania	..	..	..	..	..	..	..	..	..	..	..	..	..
108	Georgia	..	..	..	..	..	..	..	..	..	..	..	..	..
109	Kyrgyzstan	77	4.4 [b]	..	..	..	..	..	..	..	..	..	..	..
110	Azerbaijan	32	1.0 [b]	..	..	..	..	..	..	..	..	..	..	..
113	Moldova, Rep. of	23	1.5 [b]	..	..	..	..	..	..	..	..	..	..	..
118	Tajikistan	..	2.5 [b]	..	..	..	..	..	..	..	..	..	..	..
	All developing countries	..	..	..	..	..	..	..	..	..	..	..	..	..
	Industrial countries	42,547 T	..	..	..	..	..	..	..	..	..	..	..	..
	World	..	..	..	..	..	..	..	..	..	..	..	..	..
	North America	8,705 T	5.4 [d]	5.9	5.8	13	12	20	17	11	9	0.9	5.1	2.0
	Eastern Europe and CIS	12,500 T	..	..	..	..	..	..	..	..	..	..	..	..
	Western and Southern Europe	15,720 T	11.5	9.7	14.1	20	27	65	70	47	50	1.1	2.8	3.0
	OECD	37,230 T	7.1 [d]	6.8	8.0	14	14	42	40	26	50	1.2	3.8	2.1
	European Union	17,765 T	11.5 [d]	9.9	13.2	20	25	66	66	48	47	0.9	2.9	2.9
	Nordic countries	1,112 T	8.9	8.6	9.1	15	16	43	40	25	20	1.7	5.0	2.7

a. Data refer to 1993-95.
b. OECD 1997h.
c. Includes only those applying for work.
d. OECD 1997d.
Source: Column 1: ILO 1997b; OECD 1997h; column 2: OECD 1997d; 1997h; columns 3-10: OECD 1997d; columns 11 and 12: OECD 1997d; column 13: ILO 1995a.

HDI rank	Radios (per 1,000 people) 1995	Televisions (per 1,000 people) 1995	Daily news-papers (copies per 1,000 people) 1995	Printing and writing paper consumed (metric tons per 1,000 people) 1995	Main telephone lines (per 1,000 people) 1995	Public pay phones (per 1,000 people) 1995	International telephone calls (minutes per person) 1995	Fax machines (per 1,000 people) 1995	Cellular mobile telephone subscribers (per 1,000 people) 1995	Internet users (per 1,000 people) 1995	Personal computers (per 1,000 people) 1995
High human development	**1,230**	**606**	**278**	**103.8**	**510**	**4.6**	**52.2**	**37**	**82**	**23.7**	**196**
1 Canada	1,053	647	166	94.0	590	6.0	99.9	..	87	41.2	193
2 France	895	579	234	76.7	558	4.6	48.3	33	24	8.6	134
3 Norway	808	561	596	90.6	556	3.4	100.0	..	224	64.1	273
4 USA	2,092	776	218	153.9	626	5.7	59.5	..	128	38.0	328
5 Iceland	799	447	..	40.4	555	5.6	107.9	..	115	111.9	205
6 Finland	1,008	519	468	227.4	550	5.0	61.7	26	199	139.0	182
7 Netherlands	937	495	329	91.3	525	1.2	94.4	32	33	38.8	201
8 Japan	916	619	576	112.9	488	6.4	13.0	64	81	7.2	153
9 New Zealand	997	506	239	70.1	479	1.3	85.6	18	108	50.1	223
10 Sweden	882	476	460	114.7	681	3.7	108.2	..	229	51.0	193
11 Spain	314	490	102	47.9	385	1.4	27.1	..	25	3.8	82
12 Belgium	790	464	316	93.6	458	1.5	109.2	..	23	9.9	138
13 Austria	620	497	298	97.1	466	4.2	111.9	35	48	18.6	124
14 United Kingdom	1,433	612	344	104.1	503	4.9	69.5	31	98	25.6	186
15 Australia	1,304	641	257	100.5	510	4.7	52.6	26	128	55.4	276
16 Switzerland	851	461	371	108.3	613	8.3	247.1	28	64	35.5	348
17 Ireland	649	382	154	40.1	365	1.8	113.5	..	44	11.2	145
18 Denmark	1,034	536	308	115.7	613	1.6	100.7	48	157	38.3	269
19 Germany	944	550	313	95.4	494	2.0	64.1	..	46	18.3	165
20 Greece	430	442	153	20.8	493	3.9	44.3	..	26	7.6	33
21 Italy	822	436	100	61.2	434	6.7	33.3	..	67	5.2	84
22 Israel	489	303	271	52.2	418	4.4	45.0	25	53	53.5	100
26 Luxembourg	639	593	332	..	565	1.4	569.1	20	66	15.9	..
27 Malta	545	448	174	37.9	459	4.0	76.6	..	29	2.3	81
33 Portugal	245	333	41	34.2	362	3.3	30.2	..	34	9.1	60
37 Slovenia	384	374	203	27.6	309	1.1	50.5	8	14	28.6	48
39 Czech Rep.	638	406	296	28.7	237	2.0	17.7	7	5	21.3	53
42 Slovakia	570	216	244	23.5	208	1.6	11.0	8	2	5.2	41
47 Hungary	643	444	169	24.0	185	3.2	24.2	4	26	10.8	39
52 Poland	454	408	140	17.0	148	1.0	9.9	1	2	6.5	28
Medium human development	**390**	**301**	**109**	**3.6**	**155**	**1.1**	**4.5**	**1**	**1**	**1.1**	**14**
67 Bulgaria	471	359	212	4.2	306	1.8	10.0	2	3	1.2	21
68 Belarus	285	265	174	..	190	1.7	12.8	1	1	(.)	..
72 Russian Federation	340	379	122	5.5	170	1.3	1.6	0	1	1.5	18
74 Romania	211	201	299	4.5	131	1.1	3.9	1	0	0.7	5
76 Croatia	266	230	50	13.9	269	2.1	44.1	8	7	5.0	21
77 Estonia	491	411	..	19.9	277	1.9	35.7	9	21	27.0	7
79 Lithuania	401	364	134	5.0	254	1.6	14.9	1	4	..	6
80 Macedonia, FYR	183	169	25	7.1	165	0.1	21.2	1	..	0.4	..
92 Latvia	678	470	233	8.6	280	1.6	17.4	0	6	..	8
93 Kazakhstan	384	275	..	..	118	0.5	0.9	0	0	0.1	..
99 Armenia	5	241	23	..	155	0.1	13.9	..	..	0.5	..
102 Ukraine	856	233	50	(.)	161	1.1	..	..	0	0.4	6
103 Turkmenistan	81	217	..	..	71	0.2	..	..	..	..	..
104 Uzbekistan	81	183	6	..	76	0.3	..	..	0	(.)	..
105 Albania	207	89	53	3.8	12	(.)	6.3	..	..	0.1	..
108 Georgia	551	220	..	..	103	0.2	0	..	0	0.1	..
109 Kyrgyzstan	114	238	12	..	77	0.3	5.0	..	..	..	..
110 Azerbaijan	20	212	28	..	85	0.2	4.0	..	1	(.)	..
113 Moldova, Rep. of	699	300	24	1.6	131	1.1	15.2	0	..	(.)	2
118 Tajikistan	..	258	14	..	45	(.)	0.1	0	..	..	..
All developing countries	**185**	**145**	**50**	**5.2**	**39**	**0.7**	**2.8**	**..**	**4**	**0.5**	**7**
Industrial countries	**1,005**	**524**	**235**	**78.2**	**414**	**3.7**	**41.6**	**23**	**61**	**17.9**	**156**
World	**364** [a]	**228**	**115**	**20.9**	**122** [b]	**1.4**	**10.9**	**..**	**17** [b]	**4.8** [b]	**44** [b]
North America	1,990	763	213	148.0	622	5.8	63.5	..	124	38.3	315
Eastern Europe and CIS	412	317	121	6.7	158	1.1	6.5	1	2	2.6	18
Western and Southern Europe	779	505	232	78.2	487	3.6	61.2	..	53	16.7	135
OECD	1,089	543	260	89.4	457	4.4	44.6	33	70	19.8	169
European Union	880	522	243	81.6	486	3.7	58.4	..	58	17.1	138
Nordic countries	928	514	453	133.9	614	3.5	95.0	..	205	70.2	222

a. UNESCO 1998.
b. ITU 1997a.
Source: Column 1: UNESCO 1998; *column 2:* ITU 1997b; *columns 3 and 4:* UNESCO 1997d; *columns 5-7 and 9-11:* ITU 1997a; *column 8:* calculated on the basis of estimates from: ITU 1997a.

		ELECTIONS				POLITICAL PARTIES		WOMEN'S PARTICIPATION		
	Lower or single house		Upper house or senate		Voter turnout at last elections for lower or single house (%)	Parties represented in		Year women received right		Year first woman elected (E) or nominated (N) to national parliament
HDI rank	Date of last elections	Members elected (E) or appointed (A)	Date of last elections	Members elected (E) or appointed (A)		Lower or single house	Upper house or senate	To vote[a]	To stand for election[a]	
High human development										
1 Canada	06 1997	E	1994	A	69	5 [b]	2 [b]	1918 [c]	1920 [c]	1921 E
2 France	05 1997	E	09 1995	E	71	9	6 [b]	1944	1944	1945 E
3 Norway	09 1997	E	..	..	78	7 [b]	..	1913	1907	1911 N
4 USA	11 1996	E	11 1996	E	49 [d]	2 [b]	2	1920	1788	1917 E
5 Iceland	04 1995	E	..	..	87	6 [b]	..	1915	1915	1922 E
6 Finland	03 1995	E	..	..	68	7 [b]	..	1906	1906	1907 E
7 Netherlands	05 1994	E	05 1995	E	78	11	7 [b]	1919	1917	1918 E
8 Japan	10 1996	E	07 1995	E	59	7 [b]	6 [b]	1947 [e]	1947 [e]	1946 E
9 New Zealand	10 1996	E	..	..	88	6	..	1893	1919	1933 E
10 Sweden	09 1994	E	..	..	87	7	..	1921	1921	1921 E
11 Spain	03 1996	E	03 1996	E	77	8 [b]	4 [b]	1931	1931	1931 E
12 Belgium	05 1995	E	05 1995	E	91	11	10	1948 [e]	1948	1921 N
13 Austria	12 1995	E	11 1994	E	86	5	3	1918	1918	1919 E
14 United Kingdom	05 1997	E	1997 [f]	E	72	10 [b]	2 [b]	1928 [e]	1928 [e]	1918 E
15 Australia	03 1996	E	03 1996	E	96	6 [b]	4 [b]	1902 [g]	1902 [g]	1943 E
16 Switzerland	10 1995	E	10 1995	E	42	11 [b]	6	1971	1971	1971 E
17 Ireland	06 1997	E	08 1997	E+A	66	7 [b]	4 [b]	1928 [e]	1928 [e]	1918 E
18 Denmark	09 1994	E	..	..	84	8 [b]	..	1915	1915	1918 E
19 Germany	10 1994	E	1997 [f]	E	79	6	..	1918	1918	1919 E
20 Greece	09 1996	E	..	..	76	5	..	1952	1952	1952 E
21 Italy	04 1996	E	04 1996	E+A	82	7 [b]	6 [b]	1945	1945	1946 E
22 Israel	05 1996	E	..	..	79	11	..	1948	1948	1949 E
26 Luxembourg	06 1994	E	..	..	88 [d]	5	..	1919	1919	1919 E
27 Malta	10 1996	E	..	..	97	2	..	1947	1947	1966 E
33 Portugal	10 1995	E	..	..	67	4	..	1934 [h]	1934 [h]	1934 E
37 Slovenia	11 1996	E	..	..	74	7 [b]	..	1945	1945	1992 E
39 Czech Rep.	05 1996	E	11 1996	E	76	6	6 [b]	1920	1920	1992 E
42 Slovakia	10 1994	E	..	..	75	7	..	1920	1920	1992 E
47 Hungary	05 1994	E	..	..	55	8	..	1953	1958	1945 E
52 Poland	09 1997	E	09 1997	E	48	6	5 [b]	1918	1918	1919 E
Medium human development										
67 Bulgaria	04 1997	E	..	..	59	5	..	1944	1944	1945 E
68 Belarus	11 1996	E	11 1996	E+A	..	†	†	1919	1919	1990 E
72 Russian Federation	12 1995	E	1997 [f]	E	65	9 [b]	†	1918	1918	1993 E
74 Romania	11 1996	E	11 1996	E	76	6 [b]	6	1946	1946	1946 E
76 Croatia	04 1997	E	04 1997	E+A	71	5 [b]	6	1945	1945	1992 E
77 Estonia	03 1995	E	..	..	70	7	..	1918	1918	1919 E
79 Lithuania	10 1996	E	..	..	53	6 [b]	..	1921	1921	1920 N
80 Macedonia, FYR	10 1994	E	..	..	58	6 [b]	..	1946	1946	1990 E
92 Latvia	09 1995	E	..	..	72	9	..	1918	1918	†
93 Kazakhstan	12 1995	E	12 1995	E+A	76	6 [b]	4 [b]	1924	1924	1990 E
99 Armenia	07 1995	E	..	..	56	8 [b]	..	1921	1921	1990 E
102 Ukraine	03 1994	E	..	..	57	15 [b]	..	1919	1919	1990 E
103 Turkmenistan	12 1994	E	..	..	100	1	..	1927	1927	1990 E
104 Uzbekistan	12 1994	E	..	..	94	2 [b]	..	1938	1938	1990 E
105 Albania	06 1997	E	..	..	73	6 [b]	..	1920	1920	1945 E
108 Georgia	11 1995	E	..	..	68	12 [b]	..	1918	1918	1992 E
109 Kyrgyzstan	02 1995	E	02 1995	E	61	†	†	1918	1918	1990 E
110 Azerbaijan	11 1995	E	..	..	86	9 [b]	..	1921	1921	1990 E
113 Moldova, Rep. of	02 1994	E	..	..	79	4	..	1978	1978	1990 E
118 Tajikistan	02 1995	E	..	..	84	4	..	1924	1924	1990 E

† No information or confirmation available.
a. Refers to the year in which women were granted electoral rights equal to those of men. In some countries confirmation of these rights was granted later, by the constitution of the newly independent state.
b. There are also independent and other parties not sufficiently represented to constitute a parliamentary group.
c. Universal adult suffrage granted in 1950; universal rights to stand for election granted in 1960.
d. Average turnout in the 1990s. No official data are available. The figures are from International IDEA 1997.
e. Year in which women were given full voting equality with men. Non-universal suffrage existed as of 1945 in Japan, 1919 in Belgium, 1918 in the United Kingdom and 1918 in Ireland.
f. Data valid as of 1997.
g. Full franchise granted in 1962.
h. Full equality granted in 1976.
Source: IPU 1998.

HDI rank	Prisoners (per 100,000 people) 1990	Prisoners 1993	Young adult prisoners (as % of total prisoners) 1987	Young adult prisoners 1990	Intentional homicides by men (per 100,000 people) 1985-90	Drug crimes (per 100,000 people) 1980-86	Reported adult rapes (thousands) 1986	Injuries and deaths from road accidents (per 100,000 people) 1993-95	Suicides (per 100,000 people) Male 1985-94	Suicides Female 1985-94	Divorces (as % of marriages) 1992-95	Single-female-parent homes (%) 1985-91	Births to mothers aged 15-19 (%) 1992-95	One-person households headed by women aged 65 and above (as % of all households) 1992[a]
High human development	77	93	..	..	4.8	..	129.1 T	736	21	7	40	..	7.8	..
1 Canada	..	45	..	..	2.7	225	20.5	844	21	5	49	..	6.2	6
2 France	89	86	13	11	1.4	..	2.9	327	32	12	43	7	2.0	20
3 Norway	46	60	8	6	1.6	116	0.3	278	21	7	53	..	3.0	12
4 USA	..	..	..	..	12.4	234	90.4	1,283	20	5	50	8	12.8	8
5 Iceland	28	39	9	5	0.6	..	..	615	..	..	38	6	5.6	..
6 Finland	..	62	..	7	4.1	..	0.3	208	44	12	59	10	2.5	10
7 Netherlands	37	51	18	28	1.2	38	1.2	84	14	6	32	5	1.6	8
8 Japan	..	..	..	..	0.9	31	1.8	..	23	11	..	5	..	..
9 New Zealand	..	..	..	..	2.6	..	0.5	..	21	5	..	8	..	..
10 Sweden	51	66	4	5	1.7	..	1.0	247	22	10	67	6	2.1	11
11 Spain	70	115	10	6	1.7	15	1.5	321	11	3	17	3	3.8	..
12 Belgium	67	72	..	..	2.3	40	..	709	..	..	68	7	3.0	9
13 Austria	98	91	1	3	1.4	77	0.5	646	33	12	38	..	4.4	12
14 United Kingdom	96	92	25	21	1.6	..	..	555	19	6	53	10	6.5	12
15 Australia	..	..	..	..	2.5	403	2.3	..	19	5	..	..	..	..
16 Switzerland	..	81	2	..	1.1	129	0.4	411	..	..	38	4	1.0	9
17 Ireland	55	60	28	..	1.2	..	(.)	370	..	..	..	..	5.1	6
18 Denmark	62	71	..	..	1.4	176	0.6	202	..	..	37	6	2.2	11
19 Germany	85	81	..	..	1.2	..	..	639	23	9	38	8	2.8	12
20 Greece	41	68	6	..	1.2	..	0.6	311	6	1	13	..	5.1	..
21 Italy	61	89	2	1	2.5	6	0.7	465	12	4	9	2	2.7	9
22 Israel	..	..	..	..	0.5	25	0.4	697	10	4	24	..	4.0	..
26 Luxembourg	96	108	7	6	1.6	..	..	393	..	..	35	3	1.5	8
27 Malta	15	..	..	..	0.6	..	(.)	182	..	..	..	..	3.1	..
33 Portugal	84	111	10	8	2.3	13	0.2	671	12	3	19	6	7.5	..
37 Slovenia	..	..	..	..	..	..	..	436	50	14	19	..	5.1	..
39 Czech Rep.	..	..	..	..	1.3	..	..	376	..	..	57	..	11.1	10
42 Slovakia	..	136	..	..	..	..	..	229	..	..	33	..	12.3	8
47 Hungary	..	132	..	6	3.5	..	1.1	272	56	17	46	..	11.5	10
52 Poland	..	160	..	..	2.5	..	1.9	200	25	5	18	..	8.0	6
Medium human development	..	..	..	..	..	..	..	127	51	10	47	..	15.4	..
67 Bulgaria	..	99	..	..	4.0	..	0.7	117	25	10	29	..	22.6	7
68 Belarus	..	..	..	..	..	..	..	89	49	10	55	8	14.3	10
72 Russian Federation	..	..	..	..	9.0	..	..	146	74	13	62	35	17.5	..
74 Romania	..	200	..	..	..	..	..	47	..	..	23	..	17.3	6
76 Croatia	..	..	..	..	..	..	..	410	35	12	17	..	5.7	..
77 Estonia	..	..	..	..	..	..	..	150	71	15	..	..	13.7	12
79 Lithuania	..	..	..	..	..	..	..	139	82	13	46	..	12.5	..
80 Macedonia, FYR	..	..	..	..	..	..	..	167	..	..	4	..	11.0	..
92 Latvia	..	..	..	..	..	..	..	217	71	14	71	..	11.2	7
93 Kazakhstan	..	..	..	..	..	..	..	104	40	9	34	..	13.0	..
99 Armenia	..	..	..	..	..	..	..	44	4	1	17	..	18.3	..
102 Ukraine	..	..	..	..	..	..	..	105	38	9	54	..	19.5	..
103 Turkmenistan	..	..	..	..	..	..	..	506	8	3	14	..	3.0	..
104 Uzbekistan	..	..	..	..	..	..	..	..	9	3	14	..	6.0	..
105 Albania	..	..	..	..	..	..	..	19	3	2	9	..	..	..
108 Georgia	..	..	..	..	..	..	..	43	5	2	12	..	..	..
109 Kyrgyzstan	..	..	..	..	..	..	..	95	23	4	22	..	10.6	16
110 Azerbaijan	..	..	..	..	..	..	..	50	1	1	13	..	9.2	3
113 Moldova, Rep. of	..	..	..	..	..	..	..	81	30	8	45	..	19.8	..
118 Tajikistan	..	..	..	..	..	..	..	44	5	3	11	..	9.8	..
All developing countries	..	..	..	..	..	..	..	..	..	..	..	..	..	..
Industrial countries	..	..	..	..	5.4	..	..	560	29	8	42	..	10.4	..
World	..	..	..	..	..	..	..	..	..	..	..	..	..	..
North America	..	..	..	..	11.4	233	110.9 T	1,240	20	5	50	..	12.2	..
Eastern Europe and CIS	..	..	..	..	..	..	..	147	48	10	45	..	14.3	..
Western and Southern Europe	73	85	..	..	1.7	..	10.2 T	443	20	7	32	..	3.0	..
OECD	80	88	..	..	4.8	..	128.7 T	710	19	6	38	..	7.8	..
European Union	77	87	..	..	1.7	..	9.5 T	463	20	7	35	..	3.6	..
Nordic countries	53	65	..	..	2.1	..	2.2 T	239	28	9	56	..	2.4	..

a. Data refer to 1992 or a year around 1992.
Source: Columns 1-4 and 12: UNECE 1995; columns 5-7: UNDP 1994; column 8: UNECE 1997a; columns 9 and 10: WHO 1995c; columns 11 and 13: UNECE 1997b; column 14: UN 1995b.

HDI rank	Net official development assistance (ODA) disbursed US$ millions 1996	As % of GNP Average 1985/86	As % of GNP 1996	ODA as % of central government budget 1992/93	ODA per capita of donor country (1995 US$) 1985/86	ODA per capita (1995 US$) 1995/96	Multilateral ODA as % of GNP 1995/96	Share of ODA through NGOs[a] (%) 1994-95	Aid by NGOs as % of GNP 1985/86	Aid by NGOs as % of GNP 1995/96	Aid to least developed countries (as % of GNP) 1995/96
High human development	55,483 T	0.33 [b]	0.24 [b]	..	77 [b]	71 [b]	0.07 [b]	3.7 [b]	0.03 [b]	0.02 [b]	0.05 [b]
1 Canada	1,795	0.49	0.32	1.63	85	64	0.10	6.9	0.05	0.05	0.07
2 France	7,451	0.58	0.48	..	132	137	0.12	0.3	0.01	0.01	0.10
3 Norway	1,311	1.10	0.85	1.70	274	289	0.24	..	0.09	0.06	0.33
4 USA	9,377	0.23	0.12	1.82	53	31	0.03	8.3	0.04	0.03	0.02
5 Iceland	..	..	..	..	..	..	..	..	..	..	..
6 Finland	408	0.43	0.34	1.51	96	79	0.15	1.4	0.03	0	0.09
7 Netherlands	3,246	0.97	0.81	..	201	213	0.25	10.7	0.08	0.09	0.23
8 Japan	9,439	0.29	0.20	1.35	89	101	0.05	1.5	0.01	0	0.04
9 New Zealand	122	0.28	0.21	0.36	38	33	0.04	1.9	0.03	0.03	0.05
10 Sweden	1,999	0.85	0.84	..	204	201	0.24	6.5	0.07	0.01	0.23
11 Spain	1,251	0.09	0.22	0.97	21	33	0.08	..	0	0.02	0.03
12 Belgium	913	0.51	0.34	..	115	98	0.17	0.3	0.02	0.02	0.09
13 Austria	557	0.28	0.24	0.73	72	83	0.08	0.4	0.02	0.02	0.04
14 United Kingdom	3,199	0.32	0.27	..	51	54	0.13	2.0	0.04	0.04	0.07
15 Australia	1,121	0.47	0.30	1.27	73	62	0.07	1.3	0.03	0.02	0.06
16 Switzerland	1,026	0.30	0.34	3.13	130	152	0.10	10.5	0.05	0.06	0.10
17 Ireland	179	0.27	0.31	..	24	46	0.12	0.2	0.11	0.10	0.13
18 Denmark	1,772	0.85	1.04	2.51	232	325	0.43	0.5	0.02	0.02	0.31
19 Germany	7,601	0.45	0.33	..	99	94	0.12	2.8	0.06	0.05	0.07
21 Italy	2,416	0.34	0.20	0.64	52	33	0.11	0.7	0	0	0.04
26 Luxembourg	82	0.17	0.44	..	136	185	0.13	5.3	0	0	0.06
33 Portugal	218	0.06	0.21	..	9	24	0.07	0.3	0	0	0.15
North America	11,172 T	0.25	0.14	1.82	56	34	0.04	..	0.04	0.03	0.02
Eastern Europe and CIS	..	..	..	..	..	..	..	..	..	..	..
Western and Southern Europe	30,430 T	0.50	0.42	..	102	97	0.14	..	0.02	0.02	0.11
OECD[b]	55,485 T[b]	0.33 [b]	0.25 [b]	..	79 [b]	71	0.08 [b]	3.3 [b]	0.03	0.03 [b]	0.06 [b]
European Union[b]	31,293 T[b]	0.45 [b]	0.37 [b]	..	89	87	0.14	..	0.02	0.02	0.09
Nordic countries	5,490 T	0.82	0.79	1.97	202	218	0.27	..	0.05	0.02	0.24

HDI rank	Net official aid received[a] US$ millions 1990	US$ millions 1996	As % of GNP 1990	As % of GNP 1996	Per capita (US$) 1990	Per capita (US$) 1996	External debt Total (US$ millions) 1990	Total (US$ millions) 1995	As % of GNP 1990	As % of GNP 1995	Debt service ratio (debt service as % of exports of goods and services) 1990	Debt service ratio 1995
High human development	2,781 T	3,871 T	1.44	1.04	38	51	79,984 T	101,095 T	58	41	..	14.8
23 Israel	1,372	2,217	2.55	2.22	295	395	..	955	..	..	12	..
27 Malta	4	72	0.15	2.90	10	193	601	955	24	19	12	6.7
37 Slovenia	..	82	..	0.44	..	41	..	3,489	..	19	..	6.7
39 Czech Rep.	3	122	0.01	0.27	..	12	6,383	16,576	20	37	..	8.7
42 Slovakia	2	141	0.01	0.75	..	26	2,008	5,827	13	33	..	9.7
47 Hungary	67	185	0.21	0.44	7	18	21,277	31,248	67	75	39.1	39.1
52 Poland	1,322	831	2.38	0.62	35	22	49,366	42,291	89	36	27	12.3
Medium human development	812 T	4,069 T	0.08	0.82	3	12	..	164,430 T	..	26	13	5.2
67 Bulgaria	15	170	0.08	1.87	2	20	10,890	10,887	57	92	..	18.8
68 Belarus	..	74	..	0.31	..	7	..	1,648	..	8	..	3.6
72 Russian Federation	254	1,225	0.04	0.28	2	8	59,817	120,461	10	37	..	6.6
74 Romania	243	218	0.63	0.70	11	10	1,140	6,653	3	19	..	10.6
76 Croatia	..	133	..	0.71	..	28	..	3,662	..	20	35	5.7
77 Estonia	..	62	..	1.42	..	42	..	309	..	1	..	0.8
79 Lithuania	..	89	..	1.16	..	24	..	802	..	11	..	1.4
80 Macedonia, FYR	..	105	..	5.26	..	49	..	1,213	..	63	..	..
92 Latvia	..	79	..	1.50	..	32	..	462	..	8	9	1.6
93 Kazakhstan	..	124	..	0.62	..	7	..	3,712	..	18	21	4.6
99 Armenia	..	295	..	18.29	..	78	..	374	..	13	..	2.9
102 Ukraine	289	379	0.18	0.87	6	7	..	8,434	..	11	60	5.3
103 Turkmenistan	..	24	..	0.72	..	5	..	..	..	..	29	..
104 Uzbekistan	..	63	..	0.26	..	3	..	1,630	..	8	41	6.0
105 Albania	11	222	0.52	8.54	3	68	349	709	17	32	1	1.0
108 Georgia	..	318	..	7.10	..	59	..	1,189	..	52	22	..
109 Kyrgyzstan	..	232	..	13.22	..	51	..	610	..	20	..	..
110 Azerbaijan	..	106	..	2.96	..	14	..	321	..	9	..	..
113 Moldova, Rep. of	..	37	..	2.00	..	9	..	691	..	18	..	8.0
118 Tajikistan	..	113	..	5.57	..	19	..	665	..	35	23	(.)
Eastern Europe and CIS	2,207 T	5,429 T	0.20	0.74	6	14	151,230 T	263,861 T	..	31	14	8.5

Note: The top half of the table shows flows of ODA from member countries of the OECD's Development Assistance Committee (DAC), the bottom half aid flows to, and external debt of, other industrial countries.
a. On a disbursements basis.
b. Data refer to DAC countries only and are as calculated in OECD 1998.
Source: Columns 1-3 and 5-11: OECD 1998; column 4: OECD 1994; columns 12-17: OECD 1997f; columns 18-23: World Bank 1997d.

38 Military expenditure and resource use imbalances

Industrial countries

	Defence expenditure						Military expenditure (as % of combined education and health expenditure)		ODA disbursed (as % of defence expenditure)	Exports of conventional weapons (1990 prices)[a]		Total armed forces	
	US$ millions (1995 prices)		As % of GDP		Per capita (US$; 1995 prices)					US$ millions	Share[b] (%)	Thousands	Index (1985=100)
HDI rank	1985	1996	1985	1996	1985	1996	1960	1990-91	1995	1996	1992-96	1996	1996
High human development	624,583 T	533,510 T	4.1	2.6	753	591	110	30	11	17,260 T	80	4,571 T	76
1 Canada	10,688	8,387	2.2	1.5	421	295	66	15	23	157	1	71	85
2 France	44,604	46,217	4.0	3.1	808	792	131	29	18	2,101	5	399	86
3 Norway	2,826	3,689	3.1	2.4	681	844	48	22	33	..	(.)	30	81
4 USA	352,551	265,823	6.5	3.6	1,473	1,001	173	46	3	10,228	52	1,484	69
5 Iceland	..	..	..	..	..	..	(.)	(.)					
6 Finland	2,051	2,162	2.8	2.0	418	422	25	15	18	..	..	33	89
7 Netherlands	8,121	7,915	3.1	2.1	561	510	67	22	38	450	2	63	60
8 Japan	29,350	43,626	1.0	1.0	243	348	17	12	29	..	..	236	97
9 New Zealand	882	729	2.9	1.3	271	205	29	16	13	..	..	10	80
10 Sweden	4,359	5,941	3.3	2.9	522	674	30	16	28	274	1	63	95
11 Spain	10,289	8,439	2.4	1.5	267	215	126	18	16	57	(.)	207	65
12 Belgium	5,621	4,190	3.0	1.6	570	416	49	20	23	110	(.)	46	51
13 Austria	1,763	2,011	1.2	0.9	233	251	20	9	36	3	(.)	56	102
14 United Kingdom	43,536	32,764	5.2	3.0	770	561	96	40	9	1,773	6	226	69
15 Australia	7,436	8,394	3.4	2.2	472	455	46	24	14	..	..	58	82
16 Switzerland	2,636	4,479	2.1	1.6	408	633	45	14	21	105	1	27	137
17 Ireland	437	725	1.8	1.1	123	200	24	12	22	..	..	13	93
18 Denmark	2,855	2,978	2.2	1.7	558	570	37	18	52	..	..	33	111
19 Germany	48,149	38,432	3.2	1.7	634	474	67	29	18	1,464	7	358	75
20 Greece	3,180	5,465	7.0	4.8	320	520	145	71	..	..	..	168	84
21 Italy	23,462	23,289	2.3	2.2	411	402	39	21	8	158	2	325	85
22 Israel	6,899	9,359	21.2	12.1	1,630	1,624	85	106	..	168	1	175	123
26 Luxembourg	87	133	0.9	0.7	238	324	19	10	46	..	..	1	114
27 Malta	22	32	1.4	1.1	61	87	..	10	..	..	..	2	250
33 Portugal	1,674	2,853	3.1	2.8	164	289	156	32	10	..	..	54	74
37 Slovenia	..	275	..	1.8	..	137	..	..	..	10	..	..	..
39 Czech Rep.	..	988	..	2.4	..	96	60	17	..	152	1	70	..
42 Slovakia	..	438	..	2.6	..	81	..	..	..	..	(.)	43	..
47 Hungary	3,241	757	7.2	1.7	304	75	31	18	..	..	..	64	61
52 Poland	7,864	3,020	8.1	2.8	211	78	41	30	..	60	(.)	249	78
Medium human development	..	75,639 T	..	5.3	..	228	..	..	..	..	15	2,476 T	..
67 Bulgaria	2,235	335	6.6	3.3	250	40	70	29	..	..	..	104	70
68 Belarus	..	480	..	4.2	..	46	..	..	..	190	(.)	86	..
72 Russian Federation	..	69,537	..	6.5	..	470	134	132	..	4,512	13	1,270	..
74 Romania	1,905	730	4.5	2.3	84	32	47	25	..	..	..	228	121
76 Croatia	..	1,254	..	6.8	..	266	..	..	..	65	..	..	..
77 Estonia	..	106	..	2.4	..	72	..	..	..	..	..	4	..
79 Lithuania	..	122	..	4.3	..	33	..	..	..	..	..	5	..
80 Macedonia, FYR	..	..	..	..	..	..	..	..	..	..	..	..	..
92 Latvia	..	130	..	3.5	..	50	..	..	..	..	..	8	..
93 Kazakhstan	..	460	..	2.6	..	28	..	..	..	..	..	40	..
99 Armenia	..	87	..	6.2	..	23	..	..	..	..	..	57	..
102 Ukraine	..	1,306	..	3.0	..	25	..	..	..	185	1	401	..
103 Turkmenistan	..	135	..	2.8	..	30	..	..	..	..	..	18	..
104 Uzbekistan	..	412	..	3.8	..	17	..	..	..	..	..	30	..
105 Albania	258	98	5.3	6.7	87	27	..	51	..	..	..	54	134
108 Georgia	..	110	..	3.4	..	20	..	..	..	..	..	10	..
109 Kyrgyzstan	..	47	..	2.6	..	10	..	..	..	..	..	7	..
110 Azerbaijan	..	131	..	5.8	..	17	..	..	..	..	..	71	..
113 Moldova, Rep. of	..	46	..	4.2	..	11	..	..	..	..	..	12	..
118 Tajikistan	..	113	..	11.0	..	19	..	..	..	..	..	7	..
All developing countries	185,515 T	171,934 T	7.1	3.7	51	39	102	63	..	..	..	14,050 T	96
Industrial countries	628,981 T	609,149 T	4.2	2.7	728	493	110	33	..	22,147 T	94	7,047 T	78
World	814,496 T	781,093 T	4.7	2.9	182	137	109	38	..	..	..	21,152 T	91
North America	363,239 T	274,210 T	6.1	3.4	1,356	917	166	43	3	10,385 T	53	1,554 T	70
Eastern Europe and CIS	..	81,117 T	..	4.7	..	204	..	..	..	..	16	2,910 T	..
Western and Southern Europe	162,136 T	158,950 T	3.0	2.3	518	487	72	24	19	4,722 T	18	1,878 T	79
OECD	631,083 T	548,012 T	4.1	2.5	637	503	110	30	11	17,115 T	79	5,702 T	80
European Union	200,188 T	183,514 T	3.4	2.5	558	493	78	27	17	6,390 T	24	2,044 T	77
Nordic countries	12,091 T	14,770 T	2.9	2.3	537	628	34	17	33	..	..	158 T	94

a. Figures are trend indicator values.
b. Calculated using the 1992-96 total for suppliers of major conventional weapons as defined by SIPRI 1997 (excluding the former Yugoslavia).
Source: Columns 1-6 and 12: IISS 1997; *columns 7 and 8:* UNDP 1997a; *column 9:* calculated on the basis of data from IISS 1997; OECD 1998; *columns 10 and 11:* SIPRI 1997; *column 13:* calculated on the basis of data from IISS 1997.

HDI rank	Export-import ratio (exports as % of imports) 1995	Export growth rate (as % of import growth rate) 1980-94	Terms of trade (1987=100) 1995	Net foreign direct investment (as % of GNP) 1993-95	Trade (as % of GDP) 1993-95	Net workers' remittances from abroad (US$ millions) 1995	Gross international reserves (months of import coverage) 1995	Current account balance before official transfers (US$ millions) 1995
High human development	102	105	103	-0.5	38	-13,541 T	2.3	-2,573 T
1 Canada	96	92	100	-0.2	71	..	0.8	-8,693
2 France	105	105	106	(.)	43	-1,364	1.5	16,443
3 Norway	112	110	95	1.0	71	-236	..	3,645
4 USA	90	84	102	-0.6	24	-12,230	2.0	-148,230
5 Iceland	..	..	..	0.1	70	..	..	..
6 Finland	113	119	95	-1.3	68	..	2.9	5,642
7 Netherlands	110	114	103	-1.4	99	-423	2.5	16,191
8 Japan	121	133	127	-0.3	17	..	4.1	111,246
9 New Zealand	83	103	108	..	62	174	2.4	-3,778
10 Sweden	108	117	102	1.1	77	106	3.1	4,633
11 Spain	97	111	114	0.8	47	2,119	3.2	1,280
12 Belgium	106	114	101	..	143	-393	..	14,960
13 Austria	97	112	87	-0.3	77	28	2.5	-5,113
14 United Kingdom	101	94	102	-1.1	57	..	1.3	-4,632
15 Australia	80	96	101	0.5	40	..	1.9	-19,184
16 Switzerland	120	131	60	-2.3	68	-2,519	..	21,622
17 Ireland	99	130	90	0.2	136	..	2.0	1,379
18 Denmark	103	119	100	0.2	64	0	1.5	1,413
19 Germany	103	103	96	-0.8	46	-5,305	2.1	-20,976
20 Greece	61	94	111	1.2	57	2,982	7.0	-2,864
21 Italy	110	125	107	-0.3	50	98	2.4	25,706
22 Israel	72	99	109	-0.5	69	0	2.5	-5,491
26 Luxembourg	..	..	..	..	184	..	..	..
27 Malta	..	..	..	2.4	198	..	5.3	..
33 Portugal	83	126	92	1.3	66	3,348	6.2	-229
37 Slovenia	99	..	..	0.9	113	53	2.1	-37
39 Czech Rep.	94	..	86	5.7	108	0	6.5	-1,374
42 Slovakia	105	..	86	1.0	124	0	4.4	648
47 Hungary	83	34	97	10.8	67	-14	6.7	-2,535
52 Poland	90	131	109	3.1	53	35	4.9	-4,245
Medium human development	100	..	..	0.7	67	..	2.3	3,046 T
67 Bulgaria	103	123	106	1.1	94	0	..	334
68 Belarus	86	..	..	0.1	..	..	0.9	-254
72 Russian Federation	111	..	..	0.6	44	..	2.5	9,604
74 Romania	84	83	111	1.2	60	3	2.9	-1,342
76 Croatia	76	..	..	0.4	93	..	2.5	-1,712
77 Estonia	90	..	..	0.3	160	-1	2.2	-184
79 Lithuania	82	..	..	1.0	108	1	2.5	-641
80 Macedonia, FYR	60	..	..	..	86	..	1.7	..
92 Latvia	96	..	..	3.2	91	..	3.2	-27
93 Kazakhstan	90	..	..	1.3	69	..	2.8	-519
99 Armenia	41	..	..	0.3	85	12	..	-279
102 Ukraine	91	..	..	0.3	..	..	0.7	-1,152
103 Turkmenistan	..	..	..	..	..	..	..	..
104 Uzbekistan	115	..	..	0.5	125	..	..	-8
105 Albania	43	..	..	3.1	52	385	3.7	-12
108 Georgia	..	..	..	0.2	46	..	..	..
109 Kyrgyzstan	69	..	..	0.5	58	..	..	-288
110 Azerbaijan	..	..	..	3.2	66	..	..	-379
113 Moldova, Rep. of	87	..	..	1.7	78	..	2.9	-95
118 Tajikistan	..	..	..	0.8	228	..	..	..
All developing countries	91	87	97	1.8	56	37,075 T	4.3	-88,167 T
Industrial countries	102	105	103	-0.5	39	-13,141 T	2.3	473 T
World	–	102	–	-0.1	42	23,934 T	–	–
North America	91	85	102	-0.6	28	-12,230 T	1.8	-156,923 T
Eastern Europe and CIS	97	..	..	1.8	70	..	3.6	-4,497 T
Western and Southern Europe	105	111	99	-1.0	57	-1,559 T	2.3	83,732 T
OECD	102	105	103	-0.5	39	-6,109 T	2.4	-8,937 T
European Union	104	108	101	-1.0	57	1,196 T	2.1	53,833 T
Nordic countries	108	116	99	0.9	71	-130 T	2.5	15,333 T

Source: Columns 1-8: World Bank 1997d.

HDI rank	Urban population (as % of total)			Urban population annual growth rate (%)		Population in cities of more than 750,000		Largest city	Population (thousands)	
						As % of total population	As % of urban population			
	1970	1995	2015	1970-1995	1995-2015	1995	1995	City	1995	2015
High human development	72	76	81	0.9	0.6	34	44	–	–	–
1 Canada	76	77	80	1.4	1.0	41	54	Toronto	4,319	5,220
2 France	71	75	79	0.7	0.5	22	30	Paris	9,523	9,694
3 Norway	65	73	78	0.9	0.6	..	..	..	..	..
4 USA	74	76	81	1.1	1.1	42	55	New York	16,332	17,602
5 Iceland	85	91	94	1.4	1.0	..	..	..	..	..
6 Finland	50	63	71	1.3	0.7	21	33	Helsinki	1,059	1,277
7 Netherlands	86	89	91	0.8	0.3	14	16	Amsterdam	1,108	1,171
8 Japan	71	78	82	1.1	0.3	39	50	Tokyo	26,959	28,887
9 New Zealand	81	86	89	1.2	1.3	27	31	Auckland	945	1,194
10 Sweden	81	83	85	0.5	0.4	26	31	Stockholm	1,545	1,626
11 Spain	66	77	81	1.2	0.2	19	25	Madrid	4,072	4,072
12 Belgium	94	97	98	0.3	0.2	11	11	Brussels	1,122	1,123
13 Austria	65	64	69	0.2	0.6	26	40	Vienna	2,060	2,108
14 United Kingdom	89	89	91	0.2	0.2	27	30	London	7,640	7,640
15 Australia	85	85	86	1.4	1.1	58	69	Sydney	3,590	3,990
16 Switzerland	55	61	68	1.1	0.9	13	21	Zurich	909	1,108
17 Ireland	52	58	64	1.2	0.8	26	45	Dublin	911	973
18 Denmark	80	85	88	0.5	0.2	25	30	Copenhagen	1,326	1,326
19 Germany	80	87	90	0.5	0.2	44	51	Essen	6,482	6,596
20 Greece	53	59	65	1.2	0.5	39	66	Athens	3,093	1,191
21 Italy	64	67	71	0.4	0.1	23	34	Milan	4,251	4,251
22 Israel	84	91	93	2.8	1.5	36	39	Tel Aviv-Yafa	1,976	2,580
26 Luxembourg	68	89	94	1.8	0.9	..	..	..	..	..
27 Malta	77	89	93	1.4	0.8	..	..	..	..	..
33 Portugal	26	36	47	1.6	1.3	19	53	Lisbon	1,863	2,271
37 Slovenia	37	51	59	1.9	0.4	..	..	..	..	..
39 Czech Rep.	52	65	71	1.1	0.2	12	18	Prague	1,225	1,240
42 Slovakia	41	59	68	2.1	0.9	..	..	..	..	..
47 Hungary	49	65	73	1.1	0.1	20	31	Budapest	2,017	2,017
52 Poland	52	64	71	1.5	0.7	22	34	Katowice	3,425	3,651
Medium human development	55	67	72	1.5	0.5	18	27	–	–	–
67 Bulgaria	52	68	75	1.1	0.1	14	20	Sofia	1,188	1,188
68 Belarus	44	71	80	2.5	0.4	17	24	Minsk	1,784	1,903
72 Russian Federation	63	76	82	1.3	(.)	21	27	Moscow	9,269	9,299
74 Romania	42	56	65	1.6	0.6	9	17	Bucharest	2,100	2,192
76 Croatia	40	56	64	1.6	0.6	22	39	Zagreb	981	1,148
77 Estonia	65	73	79	0.8	-0.2	..	..	..	..	..
79 Lithuania	50	72	80	2.2	0.3	..	..	..	..	..
80 Macedonia, FYR	47	60	69	2.3	1.3	..	..	..	..	..
92 Latvia	62	73	79	0.9	-0.3	36	50	Riga	921	921
93 Kazakhstan	50	60	68	1.7	1.2	7	12	Alma-Ata	1,245	1,530
99 Armenia	59	69	75	2.1	1.0	35	51	Yerevan	1,278	1,478
102 Ukraine	55	70	78	1.4	0.2	19	27	Kiev	2,812	957
103 Turkmenistan	48	45	52	2.3	2.5	..	..	..	..	..
104 Uzbekistan	37	41	50	3.1	2.8	10	24	Tashkent	2,282	3,518
105 Albania	32	37	48	2.5	2.0	..	..	..	..	..
108 Georgia	48	58	68	1.4	0.9	25	42	Tbilisi	1,342	1,525
109 Kyrgyzstan	37	39	48	1.8	1.9	..	..	..	..	..
110 Azerbaijan	50	56	64	2.0	1.6	25	44	Baku	1,848	2,335
113 Moldova, Rep. of	32	52	64	2.8	1.4	17	33	Kishinev	765	988
118 Tajikistan	37	32	40	2.2	3.0	..	..	..	..	..
All developing countries	25	37	49	3.8	2.9	16	41	–	–	–
Industrial countries	67	74	79	1.1	0.6	30	40	–	–	–
World	37	45	55	2.6	2.2	19	41	–	–	–
North America	74	76	81	1.1	1.1	42	55	–	–	–
Eastern Europe and CIS	54	66	72	1.5	0.5	18	27	–	–	–
Western and Southern Europe	70	76	80	0.7	0.3	27	36	–	–	–
OECD	69	76	81	1.3	0.8	34	45	–	–	–
European Union	74	78	82	0.6	0.3	27	35	–	–	–
Nordic countries	72	78	82	0.7	0.5	25	31	–	–	–

Source: Columns 1, 3 and 8-10: UN 1996e; columns 2 and 4-7: calculated on the basis of data from UN 1996e.

41 Population trends

HDI rank	Estimated population (millions)			Annual population growth rate (%)		Total fertility rate	Contraceptive prevalence rate, any method (%)	Dependency ratio (%)	Population aged 65 and above (as % of total population)
	1970	1995	2015	1970-95	1995-2015	1995	1990-95	1995	1995
High human development	764.1 T	898.5 T	957.3 T	0.7	0.3	1.7	71	49.4	13.8
1 Canada	21.3	29.4	34.2	1.3	0.8	1.7	73	48.0	12.0
2 France	50.8	58.1	60.2	0.5	0.2	1.7	77	52.9	15.2
3 Norway	3.9	4.3	4.6	0.4	0.3	1.9	76	54.4	15.9
4 USA	210.1	267.1	310.8	1.0	0.8	2.0	71	53.1	12.6
5 Iceland	0.2	0.3	0.3	1.1	0.8	2.2	..	54.6	11.5
6 Finland	4.6	5.1	5.3	0.4	0.2	1.8	80	49.6	14.1
7 Netherlands	13.0	15.5	16.2	0.7	0.2	1.6	78	46.0	13.2
8 Japan	104.3	125.1	125.8	0.7	(.)	1.5	59	43.6	14.2
9 New Zealand	2.8	3.6	4.4	0.9	1.1	2.1	69	52.9	11.4
10 Sweden	8.0	8.8	9.2	0.4	0.3	1.9	78	56.4	17.3
11 Spain	33.8	39.6	38.9	0.6	-0.1	1.3	59	46.2	15.0
12 Belgium	9.7	10.1	10.3	0.2	0.1	1.6	79	50.5	15.8
13 Austria	7.5	8.0	8.4	0.3	0.2	1.4	71	48.1	14.7
14 United Kingdom	55.6	58.1	59.0	0.2	0.1	1.8	82	54.1	15.8
15 Australia	12.5	17.9	21.9	1.4	1.0	1.9	76	49.9	11.7
16 Switzerland	6.2	7.2	7.6	0.6	0.3	1.5	71	46.5	14.3
17 Ireland	3.0	3.5	3.7	0.7	0.2	1.9	..	55.1	11.3
18 Denmark	4.9	5.2	5.3	0.2	0.1	1.8	78	48.3	15.1
19 Germany	77.7	81.6	82.1	0.2	(.)	1.3	75	45.6	15.2
20 Greece	8.8	10.5	10.4	0.7	(.)	1.4	..	48.7	15.9
21 Italy	53.8	57.2	54.6	0.2	-0.2	1.2	78	45.0	16.1
22 Israel	3.0	5.5	7.3	2.5	1.4	2.8	..	63.3	9.5
26 Luxembourg	0.3	0.4	0.5	0.7	0.6	1.7	..	46.4	14.0
27 Malta	0.3	0.4	0.4	0.8	0.6	2.1	..	49.6	10.9
33 Portugal	9.0	9.8	9.6	0.3	-0.1	1.5	66 [a]	48.2	14.8
37 Slovenia	1.7	1.9	1.8	0.6	-0.3	1.3	..	43.9	12.4
39 Czech Rep.	9.8	10.3	9.9	0.2	-0.2	1.5	69	46.2	12.6
42 Slovakia	4.5	5.3	5.5	0.7	0.1	1.7	74	50.3	10.8
47 Hungary	10.3	10.1	9.1	-0.1	-0.5	1.6	73	47.2	14.0
52 Poland	32.5	38.6	39.7	0.7	0.2	1.8	75	51.2	11.0
Medium human development	279.4 T	334.6 T	337.4 T	0.7	(.)	1.8	..	53.6	11.0
67 Bulgaria	8.5	8.5	7.8	(.)	-0.4	1.5	76	49.2	14.5
68 Belarus	9.0	10.4	9.9	0.5	-0.2	1.5	50	52.0	12.6
72 Russian Federation	130.4	148.5	138.1	0.5	-0.4	1.4	..	49.4	12.0
74 Romania	20.3	22.7	21.8	0.5	-0.2	1.5	57	47.7	11.8
76 Croatia	4.2	4.5	4.4	0.3	-0.2	1.6	..	46.7	12.8
77 Estonia	1.4	1.5	1.3	0.4	-0.6	1.4	70	50.1	12.8
79 Lithuania	3.1	3.7	3.6	0.7	-0.2	1.6	59	51.3	12.2
80 Macedonia, FYR	1.6	2.2	2.4	1.3	0.6	2.0	..	48.8	8.1
92 Latvia	2.4	2.5	2.2	0.3	-0.7	1.5	47	51.4	13.3
93 Kazakhstan	13.1	16.8	18.7	1.0	0.5	2.4	59	58.2	7.0
99 Armenia	2.5	3.6	4.0	1.5	0.5	1.9	..	56.3	7.4
102 Ukraine	47.3	51.8	48.1	0.4	-0.4	1.5	..	51.7	14.0
103 Turkmenistan	2.2	4.1	5.7	2.5	1.7	3.8	..	77.3	4.2
104 Uzbekistan	12.0	22.8	32.3	2.6	1.8	3.7	56	79.4	4.4
105 Albania	2.1	3.4	3.9	1.9	0.8	2.7	..	58.3	5.5
108 Georgia	4.7	5.4	5.6	0.6	0.1	2.0	..	54.3	11.4
109 Kyrgyzstan	3.0	4.5	5.3	1.7	0.9	3.4	..	74.6	5.8
110 Azerbaijan	5.2	7.5	8.9	1.5	0.9	2.5	..	61.3	5.9
113 Moldova, Rep. of	3.6	4.4	4.7	0.9	0.3	2.0	..	55.5	9.3
118 Tajikistan	2.9	5.8	8.5	2.8	1.9	4.1	..	86.3	4.3
All developing countries	2,616.1 T	4,394.0 T	5,892.2 T	2.1	1.5	3.2	56	63.9	4.7
Industrial countries	1,043.5 T	1,233.1 T	1,294.7 T	0.7	0.2	1.7	70	50.5	13.1
World	3,659.6 T	5,627.1 T	7,186.9 T	1.7	1.2	2.9	58	60.8	6.5
North America	231.4 T	296.5 T	345.0 T	1.0	0.8	2.0	71	52.6	12.5
Eastern Europe and CIS	338.3 T	400.8 T	403.5 T	0.7	(.)	1.8	..	52.9	11.1
Western and Southern Europe	295.5 T	325.7 T	327.8 T	0.4	(.)	1.4	74	47.8	15.2
OECD	872.5 T	1,082.2 T	1,191.1 T	0.9	0.5	1.8	70	50.7	12.2
European Union	340.6 T	371.6 T	373.8 T	0.4	(.)	1.5	75	48.7	15.3
Nordic countries	21.7 T	23.7 T	24.7 T	0.4	0.2	1.9	78	52.7	15.8

a. Data refer to 1979-80.
Source: Columns 1-5, 8 and 9: calculated on the basis of data from UN 1996d; column 6: UN 1996d; column 7: UN 1997f.

		Electricity consumption				Commercial energy use (oil equivalent)						Net commercial energy imports (as % of energy consumption)	
		Total (millions of kilowatt-hours)	Index (1980=100)	Per capita (kilowatt-hours)		Total (1,000 metric tons)		Per capita (kg)		GDP output per kilogram (US$)[a]			
HDI rank		1995	1995	1980	1995	1980	1994	1980	1994	1980	1994	1980	1994
High human development		7,894,734 T	148	6,756	8,787	3,870,721 T	4,454,065 T	4,742	4,983	2.8	3.4	30	28
1	Canada	501,221	143	14,243	17,047	193,170	229,730	7,854	7,854	1.7	2.0	-7	-47
2	France	422,768	170	4,615	7,272	190,660	234,160	3,539	4,042	4.1	4.4	75	95
3	Norway	116,774	140	20,327	26,956	18,865	23,060	4,611	5,318	3.9	4.6	-195	-638
4	USA	3,381,546	142	10,334	12,660	1,801,000	2,037,980	7,908	7,819	2.1	2.6	14	19
5	Iceland	4,981	158	13,838	18,517	1,432	2,110	6,281	7,932	2.9	2.7	44	37
6	Finland	70,859	178	8,351	13,875	24,998	30,520	5,230	5,997	2.9	3.0	72	58
7	Netherlands	92,224	143	4,560	5,957	65,106	70,440	4,601	4,580	3.0	3.7	-10	7
8	Japan	989,935	171	4,944	7,915	347,120	481,850	2,972	3,856	5.5	6.2	88	81
9	New Zealand	34,375	156	7,061	9,653	9,202	15,070	2,956	4,245	3.4	2.8	39	15
10	Sweden	145,334	150	11,655	16,538	40,992	50,250	4,933	5,723	3.4	3.3	61	38
11	Spain	170,866	158	2,872	4,312	68,692	96,200	1,837	2,458	3.6	3.6	77	69
12	Belgium	78,500	155	5,125	7,752	46,122	51,790	4,684	5,120	2.8	3.2	83	78
13	Austria	54,117	144	4,988	6,727	23,449	26,500	3,105	3,301	4.6	5.4	67	66
14	United Kingdom	350,767	124	5,020	6,016	201,200	220,270	3,572	3,772	2.8	3.5	2	-10
15	Australia	173,404	180	6,599	9,706	70,399	95,280	4,792	5,341	2.4	2.7	-22	-83
16	Switzerland	55,803	150	5,855	7,754	20,840	25,380	3,298	3,629	7.3	7.4	66	57
17	Ireland	17,863	169	3,106	5,038	8,485	11,200	2,495	3,137	3.1	3.9	78	68
18	Denmark	35,996	139	5,054	6,892	19,488	20,700	3,804	3,977	4.4	5.5	97	28
19	Germany	539,726	..	..	6,615	359,170	336,490	4,587	4,128	..	..	49	58
20	Greece	42,348	182	2,413	4,051	15,973	23,560	1,656	2,260	2.8	2.2	77	62
21	Italy	278,533	147	3,357	4,867	139,190	154,600	2,466	2,707	4.8	5.5	86	81
22	Israel	28,790	233	3,187	5,211	8,616	14,624	2,222	2,717	3.4	3.7	98	96
26	Luxembourg	6,243	166	10,330	15,339	3,643	3,780	9,984	9,361	1.6	2.3	99	99
27	Malta	1,512	287	1,627	4,120	402	924	1,104	2,511	3.4	..	100	100
33	Portugal	34,177	200	1,750	3,482	10,291	18,090	1,054	1,827	3.5	2.8	86	88
37	Slovenia	10,996	..	..	5,712	..	5,195	..	2,612	..	..	..	51
39	Czech Rep.	58,047	..	..	5,656	29,394	39,982	2,873	3,868	..	0.8	-29	7
42	Slovakia	24,415	..	..	4,574	..	17,343	..	3,243	..	0.9	..	72
47	Hungary	36,422	117	2,920	3,604	28,322	24,450	2,645	2,383	0.8	1.0	49	47
52	Poland	136,192	112	3,419	3,532	124,500	92,537	3,499	2,401	0.5	0.7	3	-2
Medium human development		1,405,399 T	..	..	4,200	1,049,166 T	1,013,847 T	4,094	3,032	..	0.5	3	-20
67	Bulgaria	41,629	107	4,371	4,892	28,476	20,568	3,213	2,438	0.7	1.1	74	56
68	Belarus	32,077	..	..	3,099	2,385	24,772	247	2,392	..	0.8	-8	88
72	Russian Federation	840,421	..	..	5,661	750,240	595,440	5,397	4,014	0.6	0.5	(.)	-53
74	Romania	59,565	88	3,061	2,621	63,846	39,387	2,876	1,733	0.5	0.7	19	27
76	Croatia	13,359	..	..	2,965	..	6,667	..	1,395	..	..	..	43
77	Estonia	6,847	..	..	4,601	..	5,560	..	3,709	..	0.7	..	39
79	Lithuania	11,220	..	..	3,003	..	7,555	..	2,030	..	0.8	..	70
80	Macedonia, FYR	6,114	..	..	2,836	..	2,686	..	1,279	..	..	..	44
92	Latvia	6,235	..	..	2,459	..	3,997	..	1,569	..	1.2	..	90
93	Kazakhstan	73,496	..	..	4,370	76,799	56,664	5,153	3,371	..	0.3	(..)	-25
99	Armenia	5,574	..	..	1,535	1,071	1,441	346	384	4.3	1.4	100	79
102	Ukraine	191,200	..	..	3,694	108,290	165,132	2,164	3,180	..	0.4	-1	48
103	Turkmenistan	7,780	..	..	1,909	..	10,401	..	2,361	..	..	..	-191
104	Uzbekistan	46,800	..	..	2,056	..	41,825	..	1,869	..	0.3	..	0
105	Albania	4,479	139	1,204	1,324	3,058	1,093	1,145	341	0.6	2.4	(.)	3
108	Georgia	7,570	..	..	1,389	..	3,325	..	614	..	0.7	..	85
109	Kyrgyzstan	10,981	..	..	2,462	..	2,755	..	616	..	0.9	..	47
110	Azerbaijan	17,200	..	..	2,284	15,001	16,274	2,433	2,182	..	0.2	1	1
113	Moldova, Rep. of	8,892	..	..	2,004	..	4,763	..	1,095	..	..	..	100
118	Tajikistan	13,960	..	..	2,395	..	3,542	..	616	..	0.5	..	53
All developing countries		3,574,530 T	284	387	814	1,280,811 T	2,449,513 T	392	567	1.7	1.5	-94	-47
Industrial countries		9,300,133 T	147	6,601	7,542	4,919,166 T	5,467,912 T	4,587	4,452	2.3	2.8	24	19
World		12,874,663 T	174	1,566	2,290	6,200,698 T	7,917,425 T	1,431	1,429	2.2	2.4	..	..
North America		3,882,767 T	142	10,711	13,095	1,994,170 T	2,267,710 T	7,820	7,720	2.0	2.6	12	12
Eastern Europe and CIS		1,671,471 T	..	..	4,170	1,231,382 T	1,193,354 T	3,936	2,979	..	0.5	3	-14
Western and Southern Europe		2,168,624 T	157	4,488	6,659	1,057,798 T	1,179,754 T	3,412	3,635	4.0	4.4	58	53
OECD		8,265,200 T	152	5,764	7,637	4,031,877 T	4,746,937 T	4,190	4,416	2.7	3.3	29	27
European Union		2,340,321 T	150	4,330	6,298	1,217,459 T	1,348,550 T	3,425	3,640	3.6	4.1	52	54
Nordic countries		373,944 T	150	11,051	15,766	105,775 T	126,640 T	4,695	5,361	3.6	3.9	24	-82

a. Estimated real GDP (at 1987 prices) divided by kilograms of oil equivalent of commercial energy use.
Source: Columns 1-4: UN 1997b; *columns 5-12:* World Bank 1997d.

HDI rank		Land area (1,000 ha) 1995	Forest and woodland (as % of land area) 1995	Internal renewable water resources per capita (cubic metres per year) 1998	Annual rate of deforestation[a] (%) 1990-95	Trees defoliated (as % of all trees)[b] 1991	SO₂ emissions per capita (1,000 metric tons) 1992-93	CO₂ emissions Per capita (1,000 metric tons) 1980	Per capita 1995	Millions of metric tons 1980	Millions of metric tons 1995	Share of world total (%) 1995	Kg per US$ of GDP (at 1987 prices) 1992
	High human development	3,114,360 T	21.2	9,162	..	..	51.1	12.4	12.3	9,033 T	11,043 T	48.6	0.7
1	Canada	922,097	26.5	94,373	-0.1	..	105.2	17.1	14.8	421	436	1.9	0.9
2	France	55,010	27.3	3,065	-1.1	7.1	21.2	9.0	5.9	483	340	1.5	0.4
3	Norway	30,683	26.3	87,691	-0.3	19.7	8.4	22.1	16.7	90	72	0.3	0.6
4	USA	915,912	23.2	8,983	-0.3	..	78.7	19.6	20.5	4,515	5,469	24.1	1.0
5	Iceland	10,025	0.1	606,498	0	..	32.7	8.2	6.7	2	2	(.)	0.3
6	Finland	30,459	65.8	21,334	0.1	16.0	27.5	11.5	10.0	55	51	0.2	0.5
7	Netherlands	3,392	9.9	635	0	17.2	10.7	10.8	8.8	153	136	0.6	0.6
8	Japan	37,652	66.8	4,344	0.1	..	7.0	7.8	9.0	907	1,127	5.0	0.4
9	New Zealand	26,799	29.4	88,859	-0.6	..	..	5.6	7.7	18	27	0.1	0.7
10	Sweden	41,162	59.3	19,858	..	12.0	11.6	8.6	5.1	71	45	0.2	0.3
11	Spain	49,944	16.8	2,775	0	7.3	55.8	5.3	5.8	200	232	1.0	0.7
12	Belgium	30,230	2.4	822	..	17.9	9.4	12.9	10.3	127	104	0.5	0.6
13	Austria	8,273	46.9	6,857	0	7.5	9.0	6.9	7.4	52	59	0.3	0.4
14	United Kingdom	24,160	9.9	1,219	-0.5	56.7	55.0	10.4	9.3	585	542	2.4	0.8
15	Australia	768,230	5.3	18,596	(..)	..	..	13.9	16.2	203	290	1.3	1.2
16	Switzerland	3,955	28.6	5,802	0	19.0	8.2	6.5	5.4	41	39	0.2	0.2
17	Ireland	6,889	8.3	13,187	-2.7	15.0	53.1	7.4	9.1	25	32	0.1	0.8
18	Denmark	4,243	9.8	2,092	0	29.9	30.5	12.3	10.5	63	55	0.2	0.5
19	Germany	34,927	30.8	1,165	0	25.2	48.2	..	10.2	..	835	3.7	..
20	Greece	12,890	50.5	4,279	-2.3	16.9	49.2	5.4	7.3	52	76	0.3	1.5
21	Italy	29,406	22.1	2,785	-0.1	16.4	29.4	6.6	7.2	372	410	1.8	0.5
22	Israel	2,062	5.0	289	0	..	..	5.5	8.4	21	46	0.2	0.9
26	Luxembourg	2,586	..	..	..	20.8	25.3	29.0	22.8	11	9	(.)	..
27	Malta	(.)	..	..	0	..	..	3.0	4.7	1	2	(.)	..
33	Portugal	9,150	31.4	3,878	-0.9	29.6	29.1	2.8	5.3	27	52	0.2	0.9
37	Slovenia	2,012	53.5	..	0	15.9	..	..	6.1	..	12	0.1	..
39	Czech Rep.	7,728	34.0	5,694	..	41.3	149.5	..	10.9	..	112	0.5	4.4
42	Slovakia	4,808	41.4	5,745	-0.1	..	70.4	..	7.1	..	38	0.2	2.5
47	Hungary	9,234	18.6	604	-0.5	19.6	81.0	7.7	5.5	82	56	0.2	2.6
52	Poland	30,442	28.7	1,278	-0.1	45.0	70.9	12.8	8.8	456	338	1.5	6.0
	Medium human development	2,239,881 T	37.0	15,227	..	..	..	..	8.9	..	2,975 T	12.9	5.7
67	Bulgaria	11,050	29.3	2,146	..	..	120.0	8.5	6.7	75	57	0.2	2.4
68	Belarus	20,748	35.5	5,047	-1.0	..	56.5	..	5.7	..	59	0.3	4.1
72	Russian Federation	1,688,850	45.2	29,009	..	26.0	..	..	12.2	..	1,818	8.0	5.5
74	Romania	23,034	27.1	1,639	..	9.7	78.4	8.6	5.3	192	121	0.5	4.5
76	Croatia	5,592	32.6	13,663	0	..	..	..	3.8	..	17	0.1	..
77	Estonia	4,227	47.6	8,946	-1.0	28.0	..	..	11.1	..	16	0.1	4.9
79	Lithuania	6,480	30.5	3,720	-0.6	23.9	..	..	4.0	..	15	0.1	3.1
80	Macedonia, FYR	2,543	38.9	..	..	..	..	..	..	..	..	..	..
92	Latvia	6,205	46.5	7,029	-0.9	..	..	..	3.7	..	9	(.)	2.6
93	Kazakhstan	267,073	3.9	6,728	-1.9	..	..	..	13.2	..	221	1.0	12.6
99	Armenia	2,820	11.8	3,069	-2.7	..	..	..	1.0	..	4	(.)	1.8
102	Ukraine	57,935	16.0	3,838	-0.1	..	53.6	..	8.5	..	438	1.9	6.9
103	Turkmenistan	46,993	8.0	232	0	..	..	..	7.0	..	28	0.1	..
104	Uzbekistan	41,424	22.0	1,307	-2.7	..	..	..	4.4	..	99	0.4	8.5
105	Albania	2,740	38.2	2,903	0	..	14.9	1.8	0.5	5	2	(.)	1.8
108	Georgia	6,970	42.9	10,556	0	..	..	..	1.4	..	8	(.)	3.0
109	Kyrgyzstan	19,180	3.8	10,503	0	..	..	..	1.2	..	5	(.)	4.3
110	Azerbaijan	8,660	11.4	1,657	0	..	..	..	5.6	..	43	0.2	13.6
113	Moldova, Rep. of	3,297	10.8	519	0	..	..	..	2.5	..	11	(.)	..
118	Tajikistan	14,060	2.9	10,031	0	..	..	..	0.7	..	4	(.)	1.6
	All developing countries	7,494,675 T	26.0	5,975	..	..	..	1.3	2.0	4,245 T	8,636 T	37.4	2.1
	Industrial countries	5,354,241 T	27.8	10,804	..	..	52.5	12.2	11.4	9,305 T	14,018 T	61.5	1.0
	World	12,848,916 T	26.8	6918 [c]	0.3 [c]	..	..	3.4	4.1	13,551 T	22,655 T	98.9 [d]	1.2
	North America	1,838,009 T	24.9	17,450	..	..	81.3	19.4	19.9	4,936 T	5,904 T	26.0	1.0
	Eastern Europe and CIS	2,294,105 T	36.9	13,124	..	..	..	..	8.9	..	3,531 T	15.4	5.5
	Western and Southern Europe	363,224 T	30.4	5,000	..	..	33.5	7.9	7.8	1,824 T	2,550 T	11.1	0.5
	OECD	3,383,183 T	21.5	8,104	..	..	48.2	10.8	10.9	9,467 T	11,842 T	52.0	0.8
	European Union	342,721 T	30.2	2,992	..	..	37.7	8.2	8.0	2,275 T	2,978 T	13.0	0.5
	Nordic countries	116,572 T	45.4	35,306	..	..	18.8	12.5	9.5	281 T	224 T	0.9	0.5

a. A positive figure indicates a loss in forest area, a negative figure a gain.
b. Percentage of trees with greater than 25% defoliation.
c. WRI 1998.
d. The world total is less than 100% because of the omission of data for countries not reported on.
Source: Column 1: FAO 1996a; column 2: calculated on the basis of data from: FAO 1996a; column 3: WRI 1998; column 4: FAO 1997c; column 5: WRI 1998; column 6: WRI 1996a; OECD; and the U.N. Economic Commission for Europe; columns 7-12: calculated on the basis of data from CDIAC 1998.

HDI rank	Major protected areas (as % of national territory)[a] 1996	Spent fuel produced (metric tons of heavy metal)[b] 1996	Hazardous waste produced (1,000 metric tons)[c] 1991-94	Municipal waste generated (kg per person) 1995	Population served by Municipal waste services (%) 1992-95	Population served by Public sanitation services (%) 1992-95	Waste recycling (as % of apparent consumption) Paper and cardboard 1992-95	Waste recycling Glass 1992-95
High human development	**12.5**	**8,416 T**	**258,922 T**	**519**	**99**	**82**	**43**	**42**
1 Canada	9.5	1,690	5,896	630	100	91	33	17
2 France	11.6	1,200	7,000 [d]	470	100	81	38	50
3 Norway	24.2	..	500	620	98	73	41	75
4 USA	18.9	2,300	213,620	730	100	..	35	23
5 Iceland	9.4	..	6	560	99	90	30 [d]	75
6 Finland	8.3	68	559	410	75	77	57	50
7 Netherlands	11.5	14	1,520	580	100	98	77	80
8 Japan	6.8	980	..	400	100	..	51	56
9 New Zealand	23.4	..	110	..	..	..	..	..
10 Sweden	4.7	230	..	440	100	95	54	61
11 Spain	8.3	160	1,708 [d]	370	..	62	52	32
12 Belgium	2.6	137	776	470	100	..	12	67
13 Austria	28.2	..	550	480	99	76	65	76
14 United Kingdom	19.8	1,023	1,844	..	100	97	35	27
15 Australia	8.7	..	426	690 [d]	..	..	50 [d]	36
16 Switzerland	17.3	64	854	380	99	94	61	85
17 Ireland	0.8	..	248	430	..	68	12	39
18 Denmark	31.8	..	250	530	100	..	44	63
19 Germany	26.4	450	9,100	320	100	92	67	75
20 Greece	2.5	..	450	310	100	51	19	20
21 Italy	7.1	..	2,708	470	..	..	29	53
22 Israel	14.9 [e]	..	..	..	..	..	..	..
26 Luxembourg	13.9	..	180	530	100	88	..	..
27 Malta	..	..	..	..	..	..	..	..
33 Portugal	6.5	..	..	350	89	55	37	42
37 Slovenia	5.7 [e]	..	..	..	..	..	..	..
39 Czech Rep.	15.5	45	1,867	230	85	73	..	..
42 Slovakia	21.3	..	1,347	300	..	52	..	..
47 Hungary	6.8	55	3,537	420	85	43	..	..
52 Poland	9.3	..	3,866	290	..	..	..	..
Medium human development	..	..	..	..	..	..	..	..
67 Bulgaria	4.4 [e]	..	..	..	..	..	..	..
68 Belarus	4.2 [e]	..	..	..	..	..	..	..
72 Russian Federation	3.1 [e]	..	..	..	..	..	..	..
74 Romania	4.7 [e]	..	..	..	..	..	..	..
76 Croatia	6.7 [e]	..	..	..	..	..	..	..
77 Estonia	12.0 [e]	..	..	..	..	..	..	..
79 Lithuania	10.0 [e]	..	..	..	..	..	..	..
80 Macedonia, FYR	7.1 [e]	..	..	..	..	..	..	..
92 Latvia	12.5 [e]	..	..	..	..	..	..	..
93 Kazakhstan	2.7 [e]	..	..	..	..	..	..	..
99 Armenia	7.6 [e]	..	..	..	..	..	..	..
102 Ukraine	1.6 [e]	..	..	..	..	..	..	..
103 Turkmenistan	4.2 [e]	..	..	..	..	..	..	..
104 Uzbekistan	2.1 [e]	..	..	..	..	..	..	..
105 Albania	2.8 [e]	..	..	..	..	..	..	..
108 Georgia	2.8 [e]	..	..	..	..	..	..	..
109 Kyrgyzstan	3.6 [e]	..	..	..	..	..	..	..
110 Azerbaijan	5.5 [e]	..	..	..	..	..	..	..
113 Moldova, Rep. of	1.2 [e]	..	..	..	..	..	..	..
118 Tajikistan	4.2 [e]	..	..	..	..	..	..	..
All developing countries	..	..	..	..	..	..	..	..
Industrial countries	12.5 [f]	..	..	..	..	..	..	..
World	9.5 [g]	..	..	..	..	..	..	..
North America	14.2	3,990 T	219,516 T	620 [g]	100	..	35	22
Eastern Europe and CIS	..	..	..	..	..	..	..	..
Western and Southern Europe	11.4 [f]	..	26,409 T	416	99	81	48	57
OECD	12.1 [g]	8,709 T	257,575 T	510 [g]	96	77	39	38
European Union	10.9 [f]	3,282 T	26,893 T	430 [g]	99	84	45	52
Nordic countries	12.2 [f]	..	1,315 T	488	94	85	50	62

a. National classifications may differ. Includes only areas greater than 10 square kilometres except for islands. World Conservation Union (IUCN) management categories I-VI, except where otherwise noted.
b. Spent fuel arising in nuclear power plants.
c. Waste, generated mainly by industrial activities, that may lead to toxic contamination of soil, water and air if not properly managed.
d. Data refer to an earlier year or period than that specified in the column heading.
e. IUCN categories I-V.
f. IUCN categories I-VI only.
g. OECD 1997c.
Source: Column 1: OECD 1997c; WRI 1998; columns 2-8: OECD 1997c.

HDI rank	GDP (US$ billions) 1995	Agriculture (as % of GDP) 1995	Industry (as % of GDP) 1995	Services (as % of GDP) 1995	Consumption Private (as % of GDP) 1995	Consumption Government (as % of GDP) 1995	Gross domestic investment (as % of GDP) 1995	Gross domestic savings (as % of GDP) 1995	Tax revenue (as % of GDP) 1995	Central government expenditure (as % of GDP) 1995	Exports (as % of GDP) 1995	Imports (as % of GDP) 1995
High human development	22,197 T	2	31	67	60	16	23	24	..	34	19	19
1 Canada	569	..	..	..	60	19	19	21			37	35
2 France	1,536	2 [a]	27 [a]	71 [a]	60	20	18	20	38	47	23	20
3 Norway	146	..	..	..	50	21	23	29	..	39	38	32
4 USA	6,952	2 [a]	26 [a]	72 [a]	..	16	16	15	19	23	11	13
5 Iceland	..	..	..	..	60	21	15	19	..	..	36	33
6 Finland	125	6 [a]	37 [a]	57 [a]	54	21	16	24	..	44	38	30
7 Netherlands	396	3 [a]	27 [a]	70 [a]	57	14	22	29	43	51	53	46
8 Japan	5,109	2 [a]	38 [a]	60 [a]	60	10	29	31	..	..	9	8
9 New Zealand	57	..	..	..	60	15	24	26	34	36	32	30
10 Sweden	229	2 [a]	32 [a]	66 [a]	55	26	14	19	33	45	41	36
11 Spain	559	3 [a]	..	..	62	16	21	22	..	39	24	23
12 Belgium	269	2 [a]	..	..	62	15	18	24	..	53	74	69
13 Austria	233	2 [a]	34 [a]	63 [a]	55	19	27	26	..	40	38	39
14 United Kingdom	1,106	2 [a]	32 [a]	66 [a]	64	21	16	15	34	44	28	29
15 Australia	349	3 [a]	28 [a]	70 [a]	60	17	23	22	22	29	20	20
16 Switzerland	301	..	..	..	59	14	23	27	..	26	36	32
17 Ireland	61	..	..	..	57	15	13	27	..	43	75	61
18 Denmark	172	4 [a]	29 [a]	67 [a]	54	25	16	21	35	44	35	29
19 Germany	2,416	..	..	..	58	20	21	23	30	34	23	22
20 Greece	91	21	36	43	74	19	19	7	..	43	22	34
21 Italy	1,087	3 [a]	31 [a]	66	62	16	18	22	..	50	26	23
22 Israel	92	..	..	..	58	29	24	13	33	45	29	40
26 Luxembourg	..	..	..	..	..	13	..	..	..	..	96	88
27 Malta	..	..	..	..	..	..	..	..	..	..	..	..
33 Portugal	102	..	..	..	65	17	28	18	..	38	28	38
37 Slovenia	19	5	39	57	58	21	22	21	..	..	56	57
39 Czech Rep.	45	6 [a]	39 [a]	55 [a]	60	20	25	20	38	42	52	56
42 Slovakia	17	6	33	61	50	20	28	30	..	..	63	61
47 Hungary	44	8	33	59	68	11	23	21	..	..	35	37
52 Poland	118	6	39	54	63	18	17	19	37	43	28	26
Medium human development	590 T	12	37	51	61	17	24	22	..	..	27	28
67 Bulgaria	12	13	34	53	61	15	21	25	29	43	49	45
68 Belarus	21	13	35	52	58	22	25	20	..	..	43	47
72 Russian Federation	345	7	38	55	58	16	25	26	16	27	22	22
74 Romania	36	21	40	39	66	12	26	21	..	32	28	32
76 Croatia	18	12	25	62	66	33	14	1	43	47	40	53
77 Estonia	4	8	28	64	58	23	27	18	..	..	75	84
79 Lithuania	7	11	36	53	63	20	19	16	24	27	58	61
80 Macedonia, FYR	2	..	..	..	82	14	15	4	..	..	37	49
92 Latvia	6	9	31	60	65	20	21	16	23	30	43	48
93 Kazakhstan	21	12	30	57	65	15	22	19	..	..	35	37
99 Armenia	2	44	35	20	116	13	9	-29	..	..	24	62
102 Ukraine	80	18	42	41	..	..	..	..	..	..	..	..
103 Turkmenistan	..	..	..	..	..	..	..	..	..	..	..	..
104 Uzbekistan	22	33 [a]	34 [a]	34 [a]	..	..	..	..	..	..	..	..
105 Albania	2	56	21	23	93	15	17	-8	18	34	14	38
108 Georgia	2	67	22	11	103	7	3	-9	..	..	17	29
109 Kyrgyzstan	3	44	24	32	67	23	16	10	..	..	26	32
110 Azerbaijan	3	27 [a]	32 [a]	41 [a]	..	..	16	4	..	..	27	39
113 Moldova, Rep. of	4	50	28	22	81	20	7	-1	..	..	35	43
118 Tajikistan	..	..	..	..	71	11	17	18	..	..	114	114
All developing countries	4,802 T	14	36	49	60	12	28	27	..	..	27	28
Industrial countries	22,788 T	3	31	66	60	16	23	24	..	33	20	19
World	27,846 T [b]	5 [b]	33 [b]	63 [b]	63 [b]	15 [b]	23 [b]	21 [b]	..	..	21 [b]	21 [b]
North America	7,521 T	2	26	72	..	16	..	..	..	23	13	15
Eastern Europe and CIS	832 T	10	37	52	61	17	23	22	..	..	31	32
Western and Southern Europe	7,722 T	3	..	..	59	19	20	22	..	42	30	27
OECD	22,940 T	3	31	66	60	16	23	25	..	33	20	19
European Union	8,382 T	3	30	67	60	19	19	21	..	43	29	27
Nordic countries	672 T	4	32	64	54	24	17	23	..	43	38	33

Note: The percentage shares of agriculture, industry and services may not necessarily add to 100 because of rounding.
a. Data refer to a year other than that specified in the column heading.
b. World Bank 1997e.
Source: Columns 1-8: World Bank 1997e; *column 10:* calculated on the basis of data from: World Bank 1997e; *columns 9, 11 and 12;* World Bank 1997d.

HDI rank	GNP (US$ billions) 1995	GNP per capita (US$) 1995	GNP annual growth rate (%) 1980-95	GNP per capita annual growth rate (%) 1965-80	GNP per capita annual growth rate (%) 1980-95	Average annual rate of inflation (%) 1985-95	Average annual rate of inflation (%) 1995	Exports as % of GDP (% annual growth rate) 1980-94	Tax revenue as % of GDP (% annual growth rate) 1980-92	Overall budget surplus/ deficit (as % of GDP) 1980	Overall budget surplus/ deficit (as % of GDP) 1995
High human development	21,746 T	24,285	2.4	3.1	1.8	3.8	2.1	2.4	1.5	-4.3	-2.5
1 Canada	574	19,380	2.4	3.3	1.1	2.9	2.9	3.2	1.2	-3.5	..
2 France	1,451	24,990	1.9	3.7	1.4	2.8	1.7	1.9	0.4	-0.1	-5.5
3 Norway	136	31,250	2.9	3.6	2.5	3.0	2.4	2.9	-0.5	-1.7	..
4 USA	7,100	26,980	2.5	1.8	1.5	3.2	2.5	2.8	(.)	-2.8	-2.3
5 Iceland	7	24,950	2.0	..	0.9	..	2.9	-0.2	..	..	..
6 Finland	105	20,580	1.6	3.6	1.2	3.8	3.1	1.7	0.9	-2.2	-13.4
7 Netherlands	371	24,000	2.2	2.7	1.6	1.7	2.1	2.2	0.3	-4.6	-4.9
8 Japan	4,964	39,640	3.1	5.1	2.7	1.4	-0.6	1.6	2.0	-7.0	(.)
9 New Zealand	52	14,340	2.0	1.7	1.0	3.9	-1.7	2.3	0.9	-6.7	0.1
10 Sweden	210	23,750	1.1	2.0	0.7	5.5	3.9	2.5	2.0	-8.1	-6.9
11 Spain	532	13,580	2.4	4.1	2.1	6.3	4.7	3.6	2.9	-4.2	(.)
12 Belgium	251	24,710	1.8	3.6	1.6	3.2	2.1	2.4	0.2	-8.2	-0.5
13 Austria	217	26,890	2.1	4.0	1.7	3.2	2.2	2.4	0.1	-3.4	-0.1
14 United Kingdom	1,095	18,700	2.1	2.0	1.9	5.1	2.8	1.1	1.0	-4.6	0.1
15 Australia	338	18,720	2.9	2.2	1.5	3.7	(.)	3.9	2.1	-1.5	-0.1
16 Switzerland	286	40,630	1.4	1.5	0.7	3.4	0.3	1.3	..	-0.2	0.1
17 Ireland	53	14,710	3.4	2.8	3.0	2.5	1.2	4.7	1.6	-12.5	-0.2
18 Denmark	156	29,890	1.9	2.2	1.8	2.8	1.5	2.4	0.7	-2.7	-2.0
19 Germany	2,252	27,510	..	3.0	..	..	..	-0.1	0.4	..	-2.5
20 Greece	86	8,210	..	4.8	..	15.4	9.0	4.8	0.8	-0.5	-15.7
21 Italy	1,088	19,020	1.8	3.2	1.7	6.0	4.7	2.8	2.8	-10.7	-10.5
22 Israel	88	15,920	4.8	3.7	2.3	17.1	9.6	1.1	-5.4	-15.6	-2.9
26 Luxembourg	17	41,210	2.7	..	1.9	..	2.1	1.0	..	..	..
27 Malta	..	..	..	..	..	..	..	-0.3	..	..	..
33 Portugal	97	9,740	2.5	4.6	2.4	11.2	3.8	3.7	1.4	-8.5	..
37 Slovenia	16	8,200	..	..	..	..	..	..	..	..	..
39 Czech Rep.	40	3,870	..	..	..	12.2	9.1	..	..	..	0.5
42 Slovakia	16	2,950	..	..	..	10.6	9.0	..	..	..	..
47 Hungary	42	4,120	0.1	5.1	0.4	19.9	24.1	-0.3	0.1	-2.8	..
52 Poland	108	2,790	0.9	..	0.3	91.8	27.4	3.2	..	..	-2.3
Medium human development	587 T	1,750	..	..	..	..	214.7	..	..	..	..
67 Bulgaria	11	1,330	0.2	..	0.5	45.9	50.5	-11.0	..	..	-5.5
68 Belarus	21	2,070	..	..	..	..	646.5	..	..	..	..
72 Russian Federation	332	2,240	-2.9	..	-3.3	148.9	190.8	..	..	..	-10.5
74 Romania	33	1,480	-0.5	..	-0.6	68.7	35.5	-1.2	..	0.5	..
76 Croatia	16	3,250	..	..	..	..	..	..	..	..	-0.9
77 Estonia	6	2,860	..	..	..	77.2	34.5	..	..	..	1.4
79 Lithuania	7	1,900	..	..	..	..	37.2	..	..	..	..
80 Macedonia, FYR	2	860	..	..	..	..	..	..	..	..	..
92 Latvia	6	2,270	-2.5	..	-2.4	72.5	23.9	..	..	..	-4.2
93 Kazakhstan	22	1,330	..	..	..	..	161.0	..	..	..	..
99 Armenia	3	730	-4.4	..	-5.6	183.1	161.2	..	..	..	..
102 Ukraine	84	1,630	..	..	..	..	412.0	..	..	..	..
103 Turkmenistan	4	920	..	..	..	..	919.5	..	..	..	..
104 Uzbekistan	22	970	..	..	..	..	369.3	..	..	..	..
105 Albania	2	670	..	..	..	27.3	10.3	-2.7	..	..	-9.9
108 Georgia	2	440	-8.8	..	-9.2	310.0	163.4	..	..	..	..
109 Kyrgyzstan	3	700	..	..	..	..	38.5	..	..	..	..
110 Azerbaijan	4	480	..	..	..	..	609.5	..	..	..	..
113 Moldova, Rep. of	4	920	..	..	..	..	..	..	..	..	..
118 Tajikistan	2	340	..	..	..	..	226.9	..	..	..	..
All developing countries	4,745 T	1,141	4.1	3.0	2.1	127.4	24.2	3.3	..	..	-1.8
Industrial countries	22,332 T	18,158	2.2	..	1.7	9.5	9.1	2.3	..	..	-2.6
World	27,077 T	4,880 [a]	2.6	..	0.9	28.6	12.1	2.5	..	..	-2.5
North America	7,674 T	26,211	2.5	1.9	1.5	3.2	2.5	2.8	..	-2.9	-2.3
Eastern Europe and CIS	809 T	2,013	..	..	..	..	170.8	..	..	..	..
Western and Southern Europe	7,314 T	22,490	1.9	3.4	1.6	4.3	3.0	2.5	1.3	-4.7	-5.6
OECD	22,535 T	20,860	2.5	3.3	1.6	4.6	3.1	2.4	1.5	-4.3	-2.4
European Union	7,980 T	21,446	2.0	3.2	1.6	4.6	3.1	2.3	1.3	-4.9	-4.8
Nordic countries	614 T	25,803	1.8	2.7	1.4	4.0	2.8	2.4	1.0	-4.5	-7.0

a. World Bank 1997e.
Source: Columns 1-9: World Bank 1997d; *columns 10 and 11:* World Bank 1997e.

47 Regional aggregates of human development indicators

	Sub-Saharan Africa	Arab States	South Asia	East Asia	East Asia excl. China	South-East Asia and Pacific	Latin America and the Caribbean	Least developed countries	All developing countries	Eastern Europe and CIS	Industrial countries[a]	World
Table 1: Human development index												
Life expectancy (years)	50.6	63.5	61.8	69.3	71.7	64.7	69.2	51.2	62.2	68.1	74.2	63.6
Adult literacy rate	56.9	56.0	50.5	82.4	96.3	87.3	86.7	49.2	70.4	98.5	98.6	77.6
Combined first-, second- and third-level gross enrolment ratio	42	58	52	65	78	61	69	36	57	75	83	62
Real GDP per capita (PPP$)	1,407	4,454	1,724	3,359	9,934	3,852	5,982	1,008	3,068	4,109	16,337	5,990
Human development index	0.386	0.636	0.462	0.676	0.883	0.683	0.831	0.344	0.586	0.756	0.911	0.772
Table 2: Gender-related development index												
Life expectancy (years)												
Female	52.2	64.9	62.1	71.5	74.9	66.2	72.3	52.3	63.6	72.9	77.9	65.3
Male	49.1	62.2	61.4	67.4	68.3	62.4	66.1	50.0	60.7	63.3	70.4	61.9
Adult literacy rate												
Female	47.9	44.2	36.9	74.1	95.0	83.2	85.1	39.3	61.7	98.5	98.5	71.4
Male	66.2	67.2	63.2	90.3	97.5	91.8	87.7	59.2	78.8	98.6	98.8	83.7
Combined first-, second- and third-level gross enrolment ratio												
Female	38.0	52.7	43.8	62.4	76.0	59.9	68.7	30.9	53.0	76.5	84.0	58.0
Male	45.5	59.9	57.7	64.3	67.4	59.2	64.8	40.3	58.9	73.3	81.6	62.5
Share of earned income												
Female	36.2	21.4	24.8	37.7	31.5	36.6	27.7	34.3	32.4	40.4	38.0	33.7
Male	63.8	78.6	75.3	62.3	68.5	63.4	72.3	65.7	67.6	59.6	62.0	66.3
Gender-related development index	0.376	0.556	0.430	0.665	0.832	0.665	0.762	0.332	0.564	0.744	0.888	0.736
Table 3: Gender empowerment measure												
Seats in parliament held by women	..	3.4	6.3	..	..	8.6	12.1	..	8.6	..	15.3	11.8
Female administrators and managers	..	..	..	..	..	..	..	..	..	..	..	..
Female professional and technical workers	..	..	..	..	..	..	..	..	..	..	..	..
Women's share of earned income	..	23	24	38	..	34	28	..	32	..	37	33
Gender empowerment measure	..	..	..	..	..	..	..	..	..	..	..	..
Table 5: Trends in human development and per capita income												
GDP per capita (1987 US$)												
1960	492	1,012	193	98	..	281	1,122	245	330	..	7,097	1,951
1970	632	1,974	234	139	..	389	1,434	272	474	..	9,344	2,660
1980	671	2,870	365	236	2,379	615	1,959	257	685	..	11,169	3,116
1990	522	1,769	461	473	4,673	810	1,795	254	736	2,411	12,310	3,298
1995	520	..	521	725	6,185	1,063	1,902	233	867	1,601	12,764	3,417
Table 7: Human poverty profile and index												
Human poverty index	..	..	..	..	..	..	..	..	..	..	..	..
People not expected to survive to age 40 (as % of total population)	31	14	16	7	4	12	10	29	14	10	5	13
Adult illiteracy rate (%)	42.0	42.8	49.5	17.8	3.7	13.2	13.3	50.8	29.6	1.5	1.4	22.4
Without access to safe water (%)	48	21	18	32	13	35	23	43	29	..	..	..
Without access to health services (%)	48	13	22	12	..	15	21	51	20	..	..	..
Without access to sanitation (%)	55	30	64	73	..	45	29	64	58	..	..	..
Underweight children under age 5 (%)	30	17	50	16	..	34	10	39[b]	30	..	..	30[b]
Children not reaching grade 5 (%)	32	7	35	8	..	17	26	36	22	3	1	21
Refugees by country of asylum (thousands)	3,547	835	3,624	297	..	157	88	3,424	8,556	943	3,890	12,446
Real GDP per capita (1985 PPP$)												
Poorest 20%	..	..	587	747	..	1,251	933	..	768	1,505	4,811	1,759
Richest 20%	..	..	2,837	5,338	..	8,266	17,380	..	6,195	9,962	32,273	12,584
Population below income poverty line (%)												
$1 a day (1985 PPP$)	..	..	..	29.4	..	14.0	23.8	..	32.2	..	..	..
National poverty line	..	..	..	11.0	..	22.2	25.9	..	..	..	..	..
Table 8: Trends in human development												
Life expectancy (years)												
1960	39.9	45.5	43.9	47.5	54.5	45.3	55.3	39.1	46.0	66.6	68.6	50.2
1995	50.6	63.5	61.8	69.3	71.7	64.7	69.2	51.2	62.2	68.1	74.2	63.6
Infant mortality rate												
1960	166	166	163	146	84	127	107	170	149	55	39	129
1996	104	55	74	37	15	48	35	109[b]	65	26	13	60[b]
Access to safe water (%)												
1975-80	..	..	..	..	..	..	60	..	..	..	..	..
1990-96	..	..	..	..	..	..	77	57	71	..	..	..
Underweight children under age five (%)												
1975	31	20	68	26	..	46	18	..	40	..	..	..
1990-97	30	17	50	16	..	34	10	39[b]	30	..	..	30[b]
Adult literacy rate (%)												
1970	31	31	32	53	85	66	74	30	48	..	..	..
1995	57	56	51	82	96	87	87	49	70	99	99	78
Gross enrolment ratio for all levels (% age 6-23)												
1980	39	47	37	51	65	51	59	32	46	..	..	..
1995	42	58	52	65	78	61	69	36	57	75	83	62
Real GDP per capita (PPP$)												
1960	996	..	698	729	..	732	2,137	562	915	..	..	..
1995	1,407	4,454	1,724	3,359	9,934	3,852	5,982	1,008	3,068	4,109	16,337	5,990

	Sub-Saharan Africa	Arab States	South Asia	East Asia	East Asia excl. China	South-East Asia and Pacific	Latin America and the Caribbean	Least developed countries	All developing countries	Eastern Europe and CIS	Industrial countries[a]	World
Table 9: South-North gaps (index: North=100)												
Life expectancy												
1960	58	66	64	69	78	66	81	57	67	..	100	..
1995	68	86	83	93	96	87	93	69	84	..	100	..
Adult literacy												
1970	31	31	33	54	..	67	74	30	48	..	100	..
1995	58	57	51	84	98	89	88	50	71	..	100	..
Daily calorie supply per capita												
1970	74	73	69	68	89	65	83	69	71	..	100	..
1995	71	92	76	86	91	80	88	67	82	..	100	..
Access to safe water												
1975-80	..	..	..	..	..	..	60	..	..	..	100	..
1990-96	..	..	..	..	..	..	78	..	..	..	100	..
Under-five mortality rate												
1960	19	20	21	24	39	26	31	18	23	..	100	..
1996	9	21	14	35	81	23	36	10	17	..	100	..
Table 10: Women's access to education												
Female net enrolment ratio												
Primary												
1995	..	79	..	98	97	..	..	..	..	97	98	..
Index (1985=100)	..	116	..	..	..	..	..	..	..	..	..	..
Secondary												
1995	..	..	..	92	92	..	..	..	..	..	90	..
Index (1985=100)	..	..	..	..	..	..	..	..	..	..	..	..
Female tertiary students												
Per 100,000 women	228	1,063	432	441	3,244	1,204	1,668	168	679	2,737	3,717	1,369
Index (1985=100)	..	..	140	161	..	..	..	..	..	..	123	..
Female tertiary natural and applied science students (as % of female students)	..	30	..	18	18	28	31	..	..	33	27	..
Table 11: Women's participation in economic and political life												
Female administrators and managers (%)	..	..	..	..	..	..	..	..	..	37	..	..
Female professional and technical workers (%)	..	..	..	..	..	..	..	..	..	50	..	..
Female sales and service workers (%)	..	..	..	..	..	..	..	..	..	55	..	..
Female clerical workers (%)	..	..	..	..	..	..	..	..	..	69	..	..
Women in government (%)												
total	6	2	5	4	1	6	11	5	5	4	13	7
at ministerial level	7	1	4	6	3	4	7	6	5	3	11	7
at subministerial level	6	2	5	3	1	6	12	4	5	4	13	7
Female unpaid family workers (as % of total)	57	40	29	81	81	63	38	41	48	..	75	58
Female economic activity rate (as % of male rate)	74	36	48	82	70	74	51	76	64	90	79	68
Table 12: Child survival and development												
Infant mortality rate	104	55	74	37	15	48	35	109[b]	65	26	13	60[b]
Under-five mortality rate	169	73	109	46	20	68	43	171[b]	95	33	16	88[b]
Pregnant women aged 15-49 with anaemia (%)	..	..	..	..	..	..	..	..	..	..	..	..
Births attended by trained health personnel (%)	39	57	32	85	99	56	80	29[b]	58	..	99	57[b]
Low-birth-weight infants (%)	16	11	32	9	..	15	10	22	18	..	7	17
Maternal mortality rate	975	396	551	95	98	449	191	1,100[b]	488	62	30	430[b]
Mothers exclusively breast-feeding at three months (%)	31	..	47	64	..	37	38	46	45	..	..	..
Oral rehydration therapy use rate (%)	81[b]	66	71	85	..	95	59	80[b]	76[b]	..	..	76[b]
Underweight children under age 5 (%)	30	17	50	16	..	25	10	39[b]	30	..	..	30[b]
Table 13: Health profile												
One-year-olds fully immunized												
against tuberculosis (%)	70	91	94	96	80	94	93	80	89	94	92	89
against measles (%)	56	83	79	96	79	86	78	60	79	91	86	79
AIDS cases (per 100,000)	11.2	0.4	0.1	..	..	4.0	6.4	7.4	3.5	0.3	5.0	3.9
Tuberculosis cases (per 100,000)	84.2	60.5	101.6	31.1	..	87.4	47.9	69.9	68.6	51.3	27.6	59.7
Malaria cases (per 100,000)	..	125	226	6	..	1,008	249	6,765	954	..	..	..
Cigarette consumption per adult (1970-72=100)	121	159	134	243	119	147	91	156	160	..	90	115
Doctors (per 100,000)	16	107	44	116	..	19	136	14	76	354	287	122
Nurses (per 100,000)	78	180	24	94	..	75	62	26	85	809	780	241
People with disabilities (%)	..	2.0	0.8	4.9	..	1.7	..	..	2.6	..	..	..
Public expenditure on health												
as % of GNP (1960)	0.7	1.0	0.5	1.0	..	0.5	1.3	..	1.0	..	..	..
as % of GDP (1990)	2.4	2.9	1.4	2.2	..	1.0	2.4	1.9	2.0	..	..	..

	Sub-Saharan Africa	Arab States	South Asia	East Asia	East Asia excl. China	South-East Asia and Pacific	Latin America and the Carib-bean	Least developed countries	All develop-ing countries	Eastern Europe and CIS	Industrial countries[a]	World
Table 14: Food security												
Daily per capita calorie supply												
1970	2,225	2,206	2,094	2,041	2,695	1,957	2,491	2,090	2,131	..	3,016	2,337
1995	2,237	2,903	2,385	2,717	2,864	2,533	2,781	2,103	2,572	2,882	3,157	2,702
Per capita supply of cereals												
Total (kg)	119	209	165	182	158	171	124	143	165	163	130	157
Change (%), 1970-95	6	29	11	14	-21	22	6	12	14	..	1	11
Daily per capita supply of fat												
Total (grams)	47	70	44	67	74	49	78	35	58	84	117	71
Change (%), 1970-95	6	54	45	185	120	65	41	16	77	..	20	48
Daily per capita supply of protein												
Total (grams)	52	77	59	72	83	60	72	50	65	88	99	73
Change (%), 1970-95	-3	31	14	45	13	33	12	-1	25	-3	11	20
Food production per capita index (1980=100)	99	106	122	210	122	127	111	94	139	..	103	132
Food imports (as % of merchandise imports)	..	..	..	5	..	..	9	..	..	..	..	..
Food aid in cereals (thousands of metric tons)	2,324	636	1,625	..	..	205	1,134	3,290	5,935	..	..	..
Food consumption (as % of total household consumption)	..	..	..	..	..	..	..	..	..	..	..	..
Table 15: Education imbalances												
Gross enrolment ratio												
Primary												
Total	75	90	97	117	100	109	111	70	101	98	101	101
Female as % of male	80	84	78	98	101	95	98	76	87	99	99	89
Secondary												
Total	25	52	44	68	96	51	53	17	50	87	99	58
Female as % of male	76	81	66	89	103	88	109	69	81	104	102	85
Tertiary natural and applied science enrolment (as % of total tertiary)	..	..	..	37.5	38.6	27.4	28.7	..	..	43.2	32.5	..
R & D scientists and technicians (per 1,000)	..	..	0.3	0.6	2.5	..	0.4	..	0.4	3.1	3.8	1.3
Public expenditure on education												
as % of GNP												
1985	5.2	5.7	3.3	3.1	..	..	3.8	..	4.1	..	5.1	4.9
1995	6.3	5.1	3.6	2.7	3.5	..	4.5	..	3.8	4.9	5.2	4.9
as % of total government expenditure	..	..	..	..	..	..	..	..	..	..	..	..
Public expenditure (as % of all levels)												
on primary and secondary education	..	..	..	..	..	..	..	..	..	..	..	..
on higher education	..	..	..	..	..	..	..	..	..	..	..	..
Table 16: Profile of people in work												
Labour force (as % of total population)	44	34	42	59	50	48	42	47	48	50	49	48
Women's share of adult labour force												
1970	43	22	33	41	37	38	23	43	37	48	40	38
1995	47	27	34	46	41	44	35	48	41	47	44	41
Labour force in agriculture (%)												
1970	78	61	73	77	47	70	42	85	72	29	18	56
1990	67	39	62	70	23	59	26	76	61	19	10	49
Labour force in industry (%)												
1970	8	14	12	11	24	9	22	5	12	38	38	19
1990	9	22	16	16	34	14	24	9	16	39	33	20
Labour force in services (%)												
1970	14	25	15	12	29	21	36	10	17	34	45	25
1990	25	39	21	14	43	27	51	15	23	42	57	31
Real earnings per employee annual growth rate												
1970-80	..	..	..	..	..	..	..	..	..	..	..	..
1980-92	..	..	1.7	..	..	..	..	..	..	..	..	..
Table 17: Access to information and communications												
Radios (per 1,000)	166	264	88	215	707	156	384	113	185	412	1005	364[c]
Televisions (per 1,000)	35	138	55	248	255	150	223	32	145	317	524	228
Printing and writing paper consumed (metric tons per 1,000)	1.6	2.9	1.9	7.5	38.5	6.8	10.7	0.4	5.2	6.7	78.2	20.9
Post offices (per 100,000)	..	..	16.9	..	..	6.0	..	..	..	..	..	..
Main telephone lines (per 1,000)	12	49	16	49	304	29	86	3	39	158	414	122[d]
Public pay phones (per 1,000)	0.2	0.4	0.2	0.9	4.2	0.6	1.9	(.)	0.7	1.1	3.7	1.4
International telephone calls (minutes per person)	1.6	9.0	0.5	2.8	41.9	4.0	5.3	0.5	2.8	6.5	41.6	10.9
Fax machines (per 1,000)	0.2	1.5	..	0.5	..	0.3	..	0.1	..	1.2	23.2	..
Cellular mobile telephone subscribers (per 1,000)	..	3.1	0.2	4.8	..	6.7	7.5	..	3.6	1.8	61.1	16.8[d]
Internet users (per 1,000)	..	0.2	(.)	0.5	..	0.6	1.3	..	0.5	2.6	17.9	4.8[d]
Personal computers (per 1,000)	..	5.7	1.2	6.5	..	8.3	17.5	..	6.5	18.2	156.3	43.6[d]

	Sub-Saharan Africa	Arab States	South Asia	East Asia	East Asia excl. China	South-East Asia and Pacific	Latin America and the Caribbean	Least developed countries	All developing countries	Eastern Europe and CIS	Industrial countries[a]	World
Table 19: Military expenditure and resource use imbalances												
Defence expenditure												
US$ millions												
1985	9,592	65,733	31,512	41,421	14,314	15,334	18,670	5,436	185,515	..	628,981	814,496
1996	7,179	37,433	18,461	55,196	20,512	21,335	25,064	5,348	171,934	81,117	609,149	781,093
as % of GDP												
1985	3	12	15	7	..	6	2	4	7	..	4	5
1996	2	..	4	5	..	3	2	3	4	5	3	3
per capita (US$)												
1985	24	353	30	37	232	39	48	13	51	..	728	182
1996	13	151	14	42	292	43	52	10	39	204	493	137
Military expenditure (as % of combined education and health expenditure)												
1960	..	..	89	363	..	127	56	..	102	..	110	109
1990-91	44	108	61	85	..	66	29	72	63	..	33	38
Imports of conventional weapons												
US$ millions	..	..	1,754	3,684	..	1,411	..	..	..	..	..	..
Index (1991=100)	..	..	105	675	..	..	..	..	..	..	..	..
Armed forces												
Thousands	933	2,257	2,520	4,670	1,735	1,859	1,330	1,323	14,105	2,910	7,047	21,152
Index (1985=100)	105	106	115	87	118	88	100	123	96	..	78	91
Table 20: Financial inflows and outflows												
External debt												
US$ billions	224[e]	158	173	119	..	278	601	136[e]	1,583	264	..	..
as % of GNP	81[e]	..	35	17	..	50	38	113[e]	41	30	..	..
Debt service ratio												
1980	11	..	10	..	..	..	39	..	24	..	..	..
1995	15[e]	..	24	10	..	14	27	..	19	9	..	..
Net ODA received												
US$ millions	16,578[f]	5,350	5,229	2,729	112	4,663	5,571	14,235[f]	58,480 [f, g]	193	..	..
as % of 1995 GNP	5.2	1.3	1.2	0.2	(.)	0.8	0.4	14.2[f]	0.9	..	..	..
per capita (US$)	28.0[f]	23.6	4.1	2.1	1.4	9.7	14.8	25.0[f]	9.0[f]	..	..	..
Net foreign direct investment (as % of GNP)	0.8	-0.1	0.4	3.1	..	3.3	1.4	1.3	1.8	1.8	-0.5	-0.1
Trade (as % of GDP)	61	80	31	78	..	91	29	54	56	70	39	42
Export-import ratio	60	96	73	98	98	96	86	64	91	97	102	–
Terms of trade (1987=100)	95	91	134	97	..	93	95	89	97	..	103	–
Current account balance (US$ millions)	-8,901	-15,395	-9,745	-6,594	..	-13,368	-31,954	-4,999	-88,167	-4,497	473	–
Table 21: Growing urbanization												
Urban population (as % of total)												
1970	19	39	20	19	48	20	57	13	25	54	67	37
1995	32	54	28	33	76	33	73	23	37	66	74	45
2015	44	66	38	48	84	46	80	35	49	72	79	55
Urban population annual growth rate												
1970-95	5	4	4	4	3	4	3	5	4	2	1	3
1995-2015	4	3	3	3	1	3	2	5	3	1	1	2
Population in cities of more than 750,000												
as % of total population	12	22	12	14	47	10	33	10	16	18	30	19
as % of urban population	38	40	43	43	61	31	45	41	41	27	40	41
Table 22: Population trends												
Estimated population (millions)												
1970	268.2	119.9	740.7	882.1	51.4	289.4	279.8	285.7	2,616.1	338.3	1,043.5	3,659.6
1995	543.4	241.6	1,293.3	1,295.8	75.6	486.9	471.5	542.5	4,394.0	400.8	1,233.1	5,627.1
2015	919.7	371.8	1,768.0	1,498.0	88.9	636.4	618.8	873.7	5,892.2	403.5	1,294.7	7,186.9
Population growth rate												
1970-95	2.9	2.8	2.3	1.6	1.6	2.1	2.1	2.6	2.1	0.7	0.7	1.7
1995-2015	2.7	2.2	1.6	0.7	0.8	1.4	1.4	2.4	1.5	(.)	0.2	1.2
Population doubling date	2020	2023	2034	2071	2057	2038	2039	2022	2037	..	2223	2046
Crude birth rate	43.1	31.9	28.2	17.2	17.2	25.4	23.9	39.2	26.1	13.3	12.6	23.2
Crude death rate	14.9	7.7	9.2	7.1	6.1	7.7	6.5	14.1	8.7	11.8	10.1	9.0
Dependency ratio	93.2	77.2	70.2	47.7	42.2	63.4	63.1	88.8	63.9	52.9	50.5	60.8
Total fertility rate	6.0	4.4	3.5	1.9	1.8	3.0	2.8	5.3	3.2	1.8	1.7	2.9
Contraceptive prevalence rate	16	37	41	82	74	53	64	22	56	..	70	58

47 Regional aggregates of human development indicators (continued)

	Sub-Saharan Africa	Arab States	South Asia	East Asia	East Asia excl. China	South-East Asia and Pacific	Latin America and the Caribbean	Least developed countries	All developing countries	Eastern Europe and CIS	Industrial countries[a]	World
Table 23: Energy use												
Electricity consumption												
Total (millions of kilowatt-hours)	254,533	327,408	575,519	1,283,617	278,091	278,333	771,609	43,741	3,574,530	1,671,471	9,300,133	12,874,663
Index (1980=100)	173	331	357	329	312	380	212	154	284	..	147	174
Per capita (kilowatt-hours)												
1980	427	650	173	368	1,429	201	1,025	76	387	..	6,601	1,566
1995	476	1,355	445	991	3,679	572	1,636	81	814	4,170	7,542	2,290
Traditional fuels (as % of total consumption)												
1980	45	8	31	8	5	47	21	77	22	..	1	7
1995	48	3	21	5	1	30	16	84	15	2	3	7
Household energy from fuelwood (%)	..	..	..	..	..	..	..	..	..	..	..	..
Commercial energy use												
Total (millions of metric tons)												
1980	92	130	148	493	80	74	312	19	1,281	1,231	4,920	6,201
1994	131	278	363	966	175	207	445	28	2,450	1,193	5,468	7,917
Per capita (kg)												
1980	265	813	159	465	1,279	204	878	53	393	3,936	4,587	1,431
1994	251	1,178	286	753	2,340	433	960	53	568	2,979	4,452	1,429
GDP per kg (US$)												
1980	2.0	3.4	2.3	0.5	2.2	2.4	2.2	5.1	1.7	..	2.3	2.2
1994	1.9	..	1.8	1.0	2.2	2.3	2.0	5.1	1.5	0.5	2.8	2.4
Commercial energy imports (as % of energy consumption)												
1980	-124	-741	-12	5	51	-83	-28	19	-94	3	24	..
1994	-118	-305	-18	13	75	-30	-38	-97	-47	-14	19	..
Table 24: Profile of environmental degradation												
Land area (millions of hectares)	2,055	1,186	575	1,108	179	486	2,007	1,866	7,495	2,294	5,354	12,849
Forest and woodland (as % of land area)	23	4	14	14	13	50	47	23	26	37	28	27
Internal renewable water resources per capita (cubic metres per year)	6,283	546	2,854	2,228	2,178	11,895	21,497	9,940	5,975	13,124	10,804	6,918[h]
Annual fresh water withdrawals												
as % of water resources	1.5	140.2	16.4	17.0	26.8	2.0	1.9	1.4	6.3	8.2	9.5	7.3[h]
per capita (cubic metres)	132	926	658	471	649	315	510	186	496	1100	1069	626[h]
Annual rate of deforestation	..	..	..	..	..	..	..	..	..	..	..	-0.3[h]
Annual rate of reforestation	..	..	..	..	..	..	..	..	..	..	..	..
CO_2 emissions per capita (metric tons)	1.0	3.7	1.0	3.0	8.9	1.6	2.6	0.2	2.0	8.9	11.4	4.1
Loss of mangroves (%)	..	..	..	..	..	..	..	..	..	..	..	..
Table 25: National income accounts												
GDP (US$ billions)	274	381	431	1,298	600	638	1,614	93	4,801	832	22,788	27,846[i]
Agriculture (as % of GDP)	18	..	29	14	..	14	11	36	14	10	3	5[i]
Industry (as % of GDP)	31	..	27	43	..	39	33	21	36	37	31	33[i]
Services (as % of GDP)	52	..	43	43	..	47	56	43	49	52	66	63[i]
Consumption (as % of GDP)												
Private	65	..	70	50	..	55	67	..	60	61	60	63[i]
Government	17	..	11	11	..	10	13	..	12	17	16	15[i]
Gross domestic investment (as % of GDP)	19	..	23	39	..	37	20	..	28	23	23	23[i]
Gross domestic savings (as % of GDP)	17	..	20	39	..	33	20	..	27	22	24	21[i]
Tax revenue (as % of GDP)	..	..	11	..	..	..	..	..	..	..	..	..
Central government expenditure (as % of GDP)	..	..	18	..	..	16	28	..	..	..	33	..
Exports (as % of GDP)	27	..	14	39	..	43	14	..	27	31	20	21[i]
Imports (as % of GDP)	29	..	17	39	..	48	14	..	28	32	19	21[i]
Table 26: Trends in economic performance												
GNP (US$ billions)	276	401	426	1,323	578	617	1,533	100	4,745	809	22,332	27,077
GNP per capita (US$)	518	2,162	346	1,055	10,806	1,407	3,313	215	1,141	2,013	18,158	4,880[i]
GNP growth rate (1980-95)	1.6	1.5	4.6	9.3	..	6.3	1.6	2.1	4.1	..	2.2	2.6
GNP per capita growth rate												
1965-80	1.5	2.7	1.4	4.2	5.1	3.6	3.9	0.4	3.0	..	1.7	0.9
1980-95	-1.3	-1.2	2.3	7.8	..	4.3	-0.4	-0.4	2.1	..	1.7	0.9
Average annual rate of inflation												
1985-95	24.3	..	9.6	8.7	7.9	17.0	399.0	39.9	127.4	..	9.5	28.6
1995	52.8	..	17.3	10.1	5.4	8.5	41.3	102.9	24.2	170.8	9.1	12.1
Exports as % of GDP, growth rate	0.1	..	3.7	3.1	3.3	2.0	3.9	0.7	3.3	..	2.3	2.5
Tax revenue as % of GDP, growth rate	..	..	0.9	..	..	..	-1.2	..	..	..	..	..
Overall budget surplus/deficit (as % of GDP)												
1980	..	..	-6.1	..	..	-2.8	-2.1	..	..	..	..	..
1995	..	..	-5.2	-1.4	..	0.6	..	..	-1.8	..	-2.6	-2.5

Note: Columns 1-9 are for developing countries only.
a. Includes Eastern Europe and CIS.
b. UNICEF 1998b.
c. UNESCO 1998.
d. ITU 1997a.
e. World Bank 1997b.
f. OECD 1998.
g. Total net ODA to countries and territories on Part I of the OECD Development Assistance Committee List of Aid Recipients.
h. WRI 1998.
i. World Bank 1997e.

	International covenant on economic, social and cultural rights 1966	International covenant on civil and political rights 1966	International convention on the elimination of all forms of racial discrimination 1969	Convention on the prevention and punishment of the crime of genocide 1948	Convention on the rights of the child 1989	Convention on the elimination of all forms of discrimination against women 1979	Convention against torture and other cruel, inhuman or degrading treatment or punishment 1984	Convention relating to the status of refugees 1951
Afghanistan	●	●	●	●	●	○	●	
Albania					●	●		●
Algeria	●	●	●	●	●	●	●	●
Andorra					●	●		
Angola	●	●			●	●		●
Antigua and Barbuda			●		●	●	●	●
Argentina	●	●	●	●	●	●	●	●
Armenia	●	●	●	●	●	●	●	●
Australia	●	●	●	●	●	●	●	●
Austria	●	●	●	●	●	●	●	●
Azerbaijan	●	●	●	●	●	●	●	●
Bahamas			●	●	●	●		●
Bahrain			●		●	●	●	
Bangladesh			●		●	●	●	
Barbados	●	●	●	●	●	●		●
Belarus	●	●	●	●	●	●	●	
Belgium	●	●	●	●	●	●	○	●
Belize		●			●	●	●	●
Benin	●	●	○		●	●	●	●
Bhutan			○		●	●		
Bolivia	●	●	●	○	●	●	○	●
Bosnia Herzegovina	●	●	●	●	●	●	●	●
Botswana			●		●	●	●	●
Brazil	●	●	●	●	●	●	●	●
Brunei Darussalam					●			
Bulgaria	●	●	●	●	●	●	●	●
Burkina Faso			●	●	●	●	●	●
Burundi	●	●	●	●	●	●	●	●
Cambodia	●	●	●	●	●	●		●
Cameroon	●	●	●		●	●	●	●
Canada	●	●	●	●	●	●	●	●
Cape Verde	●	●	●		●	●	●	
Central African Rep.	●	●	●		●	●		●
Chad	●	●	●		●	●	●	●
Chile	●	●	●	●	●	●	●	●
China	○		●	●	●	●	●	●
Colombia	●	●	●	●	●	●	●	●
Comoros					●	●		
Congo	●	●	●		●	●		●
Cook Islands					●			
Costa Rica	●	●	●	●	●	●	●	●
Côte d'Ivoire	●	●	●	●	●	●	●	●
Croatia	●	●	●	●	●	●	●	●
Cuba			●	●	●	●	●	
Cyprus	●	●	●	●	●	●	●	●
Czech Rep.	●	●	●	●	●	●	●	●
Dem. Rep. of the Congo	●	●	●	●	●	●	●	●
Denmark	●	●	●	●	●	●	●	●
Djibouti					●			●
Dominica	●	●			●	●		●
Dominican Rep.	●	●	●	○	●	●	○	●
Ecuador	●	●	●	●	●	●	●	●
Egypt	●	●	●	●	●	●	●	●
El Salvador	●	●	●	●	●	●		●
Equatorial Guinea					●	●		
Eritrea					●			
Estonia	●	●			●	●	●	●
Ethiopia	●	●	●	●	●	●	●	●
Fiji			●		●	●		●
Finland	●	●	●	●	●	●	●	●
France	●	●	●	●	●	●	●	●
Gabon	●	●	●	●	●	●	○	●
Gambia	●	●	●	●	●	●	○	●
Georgia	●	●	●	●	●	●	●	●
Germany	●	●	●	●	●	●	●	●

	International covenant on economic, social and cultural rights 1966	International covenant on civil and political rights 1966	International convention on the elimination of all forms of racial discrimination 1969	Convention on the prevention and punishment of the crime of genocide 1948	Convention on the rights of the child 1989	Convention on the elimination of all forms of discrimination against women 1979	Convention against torture and other cruel, inhuman or degrading treatment or punishment 1984	Convention relating to the status of refugees 1951
Ghana			●	●	●	●		●
Greece	●	●	●	●	●	●	●	●
Grenada	●	●	○		●	●		●
Guatemala	●	●	●	●	●	●	●	●
Guinea	●	●	●		●	●	●	●
Guinea-Bissau	●				●	●		●
Guyana	●	●	●		●	●	●	●
Haiti		●	●	●	●	●		●
Holy See			●		●			●
Honduras	●	●		●	●	●	●	●
Hungary	●	●	●	●	●	●	●	●
Iceland	●	●	●	●	●	●	●	●
India	●	●	●	●	●	●	○	
Indonesia					●	●	○	
Iran, Islamic Rep. of	●	●	●	●	●			
Iraq	●	●	●	●	●	●		
Ireland	●	●	○	●	●	●	●	●
Israel	●	●	●	●	●	●	●	●
Italy	●	●	●	●	●	●	●	●
Jamaica	●	●	●	●	●	●		●
Japan	●	●			●	●		●
Jordan	●	●	●	●	●	●	●	
Kazakhstan					●			
Kenya	●	●			●	●	●	●
Kiribati					●			
Korea, Dem. People's Rep. of	●	●		●	●			
Korea, Rep. of	●	●	●	●	●	●	●	●
Kuwait	●	●	●	●	●	●	●	
Kyrgyzstan	●	●	●	●	●	●	●	
Lao People's Dem. Rep.			●		●	●		
Latvia	●	●	●	●	●	●		●
Lebanon	●	●	●	●	●	●		
Lesotho	●	●	●	●	●	●		●
Liberia	○	○	●	●	●	●		●
Libyan Arab Jamahiriya	●	●	●	●	●	●	●	
Liechtenstein				●	●	●	●	●
Lithuania	●	●		●	●	●	●	●
Luxembourg	●	●	●	●	●	●	●	●
Macedonia, FYR	●	●	●	●	●	●	●	●
Madagascar	●	●	●		●	●		●
Malawi	●	●	●		●	●	●	●
Malaysia				●	●	●		
Maldives			●	●	●	●		
Mali	●	●	●	●	●	●		●
Malta	●	●	●		●	●	●	●
Marshall Islands					●			
Mauritania			●		●			●
Mauritius	●	●	●		●	●	●	
Mexico	●	●	●	●	●	●	●	
Micronesia, Federal States of					●			
Moldova, Rep. of	●	●	●	●	●	●	●	
Monaco	●	●	●	●	●		●	●
Mongolia	●	●	●	●	●	●		
Morocco	●	●	●	●	●	●	●	●
Mozambique			●		●	●	●	
Myanmar				●	●	●		
Namibia	●	●	●	●	●	●	●	●
Nauru					●			
Nepal	●	●	●		●	●	●	●
Netherlands	●	●	●	●	●	●	●	●
New Zealand	●	●	●	●	●	●	○	●
Nicaragua	●	●	●	●	●	●	○	●
Niger	●	●	●		●			●
Nigeria	●	●	●		●	●	○	●
Niue					●			

	International covenant on economic, social and cultural rights 1966	International covenant on civil and political rights 1966	International convention on the elimination of all forms of racial discrimination 1969	Convention on the prevention and punishment of the crime of genocide 1948	Convention on the rights of the child 1989	Convention on the elimination of all forms of discrimination against women 1979	Convention against torture and other cruel, inhuman or degrading treatment or punishment 1984	Convention relating to the status of refugees 1951
Norway	●	●	●	●	●	●	●	●
Oman					●			
Pakistan			●	●	●	●		
Palau					●			
Panama	●	●	●	●	●	●	●	●
Papua New Guinea			●	●	●	●		●
Paraguay	●	●	●	○	●	●	●	●
Peru	●	●	●	●	●	●	●	●
Philippines	●	●	●	●	●	●	●	●
Poland	●	●	●		●	●	●	●
Portugal	●	●	●		●	●	●	●
Qatar			●		●			
Romania	●	●	●	●	●	●	●	●
Russian Federation	●	●	●	●	●	●	●	●
Rwanda	●	●	●	●	●	●		●
Saint Kitts and Nevis					●	●		
Saint Lucia					●	●		
Saint Vincent	●	●	●	●	●	●		●
Samoa (Western)					●	●		
San Marino	●	●			●			
São Tomé and Principe	○	○			●	○		●
Saudi Arabia			●	●	●		●	
Senegal	●	●	●	●	●	●	●	●
Seychelles	●	●	●	●	●	●	●	●
Sierra Leone	●	●	●		●	●	○	●
Singapore				●	●	●		●
Slovakia	●	●	●	●	●	●	●	●
Slovenia	●	●	●	●	●	●	●	●
Solomon Islands	●		●		●			●
Somalia	●	●	●		●		●	●
South Africa	○	○	○	●	●	●	○	●
Spain	●	●	●	●	●	●	●	●
Sri Lanka	●	●	●		●	●	●	●
Sudan	●	●	●		●		○	●
Suriname	●	●	●		●	●		●
Swaziland			●		●			
Sweden	●	●	●		●	●	●	●
Switzerland	●	●	●		●	●	●	●
Syrian Arab Rep.	●	●	●	●	●		●	
Tajikistan			●		●	●	●	
Tanzania, U. Rep. of	●	●	●	●	●	●		●
Thailand		●			●	●		
Togo	●	●	●	●	●	●	●	●
Tonga			●	●	●			
Trinidad and Tobago	●	●	●		●	●		●
Tunisia	●	●	●	●	●	●	●	●
Turkey			○	●	●	●	●	●
Turkmenistan	●	●	●		●			
Tuvalu					●			●
Uganda	●	●	●	●	●	●	●	●
Ukraine	●	●	●	●	●	●	●	●
United Arab Emirates			●		●			
United Kingdom	●	●	●	●	●	●	●	●
USA	○	●	●	●	○	○	●	
Uruguay	●	●	●	●	●	●	●	●
Uzbekistan	●	●	●		●	●	●	
Vanuatu					●	●		
Venezuela	●	●	●	●	●	●	●	●
Vietnam	●	●	●	●	●	●		
Yemen	●	●	●	●	●	●	●	●
Yugoslavia	●	●	●	●	●	●	●	●
Zambia	●	●	●		●	●		●
Zimbabwe	●	●	●	●	●	●		●
Total states parties	137	140	150	124	191	161	104	131
Signatures not followed by ratification	5	3	6	3	1	3	12	0
States that have not ratified and not signed	51	50	37	66	1	29	77	62

● Ratification, accession, approval, notification or succession, acceptance or definitive signature.
○ Signature not yet followed by ratification.
Note: Status is as of 1 February 1998.
Source: UN 1997d.

Primary statistical references

Brewers and Licensed Retailers Association. 1997. *Statistical Handbook 1997.* London.

CDIAC (Carbon Dioxide Information Analysis Center). 1998. Data available at http://www.cdiac.ESD. ORNL.GOV/ftp/ndp001r7. January.

Eurostat and UN (United Nations). 1995. *Women and Men in Europe and North America.* Geneva.

FAO (Food and Agriculture Organization of the United Nations). 1996a. *Production Yearbook.* FAO Statistics Series. Rome

———. 1997a. Correspondence on daily per capita calorie supply. Received July. Rome.

———. 1997b. *Report of the World Food Summit.* Rome.

———. 1997c. *The State of the World's Forests 1997.* Rome.

———. 1998. Food Balance Sheets. Available at http://apps.fao.org/lim500/nphwrap.pl? FoodBalanceSheet &Domain=FoodBalanceSheet. February.

IDEA (Institute for Democracy and Electoral Assistance). 1997. *Voter Turnout from 1945 to 1997: A Global Report.* Stockholm.

IISS (International Institute for Strategic Studies). 1993. *The Military Balance 1993–94.* London: Brasseys.

———. 1997. *The Military Balance 1997–98.* London: Oxford University Press.

ILO (International Labour Office). 1994. *World Labour Report 1994.* Geneva.

———. 1995a. *World Labour Report 1995.* Geneva.

———. 1996. *Estimates and Projections of the Economically Active Population, 1950–2010.* 4th ed. Diskette. Geneva.

———. 1997a. *World Labour Report 1997–98.* Geneva.

———. 1997b. *Yearbook of Labour Statistics 1997.* Geneva.

IPU (Inter-Parliamentary Union). 1997a. Data available at http://www.ipu.org. December.

———. 1997b. *Democracy Still in the Making.* Geneva.

———. 1998. Correspondence on political participation. Received February. Geneva

ITU (International Telecommunication Union). 1996. *World Telecommunication Indicators.* Diskette. Geneva.

———. 1997a. *World Telecommunication Development Report 1996–97.* Geneva.

———. 1997b. *World Telecommunication Indicators.* Diskette. Geneva.

Keesing's Worldwide (formerly Worldwide Government Directories). 1995. *Worldwide Government Directory with International Organizations.* Bethesda, Md.

OECD (Organisation for Economic Co-operation and Development). 1994. *Development Co-operation: Development Assistance Committee Report 1994.* Paris.

———. 1995a. *Development Co-operation: Development Assistance Committee Report 1995.* Paris.

———. 1995b. *Employment Outlook.* Paris.

———. 1995e. *OECD Health Data 1995.* Paris.

———. 1997c. *Education at a Glance 1997.* Paris.

———. 1997d. *Employment Outlook.* Paris.

———. 1997e. *Environmental Data: Compendium 1997.* Paris.

———. 1997f. *Geographical Distribution of Financial Flows to Aid Recipients.* Paris.

———. 1997h. *Short-term Economic Indicators: Transition Economies.* Paris.

———. 1998. *Development Co-operation: Development Assistance Committee Report 1997.* Paris.

OECD (Organisation for Economic Co-operation and Development) and Statistics Canada. 1995. *Literacy, Economy and Society.* Paris and Ottawa.

OECD (Organisation for Economic Co-operation and Development), Human Resource Development Canada and Statistics Canada. 1997. *Literacy Skills for the Knowledge Society: Further Results from the International Adult Literacy Survey.* Paris and Ottawa.

Psacharopolous, George, and Zafiris Tzannatos, eds. 1992. *Case Studies on Women's Employment and Pay in Latin America.* Washington, DC: World Bank.

SIPRI (Stockholm International Peace Research Institute). 1997. *SIPRI Yearbook 1997.* New York: Oxford University Press.

Smeeding, Timothy. 1997. *Financial Poverty in Developed Countries: The Evidence from the Luxembourg Income Study (LIS).* Final report to UNDP. Luxembourg.

Summers, Robert, and Alan Heston. 1991. "Penn World Tables (Mark 5): An Expanded Set of International Comparisons, 1950–1988." *Quarterly Journal of Economics* 106: 327–68.

UN (United Nations). 1993. "Statistical Chart on World Families." Statistical Division and the Secretariat for the International Year of the Family. New York.

———. 1994d. *Women's Indicators and Statistics Database.* Version 3 CD-ROM. Statistical Division. New York.

———. 1994e. "World Population Prospects 1950–2050: The 1994 Revision." Database. Population Division. New York.

———. 1995b. *The World's Women 1970–95: Trends and Statistics.* New York.

———. 1996d. "World Population Prospects 1950–2050: The 1996 Revision." Database. Population Division. New York.

———. 1996e. "World Urbanization Prospects: The 1996 Revision." Database. Population Division. New York.

———. 1997b. *Energy Statistics Yearbook 1995.* New York.

———. 1997d. *Multilateral Treaties Deposited with the Secretary-General.* New York. Available at http://www.un.org/Depts/Treaty.

———. 1997f. *World Contraceptive Use 1997.* Population Division. New York.

———. 1997i. "World Population Prospects: The 1996 Revision." Population Division. New York.

UNAIDS and WHO (Joint United Nations Programme on HIV/AIDS). 1997. *Report on the Global HIV/AIDS Epidemic.* Geneva (December).

UNCSDHA (United Nations Centre for Social Development and Humanitarian Affairs). 1995a. "Results of the Fourth United Nations Survey of Crime Trends and Operations of the Criminal Justice System (1986–90)—Interim Report by the Secretariat." Vienna.

———. 1995b. "Interim Report by the Secretariat." Vienna.

UNDP (United Nations Development Programme). 1994. *Human Development Report 1994.* New York: Oxford University Press.

———. 1995a. *Human Development Report 1995.* New York: Oxford University Press.

———. 1996a. *Human Development Report 1996.* New York: Oxford University Press.

———. 1997a. *Human Development Report 1997.* New York: Oxford University Press.

UNECE (United Nations Economic Commission for Europe). 1995. *Trends in Europe and North America: The Statistical Yearbook of the Economic Commission for Europe.* New York and Geneva.

———. 1996. Database. Geneva.

———. 1997a. *Statistics of Road Traffic Accidents in Europe and North America.* New York and Geneva.

———. 1997b. *Trends in Europe and North America 1996–97.* New York and Geneva.

UNESCO (United Nations Educational, Scientific and Cultural Organization). 1993. *World Education Report 1993.* Paris.

———. 1994. "Statistics on Illiteracy, 1994 Estimates and Projections." Paris.

———. 1995. *World Education Report 1995.* Paris.

———. 1997a. Correspondence on adult literacy. Division of Statistics. Received July. Paris.

———. 1997b. Correspondence on combined primary, secondary and tertiary enrolment. Division of Statistics. Received November. Paris.

———. 1997c. *Education Policy Analysis.* Paris.

———. 1997d. *Statistical Yearbook 1997.* Paris.

———. 1998. *World Education Report 1998.* Paris

UNHCR (United Nations High Commissioner for Refugees). 1996. "Refugees and Others of Concern to UNHCR: 1996 Statistical Overview." Geneva.

———. 1998. *The State of the World's Refugees 1997–98: A Humanitarian Agenda.* New York: Oxford University Press.

UNICEF (United Nations Children's Fund). 1997. *The State of the World's Children 1997.* New York: Oxford University Press.

———. 1998b. *The State of the World's Children 1998.* New York: Oxford University Press.

WHO (World Health Organization). 1993. *World Health Statistics Annual 1993.* Geneva.

———. 1994. *World Health Statistics Annual 1994.* Geneva.

———. 1995a. *Global Database on Child Growth 1995.* Nutrition Unit. Geneva.

———. 1995c. *World Health Statistics Annual 1995.* Geneva.

———. 1996b. *The World Health Report 1996.* Geneva.

———. 1997c. *Tobacco or Health: A Global Status Report.* Geneva.

———. 1997d. *The World Health Report 1997.* Geneva.

WHO (World Health Organization), WSSCC (Water Supply and Sanitation Collaborative Council) and UNICEF (United Nations Children's Fund). 1996. *Water Supply and Sanitation Sector Monitoring Report.* Geneva.

World Bank. 1993. *World Development Report 1993.* New York: Oxford University Press.

———. 1995b. *World Data 1995.* CD-ROM. Washington, DC.

———. 1995c. *World Development Report 1995.* New York: Oxford University Press.

———. 1996. *World Development Report 1996.* New York: Oxford University Press.

———. 1997a. Correspondence on unpublished World Bank data on GNP per capita estimates using the GDP/GNP ratio for 1995. International Economics Department. Received July. Washington, DC.

———. 1997b. *Global Development Finance.* Washington, DC.

———. 1997d. *World Development Indicators 1997.* CD-ROM. Washington, DC.

———. 1997e. *World Development Report 1997.* New York: Oxford University Press.

WRI (World Resources Institute). 1994. *World Resources 1994–95.* New York: Oxford University Press.

———. 1996a. *World Resources 1996–97.* New York: Oxford University Press.

———. 1998. *World Resources 1998–99.* New York: Oxford University Press.

Selected definitions

Administrators and managers Includes legislators, senior government administrators, traditional chiefs and heads of villages and administrators of special interest organizations. It also includes corporate managers such as chief executives and general managers as well as specialized managers and managing supervisors, according to the International Standard Classification of Occupations (ISCO-1968).

Alcohol consumption per capita Derived from sales data for beer, wine and spirits, each of which is converted to absolute alcohol based on its alcohol content. The total absolute alcohol is then divided by the population to get per capita consumption.

Births attended by trained health personnel The percentage of births attended by physicians, nurses, midwives, trained primary health care workers or trained traditional birth attendants.

Budget surplus/deficit (overall surplus/deficit) Central government current and capital revenue and official grants received, less expenditure and net government lending.

Central government expenditures Expenditures, both current and capital, by all government offices, departments, establishments and other bodies that are agencies or instruments of the central authority of a country.

Children reaching grade 5 Percentage of children starting primary school who eventually attain grade 5 (grade 4 if the duration of primary school is four years). The estimate is based on the Reconstructed Cohort Method, which uses data on enrolment and repeaters for two consecutive years.

Cigarette consumption per adult Estimated by the World Health Organization (WHO) according to this formula: the sum of production and imports minus exports divided by the population aged 15 years and older. This measure of apparent consumption has been adjusted for consumption of bidis and rolled tobacco as well as smuggling, but not for stocks kept by the trade.

CO_2 emissions Anthropogenic (human originated) carbon dioxide (CO_2) emissions stemming from the burning of fossil fuels and the production of cement. Emissions are calculated from data on the consumption of solid fuels, liquid fuels, gaseous fuels, and gas flaring. Combusion of different fuels releases CO_2 at different rates. For the same level of energy consumption, burning oil releases about 1.5 times the amount of CO_2 released by burning natural gas; coal consumption releases about twice the CO_2 of natural gas. During cement manufacturing cement is calcined to produce calcium oxide. In the process 0.498 metric ton of CO_2 is released for each ton of cement production.

Commercial energy Commercial forms of primary energy—petroleum (crude oil, natural gas liquids and oil from non-conventional sources), natural gas, solid fuels (coal, lignite and other derived fuels) and primary electricity (nuclear, hydroelectric, geothermal and other)—all converted into oil equivalents.

Commercial energy use Refers to domestic primary commercial energy supply, and is calculated as indigenous production plus imports and stock changes, minus exports and international marine bunkers.

Contraceptive prevalence rate The percentage of married women of child-bearing age who are using, or whose husbands are using, any form of contraception, whether modern or traditional.

Crude birth rate Annual number of births per 1,000 population.

Crude death rate Annual number of deaths per 1,000 population.

Current account balance The difference between (a) exports of goods and services (factor and non-factor) as well as inflows of unrequited transfers but exclusive of foreign aid and (b) imports of goods and services as well as all unrequited transfers to the rest of the world.

Daily calorie supply per capita The calorie equivalent of the net food supplies in a country, divided by the population, per day.

Debt service The sum of principal repayments and interest payments on total external debt.

Defence expenditure All expenditure, whether by defence or other departments, on the maintenance of military forces, including the purchase of military supplies and equipment, construction, recruitment, training and military aid programmes.

Deforestation The permanent clearing of forestlands for shifting cultivation, permanent agriculture or settlements; it does not include other alterations such as selective logging.

Dependency ratio The ratio of the population defined as dependent—those under 15 and over 64—to the working-age population, aged 15–64.

Disability As defined by the International Classification of Impairments, Disabilities and Handicaps (ICIDH) issued by the World Health Organization (WHO), disability is a restriction or lack of ability (resulting from impairment) to perform an activity in the manner or within the range considered normal for a human being. Impairment is defined as any loss of psychological, physiological or anatomical structure and function. The World Programme of Action concerning Disabled Persons monitors the implementation of national action to enhance the socio-economic opportunities and integration of disabled persons.

Disbursement The release of funds to, or the purchase of goods or services for, a recipient; by extension, the amount thus spent. Disbursements record the actual international transfer of financial resources or of goods or services, valued at the cost to the donor. For activities carried out in donor countries, such as training, administration or public awareness programmes, disbursement is taken to have occurred when the funds have been transferred to the service provider or the recipient. They may be recorded as gross (the total amount disbursed over a given accounting period) or net (less any repayments of loan principal during the same period).

Discouraged workers Individuals who would like to work and who are available for work, but are not actively seeking work because of a stated belief that no suitable job is available or because they do not know where to get work. The number of discouraged workers is used as an additional measure of labour market slack by the OECD.

Doctors Refers to physicians and includes all graduates of any faculty or school of medicine in any medical field (including practice, teaching, administration and research).

Earnings per employee All remuneration to employees expressed in constant prices, derived by deflating nominal earnings per employee by the country's consumer price index.

Economically active population All men or women who supply labour for the production of economic goods and services, as defined by the UN System of National Accounts, during a specified time period. According to this system, the production of economic goods and services should include all production and processing of primary products (whether for the market, for barter or for own-consumption), the production of all other goods and services for the market and, in the case of households that produce such goods and services for the market, the corresponding production for own-consumption.

Education expenditure Expenditure on the provision, management, inspection and support of pre-primary, primary and secondary schools; universities and colleges; vocational, technical and other training institutions; and general administration and subsidiary services.

Employees Includes regular employees, working proprietors, active business partners and unpaid family workers, but excludes homemakers.

Enrolment ratio (gross and net) The gross enrolment ratio is the number of students enrolled in a level of education—whether or not they belong in the relevant age group for that level—as a percentage of the population in the relevant age group for that level. The net enrolment ratio is the number of students enrolled in a level of education who belong in the relevant age group, as a percentage of the population in that age group.

Exports of goods and services The value of all goods and non-factor services provided to the rest of the world, including merchandise, freight, insurance, travel and other non-factor services.

Female-male gap A set of national, regional and other estimates in which all the figures for females are expressed in relation to the corresponding figures for males, which are indexed to equal 100.

Fertility rate (total) The average number of children that would be born alive to a woman during her lifetime, if she were to bear children at each age in accord with prevailing age-specific fertility rates.

Food aid in cereals Cereals provided by donor countries and international organizations, including the World Food Programme and the International Wheat Council, as reported for that particular crop year. Cereals include wheat, flour, bulgur, rice, coarse grain and the cereal components of blended foods.

Food consumption as a percentage of total household consumption Computed from details of GDP (expenditure at national market prices) defined in the UN System of National

Accounts, mostly as collected from the International Comparison Programme phases IV (1980) and V (1985).

Food production per capita index   The average annual quantity of food produced per capita in relation to that produced in the indexed year. Food comprises nuts, pulses, fruit, cereals, vegetables, sugar cane, sugar beets, starchy roots, edible oils, livestock and livestock products.

Future labour force replacement ratio   The population under 15 divided by a third of the population aged 15–59.

Government consumption   Includes all current expenditure for purchases of goods and services by all levels of government. Capital expenditure on national defence and security is regarded as consumption expenditure.

Gross domestic investment   Outlays on additions to the fixed assets of the economy plus net changes in the level of inventories.

Gross domestic product (GDP)   The total output of goods and services for final use produced by an economy, by both residents and non-residents, regardless of the allocation to domestic and foreign claims. It does not include deductions for depreciation of physical capital or depletion and degradation of natural resources.

Gross national product (GNP)   Comprises GDP plus net factor income from abroad, which is the income residents receive from abroad for factor services (labour and capital), less similar payments made to non-residents who contribute to the domestic economy.

Gross national product (GNP) per capita growth rates   Annual GNP per capita is expressed in current US dollars, and GNP per capita growth rates are average annual growth rates computed by fitting trend lines to the logarithmic values of GNP per capita at constant market prices for each year in the period.

Health expenditure   Public expenditure on health comprises the expenditure, both current and capital, by all government offices, departments, establishments and other bodies that are agencies or instruments of the central authority of a country on hospitals, clinics and maternity and dental centers with a major medical component; on national health and medical insurance schemes; and on family planning and preventive care. The data on health expenditure are not comparable across countries. In many economies private health services are substantial; in others public services represent the major component of total expenditure but may be financed by lower levels of government. Caution should therefore be exercised in using the data for cross-country comparisons.

Health services access   The percentage of the population that can reach appropriate local health services on foot or by local means of transport in no more than one hour.

Homicides   Includes intentional deaths (purposely inflicted by another person, including infanticide), non-intentional deaths (not purposely inflicted by another person) and manslaughter but excludes traffic accidents resulting in death.

Human priority areas   Basic education, primary health care, safe drinking water, adequate sanitation, family planning and nutrition.

Immunized   The average vaccination coverage of children under one year of age for the antigens used in the Universal Child Immunization (UCI) Programme.

Income share   The distribution of income or expenditure (or share of expenditure) accruing to percentile groups of households ranked by total household income, by per capita income or by expenditure. Shares of population quintiles and the top decile in total income or consumption expenditure are used in calculating income shares. The data sets for countries are drawn mostly from nationally representative household surveys conducted in different years during 1978–92. Data for the high-income OECD economies are based on information from the Statistical Office of the European Union (Eurostat), the Luxembourg Income Study and the OECD. Data should be interpreted with caution owing to differences between income studies in the use of income and consumption expenditure to estimate living standards.

Infant mortality rate   The annual number of deaths of infants under one year of age per 1,000 live births. More specifically, the probability of dying between birth and exactly one year of age times 1,000.

Inflation rate   Measured by the growth rate of the GDP implicit deflator for each of the periods shown. The GDP deflator is first calculated by dividing, for each year of the period, the value of GDP at current values by the value of GDP at constant values, both in national currency. This measure of inflation, like others, has limitations, but it is used because it shows annual price movements for all goods and services produced in an economy.

International reserves (gross)   Holdings of monetary gold, Special Drawing Rights (SDRs), the reserve positions of members in the International Monetary Fund (IMF) and holdings of foreign exchange under the control of monetary authorities expressed in terms of the number of months of imports of goods and services these could pay for at the current level of imports.

Internet users Based on reported estimates, derived from reported Internet access provider subscriber counts or calculated by multiplying the number of Internet hosts by an estimated multiplier.

Involuntary part-time workers Refers directly to the International Labour Organisation concept of visible underemployment and includes three groups of workers: those who usually work full-time but are working part-time because of economic slack; those who usually work part-time but are working fewer hours in their part-time job because of economic slack; and those working part-time because full-time work could not be found. The number of involuntary part-time workers is used as an additional measure of labour market slack by the OECD.

Labour force See *Economically active population.*

Least developed countries The least developed countries are those recognized by the United Nations as low-income countries encountering long-term impediments to economic growth, particularly low levels of human resource development and severe structural weaknesses. The main purpose of constructing a list of such countries is to give guidance to donor agencies and countries for allocation of foreign assistance.

Life expectancy at birth The number of years a newborn infant would live if prevailing patterns of mortality at the time of birth were to stay the same throughout the child's life.

Literacy rate (adult) The percentage of people aged 15 and above who can, with understanding, both read and write a short, simple statement on their everyday life.

Low-birth-weight infants The percentage of babies born weighing less than 2,500 grams.

Mangroves Part of the coastal ecosystems that line a quarter of the world's tropical coastlines and provide important nursery areas and habitats for fish and shellfish species. Human activities contributing to the loss and degradation of mangrove habitat include overharvesting, land clearing, mining, pollution, damming of rivers and conversion to aquaculture ponds.

Maternal mortality rate The annual number of deaths of women from pregnancy-related causes per 100,000 live births. According to the Tenth International Classification of Diseases, a maternal death is defined as the death of a woman while pregnant or within 42 days of termination of pregnancy, irrespective of the duration and the site of the pregnancy, from any causes related to or aggravated by the pregnancy or its management, but not from accidental or incidental causes. This complicated definition and the relative infrequency of maternal deaths in a short period (such as one to two years), except in very large population samples, led to misclassification and underreporting in many countries. To address this problem, the World Health Organization and the United Nations Children's Fund (UNICEF) developed a new set of estimates for 1990 that adjusted available data for underreporting and misclassification and included a model to predict values for countries with no reliable national data. These estimates should be seen as a recalculation of the previous (1991) revision rather than as indicative of trends since then. They cannot be used to monitor trends on a year-to-year basis, but provide a baseline estimate against which it will be possible to assess progress by 2003.

Military expenditure See *Defence expenditure.*

Multilateral official development assistance (ODA) Funds contributed in the form of ODA to an international institution with governmental membership that conducts all or a significant part of its activities in favour of development and aid recipient countries. A contribution by a donor to such an agency is deemed to be multilateral if it is pooled with other contributions and disbursed at the discretion of the agency. ODA received by aid recipient countries is considered multilateral if it comes from multilateral agencies such as multilateral development banks (the World Bank, regional development banks), UN agencies and regional groupings (certain European Union and Arab agencies).

Municipal waste Waste collected by municipalities or by their order, including waste originating from households, commercial activities, office buildings, schools, government buildings and small businesses that dispose of waste at the same facilities used for waste collected by municipalities.

Nurses All persons who have completed a programme of basic nursing education and are qualified and registered or authorized by the country to provide responsible and competent service for the promotion of health, prevention of illness, care of the sick and rehabilitation.

Occupation The classification of occupations brings together individuals doing similar work, irrespective of where the work is performed. Most countries have supplied data on the basis of the International Standard Classification of Occupations (ISCO). The actual content of occupational groups may differ from one country to another owing to variations in definitions and methods of data collection.

Official development assistance (ODA) Grants or loans to countries and territories on Part I of the OECD Development Assistance Committee (DAC) List of Aid Recipients (developing countries) that are undertaken by the official sector, with promotion of economic development and welfare as the main objective—and at concessional financial terms (if a loan, at least 25% grant element). Figures for total net ODA disbursed are based on OECD data for DAC member countries, multilateral organizations and Arab states.

Oral rehydration therapy use rate The percentage of all cases of diarrhoea in children under age five treated with oral rehydration salts or an appropriate household solution.

Pay phones Refers to the total number of all types of public telephones, including coin- and card-operated ones. Some countries include public phones installed in private places. No distinction is made between operational and non-operational pay phones.

Primary education Education at the first level (International Standard Classification of Education—ISCED—level 1), the main function of which is to provide the basic elements of education, such as elementary schools.

Private consumption The market value of all goods and services, including durable products (such as cars, washing machines and home computers), purchased or received as income in kind by households and non-profit institutions. It excludes purchases of dwellings but includes imputed rent for owner-occupied dwellings.

Production as a percentage of national energy reserves The data on production of energy refer to the first stage of production; thus for hard coal and lignite the data refer to mine production, and for crude oil and natural gas, to production at oil and gas wells. The data for reserves refer to proved recoverable reserves of coal, crude oil and natural gas—that is, the tonnage of the proved amount in place that can be recovered (extracted from the earth in raw form) in the future under present and expected economic conditions and existing technological limits. The ratio of production to reserves is the annual production of energy commodities as a percentage of the total proved recoverable reserves.

Professional and technical workers Physical scientists and related technicians; architects, engineers and related technicians; aircraft and ship's officers; life scientists and related technicians; medical, dental, veterinary and related workers; statisticians, mathematicians, systems analysts and related technicians; economists; accountants; jurists; teachers; workers in reli-

gion; authors, journalists and related writers; sculptors, painters, photographers and related creative artists; composers and performing artists; athletes, sportsmen and related workers; and professional, technical and related workers not elsewhere classified, according to the International Standard Classification of Occupations (ISCO-1968).

Purchasing power parity (PPP$) The purchasing power of a country's currency: the number of units of that currency required to purchase the same representative basket of goods and services (or a similar basket of goods and services) that a US dollar (the reference currency) would buy in the United States. Purchasing power parity could also be expressed in other national currencies or in Special Drawing Rights (SDRs).

Real GDP per capita (PPP$) The GDP per capita of a country converted into US dollars on the basis of the purchasing power parity of the country's currency.

Reforestation The establishment of plantations for industrial and non-industrial uses; it does not, in general, include regeneration of old tree crops, although some countries may report regeneration as reforestation.

Refugees According to the United Nations Convention Relating to the Status of Refugees and its 1967 Protocol, refugees are persons who—owing to a well-founded fear of being persecuted for reasons of race, religion, nationality, membership in a particular social group or political opinion—are outside their country of nationality and are unable or, owing to such fear, unwilling to avail themselves of the protection of that country; or who, not having a nationality and being outside the country of their former habitual residence, are unable or, owing to such fear, unwilling to return to it. According to the United Nations High Commissioner for Refugees (UNHCR), refugees also include selected groups of internally displaced persons, returnees and others of concern to or assisted by the UNHCR.

Rural-urban disparity A set of national, regional and other estimates in which all the rural figures are expressed in relation to the corresponding urban figures, which are indexed to equal 100.

Safe water access The percentage of the population with reasonable access to safe water supply, including treated surface water or untreated but uncontaminated water such as that from springs, sanitary wells and protected boreholes.

Sanitation access The percentage of the population with reasonable access to sanitary means of excreta and waste disposal, including outdoor latrines and composting.

Scientists and technicians *Scientists* refers to scientists and engineers with scientific or technological training (usually completion of third-level education) in any field of science who are engaged in professional work in research and development activities, including administrators and other high-level personnel who direct the execution of research and development activities. *Technicians* refers to persons engaged in scientific research and development activities who have received vocational or technical training for at least three years after the first stage of second-level education.

Secondary education Education at the second level (International Standard Classification of Education—ISCED—levels 2 and 3), based on at least four years of previous instruction at the first level and providing general or specialized instruction or both, such as middle school, secondary school, high school, teacher training school at this level and vocational or technical school.

Social protection Refers to OECD member countries' provision of social welfare in the areas of health, pensions, unemployment benefits and other income support schemes. This provision is intended not just to assist those in need, but also to meet economic goals by covering the social costs of economic restructuring.

South-North gap A set of national, regional and other estimates in which all figures for developing countries are expressed in relation to the corresponding average figures for all the industrial countries, indexed to equal 100.

Sulphur and nitrogen emissions Emissions of sulphur in the form of sulphur oxides and of nitrogen in the form of its various oxides, which together contribute to acid rain and adversely affect agriculture, forests, aquatic habitats and the weathering of building materials.

Tax revenue Compulsory, unrequited, non-repayable receipts for public purposes—including interest collected on tax arrears and penalties collected for non-payment or late payment of taxes—shown net of refunds and other corrective transactions.

Terms of trade The ratio of a country's index of average export prices to its index of average import prices.

Tertiary education Education at the third level (International Standard Classification of Education—ISCED—levels 5, 6 and 7), such as universities, teachers colleges and higher professional schools—requiring as a minimum condition of admission the successful completion of education at the second level or evidence of the attainment of an equivalent level of knowledge.

Total external debt The sum of public, publicly guaranteed and private non-guaranteed long-term external obligations, short-term debt and use of IMF credit. The data on debt are from the World Bank's Debtor Reporting System, supplemented by World Bank estimates. The system is concerned solely with developing economies and does not collect data on external debt for other groups of borrowers or from economies that are not members of the World Bank. Dollar figures for debt are in US dollars converted at official exchange rates.

Traditional fuels Includes fuelwood, charcoal, bagasse and animal and vegetable wastes.

Under-five mortality rate The annual number of deaths of children under age five per 1,000 live births averaged over the previous five years. More specifically, the probability of dying between birth and exactly five years of age expressed per 1,000 live births.

Underweight (moderate and severe child malnutrition) The percentage of children under age five who are below minus two standard deviations from the median birth-weight for age of the reference population.

Unemployment All persons above a specified age who are not in paid employment or self-employed, but are available and have taken specific steps to seek paid employment or self-employment.

Unpaid family workers Household members involved in unremunerated subsistence and non-market activities, such as agricultural production for household consumption, and in household enterprises producing for the market for which more than one household member provides unpaid labour.

Urban population Percentage of the population living in urban areas as defined according to the national definition used in the most recent population census.

Waste recycling The reuse of material that diverts it from the waste stream, except for recycling within industrial plants and the reuse of material as fuel. The recycling rate is the ratio of the quantity recycled to the apparent consumption.

Water resources, internal renewable The average annual flow of rivers and aquifers generated from endogenous precipitation.

Water withdrawals Includes those from non-renewable aquifers and desalting plants but does not include losses from evaporation.

KEY TO INDICATORS

Indicator	Indicator tables
A	
Agricultural production	25, 45
AIDS cases	13, 30
Alcohol consumption	30
Anaemia, % of pregnant women with	12
Armed forces, total	19, 38
B	
Births attended by health personnel	12
Births to mothers aged 15–19	36
Birth rate, crude	22
Birth-weight, low	12
Breast-feeding, at three months	12
Budget surplus/deficit	26, 46
C	
Calorie supply per capita	9, 14
South-North gap	9
Cancer	30
Carbon dioxide emissions, total	43
kg per US$ of GDP	43
per capita	24, 43
share of world total	43
Cereal, per capita supply	14
Cigarette consumption, adult	13
% of adults who smoke	30
Computers, personal	17, 34
Consumption, government	25, 45
private	25, 45
Contraceptive prevalence rate	22, 41
Current account balance	20, 39
D	
Death rate, crude	22
Debt, external, total	20, 37
as % of GNP	20, 37
Debt service ratio	20, 37
Deforestation	24, 43
trees defoliated	24
Dependency ratio	22, 41
Disabilities, people with	13, 30
Divorces	36
Doctors	13, 30
Drug crimes	36
E	
Earnings per employee, annual growth rate	16, 32
Economic activity rate, female	11, 29
Education expenditure, public, % of GNP	15, 31
as % of total government expenditure	15, 31
higher	15, 31
primary and secondary	15, 31
total, as % of GDP	31
Education index	1
Educational attainment, primary	7
Elections, date of last	18, 35
voter turnout	18, 35
Electricity consumption, total	23, 42
per capita	23, 42
Energy, commercial, total use	23, 42
GDP output per kg used	23, 42
imports, net	23, 42
per capita use	23, 42
Enrolment, all levels, total	31
Enrolment, tertiary, total	31
female	10, 28
natural and applied science	15, 31
natural and applied science, female	10, 28

Indicator	Indicator tables
Enrolment ratio, all levels	1, 2, 8
primary	15
primary, female	10, 28
primary, female ratio as % of male	15
secondary	15, 31
secondary, female	10, 28
secondary, female ratio as % of male	15
tertiary	31
Exports, % of GDP	25, 45
growth rate	26, 46
Export growth rate	39
Export-import ratio	20, 39
F	
Fat, daily per capita supply	14
Fax machines	17, 34
Fertility rate, total	22, 41
Food aid in cereals	14
Food consumption	14
Food imports	14
Food production	14
Fuel consumption, traditional	23
Fuel, spent	44
Fuelwood, as % of household energy	23
G	
GDP, total	25, 45
adjusted real per capita	1
per capita	5, 6
real (PPP$) per capita	1, 7, 8, 27
GDP index	1
GNP, total	26, 46
annual growth rate	26, 46
per capita	26, 46
per capita, annual growth rate	26, 46
Gender empowerment measure (GEM)	3, 4
Gender-related development index (GDI)	2, 4
Government expenditure, central	25, 45
H	
Health expenditure, total	30
private	30
public	13, 30
Health services, population without access to	7
Heart disease	30
Homicides by men, intentional	36
Human development index (HDI)	1, 4, 5
Human poverty index (HPI)	7, 27
I, J, K	
Illiteracy rate	7, 27
Immunization	13
Imports, as % of GDP	25, 45
Income share	2
female and male	2
women's share	3
Industrial production	25, 45
Infant mortality	8, 12, 27
Inflation	26, 46
International reserves, gross	39
Internet users	17, 34
Investment, gross domestic	25, 45
Investment, net foreign direct	20, 39
L	
Labour force, as % of population	16, 32
future replacement ratio	32
in agriculture	16, 32

Note: In addition to being shown in tables as listed, most indicators are also shown in aggregate form in table 47 for regional groups and as global aggregates.

Classification of countries

Countries in the human development aggregates

High human development
(HDI 0.800 and above)

Antigua and Barbuda	Qatar
Argentina	Saint Kitts and Nevis
Australia	Saint Lucia
Austria	Saint Vincent[b]
Bahamas	Seychelles
Bahrain	Singapore
Barbados	Slovakia
Belgium	Slovenia
Belize	Spain
Brazil	Sweden
Brunei Darussalam	Switzerland
Canada	Thailand
Chile	Trinidad and Tobago
Colombia	United Arab Emirates
Costa Rica	United Kingdom
Cyprus	Uruguay
Czech Rep.	USA
Denmark	Venezuela
Dominica	
Fiji	
Finland	
France	
Germany	
Greece	
Grenada	
Hong Kong, China[a]	
Hungary	
Iceland	
Ireland	
Israel	
Italy	
Japan	
Korea, Rep. of	
Kuwait	
Libyan Arab Jamahiriya	
Luxembourg	
Malaysia	
Malta	
Mauritius	
Mexico	
Netherlands	
New Zealand	
Norway	
Panama	
Poland	
Portugal	

Medium human development
(HDI 0.500 to 0.799)

Albania	Romania
Algeria	Russian Federation
Armenia	Samoa (Western)
Azerbaijan	Saudi Arabia
Belarus	São Tomé and Principe
Bolivia	Solomon Islands
Botswana	South Africa
Bulgaria	Sri Lanka
Cape Verde	Suriname
China	Swaziland
Congo	Syrian Arab Rep.
Croatia	Tajikistan
Cuba	Tunisia
Dominican Rep.	Turkey
Ecuador	Turkmenistan
Egypt	Ukraine
El Salvador	Uzbekistan
Estonia	Vanuatu
Gabon	Viet Nam
Georgia	Zimbabwe
Guatemala	
Guyana	
Honduras	
Indonesia	
Iran, Islamic Rep. of	
Iraq	
Jamaica	
Jordan	
Kazakhstan	
Korea, Dem. People's Rep. of	
Kyrgyzstan	
Latvia	
Lebanon	
Lithuania	
Macedonia, FYR	
Maldives	
Moldova, Rep. of	
Mongolia	
Morocco	
Namibia	
Nicaragua	
Oman	
Papua New Guinea	
Paraguay	
Peru	
Philippines	

Low human development
(HDI below 0.500)

Angola
Bangladesh
Benin
Bhutan
Burkina Faso
Burundi
Cambodia
Cameroon
Central African Rep.
Chad
Comoros
Côte d'Ivoire
Dem. Rep. of the Congo
Djibouti
Equatorial Guinea
Eritrea
Ethiopia
Gambia
Ghana
Guinea
Guinea-Bissau
Haiti
India
Kenya
Lao People's Dem. Rep.
Lesotho
Madagascar
Malawi
Mali
Mauritania
Mozambique
Myanmar
Nepal
Niger
Nigeria
Pakistan
Senegal
Sierra Leone
Sudan
Tanzania, U. Rep. of
Togo
Uganda
Yemen
Zambia

a. On 1 July 1997 Hong Kong became a Special Administrative Region of China.
b. Throughout the Report, Saint Vincent is used to refer to Saint Vincent and the Grenadines.

Countries in the income aggregates

High income (GNP per capita above $9,386 in 1995)	Middle income (GNP per capita $766 to $9,385 in 1995)		Low income (GNP per capita $765 or below in 1995)	
Andorra	Algeria	Mauritius	Afghanistan	Tajikistan
Aruba	American Samoa	Mayotte	Albania	Tanzania, U. Rep. of
Australia	Antigua and Barbuda	Mexico	Angola	Togo
Austria	Argentina	Micronesia Fed. States	Armenia	Uganda
Bahamas	Bahrain	Moldova, Rep. of	Azerbaijan	Viet Nam
Belgium	Barbados	Morocco	Bangladesh	Yemen
Bermuda	Belarus	Namibia	Benin	Zambia
Brunei Darussalam	Belize	Oman	Bhutan	Zimbabwe
Canada	Bolivia	Panama	Bosnia and Herzegovina	
Cayman Islands	Botswana	Papua New Guinea	Burkina Faso	
Channel Islands	Brazil	Paraguay	Burundi	
Cyprus	Bulgaria	Peru	Cambodia	
Denmark	Cape Verde	Philippines	Cameroon	
Faeroe Islands	Chile	Poland	Central African Rep.	
Finland	Colombia	Puerto Rico	Chad	
France	Costa Rica	Romania	China	
French Guiana	Croatia	Russian Federation	Comoros	
French Polynesia	Cuba	Samoa (Western)	Congo	
Germany	Czech Rep.	Saudi Arabia	Côte d'Ivoire	
Greenland	Djibouti	Seychelles	Dem. Rep. of the Congo	
Guam	Dominica	Slovakia	Equatorial Guinea	
Hong Kong, China	Dominican Rep.	Slovenia	Eritrea	
Iceland	Ecuador	Solomon Islands	Ethiopia	
Ireland	Egypt	South Africa	Gambia	
Israel	El Salvador	Saint Kitts	Georgia	
Italy	Estonia	Saint Lucia	Ghana	
Japan	Fiji	Saint Vincent	Guinea	
Korea, Rep. of	Gabon	Suriname	Guinea-Bissau	
Kuwait	Greece	Swaziland	Guyana	
Liechtenstein	Grenada	Syrian Arab Rep.	Haiti	
Luxembourg	Guadeloupe	Thailand	Honduras	
Macao	Guatemala	Tonga	India	
Martinique	Hungary	Trinidad and Tobago	Kenya	
Monaco	Indonesia	Tunisia	Kyrgyzstan	
N. Mariana Islands	Iran, Islamic Rep. of	Turkey	Lao People's Dem. Rep.	
Netherlands	Iraq	Turkmenistan	Liberia	
Netherlands Antilles	Isle of Man	Ukraine	Madagascar	
New Caledonia	Jamaica	Uruguay	Malawi	
New Zealand	Jordan	Uzbekistan	Mali	
Norway	Kazakhstan	Vanuatu	Mauritania	
Portugal	Kiribati	Venezuela	Mongolia	
Qatar	Korea, Dem. People's	West Bank and Gaza	Mozambique	
Réunion	Rep. of	Yugoslavia	Myanmar	
Singapore	Latvia		Nepal	
Spain	Lebanon		Nicaragua	
Sweden	Lesotho		Niger	
Switzerland	Libyan Arab Jamahiriya		Nigeria	
United Arab Emirates	Lithuania		Pakistan	
United Kingdom	Macedonia, FYR		Rwanda	
USA	Malaysia		São Tomé and Principe	
Virgin Islands (US)	Maldives		Senegal	
	Malta		Sierra Leone	
	Marshall Islands		Somalia	
			Sri Lanka	
			Sudan	

Countries in the major world aggregates

Least developed countries	All developing countries			Industrial countries
Afghanistan	Afghanistan	Gabon	Oman	Albania
Angola	Algeria	Gambia	Pakistan	Armenia
Bangladesh	Angola	Ghana	Panama	Australia
Benin	Antigua and Barbuda	Grenada	Papua New Guinea	Austria
Bhutan	Argentina	Guatemala	Paraguay	Azerbaijan
Burkina Faso	Bahamas	Guinea	Peru	Belarus
Burundi	Bahrain	Guinea-Bissau	Philippines	Belgium
Cambodia	Bangladesh	Guyana	Qatar	Bulgaria
Cape Verde	Barbados	Haiti	Rwanda	Canada
Central African Rep.	Belize	Honduras	Saint Kitts and Nevis	Croatia
Chad	Benin	Hong Kong, China	Saint Lucia	Czech Rep.
Comoros	Bhutan	India	Saint Vincent	Denmark
Dem. Rep. of the Congo	Bolivia	Indonesia	Samoa (Western)	Estonia
Djibouti	Botswana	Iran, Islamic Rep. of	São Tomé and Principe	Finland
Equatorial Guinea	Brazil	Iraq	Saudi Arabia	France
Eritrea	Brunei Darussalam	Jamaica	Senegal	Georgia
Ethiopia	Burkina Faso	Jordan	Seychelles	Germany
Gambia	Burundi	Kenya	Sierra Leone	Greece
Guinea	Cambodia	Korea, Dem. People's	Singapore	Hungary
Guinea-Bissau	Cameroon	Rep. of	Solomon Islands	Iceland
Haiti	Cape Verde	Korea, Rep. of	Somalia	Ireland
Kiribati	Central African Rep.	Kuwait	South Africa	Israel
Lao People's Dem. Rep.	Chad	Lao People's Dem. Rep.	Sri Lanka	Italy
Lesotho	Chile	Lebanon	Sudan	Japan
Liberia	China	Lesotho	Suriname	Kazakhstan
Madagascar	Colombia	Liberia	Swaziland	Kyrgyzstan
Malawi	Comoros	Libyan Arab Jamahiriya	Syrian Arab Rep.	Latvia
Maldives	Congo	Madagascar	Tanzania, U. Rep. of	Lithuania
Mali	Costa Rica	Malawi	Thailand	Luxembourg
Mauritania	Côte d'Ivoire	Malaysia	Togo	Macedonia, FYR
Mozambique	Cuba	Maldives	Trinidad and Tobago	Malta
Myanmar	Cyprus	Mali	Tunisia	Moldova, Rep. of
Nepal	Dem. Rep. of the Congo	Mauritania	Turkey	Netherlands
Niger	Djibouti	Mauritius	Uganda	New Zealand
Rwanda	Dominica	Mexico	United Arab Emirates	Norway
Samoa (Western)	Dominican Rep.	Mongolia	Uruguay	Poland
São Tomé and Principe	Ecuador	Morocco	Vanuatu	Portugal
Sierra Leone	Egypt	Mozambique	Venezuela	Romania
Solomon Islands	El Salvador	Myanmar	Viet Nam	Russian Federation
Somalia	Equatorial Guinea	Namibia	Yemen	Slovakia
Sudan	Eritrea	Nepal	Zambia	Slovenia
Tanzania, U. Rep. of	Ethiopia	Nicaragua	Zimbabwe	Spain
Togo	Fiji	Niger		Sweden
Tuvalu		Nigeria		Switzerland
Uganda				Tajikistan
Vanuatu				Turkmenistan
Yemen				Ukraine
Zimbabwe				United Kingdom
				USA
				Uzbekistan

Countries in the regional aggregates

Sub-Saharan Africa	Arab States	Asia and the Pacific and Oceania	Latin America, the Caribbean and North America	Europe

DEVELOPING COUNTRIES

Sub-Saharan Africa	Arab States	Asia and the Pacific and Oceania	Latin America, the Caribbean and North America	Europe
Angola	Algeria	**East Asia**	**Latin America and the Caribbean**	**Southern Europe**
Benin	Bahrain	China		Cyprus
Botswana	Djibouti	Hong Kong, China	Antigua and Barbuda	Turkey
Burkina Faso	Egypt	Korea, Dem. People's	Argentina	
Burundi	Iraq	Rep. of	Bahamas	**INDUSTRIAL COUNTRIES**
Cameroon	Jordan	Korea, Rep. of	Barbados	
Cape Verde	Kuwait	Mongolia	Belize	
Central African Rep.	Lebanon		Bolivia	**Eastern Europe and the Commonwealth of Independent States**
Chad	Libyan Arab Jamahiriya	**South-East Asia and the Pacific**	Brazil	
Comoros	Morocco		Chile	
Congo	Oman	Brunei Darussalam	Colombia	Albania
Côte d'Ivoire	Qatar	Cambodia	Costa Rica	Armenia
Dem. Rep. of the Congo	Saudi Arabia	Fiji	Cuba	Azerbaijan
Equatorial Guinea	Somalia	Indonesia	Dominica	Belarus
Eritrea	Sudan	Lao People's Dem. Rep.	Dominican Rep.	Bulgaria
Ethiopia	Syrian Arab Rep.	Malaysia	Ecuador	Croatia
Gabon	Tunisia	Myanmar	El Salvador	Czech Rep.
Gambia	United Arab Emirates	Papua New Guinea	Grenada	Estonia
Ghana	Yemen	Philippines	Guatemala	Georgia
Guinea		Samoa (Western)	Guyana	Hungary
Guinea-Bissau		Singapore	Haiti	Kazakhstan
Kenya		Solomon Islands	Honduras	Kyrgyzstan
Lesotho		Thailand	Jamaica	Latvia
Liberia		Vanuatu	Mexico	Lithuania
Madagascar		Viet Nam	Nicaragua	Macedonia, FYR
Malawi			Panama	Moldova, Rep. of
Mali		**South Asia**	Paraguay	Poland
Mauritania		Afghanistan	Peru	Romania
Mauritius		Bangladesh	Saint Kitts and Nevis	Russian Federation
Mozambique		Bhutan	Saint Lucia	Slovakia
Namibia		India	Saint Vincent	Slovenia
Niger		Iran, Islamic Rep. of	Suriname	Tajikistan
Nigeria		Maldives	Trinidad and Tobago	Turkmenistan
Rwanda		Nepal	Uruguay	Ukraine
São Tomé and Principe		Pakistan	Venezuela	Uzbekistan
Senegal		Sri Lanka		
Seychelles				**Western and Southern Europe**
Sierra Leone				Austria
South Africa				Belgium
Swaziland		**INDUSTRIAL COUNTRIES**		Denmark
Tanzania, U. Rep. of				Finland
Togo		Australia	**North America**	France
Uganda		Israel	Canada	Germany
Zambia		Japan	USA	Greece
Zimbabwe		New Zealand		Iceland
				Ireland
				Italy
				Luxembourg
				Malta
				Netherlands
				Norway
				Portugal
				Spain
				Sweden

Other aggregates

European Union

Austria
Belgium
Denmark
Finland
France
Germany
Greece
Ireland
Italy
Luxembourg
Netherlands
Portugal
Spain
Sweden
United Kingdom

OECD

Australia
Austria
Belgium
Canada
Czech Rep.
Denmark
Finland
France
Germany
Greece
Hungary
Iceland
Ireland
Italy
Japan
Korea, Rep. of
Luxembourg
Mexico
Netherlands
New Zealand
Norway
Poland
Portugal
Spain
Sweden
Switzerland
Turkey
United Kingdom
USA

Nordic countries

Denmark
Finland
Iceland
Norway
Sweden